TROTSKY

An Appreciation of his Life

TROTSKY

An Appreciation of his Life

by

Joel Carmichael

ST. MARTIN'S
NEW YORK

Library of Congress Cataloging in Publication Data

Carmichael, Joel.
   Trotsky.
Bibliography: p.
Includes index.
1. Trotskii, Lev, 1879-1940.
DK254.T6C37   947.084'092'4 [B]   75-9471

CONTENTS

ILLUSTRATIONS

ACKNOWLEDGMENTS:

1 The David King Collection
2 Popperfoto Ltd.

FOREWORD

Trotsky's legend has passed through three phases.

As co-founder, with Lenin, of the Soviet regime in 1917, he became a celebrity. A maker of History, creator of the Red Army, and the most versatile of the Bolshevik luminaries, he had a world reputation as statesman and thinker.

During the Twenties his prestige was clouded. The Bolshevik regime, engaged in reshaping the Soviet Union, was centralised by the Stalin dictatorship; Trotsky, a rival of Stalin's as it seemed, was presented to the public in an increasingly unfavourable light.

Banished from the Soviet Union in 1929, Trotsky became known to the 'bourgeois' world as the incarnation of revolutionary incendiarism, to political specialists as the leader of a Marxist splinter movement, and to the public at large as a somewhat eccentric journalist and historian.

In the Thirties, Soviet Orthodoxy, with its quasi-deification of Stalin, went far beyond charging Trotsky with 'deviation' from Marxism. The fabrications notorious as the 'Moscow Show Trials' of 1936–8 projected him as a demonic enemy of the Soviet regime, tirelessly plotting for the restoration of capitalism.

During the 'Purge' that was more or less veiled by the 'Show Trials', millions of people were gaoled and killed as agents of Trotsky, now an exile with no discernible influence. He was presented to the Soviet authorities as an Arch-Fiend whose henchmen, in tandem with fascist and militarist governments, were wreaking fantastic havoc within the Soviet Union. 'Trotskyism' became a synonym of Evil.

With the rise of Nazi Germany the influence of the Soviet Government among liberals and 'fellow-travellers' in Western Europe and America kept Trotsky enclosed within this satanic role until his assassination by Stalin in 1940. To this day the objects of persecution in the Soviet sphere are called amongst other things 'Trotskyites'.

Our own day has seen the third, and perhaps final phase of Trotsky's celebrity.

His reputation has risen from the ashes of the hatred, slander and, at best, baffling ambiguousness that distorted it in the aftermath of the 'Show Trials'. For many idealists discontented with regimes dedicated to radical social transformation (the Soviet Union, China, Cuba), and repelled, moreover, by what they take to be the philistinism inherent in the 'systems' of an older generation, Trotsky's name, symbolising the purity of The Revolution, has acquired a new lustre.

Trotsky was essentially, I think, a writer and speaker. Yet he was instrumental in bringing about a new order in the world. Ironically enough, Bolshevik mythology, which he played a primary role in forging, has obscured his real function.

According to that mythology, the One True Party was swept into power by the surge of The Revolution.

The reality was far less abstract, far more human.

In the First World War the German Imperial Government, its armies split by two fronts, found an opportunity to immobilise the eastern front. Supporting first the internal enemies of the Russian Government and then, after the Tsarist collapse, the opponents of the war, the Germans finally concentrated on the Bolsheviks, in the spring of 1917, as the recipients of a subsidy that launched a gigantic anti-war campaign and enabled the Bolsheviks to stage a putsch.

The Bolshevik Party and the German Imperial Government were, in fact, silent partners, each one gambling on the destruction of the other. This mutually hostile, subterranean partnership lasted until the German Imperial Government itself crumbled.

Trotsky's role in this relationship was primordial.

The news of the German subsidy came out in the summer of 1917, when Trotsky was not yet formally a Bolshevik. The scandal forced Lenin to flee and enabled Trotsky, a leader in the democratic Soviet, to stage-manage the Bolshevik putsch.

His other function, perhaps still more important, was to provide the putsch with a democratic camouflage that secured first the neutrality of the Bolsheviks' Socialist rivals, and then, in the Civil War, the allegiance of a large strata of the population. It was Trotsky, indeed, who presented the Bolshevik putsch as though it were really the assumption of power by the Soviet. He is thus responsible for the very name of the Soviet Union today.

None of this could be avowed either by the Bolsheviks, or by the German Government, or by Trotsky, least of all.

It is curious, as it seems to me, to discern these stark facts through the conventional accounts of the Bolshevik genesis, which generally have the air of exercises in the history of ideas.

Accounts of Trotsky's own life – including his own – have been warped, I believe, by an excessive identification with his ideas. Since these ideas, whatever their validity, fail to explain his career, an uncritical acceptance leads to chaos.

To disentangle Trotsky's character from his public performance I have, accordingly, been obliged to distance myself from his preconceptions.

I have done my best, also, to reduce the variety of his interests to a framework for his spiritual portrait; this entailed a substantial compression of the complex half-century spanning the First World War. I have viewed that span through the prism of Trotsky's intense personality.

Trotsky's intimate life is largely inaccessible. Yet enough has been recorded to indicate that a power of expression masked a sufferer – a virtuoso who despite remarkable bursts of activity was hamstrung by perhaps unconscious shortcomings.

Linked to the failure of his ideas, Trotsky's personal ordeal had the shape of a classic tragedy.

CHAPTER I

The Nursery

THERE ARE NOT MANY Jewish farmers in Russia; David Bronstein was one.

Brought as a child to a Jewish farming colony on the sunny flatlands north of the Black Sea in the Ukraine, he had struck out on his own and by back-breaking toil acquired a big farm – 250 acres of freehold and 50 leased.

It was only in the beginning of the nineteenth century that Jews were allowed to migrate to parts of the Ukraine, which had been absorbed into Russia only a short time before. There, as farmers, they could, for the first time in centuries, escape some of their disabilities. About forty farm colonies, of some 25,000 Jews, were spread out in the two provinces north of the Black Sea.

The Bronsteins moved to their new farm in the spring of 1879, bringing a small son and daughter, Alexander and Liza. That autumn, on 26 October, their youngest son was born. They named him Leib, in Russian Lev. Later, in other languages, he was to be called Leo and Leon as well.

Both the farm and the village nearby were named Yanovka, after a colonel who had been forced to sell them. The farmstead was a long way from anywhere. Wheatfields and sheep-pastures ran off into the distance as far as the eye could reach. The post office was fifteen miles away; the railway station was twenty-two; the nearest doctor was a night's drive. There were no newspapers or letters; telegrams – reserved for calamities – had to be brought on horseback.

During Leon's childhood the farm itself became a massive enterprise. The original thatched cottage was surrounded by new buildings. A big shed housed a workshop, the kitchen for the farm, and the quarters for labourers. There was a variety of service buildings – barns, stables, cowsheds, pigsties and countless chicken-houses. A big mill produced substantial revenue from fees paid by peasants for the service of grinding and threshing. Bronstein even developed his own international wholesale operation in Nikolayev, a small port on the Black Sea. He was able to lease large stretches of land from the spendthrift gentry, Polish and Russian noblemen living in fine houses beyond their means.

The Bronsteins were, in fact, well-to-do: their neighbours would have called them rich. By the time Leon was born the older brother and sister were attending a school in town; as a baby he had a nanny. There was going to be a music-teacher on the farm; a university education was in store for the boys. But there was not much question of luxury or leisure: throughout Leon's childhood the family lived in the same simple mud-house they had found on arrival.

Though the building that housed the machine-shop and the mill were well protected (tile roof and raised stone foundations), the family had to put up with far less: the mud walls had furrows deep enough to serve as burrows for serpents; the thatched roof teemed with sparrows; the roof was so leaky that pots and pans were routinely set out to catch the downpour, to save the mud floors from running. Indeed, of the five tiny rooms, only two had wooden floors – the 'living room', which had to be sanded every week, and the still tinier 'parlour', where the wood was actually painted. Fleas infested the mud floors of the other rooms.

Yet the house was cosy. Winter, especially, with snow mantling the house and stopping up the crevices, enveloped the little family in its own snug atmosphere.

Like all healthy farms Yanovka was a whole universe. Leon grew up together with his brother Alexander and his sisters, Liza and the younger Olga, an occasional aunt visiting during the long lazy days of summer, and, above all, the farm labourers. His friends were a nurse, a steward, a mechanic, a shepherd, the seasonal labourers.

Bronstein was quite illiterate: he learned to read only as an old man; he wanted to read what his son wrote. His physique and energy had been sufficient to take his wife away from her Jewish family, town-dwellers with a low opinion of farmers. Once harnessed to the strenuous routine of an ambitious farmer, she accepted the role; for forty-five years she toiled without let-up. Four of her eight children died in infancy; Leon was the only one to achieve distinction.

Bronstein's illiteracy, though an oddity for an able Jew, did not imply any lapse from piety. The Bronsteins made a point of travelling miles to attend synagogue services on High Holidays; on the Sabbath Leon's mother would never sew in public. She was strict enough to refuse a ride on the Sabbath even when Leon was seriously ill; a reliable Gentile had to take him to the doctor.

Until Leon was seven or eight years old a belief in God was taken for granted in the family, though according to the adult Trotsky when his father was much older he ceased pretending to believe in God. His mother would merely roll her eyes heavenward whenever such discussions came up.[1] In looks Bronstein was a 'typical Russian Jew'.[2]

It was a matter of course for the young boy to be given at least the beginnings of a Jewish education. At the age of seven he was sent to a *cheder* – a Jewish elementary school. He was introduced to his future teacher – a 'lean, wanly smiling, obsequious man' who ran a *cheder* in the little farm colony of Gromokley, a couple of miles from Yanovka. His mother had settled the business: for 'so many roubles and so many sacks of flour' he was to be taken into the school and taught Russian, arithmetic, and the Scriptures in Hebrew.

Though Leon spent some months going to this *cheder* while living in the Jewish colony with his Aunt Rachel and Uncle Abram, the whole description, written more than forty years later, is vague.

The adult Trotsky recalled that he had made no friends at the *cheder* because he spoke no Yiddish. Yet it is plain that the language of Gromokley was Yiddish, too, since that was the language of instruction in the *cheder*. Thus we are to believe that a high-spirited boy, while living for months at the house of close relatives in a community whose language was Yiddish, and going to a Yiddish-speaking school whose teacher he was fond of – he was grateful to him for having 'taught him to read and write' – did not know the language he was immersed in. This would be quite baffling even if it were to be assumed that his parents themselves never spoke to him in it.

This oddity is underscored, moreover, by the adult Trotsky's recollection that his father spoke a 'broken mixture of Russian and Ukrainian'. The languages are, after all, quite distinct: the 'mixture' seems to imply that his father's native idiom was in fact some other language – no doubt Yiddish, too, like that of Uncle Abram and Aunt

Rachel, and of the Jewish town (in Poltava Province) he had come from.

In the adult Trotsky's vague account of his family there is not much feeling. His brother and his sisters are barely mentioned; what is said about his parents is non-committal, though in its own way revealing. He was not to recall any 'display of tenderness in our family, especially during my early years'. He emphasises, instead, the 'strong comradeship of labour' between his parents.

His father was 'undoubtedly superior to my mother, both in intellect and in character. . . . He judged people by their manners, their faces and their habits, and he always judged them correctly.'

He mentions his mother without emotion. He recalls her quasi-illiteracy – 'she would read in a loud whisper from some worn novel . . . moving her toil-worn finger along the lines. She often got mixed up over the words, and would stumble over some complicated sentence. . . .' Sometimes a suggestion by one of the children would show 'her what she had been reading in a completely new light'.[3]

Tactfully put!

There is a small additional puzzle about the mother. She seems not to have 'trained' her small children properly : Leon was to say he learned from a cousin, 'how to hold a glass, how to wash'[4] only as a grown boy.

His father was 'quieter and gentler' with the children than the mother. 'My mother would often lose her temper with us, sometimes without reason, and would simply work out her fatigue or her domestic failure on her children. We always found it more rewarding to ask our father for favours.'[5]

It is, of course, impossible to tell Leon's actual feelings from this sparse account. A slightly older contemporary who met him as an adolescent was to say that young Leon actually disliked speaking of his parents and of his brothers and sisters, with the exception of the youngest, Olga.[6]

There was a contrast between the absence of 'culture' in young Leon's house and the family's aspiration towards it. The pleasure Leon's mother took in reading novels, though with such difficulty, is no doubt revealing, as is the purchase of a brokendown spinet for sixteen roubles – a substantial sum at the time – that was put to rights by a farm mechanic.

Leon's gift showed itself in childhood : he carved himself a pen with a knife and began copying some pictures of horses; he secretly wrote down coarse words picked up from the labourers. At a very early age he began to make verses: this was even more secret than the coarse words. His sister spilt the beans; when his father, to Leon's great pain, tried proudly to have him 'recite for the guests', Leon rushed from the room in agonised embarrassment.

An old-fashioned farmer, Bronstein was used to doing everything in his head, but as his holdings expanded a book-keeping system was needed. Leon soon displaced his older brother as accountant. He arranged the figures, took down what everything cost, tallied the labourer's wages, and figured profit and loss. This gave him, he was to say, the first twinge of compassion for the farm labourers; no matter how hard they worked they retained barely enough to carry them through the off-season.

As Leon began to read, he found himself more and more removed from the reality of the farm to the endless vistas opened up to young children by literature. The familiar chasm was established between things visibly at hand and imaginative constructions. On the one hand, there was the far-away life of the characters in novels – where people hovered in some ethereal medium, spoke to each other loftily about things so insubstantial as to be almost unintelligible: on the other, there was the 'real life' of the farming universe, where labourers worked their heads off, sneaked into the barn to make love, earthily denounced the frailties and iniquities of their betters, and bitterly complained about conditions of life. Leon more or less automatically took the labourers' side in disputes with his father: his emotional identification with them gave special cogency to the category of 'fairness' that children set such store by.

Later on he was, of course, to arrive at some sort of *rapprochement* between the two worlds; but even after he established a bridgehead, so to speak, between literature and life, he was to be fundamentally more at home with books: the world of the imagination embodied by books remained more substantial to him than 'real life' after all. When he was almost fifty he wrote:

The very word 'author' sounded to me as if it were uttered from some unattainable height. . . . From early years a love for words had been part of me, sometimes slackening, sometimes growing, but in general getting stronger and stronger. For me, authors, journalists, and artists were always the most attractive world, one open only to the elite.[7]

A well-written book in which one can find new ideas, and a good pen with which to communicate one's own ideas to others, for me have always been and are today the most valuable and intimate products of culture. The desire for study has never left me.[8]

This passion for the written word was consummated for a time by what may be thought of as its crystallisation – the theatre. At the age of seven Leon was inflamed by it.

One evening, while the Bronsteins were sipping tea in their little dining-room, a troupe of actors wandered in to give a performance. Leon fell to the floor transfixed while a 'Tsar' filled the crude room with bliss. A further insight into life and art was given him when he found out a few moments afterwards that the 'Tsar' was one of the hired hands.

Just as 'reading opened a new era' in his life, so his contact with the 'tree of knowledge', in the person of a cousin from the big city, abruptly channelled his energies in a new direction. This cousin, Moses Spentser, had come to the Bronstein farm to stave off tuberculosis: it was thought that life in the fresh air – milk, eggs – would be good for his health.

Spentser was a novelty in this rural milieu. He had graduated from a Russian high school and, in the idiom of the day, had 'suffered' – that is, politically. Having been barred from the university, he became a free-lance journalist, doing all sorts of hackwork: writing books for children, translating from the Greek, arranging school-texts, and so on. He was rather grand socially: he was engaged to the head of a state school for Jewish girls.

Spentser was to arouse not only his younger cousin's mind but his emotions. He gave them, perhaps, a political turn. At any rate Leon, when grown, recalled his cousin's moral outrage at seeing a shepherd struck: 'What a filthy thing!' Spentser exclaimed. 'And I felt that it was a filthy thing. I don't know whether I would have felt that without him. . . . But in any case he helped me in that, and that alone bound me to him all my life by a feeling of gratitude.'[9]

Otherwise Spentser was a 'liberal', with 'vague' humanitarian and Socialist leanings; he avoided explicit discussions.

In the spring of the following year, when Leon was nine and a half, he went to Odessa to live with Moses and his young bride while continuing his education. He arrived in the big city equipped with a brand-new suit and a big trunk with farm gifts for his relatives.

On his leaving the farm the whole family, his mother and his sisters, burst into sobs. Though in his autobiography he later described those years on the farm as 'grey' – the reader does not see quite why, it all sounds so merry! – on leaving it, in any case, he wept all the way to the main road.

Odessa was only about a century old; it had all the colour of a lively port – a medley of nationalities in which Jews numbered some thirty per cent. There were Ukrainians and Great Russians, Germans, Italians, French, and a variety of Asiatic nationalities (Tatars, Turks, Armenians, Persians, and Syrians). In a city so mongrel in composition the Jews were not singled out for discrimination. The only disadvantage they suffered was in schooling: in 1887 a *numerus clausus* cut down the number of Jewish students to ten per cent of the student population, in sharp contrast to their percentage of the population as a whole.

This prevented Leon's entry into a classical high school (*Lycée*) since with his makeshift rural schooling his marks were too low for him to get into the top ten per cent of the Jewish children who could be placed. Because of this the Spentsers got him into a more utilitarian school (*Realschule*) set up by the local German colony to give their own children a sound contemporary education based on modern languages, mathematics, and the sciences instead of classical languages and culture. By putting Leon in the preparatory class of the school the Spentsers ensured his entrance and gained a year in which he could improve his marks.

Not much time was lost. The next year Leon was in the *Realschule*, at the head of the class in mathematics and Russian, which the year before he had only just managed to scrape through. Throughout the same year, also, Spentser's help, in addition to the reading Leon had already flung himself into so energetically, was to make him far more talented at Russian 'composition' than his fellows; later on his essays would be read aloud in class.

During his first vacation he was shattered by the contrast between town and country:

I travelled homeward with the greatest impatience. My heart leaped for joy. I was longing to see everyone again and to show myself off to everyone. My father met me: I showed him my 'Five' and explained that I was in the first class now and had to have a parade uniform. We drove through the night in a van.... There was a damp breeze in the steppe; I was wrapped up in a greatcoat. Intoxicated by the change of surroundings, by the trip, by memories and impressions, I kept tirelessly talking about the school, about the bath, about my friend Kostya R., about the theatre.... My father listened, dozed off at times, started awake again and laughed contentedly.... Toward morning I fell asleep, and woke up in Yanovka. The house looked to me terribly small, the rural wheaten bread grey, the whole countryside *mine* and at the same time alien.... Between myself and what was bound up with my childhood something new had arisen like a wall.... Since this first homecoming of mine there began a sort of estrangement between myself and the family, first in trivialities, then with the years more seriously and more deeply.[10]

The compassion he felt for the peasants was sharpened, no doubt, by the new life opening up around him in the city. On his return to Yanovka for vacations he was more aware than ever of injustices.

Once on returning from the field he saw a barefooted woman, the mother of a half-witted shepherd boy, sitting timidly on the ground, leaning against the wall. She had walked miles to get a rouble that was owed her; no one was home; she waited all day for her single rouble. 'I felt a pang at the sight of that figure – the embodiment of poverty and resignation.'

Coming back home after a game of croquet, he once met his father with a small barefoot peasant, heels all black, following him, beseeching him to give him back his cow. Bronstein said:

'Your cow won't eat more than a copeck's worth of grain, but it will do ten roubles' worth of damage.' The peasant kept on; in his pleas you could hear the hate. This scene shook me to the very core of my being. The mood I had brought back from the croquet court, fringed by pear-trees, where I had triumphantly routed my sisters, was abruptly replaced by intense despair. I slipped past my father; flattened out on the bed and oblivious to everything, I sobbed away in spite of my standing as a second-year boy.

I often helped my father when wages were settled up; there were sudden brief clashes between us, suppressed by the presence of the labourers. There was never any cheating in the accounts, but the terms of the agreements were always rigidly interpreted. The labourers, particularly the older ones, would notice that the boy was on their side; that irritated my father.[11]

The adult Trotsky also gives us a more general view of his father:

I would usually go back from vacation together with my
father.... We carried our things ourselves. My father took the
heavier things; by his back and outstretched arms I could see how
heavy they were for him. I was sorry for my father, and carried
whatever I could. But when there happened to be a big case with
presents from the country for relatives in Odessa then we took a
porter. My father gave the porter a meagre tip, the porter would
be dissatisfied, and shake his head angrily. This always had the
most painful effect on me. When I would travel alone and had to
resort to porters, I would rapidly spend my pocket money; I was
always afraid of not giving enough, and looked with concern into
the porter's eyes. This was the reaction to the niggardliness of my
parents' house; it has remained with me the whole of my life.

Both in the country and in town I lived in a petty-bourgeois
milieu, where the principal effort was directed at acquisition. In
this respect I cut myself off from the countryside of my early
childhood and from the town of my school years. Instincts of
acquisition, a petty-bourgeois style of life and outlook – all these I
pushed myself away from with a powerful jolt. I kept pushing
myself away all my life.[12]

Trotsky's reaction, indeed, took the form of a lordliness about
material matters, especially money, that he was to become famous
for.

In Odessa it was not the Jews, but the Germans who were the
chief objects of discrimination, followed closely by the Ukrainians,
for different reasons. Both were targets of the large-scale 'russifica-
tion' programme launched during the nationalistic regime of
Alexander III, who came to the throne in 1881. In the eyes of the
school authorities, substantially russified by the time Leon came
along, his Jewish origins were overshadowed by the presence of
great numbers of German Lutherans and Roman Catholic Poles: he
himself was a 'star pupil'.

The Spentser household was non-religious, except for an old aunt
who 'did not count', yet some time after Leon moved in with
them – when he must have been about eleven or twelve years old –
he took up Hebrew again.

His father wanted him to 'know the Bible in the original; this was
one of the points of his parental ambition'. For several months Leon
took 'private Bible lessons with a very learned old man'. He must

have learned a good deal: they could discuss a philosophical point on the basis of the Hebrew text.

In the adult Trotsky's account this incident is quite unintelligible. Its very wording is, perhaps, revealing. After saying that his father wanted him to 'know' the Bible in the original, he goes on to say that his studies did not in the least fortify his 'ancestral faith'.[13] Thus his father's interest was not linguistic or mere vanity, but had a religious goal. Yet if his father did not *even* believe in God, what could have been the goal of his 'parental ambition'?

We seem forced to conclude that it could have been only a reflection of traditional piety, already expressed, as we know, through family attendance at synagogue, not riding on the Sabbath and so on.

Could the 'very learned old man' have been, in fact, a rabbi? Was Leon studying for his Bar Mitzvah (the Jewish coming-of-age ceremony)? The adult Trotsky is elusive: his account does not tell us why his Hebrew lessons came to an end. Did he go through the Bar Mitzvah ceremony or not? Was that the beginning of the friction with his father that was later to come to a head, so classically, in connection with a career?

It is plain, in any case, that something can be learned from Trotsky's reticence. We know that he had a low opinion of his mother on two accounts: not only was she unintelligent, and had failed, as it seems, in the most elementary aspects of child-care, but she was also ill-tempered, capricious and unfair. She could hardly have secured Trotsky's affections as a child, and had plainly failed to.

The father, too, while shrewd and good-humoured, must have been, in his son's eyes, loutish. Not only was he illiterate to the point of being unable to handle the elementary book-keeping indispensable for his business, but he was totally immersed in a way of life that Trotsky was to thrust away from himself with intense aversion. Moreover, he must have seemed to the adolescent boy a conformist hypocrite, since he faithfully attended synagogue while confessing to his son that he did not believe in God.

Trotsky's estimate of his father's piety was, to be sure, singularly primitive; it seems to have been based on the notion that an outwardly pious Jew would be hypocritical if he doubted the existence of God, as though Jews were Protestant free-thinkers. It is of a piece with his minimizing his mother's piety because of her sewing on the Sabbath only when alone.

The reading he had been launched on at the farm by his benevolent cousin turned torrential by the time he was settled in the
cousin's house in Odessa, where 'the choice of books was incomparably broader, and where there was an attentive and benevolent
guidance. I began to read voraciously; I had to be forced to go out
for walks. While walking I would live through what I had been reading and rush back to go on with it. . . . The awakening thirst for seeing
knowing, mastering, found an outlet in this insatiable swallowing up
of printed lines. . . . Everything that in later life was interesting or
fascinating, merry or sad was already contained in my reading
experience as a hint, a promise. . . .'[14]

Spentser had always wanted to be a publisher; he launched his
own firm about the time Leon came to stay with him. Later on it
became the biggest of its kind in Southern Russia. It gave Leon his
nearest approach to manual labour : he grew absorbed in the routine
of the print-shop, and adept at setting type, making lay-outs, doing
the actual printing and binding as well as correcting the galley-
proofs. He was to retain a life-long attachment to the physical
activity of arranging and looking at fresh print.

Literature disclosed the inwardness of the coarse language he had
been hearing on the farm : when his cousin was telling him a
favourite story – the opera *Faust* – Leon became aware from a change
in his voice that a 'delicate point' was coming up. But Moses 'recovered
his calm' and went on : 'Then a baby was born to Gretchen before
marriage.' They 'both felt relieved' when this point had been passed.[15]

Shortly afterwards, he was 'utterly perplexed' in reading *Oliver
Twist* by some remark about a woman not having a wedding-ring;
Moses explained 'haltingly' that when people weren't married they
wore no wedding-ring. Thereupon Leon thought of Gretchen : the
whole 'forbidden world' of human relations suddenly burst in on
him.[16]

The coarse side of life, which beforehand he had only heard
referred to grossly, was abruptly 'ennobled, rising to some higher
plane' through literature.

Leon would winnow through passages looking for apt, pointed or
colourful phrases to memorise, picking out references to abstruse
subjects, or at least subjects too abstruse for his age, and read more
mature books in order to impress his teachers. He was nimble at
absorbing an immense variety of allusions from everyday conversation in the Spentser household. By combining them he would be able
to present a formidable display of what sounded like learning,

though at the same time he was quick to feel ashamed of himself if he came up against the real thing.

Spentser had already shown him 'how to hold a glass' and 'wash himself' at the farm; in Odessa the Spentsers rounded out his general 'culture' for the first time – manners, personal hygiene, self-discipline. They turned him into a citified prig. In language especially, their tutoring the coarser elements out of his speech was to inculcate in him a lifelong finickiness.

It is perhaps significant that Leon never formed any friendships in his regular school. Indeed, he was to form hardly any personal friendships throughout his life : the number of people he was to be on a personal footing with could be counted quite easily – a handful. For that matter he had never had any attachments on the farm either, except, perhaps, to his younger sister, Olga.

> Not only in my school-years, but also in the later years of my youth nature and people took up less room in my spiritual life than books and ideas. In spite of my rural origins I was insensitive to nature. I developed an awareness and understanding of it later on, when not only my childhood, but also my first youth had been left behind. For a long time people flitted through my mind like accidental shadows. I looked into myself and into books, once again seeking myself or my future.[17]

As a schoolboy he had no interest either in the tumultuous, colourful life of the great port of Odessa; he never learned to swim or to go boating or fishing. All Odessa, in fact, was made up for him by the circumscribed area of the school, a library, the few theatres, and a few houses. There could be no question of street fights; his combativeness took on the more spiritualised forms of intellectual rivalry – he liked to shine in class.

He was a model schoolboy in all respects :

> I would rise early, hurriedly drink my morning tea, thrust into my overcoat pocket my lunch wrapped in paper, and run to school in order to get there in time for the morning prayer. I was not tardy. I sat quietly at my desk. I listened attentively and copied carefully. I worked diligently at home over my lessons. I went to bed at the prescribed hour, in order to hurry through my tea the following morning and run to school for fear of being late for the prayer. I passed from grade to grade without difficulty. Whenever I met

one of my teachers in the street, I bowed with all possible deference.[18]

Yet despite his exemplary behaviour he once found himself involved in an escapade that nearly ruined his schooling. The nascent idealism of adolescence – the awareness that the real world is not run along the lines laid down in conventional morality, literature, religion – coincided with a concrete case of injustice.

A teacher was persecuting a boy partly for being backward partly for being German. His school fellows, including Leon – though he did not particularly like the boy – banded together to straighten out the teacher: they set up a din muted by mouths kept shut as the teacher left the room. A dozen were rounded up: Leon was passed over, but was denounced by some of the others, including, curiously enough, the boy who was being avenged. One of the boys even put a nice touch to the picture of Leon as arch-culprit by reporting a petition suggested by Leon demanding that the teacher be sacked; it contained a detail of what sounds like Leon's brainpower at work – each of the mutineers was supposed to be responsible for one letter apiece of the petition so that none could be held to account.

Though there was no reason to single Leon out, and though the Spentsers intervened for him with great zeal, he was kicked out of the school. On the other hand, of the three forms of punishment – expulsion plus exclusion from *all* schools afterwards, expulsion from the *Realschule* with or without the right of re-entry – he was given the mildest: he was expelled for a year, to be admitted again if he passed some examinations. When Spentser broke the news to Leon, the latter turned 'all green' – as Spentser's wife said; but Leon did not sob and did not faint; he 'merely pined'.

In his autobiography Trotsky sums up this early disaster:

Such was the first political test of its kind that I underwent. The three groups resulting from that episode – the tale-bearers and the envious at one pole, the frank, courageous boys at the other, the neutral, vacillating mass in the middle – never disappeared even during the years that followed. I met them over and over in my life, in the most varied circumstances.[19]

The episode had dampened his interest in studies; that summer he was 'restless' with 'ever-recurring flare-ups of ill-temper'. He was in fact in the grip of adolescent torments; he describes them with poignancy:

> The snow was not yet cleared from the streets, but it was already warm. The housetops, the trees, the sparrows were throbbing with spring. The fourth-grade boy was walking home, carrying in his hand, against all the rules, a strap from his kit, because the hook was torn off. He felt that the long coat was useless and heavy. His whole body was sweating. Languor went with the sweat. The boy saw everything, primarily himself, in a new light. The spring sun suggested that there was something immeasurably mightier than the school, the inspector and the kit hanging askew on his back – mightier than studying, chess, dinners and even reading and the theatre; in general, than all everyday life. And the longing for this unfathomed something seized upon the boy's entire being down to the marrow of his bones. . . .
>
> He came home with a buzzing head, with painful music in his temples. . . . He lay down on the bed and . . . began weeping into the pillow. To justify his tears he recalled pathetic scenes from books and from his own life, as though to feed the furnace with fresh fuel; he wept with tears of spring longing. He was entering the fourteenth year of his life.[20]

Leon fell ill with an ailment he was to suffer from all his life – it was then called 'chronic catarrh of the digestive tract'. It was to flare up whenever he had 'nervous shocks'. This time, at the age of fourteen, he had to go away to the country, and in order not to fall too far behind to get a tutor. If he had had to depend on his parents for this it would have been impossible – 'they did not like extra expense at Yanovka' – but his cousin Moses handled it, finding him a down-and-out former university student, an oddball who kept alternating between revelations of his relationship with an older woman and insistence on the respect due to a teacher.

The mixture of different national elements in school, and the heterogeneity of Odessa itself, blurred any resentment Leon might have felt at the position of the Jews, who after 1881 could buy land only through straw-men. Son of a wealthy landowner, he 'belonged to the privileged class rather than to the oppressed'. In school itself, despite the limitation on the number of Jewish boys who could be admitted, he 'was always at the head of the class, and was not personally affected by such restrictions'.[21]

National inequality as such, indeed – the nastiness toward Poles, the spitefulness toward Germans, the disdain for Jews – though it may have been at the root of Leon's general discontent with the social order, was lost, he recalled, among all the other phases of social injustice.

Social contrasts shaped his mind : in his own account we can see a rationalist intelligence coagulating as it were before our eyes, cling-ing, as he thought, to a demonstrably rational causality with a lofty disdain for anything outside it. Thus it would upset him in mid-adolescence, indeed infuriate him, whenever, after grasping the validity of a general law, he came across people who disregarded it : 'When I heard boys who were studying physics and natural history repeat superstitious notions about unlucky Monday . . . I was utterly indignant.'[22]

He recalls a clear instance of ignorance repulsing science : on the farm, when people 'were spending many weary hours trying to measure the area of a field in the shape of a trapezoid I would apply Euclid and get my answer in a couple of minutes. . . . But they refused to believe it' – it had not coincided with 'practical' results. 'I would bring out my geometry textbook and swear in the name of science : I would get highly excited and use harsh words – all to no avail. People refused to see the light of reason, and this drove me to despair.

In trying to demonstrate to a gifted farm mechanic that the law of the conservation of energy proved that a perpetual machine – the mechanic's favourite hobby-horse – was out of the question, the mechanic merely laughed off his proof. 'Books are one thing, practice another,' he would say. To Leon it 'seemed incompre-hensible and unbearable that men could reject incontrovertible truth in the name of conventional errors and grotesque fantasies.'[23]

As he said :

The feeling of the superiority of the general to the particular, of law to fact, of theory to personal experience, arose within me early and grew stronger with the years. . . . Later on [this] feeling . . . became an integral part of my writing and politics. Dull empiricism, the naked cringing before a fact, sometimes merely imagined and often wrongly understood, were hateful to me. I was looking for laws beyond facts. This often led, naturally, to over-hasty and erroneous generalisations, especially in my early years when both my book-knowledge and my personal experience of life

were inadequate for generalisation. But in all fields without exception I felt myself capable of moving and acting only whenever
I held in my hands the thread of the general. The social-revolutionary radicalism that became my spiritual pivot for the whole of
my life grew out of this intellectual enmity toward pettiness,
toward empiricism, toward everything that is in general intellectually shapeless and theoretically ungeneralised.[24]

The reader of these lines – written when Trotsky was fifty, but
plainly a sincere account of his state of mind as a youth – is bound to
be struck by the religious conviction, quite unavowed, that has
seeped into this passage, especially in the sentence : 'I was looking
for laws *beyond* facts.'

Thus the longing for system seems to have fused, in the memory of
the adult Trotsky, with a fierce 'hatred of the existing order, of
injustice, of despotism', even though he had during his school years
no political views, nor any desire for them. This hatred came from
'conditions', from 'cases of injustice', from his contact with children,
servants and labourers in the country, from conversations in the
workshop, the humane atmosphere at the Spentsers, from reading,
from, in short, the whole of the 'social atmosphere'.

He was, in a word, 'opposed'. Two incidents situate the general
character of that opposition.

The son of a colonel invited Leon home for a Sunday afternoon.
He sat around with the family for three or four hours, during which
the colonel and his wife scarcely seemed to be scrutinising him;
several times he 'stumbled on something alien and alarming, even
inimical', whenever religion or the government was touched on : the
tone of 'conservative piety' was like a blow in the chest.

On another occasion he said something critical to a schoolmate
about the principal of the school. The schoolmate was sincerely
indignant :

'How can you speak of him that way?' 'But why not?' I protested,
with an astonishment that was even more sincere. 'But he's our
chief, if the chief orders you to walk on your head, you walk on
your head without criticising.' That was just how he put it. This
rounded-off formula surprised me. I did not guess at the time that
the boy was merely repeating what he had evidently often heard in
his feudal family. And though I had no views of my own I felt that

there were certain views I could no more accept than I could eat wormy food.[25]

These attitudes were counterposed by the adolescent Leon to an imaginary ideal – life in liberal Western Europe, steeped in culture, fraternal feeling, democracy and free speech.

Looking back on himself as an adolescent, the adult Trotsky recalled that he had no doubt been 'vain, choleric, and probably difficult to live with. . . . The moment he found himself at the top of his class . . . he felt he could do better than the others. . . . He would reproach himself for not having read the books mentioned by others with such assurance. . . . This was very close to vanity. The thought that he had to be better, grander, and better read kept goading him. He thought about the purpose of man in general and about his own in particular.'[26]

Here, too, the third person was easier for the adult Trotsky.

In 1896 Leon graduated from the sixth and final grade of the Odessa *Realschule*. That evening the boys rushed to the Summer Garden, where girls sang on a stage. It had been strictly out-of-bounds for them as school-boys. 'Everyone wore a necktie, had two bottles of beer on the table, and a cigarette in his mouth.'[27]

The *Realschule* did not go up to university level; in any case it was to be the end of Leon's systematic education, though he had still to finish secondary school. He had spent the first nine years of his life almost without interruption in Yanovka, and the next seven in Odessa, going back to the farm for most vacations.

His schooling had made no particular impression on him; neither teachers nor fellow students had dented his emotions beyond, perhaps, giving him a foretaste of his 'political attitudes'. He felt himself to be perfectly well equipped, according to a contemporary, for 'real life'.[28]

A quarter of a century later the Odessa *Realschule* dropped the name of St. Paul and put up Trotsky's.

CHAPTER II

The World

BY THE TIME LEON acquired his education, intense argumentation was commonplace in Russia whenever educated people came together. The reform of Tsarism had long since been incubating in the elite. The 'intelligentsia' was, in fact, permeated by the ideas associated with the French Revolution – democracy and Socialism. 'Westernisers', who thought Russia had to learn from Western Europe and 'Slavophiles', who thought she had a lofty and characteristic mission of her own, abounded in the nineteenth century.

Less than twenty years before young Bronstein's birth, in February 1861, some forty-seven million serfs had been freed; the failure to link that emancipation to a satisfactory allocation of land had created a broad arena in which the dynamic growth of Russian capitalism and the concomitant growth of an industrial working-class gave a mighty impetus to the overhauling of Tsarist society.

Russian rebelliousness, hitherto sporadic and inchoate, was transformed into a revolutionary movement led by and practically speaking composed almost exclusively of intellectuals overwhelmingly drawn from the middle and upper classes. It was this segment of the intelligentsia that evolved a messianic thrust – it was to dedicate itself to the overthrow not merely of the government but of the whole of society. For the first time in history a consciously articulated movement aimed at the realisation, through Socialism, of an apocalyptic vision.

This tide of revolutionary emotion consisted of two currents – Populism and Marxism.

Populism was more or less launched by Alexander Herzen

(1812–70). The first of the 'penitent gentry' who suffered on behalf of The People,* Herzen was a writer and agitator. He founded the first revolutionary newspaper, *The Bell,* and his rallying-cry, 'Go to The People!', addressed to students expelled from the universities in the winter of 1861, became the key slogan of the Populist movement.

The notion of Going to The People expressed two distinct emotions. One was starry-eyed love of The People that made one want to serve it: this was, no doubt, essentially a form of slumming. The other component was a determination to *force* The People to live up to its potentialities.

It was, in fact, the obvious incapacity of The People for mass action that made the coterie of frustrated intellectuals in love with The People use violence as a means of galvanising society.

Populism, after its success in assassinating Tsar Alexander II, the emancipator of the serfs, in 1881, and an abortive attempt to kill his son Alexander III in 1887, was shaped into the Socialist-Revolutionary Party, which was to remain a factor in Russian politics until shortly after the 1917 upheaval.

Marxism, which came to Russia a little later than Populism, was its principal and eventually successful rival.

The first translation of Marx's major work, *Capital,* was into Russian (1872); in 1883 the first Russian Marxist organisation, The Liberation of Labour, had been founded by a convert to Marxism from Populism, George Plekhanov, the 'father of Russian Marxism', together with Vera Zasulich, Paul Axelrod, and Lev Deutsch.

As Leon grew into adolescence The Revolution was becoming a major preoccupation of questing, educated youth. By 1896 there had been large-scale strikes; political views had been proliferating and diversifying. The Revolution was being thought about in different ways. Some future associates of young Leon, themselves only in their mid-twenties – Lenin, Martov – were in gaol at this time; they were soon to be banished to Siberia.

Leon was more or less a stranger by now to his parents; in that summer of 1896 he was, in addition, particularly out of sorts. The Revolution, as yet a little shapeless, began to seem attractive.

His father wanted him to become an engineer. There was endless bickering about the young man's career: Bronstein, opposed to pure mathematics and to The Revolution equally, must have thought the

latter a particularly grotesque notion: like well-to-do farmers
*Certain phrases, such as 'The People', 'The Revolution' etc., will retain initial capitals whenever they are meant to represent Ideas.

generally and like most of the settled Jewish community, he was thoroughly conservative.

But of course the output of dissident adolescents was high, and amongst the Jews, especially the children of the well-to-do, there was a disproportionately large number.

Most Jews in the Tsarist Empire – the largest Jewish community in history, with about five million concentrated in the areas absorbed by Tsardom after the partition of Lithuania and Poland – were quite aloof from politics. About half were in small businesses; another thirty per cent or so eked out livings as craftsmen and mechanics; the proportion of farmers was tiny.

Yet the high percentage of Jewish craftsmen and mechanics, characteristically open to new ideas, meant that the Jews were permeated by these ideas before any other community in Russia, except for the Russian intelligentsia itself, with so many roots in the aristocracy. Consequently, it was the Jewish craftsmen and mechanics who provided the initial impulse to the organisation of the masses, first among their own people and later among the Russian workers and even peasants. In fact, the big Jewish revolutionary organisation, known as the *Bund* (the Jewish General Workers' Union of Poland and Lithuania) was in the curious, well-nigh unique position among revolutionary organisations of actually having some workmen in its leadership.

On the other hand, the Jewish intellectuals and workmen were far from typical: the majority of the Jewish community was more or less solidly embedded in traditional Judaism.

It is true that tradition itself was being rapidly eroded. The Napoleonic conquests at the beginning of the nineteenth century had scattered the ideas of the French Revolution far and wide. For the first time in centuries the Ghetto was battered: in Western Europe the Jews began trickling out; in Eastern Europe the Judaism that had been feeding more or less on itself within the Jewish enclosure was being substantially eaten into by secular influences filtering in from the West in general and from emancipated Western European Jewry in particular.

Amongst the tendencies that were fragmenting the Jewish community, apart from all those committed to one version or another of The Revolution, the major two revolved around the 'Enlightenment' movement – aimed at the retention, through modernisation, of traditional Judaism – and Zionism – aimed at the restoration of a Jewish state in the 'Promised Land' of Palestine.

None of these new ideas touched Leon's immediate family. His father was simply a landowner whose conservatism was buttressed by the toil he had put into establishing himself. There was no question in his mind of any indulgence toward the 'alienation' of young Jewish adolescents; when he found one in his own family – moreover, alas! the only talented son he had – it was merely a source of pain.

It was, in fact, a classic situation. When Leon came back to the farm after graduating from secondary school, mouthing 'hazy democratic ideas', his father pricked up his ears and said with hostility: 'That's not going to happen even in three hundred years.'[1]

Leon had been going back to the family farm every summer, and sometimes during the Christmas and Easter holidays, ever since leaving it for school in Odessa. By the middle of his adolescence it was plain that he was something of a misfit in farm life. The seven years he had spent living with the Spentsers and going to the Odessa Realschule had come to an end. He was a little over sixteen and a half.

His father now thought it prudent to send Leon away from Odessa altogether, and to have him go to a secondary school in the Black Sea port of Nikolayev, where he himself had his wholesale agent for the international wheat trade and where his gifted son would be closer to the farm.

Thus, in the summer of 1896, Leon went to Nikolayev for the last year of his secondary education. He settled down in the small community; the acquaintances he had made at the Spentsers' swiftly receded into the past.

The small size of the town made it a haven for some Socialists now legally back from Siberia, where they had been exiled as members of a former Populist organisation, The People's Will. In Nikolayev 'radical' talk was commonplace.

This year was the critical year of Leon's life: 'It confronted me with the question of my place in human society.'[2]

Leon picked a boarding-house whose owner, to her great concern, had a number of Socialist children. Somewhat their junior, Leon found himself in the midst of political argumentation whose starting-point was Socialism in its Populist version.

Leon was at first hostile to the new theories. For some months he stood up for his *own* ideas, picking holes in the Populist theories of the boarding-house family.

It was doubtless only natural for his polemical verve to withstand any well-informed theory that was not his own. 'At first I showed decisive resistance in discussion to the "Socialist Utopias".' He would, he says, play the part of a 'sceptic who had passed through all that' and respond to political questions 'in a tone of ironic superiority'.

The pattern is, of course, classic, to be found in St. Paul's 'kicking against the pricks' on the eve of his own conversion, and more appropriately, perhaps, in Karl Marx's initial revulsion against Socialist theory.

In the autumn of 1896, after his first immersion in the intellectual ferment of Nikolayev, Leon went back to the family farm for the last time. He was by now getting into constant arguments about general ideas with his strong-willed father. At the moment a 'brief truce', as the adult Trotsky recalled, was in effect. In spite of this a scene took place whenever the question came up, as it was bound to, about what the boy was to do – to become an engineer or, as he now thought, a revolutionist of some kind. The scenes were violent : everyone was dejected about the future of the former 'star pupil' : his older sister Liza sat about weeping softly; the household sagged.

A way out of this impasse was thought of : Leon was to go back to Odessa with another relative, an uncle – otherwise unmentioned – who was an engineer and owned a factory there. The idea was that in the neighbourhood of a big university Leon might do something practical about studying engineering or mathematics.

The optimistic uncle, himself a former 'liberal', had thought he could make Leon see reason. They 'argued about profit and surplus profit. My uncle was stronger in making profits than in explaining them. My registration in the mathematical faculty kept being put off. I lived in Odessa and kept looking. For what? Primarily myself.'[3]

He took the last autumn ship back to Nikolayev, where he was soon arguing his head off again. This time he quickly succumbed to his new milieu :

> The ideas being carried about in the air were stronger than I, all the more so since at the bottom of my soul I wanted nothing so much as to submit to them. I rejected my pose of conservatism and veered left with an impetuousness that frightened away some of my new friends. 'Well,' said the landlady, 'I see that pointing you out to my children as an example was a waste of time.'[4]

Young Bronstein kept on attending the local secondary school, in which despite his indifference to his studies he shone with ease. He spent his time chatting with comrades and restlessly lounging about the seaport town.

Finally his life took on a new shape: a school-mate introduced him to a sort of talking-club in the garden of the school-mate's older brother, a Czech by the name of Franz Shvigovsky, in the late autumn or early winter of 1896.

Shvigovsky was a workman who had become a gardener to make a living. In him young Bronstein saw 'for the first time a workman who took in newspapers, read German, and could freely participate in the arguments between Marxists and Populists.'[5]

In the garden-salon, in fact, everything under the sun was discussed, mainly, of course, politics, which in the Russia of those days took in an endless variety. Shvigovsky himself was a source of outlawed books and of foreign newspapers; an enthusiastic Populist and anti-Marxist himself, he was full of tales of the People's Will.

Shvigovsky was described by a member of the youthful circle as belonging 'to that category of radiant people for whom you willy-nilly feel a deep attraction at the first encounter, as though you had been a friend for a very, very long time.'[6]

It was no surprise that young people flocked to a little shack in his garden that served as a focus for all sorts of talk, primarily about politics – there were endless heated arguments about whether Russia was doomed to pass through capitalism or might be able to follow a path of its own.

Broadly speaking, those who thought capitalism inevitable were Marxists; those who thought Russia might be able to bypass capitalism altogether were Populists.

The meetings in the little garden were as innocent as could be: it really was nothing but a talking-club with no thought of 'overthrow' or indeed of action of any kind, though the Gendarmerie, rather short-sighted, watched it with great suspicion.

The routine of a school, tranquillising for so many young people, had become unsatisfying. Leon was restlessly casting about for a way of his own:

Questions of personal morality ... brushed by me during a period when 'self-perfection' appeared to me to be not so much an intellectual tendency as an organic need of my spiritual growth. But this 'self-perfection' collided straightway with the question of a 'world-view' that in its turn led to a fundamental alternative – Populism or Marxism. This struggle of tendencies took hold of me

with a delay of not more than a few years in relation to the general
intellectual switch in the country. . . . I moved into this first cross-
roads on my path very little prepared politically, even for the
seventeen-year-old I was at the time. Too many questions were
presented to me all at once, heedless of the requisite order or
coherence. I thrashed about. What can be said with certainty is
this: life had already deposited in my consciousness a serious
reservoir of social protest. What did it consist of? Of compassion
for the downtrodden and of indignation at injustice. Perhaps the
latter feeling was the more powerful. . . .[7]

It was the end of Leon's youthful docility. He simply abandoned
his studies altogether; he was in fact visited by a courteous school
inspector, who on seeing that Leon's lodgings were tidy and clean
went away again, unaware of 'some illegal pamphlets lying under
my mattress'.[8]

During this seventeenth year of his life Leon picked up and
discarded a variety of ideas. He plunged into John Stuart Mill's
Logic, but came up again breathless before even reading halfway
and reached for something else. Then he plunged into Jeremy
Bentham. For several months he 'felt himself to be an unshakable
Benthamite': 'utilitarianism seemed to me the last word in human
thought.'[9]

He was looking for 'general theories', perhaps a 'system of ideas'.
There is, of course, something attractive about 'systems' that
explain everything. In adolescents, coming into a world whose
suggestion of complexity has only just been burgeoning into full
flower and that is plainly at odds, moreover, with the ideal constructions imbibed at school, the search for system can be agonising.

Those whose rebellion against their background is coupled with a
disposition that can infuse abstract ideas with emotions are particularly susceptible to the tug of systems, and particularly tormented as
they seek to implant their own new-found identity within a rounded-
off intellectual structure that will keep it propped up.

As a rationalist adolescent, consequently, Leon desperately
needed a system. At the same time, he was still hostile to Marxism –
that was too systematic!

He flung himself on the daily press: the great Moscow liberal
newspaper, The Russian News (Russkiye Vedomosti), was gone
through with a fine tooth-comb. It gave him his first glimpse of
Western European parliamentary life. In 1929 Trotsky could still

recall the account of the reply flung by a young activist at the heads
of the police entering a parliamentary building: 'I represent thirty
thousand workers and peasants of Galicia – who will dare touch
me?'[10]

Relations with his family deteriorated pell-mell during the year.
The older Bronstein, on one of his trips to Nikolayev to sell wheat,
found out about Leon's friends, with whom he was spending the
time he was supposed to be at school: he still had, after all, another
year before the university.

The ensuing scenes were tempestuous: his father gave him an
ultimatum. Leon left the boarding-houses which his father had been
paying for, and settled in with Shvigovsky, who had meanwhile
moved to a bigger garden with a bigger shack. Leon and five other
boys set up what they called a 'commune'.

For middle-class boys the Commune was a thrilling experience.
They had no proper clothes, or for that matter sheets for their beds;
they lived on strange stews made of vegetables from the garden,
sometimes fortified by cheap meat. Leon did some tutoring; the
other members of the 'commune' scraped together small sums in
various ways. A great deal of reading was done; the evening babble
in the hut was more turbulent than ever. 'We wore blue blouses,
round straw hats, and carried black canes. In town it was thought we
belonged to some secret sect. We read chaotically, looked into the
future passionately and in our own way we were happy.'[11]

Nevertheless some action gradually took shape. For instance,
when the Populist periodical *The New Word* (*Novoye Slovo*) was
taken over by Marxists – becoming the first legal Marxist periodical
in the country – Leon not only complained to the library about
stocking it, but wanted to write an indignant protest to the editors
of *The Russian News* informing them that the 'whole intellectual
and working-class masses are indignant about this reversal'. He tried
to persuade a friend to add his signature to this protest, but the
friend expressed his 'natural astonishment': '*What* intellectual and
working-class masses? At most there'll be three or four signatures,
and of these not a single worker's.' To which Leon said with
composure, 'That doesn't matter – we'll say we have thousands
anyhow.'[12]

When membership fees for a local library were raised from five to
six roubles a year, the garden-commune engaged in a political
manoeuvre. They packed the general meeting of library members
with 'radical' members, many of whom not only lacked six roubles,

but were under-age to boot, and outvoted the upper-class members
– 'officials, teachers, liberal landlords, and naval officers'. The
'democracy' won; the five-rouble fee was restored and the garden-
commune had itself elected to a new board.[13]

On Shvigovsky's initiative the young communards also founded a
'society' to get 'useful books to the people'. Leon was supposed to
help organise the 'society' to buy cheap popular pamphlets and
distribute them among the peasants: he leaped at the chance. The
society funds consisted of the meagre contributions from visitors to
the salon; the organisation, even though the pamphlets were all
legal, had to be kept very secret because of police surveillance. In
the event the Nikolayev gendarmes were to prove notably indolent,
and no more experienced than the youthful incendiaries.

This confined the activities of the small society still further;
finally, the operation proved too cramping for Leon's overflowing
energies. Yet as long as he remained a Populist there was nothing
else for him to do in Nikolayev.

He began edging away from Populism, wavering for some time
between Populism and Marxism.

For the time being the great problem was just whom to get the
pamphlets to. For the young Populists in the Commune 'The People'
naturally meant the peasantry – the majority of the population. But
where could they find a peasant who would accept the pamphlets?
Or, for that matter, who could read one?

Finally, they did come across one. Shvigovsky, up to his ears in
the activities of the little commune, had to hire a labourer and an
apprentice. The boys, overjoyed, pounced on these bona-fide representatives of The People. Indeed, since they were labourers, the
students and Franz had the option of considering them workers *too*;
in any case they were The People. The older one was especially
helpful; he asked them inflammatory questions of all kinds, about
methods of organisation, agitation, violence, plots – Revolution.

The boys did their best to answer. They read through everything
they could to help out their potential revolutionist. He, as it turned
out, was even more helpful to the local police chief. A dossier was, in
fact, rapidly built up for use against the budding rebels. The
labourer also did his own recruiting: the apprentice, too, was soon
working for the police.

Brimming over with reading, the boys started something they
called the 'Universal Knowledge Association'. Leon, in charge of
'sociology', was supposed to give a course of public lectures. His
erudition held out for two.

One of the lecturers at this impromptu university was another Jewish boy, Ilya Sokolovsky, the elder of two brothers in the Commune. He and Leon decided to write a play: they moved out of the Commune into a secret hideaway. The play was filled with social tendency and the clash of generations. The adult Trotsky recalls that though it was supposed to be Populist in out-look, the Populist hero turned out to be terribly boring, whereas the Marxist villains evolved into figures full of 'merriment, freshness and hopefulness. . . . Such was the power of the times!'[14]

Romance found expression when the revolutionary of the older generation, beaten by life, fell in love with a Marxist who responded with a merciless speech on the collapse of Populism.

The play was never finished. The young writers cooled to the central theme too quickly and abandoned the whole thing, together with their hideaway. As Trotsky was to say later, it was plain that 'in the intellectual circles' he moved in 'no one did any actual revolutionary work'. The discussions in the salon were separated by a 'vast gulf' from revolutionary organisation.

Gregory Ziv, a medical student who met Leon during the Christmas holidays of 1896 and became very friendly with him, reports that 'his abilities and his talent' had already made him the outstanding figure in the milieu.[15]

Leon's feelings were intense, yet at the same time diffuse. Though ill-at-ease with Populism, he was still repelled by precisely the element in Marxism that was later to inflame him – its 'system'. Shvigovsky was a knowledgeable anti-Marxist: he had read, he claimed, some of the 'Marxist classics', which by the end of the nineteenth century constituted a vast field. Leon found his anti-Marxism reassuring.

It was in these lively arguments in the garden-salon that young Bronstein first displayed his articulateness: he had a remarkably sarcastic tongue and a gift for debate. Describing Leon's singular glibness and, above all, his talent for 'logic', Ziv points out, on the basis of the boy's life in a provincial town as a secondary-school pupil, that he was simply incapable 'physically' of acquiring much information, especially about 'social questions'. Yet he was able, in argument, to obliterate people who knew far more. Never attracted by the laborious toil required to learn facts, Leon would take 'the most ardent part in all the arguments in Franz's "salon" literally without having read a single book either of the Populists, whom he was one of, or of the Marxists, whom he was fighting with such ferocity.' His 'brilliant memory' enabled him to snatch up the arguments of both his partisans and his adversaries, swiftly assimilate whatever he needed, and then and there present his listeners with a gifted improvisation: 'the gaps in his knowledge were filled by the firm cement of an invincible "logic".'[16]

Leon never bothered to read anything about logic either, except for Schopenhauer's well-known essay on the art of debating. This short essay gives rules for winning a debate regardless of whether one is in the right or not. In his usual tersely cynical way, Schopenhauer merely shows the moves that debaters in fact resort to for the purpose of winning, then gives his own rebuttal at the end of each paragraph.

Leon thought the book marvellous: the charm of Schopenhauer's presentation was far greater for him, says Ziv, than any number of scientific works.

Max Eastman, who saw a good deal of the adult Trotsky, confirms this estimate of Ziv's: 'like richly intellectual people who can think quickly [Leon] had a wonderful gift of bluff. He could catch so quickly the drift of an opponent's thought, with all its ... implications, that it was very difficult to overwhelm him with mere knowledge.'[17]

Though the little garden-salon throbbed with dissidence, there were no Marxists present – except for Alexandra Sokolovsky. She was much older than the others, 'at least ten years older than Leon';[18] she had been warned about Leon: his gifts were dangerous – his nimble mind, gift of the gab, and especially his knack for acid, crushing 'repartee'.

To Leon at the time, Marxism, precisely because of its claims to method and science, seemed peculiarly arid; Populism, with the romantic aura that clung to its conspiratorial heroes, each with bombs and dynamite, had an irresistible glow. In Shvigovsky's garden the great names of The People's Will were 'not heroes of legend, but living people who had been met face to face if not by these former exiles themselves then by their older friends. I had the feeling that I was a small link being inserted into a great chain.'[19]

Alexandra was bound to meet Leon. The Czech's garden was in fact the only place in Nikolayev where 'real' talk could be heard; as a Marxist she was certain to seek that out. Her two brothers, friends of Leon's and also Populists, praised him to the skies; they were looking forward to a duel.

For lack of other company, Alexandra had plunged into the maelstrom of talk in the garden. With the exception of Ziv, who lent her a hand during vacations, she singlehandedly defended Marx against the taunts of this immature Populist coterie.

Leon had also been readying himself for his 'polemics' with the much older girl. He did this much as he equipped himself during his reading when he had made lists of fine phrases, recondite allusions, and nuggets of fact to work over for effective presentation.

Later on it was to become evident that Leon's self-assurance was being eroded during these arguments. His relentlessness at the time must have been merely apparent, especially since, in view of what happened later, we are bound to assume some kindling of sexual attraction.

Both his temperament and the imminence of his conversion were highlighted at a New Year's Eve Party in December 1896.

Leon made a solemn declaration to Alexandra: he had become a Marxist! Hitherto alone in the garden-salon, she now had a formidable champion: she was overjoyed.

But when the moment came for the conventional political toasts, Leon abruptly produced a denunciation of Marxism. Ziv says it was incredibly vulgar, even obscene; in addition, Leon aimed the most ferociously disagreeable remarks at Alexandra herself as a Marxist, and he ended, 'A curse on all Marxists, and on all those who want to bring hardness and dryness into all life's relationships!'

It was plain that the sole purpose of the attack was 'to humiliate and to sting Alexandra as painfully as possible'.

Everyone was upset. Alexandra rushed off, boiling with indignation: 'I shall never, never touch hands with that boy!' she told the friend who had brought her there.[20]

These traits of young Bronstein's were, of course, obvious to the young people who knew him, but his gifts were so outstanding that his ferocity, feared that it was by opponents, was discounted:

In view of his manifest superiority to all of them and of his obvious talents, the disagreeable experiences they were subjected to were quickly forgotten; such small moral shortcomings were easily forgiven, friendly relations were maintained. The same thing happened with this little scene at the New Year's Eve Party: it was quickly forgotten by all the members of Franz's 'salon', including Alexandra; forgotten to such an extent that between her and Bronstein there swiftly arose the tenderest feelings.[21]

During this crucial segment of the critical year of 1896-7, while

Leon was being swiftly and as it were subterraneanly transformed
into his later incarnation, the conversations in Shvigovsky's salon,
while unflagging, did not have much practical significance. Nothing
was as yet being done. Though the Gendarmerie kept the salon
under surveillance it was a matter of routine, hardly to be taken
seriously.

Essentially, at this time, the talk was talk and nothing else, or
rather the talk can be seen, in retrospect, to have been a kind of
sorting out process that defined, gradually, just what it was that the
young people were looking for. Such talk-fests are, of course,
commonplace wherever intellectual adolescents meet; the difference
was that in the Russia of this period they were to give rise to
something more.

What is perhaps most striking about the profundity of Leon's
imminent conversion was the precision of the dovetailing between
his talents and his *métier*. The aptitude of his that so impressed his
contemporaries, both then and later, his gift for 'repartee', was made
to order for Marxist argumentation even more than for argument in
general. Just as he had veered away from his adolescent conservatism to take up Socialism in the form of Populism, so he was
now to veer away from his adolescent Populism and take up Socialism in the form of Marxism. His attitude to both Populism and
Marxism, in fact, was characteristic: he could learn from the give-
and-take of conversation far more readily than from study. His
'dialectical' ability was just this gift for the improvisation of an
argument, the development of a cutting edge to his talk.

Before his adolescent restlessness began in earnest, Leon's school
career had, in fact, been based on his personal brilliance. In spite of
the growing neglect of his studies he remained at the head of his
class in the Nikolayev secondary school simply because of his
brainpower – he could take everything in without the smallest effort.
Since at the time he also even lacked any interest in the sciences that
were supposed to be the secondary school's speciality, his continued
attendance until the summer of 1897 was, in fact, something of a
mystery.

Ziv explains it by inertia; since Leon had been put in school as a
small boy by his father, he simply went on going to classes. Ziv also
thought that 'it was necessary for him as water is for a fish' to
demonstrate his superiority to others: he may have had a taste for
mathematics because it was so akin to his beloved 'logic', for with
the help of mathematics, as well as of this particular 'logic' of his, he

could arrive at a semblance of truth by the power of his own mind, without wasting any time on the laborious acquisition of information. Through his own complex and skilful combinations of ideas he could not only arrive at a semblance of truth but exercise a persuasive influence over others.[22]

It is doubtless natural for energetic adolescents to funnel their rebelliousness against their immediate backgrounds – family and social – on to abstractions. To youthful rationalists it must seem that the world is there primarily in order to conform with their rationalism; when emotions infuse those abstractions a special dynamism is achieved; when they involve social change, entailing a fusion of knowledge plus power – the Marxist claim par excellence – an enthralling intellectual entity comes into being.

The idea represented by Marxism was all the more powerful since, in spite of its seeming to deal with social phenomena in a concrete way, it had organised those phenomena into an emotionally compelling schema with the added claim of being scientific and logical.

Marxism, moreover, has always exercised a special attraction because of its fusion of two potent devices.

On the one hand it concerns itself with everything, literally the whole world. Marx himself, to be sure, had been relatively modest in such matters, and did not extend his general ideas literally everywhere, even though he might have maintained that he could in fact do so, Engels, versatile journalist, had blithely undertaken to encompass the universe.

In any case the Marxist 'system', by the time it filtered down to the rank and file intelligentsia in Central Europe and Russia, constituted very nearly a full-scale organisation of values, facts and information that had the rounded-off quality of a religion; it gave all answers to all questions.

Thus when young Bronstein reviewed his ideas about such traditional occupations of young men as Life, Death and so on, it was quite natural for him to expect Marxism to provide him with enough pigeon-holes for all observable phenomena to be stuffed into, neatly docketed and numbered under the heading of 'Answers'.

The other device of Marxism, one that especially recommended itself to young Bronstein as he became aware of his special gifts – nimbleness, verbal facility, wit, high temperament, violence in language – has a marvellous simplicity.

The Dialectic has a built-in pivotality easily switched in any direction. With its technique of breakdown and recombination revolving around the thesis, its contradiction, the antithesis, and its consummation in a 'higher' form, the synthesis, it can be applied to all things, small and large.

The Dialectic was tailor-made for young Bronstein's gifts. If he had been able to stun his contemporaries in Franz's garden by the power of his 'logic' alone, he was soon to be able, after a relatively small amount of reading, to talk about everything. Moreover, since he was so intelligent, what he wrote was bound to sound intelligent. The Dialectic thus constituted a sort of frame for the Universe; as his erudition expanded he could fill in the framework more and more.

It was to be as easy for young Bronstein to make his mark on a Marxist coterie as on a Populist one – indeed, even easier, in a way, since the gimmick of the Dialectic, invested in the broad and simple outlines of Marxism in so far as it constitutes a system, gives more spring, bite and tension to the style, both written and spoken, and enables anyone with a gift for repartee to have at his disposal an instrument of trenchant rhetoric – precision-made to satisfy young Bronstein's early-expressed longing for a 'law beyond the facts'.

His gifts were now to be applied: Marxism, beginning to germinate throughout the Russian intelligentsia and gradually supplanting Populism, was superimposed in Russian conditions.

Marx's views had been tailored to the industrial West, primarily Great Britain and France, and to a lesser extent Germany. Still, by the time his theories became fashionable, toward the end of the nineteenth century, the industrial revolution had made such strides throughout Europe, including Tsarist Russia, that it had become a simple matter to manipulate Marxism for action almost anywhere.

The original theory, as outlined a little roughly by Marx and Engels when they were in their twenties, was broadly as follows.

The motor of historical progress was the technological development of the forces of production, which had already brought about the transition from feudalism to capitalism, and which were supposed to go on expanding so that ultimately – indeed, very soon, in the minds of the youthful team – they would become too powerful for the old 'husk' of capitalism.

When this happened the 'husk' would be 'burst asunder' by The Proletariat that had developed concomitantly with the development of 'bourgeois' society. The Proletariat was destined to spearhead the transition to the economy of abundance that Socialism was to bring about by properly utilising and extending the technological possibilities already developed under capitalism.

This general motor of historical progress was geared to a smaller motor, the economic structure of society itself. There the primacy of economics in the human condition as a whole implied, with respect to the capitalist 'system', that 'bourgeois society' was going to be polarised by the falling rate of profit into two camps. A smaller and smaller group of exploiters would get richer and richer and a bigger and bigger majority of society would get poorer and poorer.

The falling rate of profit and other inherent features of capitalism were supposed to *force* the exploiters – regardless of their wishes, their possible goodwill, and so on – to squeeze the increasingly large mass of the exploited manual workers so that they would finally, in sheer despair, explode in a revolutionary upheaval.

This schema was the general framework of the Marxist view of industrial society, which was of course far more advanced in Western Europe and, by the end of the nineteenth century, in the United States than in Russia. 'Logically', therefore – from the point of view of just this general forecast – The Revolution should break out in the West, where The Proletariat of the most advanced bourgeois nations would, very naturally, be the most revolutionary, since it was assumed that 'class-consciousness', or the self-awareness of The Proletariat as well as its despair, would grow together with the growth of The Proletariat itself.

At the same time, it was understood that the true leadership of The Proletariat was bound to come from the intelligentsia, that is, from 'Philosophy', in Marx's Hegel-drenched view, and from the Marxist-oriented political parties later on.

Since Marxism was regarded as 'scientific' – in harmony with the fashionable criterion of the nineteenth century and later – it was possible to treat its predictions as though they were already, in a way, facts. Discussions could accordingly be carried on not merely with a view to *bettering* society in some ideal direction, but as though a state of affairs had *already* been attained that could then be conformed with by all those in possession of the Great Key of Marxism.

For purposes of argument, a non-existent state of affairs could be taken as a starting-point. Debaters would tacitly take for granted that such a society was already *there* and crush each other with arguments derived from unavowed postulates. This applied, of course, to all forms of Socialism, but it applied to Marxism with special potency because of its claims to 'scientific' infallibility.

What was scarcely noticed, during the passionate argumentation that led people into the revolutionary movement, was precisely the role of the debaters. What material interests were these young idealists pursuing?

Young Bronstein first made his mark on a milieu of youthful middle-class Jews in rebellion against their family background and, by extension, against Society in the abstract. Their feelings of rebellion, as was only natural for ardently idealistic young people, were expressed through a mixture of ideas and moral passion.

But if The Revolution was supposed to come about when the industrial working class, its self-consciousness ripened by maddening conditions, erupted, what was the role of the middle-class intellectuals?

As we read the adult Trotsky's flat statement that 'the impulse originated within us', we perceive a crucial enigma – the relation between the individual idealist and historical events.

At the time, the 'impulse' seemed such a matter of course that there was no need to discuss it. Just as Leon gravitated, out of compassion, to the down-trodden ordinary people, so he later moved into the organisation of workers out of a desire to rectify injustice. It goes without saying that in both cases the needs of his own ego also required satisfaction.

But 'Bettering the People' against the background of a general idea plainly entailed a mystical communion with that idea. When as a young Marxist Leon went on to Better the People by guiding the forces of society in accordance with the Marxist prescription, he was still identifying himself wholeheartedly with a general idea.

Thus his own case illustrated the key element in the shaping of The Revolution. It was clear, on the basis of theory, that the working class had to do *something*: after all, they had to make The Revolution. But it was equally clear that the workers, unfortunately, were unaware of this. They did not know the theory; intellectuals had to tell them.

Yet did that not imply that the leadership of The Revolution was being taken over by the intellectuals, and not by workers at all?

It implied this only to those outside the theory. Within the theory it was an unconscious action; the intellectuals were in fact identifying themselves with the workers in so far as the workers themselves represented an idea.

For it was the *Idea* of The Proletariat, rather than the flesh-and-blood factory workers – whose attitudes seldom coincided with those of the leadership – that enabled intellectuals to carry out this primordial act of religious transsubstantiation without even noticing it.

On occasion it would be noticed. Karl Marx, too, had had to look around for some proletarians to carry out his Idea about The Proletariat's role in History; he had had to be content with a few artisans instead of factory workers, who had not yet quite come into existence. Marx had got over this hurdle, and for that matter got over his own view of classes as the decisive factor in social change, by simply declaring that Philosophy was to be the leader in this tug of cosmic forces. Given *that* point of view, why should not two middle-class intellectuals like Marx and Engels guide the upsurge of The Proletariat?

In Trotsky's case this semi-conscious identification with The Proletariat, as with The Revolution, was all the easier because of his natural gift for abstract analysis and rhetoric. The very real difficulties that were to crop up in connection with this interaction between the Idea and its Agency could be ignored for the time being because of the unconscious nature of this identification.

Meanwhile, young Bronstein, ardently enthusiastic on behalf of general reform, was about to shift into its implementation.

In the spring of 1897, when Ziv came back again to Nikolayev during the Easter vacation, the first thing he did was to go to Shvigovsky's garden. There he found Leon, just seventeen and a half.

The garden had grown far too small for him. Impatient, somewhat bored with the narrow and frustrating activities of the Populists in the garden but unwilling to 'declare himself' for Marxism, he had found a halfway stage.

His specific initiative was generated by the riots that broke out in the university towns because of the self-immolation of a woman student in the Peter-Paul Fortress in St. Petersburg. This helped crystallise the turbulence among the intellectuals that had begun in 1896 following the mass strikes of the Petersburg weavers.

The adult Trotsky recalls the event:

I was walking the street with the youngest member of our Commune, Gregory Sokolovsky, a youth of about my own age.
I said, 'We too have to start in, after all.'

'We have to start in,' answered Sokolovsky. 'But how?'

'That's just it – how? We have to find workers, not wait for any-one, not ask anyone, but find workers and start in.'

'I think we can find them,' said Sokolovsky. 'I knew a watchman on the boulevard here, a Bible student. I'll look him up.'[23]

And off he went.

The Bible sectarian Sokolovsky was looking for had moved, but he was put on to someone else from the same sect who in his turn presented him to other members. In one day, in fact, young Soko-lovsky got to know a number of workers, via the acquaintances of a woman he didn't know. He came back from his investigation 'his eyes glowing – these people are real people!'

Back in the garden young Bronstein and young Sokolovsky spread the word: contact with the workers had been established!

The next day five or six of them were sitting around a tavern. Mukhin, an electrician who was to become prominent in young Bronstein's new life, was explaining himself behind a screen of deafening sound from the automatic music machine.

A thin man with a pointed beard and a wily but apprehensive look, he watched me, screwing up his left eye and amiably looking over my beardless face.

'For me the Gospels are like a peg. I begin with religion, but switch over to life. The other day I was showing the whole truth with beans.'

'How d'you mean, beans?'

'Very simple: I lay a bean on the table – that's the Tsar; around it I lay down some more beans – those are ministers, bishops, generals; then there are the gentry and the merchants over there; and over here, in a heap, there are the ordinary people. Now I ask: "Where's the Tsar?"' He pointed to the centre 'Where are the ministers?' He pointed to those around about. 'Now just guess.'

Mukhin closed his left eye altogether and paused. 'Then I jumble all those beans up together. "Well, now," I said, "and where's the Tsar now? And the ministers? You can't tell them apart now." And that's how it should be – all the beans should be jumbled up.'

Listening to Mukhin I was sweating with ecstasy. This was the

real thing, and we had just been exercising our wits, guessing and
waiting about. . . .

'But how to jumble them up, damn them, that's the question. . . .'

From that day on we flung ourselves headlong into work.[24]

In Russia religious sectarianism was a recognised form of protest,
generally of a very mild kind : like most such Primitive Christian
sects the opposition to the *status quo* took the religious form of going
beyond the vast, heavily encrusted edifice of official religion, 'back to
the beginning' when things were simple, moral – *good*. An indi-
genous Russian outgrowth rather parallel to early Protestantism, it
provided the adolescent rebels with enough of a foothold to begin
their broad-scale campaign of conversion. The sectarians might be
pious, but they were workers.

One of the difficulties was that their dissidence had nothing
whatever to do with 'conditions'; it was rather an outcry against the
human condition as such; they longed for enlightenment, true knowledge, true justice. They took the young Jewish students in their
stride – why not reform society altogether?

The Sokolovsky family, with its contribution of four spearheaded
by the Marxist veteran Alexandra, was the biggest single contingent;
young Bronstein was the driving-force. Under his leadership the new
movement was in full swing when Ziv returned to Nikolayev;
he was approached secretly by him and asked to join the working-
class 'union' young Bronstein intended to organise.

Young Bronstein was, in fact, discarding his former somewhat
blurry Socialism, though for a while he did not feel like saying as
much. This reluctance made him want to avoid *calling* his new
organisation 'Social-Democratic' – a logical name, as Ziv thought –
and he proposed 'South Russian Workers' Union' for it instead.

The young leaders – the younger Sokolovsky, Alexandra, some of
the Communards, Ziv – became intimate, calling each other 'thou';
to show their friendship they defied the most elementary rule of
conspiracy and had their picture taken together (it was later to put
them all in jail).

Young Bronstein dressed with 'simplicity'; he sneered at Ziv's own
ordinary European-style dress (cuffs, necktie, and so on) as mere
decadence, indeed an offence against 'revolutionary purity'.[25] What
he retained from his recent Populist past was an inclination to just
this ostentatious simplicity. Now that he was head-over-heels in the
work of the organisation, he regarded 'with suspicion everyone who,

as it seemed to him, did not display the right amount of devotion to the cause'. In giving Ziv, whom he was by now intimate with, a copy of the collective photograph, he signed it: 'Faith without works is dead.' This was a signal of contempt for Ziv's determination to get his medical degree; to young Bronstein this was in and for itself a 'betrayal' of The Revolution.

In this intimate little group, absorbed in the work that young Bronstein flung himself into with his characteristic elan, there was no longer the smallest question of Populism.

Leon 'had forgotten all about his recent protest to the library; all about his recent demonstration – with his habitual, as it seemed to himself "iron" logic – of the utter impossibility of capitalism in Russia ... forgotten with an ease that was downright stupefying.'[26]

Young Bronstein was, in fact, 'through' with Populism, but he was still reluctant to take the plunge into Marxist systematics. Only very occasionally in 'intimate talks' with Ziv, would he justify this obvious contradiction by trying to get Ziv to agree that it was possible to be a Social-Democrat without subscribing to Marxism: he was still staving off complete conversion.

Ziv was sure that at this time, and indeed later, Leon really had no plans for The Revolution: he was far too taken up with his own role in it. Ziv thought it must have been this narcissistic view of himself that prevented his being troubled too much by the merely logical contradiction between his theoretical views and his practical activities: it enabled him to remain a Populist theoretically while practically – by organising workers – behaving as a Marxist.

Ziv thought young Bronstein's ambition was already unmistakably inflamed by the success of his organisation: he fancied himself a star of The Revolution whatever form it took.

He told Ziv with pride at this time that the handful of workers he had managed to get in touch with did not believe his name was Lvov (a pseudonym) but were convinced he was Ferdinand Lassalle himself. Ziv took this to be a wish fathering the thought: after all, such workers would never have heard of Lassalle, who had died thirty years before.[27]

The adult Trotsky recalls this incident of choosing a cover-name: 'this first conspiratorial lie was not easy for me; it was downright agony for me to "deceive" people you were coming together with for such a great and good cause.'[28]

Lassalle had been celebrated primarily as a speaker: it was to be a few years before young Bronstein emerged as perhaps his equal. His debut in public-speaking, which was to become his forte, has been described by Ziv.

They had arranged a little meeting for 'workers'; both were to speak, and they went over what they were going to say. Since they knew so little about anything, there was a substantial risk that their speeches might be identical: luckily they were not.

At his debut as a speaker young Bronstein showed no trace of precocity. Only ten minutes long, his speech was halting and dull. Ziv thought the size of the audience might have depressed the fiery-tempered young man – only ten people! [29]

Eastman gives more details:

> He quoted Gumpliwitz and ... John Stuart Mill ... and got himself so terribly wound up in a sliding network of unintelligible big words and receding hopes of ideas that his audience sat bathed in sympathetic perspiration.... When he finally did stop and the subject was opened for general debate nobody said a word. Nobody knew what the subject was.... Leon walked across the room and threw himself face down in the pillow on the divan. He was soaking with sweat; his shoulders heaved with shame....[30]

The little organisation was so successful in the eyes of its youthful leaders that they all, especially young Bronstein, were soon dizzied by the new perspectives. Their little milieu of relatively advanced sectarians was fertile ground for the dissemination of literature that was, in retrospect, remarkably innocuous. They had a few workers; they looked upon them as prodigies of intelligence; they would repeat their remarks to one another as parents might. To the grown Trotsky many of the more striking figures among his protégés at this time still seemed alive – a carpenter who wore a bowler and had broken with all 'mysticism' long since, and who would say, solemnly, 'I am a ratiolist' (for 'rationalist'). This same carpenter composed a 'Proletarian March' with this beginning: 'We are the alphas and omegas, the beginnings and the endings.' Another worker – a big redhead past his youth – composed in the local patois a poem in honour of the 'Great Prophet Marx'.[31]

As Ziv recalled:

> Our group was the first Social-Democratic organisation in Nikolayev. Our success had heightened our spirits so that we were

in a state of what might be called chronic enthusiasm. And the lion's share of these successes we undoubtedly owed to Bronstein, whose inexhaustible energy, many-sided resourcefulness and tirelessness knew no bounds.[32]

Thus the South Russian Workers' Union, a merger between Primitive Christians and Marxist student novices, came into being.

Young Bronstein had already made contact with the underground milieu of Odessa and some other South Russian cities; small Social-Democratic groups were springing up in many places. Every week he took the night boat to Odessa, where he would spend the day, then take the boat back the next night. He got hold of a veteran underground printing-plant organiser, and even some literature printed abroad that had been smuggled into Russia.

With all the amateurishness later recorded by the adult Trotsky, this was plainly an unusual enterprise, especially when his age is recalled – seventeen and a half.

The fact is that he was now altogether taken up with what was to be his life's vocation. Though not yet a Marxist he was already *committed*.

The South Russian Workers' Union had no schemes for upsetting society. It aimed at improving the moral tone of the workers' lives, at making them more 'cultured'. The leaders would give little lectures on the sciences at their clandestine get-togethers in the forest; they would recite, sing songs, and declaim poetry, often their own. The Communist Manifesto was also read aloud, from a mimeographed copy in very bad condition: this was the main contribution to positive activity.

Their meetings are, in fact, curiously reminiscent of the meetings described by Engels more than a generation earlier, where 'communism' was spread by Engels and Moses Hess by playing harps and reciting Shelley.

The printing techniques already acquired by young Bronstein at his cousin's house were put to use. He made a hectograph pad for offset reproductions; he personally shaped every single printed letter to make its reading as easy as possible for its semi-literate audience; a single page would take him two hours. He would produce about two hundred copies in mauve lettering, much superior to the other illegal underground sheets, which were badly printed and sometimes illegible.

Though young Bronstein's organisation was amateurish, within its limited range it had a rapid success. His handsomely turned out little leaflets seem to have had a certain effect: they were legible, even pretty; the language, all his own, was written with terse eloquence. In addition, they were effective because the bona-fide workmen who were enrolled told young Bronstein about intimate details of the primitive factory life of the region. Thus the leaflets sounded strangely knowledgeable, so that the public – as well as the police! – were given the impression of serious doings.

The organisation was also having a numerical impact: it had about two hundred members. The content of young Bronstein's hectographed leaflets, based on the exposure of factory conditions, even obliged the local police chief to do something about various infractions in the factories. Young Bronstein was enraptured.

He was encouraged, in fact, to get out an actual newspaper, also hectographed with even more of the painstaking concentration he had been devoting to the leaflets. Not only did he go on doing most of the writing, but he also made ingenious combinations of material pinched from the libraries, giving the newspaper *Our Cause* (*Nashe Delo*) a disproportionately mature air.

At the age of seventeen and a half, young Bronstein had provided an organisational, ideological, and propagandistic shape for the simple-minded enthusiasm of the Bible sectarians, which had in its turn provided the young idealists with the impetus they had needed – the awakening of The Masses 'gave the intelligentsia elan', as the adult Trotsky was to say.[33]

Success had its consequences. The police, at first somewhat incredulously, found themselves drawn in. The little organisation was penetrated by police spies – a fruitful device in all underground organisations. Only a handful were sufficient. The carpenter who had composed a ditty about the Great Prophet Marx was recruited by the police very quickly and spied away. Less than a year later, by the time the third number of *Our Cause* had been distributed, the police were ready to pounce.

In January 1898, when young Bronstein was a couple of months past eighteen, he went to deliver some papers to Shvigovsky: they were arrested together, though Shvigovsky just managed to hide the incriminating papers in the snow. Young Bronstein's younger sister Olga, who had come to warn him, had been trailed by a detective, who for good measure arrested her too. Ziv, identified from the photograph of the four leaders, was arrested on his return from Kazan with his diploma. Alexandra, who had been out of town, came back out of idealism: she did not want the workers to feel abandoned.

Altogether some two hundred people were rounded up and stuffed into the wretched Nikolayev gaol, which among other shortcomings had no way of coping with the 'politicals' that Tsarism was generally rather gentle with and kept quite distinct from common criminals.

In the spring thaws the papers Shvigovsky had hidden came out: they gave the police all they needed. To get Shvigovsky off the hook young Bronstein accepted full responsibility at the hearings. There was no trial: all decisions were made by the police.

Young Bronstein's jail term, his first, ended the torment of doubt about his career. The alternatives of engineering and pure mathematics had been replaced by The Revolution.

In his own eyes gaol brought not the smallest tinge of disgrace. On the contrary, the feeling of being close to History that he had already had as a young Populist was now reinforced; he had undergone the basic rite of initiation. How could you get into The Movement *without* going to gaol? It was a passport to immortality.

His parents took a different view, which they clung to tenaciously until their son became famous a few years later, when they gave up all hope of making him respectable. After that the Bronsteins, outstripped by events in general and more particularly by their son's break with his milieu, were simply the source of the material comforts they could provide him with in prison. For his part, with the curious remoteness, or withdrawal of interest from people he was not involved with in a 'Cause', he paid no attention to his parents at all. Materially in need for many years, Leon merely accepted from them the things he needed – money, food, blankets – without wavering in his detachment.

He was in gaol for a few weeks, sharing a huge chilly room with another young prisoner and sleeping on a straw mat that was removed at six in the morning. Since the room had no furniture, the two boys would sit on the floor huddled up in their clothes around a lukewarm little stove. Then he was put into a solitary cell in another prison in Kherson. There he spent three horrible months, with no soap or water, no change of clothing, his body eaten by lice, with one hunk of bread served for two meals and a miserable stew for dinner. In a way this was far more oppressive – Trotsky had no books and nothing to write with; he was reduced to his own resources.

To pass the time young Bronstein created logical systems – a device that enables intellectual prisoners to withstand the deadening effects of solitary confinement. He reflected on Marxism versus Populism; he even tried to construct a Marxist system out of the little he knew. He had been steadily sliding into Marxism before his arrest, while flashing about with his hectograph machine, but it had irritated him to have to surrender to the views of the much older Alexandra. In gaol, however, he more or less consummated his own conversion: alternating between versification and Marxist or pseudo-Marxist ratiocination, he combined the two by giving the words of a famous peasant song – 'Little Club' – a proletarian *leit-motif* – 'Little Machine'.

One day the gaoler – from whose revolted grimace alone young Bronstein deduced the fetidity of his own aroma – came in with some elements of civilisation sent by his parents – soap, pillow, blanket, tea, sugar, cookies. Soon afterward he was taken away from the primitive Kherson gaol to a splendid new prison in Odessa, the 'last word in technical equipment'.

Though he was also kept in solitary at Odessa, there was no lack of communications. There was, in fact, a constant exchange through the traditional tapping code. In this prison the Tsarist Government recognised 'politicals': young Bronstein was treated humanely and allowed the run of the prison library.

The library was a godsend, but all it contained, unfortunately, was works on theology and history; he became adept at the various arguments that the right-thinking might use against all the enemies of the Russian Orthodox Church – Roman Catholics, Protestants, Tolstoyans, and, especially, Darwinians. It gave him sardonic delight to read the 'codified stupidities of thousands of years' – a description of Paradise, full of details about its structure, would end: 'The precise location of Paradise is not known.'

He bickered incessantly with the warder, a Bible expert. The warder would say: 'Only for one word, one single word, "Christ's mother", instead of "God's mother", the belly of Arius the heretic was burst open.'

'And why are the bellies of heretics today still in shape?' young Bronstein would say thrustfully.

'These are ... these are different times,' the warder would answer, offended.[34]

He records a poignant detail: to see friends and relatives the prisoners were put into 'narrow wooden cages' separated from each other. When his father came to see him, he thought the cage was the permanent cell, and was so upset he could not speak. 'In answer to my questions, he only moved his bloodless lips in silence. Never will I forget his face.'

When his younger sister Olga brought him the New Testament in five languages, he began his linguistic education by the excellent method of reading the same text in different languages; to the little French and German he had learned in school was added some English and Italian. But the adult Trotsky was to recall, rather mournfully, that he never learned a single foreign language well, in spite of his sojourns in various European countries.[35]

Mere snatches of the outside world came through to the Odessa prison. The Dreyfus case, 'then at its climax, gripped us for a time by its drama'; a rumour that the French monarchy had been restored 'filled us with shame'; 'provincials in the full sense of the word, we were inclined to interpret the British war against the Boers mainly from the point of view of the inevitability of the victory of large capital over small.'[36]

The prison was filling up with people arrested with such zeal by the Tsarist gendarmes in the spring of 1898. Young Bronstein, in solitary confinement, announced a momentous experience – he had really turned Marxist at last! Via the endless chain of cell-tappers he got hold of one of Alexandra's brothers, then Ziv, then Shvigovsky: the last was livid; when Alexandra heard she was elated.

In the milieu of The Revolution, 'becoming a Marxist' was the precise equivalent of a religious conversion. It meant leading a certain kind of life, reading, studying, and discussing certain things and not other things in a certain way, frequenting certain people and not others, and – above all – sharing the same world-view, the same 'attitude'. 'Being a Marxist,' in a milieu in which everyone was something or other, was like being in a sect, inside a special enclosure with the 'petty-bourgeois philistines' howling outside.

The conversion had a natural consequence: young Bronstein switched round so completely that he became just as fanatical a devotee of Marxism as he had once been its fanatical adversary.

Some basic books were brought by Olga and by the Spentsers: young Bronstein read Plekhanov's famous essay on the 'Monistic Conception of History', some essays on historical materialism by the Italian Marxist Labriola, and, above all, Darwin, his *Origin of Species* and his *Autobiography*.

Darwin had a shattering effect on him, as indeed he had had on Marx. He wrote years later (to Max Eastman):[37]

Darwin stood for me like a mighty doorkeeper at the entrance to the temple of the universe. I was intoxicated with his minute, precise, conscientious, and at the same time powerful thought. I was the more astonished when I read that he had preserved his belief in God. I absolutely declined to understand how a theory of the origin of species by way of natural and sexual selection and a belief in God could find room in one and the same head.

It is perhaps curious to observe that just as young Bronstein was baffled by Darwin's continuing faith in God despite, as he thought, the evidence of nature, so he never seems to have observed that Darwin's methodology was the direct opposite of Marx's. It is particularly illuminating in connection with his adult recollection of his youthful longing for 'law beyond facts', especially since he re-affirms it for his own philosophy as an adult.

In this respect, too, he doubtless followed Marx, who thought his own 'systematic' approach rectified the shapeless empiricism of the otherwise admirable Darwin.

While young Bronstein had been languishing in his mouldy cell in the Kherson prison there was a meeting in Minsk, on 1 March 1898, of the Russian Social-Democratic Workers' Party. It was hardly a real meeting, consisting as it did of only nine members, most of whom were snatched by the police the moment it was over. Yet it was this abortive session that was enshrined as the very first meeting of the Party that was to have such an effect on Russia. Trotsky, who did not hear about it until later, mentions it in his autobiography with nostalgia.

Leon began his first sustained effort at composition, indeed his first book, while in the model Odessa prison. He had found himself baffled, in his ignorance, by Labriola's 'brilliance': he decided to select a specific subject – Free-Masonry – and use that as a testing-ground for his own view of historical materialism.

He started on the history of the Masons; he filled a notebook with a thousand pages, using the microscopic script developed for the underground to jot down notes and comments. As he completed a given section he would copy it out all over again on thin paper, conveying it to the other prisoners by passing it through a drain or leaving it in a special matchbox in the toilet the prisoners were marched to every morning in a fixed succession. (The stout notebook, taken into exile with him later on, was lost, to his intense regret.)

Ziv's opinion may again be of interest, with respect to the tug of Marxism on young Bronstein. Ziv had a somewhat sceptical assessment of Bronstein's scholarship. Himself convinced that Marxism was scientific, Ziv thought that with its dispassionate analysis of socio-economic forces tugging society in one direction or another it was, in fact, utterly alien to young Bronstein's character, which was preoccupied not with the evolution of social forces, but with his own role in a given historical situation.[38] Hence Ziv was now bowled over by the remarkable perfection of young Bronstein's Marxist phraseology: where on earth could he have read it? When had he had the time? Actually nowhere: he had absorbed it somehow; there it was, full-blown!

Ziv gives a curious account of Bronstein around the age of eighteen.

He thought young Bronstein's major aim in life was simply to be *first*, that all other aspects of his psyche were no more than auxiliary devices. But since he had totally ingested the idea of The Revolution, there was no conflict between The Cause and his own ego – everything that would help The Cause would also expand his own ego.

Hence his parents were just as alien to him as millions of other 'bourgeois' and non-revolutionaries. On behalf of The Cause it was perfectly all right to exploit them. Later on, even when he was more or less self-supporting, his daughters by Alexandra lived with his parents and were supported by them or by others. This was meant to leave him free of family ties, on behalf of The Cause.

Young Bronstein found it quite incomprehensible, for instance, how anyone with even the slightest profession of revolutionary interest could show any concern at all for parents, relatives, or friends. The slightest weakness in this respect was already, in his eyes, a sort of treachery to The Revolution.

Once, for instance, when Alexandra heard of the arrest of an intimate friend, she was very upset: young Bronstein was baffled by this 'sentimentality'. He even told Ziv, straight to his face that despite his liking for him he would remain quite indifferent if Ziv were arrested.

For Ziv young Bronstein had a 'hyper-trophied self-importance', a 'morbid self-esteem' that reflected his boundless egotism. He also thought him remarkably extravagant in his speech, writings and conduct, with a certain kind of pedantry (his 'logic', as Ziv puts it) that showed itself even in his fine, accurate script.

Bronstein would occasionally faint. Later on he was well known for this; he would fall down senseless for a time even during public speeches. Acquaintances explained this as due to a 'cardiac weakness', though to the outer eye Bronstein seemed remarkably healthy, with fantastic energy.

His second wife was to say that 'his nervous tension was often expressed by physical disorders before he got up to speak at meetings.'[39]

Lev Deutsch, a well-known older revolutionary and co-founder of the Liberation of Labour, who was to sponsor young Bronstein and whom Ziv got to know well in New York years later, told Ziv as an established fact that Bronstein's fainting-spells were epileptic. Ziv, a physician, records his agreement.[40]

Trotsky himself dismissed all this as legend or misunderstanding: 'I had inherited from my mother an inclination to fainting-spells when in physical pain or indisposed.'[41]

There seem to be no other data for this disability, whatever it was due to: Trotsky's energies, in any case, with their unflagging output could scarcely be considered compatible with epilepsy.

Until November 1899 young Bronstein remained in the Odessa model prison. Then he learned the results of the inquiry – a sentence of four years in Eastern Siberia. The Sokolovsky brothers and Alexandra were given the same sentence; Ziv got three years.

The greyness of solitary confinement was now replaced by the bustle of imminent departure. Wives and fiancées had special visiting privileges; it was natural for people to get married, bona fide or fictitiously.

Young Bronstein proposed to Alexandra, but since he was only just over twenty, he had to have his father's consent. Bronstein put his foot down: as far as he was concerned, Alexandra was not only a criminal who had misled his innocent son, but far too old to boot. 'Leon stormed and fought with all the energy and stubbornness he was capable of. But the old man was no less stubborn, and since he had the advantage of being on the other side of the bars he came out victorious.'[42] Leon was helpless.

The prisoners were sent to a transfer prison in Moscow, from where they were sent to Siberia as soon as there were enough of them to warrant a convoy. Since the last convoy had just gone off, the prison had to fill up again: this meant a long wait.

Life was now much better. Men were lodged in a big tower room, women in another. Politics could be argued about directly. Young

Bronstein heard the name of Lenin for the first time; in the lively discussion groups consituted by the growing crowd of political prisoners a major work of Lenin's – *The Development of Capitalism in Russia* – was read and discussed; so was the 'revisionism' of Marxism with the German Social-Democratic Eduard Bernstein (who claimed that Marxism did not necessarily imply revolution).

Around this time, before and after his 'conversion', young Bronstein didn't do much reading (this struck Ziv as very curious, for such an intelligent youth). In prison, for instance, when they were all discussing Bernstein, it was plain that he was simply ignorant. His Marxism was still only a viewpoint.

In jail his super-abundant energy made him start a novel, naturally a Marxist one; nothing came of it. Then he started up a clandestine printing-shop whose details he worked out within a frenzy of energy. Nothing came of that either.[43]

A certain bravura characterised his behaviour. In the Moscow transfer prison, for instance, an opportunity presented itself for a demonstration of revolutionary dignity:

Once, when Bronstein, I and a few others were sitting in the cell, a comrade ran in from the yard very excited; he reported that Ilya Sokolovsky and one or two others ... had been sent to solitary confinement by the commandant for not having taken off their caps when he came in. There was a general alarm. We had to react immediately; on this point there could be no argument. Bronstein instantly took charge of the situation. Against the background of the monotonous life ... the forthcoming *démarche* and the expected clash with the commandant of the prison appeared to be a great affair; Bronstein put himself in a combat mood for it. After a short conference it was decided that we would all go out into the courtyard in caps and ask the guard to give the alarm signal to call out the governor. At his appearance we would not, of course, take off our caps. The rest would be dictated by circumstances.

The guard was nonplussed, but refused to give the signal. We all crowded round him. Bronstein, standing in front of everyone, took out a watch and holding it in front of him solemnly declared to the guard: 'I give you two minutes to think it over.' When the ultimatum had expired Bronstein, pushing the baffled guard to one side, with a magnificent gesture pressed the button. Then, putting on our hats, we all went out into the courtyard. A moment later . . . the commandant, surrounded by an enormous entourage of armed guards, flew into the yard.

'Why don't you take your cap off?' he started yelling, lunging toward Bronstein, who was standing in front of everyone with the most defiant air: 'And you, why don't *you* take your cap off?' Bronstein answered with dignity.

'Off to solitary with him!'

A few husky guards seized Bronstein and carried him off to solitary confinement. . . .[44]

In personal relations this theatrical crystallisation of his high spirits took a different form. In the transfer prison, men and women were allowed to see each other, if they were married, engaged, or closely related. The regime was not very strict about visiting time or surveillance; these reunions looked like gatherings of intimates.

Ziv reports that for these informal little gatherings in gaol young Bronstein primped more than anyone else. He also showed a touching tenderness not only to Alexandra, but to all the other women who had come to see their men. One and all, reports Ziv, were 'charmed by his chivalry'.

Ziv says that after these reunions young Bronstein would go on expending his excess of 'tenderness' on all his friends in jail – kissing, caressing, and embracing them with remarkable effusiveness. At this time, in fact, he was – perhaps because of an aroused personal interest in Alexandra? – so 'tender' and warm, that a woman friend whom he wrote a particularly touching and warm letter to a little later – in 1906 – could scarcely connect him with the 'Trotsky' he was to become after the 1917 revolution.[45]

Beyond the range of his father's influence, young Bronstein could now get married: he persuaded the prison administration in Moscow to authorise his marriage, by a rabbi, to Alexandra. This is how as an adult he recalls his first marriage:

I was put ashore together with a prisoner close to me from the Nikolayev affair. Alexandra Sokolovsky had held one of the premier positions in the South Russian Workers' Union. Her profound devotion to Socialism and the total absence of any personal ambition gave her an irreproachable moral authority. Our joint work bound us closely together. In order not to be separated we had been married in the Moscow transfer prison.[46]

This somewhat astringent turn of phrase did not, perhaps, sum up their relationship. It is to be remembered, also, that when the adult Trotsky wrote this he was living with his second wife. In any case, during the long train ride to Irkutsk, on the rim of Mongolia, young Bronstein 'did not seem to take an interest in anything. He was completely taken up with A. Sokolovsky.'[47]

It was May 1900, after over two years of imprisonment, before he and Alexandra found themselves on the road to Siberia, by way of Irkutsk, then down the Lena River in a convoy of convict barges to Ust-Kut, a village of about a hundred peasant huts. Leon and Alexandra moved into a hut at the edge of the village, between the forest and the river. The village had once know 'better times – with wild orgies, thefts and murders'. Now it was quite primitive; they were plagued by cockroaches and midges.

The country itself was beautiful, yet 'in those days' Leon 'thought it a pity to waste any time or attention on nature. I lived between the forest and river, hardly noticing them. Books and personal relations absorbed me. I was studying Marx, brushing the cockroaches off the pages.'[48]

The exile was in fact a vacation, despite the harsh conditions. The young couple had nothing to do but read, talk, and meet other people – mostly fellow revolutionaries. Alexandra was soon to be taken up with first one child, then another. Their existence was well-nigh idyllic.

Society was provided by the lively interchange of the Lena River, a great artery leading northward to the famous Lena gold mines. The exiles generated by the growth of the revolutionary movement kept in constant touch with one another; they corresponded as much as they pleased, got transferred with ease, and in general led a perfectly normal, even agreeable life. Those who felt like it could hunt and shoot at their own pleasure, explore, tramp about the countryside and so on.

On top of allowing them almost complete liberty the Tsarist Government paid the exiles a small monthly allowance, which they could supplement by working. This allowance was increased when Alexandra gave birth to their two daughters, but since this did not allow for buying the books he now thirsted for, Leon took a job as clerk to an illiterate little merchant in a little place still further east. When Leon wrote 'one pound of red lead' as 'one pood' – (thirty-six pounds) – he was discharged at once; they went back to their little village on the river.

The exiles' society was naturally stratified. The elite were the old Populists, well entrenched through lengthy residence. The younger Marxists kept more to themselves. An unusual intensity developed in personal relations, doubtless a natural consequence of enforced propinquity. There were numerous suicides, often with a 'romantic' cause; suicides' graves were very common in all the larger colonies. Some of the exiles vanished in the population, particularly in the towns; a lot of them became drunkards. As Bronstein quickly saw, 'only hard intellectual work could save one'.

In Irkutsk, while on his way to Ust-Kut, he had been snapped up by the editor of a regional newspaper, *The Eastern Review*, who gave him his first bona-fide contract. As had happened so often, the newspaper, though started by Populists, sometimes came under Marxist influence; Bronstein was to be one of its most prolific correspondents. He immediately began sending off articles that were an instant and for that matter, according to Ziv, a stupefying success.[49]

He had a problem about a pen-name; he chose one that sounds, perhaps, a little arrogant – 'Antid Oto'. He says it was the first word he came across in an Italian dictionary when he started weighing different pen-names. He 'wanted to inject the Marxist antidote into the legal press.'[50]

Ziv comments sardonically on this choice of pseudonym: young Bronstein could not be 'like other people,' giving himself a straightforward, unaffected pseudonym like, for instance, Lenin and Martov, nor would he, of course, dream of using his own name – though in the milieu of the time that would have been another, different kind of unique procedure! That would have invited attention to his Jewish origins, which Ziv maintains were burdensome to him.

He was already the dyed-in-the-wool Marxist he was to remain. The rebelliousness that during the previous two years had led through a phase of sentimental Populism had landed him in a 'systematic Marxist position'. He 'had travelled far', and arrived at his intellectual destination: he was not to change his 'world-view' again.

As Trotsky was to write: 'Just as the tree feeds its leaves, flowers, and fruits with the extracts absorbed from the soil by its roots, so does the individual find food for his sentiments, even the most "sublime" ones, in the economic roots of society.'[51] This is, of course, the fundamental theme of Marxism; in his autobiography the mature Trotsky was to recall seeing a collection of the literary articles he wrote during this period of exile; they were all devoted to 'virtually one theme: the relations between the individual and society'. On seeing them collected in a single volume, Trotsky was struck upon realising that although he 'might have written them differently today' – in 1929 – he would 'not have had to change their substance'.

Trotsky was one of the very few revolutionaries who developed his gift for essay writing to the point of applying it to non-political topics. He could always make money by writing essays, articles, and reviews in a form that even from a starting point in 'classical Marxism' could be worded with sufficient generality to be read by anyone.

From a point of view taken up by him later on, the period of exile was dominated by the question of the 'revision' of Marx – i.e., by dropping the notion of revolutionary violence and concentrating on the peaceful evolution of capitalist society toward Socialism.

One reason for this 'revision' of 'revolutionary Marxism' was the revulsion of middle-class intellectuals who had originally been sympathetic to Marxism in so far as it sponsored the development of capitalism; then, when they saw that capitalism, a progressive phenomenon at a certain historical stage, also had implications that the Dialectic was bound to reject, they abandoned Marxism as itself pernicious and simply defended the capitalist order.

This anti-Marxist current of thought coalesced with another 'revisionist' current, which rejected revolutionary methods in general on the assumption that the development of capitalist society would automatically ensure the transition to Socialism as a 'ripening' of the historic process: violence would be superfluous.

Living an idyllic life, with Alexandra and their two infants, Bronstein was reflecting on all these questions, reading, studying, writing, and above all talking. They moved to a bigger colony of exiles – in Verkholensk – and en route 'settled accounts', as Marxists like to say, with anarchism. Young Bronstein came to the conclusion that it was absurdly superficial, even frivolous, as well as 'lifeless, and cowardly in its practical conclusions'.[52]

But by now news coming from the centres began to deflect the discussion; the exiles grew restive.

Two Cabinet Ministers were assassinated – one in 1901, the other in 1902. The news reached eastern Siberia fairly quickly. The feeling was that things were beginning to break up: terrorism began to be argued about. In its latest form this question of terrorism was, in fact, to create the criterion of differentiation between the Social-

Democrats and the Social-Revolutionaries, heirs of the old Populist movement, who still idealised the peasants and who believed in carrying on the grand tradition of individual murder as a means of crystallising opposition by inflaming public opinion against the iniquities of the *status quo*.

In the Far East the Marxists, after some 'individual vacillation' – there was something very glamorous about personal heroism! – plumped for mass action: 'We said, the chemistry of high explosives cannot take the place of mass action. . . . Our task is not the assassination of the Tsar's ministers, but the revolutionary overthrow of Tsarism.'[53]

The feeling of imminent action spread among the exiles; news came that new Social-Democratic organisations had sprung up even in Siberia, among the railwaymen of the Trans-Siberian Railway. Bronstein began writing 'proclamations and leaflets' in addition to his usual articles on literature and ideas.

In the summer of 1902 he began receiving books that carried, carefully concealed in their bindings, all the latest foreign publications, printed on extra-thin paper. The exiles learned that a Marxist newspaper – *The Spark* – was being published abroad. Its objective, as Trotsky put it years later, was 'the creation of a centralised organisation of professional revolutionaries who would be bound together by the iron discipline of action.' A pamphlet by Lenin, *What To Do?* dealt with this question in depth.

There was an epidemic of escapes. So many exiles had become inflamed by the prospect of action that lots had to be drawn to determine the order of escape. Sympathetic peasants would help smuggle the 'politicals' out in boats, carts, and sleighs. There was not much chance of being caught; the country was so vast and the police so scattered that the chief dangers were drowning and freezing.

An idyllic interlude in his life had come to an abrupt end. Bronstein's handwritten articles and proclamations seemed meaningless: the time had come to escape.

Though he and Alexandra now had two small daughters – the younger was only four months old – and it was plain that Alexandra was going to have a very difficult time of it, she said, as it seems, 'You must.' Trotsky recalls that it was she who 'dissipated all my doubts'.

His turn came up; buried under some hay in a peasant's cart together with another exile, he left. Alexandra played her part: for several days she kept a dummy in bed; the local inspectors accepted

her story that Bronstein was ill and couldn't be disturbed. That was
quite long enough to give him a long jump ahead of the police.

His parting with Alexandra is reported with characteristic
terseness:

> For several days after my escape she successfully hid my absence
> from the police. From abroad, I could hardly correspond with
> her. Then I was exiled for a second time. Later on we met only
> episodically. Life separated us, but we preserved indestructibly our
> intellectual kinship and our friendship.[54]

By the time young Bronstein emerged from the underground run
by the sympathetic peasants, he was transformed: he looked highly
respectable. He boarded a proper train, carrying the *Iliad* in Russian
hexameters and bearing a first-class passport that was to identify
him for the rest of his life – Trotsky, a name he says he picked at
random. He does not mention that Trotsky had been the name of an
awe-inspiring gaoler in the Odessa model prison. Ziv says that even if
that was not so, the escape was at least another occasion to soft-
pedal his Jewish origins by selecting a neutral family name.[55]

Arriving at Samara Trotsky checked in with the local 'underground', an engineer, an associate of Lenin's, who was the chief
contact-point for *The Spark* in Russia and who had the cover-name
of Kler (Krzhizhanovsky).

The escapee was put to work at once. Kler gave him the sobriquet
of The Pen – a tribute to his Siberian journalism – and sent him off
on a recruiting tour to three cities to visit some revolutionaries, some
of them already adherents to the '*Spark* group', others to be won
over. The results of the tour were meagre: 'the connections in the
south were weak, in Kharkov the address given me was wrong, in
Poltava I came up against local patriotism.'[56]

Meanwhile Lenin, to whom Kler had glowingly recommended
The Pen, was urging him to come abroad. In Kler's words, The Pen
was a 'real young eagle' – a hundred per cent for the *Spark* idea.
Lenin urged The Pen to come West at once and write for *The
Spark*.

Kler provided the money, the itinerary, and the contacts for
slipping across the Austrian border. There were no difficulties: an
official accepted Bronstein's forged passport and he made his way
along another underground route, hiding out with peasants, carried
across a river on a peasant's back so as not to arrive soaked

on the other side, carted along concealed in a chicken-cart – the usual routine for political exiles. In retrospect, of course, it looks very easy. Bronstein's only difficulty was that by the time he landed in Vienna he had given away all the money he had been supplied with by Kler.

Though only twenty-two, Bronstein regarded himself as 'representative' of the Russian revolutionaries. He took it for granted that the Marxist leaders of the mass parties of the Continent were as eager to see him as he was to see them; it seemed to him quite normal to insist on seeing Victor Adler, king-pin of the Austrian Social-Democratic Party, at an unusual hour on Sunday. Adler – later to be denounced by Trotsky for petty-bourgeois passivity – was very kind, in fact, and helped him to his next port of call, Zurich, where he woke up one of the comrades at three a.m., since he couldn't pay the taxi-fare and wouldn't wait for dawn.

By the time he got to London, his routine for awakening people was established: he woke up Lenin, too. At any rate, Krupskaya, Lenin's wife, hearing the loud triple knock agreed on, came down to avoid having the whole house disturbed.

'The Pen has come', she called out, and paid for the taxi.

CHAPTER III

The Stage

AROUND THE TURN OF the century, before the revolutionary movement was split along fairly hard-and-fast lines, a huge Russian
emigration was scattered about in Paris, London, Zurich, Geneva,
Vienna, Brussels, and Liège. These 'brotherly, enthusiastic,
and studious groups' lived agreeably Bohemian, sociable lives.
Leavened by the presence of bona-fide activists, the high spirits of
this student milieu were further heightened by an extra dimension –
commitment. 'All the revolutionary tendencies had in common an
inner certainty, a faith – to give the word its deeper value – that of
the inevitable Revolution soon to free Russia.'[1]

Young Trotsky took immediately to this gay, absorbing, colourful
life. At the age of twenty-three – Lenin himself was only nine years
older – he was at the centre of things.

He was first tried out as a speaker. Lenin sent him to lecture to
some London émigrés. His debut in Nikolayev had been pathetic:
now, abruptly and incomprehensibly, he had turned into a remarkable
speaker. Beforehand he had been practically inarticulate, a failing
encumbered by a juvenile determination to display erudition. Suddenly, he had developed a smashing attack – a remarkable production of slash, thrust, and wit, couched in a resonant, penetrating
voice that could crush adversaries and thrill audiences.

If a single feature can be said to characterise the dynamic impact
of Trotsky's writing and speaking alike, it is, perhaps, the notion of
dramatic confrontation on the one hand, and of the dialectical splitting up and reunion of constituent elements on the other. His
peculiar fusion of theatricality, cerebrality, and passion provided

him with just the right outlet for the dramatic confrontations that as a performer he could best express by means of Marxist lyricism plus invective. A favourite configuration was the combination of Marxist determinism – something moving along inevitably toward a fore-ordained climax – and of scorn for the knaves, dwarves, and slobs holding up the procession.

His physical appearance, now, harmonised with his style. An acquaintance describes his looks:

A tall, gaunt young man, he had long hair and – yellow shoes. The yellow shoes especially attracted my attention, because in those days no one in our milieu used to wear such shoes. He looked like his sister (... Kamenev's wife), though her eyes, to be sure, were black while his were light grey, but both of them had something in their faces that made them like a bird of prey. In him this was all the more striking because of his characteristic mouth – big, crooked, biting. A frightful mouth.[2]

Young Trotsky's virtuosity as an orator was to be his passport to celebrity. Many revolutionaries could write, some could speak, hardly any could speak well, only a few brilliantly. His oratorical gifts burst upon the milieu with a stunning impact. The ideas he acquired so rapidly in his earliest twenties suddenly fused with his rapidly evolving talents: the synthesis made him a first-class actor on a stage that was to dominate the Russian revolutionary movement.

Lenin was exceptionally affable to him. Though single-minded to a degree that even in that committed generation must be called extravagant, Lenin was far from stuffy. He took young Trotsky for a tour of London, speaking about it with 'admiration and detachment', pointing out the monuments of English life, consistently referring to them as 'theirs' – *their* British Museum, *their* Parliament, meaning not the English people but specifically the upper classes.[3]

Young Trotsky was eager to learn the gossip of the colony, the day-to-day politics of the émigrés. Lenin had summoned him, it turned out, as part of building up an organisation: he needed talented recruits. He asked Trotsky to turn his first lecture into an article for a theoretical Marxist organ, *The Dawn,* compared with which *The Spark* itself, quite unintelligible outside the coterie of initiates, was practically a tabloid.

Trotsky didn't feel up to it: he wrote a shorter piece for the 'popular journal' *The Spark*: it was indulgently edited a little by

Lenin, who then sent the young man off on a conventional tour
amongst the Russian exiles trickling through Western European
capitals.

Trotsky set out to canvas the émigré groups in some nearby
cities – Paris, Brussels, Liège – with the same lecture on historical
materialism he had given in London : this time he intended to use it
to collect funds for the starving 'popular journal'.

His trip to Paris changed his personal life. The first girl he
met – Natalya Sedova, a sort of unofficial factotum for visiting
speakers – was smitten at once.

Natalya was characteristic of the 'penitent gentry'. She had been
involved in a conspiracy to circulate prohibited books at Moscow
University; she went on to study in Geneva. Like so many girls her
age she was an established rebel, swept by idealism into the
blossoming revolutionary movement, where she gladly devoted herself to the chores required of its mediocre, willing juniors.

At the time (1902) Natalya used to eat in a small flat in Rue
Lalande; she and some of the comrades would pool their resources
to make living cheaper. Julius Martov – aged twenty-nine – used to
go there; it was he who heralded Trotsky's arrival.

Trotsky was now twenty-three : as Natalya was to say in the *Diary*
she kept for many years : 'His vitality, his liveliness of mind, his
capacity for work' made him stand out.

Natalya thought him terribly young – he was her own age very
nearly – to be touted as a 'leading theoretician' – a word heavy with
glamour. At the same time, to her bewilderment, he was jaunty and
insouciant : she got him a room in her own boarding-house; he spent
his time whistling when he was supposed to be slaving over his
lecture.

Trotsky's first lecture in Paris went off well too; 'the colony was
delighted, the young *Spark*-man exceeded all expectations.'

When the lecture was over the young Marxists set out to see Paris;
Their expedition might have been a conventional idyll – as of course
it was – but at the same time it was highly edifying, too. Natalya
kept recommending to Trotsky the history-laden sights of Paris as
well as all its other charms – beauty, culture – while Trotsky
defended himself as provincials often do : 'Paris resembles Odessa,'
he said, 'but Odessa is better.'[4]

They eventually set up house in the airy quarter 'our emigration'
was attached to (Rue Gassendi). She received from her family
twenty roubles a month, or fifty francs; Trotsky earned as much by

his pen. 'This gave us a very slender budget, but we had Paris, the comradeship of the refugees, the unflagging preoccupation with Russia, and the great ideas we were living for. . . .'⁵

Trotsky's later comment has the terseness reserved for such relations: 'I was incomparably more attentive to familiarising myself with Paris than I had been with London, because of the influence of N. I. Sedova.'⁶

Natalya was to be at his side for the rest of his life, despite some fleeting affairs of his. His relationship with Alexandra had not, perhaps, been very deep; he had been very young; it had lasted a very short time. Although she remained his legal wife, retaining the name Bronstein, he never supported her or their two children. It was in fact his father, who had so disapproved of the marriage to begin with, who provided money whenever necessary.

Russian Marxists did not make much ado about monogamy, yet they generally maintained monogamous marriages with remarkable fidelity, referring to their wives, whether or not legally married to them, as their 'life-companions'.

For the time being, however, Trotsky had not quite left London. After his first lecture tour he returned there, to be plunged into the tensions of the 'Spark group'. Young Trotsky was at first immersed in the little group around the journal. As he put it later, he 'fell in love with The Spark,' that is, the idea and the fact taken together independently of shadings, disagreements, and disputes. For a short time he remained unaware, it would seem, of the dense mesh of controversy – thought of by outsiders, unkindly, no doubt, as logic-chopping, quibbling, casuistry – that went into practically all general statements. His native argumentativeness was overshadowed for the time being, perhaps, by the deference due the greater experience of his seniors.

There were six editors of this 'popular journal', more or less evenly divided by age: the three younger ones – Lenin, Martov, and Potresov – would tend to vote against the three older ones – Plekhanov, Axelrod, and Zasulich.

Trotsky had arrived at an opportune time for Lenin, who proposed him soon after his arrival as a new member of the board, which by creating a seventh vote would obviously have given Lenin the upper hand. While the personnel of The Spark as a whole would be increased, Lenin's relative share also would – to put it in practical terms. In addition, there were frictions between the various segments of the small editorial board. Plekhanov and Lenin, more or less the leaders of their respective 'generations', were temperamentally antagonistic.

Plekhanov, much older than Lenin, had a great reputation amongst the Russian émigrés for style and erudition. His authority was considerable – he had been close to Engels! As a brilliant writer, indeed, a philosopher, his celebrity went beyond the Russian movement. He had an elegant 'bourgeois' style, to boot; he would use a sort of condescending irony to counter the bulldog-like diligence and flatness of Lenin's style, as well as his insistence on hard work, detail, and action. Lenin, now over thirty, his character fully formed – he had been called 'The Old Man' by juniors since the age of twenty-five! – and with a brain he had been stuffing since adolescence, naturally found this attitude annoying.

Another member of the older generation was the celebrated former terrorist Vera Zasulich, a correspondent of Marx himself and long since converted to Marxism. The translator of *The Communist Manifesto* into Russian and a co-founder of the Liberation of Labour Group, she had attempted to assassinate a Tsarist functionary (Trepov) before Trotsky was born.

Martov had been born Tsederbaum: his family had been well known in the Hebrew-language revival among Russian Jews of the generation before. He had helped found the *Bund*; afterwards he had turned against the idea of Jewish autonomy in the labour movement and together with Lenin had founded the *Fighting Union for the Liberation of the Working Class* in St. Petersburg in 1895. He and Lenin had gone into exile and formed an association with the older exiles for the establishment of *The Spark*.

Temperamentally, also, Lenin and Martov were a little incompatible, though it was rather Martov who felt ill at ease with Lenin: to his dying day Lenin retained a singular affection for Martov. Later on, Trotsky summed up the psychological atmosphere between the two men – Lenin's 'hardness' and Martov's 'softness':

Lenin would glance at Martov with a critical and slightly suspicious eye, while Martov, feeling this glance would look down and a narrow shoulder would twitch nervously.... Lenin would look beyond Martov as he talked, while Martov's eyes grew glassy behind his drooping and never quite clean pince-nez.[7]

Antagonisms, while of course obvious to the men themselves, were difficult to refer to. All sentiment was overlaid by theory, and in theory they were 'classical Marxists'. On the other hand, situations kept changing: different tactics, different strategy might be called for; theory itself was not so very simple, after all, and had to be constantly reinterpreted.

At the same time, it was only natural for theory to be used by practice: persuading someone of your theory meant getting him on your side, and it was, in spite of everything, *your* side.

Hence Lenin's remarkable stubbornness tended to have organisational as well as theoretical consequences. In this respect he stood out among his associates, though even here the differences were far from clear – the fact of organisation, too, had to be interpreted as part of theory!

It was understood that Martov handled the writing side of *The Spark*, while Lenin specialised in the politics and, above all, in the organisation underlying the little newspaper. Practically speaking, Lenin was its mainstay.

Indefatigable, and a remarkably prolific writer, Lenin devoted himself, aside from study, to organisational work. He seldom took part in the practically endless argumentation characteristic of the émigré colonies; his interest in discussion was essentially as a prologue to some kind of action; this was also one of the outstanding traits of his oratory.

Plekhanov disliked young Trotsky on sight. The dislike, soon mutual, bloomed into aversion, perhaps because they had the same sort of highhanded contentiousness, polemical brilliance, and theatrical presence, and were equally narcissistic. Plekhanov may also have had a touch of plain, old-fashioned, 'vulgar' anti-Semitism; he was 'ambivalent' about the Jews.[8]

Though affable and charming, Lenin was not very accessible. On top of his practical activities he had a genuine household, run by his wife, Krupskaya. He could not be hobnobbed with so matter-of-factly; seeing him, as Trotsky said, was always a bit of an 'event'.

Because of this Trotsky was closer to the more easy-going Martov. The Bohemian aspect of the revolutionary movement suited both of them. They would spend time together chatting in cafés and restaurants both in London and later on in Geneva: they would be joined by Zasulich, a chain-smoker and tea-drinker, mountainous, untidy, muddle-headed, sincere, and hard-working.

Aside from his dislike of Trotsky, Plekhanov saw no reason to have Lenin take on a recruit for his own purposes. His acumen, fortified by his distaste for Trotsky, enabled him to pierce through Lenin's touting of Trotsky's 'gifts' by asking the simple question – gifts for what? In fact, Plekhanov's opposition kept Trotsky off the editorial board.

The somewhat diffuse revolutionary movement was about to crystallise in an organised form; some nine months after Trotsky's arrival in Western Europe a number of delegates came together to form the Russian Social-Democratic Workers' Party. Trotsky stayed on in Western Europe to attend the Congress, as part of a little plan of Lenin's.

Without his knowing it, Trotsky was being *handled*. The ill-staffed and penurious revolutionary Russian underground had asked for his return; but since Lenin needed him on *The Spark* he told the underground centre, without telling Trotsky, that the latter seemed unwilling to go back.[9]

The Congress, held in Brussels on 30 July 1903, was to lay the organisational foundations of the Russian Marxist movement for a long time to come. It was supposed to unite the fragmentary, tenuous 'groups' and 'organisations' of the revolutionary movement, whose general aim was to articulate and guide to victory The Revolution, felt by everyone to be fairly imminent.

This reunion, despite the sentimental or symbolic function of the tiny convention whose nine members had met in Minsk in 1898 and been collared by the police out of hand, was the real Founding Congress, though out of deference to the symbol it was called the Second.

About sixty delegates, a motley group, came together in a vermin-infested warehouse in the rear section of the Socialist *Maison du Peuple* in Brussels. Practically all of these founding members of a 'workers' party' were intellectuals of one kind or another, mostly from the émigré colonies. Four of them had at one time been workmen: ornamental exceptions, they influenced no one.

The meeting was supposed to be kept very secret, but the police learned about it immediately from a Tsarist agent on the Ways and Means Committee who was, characteristically, trusted by Lenin.

Trotsky, a young man not yet twenty-four, by now with a small reputation as speaker and writer associated with the 'Spark-group', came in from Geneva, one of the most important way-stations on the revolutionary lecture circuit; he represented a somewhat impromptu 'organisation' – the 'Siberian Social-Democratic Workers' Union'.

The 'Spark-group', led by Lenin, had a majority – thirty-three out of the fifty-one official votes – and it was a majority that consisted in the main of people already chosen by Lenin himself; he himself had sent many of them to Russia in order for them to be sent *back* to the Brussels congress by some local organisation in Russia.

Since it was to be practically impossible even at the centre to understand the fine points of the issues involved, or for that matter the issues themselves, there was no question of such agents representing the 'views' of little coteries in far-away Russia. This meant that from the very start it was routine for the 'centre' to dictate its own 'representation', despite its formal obeisance to the notion of democracy.

The number of votes allocated to the Jewish *Bund*, by far the biggest and most effectively organised working-class body in Russia, was significant. Its five votes did not remotely reflect its real influence.

The Congress was soon enmeshed in a complex tangle whose elements were largely unconscious.

As a young man, Karl Marx had said that the time had come not merely to understand the world, but to change it. 'Classical Marxism', accordingly, placed its emphasis on a dual approach to history.

On the one hand, it analysed and explained the gradual, impersonal ripening of socio-economic forces leading inevitably to a Socialist transformation of society; on the other hand it contained an element of human will-power. Linked to the impersonal and inevitable unfolding of these socio-economic forces, this element of will made the transformation depend on human action – the conscious, cerebral decision of an elite to bring about the Great Transition by the armed seizure of power by The Proletariat or, of course, its 'representatives'.

One of the reasons this rather obvious contrast, or at least distinction, between the two views could never appear nakedly, and so be clarified rationally, was that both attitudes had always been implicit in Marx's own formulation, which he regarded as unitary. Hence neither Marx nor Engels had ever elucidated the following discrepancy.

Both the transition to Socialism and the seizure of power to bring it about were considered inevitable. Their conjunction was also taken for granted. Derived from Hegel, Marx's fundamental philosophical stance, despite qualifications of detail, assumed that the motive force behind the tug of History was the clash of ideas, *exemplified* by human agents. Also, young Marx had merely been constructing an essentially logical schema – timeless – which, insofar as it remained *a mere schema* did not require the necessary modulations of a real-life situation.

The moment that real life supplemented the logical timelessness of Marx's schema a contradiction became manifest. If the transition to Socialism was inevitable, why was it necessary to seize power by force? Contrariwise, if it was necessary to seize power by force, how could the transition to Socialism be inevitable? A contest for power, after all, implies the possibility of losing the contest; hence the notion of inevitability is contaminated by this empirical element of earth-bound, human contingency.

This contradiction went unnoticed during most of Marx's lifetime, partly because the theory, though couched in timeless terms, was elaborated during Marx's messianically fervent youth – before the debacle of 1848 – when it seemed to him that the whole European order was about to be cataclysmically transformed. But after 1848, as the slowly, then swiftly growing Marxist movement accustomed itself to a widening of the gap between its desires and their fulfilments, the relationship of the means to the ends had to be gone into in detail.

There was still another ambiguous idea, also rooted in the common-sense perception that a revolution had to be made by people.

It was another cliché of Marxism inherited from Hegel that 'Philosophy' was the natural conductor of the subterranean surges of History. In the case of Hegel this had meant Philosophers proper; in the case of Marx, it meant those who had mastered his own Great Key; by the turn of the century this naturally meant The Revolutionary Party, which alone had the understanding of the Great Key and the will to turn that key in the door of History.

At the Congress, Lenin summed up this idea in a more or less throwaway style: 'Aside from the influence of the Social-Democracy there is no conscious activity of the workers.'[10]

Another ambiguity in Marxism was aired in a key sentence: 'The essential condition for the social revolution is the Dictatorship of the Proletariat, i.e., the conquest of such power by the proletariat as will allow it to suppress all attempts at resistance on the part of the exploiters'.[11]

This statement accompanied much talk in the rest of the draft programme about a 'democratic republic', a 'constituent assembly' to be elected by free, equal, direct, secret and universal suffrage and so on.

The elusiveness of this question was such that the difficulties emerged, obscurely though unmistakably, in the very definition of the Party itself: the phraseology that was to bring about the split was only dimly felt to be of consequence.

This was Lenin's wording of the celebrated Paragraph One of the draft statutes of the projected unitary party: 'A member of ... the Party is any person who accepts its programme, supports the Party with material means, and personally participates in one of its organisations.'[12]

The other draft for the basic statutes, submitted by Martov, was almost identical: the difference was that instead of the phrase 'personally participate', Martov said: 'cooperates personally and regularly under the guidance of one of the organisations.'[13]

A moment's reflection will indicate that there is a substantial difference behind the two formulations. It is a difference, however, not of *ideas* but of *organisation*, and at this stage in the evolution of the Russian movement, before the significance of organisation was clear, the difference between the two drafts seemed well-nigh negligible; Martov was ready to give up his own wording.

Lenin's phrase implied a team of people, i.e., an organisation, Martov's no more than a state of mind. But the fundamental confusion, altogether unavowed, as to whether History or People were the guide made this point obscure. It was not, indeed until much later – in 1917 – that its importance was to become manifest.

Two other vital questions – ultimately, though as yet unsuspectedly linked to the streamlining of the Party – also created immense heat.

The first was the question of how to define the *Bund*'s relationship to the Party now in formation. This was fundamental, partly because of the *Bund*'s importance, and partly because it raised once again the primary question of organisation: who was to run what?

The *Bund* was the only rival to Zionism among the slowly awakening masses of Eastern European Jews. Both movements were soliciting the allegiance of all those Jews in the Tsarist Empire – some five million – who wanted to become substantially secularised without losing their Jewish identity.

In trying to organise Russian workers, the *Bund* had learned that the Jewish workers had far more advanced ideas; thus it shelved the idea it had begun with, that the education of Russian workers would help the Jews solve their own specific problem, and, as part of its struggle against Zionism, adopted the Yiddish language and also the ideology of national autonomy.

At the Second Congress, accordingly, the *Bund* was eager to have the Jews recognised as an autonomous minority, and itself as its official representative. This implied, of course, in view of the numerous other nationalities in Tsarist Russia, that the Party would ultimately be no more than a federation of national parties; furthermore, that each nationality would retain its own right of self-determination.

Lenin was determined to obliterate this notion: it ran counter to his faith in centralisation as a method of rule, both in a political party and in the State. In addition, his theory of national self-determination had nothing to do with culture, but with territory, a theory that ruled out Jewish nationality and was later on to have fateful consequences for Jews in the Soviet Union.

The *Bund*'s view was smashed: Lenin was assisted in this clash by a number of Jews, including Martov – a former Bundist – Axelrod, and Trotsky, who on this point supported Lenin wholeheartedly.

It was in this debate on the question of the *Bund* that Trotsky, almost uniquely, spoke as a Jew and on a 'Jewish' issue. The issue transcended, to be sure, Russian Jewry: in the nature of things the concept of ethnic representation affected the constitution of the Russian Social-Democratic Party.

Trotsky was in favour of the disappearance of the Jews. Since Marxists were both against religion and also, theoretically, against nationalism, they naturally opposed the very existence of the Jews, which they explained as due to a combination of religion plus bogus nationalism, at this time Zionism. For Trotsky, at the age of twenty-three, and for most of his life, the solution to the Jewish problem lay in the blanket internationalisation of society, which required, naturally, total confidence between Jews and Gentiles during the process of merging. Against the background of the horrible Kishineff pogrom, which had taken place only a few months before the Congress, Trotsky's contention had an element of macabre comedy.

Even aside from the potentialities of organised anti-Semitism one can perceive a characteristic cerebralism in the unreality of his prerequisite for the solution of the 'Jewish problem' – the homogenisation of the world plus the vanishing of anti-Semitism.

Trotsky's early grasp of Marxism may be illuminated by the speech he made during the discussion of the paragraph on the 'Dictatorship of the Proletariat'. It conflates two distinct ideas with disconcerting glibness – the idea of dictatorship and the principle of democracy.

In the basic Marxist schema – stripped of reservations and exceptions – the notion was that in the nature of things The Proletariat would grow bigger and bigger and poorer and poorer. This growing poverty plus the attendant despair was, as indicated, supposed to make The Proletariat finally bring about Socialism.

As far as numbers were concerned, there was, to be sure, a trifling discrepancy in the Communist Manifesto; there Marx and Engels had said that the peasants came to 'far more than half the population', though at the same time, somehow, 'private property has already been eliminated with respect to nine-tenths of the population', while on the other hand the movement of The Proletariat was already – in 1848! – said to be 'of' the overwhelming majority as well as 'for' it.

These details were brushed aside by the youthful Trotsky:

The rule of the working-class was inconceivable until the great mass of them were united in desiring it. Then they would be an overwhelming majority. This would not be the dictatorship of a little band of conspirators or a minority party, but of the immense majority in the interests of the immense majority, to prevent counter-revolution. In short, it would represent the victory of true democracy.[14]

This youthful formulation represents, of course, one version of the ambiguity that Marx, in his own youthful euphoria, had not bothered to clarify; it was later to create 'theoretical difficulties'.

The question of 'Economism' – in the jargon of the milieu – created another knotty tangle at the Founding Congress: Trotsky was to distinguish himself in the passionate debates on this point too.

Broadly, 'Economism' was another aspect of the view that the playing out of subterranean historical forces would take care of themselves: the 'Economists' believed in economic reforms and in a general, large-scale struggle for trades-unions: they attacked the primacy accorded by the *Spark*-group to the whole idea of revolutionary *politics*.

Trotsky pounced on the 'Economists' with such violence that he was given the nickname of 'Lenin's cudgel'.[15]

During the lively polemics around this theme Trotsky also

defended an extreme form of the idea that the control of the Party by its own leadership should be streamlined; he wanted the statutes to be formulated to reflect the 'leadership's organised distrust' of the membership.

This is, of course, a classic expression of 'elitism'. It was just this pregnant idea that was very quickly to become Lenin's trademark: it had also, curiously, been adumbrated, very succinctly, with all the details characteristic of Lenin's own view, in an essay written by Trotsky in 1901. Against the background of chaos in the revolutionary movement and of diffuse organisational proliferation, he had defended the concept of a Central Committee with the power to expel or dissolve any recalcitrant organisation: 'The Central Committee will cut off its relations with [the undisciplined organisation] and thus cut off that organisation from the entire world of The Revolution.'[16]

Thus, at the age of twenty-two, Trotsky had expressed views that he was savagely to attack in the case of Lenin and to identify himself with again only very much later, during the turmoil of 1917.

The *general* idea of the supremacy of the Party, advocated by Trotsky, too, as early as 1901, before the split at the Founding Congress of 1903, was such a cliché of Marxism, that, as Martov, Lenin's chief rival, was to put it, *all* Socialists believed in centralisation vis-à-vis the 'shapelessness and federative looseness' of the pre-1903 movement.

Yet so intertangled and exquisitely nuanced was the clash of theory at the Founding Congress that it was Plekhanov and the Mensheviks who defended the concept of the proletarian dictatorship even more than Lenin. Plekhanov, for instance, came out squarely for the concept of *salus revolutionis suprema lex* – in a 'revolutionary situation' the Marxists would gladly annihilate all civil liberties if that was called for by The Revolution.

The major questions of the Founding Congress, in short, all revolved around this primordial question – the relationship between the revolutionary Idea and its Agency.

Plainly, the difficulties were endless. Within the framework of classical Marxism this whole cluster of propositions stemming from the central notion of the human control of an inevitable cosmic development simply could not be rationally coped with.

It was difficult, indeed impossible to say just what those human beings – revolutionaries – should do, how they should do it, whom they were responsible to, and, above all, what their proper relation was to each other.

If the supremacy of the Party, for instance, was more than a cliché, did it mean that the Party was in its *nature* dictatorial? Was it the servant of The Proletariat? Its master? Were the interests of the Party similar to the interests of the working-class? Identical?

And in any case, if Marxism was a true reflection of reality, just why were there these uncertainties? Did the Party have free will? Was it forced to follow History according to the Great Key? Could it, above all, change History? And if that was so, where was the inevitability?

Since the resolution of all such questions was, in 1903, not even conceivable, no one at that time foresaw the thorny potentialities of this particular ambiguity. The Russian revolutionaries were in their own minds still so far from exercising power that it would have been a waste of time even to think about it.

The Congress was, in fact, wrestling with the fundamental ambiguity or confusion of the Hegelian heritage of Marxism: are Ideas autonomous? Or must they be implemented?

But this wrestling was thoroughly unconscious. On the one hand, the titanic forces of History – the ascension onward and upward, powered by the tug of improving technology – were to bring about Socialism; on the other, it had to be brought about, naturally, by people – by The Proletariat.

And where, indeed, *was* The Proletariat? The people discussing all this were not workers, after all; nor could any worker even have hoped to understand their idiom.

Possibly the strangest thing about the fundamental result of the Founding Congress – the *de facto* party split – was that it was so hard to understand what had happened.

The spitefulness the Congress was steeped in was hard to express, since the debates were naturally expressed in a form of rationalistic argument – logic based on the authority of the Marxist scriptures. But since the reality that logic was seeking to encompass was far too fluid, the delegates had the air of shadow-boxing.

Later, by the time the Party had split into autonomous Bolshevik and Menshevik factions, it was natural to talk as though the split had taken place because of differing interpretations of the celebrated Paragraph One of the Party statutes. Yet the venomous atmosphere of the Congress had little to do, in fact, with either policy or

organisation. What had poisoned the debates was really Lenin's
proposal to cut down the number of *Spark* editors.

Martov, for instance, wanted the Committee that decided the
agenda of the Congress – what it would discuss – to represent the
various groups actually at the Congress. For him it was a matter of
saving time by making prior agreements between groups whose existence was already accepted.

Lenin, on the other hand, wanted a very small core – three people,
all from *The Spark* – to decide everything. He made this motion in
the preliminary discussion of the caucus; since the *Spark* group had
a majority the motion was passed. Lenin and his two other candidates – Plekhanov and Martov – were thus elected to the presidium.

Lenin's point in this was, he said, to make the *Spark* organisation
more efficient by circumventing the problem of the deadlock
between an even number of editors (as he had tried to do before, by
proposing Trotsky himself, only to be blocked at that time by
Plekhanov's veto).

It was plain, after all, that the other three editors – Zasulich,
Axelrod, and Potresov – were not very useful to the organisation and
still less to the paper; they were bad writers.

Trotsky, chilled or perhaps frustrated by Lenin's 'hardness',
professed to be indignant at the proposal. The idea of excluding two
luminaries like Axelrod and Zasulich, by now, moreover, his intimates, seemed to inflame him.

It was, in fact, just this proposal that let loose a flood of venom – it
was a 'family scandal'. The dissolution of the tight little *Spark* group
instantly became entangled with all sorts of other organisational
questions, of which the cardinal one was the wording of Paragraph
one on the requirements for membership.

By the time the wording of this paragraph came up for discussion
the Congress was already honeycombed with spitefulness that was
reflected in an incredible amount of recrimination concerning
antique squabbles heightened by a maximum suspiciousness of
personal motives. Not merely would the wording of a given paragraph, say, be raked over, but its remotest implications would be so
malevolently dissected that agreement became impossible.

At the same time the fury of the wrangling concealed the personal
or temperamental factor.

As theory descended into the sphere of practicality – after all,
theory and practice were held to be one – the role of character
became predominant. Thus it was plain that the determination to

create one's own organisation, one's own apparatus, was essentially
– quite apart from theory – a reflection of positive *will*. Conversely,
the principle that what would be decisive would be not individual
human action, but the broad subterranean tug of History, could
obviously likewise be a reflection of a passive dependence on
uncontrollable events.

For those who accepted the cogency of Marxist doctrine it was
possible either to wait for the transition to Socialism as a result of
the ripening of the forces of production etc., or else to accelerate the
transition through an act of leadership in which violence was merely
one element.

Historically, the democratically based, mass Socialist parties of
the Continent, notably in Germany, adopted a 'passive' line:
they took for granted the concept of the gradual ripening of society,
including the working class, toward the inevitable Great Transition
to Socialism. Since this whole process was necessarily long-range, no
revolution, plainly, was called for at all. It was this attitude that had
been enshrined in Bernstein's 'revision' of Marxism, though of course
it found its 'justification' in the writings of Marx and Engels.

The other point of view – the seizure of power by an elite to bring
about the Great Transition – was of course discussed, but in
practice nothing could be done about it until Lenin himself took
action in 1917.

From this point of view – the point of view that, as we can see
with hindsight, was decisive in 1917 – Lenin's 'hardness' was not
merely a stubborn insistence on principle, but the sign of a more
fundamental quality of character – his willingness to direct events.

His chief theoretical opponent, Martov, for instance, was just as
uncompromising a Marxist *theoretically*; but he did not feel at ease
as a director of History; he was rather an observer, as it were
commentator.

None of this could be avowed, or at least put in theoretical
language. Lenin could never have admitted, doubtless even to himself, that he *wanted* to direct events – no doubt it seemed to him that
this was simply the best way to further The Revolution.

Thus, in these theoretical discussions two different *kinds* of fact
were being accomplished. One was that certain opinions were pro-
moted: this was the theoretical discussion, full-blown and endless.
The other was that certain relations between individuals were being
decided – this was to lead to the evolution of power-structures.

In one way, for instance, agreeing, say, with Lenin meant no more than that – both of you simply shared the same views. From the other point of view, however, agreeing with Lenin meant that you were on his side, and, since it was a political structure whose foundations were being laid at the 1903 Congress, that might mean, further, that you were a member of *his* organisation.

This is, of course, the most elementary thing in all organisation – a child is as aware of social hierarchy as chickens of pecking-order. Yet it was just this blatant fact of life that was obscured by the scholastic idiom of Russian Marxism.

Amidst the confused embitterment of the Congress as a whole Trotsky did something that was to have a fateful effect on his career. In the tangled squabble over Paragraph One of the statutes he came out as an opponent of Lenin's.

This was in spite of his own 'position' on organisation, as revealed not only in 1901, but also at the Founding Congress itself, during his attack on the 'Economists', when the idea he championed – a streamlined Party leadership independent of its members – was essentially the same as Lenin's in all respects.

Thus, in opposing Lenin on the question of the definition of the membership, he was upholding the 'general' view of Marxism, so to speak, as an unorganised, more or less instinctual expression of 'class' impulses. He was charging Lenin with a desire to create an exclusive caucus of conspirators, instead of a general party of the working class. His view could be regarded, of course, as the more 'naive' aspect of Marxism – in which the Idea reflected a total confidence in the workers' 'class consciousness'.

As against this 'naive' confidence in Marx's general scheme, Lenin's 'narrow' view of the Party contained an element of horse-sense that had the charm of coinciding with the Dialectic. The working class, too, was in the grip of 'dialectical contradictions'! It was impossible to speak of its having unitary goal, will-power, or insight, since as a class it was often vacillating, confused, and short-sighted. A party that let in *all* working-class sympathisers would be letting in countless elements of disruption. Because of this, the Party, in order to lead the amorphous mass of workers, had to stand outside them and organise itself as a 'vanguard'.

It should have been easy for young Trotsky to unite his previous support for Party centralisation with this element of horse-sense and, more important, perhaps, with the factor of *will*. Yet inflamed, as he sounded, by Lenin's callousness toward the veterans of the old *Spark* group, he attacked Lenin with peculiar hostility on what seemed to be the theoretical question underlying the definition of Party membership. He remained obdurate even when Lenin made a special effort to talk him around, criticising him for no more than youthful inexperience – a singularly mild criticism for this passion-charged Congress!

His hostility to Lenin at this juncture can scarcely be ascribed either to theory or to youthful sentimentality on behalf of the older members of *The Spark*. The roots of disagreement lay in character.

Trotsky, too, after all, inclined to the 'voluntaristic' element in Marxism – the determination to make sure that what was supposed to happen did happen. Thus this particular aspect of his character might have been thought to propel him into a close alliance with the older man who had been so indulgent to him.

Yet at the Founding Congress, and in the movement in general, Trotsky had a special problem. Just because of his gifts, and because of his high spirits, he must have been considering – consciously or not – methods of being first. And at the Congress this problem was bound to be beyond him.

To begin with, he was too young: Lenin's prestige meant that he could not be dislodged by a mere newcomer. In addition, Lenin's own single-mindedness, the very 'hardness' that Trotsky was later to admire, implied for Trotsky personally a permanent role of subordination. The reverence he professed for the other members of the *Spark* group (except Plekhanov) could easily co-exist with the perception that their 'softness' might ultimately give way to his primacy.

It would have been far more natural for him to stay at Lenin's side. On the central issue between them Trotsky did agree with Lenin both before and after: his having emphasized the paramount role of organisations while still a novice in Siberia implied a precocious, seemingly temperamental alignment with Lenin's 'position'.

Lenin himself was unaware of this merely logical confusion in Marx's original scheme. The consequences of that confusion were to be a long time in manifesting themselves; he was not to *express* the despotic idea attributed to him by Trotsky for a long time to come – indeed, not until 1917.

Thus the Founding Congress gave birth not to a unitary party, but to two different and generally antipathetic 'factions', really two different parties. At the very moment of conception the Social-Democratic Russian Workers' Party became, in fact, twins.

Initially, the Congress passed Martov's 'soft' wording of the statute, but the Congress majority was weakened almost at once by the total withdrawal of both the *Bund* and the 'Economists'. Hence, after their withdrawal, when Lenin made his proposal for the reduction of the *Spark* staff, he managed to get a tiny majority (two votes), as he also did for his own candidates to the Central Committees.

This vote gave rise to the two names soon to become famous as the two branches of the Russian Social-Democratic Workers' Party – the Bolsheviks, meaning 'majority-men', and Mensheviks, meaning 'minority-men', though the literal significance of the two words was lost almost immediately and in any case could never have had any stable meaning: generally the Mensheviks had a bigger following.

The split into the two branches had come about for such apparently trivial reasons, and the two branches were to go on for many years – till well after 1917 – claiming the identical party platform and identical principles of both policy and organisation, that it was practically impossible to discern the formal difference. For years Trotsky was to keep himself apart from the Bolsheviks organisationally, calling them 'splitters'. Nevertheless, he was to be plagued by the *de facto* psychological affinity inherent in his 'voluntaristic' mode of speech.

The split between the two branches was basic, yet at the same time intangible – intangible, at least, so long as the slightly differing formulae were not tested by the experience of power: *then* the Marxist desideratum of combining 'theory and practice' gave a somewhat unexpected answer! It was to turn out that the will-power of the Bolsheviks made them ready to mould events; it was Bolshevik decisiveness that proved to be fundamental.

Meanwhile, not only was the intellectual – as opposed to the characteristic – distinction between Bolsheviks and Mensheviks fine-grained to the point of invisibility, but it was further blurred by Tsarist conditions.

Temperamentally and intellectually, the Mensheviks were a replica of the democratic, mass Socialist parties of the rest of the Continent. Against a parliamentary background, like that of Western Europe, it would doubtless have been natural for them to identify themselves quite openly with the passive ingredient in the Marxist schema for the transition to Socialism – the general 'ripening' of the working class within the gradual evolution of capitalist society – rather than with the putschist element in Marxism – the seizure of power by an elite acting 'on behalf' of The Proletariat.

But as an underground party organisation they were blocked from giving expression to any form of 'revolutionary Marxism' at all. Within the underground movement they could come out against the autocracy only by harping on their 'revolutionary' intransigence as part of Marxist orthodoxy.

This deposited a further layer of obscurity and indirection over the clear expression of opinion; the conflict of tendencies within the Russian Socialist movement grew more and more casuistic.

This blindness to the fundamental issues underlying the squabbling doubtless accounts for the remarkably lush disputatiousness. There was agreement, it seemed, on all *fundamental* points; yet the trivial points held up the Congress until all the money it needed – contributed by the middle-class sympathisers of the middle-class revolutionists! – had been frittered away.

The heat in the verminous warehouse was prostrating. The wrangling would last into the dawn. The delegates simmered with rage. The whole Congress was permeated by a miasma of violent emotion.

In the rationalist idiom of Marxism only ideas and logic are supposed to be meaningful; it was difficult, in the verbosity of the Congress and its aftermath, to formulate unavowed aversions, ambitions and prejudices openly. Yet their repression inevitably built up an enormous reservoir of bitterness.

After the Congress disputes about the management of *The Spark* went on bubbling away. There were endless frictions between Trotsky and the Mensheviks too, yet they did not make him lean toward Lenin – quite the contrary.

After the Founding Congress was over Trotsky subjected the 'Jewish question' to a more serious scrutiny. The rationalist framework his Marxism had obliged him to apply to it could not have reflected his true feelings. He was, in fact, preoccupied with this 'question' in his own way; he was to write about it more than any other revolutionary.[17]

His description of a pogrom written around this time, for instance, contained an element of pathos that somehow sounds purely personal; the reader feels he detects a specifically 'Jewish' strand in an outburst that can otherwise be thought of as neutrally humanitarian.[18]

His hostility to Zionism must also have been rooted in a profound *interest*. He seems to have gone from the Founding Congress in London to a quite different Congress – the celebrated Zionist Congress that sat in Basle, Switzerland in the summer of 1903. There he witnessed[19] the passionate turmoil that had broken out in the Zionist movement about the British-controlled territory of Uganda, which seemed to many Zionists an alternative to Palestine as a homeland for the Jews.

He wrote a murderous attack on Zionism (for *The Spark*) in the characteristic 'slashing' style of the milieu; regarding Zionism as already exploded, he castigated both Theodor Herzl, the founder of political Zionism, as a 'shameless adventurer', and the 'romanticists of Zion' for their 'hysterical sobbings'.[20]

But his interest in Jewish affairs, however profound, remained peripheral to his activities. His political orbit remained within the revolutionary movement; in August 1904, a few months after leaving *The Spark* (in April), he went on with the attack he had made on Lenin at the Founding Congress as a 'disorganiser' of the Party. He now systemised his opposition in a substantial brochure, one hundred densely printed pages dedicated to his 'dear teacher', Axelrod, called *Our Political Tasks*.

This brochure formulated an idea of Trotsky's that summed up this whole relationship between an Idea and its Agency. His conflict with Lenin gave him, as it seems, a remarkable insight into the evolution of the Bolshevik Party. Much later on, he was to abandon his prescience in favour of action, but for the time being it served him by justifying in theory his temperamental distaste for Lenin.

Denouncing Lenin for his overemphasis on a party that was to incarnate the 'revolutionary intelligentsia' instead of the working-class, Trotsky derided the idea that such intellectuals would then lead an unripe, timorous working-class movement into revolution. This was ultimately, as he thought, dependent on the notion of an 'orthodox theocracy' designed for a party that was meant to 'substitute itself for the working classes' independently of any action or even thought on the part of the working classes themselves.

Trotsky coined this word 'surrogatism' or 'substitutism' (*zamestitelstvo*): it sums up with striking accuracy a psychological process that far transcends the Party disputes of 1903 and afterwards. It sums up, in fact, the very notion of intellectuals, say, representing the interests of the workers and finally becoming in this sense the workers *tout court*.

Here is, according to Trotsky, the cardinal consequence of 'surrogatism':

> Lenin's methods lead to this: the party organisation (the caucus) at first substitutes itself for the party as a whole; then the Central Committee substitutes itself for the organisation; and finally a single 'dictator' substitutes himself for the Central Committee.[21]

He then counterposes to this his own (and Axelrod's) view:

> The party must seek the guarantee of its stability in its own base, in an active and self-reliant proletariat, and not in its top caucus, which the revolution ... may suddenly sweep away with its wing.[22]

This formulation forecasts more or less exactly what happened: Trotsky's notion of 'surrogatism' was the fundamental bridge-concept between the mythology of the evolving Bolshevik Party and its actual behaviour, so that from its very inception down to our own day the Party has been able to claim, quite sincerely, to *be* the working class by virtue of this theory of representation. The dictator who eventually appeared could, within the framework of this mythology, present himself to the Party and to the world – perhaps also to himself! – as himself constituting the Party by virtue of representing the Politburo, which represented the Central Committee, which represented the Party, which represented the working class. By merely disavowing this unconscious psychological process the Party – or the caucus controlling the Party, or the dictator controlling the caucus – could very naturally act with integrity and composure.

A few years later, in 1912, Trotsky gave a sharpened expression of this view in a lengthy essay he wrote for his chief journalistic standby, the big liberal Russian newspaper *Kiev Thought*. There, in a characteristic effort to place his generalisations against a broad historical background, he traced this process of 'surrogatism' in Russian history as a whole, or more precisely in the intelligentsia's efforts to lead political movements, in which various intellectuals 'express' the ideas of others – the aristocratic Decembrists in 1825 'representing' the ideas of a middle class that had not even come into existence, the Populists representing an inert peasantry, and most recently, the Marxist intelligentsia that was now thinking of making

itself the self-appointed spokesman for a working class that could not
yet speak for itself.

He crystallised this whole summing up – both trenchant and
accurate – in the charge that all such intellectuals, instead of looking
at the interests of a real class, where in fact merely being seduced by
the Idea of the class – an Idea that justified, of course, their own
claim to paramountcy. (Much later Trotsky was to abandon this
whole view of things; by 1917 he was to make, in fact, a complete
right-about-face.)

In this curiously violent pamphlet, written in 1904, Trotsky made
much of an analogy with the French Revolution, a favourite pastime
of Marxists, especially in Russia. After giving an entertaining satire
of Lenin's style, he identified him as a 'Jacobin' in contrast to a
'Social-Democrat'.

In the framework of the analogy this was merely another way of
saying that Lenin was trying to manipulate the working class by
means of his organisational obsession instead of allowing its spontaneous impulses free play.

Trotsky thought 'Jacobinism' essentially pessimistic, since it
lacked confidence in the potentialities of The Revolution: under
modern conditions, with the titanic technological developments of
society accompanied by the unprecedented expansion of the industrial working class, no one could seriously claim that Socialism was
still a utopia. Hence the 'optimism' of the Social-Democrats, who
thought the independent action of an elite superfluous, was no more
than a reflection of the Zeitgeist.

Thus it was the Jacobins who were the true pessimists – they
could not imagine that their own view of the world could prevail;
they saw themselves outside reality, separated from others – that is
why the dividing-line had to be drawn by the blade of the
guillotine!

> The Jacobins were Utopians; we aspire to express the objective
> trend. They were idealists ... we are materialists ... they were
> rationalists, we are dialectitians ... They chopped off heads, we
> enlighten them with class consciousness ... Marx's lion head
> would have been the first to roll under the guillotine.[23]

With this view Trotsky represented, of course, the positive, self-
assured 'optimism' of early 'classical Marxism', with its euphoric and
essentially religious faith that History was fundamentally on the right

track and that all would be well for those who grasped its inwardness.

Lenin, to be sure, had the same faith, but in him it was associated with an equal faith in the obvious necessity of a modality for History to work through – the modality of an apparatus. That he could think this even when there could still be no question in his mind of using his organisation to take power was, perhaps, a stroke of luck: the apparatus created by the necessity for working underground effectively was to be in existence when the question did arise, later on, of actually taking power in a situation that had meanwhile turned favourable.

But how could this point be articulated clearly? And what place did it leave for personal animosity, spite and ambition?

Perhaps the slipperiness inherent in expounding in the idiom of rationalism these subleties of faith explains the curious ferocity of Trotsky's prose in *Our Political Tasks*. In this pamphlet his style, always trenchant, was studded with stings aimed at Lenin: 'Hideous', 'dissolute', 'demagogical' 'adroit statistician', 'slovenly lawyer', 'malicious and morally repulsive'. Such epithets – routine, to be sure, in the polemical style of the milieu – were nevertheless bound to chill.

It was doubtless the personal repugnance Trotsky now felt toward Lenin that explains the remarkably ferocious tone of the pamphlet. It was, in fact, the most systematic onslaught on Lenin hitherto made, even in a movement in which 'annihilating' rhetoric had been conventional since Marx himself.

Politically this early episode in Trotsky's life – his savage hostility at the Congress, reinforced by his polemical writings – was to have far-reaching consequences. His pamphlet laid the groundwork for his subsequent alienation from the fundamental groupings in the movement.

Until 1917 Trotsky was to be very nearly a lone wolf. His violent attack on Lenin naturally led to his being looked upon by Lenin's entourage as a particularly virulent Menshevik. Among the Mensheviks, on the other hand, he was equally out-of-place: his voluntaristic style, his youth, his ineptitude in personal relations made him ill-at-ease as a 'faction member' there too.

Trotsky's only hope, organisationally, was to reconcile both wings of the Party; had he done that he would, of course, have been in a strong position.

After writing his savage *Our Political Tasks*, but before publication, for instance, there were signs of reconciliation. Lenin seemed to

have been isolated by the successful Menshevik reaction, aided by
Plekhanov; even some of his factional associates regarded his
attitude as merely personal, and seemed willing to make peace.

Accordingly, when Trotsky wrote a preface to his pamphlet it
might have seemed that the crisis in the Party was over, and that the
hotheads on both sides had been bypassed. Trotsky wrote as much in
his Preface; he called on the Mensheviks to make peace with the
Bolsheviks – minus Lenin, to be sure, but still to make peace. If he
believed that there was of course no point in publishing his pamphlet at all; it would merely poison relations still further.

Yet he was strangely intransigent: after writing a Preface that
obviated the brochure, he published it *anyhow*. In the event, while
calling on the Mensheviks and Bolsheviks to make peace, he was
effectively excluding himself from any contact with the Bolsheviks.

He was encapsulated within a cul-de-sac. This was not, to be sure,
very evident at the time, since the whole of this embittered controversy involved only a few dozen people; if it were not for its historic
consequences it would have to be summed up, in fact, as a tempest
in a teapot.

The life the revolutionaries led was essentially a Bohemian one;
nothing was more natural than roaming about from one colony of
émigrés to another, writing an odd article for some revolutionary
periodical of varying degrees of partisanship, and doing so from any
one of half a dozen cities.

After Trotsky had been ousted from *The Spark* and was more or
less on the oust with both factions of the Party, he left Geneva for
Munich, where he stayed at the house of a most unusual figure in the
revolutionary movement – Alexander Israel Helphand. A little later
Natalya joined him.

Well known under his pen-name, 'Parvus', Helphand had been
born into a lower-middle-class Jewish family in the province of
Minsk, where Jews made up more than half the population. Like
Trotsky he had grown up in Odessa.

Having managed to acquire an education in Switzerland, 'Parvus'
could write authoritatively on many subjects, including technical
economics, and was an established contributor to the outstanding
Socialist periodical in Europe, Karl Kautsky's *Neue Zeit*. At this time
he was thirty-seven, twelve years older than Trotsky: they became
friends.

Trotsky had great respect for Helphand's mind. He thought him
not merely 'the most eminent Marxist figure at the turn of the

century', but also 'with his fearless thinking and his virile, muscular style a really remarkable writer.'[24] On the other hand, 'there was always something mad and unreliable about him. In addition to all his other ambitions, this revolutionary was enthralled by a surprising dream – to get rich ... Thoughts of The Revolution were interwoven with thoughts of wealth in the heavy fleshy head of this bulldog.'[25]

Helphand was in fact to have a remarkable career as doubtless the only multi-millionaire in history who was a genuine Marxist.

At this time, however, he was still a journalist, an authoritative figure in the German Socialist movement and hence of special weight for the Russian revolutionaries. He published a review of his own (Aus der Weltpolitik) in which he achieved the distinction of making a Marxist prophecy that came true: in 1895 he began predicting a war between Russia and Japan and, moreover, a revolution that would come out of it. Both things happened in 1904–5.

Helphand is of particular importance from the point of view of practical Marxism because he and Trotsky collaborated – it is hard to know who owed what to whom in any detail – on a theory that was to play a role in Bolshevik politics.

Helphand's central notion was expressed in a series of articles on 'War and The Revolution' in The Spark.[26] He took as his main point a Marxist cliché – that the nation-state evolved under capitalism had become outmoded – and gave it an original twist by advancing the presumed date of realisation: he thought the nation-state would collapse in an imminent upheaval. He analysed the whole phenomenon as part of the international division of labour, in which a vast international struggle between capitalist nation-states, triggered by the Russo-Japanese war of 1904, would ultimately lead to a political overturn in Russia itself. He considered that The Russian Revolution, breaking out as one of the consequences of the world-wide debacle of nationally articulated capitalism, would shake up the Bourgeois world; in consequence the 'Russian Proletariat may well play the role of the vanguard of social revolution'.[27]

This was the starting point of Trotsky's theory of 'Permanent Revolution'. Helphand had restricted himself to predicting political upheaval and to a role for the Russian Proletariat as 'vanguard' of The Revolution: he had not spoken about an actual 'Socialist' Revolution in Russia: all Marxists still believed that in and for itself a Revolution in Russia was bound to be 'Bourgeois' because of the country's agrarian, backward, and indeed semi-feudal condition.

Trotsky took Helphand's prediction as a starting point for a twist of his own. He predicted that, just *because* the Russian bourgeoisie was so feeble, once the upheaval took place it would find itself incapable even of carrying through its *own* Revolution, and that it would thus be necessary for the Russian working class to establish a proletarian dictatorship in order to bring about the Bourgeois Revolution itself, regardless of whether or not The Revolution had as *yet* broken out in the West.

The elaboration of this theory was not to play a role until much later, during the turmoil of 1917, when a version of it was to be taken up by Lenin.

At the time that Trotsky jointly with Helphand evolved this theory of Permanent Revolution it was attacked by Lenin very violently – all Lenin's attacks, to be sure, were violent!

In the course of his diatribe Lenin remarked that he thought the view that the 'maximum programme, the conquest of power for a Socialist revolution, can be achieved immediately', was 'absurd, semi-anarchist'. He repeated the common-sense observation that since hardly any of the workers understood the first thing about Socialism it was ridiculous to expect them to make a Socialist Revolution. And this understanding of theirs was, after all, a 'subjective condition indissolubly connected with the objective condition' of the 'present degree of economic development of Russia'.

> We are all convinced that the emancipation of the workers can only be brought about by the workers themselves; a Socialist revolution is out of the question unless the masses become class-conscious, organised, trained and educated by open class struggle against the entire Bourgeoisie. In answer to the anarchist objections that we are delaying the Socialist Revolution, we shall say: we are not delaying it, but are taking the first steps in its direction, using the only means that are possible along the only right path, namely the path of a democratic republic.

Lenin ended this paragraph with an unusually prescient remark – which he was, to be sure, soon to disregard: 'Whoever wants to approach Socialism by any other path than that of political democracy will inevitably arrive at absurd and reactionary conclusions both economic and political.'[28]

When properly connected, this harmonises with Trotsky's remark the year before (1904) (see page 91):

The organisation of the Party will take the place of the Party itself; the Central Committee will take the place of the organisation; and finally, the Dictator will take the place of the Central Committee.

In this case, to be sure, both men were saying the same thing – the one within the context of the party, the other within the context of a state. If the Party were to become the State, of course, both pernicious situations would coalesce.

Neither Trotsky nor Lenin ever foresaw the fruition of such a coalescence. No Russian Marxist could have been expected to foresee at that time the structural consequences of a situation inherently inconceivable – Socialist power in a peasant society. Trotsky was merely applying logic to an analysis of a theoretical proposition. It was to be his tragedy – much later – that the extrapolation of this consequence of logic was to find an embodiment in reality!

Meanwhile, his organisational allegiance remained obscure : even when he broke with the Mensheviks formally by writing a letter to *The Spark* (at the end of September 1904) the letter was not published. Thus in the somewhat fluid medium of the movement he remained linked to them.

In any case these skirmishings were now to be overshadowed by a large-scale fact – a shake-up of the Russian State.

On 9 January 1905 a big procession, led by a priest, made its way to the Winter Palace of the Tsar in St. Petersburg. It was quite peaceful : the marchers were carrying a variety of pious emblems – ikons, church banners and portraits of the Tsar. They intended to submit a modest petition imploring the Tsar's help. (The priest, a Father Gapon, later turned out to be an agent of the Gendarmerie; he was supposed to infiltrate the working-class movement in order to combat Socialism with the help of religion.)

The Tsar and his advisers made a fateful blunder: the troops protecting the Winter Palace were ordered to shoot into the throng; the peaceful parade turned into a shambles, instantly notorious as 'Bloody Sunday', Amidst the frictions generated by the Russo-Japanese war, which had broken out in 1904, the symbol of Bloody Sunday had immense potential.

Trotsky heard about the shambles on his return to Geneva from one of his numerous speaking trips. When he heard Martov describing the march on the Winter Palace, 'he turned pale; grew dizzy, and very nearly fainted . . .'[29]

This emotional tension, though chronic with Trotsky, in this case had an objective justification. The news of Bloody Sunday came on the heels of some optimistic forecasts of his own, generated by the Russo-Japanese war.

The conflict with Japan had sadly disoriented the Tsarist Government; its discomfiture created a fissure that the influences not only of Liberalism but of Socialism now began to seep through.

In July 1904, after the assassination (by a Social-Revolutionary) of Plehve, the Tsarist Minister responsible for policy in the Far East, there was a reaction that toned down his tough tactics against the Liberal and quasi-Liberal gentry. Plehve was succeeded by a minister who restored the status of the *Zemstvos* (semi-representative Liberal bodies) and permitted them to convene a national assembly in November 1904.

This gave rise to a flood of Liberal oratory throughout the country, at an extended series of 'banquets' at which it was possible not only for the Liberals and middle-class spokesmen to speak up, but also Socialists. It was natural for the government to come in for harsh words at these banquets.

Even in the torrents of anti-government speechifying it was plain that the Liberals and the Socialists had somewhat different aims. But the very possibility of speaking up legally, side by side with middle-class and upper-class Liberals, in its turn brought about a further split in the Socialist movement. Collaboration with the Liberals became a concrete possibility that fitted in both with the concept of 'Legal Marxism' and with the general perspective of the 'ripening' of the working class for Socialism through the 'ripening' of society as a whole.

Many Mensheviks inclined toward this view; it entailed, of course, a compromise with Liberal and middle-class elements for the purpose of broadening the capitalist foundations of society in order, eventually, to create the prerequisites for Socialism.

Marxists in general were against Populist terrorism, as well as against Socialism based on the communalism of the old-fashioned peasant villages. Hence it was possible for 'Legal Marxists' to remain Marxist while fighting both approaches. On the other hand, this naturally converged with middle-class demands in general. Yet the Legal Marxists (whose chief organ since 1902 had been Peter

Struve's *Emancipation*, published in Stuttgart and later in Paris)
failed to go on to sponsor proletarian Socialism.

It was at this point that Legal Marxism abandoned what had been
a reasonable convergence of views with *The Spark*: the Legal
Marxists were becoming liberals, just as in their conflicts with the
Bolsheviks the Mensheviks, too, were moving toward collaboration
with the Liberals.

Trotsky had been extremely optimistic. In November and
December 1904 he had published a pamphlet attacking the Mensheviks' 'indulgence' of Russian Liberalism; it contained an inflammatory forecast of an imminent upheaval in Russia – a view heavily
discounted by most of his associates.

Trotsky's passionate lyricism facilitates his assessment both as a
leader and as an historian:

Tear the workers away from the machines and benches, lead
them out the factory gates into the street, direct them into nearby
factories, proclaim a work-stoppage there, carry new masses into
the street. In this way, growing from workshop to workshop, from
factory to factory, flinging aside all police obstacles and attracting
passers-by by speeches and appeals, swallowing up groups
encountered en route, filling up the streets, seizing all suitable
buildings for meetings of the people, entrenching yourselves in
these buildings, using them for uninterrupted revolutionary mass-
meetings with a constantly self-renewing audience, you will bring
order into the movement of the masses, heightening their mood,
explaining to them the aim and the meaning of what is going
on – thus finally turning the city into a revolutionary camp – such,
by and large, is the plan of action.[30]

It is only too plain that this whole notion of the 'plan of action' has
a dream-like glow. All details are smothered in the assumption that
just such a spontaneous movement will come about and will be
'directed' by someone.

But it was a dream that demanded of the dreamer some public
action – 'haranguing and attracting passers-by'. Hence when Trotsky
heard about Bloody Sunday from Martov, he was exhilarated.

What had seemed to his associates to be mere euphoria now
looked altogether justified. Things were moving at last. All the
émigrés were entranced by the convergence between History and
their own ideas.

Younger and more impetuous, Trotsky decided to leap into action, though he had no organisational attachment and no plan. There was also some danger inherent in a return to Russia: he risked capture as a fugitive from Siberian exile; he might even be sent to hard labour.

But in February 1905 doubts were impossible: 'I could remain abroad no longer. Ever since the Congress I had had no connection with the Bolsheviks. I had broken organisationally with the Mensheviks. The only thing left for me to do was to act on my own account.'[31] This was, in fact, to remain the keynote of his career until 1917.

The first thing he did was to send Natalya on ahead to arrange for living quarters, which of course had to be done secretly.

The second thing was to consolidate his 'theoretical position'. He hastened back to Munich to show Helphand the proofs of the pamphlet that had made the Mensheviks hem and haw. Helphand read them with mounting enthusiasm; he was so inflamed by the substance of the pamphlet, especially by its topicality, that he subscribed to it at once. It seemed to be the first time that a theoretical analysis of history was intertwined with practical opportunity.

Helphand agreed to write a preface to Trotsky's pamphlet; it was to have a prophetic element – it was the first time the claim was made that a Marxist group could even think of 'taking power' in Russia.

This was Helphand's conclusion in his Preface to Trotsky's pamphlet; it went beyond Trotsky's own boldness at this time:

> The Revolutionary Provisional Government of Russia will be the government of a workers' democracy. . . . As the Social Democratic party is at the head of the revolutionary movement . . . this government will be social-democratic . . . a coherent government with a social-democratic majority.[32]

Both Bolsheviks and Mensheviks opposed this prophetic conclusion, though for slightly different reasons.

The Mensheviks thought it out of the question for a revolutionary party representing proletarian interests to participate in a Bourgeois Revolution aimed merely against absolutism, feudalism etc., and not at Socialism. It was up to The Bourgeoisie alone to head its own revolution; the workers' party should be no more than the workers' watchdog.

Lenin also thought the revolution in Russia was to be Bourgeois, in so far as Socialism was beyond its scope; but he did not think The

Bourgeoisie *itself* was really revolutionary. Hence he thought it was up to a Socialist party to enter into any revolutionary government, though he was strongly opposed to the notion that such a government could ever be Social-Democratic.

This is how he demolished such a possibility:

This *cannot be*, if what we are thinking of are not accidental, ephemeral episodes, but a revolutionary dictatorship that is at all lasting, that is at all capable of leaving some trace in history. It cannot be, because only a revolutionary dictatorship based on the vast majority of the people can be at all stable.... But the Russian proletariat is now a minority of the population.... It would be extemely harmful to have any illusions whatever about this.[33]

For Marxists there was no way of accommodating a point that had been made by Helphand merely on the basis of common sense. Even in this daring conclusion he was not, after all, recommending an actual 'Dictatorship of the Proletariat', but merely a 'workers' government', on the theory that if the industrial working class were in fact to be instrumental, in overthrowing The Bourgeoisie its delegates would naturally have a decisive voice in any provisional government.

This was common sense, but it was not Marxism. How, in fact, could this simple observation of Helphand's – assuming it became a reality – dovetail with the 'general Marxist' view that *any* revolution in Russia was simply bound to be 'bourgeois' in its nature? On the other hand, how could a mere minority of the country – the industrial working class – govern a country democratically? At this time not only Liberals but all Marxists, after all, believed in 'representative democratic' government.

Though neither Trotsky nor Helphand was able to reconcile these two somewhat disparate ideas, Trotsky was exhilarated by the general elan. After spending a few weeks with Helphand in Munich writing more articles that articulated both a lyrical view of The Revolution as a whole and at the same time a rationalist analysis of the techniques that had to be developed, he followed Natalya to Kiev, which was more or less the focal point of a Marxist 'underground', and where the police were less active.

He immediately ran into an outstanding member of the tiny Bolshevik hierarchy, Leonid Krasin, a well-to-do engineer who acted as fund-raiser for the Bolsheviks but who, because of his personal belief in the reconciliation of the two halves of the Party, was at this point sympathetic to Trotsky.

There is some suggestion that Trotsky had some relations with the Jewish 'self-defence' units set up against pogroms; a Jewish student remembered him for this, as well as for 'directing revolutionary operations throughout the Ukraine . . . from his apartment [sic] in Kiev'.[34] As before, however, these Jewish interests, whatever they might have amounted to, were peripheral.

Trotsky took the odd name of 'Ensign Arbuzov'. He spent hours secluded with strange visitors and the rest of the time reading newspapers and books. To avoid the police he had to keep moving; sometimes he would be asked to leave his lodgings, sometimes he would be taken care of.

Later he recalled taking refuge in an eye-hospital as a patient: the ward-physician knew about him, as did some of his assistants, but a nurse was overzealous – she advised him not to read and write so much and above all to take eye-drops and foot-baths.

In the spring he left for St. Petersburg with Krasin, well ahead of the other émigrés, who were uncertain about what was going on in Russia and had remained in Western Europe sitting about. Thus Trotsky had something of a head start.

But in Petersburg there was no chance for real action either. By the time he arrived there the hullabaloo over Bloody Sunday had subsided. The police seemed to have successfully curbed the agitation of the clandestine Marxist coteries. What had assumed importance, instead, was a strong movement among Liberals on behalf of constitutional monarchy and general reforms. Not until much later that year, after the Japanese defeat of Russia, were Marxists again to become a factor.

Trotsky and Natalya were soon obliged to leave Petersburg again. They had been living with a colonel, who together with his sons 'sympathised' with the revolutionaries – a middle-class fashion in Tsarist Russia as elsewhere. Trotsky's 'official' name was Vikentyev: he and Natalya were passing themselves off as landowners. To the local revolutionaries he was known as Peter Petrovich.

Natalya was picked up by the police during a Cossack raid on a May First meeting in the woods; she was gaoled for six months and then deported to Tver under police surveillance. Trotsky, learning that his underground coterie had been penetrated by a Tsarist agent who knew him by sight, fled to Finland, to a tranquil environment of 'hills, lakes, pine-trees, clear autumn air, repose'. When summer was over, Trotsky was completely alone in the big hotel, waited on by a young boy. The snow fell. The place was quite dead; not a sound could be heard. In the evenings the postman would bring a bundle of newspapers from Petersburg. Trotsky took long walks.

In mid-October this tranquillity changed overnight. There was news of a general strike in St. Petersburg. 'In the calm of the hotel the rustling of the newspapers resounded in my ears like the thunder of avalanches. . . . The Revolution was in full swing.'[35]

Trotsky rushed back to Petersburg on horseback; the following evening he made his first appearance in a genuinely public arena – an impromptu mass-meeting.

This was a great change from his life beforehand, which had been spent in a closed circle speaking to handfuls of people in a specialised jargon. For the first time he had occasion to address not just Marxists, general Socialists or Populists, but ordinary people, most of them quite ignorant of or indifferent to the special idiom of the revolutionaries. It was to launch him on his own special path as a 'public' revolutionary.

For a time he was helped by the condition of Russian Marxism. The practical ideas of both factions in the Marxist party had not quite jelled. In addition, Mensheviks and Bolsheviks were hampered by their split, although the split had not lasted long enough for them to elaborate their own individual party structures.

At the same time Trotsky, just because he was relatively free of organisational connections, was able to 'express' the *general* aims of The Revolution in its 'public' phase. Thus he could present himself to nonpartisan masses more easily than other Marxists.

His looks were now striking: he was an 'elegantly dressed, cultivated gentleman with a very important look about him; it was hard to recognise Lyova Bronstein with his careless shirt and other attributes of a bygone simplicity.'[36]

A later associate, who was to become something of a friend, Lunacharsky (the first Soviet Commissar for Education), remarked, after the January events of 1905:

Trotsky was at that time extraordinarily elegant, in contrast to all of us, and very handsome. This elegance of his, and especially a sort of carelessly condescending manner of speaking to no matter who struck me very disagreeably. With great malevolence I looked at this dandy, with one leg slung over the other, dashing off with a pencil an outline of an impromptu speech.[37]

Natalya, with somewhat more sympathy, was to recall his 'strapping build, abundant dark, rebellious shock of hair and small moustache. He had strong features in a bony face; his blue eyes expressed the joy of life.'[38]

*   *   *

The starting point of the St. Petersburg strike had been the printers' insistence on improved conditions (less work and higher wages), but the mood had caught on in some other industries and even overflowed into the countryside. The clandestine Socialist coteries were taken by surprise: economic demands were soon accompanied by demands for constitutional reforms.

The strikes gave rise to an institution that was to achieve celebrity the Soviet (Council) of Workers' Deputies.

The handful of Bolsheviks in the capital had had nothing to do with the formation of the Soviet. At that stage in Bolshevik development, in fact, the Soviet was frowned on. The Bolsheviks thought it would compete with them, since at this time Marxists hoped to create a mass party. Hence, as a general institution the Soviet was suspect.

It came into being, curiously enough, as an effect of a Tsarist directive. After the fiasco of Bloody Sunday in January, the Tsar had set up a commission of enquiry that called for a hearing of workers' complaints to be transmitted by delegates elected in the factories. Nothing was done until strikers from about fifty print-shops gave the deputies instructions to create a Council; this established a core that was soon increased by workers' deputies from other industries.

This was the paradigm for the 1905 Soviet. Up to then the working class had been constitutionally voteless; thus the Soviet played a role as legal mouthpiece for a substantial segment of the population. Nearly half the Petersburg workers – some 200,000 – had taken part in electing to it hundreds of deputies (400–560).

The complexion of the Soviet was very vague; the Marxists were in two minds about participating at all. While they were still wrangling about it the Tsar issued a Manifesto yielding the main points of a general constitutional reform and a universal vote.

The abruptness of the announcement and the content of the

Manifesto gave rise to some public excitement; jubilant throngs roamed the streets. The Manifesto seemed to embody a painless surrender.

On 18 October Trotsky joined a big, cheerful crowd on its way towards the Technological Institute. It was being curbed by mounted gendarmes, but nothing much happened; occasionally the gendarmes jostled people. Youthful factory-workers tore down dynastic banners – red, white, and blue – from houses and replaced them with jagged flags. When the police and gendarmes barred the way to the Institute, the throng flowed on to the University grounds, the usual place for mass-meetings, and into the courtyard to join the crowds being harangued.

Trotsky had made his first appearance in the Soviet the day before; he had presented himself there as representing the Mensheviks. He had called himself 'Yanovsky', i.e., from the Yanovka farm named after the colonel who had sold it to his father. A handful of individuals also knew him to be the same Trotsky who wrote for *The Spark* and who was also called Peter Petrovich.

Now he edged himself through the crowd to the balcony to make his first speech to a non-Party audience:

Many tens of thousands of people, not yet cooled off by the struggle and drunk with the enthusiasm of the initial victory, were standing in front of the Petersburg University. I yelled down to them from the balcony that the half-victory was unreliable, that the enemy was irreconcilable, that a trap was lying in wait for us; I tore up the Tsar's Manifesto and let it flutter with the wind.[39]

Trotsky is remarkably terse about this first intervention in mass politics: this speech, followed by others, was to magnify his name.

Helphand, also inflamed by the events, arrived in St. Petersburg toward the end of October, and became a member of the Soviet. He and Trotsky immediately became outstanding; Lenin and Martov did not arrive until November, after a general amnesty for political offenders had been declared by the Tsar (30 October). By the time they arrived, Trotsky and Helphand were an effective team.

During the Soviet's brief existence – it lasted fifty days – Trotsky was incredibly energetic. Early in November he and Helphand got hold of *The Russian Gazette*, a small, hitherto negligible Liberal daily, and turned it into a spectacularly successful mass organ, doubtless the first popular Socialist newspaper in Russia. In addition, Trotsky wrote for the Soviet's own somewhat shapeless organ, *Izvestia*, which, couched in a primitive, popular style, appeared only spasmodically, and a little while later for a big daily called *The Beginning*, an organ of the Mensheviks.

Thus, at the age of twenty-six, he was in a position to request articles from the most famous European Socialists – Bebel, Kautsky, Rosa Luxemburg, Franz Mehring, as well as Plekhanov.

As a popular journalist Trotsky was an immense success. Not only did he build up the circulation of *The Russian Gazette* from 30,000 to 100,000 in the space of a few days, and in the space of a month up to half a million, but he even turned the Menshevik paper *The Beginning* into what amounted to his own organ, since the Mensheviks had made him many theoretical concessions (sponsoring in effect his and Helphand's private theory of Permanent Revolution and barring any deals with the chief Liberal party, the Constitutional Democrats, or Kadets).

The Beginning had far more impact than the Bolshevik press, despite the availability of Gorky and Lunacharsky as well as of Lenin. The Bolshevik periodical, *New Life*, had a circulation of only 50,000.

Natalya could now come back to Petersburg. She and Trotsky, still known as Vikentyev, moved to a rented room belonging to a stock-exchange speculator who was forced to rent out rooms because business was so bad.

The Soviet was quite powerless. Though supported by Bolsheviks, Mensheviks and Social Revolutionaries, it was essentially still-born. Its intransigent demands on behalf of so many workers in the capital remained *demands put to the authorities*. It could do nothing to implement them.

The politically conscious groups were not armed; their enthusiasm lacked both consistent thought and organisational ability.

Hence the question of arms remained, very evidently, vital. The capital was, after all, filled with soldiers as yet quite untouched even by the shapeless political agitation, which in any case was itself split between liberal and middle-class elements that were intent merely on the constitutionalisation of the monarchy, while the factory workers who had started the strike, though doubtless in favour of a republic, were more concerned about economics.

The Soviet was hamstrung. There was no way for it to express a political will of its own, even if it had had one. At the same time, its existence provided a forum in which dangerous sentiments, by being highly publicised, could easily be punished. Since this was so, it was obliged to move carefully from the very outset. Indeed one of Trotsky's most striking features at this time was his realism; his rhetoric remained subordinate to common sense.

Only a couple of days after the Tsar's Manifesto he put up a strong case for stopping the strike, which was done. A few days later, when it was learned that the Gendarmerie were preparing to crush a funeral for the casualties of the strike, and in addition that a pogrom against Jews was being planned by the Tsarist Secret Police, the funeral was cancelled too. The most the Soviet could undertake was to use the crude militia to forestall a pogrom. The militia already in existence – improvised 'squads' meant to defend the Soviet itself – generally had only rough clubs made of wood or iron, very rarely revolvers.

The Soviet was, in fact, reduced to mere agitation: to Trotsky this function was fundamental. When it was announced, for instance, that despite the assurance proclaimed in the Manifesto, censorship was to continue, the printers in their turn announced that no books or periodicals submitted for news censorship would be printed. This created a relatively free press for the first time in Russian history. To implement their demand for an eight-hour day, the factory workers began applying it in their own workshops and factories.

Since such initiatives could not be sustained, Trotsky was in the paradoxical position of standing out as the Soviet's premier speaker in expressing its *general* defiance while nevertheless stopping the general strike, cancelling the funeral, and in the case of the eight-hour day, reminding the Soviet that it simply could not go on with it: it had prompted a lock-out of 100,000 workers.

In 1905, before effective action was, perhaps, even possible, Trotsky's long-range theoretical views prevented him from embarking on merely adventurous schemes. There was, after all, simply no background for a serious attack on Tsarism. Trotsky's 'moderation' was thus a way of remaining anchored to that primary fact while allowing his imagination to soar into the future.

The eight-hour day, for instance, had been considered chimerical even in Western Europe. Yet partly as a result of the psychological preparations inherent in the 1905 Soviet, it was to figure as a primary working-class demand until 1917. By modulating his support of the general strike so as to make that support a method of clarifying to the entourage of the political parties just what it implied, he also pinpointed a general analysis of society. In this way he imperceptibly altered the world-view of the workers themselves, and readied them, to some extent, for radical developments.

In fact, all the Soviet's goals were so remote from realisation at this time that in a certain sense promoting them was not really risky at all – at least, not in terms of action.

A combination of euphoria and realism may be seen, for instance, in a statement made by Trotsky as spokesman for the Executive collectively, on 5 November, when he called for putting a stop to a second general strike. He pointed out that, in the nature of things, a general strike should lead to a *coup d'état*, which, since the Soviet was plainly not ready for it, could not be made; hence, since the strike could not be carried on properly it had to be called off.

In Trotsky's eyes this realism was justified by his assessment of the current situation. Later on, in some other era, the strikers would be joined, no doubt, by railway and communications workers who 'with the steel of rails and with telegraph wire would bind together all revolutionary bulwarks of the country into a single whole. This would enable us to arouse the whole of Russia within twenty-four hours when necessary.'[40]

This is the far-reaching, epoch-making prediction of 'classical Marxism – there will come a time when . . .

The Soviet, which had taken shape overnight, dissolved almost as rapidly. Some leaders were arrested on 22 November, after the censorship was re-imposed: the chairman was one. Trotsky was elected one of a trio of co-chairmen. Speaking on this occasion, too, he played a dual role – moderate, in the sense of opposing some terrorist suggestions for reprisals against Tsarist Ministers (made, characteristically, by Social-Revolutionaries), and extremist, in favour of an armed uprising.

This proposal for an armed uprising was, of course, dangerous as well as futile: both arms and organisations were totally lacking. In Trotsky's mind, it was merely another way of 'radicalising' the workers' psychology.

Just as he justified the abandonment of the campaign for the eight-hour day by claiming it to have been a technique *not* for 'winning the eight-hour day for the working class but the working class for the eight-hour day', so he now came out for an armed uprising *not* in order to bring it about, but to lend the mere possibility of it a sense of immediacy in the minds of the more extremist workers by investing it with a matter-of-fact atmosphere.

The Soviet not only called for an armed uprising, the idea advocated by Trotsky, it also issued a so-called Financial Manifesto composed by Helphand, a lengthy denunciation of everything in the administration, culminating in a summons to 'the people' not to accept banknotes, not to pay taxes, to take their money out of the bank, and so on.

Both the Financial Manifesto and the call for an armed uprising were plainly beyond the resources of the Soviet. They were, in fact, a mere reflection of the reality that the Soviet could not, in its nature, accomplish anything at all. They were obviously a mere surrogate for action, the more so since the words of the Financial Manifesto – 'there is only one way . . . to overthrow the government, to deny it . . . its revenue' – obviously contradicted the claims put forth for the other 'only way' mentioned – the armed uprising.

Trotsky was juggling words, or perhaps ideas. It was plain that, from the point of view of at least *immediate* realism, while the demand for an eight-hour day was a way of radicalising workers' psychology by making the extreme sound moderate, the idea of both the Financial Manifesto and the armed uprising was just as dangerous as a general strike, even more so. Legally, in any case, the call to an armed uprising would certainly prejudice a court!

A courtroom was, in fact, already at hand. The Government finally intervened. On 3 December the police descended on the Soviet. The Executive was in session under Trotsky's chairmanship, when word was received. It decided to carry on with business as usual, though without resisting. The police were accompanied by the Guards, the Cossacks and the gendarmes.

There was a pounding of boots; sabres were heard clanking. On a balcony Trotsky ordered everyone to surrender at once, and to break their revolver locks before handing them over. 'We declare beforehand that only an agent provocateur or a policeman will fire a shot here!'[41] Then he went back to his seat in the Executive.

A unit of policemen and soldiers occupied the corridor outside: an officer came into the Executive's room while someone was speaking. Facing the Executive, the officer started reading out the warrant for arrest.

Trotsky pulled him up short: 'Please don't interfere with the speaker. If you wish to take the floor, you must give your name; I shall ask the meeting whether it wishes to listen to you'.[42]

The officer waited, nonplussed. When the speaker finished,

Trotsky asked the Executive whether the officer should be permitted to make a statement 'as a matter of information'. The officer was then permitted to read out the warrant; Trotsky moved that it be acknowledged and the next business taken up. Someone else got up to speak.

The baffled officer stammered out an 'Excuse me' to Trotsky, who again took a sharp tone: 'Please don't interfere; you have had the floor; you have made your statement; we have acknowledged it.' He then turned to the Executive: 'Does the meeting wish to have further dealing with the policeman?' 'No!' 'Then please leave the hall!' said Trotsky.

The officer, flummoxed, mumbled and left. Trotsky then called on everyone to get rid of all documents and to withhold names from the police.

A few minutes later the officer returned, followed by a platoon: when a speaker started addressing the soldiers in his own way, appealing with 'revolutionary pathos' to the solidarity that ought to prevail between soldiers and workers just when the Tsar was actually breaking the promise he had given in the October Manifesto, the officer led them all out again and stationed them in the corridor.

Finally a big police unit arrived. Full of sang-froid, Trotsky said: 'I declare the meeting of the Executive closed.'

The Soviet had passed into history and, more important, into mythology.

CHAPTER IV

The Free-Lance

1905 MADE TROTSKY a celebrity. Despite his pseudonyms the Socialist 'professionals' knew who he was; within the emigration he was now a public figure. His eminence, even though it was restricted to the Soviet and had lasted only a couple of months, was indisputable. His bearing at the trial of the Soviet leaders was to epitomise his theatrical effectiveness.

Lunacharsky summed it up:

> Trotsky came out of the 1905 revolution with the greatest gain in the way of popularity; essentially neither Lenin nor Martov gained anything. ... From that time on Trotsky was in the first rank. In spite of his youth he was the most prepared; least of all was there the stamp of a certain émigré narrowness that ... at that time hampered even Lenin. ... I recall someone saying in Lenin's presence: 'Now the strong man ... is Trotsky.' Lenin seemed to scowl for a second, then he said : 'Oh well, Trotsky has earned that with his tireless, brilliant work.'[1]

Yet despite Lenin's epigram characterising the shake-up of 1905 as a 'dress-rehearsal' for 1917, all the accounts of it in the luxuriant, intelligent St. Petersburg press[2] of the time make it plain that it was no more than a trivial episode in the busy life of the capital.

It was, in fact, to be the Bolshevik victory of 1917 that in retrospect makes the 1905 Soviet important. Its magnification from the point of view of Bolshevik mythology was inevitable – it provided a paradigm for elite strategy, and more especially for its camouflage.

Before the 1905 Soviet all the émigré colonies scattered about Western Europe had been no more than discussion groups; attempts were made to 'organise' followings in Russia, to be sure, but if one recalls how the great bulk of the exiled intelligentsia lived, it is plain that only a fraction of its energies went into political organisation. Most of the time was spent analysing theory in the relentlessly talkative atmosphere of a coterie.

The Soviet, however, regardless of what it *actually* was, could plainly become a symbol of a different kind of politics – the politics, ultimately, of democratic action. The mere fact that it involved the *de facto* enfranchisement of a hitherto disenfranchised segment of the public implied a different sort of political activity – the activity of expressing, shaping, and conveying broad attitudes toward public questions.

The possibility of open agitation in a legal, democratic arena had come about so quickly that the underground leaders were quite unprepared : they had failed to digest the possibilities of the medium. Lenin had, to be sure, been moulding a small organisation, but it still did not amount to much; also, he was still unsure about how to deal with 'outsiders' – i.e., ordinary people.

Trotsky was completely at home : it was precisely a democratic medium, in fact, that suited his nature. His oratorical ability as well as his aesthetic talents, combined with his animal energy and his gift for couching generalisations in simple, emotional terms, made him an ideal mass speaker.

The democratic atmosphere of the legal Soviet heightened Trotsky's eminence in another way. Bolsheviks and Mensheviks concluded that their 'theoretical' wrangles had been senseless commotions due to their clandestine existence; with the emergence of the Party above-ground, bickering about conspiratorial techniques became superfluous.

Had the schism in the Party been overcome, had it become an organisation of masses, Trotsky as a maverick might have been able to play a role in it. But the Party was thrust back into the underground at once : Bolsheviks and Mensheviks resumed their envenomed rivalry.

Trotsky himself, according to Ziv, did not have the smallest interest in their theoretical squabbling. What counted for him was a broad arena in which he could display his personal virtuosity. But, since a Marxist's activity had to be clothed in theory, it was Trotsky's misfortune to be stuck with a theory that meant little to him.

It was plain to Ziv, who shared his prison once again in the aftermath of the 1905 upheaval, that though Trotsky was, so to speak, a 'Bolshevik by nature', he had become a 'Menshevik by necessity'. He put this conclusion to Trotsky himself during one of their intimate nocturnal chats: 'How can you, as a Marxist, not see that it is precisely the Mensheviks who are the real Marxists, and that the Bolsheviks are totally alien to Marxist thought?'

Since Trotsky was now linked with the Mensheviks, he was bound to accept the justice of this remark, says Ziv (how else, indeed, could he have remained a Menshevik?) and to agree that Lenin was no Marxist. On the other hand, young Trotsky added, the Mensheviks were quite incapable of any lively political action, whereas the Bolsheviks were always capable of adopting a 'real, healthy' tactic. 'In his words . . . there was a clear echo of the ardent sympathy he had for the Bolsheviks, who were close to him in spirit, and his ill-concealed antipathy for the Mensheviks, who were thoroughly alien to him.'[3]

Throughout the 1905 period, in any case, Trotsky's hostility to Lenin kept him excluded from the relatively tight little group around Lenin. Since their estrangement, Lenin had referred to Trotsky in a variety of phrases that all boiled down to 'chatterbox': 'hollow bell', 'revolutionary balalaika', 'phrase-monger', and so on. In a more expansive mood he would refer to him as typical of 'half-baked seminarist rhetoricians', 'university lecturers prattling about Marxism', and 'shyster lawyers'.[4]

Trotsky spent fifteen pleasant months in gaol. The Soviet leaders were treated with characteristic indulgence – put in unlocked cells and cosseted. They could walk about, receive books and visitors and carry on scarcely veiled agitation.

Trotsky was sent all the books he wanted: he wrote as much as he liked, smuggling everything out in his lawyer's brief-cases; he was visited twice a week by Natalya.

For relaxation I read the classics of European literature. Stretched out on the prison cot, I devoured them with a feeling of physical pleasure, like that of a gourmet sipping a fine wine or drawing on a fragrant cigar. These were the finest moments. My preoccupation with the classics has left traces, in the form of quotations and epigrams, throughout my writings of that period. It was at that time that I became familiar with the *grands seigneurs* of the French novel in the original. The art of story-telling is primarily a French art. Though I know German well, perhaps better than French, especially in areas of technical terminology, I read French *belles-lettres* more easily than German. To this day I have preserved my love for the French novel.[5]

The defendants were given all the leisure they needed to prepare their defence, which they were allowed to keep secret until the trial. To convey their views to the public they had assigned each other various roles: Trotsky was to defend the idea of an armed uprising. During the preliminary investigations he made no statement at all.

The trial kept being postponed; the Government was uneasy. The defeat at the hands of Japan had shaken things up; there were numerous small mutinies all over the country. In addition to some strikes in St. Petersburg, there was a very big strike in Moscow.

Parliamentary elections were held in March 1906; these were boycotted by the Socialists, but the Constitutional Democrats – Liberals – made a very good showing.

The trial was not held until September 1906, after the morale of the Government had been restored. It went on for a few weeks in a civil court (which meant no one was going to be executed). A whole troop of lawyers appeared on behalf of the defendants. The audience, made up of about a hundred people, included Trotsky's parents.

Trotsky was referred to as 'Leo, son of David Bronstein, a colonist (in Kherson Province).' Occasionally 'Trotsky' would appear in brackets.

A variety of witnesses – 250 – pieced together the record of the Soviet. Tens of thousands of workers signed petitions and sent them in to the court. The defendants were also pampered by the general public: Trotsky wrote of a constant stream of newspapers, letters, boxes of sweets, and above all flowers. The prosecution finally abandoned some of the initial charges (instigation of general strikes and manifestations) and concentrated on a single charge – armed insurrection.

The courtroom, in these lenient conditions, was a natural rostrum. Trotsky, having encouraged all the defendants to take up an attitude of blanket defiance, had a grand occasion to turn the trial into a demonstration of faith.

He made a speech – drawn from similar speeches made by Marx and Lassalle in the debacle of 1848 – summing up the phenomenon of an armed uprising as a tidal wave that revolutionaries, with their superior insight, merely foresee: they do not *plot*.

His speech impressed the courtroom (the prosecutor himself congratulated Trotsky) and generated so much emotion that the defence lawyers asked for an adjournment. During the adjournment Trotsky was thronged round by the lawyers and the public; his mother, who had been sitting there sobbing away, while his father stared at him, thought the respect he was being treated with meant that things were going to turn out all right.

When the verdict was in, the Soviet itself was declared blameless of insurrection; but Trotsky and fourteen other defendants were deprived of all civil rights and sentenced to Siberian exile for life. Of the other 300 people arrested with Trotsky after the 1905 upheaval, 284 were released; only two were given brief terms in jail.

Sentenced on 2 November, the convicts left for Siberia at dawn on 5 January 1907. After having spent their last night at a 'passionate game of chess', they had barely gone to sleep when they were awakened to leave, sending the 'Petersburg workers' an exhortation in farewell.

Many of the prisoners had their families with them; they were treated with indulgence, though the car they were in had a heavy escort of gendarmes and they were not told where they were going until they were nearly there. At the Urals they changed escorts and went on toward Tobolsk in forty horse-drawn sledges. Since they travelled only when the sun was up, progress was very slow. The caravan of sledges was constantly being greeted by little colonies of exiles, singing and waving red banners.

Three weeks later they arrived at Tobolsk, where they got a great shock: their destination was Obdorsk, a little penal colony on the Arctic Circle almost 1,000 miles from a railway and 500 from a telegraph outpost. The route to the colony trailed along a river across wastes of snow and ice, the notorious tundra and the taiga, with nothing to be seen except a sprinkling of Mongol dwellings.

Trotsky, who had been writing constantly to Natalya, now told her to join him in the Arctic Circle, bringing along all the literature and paper she could.

The question of escape was tricky: Trotsky was now so well known that he would automatically be given three years at hard labour if caught; also, it was a point of honour among the political prisoners not to embarrass their escorts by running away while in transit.

When he got to Berezov, the last way-station before the big jump to the Arctic Circle, the idea of escape cropped up anyhow. An exiled physician showed him how to pretend he had sciatica; this would help him avoid the final leg of the trip to Obdorsk; he could stay on in a hospital without much surveillance. The pretence called for a great deal of resolution, but he could get away with it if he used all his self-control: it would save him a tremendous trip across the icy wilderness.

He took a chance on the physician's advice. A friendly peasant was willing to help and found him a native guide, a drunkard, who knew the passes across the tundra and the right dialects. Trotsky gave the guide money for the reindeer and for the furs they needed.

Trotsky's show of sciatica went off well. Since it was considered axiomatic that the ailment could not be checked up on and since in that season there was no fear of anyone's escaping, Trotsky had complete freedom in the hospital. He could often leave for hours at a time whenever he 'felt better'.

The escape was scheduled for a Sunday midnight, when the local authorities were giving an amateur play. Trotsky, encountering the local police chief during an intermission, told him he was feeling much better: he would soon be able to travel on to Obdorsk.

The escape, covering some 700 kilometres, lasted eight days of more or less constant travel. The guide, continually drunk, kept dozing off: to Trotsky's alarm the sleigh would wander into snowdrifts. Trotsky himself had nothing to eat or drink, and he could not afford to go to sleep, for then the guide would vanish into one of the Mongol huts and tents scattered far and wide. Trotsky would find him drinking his head off with the Mongols, both men and whole families, or stretched out dead drunk. And when the reindeer tired, Trotsky had to go off hunting for some other ones together with the Mongols. In spite of these difficulties, Trotsky was indefatigably literary. He made notes on all he came across – the icy wastes, the life of the Mongols, animal habits, everything.

As Trotsky and his drunken guide neared the Urals they encountered more and more people. Their curiosity was alarming; but Trotsky successfully passed himself off as a merchant or explorer on his way home from a polar expedition.

In Bogoslovsk, the head of the single-track railway, he got on the train, and in a burst of exhilaration went directly on by rail towards St. Petersburg.

He was still far from safe; as an outlandish-looking person he could have been picked up at once on the basis of a mere wire.

I felt full of apprehension. But when after a day I found myself in the comfortable car of the Perm railway I suddenly felt I had won. The train was passing through the same stations where we had been met with such pomp by gendarmes.... But now my path lay in the opposite direction, and I was travelling with different feelings. For the first few minutes the roomy and almost empty railway cars seemed to me too cramped and stuffy. I went out on to the platform, where there was a wind blowing and it was dark; and from my chest threw out a loud cry – of joy and freedom![6]

At the first stop he wired Natalya, who was living together with their infant son in a Finnish town near St. Petersburg; she thought he was still on his way to the Arctic Circle. The trip to Berezov, after all, had lasted over a month; he had come the whole way back in eleven days. She had even received a long letter that same day from him en route in which he had asked her to take along various things he needed, books etc., when she set out for the Arctic.

Natalya, 'beside herself with joy and excitement', was a little perplexed by his having left out the name of the station where she was to meet him. The wire had told her merely to meet him at the 'station where the trains met'. Thus Natalya set out with her infant son at night without knowing just where she was going to. Entering a compartment full of landowners taking delicacies of all kinds back to their estates for Shrovetide, she listened to their talk of caviar and wine. At last, they mentioned the right station – Samino!

When the trains going in opposite directions came to a stop in Samino, Natalya rushed to the platform to look for Trotsky: no one! She rushed into the other train – no one! She ran through all the cars – no one! Suddenly she saw Trotsky's fur coat in a compartment: she rushed out again – there he was! He was coming out of the waiting-room where he had darted in to look for her. Annoyed by the garbling of the wire, he wanted to make a fuss about it; Natalya had to dissuade him.

They both got back into the train and quite openly, with Trotsky 'talking and laughing out loud' – the 'best protection' – set out for St. Petersburg, where they stayed for a short while before going on to Finland, a natural haven for enemies of the Russian Government.

There Trotsky was clapped on the back by Lenin and Martov for his conduct at the trial: he wrote a lively account of his escape from Siberia (*There and Back*) that was to bring him in some money.

Once again Trotsky was to try his hand at organised politics, this time as a celebrity. He went off to London for another Party Congress, a secret one, leaving behind Natalya and their small son. The Party was so poverty-stricken that some money was borrowed from a liberal English businessman; the Congress was held in April in a London Brotherhood Church.

The last Congress to be attended by both Mensheviks and Bolsheviks, it was, with some 350 participants, six times as large as the Founding Congress in 1903. Despite the psychological slump in Russia, morale was high.

For Trotsky, the situation was worse than it had been in 1903: the two major factions now had more or less fixed profiles. The leaders were all there in force; there was no room, in a way, for Trotsky, perhaps just because of his celebrity, which made it difficult for him to fit into either of the factions. Thus the 'conciliationism' associated with him was now his 'tendency'; he could speak 'in its name' and not merely as an individual. Later on he was to be its sole representative: in an acid phrase of Martov's he turned up everywhere with his own folding-chair.[7]

In theory, too, Trotsky had elaborated a characteristic position: he was now a champion of his patented 'Permanent Revolution', which despite his age gave him a vantage-point from which he could exploit the renown he had acquired as an orator in 1905. It also enabled him to lecture both Mensheviks and Bolsheviks from the heights of his special 'position'.

The collapse of 1905 had polarised most Russian Marxists into two different tendencies, both reflecting various attitudes to the central question of all Marxist practice: whether to escort or to guide The (inevitable) Revolution.

One ambition was to scrap the clandestine movement altogether; its antithesis consisted of those who were against any concessions to the victorious 'reaction' in Tsarist society.

Those who wanted to dismantle the underground organisations were called 'Liquidators'; those who wanted to insulate themselves against the 'bourgeois' influences of reviving Tsarism were known as 'Boycotters'.

Trotsky opposed both these movements. In this he concurred with Lenin: both thought that a secret underground apparatus was indispensable and at the same time that all legal institutions in Russia ought to be systematically infiltrated.

But because of the solidification of the factions that had occurred since the Founding Congress of 1903, it was to prove impossible for Trotsky to promote either his own 'position' or his own status. He was speaking not to a general audience, but to partisans. The debates, though long-winded and stuffed with fine points, were not carried on with the happy-go-lucky diffuseness of an open debating society, but within a factional structure consistently underestimated by Trotsky.

Like all Russian Marxists in the aftermath of 1905, Trotsky was incapable of assessing the real element that ensured the Bolshevik victory in 1917 – *organisation*. Marxists thought they were predicting the future: at that time it would have been merely whimsical, perhaps vainglorious to claim that the prophecies they were making might be self-fulfilling.

Yet granted the applicability of Permanent Revolution – Trotsky's contribution to Marxism – it was plain that in any turbulent situation it was Trotsky's approach that would eventually lead to a 'Bolshevik' turn, that is, to the creation of an organisation to guide, or rather to create events, and not a 'Menshevik' turn, which regardless of theory was based on the psychological predisposition of the Mensheviks to passivity.

The difficulty with these options, however, was that they remained insulated within the abstractions of theory: on the human plane Trotsky could not surmount the combination of the factional split and his own aloofness. He remained friendlier, personally, with Martov at a point when he was politically, close enough to Lenin to have made no bones about joining his faction. But the venom that was still latent from the time of his wrangle with Lenin made it impossible to establish any close political links; when that venom was brought to the surface again at the London Congress, it precluded any *rapprochement*.

One of the most virulent interchanges at the Congress revolved around the scandalous 'expropriations', a euphemism for highway robbery, much specialised in by Lenin's faction. In these one 'Koba', born Djugashvili, and present at the London Congress as 'Ivanovich', had distinguished himself. A short, swarthy, pock-marked Georgian from the Caucasus, 'Ivanovich' was mute throughout the Congress. Trotsky was not to recall seeing him in London; he remembered Trotsky.

These bandit squads of Lenin's had been devastating the countryside in south-eastern Russia, especially the Caucasus Mountains. The Mensheviks denounced the 'exes' as out-and-out piracy; their moral indignation swung the Congress, which otherwise was under Lenin's authority, to forbid them. Lenin personally was very evasive about the whole subject; the expropriations were a first-rate source of funds.

Trotsky sided with the Mensheviks. Later, he went further, denouncing the practice in the 'foreign' Socialist press of Western Europe.

During the Congress Lenin made some further attempts to attract Trotsky. He went out of his way to show him that in Trotsky's exposition of Permanent Revolution the point championing an alliance between the workers and peasants put Trotsky in the Bolshevik camp. This approach failed. When Trotsky then attacked the 'exes' alongside the Mensheviks, the ferocious vilification characteristic of Marxists who are not allies was routine once again. Trotsky, in fact, kept snarling at Lenin even when there was no discernible cause; after the Congress there seemed no prospect of any alliance.

After the Congress Trotsky went to Berlin, where he was reunited with his family. Helphand, whose sentence after the 1905 affair had been embarrassingly negligble (three years' exile) had also come back from Siberia to Berlin; he had arranged for publication in German of Trotsky's account of his Siberian escape.

Trotsky's articles had been coming out in German, where the Socialist press was already making a great to-do about his dramatic conduct at the trial of the Soviet. By now Trotsky was earning respectable sums of money from his journalism; his prolific output produced an income that enabled him to support his small family, especially since his daughters by Alexandra were being paid for by his father.

It was a simple matter for Trotsky, with his rhetorical flexibility, to compose articles for a German public; he would clarify the problems of Russian Socialism from his own point of view; that is, he would use the forum of the German Socialist press as his own rostrum. To a German and, indeed, a general European audience, Trotsky's status as a maverick was particularly attractive : he could seem to be, and in a way was uncommitted to the two major factions whose squabbles, even to Marxist scholastics, were remarkably impenetrable.

The virulent scholasticism of the Russian exiles was notorious throughout the Socialist movement. Jaurès had made a point of instructing the staff of the French Socialist newspaper, *Humanité*, to deny the Russian Party any space, since the paper would inevitably be flooded by obscure statements from contending factions.[8]

Trotsky was relatively free of this vice. His lucid, witty, vigorous style ensured him a readership among European Socialists as well as the liberal Russian public.

Helphand introduced his protégé to the Socialist Party leaders, of whom the most notable was Karl Kautsky, a patriarch of Marxist Socialism on the Continent. Trotsky went to Kautsky's house very often, chatting about Socialism with the most venerable leaders of the German Party.

In German Socialism Trotsky aligned himself with the orthodox Marxists who were in what the 'radicals' called the centre: he remained somewhat aloof from Karl Liebknecht and also from Rosa Luxemburg, whom he 'admired from afar' but did not become friendly with.

At the end of the summer of 1907, Trotsky, Natalya, and Helphand went on a walking tour in Saxon Switzerland. In his *Life* Trotsky gives an engaging account of the marvellous days, the chill of the mornings, the milk, the mountain air. He and Natalya were almost killed clambering down into the valley without a path. They came out into a little village in Czechoslovakia, Hirschberg, a 'resort for small functionaries', where they spent a few weeks. 'Whenever money was running out – which happened periodically – Helphand or I would hastily write an article for the Social-Democratic Press.'[9]

A couple of months later Trotsky moved to Vienna, since he could not obtain a residence permit for Berlin and wanted to stay within the orbit of German-speaking socialism. Natalya, who had gone back to St. Petersburg for their small son, joined him in Vienna a little later; there they stayed at first in a small suburb, Hütteldorf, where they could afford a villa by taking it out of season. 'Through the windows you could see the mountains in their dark-red autumnal colours, and by a small door get out into the open without touching the street.'[10] Later they moved to Sievering, the 'people's' section. They were to stay on in Vienna until 1914.

Trotsky resumed his pen-name, Antid Oto; throughout these pre-war years he wrote a great deal for many Russian Liberal periodicals – chiefly *Kiev Thought*, with which he had a permanent connection – as well as another half-dozen papers in Russian, German, and French. Despite occasional money crises – rent at the end of each

month, bailiff's notices, sometimes selling their books – Trotsky and
Natalya managed on the whole quite well. They kept very busy;
aside from talking politics, their chief relaxation was an occasional
excursion into the splendid woods around Vienna.

They were partly supported, also, by Trotsky's father, who had
meanwhile become quite rich. Their second son, Sergei, almost two
years younger than Sedov, was born in Vienna.

Trotsky was very much of a family man; he helped out in the
house and in the care of the small boys. For some time, despite his
unusual load of work, he managed to help the boys in their studies.
From his very first exile on, his parents had begun travelling abroad
to see him; they had visited him and Natalya in Paris, and then made
a trip to Vienna, too, with his older daughter, who at this time was
living with them in the country. By this time they had reconciled
themselves to his career: what clinched their indulgence was seeing
the first book of his to appear in German.

His mother had fallen ill with a serious illness (actinomycosis)
that

> she endured for the last ten years of her life; to her it was merely
> another burden to bear, she never stopped working. At the age of
> sixty a kidney was removed; for a few months afterwards, to the
> amazement of the medical authorities, she blossomed and became,
> indeed, a sensation in the medical world. But a few months later
> the disease killed her; she died in Yanovka.[11]

When Sedov, the older boy, began school, the question of religious
instruction arose. By law, children up to the age of fourteen had to
be brought up in the religion of their fathers. Since Trotsky and
Natalya had no religion noted in their papers, they chose Protestantism for their children; this seemed to them the most easily endurable
for their 'shoulders and souls'.

The children spoke Russian and German: in kindergarten and at
school they would speak German and go on speaking it together; but
whenever addressed by Natalya or Trotsky they would answer in
Russian; if their parents spoke to them in German they were embarrassed and would reply in Russian anyhow. Toward the end of their
stay there they even developed a splendid command of the Viennese
dialect.

The years in Vienna gave Trotsky ample scope for his great
variety of interests, very unusual for a Marxist professional. He was,

for instance, practically the only Russian Marxist who ever read Freud. He was introduced to psychoanalysis through the emotional disturbances of an assistant, Yoffe, a patient of Freud's former pupil, Alfred Adler: 'Through Yoffe I became familiar with the problems of psychoanalysis, which attracted me extraordinarily, though a great deal in this area is still unclear and shaky, and opens a path to fantasy and caprice.'[12]

On trips he heard the celebrated French Socialist, Jaurès:

I heard Jaurès speak at Paris mass-meetings, at international congresses and in committees. And I always listened to him as though it were for the first time.... Fundamentally he never repeated himself, he always found himself all over again, always mobilised anew the subterranean sources of his own spirit. There was in him, together with a mighty force as elemental as a waterfall, a great gentleness that lit up his face like a reflection of a higher spiritual culture. He would bring rocks hurtling down, would thunder and move the earth, but he never deafened himself; he was always standing on guard to pick up with a sensitive ear every echo, snatch it up, parry objections, sometimes mercilessly, like a hurricane, sweep away all resistance, sometimes as generously and gently as a tutor, as an elder brother....[13]

In the pages of *Kiev Thought* he discussed literature, painting, poetry, politics – everything.

His reputation as a journalist was solid enough to enable him to handle delicate subjects from a characteristic point of view. He devoted an article to the celebrated 'blood-libel' trial of a Russian Jew called Beilis in *Die Neue Zit* in 1913. This trial, which for the first time in a modern European country paraded the ancient attack on the Jews (to the effect that they used the blood of a Christian child for ritual purposes) was gone into by Trotsky at great length. It enabled him, as in his descriptions of pogroms, to utilise a plainly personal note of indignation in the service of his Marxism.[14]

Much later Trotsky was to write about this Viennese period of his life with a great deal of disdain, even contempt, for the German Socialists who in his eyes had become arrant reformists; while he was there he seems to have had a very good time in the busy, amusing, colourful life of the city. Vienna had of course a marvellously rich culture, with just the right mixture for gifted outsiders to make a variety of sardonic comments on the decadence of an aristocratic

society. So-called 'Austro-Marxism', which had given the European Socialist movement a special flavour, had pried loose the
hold of the Church sufficiently to allow a lively play of expression
and a fruitful intellectual interchange in the arts and sciences. The
effervescence was, moreover, remarkably accessible, with countless
cafés, meetings and artistic coteries discussing everything under the
sun from life at court to the latest painting, play or *feuilleton*.
Trotsky was like a fish in water.

A member of the local Social-Democratic Party, he attended
meetings, wrote articles for the local Socialist press, and chatted
with friends and acquaintances in cafés. He was on friendly terms
with many of the local Socialist leaders, notably Victor Adler himself, whom he had woken up one Sunday morning on his way to
London from Siberia in 1902. He wrote of Adler with unmistakable
warmth and affection. He was also friendly with Rudolf Hilferding,
the great brain of 'Austro-Marxism'.

The Russian Marxists were, very naturally, 'under the spell' of the
new majestic German Social-Democracy – so organised, so institutionalised, so learned. In Trotsky's words, the 'German Social-
Democracy was mother, teacher, and living example for us Russians.
We idealised it from a distance.'[15]

It gave Trotsky pleasure to recall that once in Berlin, when
Mehring, the celebrated biographer of Marx, on hearing Hilferding
refer to the German Leftwing as 'revolutionaries', burst out: ' "*We*
are revolutionaries? Bah! Those are revolutionaries!*"*, and he nodded
in my direction.'[16]

Nevertheless – if Trotsky's comments on this period of his life are
to be taken at face value – he was utterly alienated the moment he
came into personal contact with the men who incarnated the grand
traditions of Marxism : he found nearly all of them repellent.
Whatever their theoretical pre-eminence, they struck him as philistine routineers and petty bureaucrats: Hilferding himself, for
instance, 'was a literary official in the service of the German Party –
and no more.'[17] Recalling an encounter with him, Ramsay Macdonald the British Socialist, and Eduard Bernstein, Trotsky comments : 'I asked myself which of these three men stood furthest from
what I had been accustomed to call Socialism.'[18]

Trotsky was always baffled by the failure of Marxists to understand Marxism. In encountering the learned doctors of the Marxist
science he was surprised to find them 'absolutely incapable of

handling Marx's method the moment they came to the big problems of politics, especially its revolutionary turns.'

In fact all such men were 'strangers' to Trotsky: when they spoke informally they revealed 'either undisguised chauvinism, or the bragging of a petty proprietor, or holy terror of the police, or vileness toward women. In amazement I often exclaimed: "What revolutionaries!" ' [19]

This disdain was not necessarily mean-minded; it was rooted in Trotsky's innermost being. Just as he was convinced that the only thing that lent meaning to personal existence was a great super-human purpose that a man was ready to pay for with his life,[20] just as he was made spiritually uncomfortable by the 'niggling' aspect of life as expressed in the adoration of mere 'facts', so he had the deepest contempt for the unheroic.

Writing about his disillusionment with the 'Austro-Marxists', he reveals something fundamental in himself, a little indirectly, in what he says of his ideal men, Marx and Engels:

The correspondence between Marx and Engels was the most useful of books and the one closest to me – the greatest and most trustworthy test not so much of my views as of my feeling for the world as a whole. The Viennese leaders of the Social-Democracy were using the same formulas I was using, but it was enough to move any one of these formulas five degrees around on its axis and it turned out that we were putting together an altogether different content into the same concepts.... The correspondence between Marx and Engels was for me not a theoretical but a psychological revelation. *Toutes proportions gardées*, I was convinced on every page that I was bound to these two by a direct psychological kinship. Their attitude to men and ideas was close to my own. I guessed what they left unsaid, I shared their sympathies; together with them I felt indignation and hatred. Marx and Engels were revolutionaries through and through, they lacked even a shadow of sectarianism or asceticism. Both of them, especially Engels, could at any time say of themselves that nothing human was alien to them. But their revolutionary outlook, which had entered into their very nerves, always raised them above the accidents of fate and the handiwork of man. Pettiness was out of place not only with themselves but with their presences. Vulgarity could not cling even to their boot-soles. Their evaluations, their sympathies, their jokes, even when routine, are always imbued with the mountain air of spiritual nobility. They may refer to someone murderously, but they will not gossip. They can be merciless, but not treacherous. For external gloss, for titles, rank or office they have only a tranquil contempt. What philistines and vulgarians considered aristocratic in them was in fact only their revolutionary superiority, whose most important feature is a total, organic independence of official public opinion always and under all conditions. In reading their letters I felt, even more clearly than in reading their works, that what bound me intimately to the work of Marx and Engels was what opposed me irreconcilably to the Austro-Marxists.[21]

This is striking, since even the expurgated edition of the Marx–Engels correspondence read by Trotsky – years before the full version was published in the Soviet Union – reveals spite, envy and pettiness. Rivals, outsiders, and even friends are belittled, sneered at and gossiped about in the coarsest way.

Noticing only the intellectual fireworks and the idealistic hopes, disregarding the all-too-human men behind the masks, Trotsky is plainly giving us his own self-image.

Trotsky was quite aware of his shortcomings in comparison with these erudite Social-Democrats: he considered himself provincial and ignorant, with his scraps of information gathered at random by a vigorous but impulsive mind guided only by the Great Key.

While actually rubbing shoulders with these luminaries, it was, of course, reasonable for him to overlook their unheroic routinism, vulgar opportunism, and corrosive cynicism by assuming that the tidal wave of The Revolution would sweep all that aside. Marxists were bound to pay at least lip-service to the Great Change that would inevitably take place; it was natural for Trotsky to take it for granted that the upthrust of The Revolution, once it got started, would make short work of the vacillation, complacency, stupidity and general worthlessness of the leaders.

The Russian Government recovered quickly; by the summer of 1907 the obdurate element of the Tsarist regime had resumed full command. The Second Duma, dispersed under Stolypin, was followed by a Third based on a very restricted electorate. The Social-Democrats who had been members of the Second Duma were banished to Siberia, the rank-and-file were completely repressed, many thousands of individuals being executed; various revolutionary associations and the press were naturally prohibited; moderates were harassed.

Against this background Socialism went out of fashion: Russian public opinion, which optimists in 1905 had thought receptive to Socialist ideas, had veered about. Most of the exiles, except for leaders like Lenin and Martov and their immediate entourages, now reverted to the semi-political, semi-intellectual activities of the Bohemian emigration.

Trotsky was characteristically optimistic: he was sure the convalescence of Tsarism was superficial. The 1905 upheaval, which despite general Marxist predictions had come about so unexpectedly, was bound to have been the harbinger of a second revolution, equally inevitable but now to be looked forward to with far more definiteness.

His productivity had encompassed, of course, revolutionary journalism. In October 1908 he took over *Pravda*, a Russian periodical that had been issued irregularly since 1903. It had been the organ of some Ukrainian Mensheviks. Now it became his, in so far as it could transcend its financial problems.

The money made from Trotsky's European journalism went into postage and printing costs; Trotsky would sell his books and hock personal possessions to send bundles of the little paper across the border into Russia. Sometimes the big German Party would lend them money; then Natalya would retrieve some of the items she had hocked, and for a while the paper would come out once a fortnight as it was supposed to. In 1909 Trotsky did his best to get the Bolsheviks to help support *Pravda*, but Lenin would not do so unless a Bolshevik became co-editor. On Trotsky's refusal, Lenin instructed the Bolshevik print-shop in Geneva not to print *Pravda* except on a commercial basis. Nevertheless, the paper produced an echo in Russia; it was mentioned in the reports of the Tsarist Secret Police.[22]

The contributors to the paper were a motley cluster of students and scholars. Since Trotsky as a would-be conciliator hovered above Bolsheviks and Mensheviks, and since he also had a natural belief in getting through to the masses, *Pravda* avoided heavy-handed discussions of theory. Thus its simple explanations, aiming at unity, made it more widely read than it might have been otherwise. But clarity alone could not much influence the two branches of a party that reflected, after all, a certain movement. It was, in fact, this side of Trotsky – his allegiance to the Idea of The Party, as expressed in its unity – that frustrated him within the real party. It was during just this period of stagnation, between 1907–17, that Trotsky's isolation was consolidated.

A truce was reached in Paris in January 1910. Both Bolsheviks and Mensheviks had seemed to agree that each faction would get rid of its hotheads. For the Bolsheviks these were the 'Boycotters', intransigent against co-operation with all 'bourgeois' institutions in Russia; for the Mensheviks these were the 'Liquidators', intransigently for the 'Liquidation' of the underground.

It looked as though Trotsky's 'conciliatory' line had been successful: both factions were to pool their resources and publishing enterprises (under the surveillance of the German Socialists, Kautsky, Mehring, and Clara Zetkin); Trotsky's *Pravda* in Vienna was praised and promised subsidies.

Yet the whole arrangement collapsed only a few weeks later: it did not reflect the real background. If the Mensheviks had expelled their Liquidators they would have lost the support of a big segment of their following while leaving untouched the Bolshevik predominance in the underground.

When the Bolsheviks then made the reasonable point that, since both factions had agreed to support the underground, any particular member who really opposed it should not be in the Party at all, the only possible Menshevik response to this was based on a very broad principle – the right to dissent. Lenin's retort to this was mere commonsense: dissent, while permissible in theory, *in this case* would hamper the functioning of the underground – that was, after all, supposed to be clandestine!

In this curiously intricate imbroglio – arguments pro and con could be and were interminable – Trotsky was simultaneously a sponsor of Party unity and also, on the other hand, as a *correct principle*, of tolerance of dissent. Thus, by defending the Mensheviks on this point he kept himself insulated against the Bolsheviks.

At the same time, the points on which he *agreed* with the Bolsheviks were far more important both to him and to the future of the Party; he believed, for instance, not only in the underground, but in the perniciousness of Liberals.

His defence of the Mensheviks' right to dissent as a matter of principle linked him to them with respect to the toleration of Liberalism and to a split attitude on the underground. Accordingly, he found himself defending Mensheviks in a situation in which he was, fundamentally, far more in accord with the Bolsheviks.

Humanly speaking, the explanation of this wayward and some-what self-destructive selection of principles was quite simple: he was keeping himself out of Lenin's orbit. By following his own line, and merely allying himself with the Mensheviks, he remained his own man.

This had an essentially irrelevant but pernicious side-effect. Since Trotsky was considered *some sort* of Menshevik, after all, he could attack the Mensheviks only in private correspondence, while in public he would turn the full battery of his ferocious style on Lenin and the Bolsheviks, on every item they disagreed on, even though his discords with the Mensheviks were far more fundamental.

This factor envenomed relations between him and the Bolsheviks for a long time; it was to have a permanent effect on his fortunes.

Only a few months after the Paris truce of 1910, Trotsky broke off all relations with the Central Committee. By now *Lenin* was in a strong enough position to appeal for Party unity above all: Trotsky savagely condemned the 'conspiracy of the (Bolshevik) clique against the Russian Social-Democratic Party.... Lenin's circle, which wants to place itself above the Party, will find itself outside it.'[23]

In addition, it was natural for him to generalise the 'struggle' by airing it in the German press: this created a furore among the Russian delegates to a Congress of the Second International that met in Copenhagen in October 1910.

By 1912 the schism was consummated: Lenin announced in Prague that the Bolshevik faction of the Party was the whole Party. In his little newspaper, *Pravda*, Trotsky attacked Lenin and the whole enterprise; his attacks became even more strident when Lenin started up a daily periodical by the same name in – St. Petersburg!

Trotsky thought the title *Pravda* somehow belonged to him; Lenin took the view that since Trotsky's *Pravda* had been subsidised by the Central Committee they had a right to look upon it as a political organ and not a private publication.

Curiously enough, the St. Petersburg *Pravda* came out first under the editorship of Joseph Djugashvili, at the time hardly known to anyone outside the inner circle of Bolsheviks, and who had made his first public appearance at the London conference in 1907, when the 'exes' had come under attack.

Livid with rage, Trotsky stopped publishing the *Pravda* he had made so characteristically his own; the other *Pravda* has remained in existence – with some changes! – down to our own day.

The mere possibility of launching a Marxist paper in St. Petersburg – the Mensheviks did, too – was a symptom of the changing times. The repression in Russia was largely over. Younger people had begun streaming into the few surviving workers' clubs, associations, trade-unions and so on, as well as into the underground. It had become increasingly easy to speak up.

The absence of repression implied the upsuge of Liberal and revolutionary forces in Russia; Trotsky could reasonably imagine that that alone would give the Party more public attraction; hence unity might really be a practical possibility.

This also proved chimerical: factional arguments could not be constrained by a broadening of the arena. The new freedom in Russia, for instance, merely reinforced the arguments both of those who wanted to abolish the underground – they said it was no longer needed – and of those who wanted to strengthen it – *they* said it could now be still *more* effective, also that its mere existence frightened the government into allowing still more open agitation.

It was plain, in any case, that the Bolshevik and Menshevik factions had now evolved into functional independence.

Lenin's coterie especially, with years of organising behind it, was now by far the predominant element in the clandestine movement; the Mensheviks, with so many leaders against clandestine organisation on principle, had dislodged themselves from such activities and were floating on the waves of open opinion.

Trotsky made one more attempt to play his unity card: in August 1912 he persuaded the so-called 'Organisation Committee' – set up early in the year as a counterploy to Lenin's announcement in Prague that the Bolsheviks were in *The* Party – to convoke a Social-Democratic Conference in Vienna. Lenin's group naturally paid it no attention, beyond banning attendance at it.

This abortive group – known as the 'August Bloc' – consisted of some Mensheviks, a few hard-core intransigents like the 'Boycotters', and a few Bolsheviks opposed to Lenin's ban on the Conference, as well as the Jewish *Bund* and a few of Trotsky's sympathisers. As spokesman for this somewhat motley assortment, Trotsky denounced Lenin right and left as a 'disorganiser'.

Both factions now realised that there was no hope of uniting the Party under the leadership of either one. It suited Lenin to make a point of emphasising the split in order to aggrandise his own group. In public, on the other hand, the Mensheviks soft-pedalled the irreversibility of the split; they wanted to 'blame' Lenin for its continuation.

Lunacharsky gives a sidelight into the atmosphere of the revolutionary movement during the phase when it had already begun jelling into factions, but had not yet become altogether rigid: he had invited Trotsky, soon after the Copenhagen Congress in 1910, to a school organised by some Bolsheviks in Bologna for some practical journalism and also for lecturing. Trotsky stayed in Bologna a month: following his own 'line' he tried to persuade Bolsheviks to take a moderate, though to him 'left' line on conciliation. This failed, but his exceptionally talented lectures were very successful with the students. 'In general,' said Lunacharsky, 'throughout his stay there Trotsky was exceptionally merry, brilliant, and extraordinarily loyal with respect to us; he left the best souvenirs with all of us. He was one of the ablest workers we had.'[24]

The abortive 'August Bloc', almost Trotsky's last effort in émigré politics, was a brief break in his busy life as a writer and journalist. Soon afterwards he undertook a major trip through the Balkans for his newspaper.

Trotsky had gone to the Balkans once before, in July 1910, to attend a Pan-Slav conference. Since then he had often made brief visits to Belgrade and Sofia, and had become, in fact, something of a Balkan 'specialist'.

In October 1912, shortly after the adventure of the 'August Bloc', he investigated once again the countless plagues of Balkan political life. His reportage, on the first Balkan War of 1912 (South Slavs against the Turks), was in the best style of Central European and pre-revolutionary Russian journalism. An article would be a dense little essay, artistically combining an unusual concentration of 'background material' with reportorial flashes, vignettes of people and reflections, conveyed by Trotsky's colourful, incisive writing. As a journalist he was unusually thorough – interviewing officials, collecting data on logistical problems, army training, military tactics, while at the same time describing the horrors of the war itself. He immersed himself in the blood and filth of the hospitals and prisoners' camps, the bourgeois hotels, the cafés, the horrifying Balkan slums.

He put the finishing touches on his journalistic role by denouncing Bulgarian atrocities against the Turks at a time when it suited Liberal opinion in Russia to soft-pedal them. This got him into trouble with the Bulgarians while having no effect on the Turks; they did not, after all, read Russian.

His reportage kindled a long-drawn-out, venomous squabble in the Russian Liberal press; it lasted for months, coming to an abrupt end only when the Bulgarians and Serbs beat the Turks and instantly turned on each other, whereupon the Russians, championing the Serbs, naturally began denouncing the Bulgarians. Trotsky played the dashing newspaper man, frank and fearless.

After a short stay back in Vienna – he found the Mensheviks very pleased with the split in the Party, and his conciliatory opinions now quite unfashionable even rhetorically – he went back to the Balkans once again as a spectator, this time of the Second Balkan War.

In this second clash it was natural for him to defend the Bulgarians, since Serbia and Greece together were now plundering Bulgaria; he wrote some more articles on the Balkans, including a very successful grand reportage on Rumania.

If Trotsky's activities during the decade before 1917 are considered in the perspective of his personal life, journalism manifestly accounts for the bulk of his time. It was only from the much later perspective of 1917, when he became a world-figure, that this decade could be presented as a mere interlude in his career. Trotsky's glossing over of this in 1929, after his exile, is plainly apologetic: 'During the years of the reaction my work consisted very largely of interpreting the revolution of 1905 and of breaking theoretical ground for the next revolution.'[25]

Yet it is plain that the decade before 1917 saw no particular change in the theory of The Revolution. For that matter, there was no real change either before or after the Founding Congress of 1903, nor did Trotsky add anything to his own formulation of Permanent Revolution, elaborated around 1905.

What was to prevail, after the breakdown of the traditional order in 1917 cleared the way for innovations, was not so much theory as the efficacy of organisations. This was why Trotsky's aversion to organisational commitment during the decade was to have a fateful effect on his career.

His passivity vis-à-vis the idea of an underground apparatus that he favoured, in theory, may have been the keynote of his attitude toward practical politics. His purely theoretical sponsorship of the idea did not entail any action aimed at implementing it. While Trotsky led the life of a free-lance journalist throughout the decade, with only an occasional foray, invariably fruitless, into the area of organisation, both the big factions were building up mini-'apparatuses' that, with hindsight, we can see were decisive at crucial moments.

It was during this period of general stagnation that Lenin put together his general staff, headed up by those who were later to become famous together with the Party – Zinoviev, Kamenev, and Stalin. Quite unknown outside the Party, the last was acquiring a reputation as a 'practical'. Looked down on by the Party eagles – the thinkers, speakers, and writers – the 'practicals' were soon to achieve cardinal importance.

Of the two activities imposed on the Russian movement of dissidence by its clandestine existence – the luxuriance of discussion and the concentration of organisation – it was the second that won out. The small general staff created by Lenin in the underground was to develop an unsuspected potential *merely because it existed at a given moment.* This was the true achievement of Lenin before 1917, the period that for the public side of The Revolution was so sterile.

Throughout this period Trotsky was a writer and talker – essentially a spectator. From the vantage-point of the Bolshevik success in 1917, his politics was really no more than a hobby. In marked contrast with the organisational dynamism he had shown as an adolescent in Nikolayev, he had gravitated instinctively after his first exile toward the 'public' side of life – speaking and writing for people in the abstract instead of steeping himself in the drudgery of detail and of close relations with peers.

It was as a *public* figure, in fact, that he had become famous in 1905. He had not been a 'professional revolutionary' at all, but an amateur whose gifts had, through the democratic process, whirled him aloft.

Though he himself avoided distinguishing between the two activities – to him all seemed to be a seamless web of striving on behalf of The Revolution – something must have turned him from a zealous 'practical' at the age of seventeen and a half into a public virtuoso.

If we assume that the display of his personality was vital for his self-expression, we can see how natural it was, as his character hardened into its characteristic aloofness, for him to have exploited the gifts that transformed him from an intelligent, industrious adolescent into a brilliant artist. Not merely the donkey-work inherent in organisation, but the complications of working with others, of finding his own place in a hierarchy, fell far behind the glamour of public performance.

His short-lived blossoming as an independent 'practical' came to an end, in fact, when he grew out of a family-like adolescent milieu into an adult world of large groups, in which hierarchies are the natural medium. As his rebelliousness, natural for so many high-spirited children in a middle-class milieu, came to dovetail with the aspirations of others and became a social activity, so it seemed to him natural to soar beyond his *merely* practical work into the exposition of ideas. In this transition from drudgery to glamour it is difficult to withstand the impression that Trotsky's primary gift – his oratory – was the specific function that crystallised this metamorphosis.

And it was, fatefully, this change of course that produced the contrast between his organisational lethargy before 1917 and the mole-like activity of his future colleagues, rivals and enemies.

It was in Vienna that Trotsky first saw Stalin to speak to. In February 1913, while Trotsky was visiting a former assistant, Skobelev, a Menshevik who had been in the Duma, a man suddenly entered the room they were sitting in. He was pockmarked, with a swarthy complexion and – as Trotsky was to recall twenty-seven years later – 'yellow' eyes in his 'dim but not commonplace' face, which had a look of 'morose concentration' and animosity. Skobelev introduced him to Trotsky as Djugashvili, a Caucasian who had just been put on to the Bolshevik Central Committee. This gave him considerable political weight.

Trotsky was later to say he had been chilled by Stalin's atmosphere, enough, indeed, to remember it many years later.[26]

After seeing Trotsky at the Party Congress in London in 1907, Stalin had referred to Trotsky's 'beautiful uselessness', and shortly before this accidental meeting with Trotsky in Vienna, as the undisclosed editor of the new St. Petersburg *Pravda*, he had mentioned Trotsky in an article calling him a 'noisy champion with fake muscles'; it was this article that he signed for the first time as 'Stalin'.[27]

Trotsky was still living in Vienna when the First World War broke out on 2 August 1914.

That day he wandered about the boulevards: throngs of people were yelling 'Death to the Serbs!' Sergei, aged six, came back with a black eye for crying out 'Long live the Serbs!'[28]

The Great Powers were on a war footing; mobilisation was in full swing. Jaurès was assassinated – by a Right-wing 'patriot'. The Congress of the Second International was cancelled.

Victor Adler took Trotsky to police headquarters to see how Russian subjects were going to be treated. It was simple – they were to be interned out of hand.

Trotsky, Natalya and the two boys took off at once for Zurich, a natural haven for outsiders.

The First World War smashed, among other things, the Socialist ideal of unity and the prospect of Socialism becoming the saviour of European civilisation. With no exceptions to speak of, the national divisions of the Second International succumbed to the martial spirit spreading so rapidly throughout Europe.

For the Russian Social-Democrats this was a great shock; the exiles were flabbergasted by the chauvinism of the other European Socialists, who at one stroke tossed overboard their innumerable condemnations of militarism, their fervent vows of internationalism, their solidarity as Socialists. They told their millions of followers that it was their duty – their Socialist duty, too! – to slaughter the 'national foe'.

Some Russian Socialists later changed their minds and defended their own 'national' Tsarist Government, but at the time this outbreak of nationalism alienated substantial numbers from the Second International.

For a while the chronic bickering between the different coteries of the Russian movement was superseded by the all-inclusive fact of the war and the attendant 'ideological collapse' of the Second International. Martov's and Lenin's entourages vilified the formerly revered leaders of the Second International as renegades of the foulest description; Trotsky joined the chorus of abuse. Amongst the exiles, Plekhanov, on the other hand, who had formerly been linked to Martov, entered the patriotic camp, finding, inevitably, the same Marxist arguments for his Tsarist patriotism as the German Social-Democrats had found for their own zeal on behalf of the German Empire. (Plekhanov's theory was that the Romanovs were *nothing* compared with the Hohenzollerns and Habsburgs as obstacles to the march of history.)

Trotsky's denunciation of the Socialist betrayal was aimed primarily at the party he was closest to – the German Social-Democracy, which up to then had been, for the Russian revolutionaries, 'The Party'. He expressed his outrage in Zurich in an essay – *War and the International* – that came out in November 1914 in German; he was sentenced *in absentia* to several months in gaol.

In *My Life* he recalls with a tinge of pleasure that when this essay was brought out in New York by some enterprising publisher after Trotsky had become world-famous, Woodrow Wilson himself, by his own account, asked for the proofs by telephone; he was composing his Fourteen Points at the time and could not bear the thought that the Bolsheviks had anticipated his 'best formulas'.[29]

Trotsky's well-anchored friendship with Helphand, the chief inspirer, after all, of Permanent Revolution, was also smashed by the war: Helphand, too, had thought of some good reasons for supporting German civilisation.

Helphand had, in fact, two quite different justifications for supporting the German side – one open, one secret.

He had an excellent Marxist justification for championing German parliamentary democracy, anchored in a huge industrial working class, against feudal Tsarism, with its backward society and gigantic peasantry. This was the general line of those Marxists who defended Germany, including, of course, the German Marxists.

In addition he had a perhaps more practical, and in any case more personal and far more grandiose aim – a concrete scheme for toppling Tsarism and promoting The Revolution via a German victory.

In November 1910 he had moved to Constantinople, where he had laid the foundations of a substantial fortune by business operations in the Balkans. By 1912, the beginning of the Balkan wars, he was already very successful, apparently, as a trader in commodities and a representative of some European business combines.[30] During the First World War he was to become, in addition, a remarkably nimble war-profiteer; his theoretical understanding of capitalism proved to be very practical.

He was by now accustomed to a life of great luxury: champagne and women surged back and forth against a background of big business deals. His appearance, too – a high forehead accentuated by baldness, a corpulent upper body mounted on short, spindly legs – completed a personality that was both grotesque and, because of his brainpower, compelling.

His Socialist connections had been very useful. His name was well known to the Serbian, Rumanian, and Bulgarian Socialists, for whom the Ottoman capital was a natural meeting-point. He had been particularly friendly with Rakovsky, a rich Bulgarian Socialist who had become a great friend of Trotsky's during the latter's journalistic junkets through the Balkans.

Early in January 1916 Helphand had been introduced to the German Ambassador to the Ottoman Empire. At their meeting he had pointed out that the 'interests of the German Government are identical with those of the Russian revolutionaries', and that he, Helphand, saw it as his duty to 'create unity' among those revolutionaries in order to 'organise a rising on a broad basis' against the Tsarist regime. A corollary was that he be given substantial sums for transmission to revolutionary groups, primarily the Bolsheviks, to carry on propaganda and agitations.[31]

His conversation in January had been followed up in March by a remarkable memorandum outlining in some detail the steps he thought necessary for the break-up of the Tsarist Empire; he proposed a twin policy of support for the Russian revolutionaries and for the minority nations working for independence.[32]

On the face of it this was a tempting proposal; it was, in fact, wholeheartedly accepted by competent elements in the German Foreign Office and on the General Staff.[33]

This was the first of Helphand's numerous contacts with German officialdom. His business network, which became a small empire, was to provide a natural channel for funds.

None of this came out until later during the war; it was to be hotly denied by all the revolutionaries concerned.

At the time Trotsky seemed to think that Helphand had simply become a devotee of German civilisation; this was, to be sure, enough to warrant a rupture. Acknowledging that he owed to Helphand the 'lion's share' of his own 'diagnosis and prognosis of events', Trotsky sadly interred him : 'Helphand is no more. A political Falstaff is now roaming the Balkans, and he slanders his own deceased double.'[34]

Yet his real relations with Helphand must have been far more complex, perhaps just because they could not be disclosed. There was a curious reversal of his general political 'line' around this time that was hard to explain at the time; it is understandable only in connection with the 'German money'.

Trotsky stayed in Zurich with Natalya and the children for only a couple of months; then he moved on to Paris alone on 19 November 1914 as war correspondent for *Kiev Thought*, his chief source of income. The family followed in May 1915; they took a house outside Paris in Sèvres, where the boys went to school. The weather that spring was marvellous, but the growing number of women in black was very depressing. Later on they moved to Paris, to a little street near the Place d'Italie, in a 'people's' quarter; the only relaxation they had was strolling about the rapidly emptying streets of Paris.

In Paris Trotsky worked with Martov on an anti-war paper for Russian émigrés, called *The Voice*; the little paper was banned by the censorship and collapsed on 15 January 1915, some six or seven weeks after Trotsky's arrival. It was replaced almost immediately (29 January 1915) by a tiny sheet of two, occasionally four pages, called *Our Word*, also edited by Trotsky and Martov.

They had been invited to collaborate in this enterprise by Antonov-Ovseyenko, a former Tsarist officer, who had led his unit in a mutiny in 1905 and escaped a death sentence by going underground. (He was to play a role, under Trotsky's orders, in the Bolshevik putsch in 1917.) In Paris 1915 he showed unusual energy in keeping the little newspaper going. Despite the presence of Martov as co-editor the paper soon became known as Trotsky's mouthpiece. He worked on it with his usual concentration, writing generally until three in the morning; his little boys would hand in his articles to the printer on their way to school.

Now, while the articles he was writing for his Paris paper were against the war generally, he also seemed to be concentrating on the iniquities of the Allies, especially France and Russia, which he vilified with characteristic virulence. He was so violent on this score that Russian émigrés in New York were convinced he was an out-and-out German agent. Writing in *The Voice*, for instance, he never mentioned the sinking of the *Lusitania*; this had outraged the Russian exiles in America, themselves, to be sure, doubtless enthralled by Allied propaganda.

Trotsky in fact spent his time castigating the French government. L. G. Deutsch, his old friend and sponsor, went so far as to say to Ziv: 'If I didn't know Trotsky personally, I'd have no doubt he was in the pay of the German government.'[35] Ziv himself thought Trotsky's 'pro-German' attitude due to his admiration for German efficiency: Trotsky considered Germany the only power that could unify the Continent, indeed, the whole world.

The fact is that *Our Word* was largely financed by Rakovsky,[36] himself a recipient of German funds aimed at getting Rumania out of the war.[37] Rakovsky's connection with Helphand may have reinforced his own position with the Germans. Thus, it is likely that *Our Word* was subsidised indirectly by the German Government.

It was all the easier to camouflage this support intellectually since it obviously 'sounded' all right for a Marxist to be attacking the French Government on French soil, especially since in the nature of *Our Word* it was bound to represent many shadings. The need for the 'right' position on the war lacerated the whole of the Russian Socialist movement; endless nuances were expressed on the grand themes of The Revolution and how it would be affected by 'social-patriotism' on an international scale.

(An echo of this connection between the Imperial German Government and the Russian revolutionaries was sounded in the third Moscow 'Show Trial', in 1938. This trial, like its predecessors, made occasional use of minor factual details to pad the fabrication. Rakovsky, a prisoner in this 'Show Trial', mentions working for the Germans, and also refers to lists of firms and newspapers in Rumania that were supposed to be bribed to get Rumania out of the war against Germany.)[37]

It is doubtless significant, also, that with the exception of Martov all the contributors most closely connected with *Our Word*[38] were to join Lenin in 1917.

On 14 February 1915 Trotsky published his old differences with the Mensheviks – hitherto reserved for private correspondence and conversations. His last formal connection with them (the 'August Bloc') was neutralised.

In the mini-universe of the Russian emigration this constituted a clearing of the way that was ultimately to make it easier for Trotsky, having disavowed his previous alignments, to be absorbed by the Bolshevik Party.

In the summer of 1915 the heated discussions of the 'position on the war' among the anti-war Russian Socialists achieved some organisational expression in Zimmerwald, Switzerland, where an international conference assembled. The conference, the first since the start of the war, was the only public occasion of this decade, which in the revolutionary movement was so quiescent, in which Trotsky played a role.

There is some obscurity about the origins of the conference. Ostensibly it was convoked by Emile Vandervelde, a Belgian Socialist, President of the Second International, who after rejecting a suggestion made by an Italian Socialist deputy (Ordino Morgari) that the Executive of the International come together, had asked the Russian and Swiss Socialists, outside the immediate orbit of the Allies, to meet independently.

Yet there seem to be indications[39] that it had been arranged behind the scenes by two Polish Jewish intimates of Lenin (Radek and Haniecki) and by Robert Grimm, a Swiss Socialist (later arrested and expelled from Russia in 1917 as a German agent), with the connivance of the German Government.

In any case, the conference was quite unrepresentative of the Socialist movement in Europe; it has been magnified extravagantly in Bolshevik mythology. The only important Socialist party that was invited was the Italian; the other participants represented only themselves or fragments of émigré Socialist groups. The Swiss Socialist Party was not even informed of it; most curiously, the heads of the anti-war Socialist opposition in Germany itself – Karl Kautsky, Eduard Bernstein, and Huge Haase – were not invited; they, too, learned about it after it was all over.

Lenin and Zinoviev came 'for' the Bolsheviks; Martov and Axelrod for the Mensheviks. Poland was 'represented' by Radek and Haniecki. Trotsky represented *Our Word*; in the teeth of Lenin's protests he was given full voting rights. All in all some thirty-eight Socialists came together from eleven countries that were either in the war or neutral.

Though Lenin was present as a Bolshevik representative, he emerged for the first time as head of an international, not merely a Russian tendency. Lenin's views were those of 'revolutionary defeatism': the 'imperialist war' should be 'turned into civil war' and another International, the Third, should be proclaimed. The majority of those attending the Zimmerwald conference were, however, mere pacifists.

Trotsky himself was against 'revolutionary defeatism': his own formula was that it would be better for Socialism if the war ended 'without victors and vanquished'. He was selected to compose the 'Zimmerwald Manifesto', which with conventional pathos – the affliction of Europe was blamed on the 'capitalist system', especially on the governments and the renegade Socialist mass parties – summoned The Proletariat to put a stop to the blood-bath.

But the need for compromise naturally blunted the practical point of the Manifesto: it did not accept Lenin's formula of civil war as a means of halting the 'imperialist war' nor his insistence on a new International; this meant that Lenin's group was set apart from the other participants at Zimmerwald.

Trotsky had still not given up hope of somehow playing an

independent role. There was a revealing indication of this from Lenin himself.

During the Zimmerwald Conference Angelica Balabanoff, a Russian Marxist who had settled in Italy and played a role in Italian politics, had heard Trotsky express even more irreconcilable 'Leninist' views on specific points than Lenin himself; she asked Lenin point-blank just what the differences between himself and Trotsky amounted to: ' "Why does he hold apart from your group?" "Don't you know?" Lenin answered curtly, astonished and irritated at my naiveté, "ambition, ambition, ambition!" ' [40]

The 'Zimmerwald Movement', in itself a cluster of slightly disparate tendencies, was soon to be sundered even more than at the actual conference. As other Russian Marxists succumbed to the tug of emotion and reasoned their way into patriotism, Lenin's little group was increasingly isolated.

These switches of opinion in the atmosphere of the revolutionary movement involved basic loyalties. No opinions were 'mere' opinions: 'breaking with' someone because of changes in view was not only commonplace but more or less *de rigueur*; Trotsky now found himself 'breaking with' many veteran Marxists with whom Lenin was at odds and in consequence edging closer to Lenin's theoretical 'position'. Lenin's 'position' – on the basis of theory alone – represented a rather natural strong-point for Trotsky's own evolution; hence Trotsky's reluctance to join him must be explained not by theory but by the play of personal relations – the 'ambition' that Lenin himself took for granted.

The real differences between the exiled groups of Socialists had little to do with theory, despite their obsession with it. In fact, from the very foundation of the Russian Social-Democratic Party to the Bolshevik putsch there were no real innovations of theory at all. As before 1905, the endless discussions in the emigration were quite irrelevant to the crucial political situation in 1917 that came about independently of Marxist initiative and was only later encompassed by theory.

Lenin's 'hard' line in politics – his voluntarism-cum-exclusiveness – performed two real functions. It kept his followers, during the First World War, from being contaminated by patriotism or war fever, and above all, from an organisation point of view – it made Lenin's coterie *special*.

To keep it special the appeal to theory was, to be sure, also vital:

Lenin's personal authority was accompanied by, indeed transmitted through his interpretation of the Marxist scriptures. The thrust-and-parry of theory was indispensable for the shaping of a true elite.

Trotsky was still living off the liberal newspaper *Kiev Thought*: since the newspaper was patriotic Trotsky had to do a good deal of pussyfooting, i.e., distort or conceal his own views in order not to sour his relationship with the management. Only those parts of his writing that seemed to attack the Central Powers could get printed.

This naturally impelled him to concentrate on more or less 'objective' reporting, including military analyses: he became, in fact, a military correspondent as well as reporter. Just as he had flung himself with remarkable energy into his day-to-day journalism in the Balkans and elsewhere, so he now performed the role of a seasoned correspondent – roaming about France, to the south and the west, sketching in local colour, atmosphere, 'impressions', and so on. He visited hospitals and hung about with soldiers, soaking up their talk in cafés and other places. His unflagging attendance in Paris cafés, where it was possible to read the world's press all day long for the price of a cup of coffee and to chat with friends and acquaintances about politics, generally at the famous Café Rotonde in Montparnasse (where Martov was practically renting a chair), enabled him to keep abreast of everything. He also read serious military literature.

His role as military correspondent was peculiarly congenial. It was of course a mere commonplace for a Marxist, taking the 'long' as well as the 'deep view', to see beyond the interplay of externalia into their fundamental causes. Trotsky was further helped by a literary gift for psychological observation; this enabled him to combine analyses of causes with the psychological atmosphere of collectivities. He could convey a vivid impression of national morale.

Trotsky's later misfortunes were to lead to the partial eclipse of some of his most distinguished writing, of which his military analyses, especially, only recently collected and translated, retain an historic interest. It was he, after all, who was to create an army.

However 'objective' Trotsky's military writings were, however, he was bound to fall foul of the French Government because of his attacks on the Allies. Nudged a little by the Russian Government, the French abruptly lost patience with Trotsky. On 15 September 1916 they shut down *Our World*; the following day Trotsky was told he and his family had to leave the country.

Since Trotsky was afraid of being shipped back to Russia, he did his best to return to Switzerland, or alternatively to go to Italy or Scandinavia via England. He kept trying for six weeks until a couple of policemen forcibly put him across the Spanish border on 30 October 1916.

He still hoped to get to Italy, but his stay in Spain was complicated by the French informing the Spanish police that he was a 'dangerous anarchist'. A couple of weeks later he was arrested and gaoled.

While being hustled through Spain his sense of humour leaped to the surface, as it often did in times of stress: lying on his 'repulsive bed', surrounded by 'heavy prison odours', 'his clothes all buttoned' he suddenly realised 'the full incongruity of what had happened. In a prison – in Madrid! I had never dreamed of such a thing.... In Madrid! I lay on the bed in the Madrid "model prison" and laughed with all my might, laughed till I fell asleep.'[41]

There was a maddening delay; he had to dawdle about while friends in Italy and Switzerland did their best to get him entry permits. He spent some six weeks in Cadiz, reading omnivorously as usual in an old library; he was supposed to be put aboard the first ship leaving the country, but when one turned up whose destination was Cuba he protested so vigorously that he was permitted to wait for one headed for the States.

Toward the end of December he was escorted by the police to Barcelona, where Natalya and the two boys had finally turned up: a few days later, on Christmas Day 1916, they all embarked for New York. The trip took two and a half weeks.

A friend and future associate, Nikolai Bukharin, was there to meet him. As Natalya was to recall, 'Bukharin received us with open arms. Twenty-nine, vivacity itself, an open laughing face, an affectionate nature, a gay speaker full of humour.'[42]

Hardly off the boat, they were hustled off by him at nine in the evening just to see the beautiful public library. The next day Trotsky set to work on *The New World*, a local periodical in Russian.

Trotsky was given a tremendous welcome by the New York colony of émigrés and Socialists. By now he was one of the most celebrated figures of the Socialist movement in Russia, especially distinguished, moreover, as the author of the Zimmerwald Manifesto. He was an ideal newcomer for the overwhelmingly anti-militarist Russian colony, most of whom in New York were in fact Jews. His arrival was noted everywhere, even in the 'bourgeois' press.

The little family moved into a small flat in the Bronx, New York. It cost eighteen dollars a month, and was

> fitted out with conveniences that for European habits were un-
> heard of: electricity, a gas oven, a bathroom, a telephone, an
> automatic dumb-waiter to bring food up and another one to take
> the garbage bin. All this captured our boys in favour of New York.
> For a while the telephone was the centre of their lives. We had not
> had this martial instrument either in Vienna or in Paris.[43]

Trotsky soon found the class-struggle in New York: the coloured janitor vanished with the rent-money they had given him for three months in advance; he had also had charge of all their belongings; Natalya had not got a receipt; they were very upset. But it quickly turned out that the janitor had not only safeguarded their things, but had tucked the rent-money in one of the cases. Out of hatred for the owner of the building and solidarity for the poor tenants, he had stolen only the money of the people who had receipts!

> Truly a splendid fellow! My wife and I were deeply moved by
> his concern and retained a grateful memory of him. The sympto-
> matic significance of this little adventure seemed to me very great.
> It was as though a little corner of the 'black' problem in the
> United States had been disclosed to me.[44]

As usual, Trotsky earned his living by lecturing and writing. Years later many legends sprang up about his short stay in New York: he was supposed to have been a tailor, a dish washer, a bit player in films, and so on. All these stories – revolving around the assumption that he was a typical Jew (the 'tailor' is, of course, archetypal) – are poppycock. Trotsky denied them all, nor are they mentioned in any other reliable source.

A star 'attraction', his presence at a ball would justify charging more money.[45] 'A mass-meeting would sometimes be delayed for several hours because Trotsky, who was attending a number of simultaneous mass-meetings, was physically incapable of getting anywhere on time.'[46]

In the little New York colony Trotsky's behaviour made a certain impression. They were all struck, Ziv says, by his aloofness. He would speak, be applauded, and then vanish not into the crowd, in the usual fashion of the movement, but elsewhere: ordinary people would never see him, only 'leaders'. He behaved in fact like an august official, never allowing the distance to be forgotten between him and, say, an interviewer.

According to Ziv, this whole technique – if it was one, and not simply the man himself – actually worked. Even those displeased by Trotsky's remoteness were in awe of it: even Ziv, a boyhood friend, found himself impressed by the fact that he too was going to see Trotsky![47]

Trotsky was in the United States only a couple of months; he could hardly be expected to see much of America, nor did he: he was restricted to the parochial life of the Socialist émigrés. In a few cities on the eastern seaboard he lectured to various Socialists who spoke German or Russian (Latvian, German, Russian, Finnish and Jewish groups).

He was steeped as always in Marxist metaphor. It had always been a great conundrum for Marxists why the most highly developed industry in the world should not have evolved the most highly developed 'class consciousness' in its working class. Trotsky was never to give up hope that this would happen from one moment to the next; it was a constant theme of his remarks on America.

The realities were quite different. There was a particularly startling contrast between Marxist hopefulness and the *de facto* situation amongst the immigrants. Socialism had made a little headway among Americans, but not Marxism: American Socialism seemed to Trotsky parochial, shallow and philistine. He described Morris Hillquit as the 'Babbitt of all Babbitts – the ideal Socialist leader for prosperous dentists.'[48]

Eugene Debs was an exception. To Trotsky he was 'a sincere revolutionary, though a romantic and a preacher, absolutely no political person and no leader', but 'distinguished by an unquenchable little flame of Socialist idealism.' Whenever they met, Debs – not a 'dry one' – would 'embrace and kiss' Trotsky.

The American excursion was cut short by news of the February 1917 upset in Petrograd, described by the defective wire services as 'breadline riots'.

Trotsky took it for granted that the Grand Overturn had erupted and that the news from Petrograd heralded not merely the Russian but at the very least the European Revolution. He immediately conceived it in the broadest possible terms: he forecast that it would inevitably and immediately sweep throughout Europe, in particular throughout Germany. Not only during the first period of the new era, but for years afterwards – indeed, until his death – he found it inconceivable that The Revolution could remain confined to a backward peasant country like Russia; he thought it bound to besiege and eventually to engulf the whole capitalist world.

A fortnight after the news of the Petersburg 'riots' Trotsky, Natalya, and the two boys sailed for Russia. Although for the first time in his life Trotsky had bonafide documents, he nevertheless was forcibly removed from the ship by British police when it docked at Halifax, Nova Scotia a few days later. He was interned; Natalya and the boys were put under strict custody. He started cabling again – to the new Russian Government and to the British authorities. The cables were suppressed at the source.

His detention soon became a factor in the internal politics of the new Russian regime, since one half of it – the newly reconstituted Soviet run by Mensheviks – insisted on his immediate release. There were, in fact, protests throughout the country; as a chairman of the 1905 Soviet, Trotsky was known to all veterans of the Left-wing parties.

There was something mysterious about his detention. From the British point of view, it was only reasonable to detain a sworn enemy of the war and of the Allies; the oddity was the lengthy delay before the new Russian Government intervened on his behalf.

There are indications that, at the time, Trotsky suspected a strong reluctance on the part of both Bolsheviks and Mensheviks to help him. On his arrival in Russia, for instance, Angelica Balabanoff thought he was in

a bad mood. . . . Both Mensheviks and Bolsheviks regarded him with rancour and distrust, possibly in memory of the bitter polemics . . . in the past and partly, no doubt, out of fear of the competition offered by such an effective writer and orator. . . . Trotsky was particularly bitter because he assumed that his political adversaries, in order to keep him out of the political arena in Russia as long as possible, had failed to bring sufficient pressure to bear upon the Allied authorities. . . . In my conversation with them they displayed quite as much hatred of Trotsky as he did of them.[49]

The detention lasted almost a month. At first he held mass meetings among the 800 German prisoners-of-war in the camp, but his successful speeches annoyed the German officers, who persuaded the commandant to stop him.

At last Miliukov, the 'bourgeois' Foreign Minister of the new regime, was obliged to intervene: Trotsky's return could not be opposed openly by any prominent groups in Russia. The release came through; some three weeks later, exactly a month after Lenin, Trotsky arrived in Petrograd.

This month-long delay had fateful consequences. During a period of effervescence, in which groups already in existence were solidifying, Trotsky was out of circulation.

He was not even met by any of the revolutionary leaders on his arrival at the Russian frontier, but by a rank-and-file Bolshevik assigned the formal task of keeping up appearances – Trotsky was still, after all, an eminent Social-Democrat!

He doubtless thought that it might turn out not to matter: in Petrograd itself a throng waving red banners carried him away from the train on their shoulders.

He was on stage once again.

CHAPTER V

The Star

THE VAST AREA created by the turbulence in Petrograd in 1917 lacked the fluidity that had served Trotsky's talents before. This time it was organised.

The breakdown of the Tsarist regime had taken place with stunning rapidity. For a time it seemed to the Russian revolutionaries as though there were no limits to their dreams.

The breakdown itself was a sort of negative occurrence. It seemed to have come about 'spontaneously'; no political group in any case had done anything to cause it. All the Left-wing political leaders were away; there was no mass action of any kind – neither strikes, nor demonstrations, nor uprisings.

Yet in three days the 400-year-old Romanov dynasty had been obliterated. Its place was taken, on the same day and in the same building, by two organisations that together constituted a new regime.

One was the Provisional Government, composed of elements of the former parliamentary body, the Duma; the other was the Soviet of Workers' and Peasants' Deputies, composed of a variety of Left-wing elements – intellectuals and representatives of workers' and peasants' organisations.

Formally, the Provisional Government was *the* Government; the Soviet was, at first, merely supposed to supervise it. Yet as a matter of fact the Soviet had all the powers required for any government. Since it represented all the organisations of the working class and peasantry, it was impossible to take a train, send a wire, distribute bread, manufacture a pair of shoes, run a machine, or give orders to soldiers without its authorisation.

The regime was, in fact, a Dual Power; it was to last some eight months.

It was Socialist theory that had led to this paradoxical situation, in which the sovereign body, the Provisional Government, was powerless, while a subordinate body, the Soviet, controlled all practical affairs.

For in Marxist eyes the Tsarist breakdown constituted the opening of The Revolution. From the point of view of Marxism, indeed, the very fact that Tsarism had collapsed of itself, and not because of any conscious political action, seemed to conform with the Marxist schema; impersonal socio-economic forces had worked themselves out.

Yet the general schema of Marxism seemed to reveal a flaw when applied this time to Russia: it was curious, and slightly inexplicable, that The Revolution had broken out not in Berlin, Manchester, Paris or Detroit, as it should have, but in Petrograd – the capital of a backward agricultural country.

This confronted the Marxist leaders of the Soviet with a peculiar problem. They were the acknowledged leaders of the complex of working class and peasant organisations represented in the Soviet without whose assent, during the months following the Tsarist breakdown in February 1917, it was impossible to carry out the most elementary acts of the administration.

Yet the Soviet was incapable of taking power, that is, of *proclaiming* its own authority, and political authority becomes such, after all, only when it is acknowledged to be such.

It was here that the Marxist orientation of the Soviet paralysed its leaders: If Russia, by Marxist criteria, was ripe only for a 'bourgeois' revolution, how could a Socialist party take power? To do what?

If any form of mass action was strangely absent from the incredibly swift dissolution of the Tsarist regime, then there was, if possible, still less action on the part of any 'bourgeois' institutions. What the 'bourgeoisie' did, in fact, was to acknowledge the elimination of the Tsar and institute some socio-economic reforms that did not alter the actual 'class structure' of the country.

The principal immediate result of the Tsarist collapse was the creation of a democratic society. Overnight Russia became remarkably free – there was freedom of speech, press, assembly; there was democratic representation. The underground vanished:

Russian revolutionaries of all kinds came to the surface and agitated
in free competition with their rivals. The Marxists, too, acquired a
democratic electorate; they vied for influence, authority and votes
with all other tendencies. The Marxist party, to be sure, in both
Bolshevik and Menshevik factions, retained its executive structure,
so to speak, but in its approach to society at large it could present a
public face as well.

It was this achievement, indeed, that constituted the essence of a
'bourgeois' revolution; as the paramount consequence of the toppling of the dynasty, it was enough to enable Marxists to look on it as
the liquidation of feudal Tsarism and as the harbinger of a new
era.

And since from this point of view, a further Socialist revolution
was precluded by Russia's backwardness, a Socialist party would
merely be compromising itself in the eyes of its followers by taking
power in order to defend what was – by agreed-on definition – a
'bourgeois' revolution. In short, all a sincere Socialist party could do
was to supervise the 'bourgeois' government to make sure it did not
deviate from the Marxist prescription.

By the beginning of May, at the time of Trotsky's arrival, that
theory had worn thin.

It had been possible, at first, for the Socialist parties represented
in the Soviet, in harmony with their theory, to abstain from the
responsibilities of government. But the refusal of the Mensheviks
and Social Revolutionaries to *join* the government while proclaiming
their *support* for it, had put the Socialists into an impossibly equivocal situation. The Provisional Government was in favour of the war,
but it depended for its existence on the support of the Soviet, which
was bound to tell its own followers that while in the midst of
supporting the pro-war government it was itself rather *against* the
war. Similarly, Prince Lvov's regime – the first government to
emerge from the collapse of February 1917 – was bound to try to
restore the old Tsarist governmental machinery, even though the
Soviet plainly controlled all administration.

The Soviet was, in short, bogged down in contradictory attitudes
stemming from a basic logical contradiction – holding *de facto*
power without exercising it, or, put in another way, being morally
committed to the support of an otherwise helpless organism that
through that very support was empowered to follow policies the
Soviet's own following was against.

Consequently, when the Provisional Government ran into a maelstrom through the resignation of the War Minister and the Foreign Minister in April, the Soviet leaders had to reinforce their moral support of the Provisional Government by actually joining it.

Trotsky had arrived in the midst of this governmental shifting of position, just as the first Coalition was formed between the ruling party of the Provisional Government, the Kadets, and the Socialist leaders of the Soviet. The Coalition had been formally constructed of ten 'capitalist' and six Socialist Ministers: as the leading group the Kadets naturally put forth their own programme, which the Socialists supported while doing their best to make it digestible for their own following. When Trotsky appeared this issue had been settled: the Socialist Ministers were asking their followers in the Soviet to support them.

Trotsky and Natalya had arrived quite penniless; Natalya set about looking for lodgings while Trotsky rushed off to the Smolny Institute, a former finishing-school for young noble-women that was now the headquarters of the Soviet.

Trotsky, whose welcome by the Soviet was enthusiastic – in contrast with his welcome by the Executive – was given the floor.

As a chairman of the 1905 Soviet that had been revived in 1917, he might have expected an invitation to become part of the Executive as a matter of course, but the Mensheviks and Social-Revolutionaries running the Soviet would agree to no more than his admission as a non-voting associate.

The rancorous bickering of the preceding decade had had its effect; the lines between the formerly somewhat fluid divisions within the movement were now far firmer. Still in a 'bad mood' about his detention in Nova Scotia, Trotsky himself interpreted his chilly reception by the leaders as due to factional rivalry.

At his first appearance he had not yet made up his mind on just what 'line' to take on the question of support for the Socialists' entry into the 'bourgeois' government. He was not sure of his audience, and, far more important, he was necessarily being called upon not as a member of any group, but as an individual.

Sukhanov, a 'wild' or non-party Menshevik who wrote the chief memoir of the upheaval of 1917, describes Trotsky's first public appearance on his return to Russia:

Trotsky had already been pointed out; the hall resounded with cries of 'Trotsky! We want Comrade Trotsky!'
It was the famous orator's first appearance on a revolutionary

tribune. He was warmly greeted. And, with characteristic brilliance, he made his first speech on the Russian Revolution and its
influence in Europe and overseas. He spoke of proletarian solidarity and the international struggle for peace; but he also
touched on the coalition. In mild and cautious terms, not characteristic of him, he pointed out the practical fruitlessness and
erroneousness in principle of the step that had been taken.

Trotsky was visibly disturbed at this début under the neutral
gaze of an unknown crowd and to the accompaniment of the hostile
exclamations of a couple of dozen 'Social-traitors'. From the outset
he did not expect any sympathy. And to make it worse – his cuff
kept constantly shooting out of his sleeve and threatening to fall
on the heads of his nearest listeners. Trotsky kept on settling it
back in place, but the wilful cuff would shoot out again – and it
distracted and irritated him.[1]

Trotsky was plainly doing his best to be conciliatory, but two of
the themes – that a Coalition would not wipe out the Dual Power,
which should be superseded by the Soviet – recalled Lenin's own
agitational angle around this time.

Trotsky had, in fact, come late in still another way. Not merely
was he now isolated with respect to the main factions of the Party,
but a cardinal element of his patented theory, 'Permanent Revolution', had been quietly taken over by Lenin.

Because of his isolation just beforehand, Trotsky was not, apparently, quite aware of this. Yet it was to be the major theoretical and,
in this case, practical development of the whole period of break-up
prior to the Bolshevik putsch, for which it was, indeed, an indispensable stage.

Lenin had arrived in Petrograd just a month before, in circumstances that in the nature of things were acutely embarrassing for
any Russian and for a Russian Marxist even more so – he and some
other revolutionaries had been provided with a 'sealed train' by the
German General Staff, crossing Germany from their exile in Switzerland. On his arrival Lenin had compounded the embarrassment, and
had stupefied his own followers, as well as his fellow-revolutionaries
in general and for that matter his enemies, by switching as it seemed
overnight his view of the Bolshevik role in the Tsarist breakdown.

Before his arrival the Bolsheviks had had more or less the same
attitude as other Marxists on this question of The Revolution in
peasant Russia. They, too, took it for granted that this phase of The

Revolution was 'bourgeois' and accordingly, that a Socialist party could do no more than tend the interests of The Proletariat while keeping an eye on the handling of The 'Bourgeois' Revolution by The Bourgeoisie.

The first thing Lenin did on arrival was simply to drop this whole conception – a banality for years – and declare outright that The Bourgeoisie too had to be overthrown by The Proletariat in order for The Bourgeois Revolution itself to be accomplished.

His followers were flabbergasted. Sukhanov describes Lenin's opening speech in April at the Finland Station; it was in the form of a reply to Chkheidze, a Menshevik now chairman of the Soviet:

Lenin came, or rather ran, into the room. He wore a round cap, his face looked frozen, and there was a magnificent bouquet in his hands. Running to the middle of the room, he stopped in front of Chkheidze as though colliding with a completely unexpected obstacle. And Chkheidze, still glum, pronounced the following 'speech of welcome' with not only the spirit and wording but also the tone of a sermon:

'Comrade Lenin, in the name of the Petersburg Soviet and of the whole revolution we welcome you to Russia.... But – we think that the principal task of the revolutionary democracy is now the defence of the revolution from any encroachments either from within or from without. We consider that what this goal requires is not disunion, but the closing of democratic ranks. We hope you will pursue these goals together with us.'

Chkheidze stopped speaking. I was dumbfounded with surprise: really, what attitude could be taken to this 'welcome' and to that delicious 'But – '?

But Lenin plainly knew exactly how to behave. He stood there as though nothing taking place had the slightest connection with him – looking about him, examining the persons round him and even the ceiling of the imperial waiting-room, adjusting his bouquet (rather out of tune with his whole appearance), and then, turning away from the delegation altogether, he made this 'reply':

'Dear Comrades, soldiers, sailors, and workers! I am happy to greet in your persons the victorious Russian revolution, and greet you as the vanguard of the world-wide proletarian army. . . . The piratical imperialist war is the beginning of civil war throughout Europe. . . . The hour is not far distant when at the call of our comrade, Karl Liebknecht, the peoples will turn their arms

against their own capitalist exploiters. . . . The world-wide Socialist
revolution has already dawned. . . . Germany is seething. . . . Any
day now the whole of European capitalism may crash. The Russian
revolution accomplished by you has prepared the way and opened
a new epoch. Long live the world-wide Socialist revolution!'

It was very interesting! Suddenly, before the eyes of all of us,
completely swallowed up by the routine drudgery of the revolution, there was presented a bright, blinding, exotic beacon, obliterating everything we 'lived by'. Lenin's voice, heard straight from
the train, was a 'voice from outside'. There had broken in upon us
in the revolution a note that was novel, harsh, and somewhat
deafening.[2]

Sukhanov goes on to describe the stunning effect of his speech,
later that same day, at the Bolshevik headquarters (the former house
of a ballet star, the Tsar's mistress):

The apartments of the famous ballerina had a rather strange
and inappropriate look. The exquisite ceilings and walls were out
of all harmony with the unpretentious furnishings, the primitive
tables, chairs, and benches set casually about as required by
business. There was very little furniture. Kshesinskaya's movable
property had been put away somewhere, and it was only here and
there that the remains of former grandeur were visible, in the
display of flowers and a few examples of artistic furniture and
ornaments.

Then the celebrated master of the order himself rose to reply. I
shall never forget that thunder-like speech, which startled and
amazed not only me, a heretic who had accidentally dropped in,
but all the true believers. I am certain that no one had expected
anything of the sort. It seemed as though all the elements had
risen from their abodes, and the spirit of universal destruction,
knowing neither barriers nor doubts, neither human difficulties
nor human calculations, was hovering around Kshesinskaya's
reception-room above the heads of the bewitched disciples.

Lenin was in general a very good orator – not an orator of the
consummate, rounded phrase or of the luminous image, or of
absorbing pathos, or of the pointed witticism, but an orator of
enormous impact and power, breaking down complicated systems
into the simplest and most generally accessible elements, and

hammering, hammering, hammering them into the heads of his audience until he took them captive.

. . . Everything touching on what had hitherto been called scientific Socialism Lenin ignored just as completely as he destroyed the foundations of the current Social-Democratic programme and tactics. Extremely remarkable. . . .

Lenin ended his speech. The pupils delightedly, unanimously, lengthily applauded their teacher. On the faces of the majority there was nothing but rapture; not the shadow of a doubt. Happy, innocent souls! But the literate ones, clapping loud and long, seemed to stare strangely in front of them; or else their eyes roved about unseeingly, showing complete confusion: the teacher had given the minds of his Marxist disciples some work to do.

I looked for Kamenev ... but in answer to my question as to what he had to say about all this, he merely shrugged his shoulders: 'Wait, just wait!'

As an infidel, I turned to another and then a third of the faithful: after all, I *ought* to understand – what was this really all about? The people I talked to grinned and shook their heads, without the slightest idea of what to say.

I went out into the street. I felt as though I had been beaten about the head that night with flails.[3]

Shortly afterwards, at a 'unity meeting' of Marxists, Lenin dumbfounded the non-Bolshevik Marxists as well:

They weren't only stunned: each new word of Lenin's filled them with indignation. Protests and exclamations of outrage began to be heard. It wasn't only a question of the inappropriateness of such a speech at a 'unifying' conference, it was also that together with the idea of unity the foundations of the Social-Democratic programme and of Marxist theory were spat upon. . . . I remember Bogdanov, who was sitting opposite me, on the 'Ministerial bench', two steps away from the platform: 'This is the raving of a madman! It's indecent to applaud this clap-trap!' he cried out, livid with rage and contempt, turning to the audience. 'You ought to be ashamed of yourselves! Marxists!'

The real Bolsheviks also made no bones – at least in private conversations behind the scenes – about Lenin's 'abstractness'. One even expressed the idea that Lenin's speech had removed the differences within the Social-Democracy, for with respect to

Lenin's position there could be no differences between Bolsheviks and Mensheviks.

The Bolshevik sect was still in a state of bafflement and perplexity. And the support Lenin found may underline more clearly than anything else his complete intellectual isolation, not only among Social-Democrats in general but also among his own disciples.[4]

In a conversation Sukhanov had at this time with Miliukov, the Foreign Minister and leader of the Kadet Party (the 'bourgeois' party par excellence), they both agreed that Lenin's views were not dangerous as yet to the 'bourgeois' government, since they were 'unacceptable' to everyone. But they both thought he would change, become more 'Marxist', and *then* would be dangerous:

> We refused to admit that Lenin might stick to his abstractions. Still less did we admit that through these abstractions Lenin would be able to conquer not only the revolution, not only all its active masses, not only the whole Soviet – but even his own Bolsheviks.
> We were cruelly mistaken. . . .[5]

In essence, Lenin's views at this time reproduced Trotsky's own 'Permanent Revolution'. By claiming that in a backward agricultural country The Bourgeoisie was too weak to make its own revolution, and hence that The Proletariat would have to make The 'Bourgeois' Revolution itself and then go on to extend it until The Proletariat in the advanced capitalist countries could catch up with it *later* and themselves carry the full burden of the Socialist transformation of society, Trotsky's theory provided the basis, in fact, for a Socialist party in a peasant country to take power *then and there*.

It was true that in the past Lenin had fought this theory, too, tooth and nail as he fought everything he disagreed with. Now, however, without saying so, he had borrowed Trotsky's theoretical formulation and from the moment of his arrival in Russia in April 1917 acted on it.

Hence there was no longer any 'theoretical' reason for Trotsky not to collaborate with Lenin, all the more so since Trotsky, in spite of his virtuosity as a speaker and writer, had no real following and was, in fact, no more than an individual star appealing abstractly as it were to a large audience rather than as the spokesman for one of the party organisations that made up the Soviet. Lenin for his part had no reason not to accept the services of a gifted free-lance, nine years his junior, and moreover a Jew: there could be no question of rivalry *within* the Party.

Perhaps the cardinal factor in Lenin's assimilation of Trotsky's viewpoint was his euphoric assessment of The Revolution. Convinced that The Revolution was about to break out all over at least the Continent, Lenin could look upon Russia as merely one link in the general chain – if Europe as a whole was 'ripe' for Socialism it no longer mattered that Russia, merely part of Europe, might not have been. It was possible to look upon a seizure of power in Russia as a means of breaking the back of at least one big capitalist class, while rushing toward The Revolution along with the Continent as a whole.

It was thus from this international point of view, hitherto rather characteristic of Trotsky, that Lenin could now envisage The Revolution bursting the bounds of the 'bourgeois' phase in Russia and thus go on to the justifiability of the 'proletarian' dictatorship as a means of smashing the capitalist as well as the landowning class.

Hence Trotsky was, organisationally, in a baffling position; the only party he was now close to spiritually was not accessible to him on his own terms.

Sukhanov has described the 'atmosphere' of the Bolshevik Party then:

> From time to time some characteristic traits of the Bolshevik 'way of life' and of specific methods of Bolshevik party work, all of which I found very curious, slipped out. It became quite obvious that all Bolshevik work was held within the iron framework of a foreign spiritual centre, without which the party workers would have felt themselves to be completely helpless, which at the same time they felt proud of, and which the best amongst them felt themselves to be the devoted servitors of, like knights of the Holy Grail.[6]

This lay order, essentially a conspiratorial nucleus, was no longer tussling with rival sects; the arena created by the collapse of Tsarism enabled it to appeal to a general audience.

For that general audience there was no question, of course, of Marxist theory. Slippery even for its adepts, Marxism could not be unloaded wholesale.

Thus the decades of elaborating the theories of Marx and Engels,

the unflagging contentiousness in tailoring those theories to constantly changing circumstances, were to prove quite irrelevant as
far as the general public was concerned. Whatever the function
performed by theory in welding together the conspiratorial nucleus,
theory was kept entirely in the background when it came to Bolshevik propaganda and agitation, Bolshevik slogans, Bolshevik rhetoric,
Bolshevik passion.

The Bolsheviks had, in short, been acquiring a following as well as
a membership. Bolshevik views were no longer worded in the
scholastic form appropriate to a Marxist cloister, but in accordance
with the requirements of mass manipulation.

This public dimension of the Bolshevik Party was tightly
controlled by the nucleus, and in the hurly-burly of 1917 the most
formidable of all obstacles to what might have been Trotsky's hopes
of pre-eminence was, perhaps, the fact of Lenin. Recalling him on
the very brink of his apotheosis as founder of the Soviet State,
Sukhanov explains his primacy:

> Lenin is an extraordinary phenomenon, a man of absolutely
> exceptional intellectual power; he is of first-class world magnitude
> in calibre. For he represents an unusually happy combination of
> theoretician and popular leader. If still other epithets were needed
> I shouldn't hesitate to call Lenin a genius.
>
> A genius, as is well known, is an abnormal person. More
> concretely, he is very often a man with an extremely limited area
> of intellectual activity, in which area this activity is carried on
> with unusual power and productivity. A genius can very often be
> extremely narrow-minded, with no understanding or grasp of the
> simplest and most generally accessible things.
>
> In addition to these internal and, so to speak, theoretical quali-
> ties of Lenin's, as well as his genius, the following circumstance
> also played a primary role in his victory over the old Marxist
> Bolsheviks. In practice Lenin had been historically the exclusive,
> sole, and unchallenged head of the party for many years, since the
> day of its emergence. The Bolshevik Party was the work of his
> hands, and his alone. The very thought of going against Lenin was
> frightening and odious.
>
> Lenin the genius was an historic figure – this is one side of the
> matter. The other is that, except Lenin, there was nothing and no
> one in the party. The few massive generals without Lenin were
> nothing, like the few immense planets without the sun (for the

moment I leave aside Trotsky, who at that time was still outside
the ranks of the order, that is, in the camp of the 'enemies of the
proletariat, lackeys of the bourgeoisie', etc.).

In the First International, according to the well-known description, there was Marx high up in the clouds; then for a long, long
way down there was nothing; then, also at a great height, there
was Engels; then again for a long, long way there was nothing,
and finally there was Liebknecht sitting there, etc.

But in the Bolshevik Party Lenin the Thunderer sat in the
clouds and then – there was absolutely nothing right down to the
ground. And on the ground, amongst the party rankers and officers
a few generals could be distinguished – and even then I daresay
not individually but rather in couples or combinations. There
could be neither independent thinking nor organisational base in
the Bolshevik Party without Lenin.[7]

Trotsky's dilemma – the problem of a fitting role – was compounded by Lenin's radical switch-about in theory; it meant that
Trotsky now had no characteristic angle of his own. He could not,
after all, take much advantage of Lenin's right-about-face on this
question of the goal of a Marxist party in a revolution. Against the
background of the embittered polemics of a whole decade, it would
have been quite futile for Trotsky to point this out.

Trotsky was now plunged into a maelstrom with nothing to cling
to but his personal gifts – he had neither an organisation to speak of
nor a characteristic view of events that might create a following.

The importance of this whole issue was all the greater because of
the instability in Russian society revealed by the Tsarist breakdown: Lenin's switch-about, implying that The Revolution was
bound to transcend any 'bourgeois' reform of society, naturally
posed the crucial problem of politics – power.

Thus, in the short run, Trotsky was now confronted by the
decisive question of organisation: which group was he to join?

These theoretical convergences, after all, were completely negligible in the power-relationships of the two men. Trotsky might feel
smug, if he chose to, at his having preceded Lenin chronologically in
the formulation of the same view. That didn't matter.

What mattered was that Lenin had a *party*. Nor was there any
need for him to give Trotsky 'credit' for a theoretical device: the
elaboration of one view into another by 'Marxist methods' was

commonplace, and always put forth as a reflection of changing circumstances.

Lenin need have felt no qualms; nor did he. In April, for instance, on being castigated for his 'Trotskyism' on this point by Trotsky's brother-in-law, Kamenev, he had been quite indifferent.

In spite of his general isolation Trotsky did have a following, the 'Inter-Districtites', a small coterie, neither Bolshevik nor Menshevik, he had been mentor to since its emergence in 1913. It had a little support in a few working-class boroughs of Petrograd, nowhere else, and was now united by a few broad views – against the war, against the 'bourgeois' Provisional Government, etc.

It was difficult, from a theoretical point of view, to distinguish the Inter-District Organisation from the Bolsheviks who were making inroads into its potential clientele. By the time Trotsky appeared in May, and was soon afterwards invited to a welcoming party organised by the Inter-Districtites and the Bolsheviks, the question of a merger had become the dominant issue.

Aside from the Inter-Districtites, Trotsky had no organisation at all. He did have a cluster of as it were editorial collaborators, many talented journalists who had written for various papers Trotsky had edited, such as Lunacharsky, Ryazanov, Yoffe and others, some of whom were to become well known, but while the coterie of writers, some of whom, like Ryazanov, were also 'thinkers' or at least scholars, might be called the flower of the movement, they could not be called leaders.

Trotsky, who had not seen Lenin since a chilly encounter in Zimmerwald in 1915, met him at the meeting of the Bolsheviks and Inter-Districtites on 10 May.

At this meeting Trotsky agreed that any reunion between Bolsheviks and Mensheviks no longer made sense. This in itself implied, of course, that he was now inclining toward the Bolsheviks. When he asked Lenin whether he still believed that The Revolution still had to be confined to its 'bourgeois' phase – indicating his unawareness of Lenin's switch-about of the preceding month – Lenin answered, in harmony with his new line, that the Bolsheviks were now aiming at a 'proletarian' dictatorship.

Lenin then proposed to Trotsky that he and his little entourage come into the Bolshevik Party immediately; he even offered them leading posts in the Bolshevik institutions and on *Pravda*. Trotsky found this objectionable; and since he could not because of the past call himself a 'Bolshevik' he suggested that a new party be formed, through a merger of their respective organisations, at a congress that would also proclaim a new name.

Had Trotsky managed to pull this off it would, of course, have been a great coup. At such a congress the Bolsheviks, by far the dominant force, would be sponsoring Trotsky as an equal; this, combined with the symbolic power of a new name, would have the effect, psychologically, of promoting Trotsky's influence both personally and factionally.

Such a lopsided 'merger' was plainly unthinkable; for his part Trotsky baulked at Lenin's 'offer'. For the time being the idea of any joining of the unequal forces was dropped.

Organisationally, now, Trotsky was at loose ends: a half-hearted attempt to find a mouthpiece in Gorky's periodical, *New Life*, which hung in the same limbo between Bolsheviks and Mensheviks as Trotsky himself, came to nothing. He tried starting a newspaper of his own, *Forwards*: it was to put out only sixteen numbers, appearing spasmodically.

Trotsky in fact was to exercise his influence essentially through his unique gift – the spoken voice. Isolated for the time being from all organisational connections, and with a vast mass of people churned up by new ideas following the collapse of the Tsarist regime, Trotsky as a speaker became a factor in moulding the mood of Petrograd.

For months the whole city had been bubbling over with talk: there were more or less constant mass-meetings in one part of the city or another, and an insatiable audience to speak at. By the end of May Trotsky and Lunacharsky, also a talented speaker as well as writer, were the most popular among the Left-wing supporters of the Soviet.

It is of course well-nigh hopeless to convey in print the effect of oratory. In the case of Trotsky the attempt seems essential; it was his oratory, primarily, that accounts for much of his career. Lunacharsky describes it:

I consider Trotsky very nearly the greatest orator of our times. In my day I've listened to all sorts of the greatest parliamentary and popular tribunes of Socialism and a very great many of the celebrated orators of the bourgeois world, and I should find it difficult to name any one of them, aside from Jaurès ... whom I could place next to Trotsky.

A striking appearance, beautiful broad gestures, a powerfully rhythmic speech, a loud, utterly tireless voice, remarkable coherence, a literary turn of phrase, a luxuriance of images, a stinging irony, a soaring pathos, a completely extraordinary logic of genuinely iron-like incisiveness – such are the qualities of Trotsky's oratory. He can speak in a lapidary style, throw out a few unusually accurate shafts and can give the most majestic political speech ... I've seen Trotsky speaking for 2½–3 hours before a completely silent audience, standing on its feet to boot, listening as though enthralled to a vast political treatise. Everything Trotsky said was in most cases familiar to me: for that matter, indeed, every agitator is of course bound to repeat again and again very many of his ideas before new audiences, but every single time Trotsky presents the selfsame idea in a new dress. . . . Trotsky is a great agitator. His articles and books constitute, so to speak, congealed speech – he is a writer in his oratory and an orator in his writing.[8]

Trotsky himself describes the wellsprings of this great gift:

Every authentic orator knows moments when something more powerful than himself in his ordinary hours speaks out of his mouth. That is 'inspiration'. It arises out of the loftiest creative concentration of all his powers. The unconscious rises out of a profound recess and subjugates the conscious labour of thought, fusing with it into a higher unity.[9]

At the Cirque Moderne he spoke fairly regularly to vast throngs. It was in the presence of these enormous masses of people, few of them Marxists or even 'professional revolutionaries', that Trotsky's gift could be given full expression. It was there that his non-intellectual, emotional, artistic and lyrical side could be amply displayed: he could succumb, as he was later to indicate, to the upwelling from his unconscious, to the torrent of emotion that harmonised with the inarticulate tension of the 'dark masses' in front of him and that obliterated all his purely cerebral decisions about 'opening sentences', 'lines of argument' and political 'points'. He voiced the emotions of a shapeless crowd.

All this is, of course, another way of indicating the difference between an orator and a debater.

There was such a crush more or less constantly at the Cirque Moderne that it was impossible for Trotsky to walk to the rostrum: he had to be carried on people's hands over the heads of the throng.

He would occasionally catch a glimpse of his two daughters, Zinaida and Nina, watching their famous father with the ardent eyes of adolescent girls.[10]

The public period of the Russian breakdown was in fact Trotsky's best medium: the effervescence of ideas, of talk, of plans and projects of all kinds was so intense that an orator like Trotsky, who could talk to all kinds of people and in Sukhanov's words 'warm up' audiences with remarkable skill, was altogether in his element. In a situation where people were preoccupied by public activities, by mass-meetings, by collective projections, by images, attractive orators were naturally at a premium.

Publicly, Trotsky was far more *there* than Lenin himself: here is an assessment of Lunacharsky's:

Under the influence of the vast range [of the agitational work of the spring of 1917] and of its dazzling success some people close to Trotsky were even inclined to see in him the genuine prime leader of the Russian revolution. Thus the late M. S. Uritsky once said to me: 'Here the great revolution has come, and there is a feeling that, however able Lenin is, he is beginning to fade alongside the genius of Trotsky.'

This assessment was proved incorrect not because it exaggerated Trotsky's gifts and ability, but because at that time the dimensions of Lenin's own statesmanlike genius were still unclear. Really, after the initial thunderlike success of his entry into Russia, and before the July Days, Lenin was to some extent eclipsed: he spoke seldom, didn't write much, but was mainly running organisational work in the Bolshevik camp while Trotsky was thundering in Petrograd at the mass-meetings.[11]

Just this 'thundering' of Trotsky's at the mass-meetings made him the star of this whole period. He incarnated par excellence the public aspect of the Revolution, and since even the chief actors in this drama were inevitably mesmerised by the heroic realisation of the Idea, Trotsky's stature was correspondingly magnified.

In any case, however, since for the time being there was 'nothing to do' for Trotsky but to join hands with Lenin, he was obliged to do so soon enough.

By July it was plainer than ever that there could be no question of changing the Party's name so as to make Trotsky's entry a 'merger':

he was now supposed to join the Bolsheviks formally at their sixth Congress.

But the formal union – or rather the absorption of Trotsky and his entourage by the Bolsheviks – was delayed by the singular phenomenon of the 'July Days' – singular because it is not so very clear what happened, or, more precisely, just how ripe was the Bolsheviks' determination to make a putsch.

The 'July Days' followed from the central dilemma of the regime – the curiously obdurate refusal of the Soviet leaders to exercise the sovereignty they could not avoid possessing. In the nature of things this dilemma kept being sharpened by events. It became routine for the Soviet Left wing – represented by the Bolsheviks and by Trotsky together with his small entourage – to call upon the Soviet leadership – represented by the Mensheviks and the Social Revolutionaries – to 'take power' – i.e., to exercise and proclaim the power already in their hands.

During the three weeks that the first All-Russian Congress of the Soviets was in session (from early June on), it became plain that the immense support being given the Soviet as a whole was split along general lines: the moderate Socialists (Mensheviks and Social-Revolutionaries), who had about five-sixths of the delegates, represented a wide range, including peasants and many soldiers, themselves generally peasants, while the extreme Left drew its following almost exclusively from the working-class districts of the big cities.

Just before the Congress met a city election for Petrograd had dealt a staggering blow to the Kadet Party that controlled the Government; half the ballots went to the Mensheviks. This victory for the Mensheviks was interpreted by the Bolsheviks as a swing Leftward on the part of the city population as a whole, hence as a hopeful omen for themselves.

Now, Lenin had already laid it down that in the general perspective, The Revolution was going to burst the bounds of its 'bourgeois' phase and go on to a purely Socialist phase. At the time he had established this point – of fundamental importance for his Marxist partisans – he had not yet moved forward to a declaration that it was the Bolsheviks themselves who would take power. Still a small minority within the Soviet itself, and furthermore not claiming to represent, even potentially, more than a minority of the population, it would have been impossible to justify such an ambition in traditional Marxist terms.

At the June All-Russian Soviet Congress, however, Lenin displayed a new perspective to the Congress, whose delegates came from all parts of the country.

When a speaker defended the Coalition between the Soviet and the Provisional Government, by challenging the delegates to come out openly and dare to point to any party that was ready to take the power *alone*, Lenin intervened from the floor, to say that his own was *quite* ready!

Lenin's interjection was considered highly comical – most of the delegates burst out laughing. The headway being made by the Bolsheviks in Petrograd was not appreciated.

Yet even then Lenin's intentions did not seem concentrated on an actual seizure of power: Bolshevik influence still had to be increased within the Soviet; later on, perhaps, the question of taking power, with the Soviet as a cover and a base, could be considered. Consequently Bolshevik sloganeering still did not aim at the Government itself – i.e., it was not 'Down with the Government!', simply 'Down with the Ten Capitalist Ministers'. But that meant 'All Power to the Soviets!' a slogan that was acutely painful for the Soviet leaders who had staked their careers on continuing the alliance with the Kadets in the 'bourgeois' Provisional Government in the name of the theory of The 'Bourgeois' Revolution.

At bottom their attitude was, no doubt, an illustration of congenital diffidence, of a perfectly ordinary, conventional kind, on the part of the middle-class leaders of the Soviet – they lacked the arrogance to rule! Trotsky was to make much of this 'petty-bourgeois' reluctance to assume authority.

A demonstration had been called by the Soviet for 18 June, designed to show public support for the Soviet *as a whole*, after the Soviet Executive had forbidden the Bolsheviks to hold a parade of their own the week before. The demonstration turned into a parade that in spite of everything marched under 'Bolshevik' slogans – e.g., 'Down with the Ten Capitalist Ministers!' 'Down with the War!' 'All Power to the Soviets!'

The Bolsheviks' slogans were calculated to reflect as far as possible very broad, general attitudes held by their potential clientele: opposition to the war was their most popular card.

These attractively streamlined slogans naturally fanned the unrest that had been growing apace among both the factory-workers and the soldiers.

During the last week of June a strike was threatened at the huge Putilov metal-works, together with the support of some other factories and some labour organisations. Economic demands were put forward, including the control of production, now vital in the minds of many workers because of the irresistibly rising cost of living.

In addition many soldiers, now being claimed for the increasingly obvious futility of the front, were chafing audibly: on 21 June, for instance, the First Machine-Gun Regiment – emotionally very 'Bolshevik' for some time – had refused to send its full quota to the front; they threatened that if the Soviet tried to force them they would not hesitate to 'dissolve by armed force the Provisional Government and the organisations that support it'.

This was a clear instance of hostility to the *Soviet itself*, the beginning of a switch away from the slogan, so popular during May and June, of 'All Power to the Soviets'. It marked, in fact, an overt split in attitude:

On the one hand the Soviet was unreliable, even traitorous, *because* of its spineless leadership: on the other it was authoritative because it represented the feelings of The Masses *despite* its leadership.

On 2 July the First Machine-Gun Regiment had a farewell meeting for military units leaving for the front. Trotsky was one of the main speakers; he and others harped on the need for exclusive Soviet power as the only way to get Russia out of the war.

Some Kadet Ministers resigned. Parades began. An armed demonstration was announced for the next day by the First Machine-Gunners; other regiments were summoned and harangued to co-operate. That evening the Machine-Gunners and another regiment set out for the Bolshevik headquarters; but were deflected to the Tauride Palace, now the residency of the central Soviet bodies.

Here is Sukhanov's description of the tension at the beginning of July:

Meanwhile the movement was already pouring through the city. The tempest was unleashed. Everywhere in the factories the same thing was going on: workers' and soldiers' delegations would turn up, refer to 'all the others', and demand in someone's name that they 'come out'. Only a minority, of course, demonstrated, but everywhere work was abandoned. Trains ceased to leave from the Finland Station. In the barracks short mass-meetings took place, and then from all sides enormous detachments of armed soldiers made their way towards the centre – some of them

to the Tauride Palace. Some started shooting into the air: the rifles
went off by themselves.

From early evening, lorries and cars began to rush about the
city. In them were civilians and soldiers with rifles at the trail and
with frightened-fierce faces. Where they came hurtling from and
why – no one knew.

The city fairly quickly took on the look of the last days of
February. Since then four months of revolution and liberty had
passed. The garrison of the capital, and even more the proletariat,
were now strongly organised. But the movement appeared to have
no more 'consciousness', discipline, or order. Elemental forces
raged.

One of the insurgent regiments, led by a Bolshevik lieutenant,
was moving along the Nevsky. It was an imposing armed force.
It was probably enough to hold the city – unless it came up against
a similar armed force. The head of the regiment had started to turn
into the Liteiny, when some shots were heard from Znamensky
Square. The commander of the column, who was riding in a car,
turned around and saw the heels of the soldiers, running off in all
directions. A few seconds later the car was left alone in the middle
of a jeering crowd on the Nevsky Prospect. There were no casualties. . . . Something similar was going on at this time at various
points of the capital.

The insurgent army didn't know where it should go, or why. It
had nothing but a 'mood'.[12]

There was, in short, an army – shapeless, perhaps, leaderless, but
an army – roaming the city on 3 July. It was plainly annoyed, not so
much with the Provisional Government as with the Soviet that
propped it up. Its mood was roughly expressed by a worker who
waved his fist at a Social-Revolutionary Government Minister and
yelled out in a frenzy: 'You son of a bitch – take the power when
they give it to you!'

After the commotion of the third, the street movement reached its
peak the next day – Lenin came back that morning from a short
trip – when the Bolsheviks staged what they called a 'peaceful
armed demonstration' to support the now classic slogan – 'All Power
to the Soviets'.

The 'peaceful demonstration' was instantly made explosive:
20,000 armed sailors from Kronstadt joined the parade on the morn-

ing of the fourth; they paraded straight to the Bolshevik headquarters.

Lenin spoke to them a little warily. He avoided committing himself, merely recommending that the sailors be 'firm and watchful': the Soviets would duly be given power.

The evaluation of all this is made difficult by the Bolsheviks' subsequent denial of all responsibility for the disorders, which they claimed were a 'spontaneous' eruption of the anger of The Masses, though the armed sailors were undeniably the most prominent and dangerous element in the disturbances, and their Kronstadt fortress had long been known as the most violently intransigent single unit of the armed forces.

There was in any case a big, infuriated throng around the Soviet headquarters in the Tauride Palace on 4 July. The crowd, with the armed Kronstadt sailors a nucleus of violence, threatened the Socialists in the Palace with physical violence; they refused to disperse unless the Coalition with the Provisional Government was disavowed.

Trotsky responded. According to Sukhanov:

Trotsky, two steps below us, climbed up on the bonnet of a car. The mob was in turmoil as far as the eye could reach. Around the motor-car a number of sailors with rather savage faces were particularly violent. Chernov, who had plainly lost all presence of mind, was in the back seat.

All Kronstadt knew Trotsky and, one would have thought, trusted him. But he began to speak and the crowd did not subside. If a shot had been fired nearby at that moment by way of provocation, a tremendous slaughter might have occurred, and all of us, including perhaps Trotsky, might have been torn to shreds. Trotsky, excited and not finding words in this savage atmosphere, could barely make the nearest rows listen to him.

'You hurried here, Red Kronstadters, as soon as you heard the revolution was in danger! Red Kronstadt has once again shown itself to be the champion of the proletarian cause. Long live Red Kronstadt, the glory and pride of the revolution! ...'

Nevertheless he was listened to with hostility. When he tried to pass on to Chernov himself, the ranks around the car again began raging.

'You've come to declare your will and show the Soviet that the working class no longer wants to see the bourgeoisie in power. But why hurt your own cause by petty acts of violence against casual individuals? Individuals are not worthy of your attention.... Every one of you has demonstrated his devotion to the revolution. Every one of you is ready to lay down his life for it. Give me your hand, Comrade! Your hand, brother!'

Trotsky stretched his hand down to a sailor who was protesting with especial violence. But the latter firmly refused to respond, and moved his hand – the one not holding a rifle – out of reach. If these were people alien to the revolution or outright *provocateurs*, to them Trotsky was just as bad as Chernov, or much worse: they might be waiting only for an opportunity to settle accounts with both advocate and defendant. But I think they were Kronstadt naval ratings who had, in their own judgement, accepted Bolshevik ideas. It seemed to me that the sailor, who must have heard Trotsky in Kronstadt more than once, now had a real feeling that he was a traitor: he remembered his previous speeches and was confused. Let Chernov go? Then why had he been summoned?

Not knowing what to do, the Kronstadters released Chernov.[13]

Chernov was in a state of semi-collapse; Trotsky, white as a sheet and in a cold sweat, half-carried him into the Palace.

The size of the mob, its high temper, and the threat of violence had an upsetting effect on the capital. Throughout the city there were riots and clashes. The mob that had been so stimulated by the Bolsheviks was now being restrained by them, but since the manifestations had no object, and since the insurrection had been called off, no outlet was provided for the passions of the multitude. They were gradually beginning to drift apart when some frontline troops entered the city.

Now the countless Right-wing elements in the capital, quiescent since the first days of the upheaval, were stimulated in their turn by the news, which arrived at this moment, that the most recent offensive at the front had been a fiasco. This news was linked to a shattering revelation – the Bolsheviks were German agents! The news was published in the patriotic press in the form of some documents indicating that Lenin had been subsidised by the German General Staff.[14]

In short, high treason in wartime. Everyone involved was in mortal peril.

The revelations of the German subsidy had a devastating effect.

Both the 'sealed train' and Lenin's anti-war agitation were, after all, notorious.

The reaction to the violence sponsored by the Bolsheviks was bound to be violent. The convergence between the fiasco at the front – a terrible embarrassment for the Army, the Right wing, and the Government as a whole – and the enduring, now intensified alarm over the social breakdown, produced a tidal wave of fury.

Warrants were issued forthwith for the arrest of Lenin, Zinoviev and Kamenev. Lenin bolted to a hideaway; his two intimates likewise.

The disclosure of Lenin's relations with the German Government had come at the worst possible time – after an attempted putsch had misfired. Lenin was both exposed and powerless.

He was still supported, to be sure, by the 'Soviet democracy', as a matter of solidarity. Whatever his differences with the other Soviet leaders, they none of them thought he was an actual German 'agent', even though it was obvious to everyone, in a way, that the Germans *must* have been giving the Bolsheviks money. When Stalin, for instance, in a state of high nervous tension, was sent to ask Tsereteli and Chkheidze to use their positions as Soviet leaders to request the press not to disclose the German connection, it seemed to the two Soviet leaders, bitter opponents of Lenin's, a matter of course to comply. (The disclosures were published in the press, indeed, only because one extremist Right-wing publication declined to co-operate.)[15]

In any case, since the Bolsheviks were members of the Soviet, discrediting them would harm the Soviet, too; it would in fact, play into the hands of the Provisional Government, and especially of the Right wing. Hence, since it was thought difficult to *demonstrate* the Bolshevik-German connection legally – the transmission belt was very round-about and well camouflaged – and since the primary iniquity of the Bolsheviks lay in what they were doing *openly* – promoting the collapse at the front – many Socialist anti-Bolsheviks were altogether sceptical about the practicability of a police enquiry at the time.[16]

From a practical point of view their scepticism was well-founded. The actual documents released by the Provisional Government in the summer of 1917 were remarkably puerile (the connection between Lenin and the German General Staff was supposed to be established via a junior officer, released from a prisoner-of-war camp in Germany, who had been sent to Russia with money in order to foment disaffection!).

The documents were, in fact, preposterous enough to make it seem likely that Lenin himself had 'leaked' them, in order to discredit in advance any authentic disclosures. The true documentation was not to emerge until after the Second World War.

The German subsidy was enormous. Eduard Bernstein – whose probity and acumen were never challenged – said later (in 1921) that it came to more than *fifty million gold marks*.* It enabled the Bolsheviks to maintain a huge daily press throughout the country – plainly far beyond the resources of the Party's membership dues – and to make potent propaganda in the public arena.

No doubt Helphand was the principal channel. He had become a Prussian citizen, and was acknowledged to be either an 'agent' or an 'ally' of the German Government. The suggestions he had made in the winter and spring of 1915 had borne fruit (see page 137); he had been given large sums for transmission to anti-war elements in Russia, of which the Bolsheviks, by the spring of 1917, were the only serious one.[17]

Lenin's circumstances had changed radically in the early part of 1917. Before the arrangement about the 'sealed train' he felt 'stoppered up in a bottle'; he would gladly, he said, have made a pact with the Devil if necessary to get to Petrograd.[18]

The change in his situation must have been abrupt. He had not even had time to prepare his followers in Petrograd for his sudden 'theoretical' switch, proclaimed in a systematic way for the first time when he got to Petrograd in April 1917 and vividly recorded, together with the stupefaction of his immediate entourage, by Sukhanov (see pages 153–6).

There was, in short, a convergence at last between 'theory' and practice! Marxist theory, appropriately modified by Lenin in a variant paralleling Trotsky's, was implemented practically by the German subsidy aimed at the immobilisation of the eastern front.

It was surely one of the most silent partnerships in history. Neither side has ever avowed it, then or later.

For the Bolsheviks it was not only a matter of life and death in the beginning – high treason in wartime – it also represented the crux of their 'revolutionary honour' – taking money from imperialists. And

---

*The equivalent of about two thousand million Deutschmarks today, or two hundred and thirty-five million pounds, or six hundred and sixty-six million dollars. J.C.

taking it no longer to subvert Tsarism, but to subvert institutions that had arisen through its collapse.

For the German General Staff, while the question of honour was irrelevant – why not subvert an enemy from within? – the German defeat and the consequent establishment of the Bolshevik regime, with its undreamt of potentialities for upheaval throughout the world, made what might otherwise have been a shrewd stratagem a source of acute embarrassment. This, no doubt, explains the reticence of some key figures[19] in discussing activities documented by their own memoranda.

More generally, many observers of Russian affairs, even those hostile to the Bolsheviks and for that matter to Marxism, have been reluctant to accept the evidence of the partnership. This reluctance is based, ultimately, on faith in Lenin's integrity; they reason that Lenin could never have become an 'agent' of the German Government.

This would seem to invert the relationship: it was precisely Lenin's unwavering intransigence, more particularly his determination to stop the war as a way of promoting The Revolution, that made the German Government see in him not an agent, but the *ally* they needed to immobilise the eastern front.

It would seem obvious, in fact, as Helphand had pointed out to the German Ambassador in January 1915, and written in greater detail in his remarkable memorandum of March, that the overthrow of the Tsarist Government, and after its collapse in 1917, the paralysing of the new regime's armed forces, constituted aims common both to the German Government and to the Russian revolutionaries, or at least, in the second phase, to the Bolsheviks. An identity of aims had brought about a bona fide convergence of behaviour – why not become allies?

Plainly, this had nothing to do with Lenin's integrity, with his being too 'revolutionary' to disdain such help. The over-emphasis on this moral, or psychological question on the part of many students of history would seem misplaced.

There remains, to be sure, a question of integrity with respect to Lenin's motivation. This has nothing to do with his view of Tsarism, but with his attitude toward the Provisional Government and the Soviet that had taken Tsarism's place.

The Germans wanted to immobilise the eastern front. At first that goal involved crippling the Russian Government; then, after the Tsarist collapse in February, it involved the elimination of the new regime from the war. In the one case as in the other the immobilisation of the front remained paramount.

But once the Tsarist Government had vanished, what could be the Marxist justification of sabotaging the new, 'revolutionary' regime?

Alone among all 'revolutionary Socialists', accordingly, it was the Bolsheviks who went on working for the paralysis of the new regime, as of the old, vis-à-vis the German Government. Hence, their activity could be justified only as a drive for the victory of the – Bolsheviks!

Looked at from this point of view, accordingly, this gamble, in which each side was speculating on the collapse of the other, was perfectly 'proper' for Lenin, just as it was 'proper' for him to accept Ludendorff's sealed train.

In retrospect, what seems important historically is not at all the Bolsheviks' 'revolutionary honour', but the legitimacy of their enterprise.

The German subsidy was so enormous that it could have been, and on balance no doubt was a prime factor in the Bolshevik victory.

The conjuncture was delicate; relationships were shifting; margins were narrow; contingencies were slippery.

It must be recalled that the German money went in the main to the network of Bolshevik newspapers created overnight by the Party throughout Russia; these newspapers – forty-one! – were engaged in penetrating public opinion with a cluster of thoroughly 'general', that is, non-Marxist slogans – basically a termination of the war, buttressed by the theme of 'Bread and Land'.

What this press barrage accomplished was on the one hand the conditioning of the population as a whole to these very popular themes, and, as a corollary, the conditioning of the population to accept the Bolsheviks as a respectable group, merely the most forthright among the other respectable parties in the respectable Soviet.

And since the Bolsheviks were to function under the camouflage of the Soviet, the effectiveness of this broad-gauge press campaign can scarcely be overestimated.

Looked at once again from Lenin's point of view, the putsch was conceived of as no more than a preamble of the World Revolution. Thus the structure of the operation in his own mind must have been something like this:

Behind a barrage of propaganda for general objectives, quite unrelated to specific Marxist aims, the Bolsheviks would seize power, hold it until the World Revolution, specifically in the form of a large-scale German insurrection, would turn the world upside down and incidentally sweep away their provisional sponsors – the German Government. Thus this secret, hostile alliance – in which each side was gambling on the destruction of the other – was to play a merely ephemeral, tactical role in the unfolding of the grand historical process.

Trotsky's treatment of this question of the 'German money' is singularly disingenuous, both in his *History of the Russian Revolution* and in his autobiography (to say nothing of his public utterances in the heat of the fray!).

In his *History*, for instance, he quotes Sukhanov, who like the public at large was quite taken in by the Bolsheviks' protestations of innocence.

Sukhanov found Lenin's behaviour simply unbelievable:

> Besides the accusation of insurrection, a monstrous slander, believed by hundreds of thousands and millions of people, had been directed at Lenin. Lenin was accused of the crime, vile and shameful from every point of view, of being in the pay of the German General Staff.... It was impossible *simply to ignore this*.... But Lenin *went into hiding* with *such* a charge hanging over him.
>
> This was something quite special, unexampled and incomprehensible. Any other mortal would have demanded an investigation and trial even in the most unfavourable conditions. Any other mortal would personally and publicly have done everything possible ... to rehabilitate himself ...
>
> I consider that ... Lenin's disappearance must lie at the very root of any description of the personality of the future ruler of Russia. In the whole world only he could have behaved thus.[20]

Trotsky retorts: 'Yes, "any other mortal," ' then draws a pious moral: 'But no other mortal could have become an object of such raging hatred to the ruling classes.'[21]

Yet Sukhanov himself has shown up the stupidity of this view:

> Was (Lenin) in any real danger? Absurd, in the summer of 1917! There could be no question of lynch-law, of the death penalty, or of hard labour ... Lenin risked absolutely nothing but imprisonment. The example of his comrades completely confirms

all this. Many of them were arrested and put on trial for the same crimes. They safely sat out six weeks or two months in prison and went on with their writing there. With their martyrs' haloes they served as an inexhaustible source of agitation.... Then, without the slightest evil consequences, they returned to their posts.[22]

This background explains a small point, otherwise incomprehensible, in Trotsky's *History*, when he records Lenin's asking him, on 5 July : 'Aren't they getting ready to shoot us all?'[23]

This can be understood only if it is taken for granted that the charges were in essence *true*, and hence that Lenin could not risk a systematic enquiry; it also explains, of course, Lenin's determination to take to his heels.

The rest of Trotsky's discussion of this question is, if possible, still more disingenuous, not to say deceitful. In his *History* he discusses everything under the sun in connection with the disclosures in July 1917 – the French Revolution, Isaac Newton, Rasputin, anti-Semitism – yet says nothing whatever about Bernstein's articles in 1921,[24] which mention the dimensions of the German subsidy and for that matter Trotsky's own relationship to the Germans. Similarly in his autobiography, where he tears to pieces Kerensky's account of the matter (published in 1928[25]); there too his heavy-handed sarcasm is satisfied with demolishing Kerensky's defectively documented and badly presented version.

Trotsky was, no doubt, performing one more service for The Revolution. But it is hardly possible to imagine that he was unaware of the subsidy during the summer of 1917, when he was taken into the Bolshevik Party, and later after he became a top official in the new Bolshevik government. Trotsky was, no doubt, defending his own 'revolutionary honour' as well as the Bolshevik Party's.

Thus the argument he advances in his autobiography was bound to accommodate the well-known fact that Ludendorff had provided the revolutionaries with the 'sealed train' that had brought them to Russia in April.

Trotsky sums up the transaction :

On Ludendorff's part this was an adventure arising out of Germany's grave military situation. Lenin was taking advantage of Ludendorff's calculations while keeping to his own. Ludendorff said to himself : 'Lenin will overthrow the patriots, then I'll strangle Lenin and his friends.' Lenin said to himself : 'I'll travel by Ludendorff's train, then pay him for the service in my own way.'[26]

Now, this argument seems contrived to accommodate both the 'sealed train' and, tacitly, a *potential* charge that money had changed hands.

No one could claim, after all, that Lenin had elaborated his characteristic views on behalf of Germany. Consequently, if he accepted a sealed train from Ludendorff, why should he not accept money? One service is like the other. The subsequent German defeat and Bolshevik victory made it possible, in principle, to reconcile Bolshevik theories and German money. History proved to have been on the side of the Bolsheviks!

Thus the *shape* of Trotsky's argument might be thought to contain a defence both against the well-publicised charge revolving around the 'sealed train' and a charge about the German subsidy if that should happen to leak out.

It obviously bypasses the true 'charge', which would have been that the Bolshevik victory was to some extent *due* to German assistance.

What makes Trotsky's camouflage in this matter particularly piquant is that it also conceals a cardinal factor of his career.

It was the German subsidy that catapulted him into the leadership of the Bolshevik Party at a crucial moment.

Lenin, obliged to take to his heels by the scandal of the 'July Days', had to relinquish the tactical and, in some respects, indeed, the strategic command. Trotsky could assume a co-command, despite his newness on the scene and his unpopularity with the Bolshevik summit, because of his primacy in the democratic arena – more particularly, his chairmanship of the Petrograd Soviet, which he was elected to before the putsch.

Trotsky soared into his stellar role, indeed, not only because of his gifts, but because the unavowable disqualification of the Bolsheviks' real leader at a crucial moment had cleared the stage for a stand-in.

This was, no doubt, to influence relations with his new-found team-mates.

With Lenin in hiding, Trotsky could 'take over'.

Since he was not yet a Bolshevik officially, and there was no evidence at all against him personally as a German agent, he was not arrested at once. But his former friendship with Helphand was used against him; in addition a newspaper published by Miliukov reported that he had been given ten thousand dollars by some German-Americans to carry on a defeatist campaign in Russia.

Now he identified himself in public with 'Comrades' Lenin, Zinoviev, and Kamenev, in the third of three Open Letters – one of his favourite literary media – addressed to the Provisional Government. After demanding to be arrested he hid out in a friend's flat, to be sure – giving rise to a quip, by Theodor Dan, to the effect that he hadn't 'left his address',[27] but after a few days' hiding he reappeared in public as a vociferous champion of Lenin and the Bolsheviks.

For the moment his efforts were bound to fail: even the Socialists who thought it unlikely that Lenin was a German 'agent' thought it very likely that he had attempted a putsch that had simply miscarried, forcing Lenin to damp down the movement and deny the whole thing. In any case they thought his sabotage of the war outrageous.

A couple of weeks later Trotsky and Lunacharsky were jailed in the same prison where Trotsky had been held after the 1905 fiasco.

Their arrest inflamed the Soviet. When Sukhanov reported it to a mass-meeting of Mensheviks at Trotsky's favourite stage, the Cirque Moderne, there was a 'storm of indignation'.

The complexities in the position of the Soviet were mounting at an increasing pace and in a characteristically paradoxical manner: at the height of the 'July Days', with mob turbulence slipping out of the control even of the Bolsheviks who had been stimulating it, the Socialist Ministers, cringing fearfully in the Soviet headquarters, were in fact shielded by the 'loyal' troops of the Provisional Government.

But with the hope held out to the Right wing by the shaking up of the 'July Days' the polarisation between Right and Left, masked by the Socialists' decision to sponsor the Provisional Government, came to the fore once again in an acute form.

All Socialists were now plainly subversive from the point of view of the 'bourgeois' parties that regarded the very Soviet as a criminal infringement on sovereignty. Whereas beforehand the Socialists had seemed to be necessary as a shield for the Provisional Government, now they themselves seemed vulnerable to firm treatment from the Right.

The non-Bolshevik Socialists were being gored, in fact, more painfully than before by their own dilemma: the support for a regime whose principles and behaviour repelled both themselves and their following. The Mensheviks and Social Revolutionaries were *for*, say, the rights of the army rank-and-file, as they naturally were *for* the Soviets themselves. But at the same time they believed in using their position within the Soviets and in the minds of their vast following amongst the peasants and soldiers to protect a regime, the Provisional Government, that still believed in the war, in the traditions of the army, and in its own exclusive sovereignty.

Thus, as conditions deteriorated, as the war became more and more maddening, and as the Bolsheviks were provided with intolerable situations that gave them effective slogans, the chasm between Right and Left began yawning more and more, and finally became too much for even the most agile rhetoricians to straddle.

Among the conservative, anti-revolutionary forces there was a widespread longing for a dictatorial hand.

A second Coalition Government headed by Kerensky was formed after the 'July Days'; the Socialists dominated it at the precise moment that they had become weaker than ever before, having had their support eroded somewhat on the Left by the Bolsheviks and having now lost even the illusory authority of the Provisional Government itself.

Kornilov, a general appointed Commander-in-Chief by Kerensky and regarded with great hopefulness by conservatives, attempted to settle the situation in his own way. On 24 August, he made an open move at the head of his troops against both the Provisional Government, and especially, the Soviet.

Trotsky, still in gaol, where he had been pouring out a flood of articles and pamphlets, was now in extreme danger. If Kornilov's troops won there could hardly be any doubt but that Trotsky and his associates would be killed out of hand. (Kresty prison was in fact filled with men soon to emerge as leading figures in the October putsch and later on in the Bolshevik war commissariat.)

From the other point of view, of course, Kornilov's enterprise implied another possibility if Kornilov was undone – a favourable swing in the opposite direction. The Bolsheviks were, in fact, necessary for this, since the other Socialists could hardly go on attacking the Bolsheviks in the face of an armed reaction from the Right. This was, in short, a reversal of the situation they had been in during the 'July Days', when the Socialists had thought they needed the loyal troops and generals to shield them against insurgents led by Bolsheviks.

In fact the Government was obliged to turn at once to the Bolsheviks and the Red Guards, haphazard units of armed workers impro-

vised by them. At the very moment that the Bolshevik leaders were
in gaol or in hiding on charges of complicity with the Germans, the
Red Guards were being given guns, while Kerensky was calling upon
the Kronstadt sailors, the most tempestuous element in the Bolshevik camp and the prime incendiaries of the 'July Days', to rush to the
defence of the Provisional Government.

Trotsky's imprisonment as a German agent was lent a farcical
grace-note: during the very process of interrogation he was visited
by a delegation of Kronstadt sailors asking for his advice on what to
do – should they stop Kornilov by defending Kerensky or kill both of
them?

Trotsky, referring to his defence of the sailors in the Soviet in
May, reminded them how he said at the time that in case of any
counter-revolutionary attempts the 'Kronstadt sailors would come
and fight and die with us': on the basis of this promise he now said
that they must, for the time being, help stop Kornilov even by
helping Kerensky, whose goose they would soon be able to cook in
any case. Trotsky's prestige with the sailors was so high they followed
what were in effect instructions and moved off to join in the general
resistance to Kornilov's troops.

By this time the Bolsheviks and their now far more numerous
sympathisers had recovered from the disarray following the 'July
Days'.

The resentment of Kornilov's well-advertised decision to 'disperse
the Soviet' once and for all, after an announcement that he was going
to put the operation in the hands of a general who would gladly
'hang every member', had the effect of paralysing the whole Kornilov
enterprise. Just as the Provisional Government had been dependent,
even for its routine functioning, on the goodwill of the workers
holding key positions, for instance in the railways and telegraph
stations, so, too, was Kornilov's operation open to systematic
sabotage.

The troops themselves moved through a dense fog of agitation,
fanned by all the Left-wing parties and spearheaded by the tight
Bolshevik organisation, that hindered all movement and ultimately
dissolved the army units.

The consent of the railway men, for instance, was indispensable to
the movement of troops; where they could not refuse it outright, the
workers would simply hold up the trains. The upshot was that
Kornilov's people could not prepare any effective time-tables. His
generals could not communicate with one another, while at every

station throngs of local workers and garrison soldiers would envelope Kornilov's troops, harangue them, and swiftly damp down their morale.

Against a background of popular approval the Left-wing leaders found it child's play to funnel their agitation into effective channels.

It was only natural for the Bolsheviks to become the chief lever in the anti-Kornilov organisation. The Committee for the Struggle Against Counter-revolution, which Kerensky had been obliged to authorise and which now consisted of Bolsheviks, Mensheviks, and Social-Revolutionaries, had arranged for the formation of an armed workers' militia, a revival, essentially, of the Red Guard that had been suppressed after the 'July Days': from 27 August on only a few days were needed to collect some 25,000 recruits.

This Committee simply dissolved Kornilov's forces, with scarcely a casualty.

At the same time, since the Kornilov enterprise was plainly not only in earnest but actually reflected a situation in which conservative and middle-class opinion was in a genuine panic because of the broadening of revolutionary ideas and propaganda, the success of Kornilov, or someone like him, would plainly have reversed the situation once and for all. It would doubtless have restored the monarchy and also wiped out the Socialists in general and the Bolsheviks in particular.

By failing so ignominiously, on the other hand, the Kornilov would-be putsch simultaneously heightened the morale of the Left wing, consolidated it under its extremist leadership, the Bolsheviks, and thus paved the way for *their* putsch some weeks later. It was of great significance, for instance, that the moment the Kornilov movement evaporated the key Soviets – Petrograd and Moscow – gave a majority vote to resolutions with a Bolshevik wording.

On the superficial political level the immediate results can be simply summed up: the Government dissolved. The Kadet Ministers on the one hand resigned, out of irritation with Kerensky's enforced action against Kornilov; the Socialist Ministers, on the other hand, left the Government because they thought Kerensky's role had been fishy. Kerensky, left with a shattered administration, grew more and more frantic. The central authority had evaporated: Kerensky's 'government', a small colourless committee called the 'Directorate', plainly lacked support.

The 'case' against Trotsky was so flimsy, and the normal routine of the prosecutor's office was so manifestly at variance with what was happening outside the gaol, that *they* finally gave up: on 4 September Trotsky was released, though only on bail.

While in gaol Trotsky, now regarded by the public unambiguously as a Bolshevik, had become one in fact: he had been elected to the Central Committee of the Party, and during the seven-week period that elapsed before the successful Bolshevik bid for power towards the end of October he was not merely known as a Bolshevik but, because of his remarkable performance during these seven weeks, regarded as the Bolshevik par excellence. Lenin was now completely out of sight; it was Trotsky who was in the limelight well-nigh alone. His identification with the Bolsheviks was complete; their joint enterprise began gathering momentum.

From gaol Trotsky rushed to the Smolny Institute, to sit in on a meeting of the Committee for the Struggle against Counter-Revolution.

With the Kornilov affair finished there no longer seemed any reason for the Mensheviks and Social-Revolutionaries to cling to the idea of a Coalition with the Kadets. After all, some Kadets had sponsored Kornilov: also, they were visibly losing their following. In the Soviet, accordingly, Trotsky and other Bolsheviks hammered away at the idea of a Socialist government; this time they carried the vote: on 9 September a Bolshevik resolution, moved by Trotsky, of no confidence in the Menshevik 'Presidium' of the Soviet, won a majority; it was the first time a Bolshevik motion had been so successful.

The Bolshevik tide was in full spate; by the beginning of September Bolsheviks already controlled majorities in Petrograd, Moscow, and some other industrial centres; they could reasonably look forward to becoming the major party at the scheduled Congress of Soviets.

In mid-September the Mensheviks and their allies tried to counter the Bolshevik tide by convening a 'Democratic Conference,' not of elected delegates, but of appointees from various non-political bodies known to be against the Bolsheviks. The Mensheviks were so disoriented that instead of convoking a Constituent Assembly immediately they left this plainly democratic idea to the Bolsheviks as their principal 'constitutional' slogan. The Soviets, which consisted of political parties claiming to represent the industrial working class, the army, and the peasantry (including the peasant army) did not quite represent a 'national' idea; yet the Coalition Governments had constantly put off the Constituent Assembly, a *sine qua non* since the inception of the revolutionary movement, and the Mensheviks had gone along with this.

The soft-pedalling of the Constituent Assembly had been another price the Mensheviks had been willing to pay the Kadets in order to keep The 'Bourgeois' Revolution in its proper niche. The Kadets had been against the Assembly for common-sense reasons: they were afraid, understandably, that it would be too radical.

It suited the Bolsheviks at this time to put forth two slogans that, by implication, were thoroughly contradictory, though of course they could be reconciled by casuistry. The Bolsheviks had been clamouring both for 'All Power to the Soviets' and for a Constituent Assembly that was logically, constitutionally, and politically its antithesis.

The Democratic Conference, which led to a so-called 'Pre-Parliament,' was a way out of this impasse; it provided the Mensheviks and their allies with a sort of pseudo-parliament that had the happy feature of not being encumbered by a ballot.

As chief Bolshevik spokesman, it was Trotsky's business to boycott the Conference after presenting it as a farce. He made one of his most effective speeches, concentrated on a denunciation of the 'unrepresentative' character of the Conference; after making this point with great force Trotsky demonstratively headed a walk-out of the Bolsheviks.

On 23 September, a few days after leading the Bolsheviks out of the Democratic Conference, Trotsky was elected president of the Petrograd Soviet. After reminding this audience that it was not he who was taking the former chairman's (Chkheidze's) place, but vice-versa, since he himself had been a chairman of the Petersburg Soviet in 1905, he then, according to Sukhanov, added a few words, not thinking that in time he would have to disregard them and create a theory to justify their opposite. He said:

'We are all party people, and we shall have to cross swords more than once. But we shall guide the work of the Petersburg Soviet in a spirit of justice and complete independence for all factions; the hand of the Praesidium will never oppress the minority.'

Heavens! What liberal views! What self-mockery! But the point is that about three years later, while exchanging reminiscences with me, Trotsky, thinking back to this moment, exclaimed dreamily: 'What a happy time!'[28]

Throughout this period of 1917 – the most intensely active of Trotsky's life – there was, of course, no question of 'private life'. Politics consumed his every moment.

During the two months before the October putsch, Trotsky, Natalya and the boys lived in a single room in the 'middle-class' quarter around the Tauride Palace and ate official rations. They had no distractions and no rest; they had no time to receive or to make visits. All personal relations were replaced by 'contacts' with 'militants', colleagues and so on.

When Trotsky was elected Chairman of the Soviet at the end of September he would leave this little room early in the morning, and work in the Smolny Chairman's office. Natalya has left a note of its 'working-atmosphere':

It was a big, square room, naked, sketchily furnished, and thronged daily by hundreds of delegates from various organisations. . . . The staircases were covered with heaps of sunflower seed shells; placards and hand-written notices were hanging all over the walls; a mob in caps and dark-green tunics kept circulating through the corridors. The telephones kept squeaking without let-up. . . . Leon Davidovich struggled to spare his energies without sparing himself. He was always preoccupied with struggling against overwork, with disciplining himself in his work in order to get himself a 'maximum yield'.

At that time the fashion was rather toward careless dress: he never followed it. Without worrying about elegance, with no understanding that one might ask oneself a question about the nuance of a necktie, he had an innate concern for correctness, and a horror – for himself above all – of any sartorial slackness as well as of any other kind of slackness.

He would eat at the Soviet refectory, a big hall furnished with wooden tables and benches. Indifferent clear soups – cabbage, fish, gruel, stewed fruits, tea. He didn't drink.

He was a little taller than the average, not corpulent but well-built. He had fair skin, set off by abundant shock of dark hair, a little moustache and a goatee. His pince-nez sharpened his gaze.[29]

This was a couple of months before Trotsky's thirty-eighth birth-

day. His nerves were strained to their highest pitch; he was walking
about 'like an electric battery, each contact with him brought forth a
discharge'.[30]

Yet if the Revolution-as-Idea was to be realised a certain procedure had to be applied.

CHAPTER VI

The Gamble

ON HIS RETURN TO Russia in April, Lenin had dropped his traditional perspective and veered over to the idea that it was possible for the working class to conduct The Revolution through its 'bourgeois' phase; by September he thought the situation ripe for the Bolshevik Party itself, 'representing' the vanguard of the Russian Proletariat, to seize power 'on its behalf' and 'in the interests' of The Revolution. With that as a starting-point a specific action was needed – conspiracy. A putsch naturally required secrecy and precision.

Lenin was still hiding in Finland: from there he sent the Central Committee a letter confronting it with the general proposal for a putsch: in view of the widespread change of mood, the upsurge of peasant rebelliousness and the frustration plainly felt by the soldiers at large, now was the moment to move from generalisation to action.

On 6 September, when Trotsky had first appeared in the Bolshevik Central Committee, this question had just been raised. The Central Committee was not yet persuaded; Zinoviev opposed a putsch and had asked them to authorise his leaving the hide-out he shared with Lenin and appearing in public in order to display his falling-out with Lenin.

Though Trotsky, now an ardent Bolshevik, had been accepted into the Party without apparent qualification there had, in fact, been some little hemming and hawing about it. At the very time that he had seemed – in public – to be the incarnation of Bolshevism, the Party veterans had had misgivings. Soon after Trotsky's arrival Lenin had failed to persuade his Party to let Trotsky have an appropriate post in the Bolshevik press; even on 4 August, while Trotsky was still in gaol, he was turned down for a post on a central editorial board for all Bolshevik newspapers by a general vote (eleven to ten);[1] it was not, in fact, until a couple of days after he got out of gaol that he was without opposition finally made one of the Party's principal editors. Consequently, he had at first behaved rather circumspectly: he did not leap into the intra-Party debate with his usual elan. Aside from questions of presentation and public relations, however, the paramount question remained – should the Bolsheviks do it at all?

Lenin's two chief lieutenants – Zinoviev and Kamenev – were violently opposed to the whole project: they thought it gross 'adventurism' – not rooted in the Marxist view of the grand tug of historical forces, but arising out of personal caprice.

Two issues were vital – one was the prospect of success of the putsch *qua* putsch, the other – for Marxists, of cardinal importance – was the promotion of The Revolution.

From the narrow viewpoint of preparation the question was relatively simple: could the Bolsheviks muster enough support to ensure the technical execution of a *coup d'état* against the existing opposition?

Here Zinoviev and Kamenev, merely faint-hearted, showed bad judgment: they thought a putsch suicidal. Yet it is plain – not only with our hindsight, but at the time – that Kerensky's forces were so demoralised that the Bolsheviks had at least a very good chance of getting away with it. In the event, the operation turned out to be child's play. There was, for all practical purposes, no resistance whatever.

From a long-range perspective, on the other hand, the real justification of the seizure of power, for both Lenin and Trotsky, was the imminence of the Grand Overturn – The Revolution on a world or at least on a continental scale.

Both were convinced that the European revolution was absolutely bound to occur in the immediate future. Trotsky had long been saying that a Socialist Revolution in Russia could be no more than an overture to a European explosion (this was, in fact, part of his Permanent Revolution). Lenin had an identical view: a recent mutiny in the Geman navy was interpreted by him as a sure sign of the general and universal upheaval that was just around the corner, or really, rather, was already *there*. Lenin's speeches and statements throughout this period all rotated around this theme.

He considered a revolt in the German navy 'an extreme manifestation of the growth throughout Europe of the World Socialist
Revolution'.[2]

The presence within *all* European states of revolutionary and
Socialist proletarian masses is a fact. The ripening and the inevitability of the world Socialist Revolution is indubitable.[3]

We stand on the threshold of world proletarian Revolution.[4]

The ripening of the world revolution is incontestable. . . . We
shall be real traitors to the International if, at such a moment, in
such favourable circumstances, we respond to such an appeal
from the German revolutionaries (i.e., in the German navy) *only*
– by resolutions.[5]

The international situation gives us a number of objective data
showing that if we act now we shall have on our side the whole of
proletarian Europe.[6]

Thus it was in a mood of messianic elation, allied to his realistic
assessment of practical possibilities, that Lenin, supported by
Trotsky, moved the Bolshevik Party.

Zinoviev and Kamenev were always to suffer from their initial
faint-heartedness: it was always to be a 'charge' that could be
thrown up to them.

As for the long-range results, a discussion of those would no doubt
be interminable. The failure of The Revolution to appear in Europe
on schedule was to mean the *de facto* isolation of the Soviet Union,
and more particularly of the Bolshevik Party, which in its turn
meant that it was to remain a tiny minority committed to a sweeping
social transformation. This was to entail portentous consequences,
still some distance in the future.

Lenin and Trotsky had quite different approaches to the 'constitutional' aspect of the putsch.

Lenin thought the crucial factors were so delicate, also so
dynamic, that points of timing and tactics were bound to outweigh
merely constitutional questions, i.e., what the putsch *was* – who was
making it on whose behalf. Though not at all dogmatic about details
(he thought the putsch could just as well be launched in Moscow or

even in Finland), Lenin wanted the Bolsheviks to seize power openly *as Bolsheviks.*

Trotsky was far more 'diplomatic'. His circumspection, though partly traceable to his position as a Bolshevik novice, was inherent in his role as chairman of the Petrograd Soviet. He thought it common sense to benefit by pro-Bolshevik opinion.

He wanted to synchronise the putsch with the forthcoming Congress of the Soviets, which should be handed the power that would meanwhile have been captured by the Bolshevik Party. As part of this general idea he thought the putsch itself should be carried out by the Bolsheviks *in the name* of the Petrograd Soviet and by means of its apparatus. Since the Soviet already had a Bolshevik majority, and he was its chairman, this was plainly a matter of window-dressing; whatever the name, the same people would be involved.

If that were done, it could, of course be presented to the public and to the other political parties as an enterprise that was not Bolshevik *at all,* but was a mere implementation of the slogan that had already found some popular support – 'All Power to the Soviets'.

Thus Trotsky, by elaborating the 'public-relations' aspect of the putsch, was responsible for the primary mystification underlying the name of the regime, the Soviet Union, that endures to this day: namely, the notion that the Bolsheviks 'represented' the masses via an electoral principle.

Hence there was no contradiction between these 'nuanced' differences of approach to the 'constitutional' question: both Lenin and Trotsky assumed that the Bolshevik Party would hold the real power and that the Congress of Soviets would be the 'constitutional' locus of that power. It was naturally taken for granted that this would work only so long as the Bolsheviks had a majority in the Congress.

As it was to turn out, it was just this question of 'public relations' that governed all preparations for the putsch. The technical nub of the operation, the seizure of power itself, was to constitute an altogether minor aspect of it.

It is doubtless ironical that all the subtleties of ratiocination, all the logic-chopping of Marxist 'dialectics' needed to defend a 'position' vis-à-vis one's own followers was quite irrelevant to the appeal made by the Bolsheviks to the public. Telling peasants or workers of the Dialectic, of a 'Bourgeois' as opposed to a 'Socialist' revolution, of the means of production, of The Revolution as a whole, was out of the question. In public the problem was simpler.

People were sick and tired of the war: the Bolsheviks called for peace.

Everything, especially food, was in short supply: the Bolsheviks called for bread.

Huge numbers of peasants wanted a redistribution of land: the Bolsheviks called for land.

These three demands – none of them Bolshevik or even Marxist – made up the slogan that the Bolsheviks put forth to secure the support of the public.

During September, in any case, the basic decision was not made: Lenin failed to carry the whole of the Party leadership. Even at the end of the month, when Kerensky called a meeting of the 'Pre-Parliament', practically the sole result of the Democratic Conference, the Bolsheviks were not in accord on how to deal with it. Those for the putsch were for the boycott of the Pre-Parliament: those against the putsch wanted to use the Pre-Parliament as a forum. Most of the Bolsheviks who were actually delegates to the Pre-Parliament itself wanted to appear in the debating there.

The Central Committee was not yet united.

One of the principal oddities throughout this strange interval of hesitation – all of which naturally percolated outside the ranks of the Party and was doubtless well known to the Government – was that since Lenin was in hiding his place as the most authoritative Bolshevik was occupied by Trotsky, at least as far as the public was concerned. In effect this turned a man who had been an implacable opponent of the Bolsheviks for fifteen years into their most authoritative spokesman.

Just as Trotsky had been hopelessly disadvantaged by his absence from Petrograd during the crucial beginnings of 1917, so he now benefited by Lenin's physical absence from the scene of action in the autumn. All the advantages of the Bolshevik organisation reinforced his own public position. From the point of view of Trotsky's career, Lenin's absence might be called a dividend of the German subsidy!

It was, in fact, Trotsky who conceived and executed the *coup d'état*, supported by the Party press and apparatus and his position as the elected chairman of the Petrograd Soviet.

Trotsky's broad public design for the putsch was simple enough – there was no such thing! Throughout the preparatory phases of the putsch – the phases in which psychological warfare necessarily

played a paramount role – he masked all his actions in such a way as
also to be able to present them as governed by some quite different
and, of course, innocuous point of view. Afterwards, it would be
possible to envisage the whole operation as a unit, but any particular
move seemed at the moment to have a quite different and eminently
justifiable rationale. None of the observers working for the Provisional Government, its General Staff, and least of all the numerous
foreign bodies on the spot – the various embassies, missions, and so
on – had the slightest inkling that anything was afoot.

Trotsky's task was enormously facilitated by the general deterio-
ration of the economy and by the disastrous military situation. The
economic position was so bad that urban food supplies collapsed;
there was constant turmoil in the countryside, with intermittent
peasant riots, burnings of mansions and so on. On the front the army
was humiliated again and again. The likelihood that the capital
would come under direct attack grew constantly.

What helped Trotsky most in his preparations for the putsch was
that, from the military point of view, Petrograd was both the capital
of the country and, coincidentally, its 'revolutionary' capital. Hence
the promotion of The Revolution could be presented as the defence
of the national capital. It was an admirable mask for Bolshevik
operations, all the more effective since it was, after all, quite sincere.

On 6 October, for instance, Trotsky told the Soldiers' Section of
the Soviet : 'If the Provisional Government is incapable of defending
Petrograd, then it ought to conclude peace or make room for another
government.'[7] When he told the Pre-Parliament the following day
that the 'idea of surrendering the revolutionary capital to German
troops was a natural link in a . . . counter-revolutionary conspiracy,'
his speech gave natural camouflage to the prime Bolshevik objective,
while at the same time it could be understood as a combination of
revolutionary fervour and old-fashioned patriotism.

Trotsky was able to achieve this effect despite his leading a walk-
out from the Pre-Parliament.

This time, by walking out of a more or less elected gathering at
the head of the Bolshevik delegation, Trotsky was making it plain
that the die was already cast for a unilateral *démarche* on the part of
the Bolsheviks. Against the turbulent background of the moment the
mere fact of the ostentatious exodous was of cardinal significance. As
Sukhanov said :

From their point of view the ones who left were logical enough.

If they were *on the other side* of this entire order, then there was really nothing for them to do in the Pre-Parliament. But ... if there was nothing for them to do there and they left, consequently – they were *on the other side*. There was only one road for them out of the Pre-Parliament – to the barricades. If they cast away the 'ballot' they must take up the rifle. And that, indeed, is what happened.[8]

It was this question of the defence of the capital – simultaneously 'revolutionary' and national – that framed the duel between Trotsky and Kerensky. Just as Kerensky was doing his best to redistribute the troops in Petrograd in order to get rid of the most politically-minded regiments, so it was Trotsky's concern to keep them there, ostensibly for the defence of the city: both attitudes could naturally be championed, from the point of view of defence in general.

Kerensky's attempts to redistribute troops, manifested after the Government's denial of charges that it was going to leave Petrograd, naturally made the Soviet and its following very suspicious. On 9 October Trotsky proposed that the full Soviet take a hand in this whole question; it could do this legitimately, of course, since it had already declared its own direct role in the defence of the capital. Thus Trotsky, without seeming to, raised a first-class political question: who controlled the capital garrison?

On 9 October, also, a new body was formed: the Military Revolutionary Committee. This *seemed* to be an extension of the Committee for the Struggle Against Counter-Revolution, which the Mensheviks had put together at the time of the Kornilov threat. Though the formal chairman of the new Military Revolutionary Committee was Vlazimir, a youthful (eighteen years old!) Left Social-Revolutionary, it was Trotsky who, as chairman of the Soviet, was its real head. This Committee was to be the executor of the putsch.

At first the Committee's ostensible purpose was simply to arrange for the defence of the city. It had a number of clearly defined functions: determination of the magnitude of the defence garrison, liaison with the northern front, the Baltic Fleet and the Finnish garrison, calculation of manpower and ammunition on hand; the plan of defence; securing discipline in the public at large. A committee with such functions could plainly do much.

What is perhaps strange about this sparring in what may be called the field of public relations was that up to then the actual decision itself had not yet been made : Lenin had persuaded his Party that it must aim at power, but the act itself had not been agreed upon. It was possible for Trotsky to go on for a time in his public capacity, well served in his various proposals by his function as Chairman of the Soviet.

Things came to a head on 10 October, the day after the Military Revolutionary Committee had been set up in the Soviet under Trotsky's control.

Lenin's insistence on boycotting the Pre-Parliament had borne fruit. After Trotsky had flung his rejection of the electoral process at the heads of the Pre-Parliament and had ostentatiously led the Bolshevik delegation out of it, it was obvious that the Party now had to make up its mind once and for all. In Lenin's terms it was now 'criminal' and 'treasonable' to wait any longer for the forthcoming Congress of Soviets.

The crucial meeting was held, curiously enough, in the flat of none other than – Sukhanov! He was now rather hostile to the Bolsheviks – as a matter of current tactics, to be sure – but his wife was one of the faithful; she had taken advantage of his attendance at some meetings to give him, as he records, a 'piece of friendly, disinterested advice – not to inconvenience myself by a further journey after work.' A curious variation on the classical jokes about adultery!

In any case, as Sukhanov goes on to report,

> For such a cardinal session not only did people come from Moscow, but the Lord of Hosts himself, with his henchman, crept out of the underground. Lenin appeared in a wig, but without his beard : Zinoviev appeared with a beard but without his shock of hair. The meeting went on for about ten hours, until about 3 o'clock in the morning. Half the exalted guests had to sleep over in the flat somehow.[9]

Lenin hammered away in favour of an immediate putsch : out of the twelve people present (of the twenty-one on the full Central Committee) only two voted against it – Zinoviev and Kamenev.

It was this meeting that created the first Political Bureau (Politburo) of the Party : it consisted of Lenin, Zinoviev, Kamenev, Trotsky, Stalin, Sokolnikov, and Bubnov. It was supposed to guide the putsch from one day to the next.

In the event, all the work inevitably devolved on Trotsky : Lenin left for his Finnish hide-out after the meeting, Zinoviev and

Kamenev opposed the putsch in public, appealing to the rank-and-file of the Party against the very decision; Stalin was absorbed by editorial work. There was no one but Trotsky to run things:

> Trotsky, tearing himself away from work on the revolutionary staff, personally rushed from the Obukhovsky plant to the Trubochny, from the Putilov to the Baltic works, from the riding-school to the barracks; he seemed to be speaking at all points simultaneously. His influence, both among the masses and on the staff, was overwhelming. He was the central figure of those days and the principal hero of this remarkable page of history.[10]

But though the fateful meeting of 10 October had decided on the putsch, the details, including the paramount item of timing, had not yet been fixed. For the time being, the warfare remained psychological; indeed, there was now to be a short period of quasi-public actions, all quite unmistakable, yet not somehow registering on the consciousness of the enemy as being what they in fact were.

On 13 October a sort of reconnaissance effort was made in the opaque medium of the skirmishing and counter-skirmishing being carried on both by Trotsky plus the Soviet and the Government plus Kerensky: the Military Revolutionary Committee informed the Petrograd Military District Commander (Polkonikov) that no order of his would be valid unless counter-signed by the Military Revolutionary Committee. On being told so openly that his authority was being denied, the District Commander might have arrested all the delegates of the Military Revolutionary Committee out of hand. Yet he could not – he was aware of his helplessness.

Contrariwise, the Military Revolutionary Committee could, presumably, have arrested *him*. Why not, after all?

Thus, on the thirteenth nothing seemed to be happening; it was as though basic political actions were being carried out in a sort of dream, where causes need not bring about effects. Two days later the regimental committees of the Petrograd army garrison convened in the Smolny, the Soviet headquarters: they forbade any unit to leave the city without the specific permission of the Soviet.

Two 'symbolic' acts took place the same week that in a way settled, as it were, the public issue: on 16 October the city garrison officially declared that they would not leave Petrograd; that is, they announced their refusal to obey the orders of Kerensky, the head of the Government. This was, of course, sedition.

The same day Trotsky, as chief of the Military Revolutionary
Committee, gave a written order to the arsenals to issue 5,000 rifles to
the Red Guards.

The Red Guards – who with the sailors were to be the chief prop
of the putsch – had been recruited under the aegis of the Socialist
parties collaborating with factory-committees and the trades-unions.
At the time of the putsch there were about 20,000 of them in
Petrograd, some in nearly every factory. They had been in training
ever since the Kornilov would-be coup.

The acceptance of Trotsky's signature by the city garrison meant
that it accepted the orders of the Military Revolutionary Committee
formally and substantively.

Both these acts of defiance were quite open; yet they provoked
no response whatever.

It was while these two open acts of sedition were being
performed, on 16 October, that the Central Committee met once
again; Lenin reappeared in heavy disguise, to demand that the
decision taken on 10 October be confirmed and that a summons to
action be issued immediately.

Once again the matter was discussed in substance – should there
be a putsch at all? Even at this late hour it was possible to discuss
the actual decision – it *seemed* to have been taken, yet *not quite*. It
was possible for Zinoviev and Kamenev, for instance, to go over their
opposition to the whole enterprise once again, and for Stalin to
advance in its support the notion that the Soviet was already 'on the
road to insurrection'* and to reprimand the others for not having
enough faith in The Revolution. Some local leaders spoke about the
apathy of the masses and recommended different dates; even Krylenko, the head of the military section, the Party unit supposed to
guide the putsch, could still say that only a minority of his section
backed the putsch, and even then only with the idea that the move
should be made not by the Party at all, but by the Soviet, i.e., in
accord with Trotsky. The conference of 16 October ended with
Lenin finally making a concession to Trotsky's desire to generalise
the initiative; the resolution read that the 'Central Committee *and
the Soviet should in due time indicate the favourable attack.'*[11]†

The date set at the conference, 20 October, was provisional,
selected because it was supposed to be the day before the opening of
the Congress of the Soviets. It left only four days for preparation.

*My emphasis. J.C.
†Italics mine. J.C.

Even then, with so little time left, Zinoviev and Kamenev did something very unusual. They published a categorical denunciation of the whole project, and they did so in a non-Party newspaper (Gorky's *New Life*). This was a completely public act, altogether outside the Party milieu, plainly an alarm to enemies.

Lenin was furious. Calling them 'strikebreakers of the revolution', he insisted that they be expelled from the Party. Nothing happened; he did not insist strongly enough.

Lenin's position was complicated by the way he ran the Party. Anyone could vote against him and so on; the discussion of what to do about Zinoviev and Kamenev went on for some time. Trotsky, for instance, suggested that Kamenev's resignation be accepted but that he be kept on. The Bolshevik Party at this time was not yet strait-jacketed; the mere fact that outstanding vacillators like Zinoviev and Kamenev could vote against Lenin is itself illuminating.

The next day the Mensheviks still running the Central Executive Committee of the Soviet put off the Congress of Soviets another few days – more time for Trotsky and the Bolsheviks.

In his statements as Chairman of the Petrograd Soviet, meanwhile, Trotsky kept emphasising the needs of defence and giving the impression that nothing else was involved. By putting all positive acts in the perspective of defence Trotsky could sanction very nearly anything without spoiling the camouflage. On 18 October he came out finally for armed action, too, by claiming that it was purely defensive:

> We are hiding nothing. In the name of the Soviet I declare: no armed actions have been planned by us. But if in the course of events an action were planned, then workers and soldiers would come out at its call as one man. . . . The Petrograd Soviet will go on organising and arming the workers' guard. . . . We must be at the ready. We are entering a period of the most acute struggle. We must be in constant expectation of an attack on the part of the counter-revolution. But – we shall respond with a counter-attack that will be merciless and that we shall carry on to the end.[12]

The fluidity of the situation was demonstrated in the support instantly given this statement of Trotsky's by Zinoviev and Kamenev, the two main Bolshevik opponents of the putsch.

For their part Zinoviev and Kamenev imagined their public support of an ostensibly defensive measure to be a sort of ruse – *they* thought it would obviate the putsch by congealing the Bolsheviks, as it were, in a purely defensive stance. Contrariwise, the Bolsheviks' enemies thought that if Lenin's two cronies supported such a defensive statement by Trotsky there was, in fact, no likelihood of a putsch after all.

Things had begun moving so rapidly, and so much depended on atmospheric psychological warfare, that Lenin, too, was distracted by Trotsky's legerdemain.

Trotsky saw him immediately after the speech – both evasive and obfuscatory – about the two questions asked him concerning the rumours about a putsch and his order for the 5,000 rifles. Lenin was so remote from the day-to-day conduct of the preliminaries to the putsch that he had to be reassured, sometimes generally not very effectively, at every turn.

Throughout this whole strange period of hesitation, Lenin's attitude toward Trotsky had been slightly equivocal. Trotsky's insistence that the putsch coincide with the Congress of Soviets seemed to him highly dangerous, far more so, in fact, than the outright rejection of the whole idea by Zinoviev and Kamenev. Since in its very nature a putsch depended on timing, it was natural for Lenin in his communications to the Central Committee to condemn Trotsky's tactics as actually 'treasonable'.

By building up the 'atmosphere' within the Soviet it was possible for Trotsky to convey *general* orders to executive agencies in such a way as to justify, later on, *specific* action initiated by himself. On 21 October, for instance, Trotsky put a motion through the Soviet telling the garrison to obey only the Military Revolutionary Committee, headed by himself: here is how he put it to the committees representing the garrison regiments:

The garrison declares: The time for words has passed. The country is on the brink of disaster. The army is demanding peace, the peasants are demanding land, the workers are demanding work and bread. The coalition government is against the people. It is an instrument in the hands of the people's enemies. The time for words has passed. The All-Russian Congress of Soviets must take the power into its own hands and secure, land, and bread to the people.... The Petrograd garrison solemnly promises the All-Russian Congress to put at its disposal all its forces, to the last man, to fight for these demands. Rely on us.... We are at our posts, ready to conquer or to die.[13]

This time the ceremoniousness of this phraseology – a speciality of Trotsky's – had as a background what by now was the assurance of the garrison that all was going very well, that the support given to the Soviet signified merely an imminent defeat for Kerensky, a defeat that would mean the end of the war. This was why the garrison had, after all, subordinated itself to the Soviet.

Trotsky was still not *claiming* that the Military Revolutionary Committee had already obviated the military command. The Committee's commissars, seconded to the General Staff, presumably by way of liaison, were behaving with routine decorum.

Yet it is plain that the garrison's decision implied something fundamental – the issue of sovereignty. The garrison was saying, quite plainly, that the Soviet was the sole authority in the country and the Military Revolutionary Committee its direct agent. This could mean only one thing: the Provisional Government was already overthrown – the Dual Power that had endured for eight months was done with and the Soviet was now the government. *Nevertheless,* nothing happened.

Now the significance of all these obvious moves became still more obvious: on 22 October the Military Revolutionary Committee implemented the vote of the day before in a proclamation saying: 'No orders to the garrison not signed by the Committee are valid'.

This was a vast change. Unambiguously, and above all *on its own authority,* it was proclaiming that the Provisional Government was definitely extinguished.

Psychologically, nevertheless, the situation remained unchanged – the new authority had to be acknowledged. What was in essence a putsch made by the Petrograd garrison on 21 October had to be institutionalised. Here is how Sukhanov describes it:

In actual fact the overturn was accomplished the moment the Petersburg garrison acknowledged the Soviet as its supreme authority and the Military Revolutionary Committee as its direct command. Such a decision, as we know, was made at the meeting of the garrison representatives on 21 October. But in the unprecedented setting this act may be said to have had an *abstract character.* No one took it for a *coup d'état.*

And no wonder. The decision, after all, did not really change the situation: even earlier the Government had had no real power or authority. The real power in the capital had already been in the hands of the Bolsheviks of the Petersburg Soviet long before, and nevertheless the Winter Palace had remained the Government, and Smolny – a private institution. Now the garrison had declared officially, *urbi et orbi*, that it did not recognise the Government and was subject to the Soviet. But did it matter what was said in Smolny, where there was nobody but Bolsheviks?

Nevertheless, this is a fact: by 21 October the Provisional Government had already been overthrown, and was non-existent in the territory of the capital. Kerensky and his colleagues, calling themselves Ministers, were still completely at liberty, busy with something or other in the Winter Palace; in many parts of the country they were still recognised as the Government (wherever the Soviets were not Bolshevik), and in addition they might still have some real support outside the capital and theoretically speaking have been able to destroy the Bolsheviks and their Petersburg garrison together. The main thing, however, was that no new power had been proclaimed, and the situation was transitional. It was the same as on 28 February, when the capital garrison turned against the Tsarist Government but there was no new Government; when Tsar Nicholas was at liberty and busy at Headquarters; when his authority was still recognised in many parts of the country and he could still find loyal troops to crush the insurgent capital.

Nevertheless the Government was already overthrown on 21 October, as Tsar Nicholas had been on 28 February. What remained now was essentially to *complete* what had been done – first of all, to make the overturn official by proclaiming a new government, and secondly, to liquidate *de facto* the pretenders to power, thus achieving general acknowledgment of the accomplished fact.

The significance of what was accomplished on 21 October was obscure not only to the man-in-the-street and the spectator; it was not clear to the revolutionary leaders themselves. Glance into the memoirs of one of the chief figures of the October Days, Antonov-Ovseyenko, secretary of the Military Revolutionary Committee. You'll see a complete 'unawareness' of the internal evolution of events. This gave rise to a lack of system and orderliness in the external, military-technical measures of the Bolsheviks. It might have ended for them much less successfully if they had been dealing with a different adversary. It was luck that the adversary was not only unaware, but completely blind; and not only blind, but equal to zero with respect to real power. . . .

But here's what must be taken into account: neither Smolny nor the Winter Palace could be fully aware of the meaning of events. It was obscured by the historical position of the Soviet in the revolution. A confusion of ideas inevitably flowed from the fact that for half a year the totality of real power had been in the hands of the Soviet, while at the same time there existed a Government, and indeed an independent and sovereign one. The Soviet, by tradition, did not acknowledge that it was a government; and the Government, by tradition, did not acknowledge that it was a mere sham. . . . How many times, after all, had even the garrison passed resolutions almost identical with its vote on 21 October? How many times had it sworn allegiance to the Soviet, both after the July events and during the Kornilov revolt? How could one tell that now something completely different had taken place?[14]

Hence, since the acknowledgment of authority is the essence of authority, the Soviet lacked true authority, whereas, contrariwise, the Provisional Government, despite the helplessness that by October was well-nigh complete, still retained theoretical, hence factual authority – up to a point.

In a word the Soviet, now controlled by Bolsheviks, was the *real* government, though still *not quite*: those who still thought the Smolny headquarters of the Bolsheviks a 'private' institution also thought the Provisional Government was still functioning.

And it was just at this gap in the civic fabric – the gap between institutions and mythology – that the knife-thrust of a putsch had to make the Bolshevik headquarters 'public' – a real government, with power *plus* authority.

Trotsky's role in these developments was of paramount consequence, from the point of view of psychology as well as of technique.

On 22 October – the 'Day of the Petrograd Soviet' – a vast throng of 'democratic' Petrograd (i.e., the plebs of the city) was supposed to move on to join the endless number of mass meetings throughout Petrograd. It was conceived of as a form of psychological warfare: as Trotsky said, it was to carry out a 'gigantic review without clashes, without employing weapons, without even showing them.'

The Military Revolutionary Committee had determined to key up the masses by a demonstration of strength, by wiping out the depressing effect of the 'July Days' and showing up the feebleness of the upper classes and the Government.

The same day Trotsky made one of his effective speeches to a huge mass-meeting in the People's House: by now, as our principal eyewitness, Sukhanov, reports,

The whole point lay in the mood. The political conclusions had long been familiar. They could be condensed, as long as there were enough highlights.

Trotsky did this – with enough highlights. The Soviet régime was not only called upon to put an end to the suffering of the trenches. It would give land and heal the internal disorder. Once again the recipes against hunger were repeated: a soldier, a sailor, and a working girl, would requisition bread from those who had it and distribute it gratis to the cities and front. But Trotsky went even further on this decisive 'Day of the Petersburg Soviet'.

'The Soviet Government will give everything the country contains to the poor and the men in the trenches. You, bourgeois, have got two fur caps! – give one of them to the soldier, who's freezing in the trenches. Have you got warm boots? Stay at home. The worker needs your boots. . . .'

They were very good and just ideas. They could not but excite the enthusiasm of a crowd who had been reared on the Tsarist whip. In any case, I certify as a direct witness that this was what was said on this last day.

All round me was a mood bordering on ecstasy. It seemed as though the crowd, spontaneously and of its own accord, would break into some religious hymn. Trotsky formulated a brief and general resolution, or pronounced some general formula like 'we will defend the worker-peasant cause to the last drop of our blood'.

Who was – for? The crowd of thousands, as one man, raised their hands. I saw raised hands and burning eyes of men, women, youths, soldiers, peasants, and – typically lower-middle-class faces. Were they in spiritual transports? Did they see, through the raised curtain, a corner of the 'righteous land' of their longing? Or were they penetrated by a consciousness of the *political occasion*, under the influence of the political agitation of a *Socialist*? Ask no questions! Accept it as it was. . . .

Trotsky went on speaking. The innumerable crowd went on holding their hands up. Trotsky rapped out the words: 'Let this

vote of yours be your vow – with all your strength and at any
sacrifice to support the Soviet that has taken on itself the glorious
burden of bringing to a conclusion the victory of the revolution
and of giving land, bread, and peace!'

The vast crowd was holding up its hands. It agreed. It vowed.
Once again, accept this as it was. With an unusual feeling of
oppression I looked on at this really magnificent scene.

Trotsky finished. Someone else went out on to the stage. But
there was no point in waiting and looking any more.

Throughout Petersburg more or less the same thing was going
on. Everywhere there were final reviews and final vows.
Thousands, tens of thousands and hundreds of thousands of
people. . . . This, actually, was already an insurrection. Things had
started. . . .[15]

Trotsky's oratory, with its unusual combination of lyricism, emotion, and logic, powered by his passionate theatricality, itself served
as a mask for the technical measures still needed to transform the
mood of the Petrograd partisans of the Bolsheviks into a political
reality. Since Trotsky always tended to speak 'magnificently', his
speaking 'magnificently' now did not necessarily signify a 'magnificent' occasion: it could have been just another speech!

But by 'fanning the mood' of the politically active elements in
Petrograd, Trotsky was providing a matrix necessary for the putsch.
This matrix enabled the putsch to acquire the flesh-and-blood of a
new social organism.

When the mood had been fanned sufficiently, the operation could
proceed. It was of striking simplicity: troops had only to occupy
certain key positions in the city.

By 23 October a list had been drawn up and liaison between
the headquarters of the putsch and the city garrison ensured. There
was only one area of uncertainty – the Peter-Paul Fortress, the celebrated political prison on a small island in the middle of the Neva
River. It had a first-class arsenal, including 100,000 rifles; its guns
were aimed directly at the Winter Palace. Some artillerymen were
stationed there as a garrison, and some bicycle troops hitherto
thought of by the Provisional Government as trustworthy. The
bicyclists had been brought to the city during the July riots to
restore order.

The Peter-Paul presented a unique and crucial problem. The
Commissar assigned to the Fortress told Smolny that his credentials

had not been accepted and that he had, in fact, been threatened with arrest. It had to be assumed that the Fortress was an enemy point. But taking the Fortress by force through an overt move by the Bolsheviks was extremely dangerous. Unlike the other crucial targets the Fortress was physically formidable : it might even serve to shelter the Government, which might then be saved by front-line troops – if it could hold out long enough. The Fortress had to be seized at once, before the Government stopped palavering.

Trotsky settled the question. When it was suggested that a trust-worthy battalion be despatched to disarm the garrison – a very risky business and an overt act of war to boot – Trotsky proposed to go at once himself to *talk* the Peter-Paul garrison into surrendering. This was altogether in accordance with his tactics, which until now had been so successful. It was not risky – except, perhaps, for Trotsky! – and might very well escape the attention of the bemused Government.

The lively speeches made by both Trotsky and Lashevich (a non-Bolshevik) were received with enthusiasm; the garrison voted nearly unanimously to support the Soviet regime against the 'bourgeois' Government. Without firing a shot Trotsky had swung the Peter-Paul garrison over to the Military Revolutionary Committee.

The Bolsheviks had another 100,000 rifles; the Red Guards were issued with a great many.

To this quite decisive event, the Government also failed to react.

Smolny, the Bolshevik headquarters, now had a quite different look from the time the Central Executive Committee of the Soviet had sat there :

Smolny hummed with a new crowd, quite grey in aspect. Every-thing was dirty and untidy and smelt of cheap tobacco, boots, and damp greatcoats. Armed groups of soldiers, sailors, and workers scurried about everywhere. Grey wolves lived in Smolny now, and they were going on with their work.[16]

What was, of course, most incomprehensible about the clash between Kerensky's Government and the Military Revolutionary Committee was the Government's apathy.

The Government were, to be sure, hanging more or less nerveless in the void of their institutional isolation; Kerensky did not move until the night of the twenty-third, despite the all-too-obvious and indeed undisguised fact that since the twentieth the Bolsheviks had in fact been carrying out one step after another of an unmistakable putsch. At six in the morning of the twenty-fourth Polkovnikov sent a few military cadets to perform a decisive act – they closed down two newspapers! They broke up the type, put seals on the presses, and destroyed the numbers already in print.

The Military Revolutionary Committee were instantly informed: a working girl and someone from the print-shop asked for an escort to break the seals on one of the newspapers and carry on with the paper. Trotsky was told at once: in his *History* he was to write: 'A piece of official sealing wax on the door of the Bolshevik editorial room as a military measure, that was not much. But what a magnificent signal for battle!'[17]

Then and there Trotsky simply signed an order for some riflemen and sappers to provide a guard for the Bolshevik facilities.

In this way, at a moment when Smolny, the real headquarters of its enemy, had already claimed all the powers of sovereignty, the legal Government did no more than shut down two organs of the new regime as though they were doing nothing but *sponsoring* a putsch.

Smolny itself, on the other hand, did not draw the obvious conclusions from its assumption of sovereignty – it took no direct measures against the Provisional Government.

Nevertheless, with the Government finally responding, however pathetically, something did have to be done: this dreamlike state of colliding with each other as it were under water, soundlessly, obviously had to be stopped.

That same morning of the twenty-fourth, after the Bolshevik newspapers had been shut down and swiftly reopened, Smolny itself was turned into a heavy armed fortress. The Bolsheviks called a final meeting of the Central Committee: all were there but Lenin, Zinoviev, and, rather puzzlingly, Stalin. Trotsky proposed allocating functions – each member was given a special job: liaison with the railwaymen and workers in posts and telegraph offices, food supply, and intelligence. Two members of the Bolshevik Central Committee from Moscow attended the conference; one was sent back immediately to co-ordinate activities between Moscow and Petrograd.

The Government also took action. It sent off the cruiser *Aurora*, which had been moored close to the Winter Palace, and stationed a battalion – of women! – in the Winter Palace itself, which was now in fact defended only by these women together with some military cadets and a few Cossacks. They also posted military cadets at

various points in the city, raised the bridges to isolate the workers'
section on the other side of the Neva River, and cut off the Smolny's
telephones.

These trivial measures were immediately reversed by the Military
Revolutionary Committee.

The military element of the putsch was the decisive one; it was
also the simplest. It was in the hands of three men under Trotsky,
including Antonov-Ovseyenko.

It was decided to assault the Winter Palace on the night of the
twenty-fourth, using the Kronstadt sailors and the Red Guard from
the Vyborg workers' quarter, in addition to the crews of the *Aurora*
and some torpedo boats. The Winter Palace operation might – just
possibly – have involved some risk: troops with elan were needed.
Other troops, who were supposed to attend to more routine matters,
such as the mere surveillance of the military schools and the Cossack
barracks, did not have to emerge from the languor characteristic of a
garrison.

The assault had to be put off for a moment: the sailors had been
held up. The Winter Palace was not to be taken, in fact, until the
evening of the twenty-fifth, though technically, so to speak, it would
have been child's play to take it at any time, since the Women's
Battalion and the random assortment of Cossacks and military
cadets could hardly have withstood a force of any size. Indeed, the
whole Provisional Government had no more than one or two
thousand soldiers it could depend on.

It was in fact not until the day and the evening of the twenty-
fourth that Smolny itself was finally defended: it had taken that
long to shield the actual staff of the putsch! Moreover, the quality
of the defence was more than dubious: the soldiers were not ill-
disposed, on the other hand they could scarcely be called trust-
worthy; the smallest risk might have dispersed them. The workers,
on the other hand, who had far more political zeal, were total
novices: as Sukhanov says, they had 'never smelt gunpowder in
their lives'.

But only a day later the scene was quite different:

Smolny now had a quite impregnable look. Detachments of
sailors, soldiers and armed workers were posted around and
inside the enormous building. There were quite a few machine-
guns in the square, besides the cannon. Lorries, on which were
crowded people with rifles and other weapons, were making a

deafening racket. Now it was no longer possible to arrest the Military Revolutionary Committee, or bring up a detachment of 500 men to *occupy* this nest of insurgents. Now Smolny could only be *besieged and stormed.* This would no longer have been a simple 'measure' of a powerful Government, but an act of civil war. If the Government had massed enough strength, with artillery and the activity and skill of Government troops, I don't think success would have been completely excluded as yet. The chances, however, had grown infinitely smaller. The moment had been missed.[18]

By the night of the twenty-fourth, it was possible for Trotsky to report, in public, in a perfectly 'normal' way, all the actions that the Bolsheviks, now the leaders of the Soviet, were accepting full responsibility for: it was easy to state matter-of-factly that the reopening of the Bolshevik printshops and the recall of the *Aurora* were the first initial Bolshevik victories in a clash of arms that by now had become, so to speak, official.

Not only that: it was possible for him to do this under the mantle, as it were, of official action; he could declare that the Government was now in fact the Soviet itself – the Bolshevik majority was a happy accident.

Simultaneously, however, all the publicity Trotsky was trumpeting forth to the world concealed a double bluff – the Military Revolutionary Committee was carrying out conspiratorial operations *too.* At the very moment that Trotsky was speaking in his public capacity as Chairman of the Soviet his men were fleshing out his public statements with power.

While the palavering was still going on in the public institutions of both the Soviet and the Provisional Government, with Kerensky vainly trying to assemble enough material force to give his legal sovereignty some apparatus of actual constraint, the Military Revolutionary Committee, run by a trio of relative amateurs, was seizing a number of nodal points:

At two a.m. of the twenty-fifth two of the chief railway stations were taken; by three-thirty a.m. the *Aurora* had dropped anchor near the Nicholas Bridge after the crew and the military cadets stationed on the bridge had been dispersed by the crew; by sunrise some torpedo boats had arrived from Helsingfors; by six a.m. the State Bank was taken; by seven a.m. the central telephone exchange had been occupied, giving the Committee control of the telephones of the Winter Palace and the General Staff headquarters, which were immediately cut off. A patrol was stationed close to the government centre, at the Palace Bridge.

All points of support had evaporated; Kerensky was simply paralysed. There was nothing for him to do but keep frantically flitting back and forth between fruitless conferences with his Ministers in the Winter Palace and equally fruitless conferences on the other side of the Palace Square with staff officers – nothing could be done.

Even at the moment the putsch was actually being carried out – by the occupation of these strategic points in the city – Trotsky covered the technical aspects of the operation with a blanket of simultaneously authoritative and vague generalisations: his celebrated Order No. 1 was issued during the night and morning of the twenty-fourth-twenty-fifth :

The Petrograd Soviet is in imminent danger. Last night the counter-revolutionary conspirators tried to call the cadets and the shock battalions into Petrograd. You are hereby ordered to prepare your regiment for action. Await further orders. All procrastination and hesitation will be regarded as treason to the revolution.[19]

This could still be understood as a moral summons; in effect, it disarmed suspicion.

The dissolution of the Provisional Government took, quite literally, no more than a few hours and resulted in no casualties to speak of, possibly 'about ten'.[20]

By the morning of the twenty-fifth Kerensky had already been obliged to flee in a motor-car he had requisitioned from the United States Embassy. At noon of the same day Trotsky once again reported to the Petrograd Soviet, this time *post facto*, since everything had taken place so swiftly – all Petrograd except the Winter Palace, where Kerensky's Ministers were holed up, was now controlled by the Military Revolutionary Committee, i.e, by Trotsky himself as its head and hence of the Bolshevik Party. The Pre-Parliament had simply been dispersed; a few other Ministers had been put under arrest.

Throughout all this rather muted turbulence Lenin himself had been altogether superfluous, as far as his role in the putsch proper was concerned. On the evening of the twenty-fourth he re-appeared in Smolny, still in dense disguise; he was so far removed from the events, now unfolding with lightning-like speed, that as he furtively proceeded to the Smolny from his hide-out in the Vyborg suburb of the city he could not grasp the *fait accompli*.

He was still mistrustful; he seemed to have believed some newspaper accounts of 'friendly negotiations' between the Military Revolutionary Committee and Kerensky's Staff.

It was plain that the putsch had been conceived, designed, and executed by Trotsky, in his dual capacity as the public spokesman of the Soviet and as the conspiratorial commander of the forces carrying out the putsch. Lenin naturally saw this.

Trotsky had carried it all through without consulting Lenin, since in the nature of things Lenin could do nothing to affect decisions that had to be taken instantaneously; for that matter, he had been too remote to contribute anything to the operational plan. His remoteness from the scene of action, added to his long-time mistrustfulness of Trotsky as a political ally and his more recent doubts of him as a Party colleague, made him look at the putsch somewhat incredulously. Only after witnessing its rapid, dreamlike success, after seeing the atmosphere of composure plus exhaustion in the Smolny leaders – filthy and drained – was it plain : the tremendous gamble had come off. His formula for admitting this was characteristically realistic, though modest : the putsch could, 'of course, be carried out their way, too' – as long as it worked!

The Bolsheviks already had a majority at the Congress of Soviets, though legally they were, of course, merely one of its elements. In theory, accordingly, if they had handed the power over to the Soviets they would have had to form some sort of coalition with the other elements, since no provision had ever been made for any element to suppress the others.

But the Mensheviks insisted on boycotting the Congress because the Bolsheviks had made a putsch, which was now being consummated by the 'storming' of the Winter Palace.

Trotsky, having led the movement that had in effect smashed the framework of the Soviets and provoked the Menshevik boycott, could now take advantage of the headstrong Menshevik action in order to justify the Bolshevik initiative : he delivered a classic reply to the Mensheviks' furious speeches :

'A rising of the masses of the people,' Trotsky rapped out, 'needs no justification. What has happened is an insurrection, and not a conspiracy. We hardened the revolutionary energy of the Peters-

burg workers and soldiers. We openly forged the will of the
masses for an insurrection, and not a conspiracy. The masses of
the people followed our banner and our insurrection was victorious. And now we are told: renounce your victory, make concessions, compromise. With whom? I ask: with whom ought we to
compromise? With those wretched groups who have left us or
who are making this proposal? But after all we've had a full view
of them. No one in Russia is with them any longer. A compromise
is supposed to be made, as between two equal sides, by the
millions of workers and peasants represented in this Congress,
whom they are ready, not for the first time or the last, to barter
away as the bourgeoisie sees fit. No, here no compromise is
possible. To those who have left and to those who tell us to do this
we must say: you are miserable bankrupts, your role is played
out; go where you ought to be: into the dustbin of history!'[21]

At the very moment of personally consummating, together with a
handful of aides, a state overturn, Trotsky could feel sincerely
'representative' of the masses.

The final stage in the material dismantling of the Provisional
Government, consummating its spiritual obliteration, was absurdly
simple. Beginning around six-thirty p.m., on 25 October, the Winter
Palace was occupied practically painlessly. The Cossacks and the
military cadets had been slipping furtively out of the Palace and
disappearing. A few armoured cars were brought to the Palace
Square by the Military Revolutionary Committee, surrounding the
Palace completely.

At about nine p.m. a blank shot was fired by the *Aurora*; there was
a little quite harmless rifle and machine-gun fire for an hour or so.
When the Women's Shock-battalion tried to leave, theoretically to
rescue a general trapped at staff headquarters, the besiegers simply
scooped them in, apparently raping a few and sending the whole
battalion back to its base – out of business.

The Ministers, having nothing whatever to do, had been hanging
about in one of the rooms, darkened and silent. As Sukhanov says,
they were 'languishing in torment':

Outside the walls they were shooting as before; it was after 1
o'clock.

Again an uproar. It kept growing, nearer and nearer, up to the
very doors. It was clear the Palace was being stormed and taken. A

cadet rushed in to the Ministers and, drawing himself up, reported: 'Ready to defend ourselves to the last man. What are the Provisional Government's orders?'

'It's no use. We give up. No bloodshed! We suppose the Palace is already occupied?'

'Yes. Everyone's surrendered. Only this room is being held.'

'Tell them we don't want bloodshed and give up. We yield to force. . . .'

'Go, hurry, hurry! We don't want bloodshed!'

'Let's sit down at the table,' said the Ministers, and sat down, in order to look like busy statesmen.

The doors were flung open, and the room filled up at once with armed men, headed by Antonov himself. Palchinsky adroitly hastened forward: 'Gentlemen, we've just come to an agreement with your people on the 'phone. Just wait one moment, you haven't heard the latest!'

The chiefs of the detachment were within a hair's breadth of being disconcerted, but they pulled themselves together at once.

'Members of the Provisional Government!' shouted Antonov, 'I declare you under arrest! I'm a member of the Military Revolutionary Committee!'

'The members of the Provisional Government yield to force and surrender in order to avoid bloodshed,' said Konovalov.

The temper of the mob that had burst in, armed to the teeth, was extremely high, vengeful, furious, and impetuous. Antonov tried to calm the particularly hot-headed soldiers and sailors, but lacked sufficient authority. They set about drawing up an official report, while the Ministers began to 'agitate' at the victors. . . . Tempers would rise, then subside. The report that Kerensky was not around had a powerful effect. There were shouts that the others must be slaughtered so that they wouldn't flee after Kerensky.

After rather lengthy proceedings, with interrogations, roll-calls, and the making of lists, the column of prisoners moved out, in the direction of the Peter-Paul Fortress. In the darkness, between 2 and 3 o'clock in the morning, in the midst of a dense excited mob, the column moved along the Milliony and over Trinity Bridge. More than once the lives of the former Ministers hung by a hair. But it went off without a lynching.[22]

Trotsky's exertion had been titanic. He records a moment of

repose during the night of the twenty-fourth, when victory was assured:

> All is well. Couldn't be better. The telephone can be left. I sit down on a sofa. The nervous tension slackens. And just because of that a dense wave of fatigue pounds my head. 'Give me a cigarette,' I say to Kamenev. In those years I still smoked, though not regularly. I inhale deeply twice and barely have time to tell myself: 'That's all I needed!' when I lose consciousness. I had inherited from my mother a tendency to fainting-spells whenever ill or in physical pain. It was this that made an American physician say I was epileptic. Coming to, I see Kamenev's frightened face above me. 'Perhaps I ought to get some medicine?' he asks. After thinking a moment I reply: 'It would be much better to get something to eat.' I try to remember when I last ate: I can't. In any case it wasn't yesterday.[23]

Trotsky also records an intimate scene of the following night, after Lenin's arrival:

> Late in the evening, waiting for the session of the Congress of Soviets to open, Lenin and I were resting in an empty room near the meeting hall, where there was nothing but some chairs. Someone had put down a blanket for us on the floor, someone – apparently Lenin's sister – had brought us some pillows. We were lying side by side, bodies and souls relaxing like a spring that has been stretched too tight. It was a well deserved rest. We could not sleep. We were chatting in half-whispers. Lenin had finally reconciled himself only now to the postponement of the insurrection. There were notes of special gaiety in his voice. He asked me about the sentry units stationed everywhere, made up of a mixture of Red Guards, sailors and soldiers. 'What a magnificent picture: a worker with a rifle side by side at the fire with a soldier!' he repeated with deep feeling. 'Finally, workers and soldiers have been brought together!' Then he suddenly burst out: 'And the Winter Palace? Really not taken yet? If only nothing happens, what?' I started getting up to phone about the course of the operations, but he held me back. 'Lie down, I'll send someone.' But there was no question of lying down for long.[24]

Natalya has left a more personal account of the glorious feeling of the morning after:

Those days, those nights have left me a memory of lucid delirium. So many things were happening, all mixed up, that it was extremely difficult later on to restore more or less their order. . . . Everything was going on that morning of the 26th. No one had slept except for moments, nervously, ears pricked. We took literally a strict minimum of sleep, in order not to fall down exhausted. The hours and the days passed in an activity that was passionately purposeful but bubbling over and full of improvisations. . . . I went back to Smolny. I saw nothing but faces slack with fatigue, smudged by a stubble of beards, with circles under puffy eyes. Trotsky's face was drawn; he was pale, exhausted, overexcited. But an immense and austere joy dominated all other feelings.[25]

The Bolsheviks were in power.

CHAPTER VII

The Pinnacle

THE BOLSHEVIKS WERE in power. Yet that was still not quite obvious. The putsch had taken place so rapidly, it was so much the antithesis of The Revolution, that it was not at all clear to the man in the street that the Bolsheviks – up to the night before merely one party among many – were now ruling the country.

The leadership of the Party, too, was still groping: it faced a general problem – who was to do what?

Trotsky had been both the architect of the seizure of power and its spiritual inspiration. Publicly he was better known than Lenin at this time and very nearly as important even for the Party rank-and-file. It was possible, in fact, for an acute French observer, Jacques Sadoul, to say he 'dominated the insurrection, of which he was the soul of steel, while Lenin remained rather its theoretician.'[1]

Nevertheless, despite the glamour of Trotsky's role in the putsch, it was plain that what had been required was not personal virtuosity, but the Party staff that Lenin had spent some fifteen years in putting together and that Trotsky had merely joined at more or less the last moment.

The putsch was founded on a sort of tripod – its technical performance, its Marxist justification, and its public presentation. The pivot of the tripod was the Party apparatus. All unconsciously, perhaps, Lenin, in his preoccupation with forging an instrument to accommodate the surge of History, had forged one to carry out, on a conspiratorial basis, a transfer of power to a small group equipped with a theory of moral justification, an apparatus of adjutants, and a network of propaganda media. It was the fusion of these elements that enabled the core of the Party, having explained and justified to itself its decision, to keep the reasons for the decision itself totally hidden and to come before the public at large – including recently acquired sympathisers and partisans – with a platform of generalities – the celebrated slogan of 'Bread, Peace and Land'.

But the seizure of power had called for such concentration of energies that the Bolsheviks had had no time to consider the problems of actual government. Everything was, perhaps inevitably, improvised.

Trotsky records fumbling for a name – what *should* such a regime be called?

'What shall we call it?' Lenin reflects aloud. 'As long as it's not "ministers" – a repulsive, worn-out word.'

'We might say "Commissars",' I suggest, 'only there are too many commissars now. Maybe Supreme Commissars? ... No, "Supreme" sounds bad. Maybe "People's Commissars"?'

' "People's Commissars"? Yes, that might work,' Lenin agrees. 'And the government as a whole?'

'Soviet, of course – "The Council of People's Commissars", eh?' I ask.

' "Council of People's Commissars",' Lenin repeats : 'excellent – what a marvellous smell of revolution!'[2]

The irony that what Trotsky was always to present as a movement of the Masses could find itself summed up, as a function of literary style, in a private conference between two individuals, does not seem to have been noticed by Trotsky himself. To put it baldly, a handful of people were now in charge.

The psychological background was now, in fact, altogether different. Here is Trotsky's account of it :

Lenin has not yet had time to change his collar, but his eyes are very wide awake, even though his face looks so tired. He looks softly at me, with that sort of awkward shyness that with him indicates intimacy.

'You know,' he said hesitatingly, 'from persecution and life underground, to come so suddenly to power . . .' He pauses for the right word. '*Es schwindelt*,' he concludes, changing suddenly to German and circling his hand around his head. We look at each other and laugh a little. All this takes only a minute or two; then a simple 'passing on to the next item of business'.[3]

Trotsky reports that Lenin, at one of the first sessions of the Central Committee, suggested him as chairman of the Council of People's Commissars, evidently the equivalent of chief of state. This is confirmed indirectly by Sukhanov's report of a remark made by Lunacharsky, who was to become the Commissar of Education: Lunacharsky's explanation was that Lenin wanted to attend to Party affairs![4]

Trotsky protested vehemently: the suggestion seemed to him altogether inappropriate. Lenin then insisted, saying it was perfectly suitable – after all, Trotsky had been Chairman of the Petrograd Soviet that in theory had seized power.

In the first few 'dizzying' moments of triumph Lenin and Trotsky might still have assumed that there was some difference between 'Party affairs' and the Government. In that case, the explanation of Lenin's proposal could only be that Trotsky was to become a figurehead. It is hardly imaginable that Lenin was going to relinquish power on behalf of the Bolshevik Party, which had, after all, *really* taken power.

In any case, when Trotsky turned down the proposal and Lenin agreed to take his natural place as chairman of the Soviet of People's Commissars, Trotsky was then proposed by Lenin as Commissar for International Affairs. As Lenin put it, 'the struggle against the counter-revolution is now the chief thing': since the Bolsheviks knew that their long-range plans were bound to make them fall foul of the population as a whole the post had a certain importance.

In rejecting this second proposal Trotsky referred to his Jewish origins – 'Why give enemies one more such weapon as my Jewishness?' he said. Lenin, almost indignant, said: 'We have here a great international revolution, what importance can such trivialities have now?' After a 'semi-jocular' conversation, Trotsky clinched his point by saying, 'Why create a superfluous complication at the very outset?'[5]

Throughout these discussions it is plain that the Petrograd Soviet itself, which for the Bolsheviks had never been more than a façade, had lost its point the moment they wielded power openly. Trotsky's pre-eminent position as its chairman was obsolete: now he was one of a team.

Though a newcomer to the Party and, moreover, one who for

fifteen years had been sniping at the Bolsheviks and Lenin, Trotsky's performance during the turmoil preceding the putsch had been so distinguished that it seemed to be quite natural for him to have emerged as the Party's chief spokesman after Lenin. The Politburo tentatively put together before the putsch had proved abortive: its place was taken by a 'Bureau of the Central Committee' made up of only four men, Lenin, Trotsky, Stalin, and Sverdlov. Stalin, unknown outside the ranks of the Party and regarded as a mere 'practical', was responsible for organisation together with Sverdlov.

Sverdlov, essentially an organisation specialist and Stalin's predecessor in the office of General Secretary of the Party, though it was not yet called that, had familiarised Trotsky with the internal regime of the Party, its functioning as an apparatus. To Trotsky this was never of the smallest interest. In fact, his indifference to all matters of Party organisation must be the explanation of his singular remark in his book on Stalin, to the effect that until the October putsch was over he was unaware of him.[6] Since Stalin was both the editor of the Party newspapers, as well as an outstanding member of the Central Committee, Trotsky's remark – if not wishful thinking – is intelligible only as a reflection of his indifference to bureaucratic detail, well known from other sources.

Trotsky persuaded some of the other newborn 'People's Commissars' to support this Jewish diffidence of his, notably Sverdlov, also a Jew. Lenin gave in with a shrug, saying they 'would in any case all be fighting the Counter-revolution regardless of offices'.

Trotsky's own desire was to go back to journalism – this time, as a Marxist might say, on a higher plane – as director of the press! But the new Politburo was against this: 'Comrade Trotsky was to be counterposed to Europe' as Commissar for Foreign Affairs.

Improvisation pervaded, indeed, the entire government. Smolny Institute was practically bereft of all stenographers; typewriters were few and far between, telephones equally so. The Bolsheviks would dash back and forth between their tiny little offices, living at the canteen on the cabbage soup and coarse black bread of the Russian countryside.

Trotsky describes the Smolny work-rooms he shared with Lenin. The corridor that connected, or as Trotsky said, 'separated' them was so long that Lenin suggested communicating by bicycle. They were in fact linked by a telephone; nevertheless, Trotsky went back and forth several times a day for flash conferences on the endless problems that engulfed them. A young sailor who called himself Lenin's secretary trotted from Lenin to Trotsky with chits containing two or three terse remarks, the most vital words being underlined two or three times, followed by a sharply worded question. These little notes frequently accompanied draft decrees demanding an urgent response.

They were all living in the Smolny: Trotsky, Natalya and their two little boys had moved into a couple of rooms there from their former cramped lodgings.

Sadoul has recorded the atmosphere of the Trotsky household during these early days:

> Trotsky seems tired out, nervous, and admits it. Since 20 October he has not been home. His wife, a sweet little militant, lively, graceful, told me that the tenants of their building had been threatening to kill her husband. No one is a prophet in his own quarter, but isn't it amusing to think that this pitiless dictator, this lord of all the Russias, doesn't dare sleep at home for fear of his janitor's broom?
>
> Trotsky has two charming children, two boys of ten and twelve, who come in to disturb their papa from time to time and show him their admiration, plainly shared by the formidable leader himself.[7]

At first there was not the smallest assurance that the new regime would survive. The Bolsheviks, realising what a small minority they were throughout the country, considered themselves to be hanging by a thread. Because of this Lenin wanted to utilise his power as long as possible by telling the public at large just what the Bolsheviks stood for. His 'decrees' were, as Trotsky said, no more than a form of propaganda, especially since at the outset there was not even the shadow of an administration. Similarly, he used the whole of the governmental power to publish the classics of Socialism and materialism, in order, as Trotsky said, to 'fasten what had happened in the imagination of the masses, to leave behind as deep a furrow as possible in the people's memory'.[8]

Of paramount importance was the war. The Bolsheviks were determined to get out of it as quickly as possible. This was a matter of common sense as well as of ideology – the country was exhausted. Their determination to make peace took the form of an appeal addressed simultaneously to governments and to peoples; the former were called upon to make peace and the latter to overthrow the former. The first demand was a consequence of the Bolsheviks' weakness and the *de facto* necessity of saving their necks; the second was an echo of their faith that an imminent social upheaval abroad would shore up their position in Russia.

The Germans, too, saw the survival of the Bolsheviks at this time as desirable, indeed, indispensable: only they could be depended on to get Russia out of the war and keep it out. Thus they felt obliged to go on extending material aid to the Bolsheviks at the very moment they were engaged in negotiations that were to impose a great strain on the Bolsheviks. The German Minister in Moscow, Count Mirbach, kept sending memoranda to the State Secretary in Berlin, Richard von Kühlmann, asking for money to prop up the Bolsheviks; Kühlmann agreed entirely with this approach and recommended still larger sums whenever necessary.

Immediately after the putsch, for instance, the German Treasury set aside fifteen million marks for political aims in Russia, with another two million via the German Legation in Stockholm. In these relations Helphand had once again become a key intermediary. (Lenin and Trotsky concurred in keeping him out of Russia; his assistance in the past was now an embarrassment.)

The ambiguous relations between the German Government and the Bolsheviks were to last until the German defeat in November 1918.[9]

It was only natural for the Allies to regard the Bolsheviks as German agents and in any case enemies. There was no reason to disbelieve the rumours, by now rife, that the putsch was the handiwork of the Germans.

On the domestic side Trotsky had a smaller problem: he was in effect boycotted by his own department of Foreign Affairs, because he was determined to publish the secret treaties between the Tsarist Government and its Allies, a source of embarrassment to one and all. (Tsarist policy had aimed at the conquest of Constantinople as well as of Galicia.)

It was natural, in short, for the new regime to fall foul of the Allied Governments, which formally denounced the Bolshevik regime as illegitimate: they threatened a Japanese advance in the east if Russia got out of the war. The Allies at once, in fact, displayed extreme hostility toward the new regime: Trotsky had presented them, through their representatives, with a quite common-sense appeal not to force the new regime to accept *any* German terms, but the Allied Governments, a little unrealistic, as it turned out, about the stability of the parvenu regime, were quite inelastic.

The Germans, in any case, were eager to come to terms; by 14

November an armistice was agreed on principle. Krylenko, the Party's military expert, who had been a Tsarist ensign, had been appointed commander-in-chief: he ordered a ceasefire and also gave orders for 'fraternisation' between the soldiers on both sides of the front.

Trotsky transferred his high, emotional-cum-polemical style to his new office as Foreign Commissar; he deliberately used the rhetoric of The Revolution as a means of spreading it at the very moment he was obliged to carry on old-line negotiations with governments he was hoping to destroy.

Trotsky was far from high-handed in dealing with the representatives of the big governments. In individual situations he responded with courtesy and common sense. His objective remained, of course, the presentation of a lofty goal to as large a multitude as possible, in the hope that The Revolution buttressing the Bolshevik putsch would take place quickly. In opening negotiations with the Germans, for instance, he insisted that no German troops be re-deployed against the West, and that the Bolsheviks be permitted to carry on revolutionary propaganda among the German and Austrian soldiers.

He was optimistic about the 'possibility of a general armistice and universal peace'. At the beginning of the war he had correctly foreseen that trench warfare was in its nature a deadlock. Even America's entry into the war – a decisive factor, as it quickly turned out – did not modify his optimism: he thought neither side could possibly win, which gave his haughty approach to the Germans a certain rationale. It was also natural, on the other hand, for the Bolsheviks to fear that the two warring camps might join together against The Revolution. It thus became essential, in Lenin's opinion, that there should be a separate peace in the east before the *Entente* made a peace of its own with the Central Powers. This possibility was also very much in the minds of the Germans; in their clandestine support of the Bolsheviks they were aware of the latter's desperate situation.

This 'foreign problem', was merely the prelude to the Bolsheviks' stabilisation of domestic affairs.

A civil war loomed up immediately after the putsch. Within a month the organisation of the White armies was in train along the Don River; Cossacks were rising. In the capital itself there was a mutiny of a middle-class party (the 'Kadets') and some Right-wing Social-Revolutionaries.

By 28 November Trotsky outlawed the Kadets; it was the outset of what almost immediately became a movement of terrorism, no doubt inevitable in any seizure of power and all the more because of the Bolsheviks' isolation in the country.

The Bolsheviks had found it simple to settle the other domestic problem: what to do with their rivals and former allies on the Left wing – the Mensheviks and Social-Revolutionaries.

They had stood blandly on their claim that they 'represented' the Soviet by virtue of constituting its current majority; they said they would be delighted to collaborate with the losers the moment they agreed to accept the Soviet, with its Bolshevik majority, as sovereign.

'Constitutionalism' had suited the Bolsheviks very well, especially since it was obvious that the other Socialists would, in fact, be acquiescing instantly in their self-obliteration.

The issue was plainly academic; there was not the smallest prospect of the Bolsheviks' surrendering their monopoly. Yet a concern for appearances kept the dialogue alive.

Trotsky had concurred with Lenin completely on this question of the Bolshevik monopoly, though there still seemed no need to repress the other Socialists; after Martov interceded with the Bolsheviks for the release of the arrested Socialist Ministers – he was heard, according to Sukhanov, 'with chilly reserve' – they were taken out of gaol and put under house arrest.

In any case the whole discussion had come to an end only a few days after the putsch, on 3 November, when the two outstanding Mensheviks (Martov and Abramovich) said that all negotiations were banned as long as the arrests being made went on and the shutdown of the press, imposed by the Bolsheviks at once, was not lifted. Since the Bolsheviks had set about defending themselves and their new regime and were, in fact, – with rumours of Cossack advances, of the formation of White Guard units and so on – already well advanced on the path to civil war, this, too, had been academic: nothing could ever have come of it.

The terror initiated by Trotsky on 28 November, with his banning of the Kadets, had been highlighted by a phrase of his: 'We have made a modest beginning.' He added to this a comment that in the 'French Revolution the Jacobins guillotined better men ... for opposing the people's will. We have executed nobody and are not about to do so. But there are moments of popular fury. . . .'[10]

The mere juxtaposition of the classical phrase, 'the people's will',

and the assurance that the Bolsheviks had 'no intention' of killing
their opponents was plainly menacing.

Even if one limited oneself to the political spectrum in Russia as a
whole, it was plain that the Bolshevik monopoly entailed the alienation of countless groups and parties that might not have been inflamed by mere theory but were bound to respond to repression.

The Socialist parties represented many political shadings, for
instance, that enabled them to collaborate with the Kadets perfectly
comfortably; indeed, all the Socialists, including the Bolsheviks until
Lenin's arrival in April, had been unquestioningly in favour of such
collaboration. The Kadets, on the other hand, were in their own way
monarchists; this implied sympathy for the old regime – naturally
with modifications – and hence, once the parvenu Bolshevik power
was established, a *de facto* alliance between them and the out-and-
out monarchists.

Consequently, by outlawing the Kadets, the Bolsheviks automatically, like knocking down a series of bowling pins, irremediably
alienated well-nigh the totality of the population: the spectrum of
allegiance, beginning with the extreme Right wing, was interlocked
in a series of stages with groups that through the inclusion of the
peasant Social-Revolutionary Party encompassed all Russia.

Hence the Civil War was an inevitability that could have been
forestalled only by abandoning the Bolshevik monopoly. Since the
notion of 'enemies of the people' was in its very nature elastic
enough to encompass practically everyone, the use of it against the
Kadets was an implicit menace to the public at large.

But for the time being getting out of the war with Germany had
first priority; something had to be done at once.

Here the Bolsheviks, euphoric Marxists, had a peculiar problem.

In their eyes the putsch was not a mere putsch, but the initial
phase of The Revolution they were confidently expecting all over
Europe. Hence the dilemma they seemed to be in – to wait for The
Revolution to surge forward before they made peace, or to extend it
themselves by means of peace – was in its nature temporary, to be
superseded sooner or later by the irresistible, inevitable, cosmic
surge.

It is this conception of the cosmic surge that explains the curious
line followed by Trotsky during the peace negotiations with the
Germans that were initiated at Brest-Litovsk on 9 December, and
were brought to the stage where Trotsky himself could appear, on 24
or 25 December 1917, just two months after the putsch.

On the way to the town of Brest-Litovsk Trotsky saw what was obvious: the Russian soldiers had faded away; their trenches were simply empty. The Bolsheviks were materially helpless.

Trotsky arrived accompanied by the veteran Bolshevik journalist, Karl Radek, clever, talkative and amusing, though notoriously frivolous and in fact characterless.

Properly speaking, the Bolsheviks had no choice whatever: they could not possibly withstand a German advance. On the other hand, it was embarrassing to negotiate with the agents of a militaristic, imperialist power. The only way out of this dilemma continued to be hope – the confident, even desperate assumption that the Bolsheviks would be bailed out at any moment by the next groundswell of The Revolution.

The Bolshevik negotiators had lacked the self-assurance and *savoir-faire* to hold their own against the upper-class Germans and Austrians, who for their part had been leaning over backwards to show off their charm. Before Trotsky's arrival Kühlmann, now German Foreign Minister, had been masterminding the negotiations.

Trotsky's first act was to ban the social graciousness of the proceedings. He wanted to eliminate once and for all the old tradition that war is a gentleman's game and that even in defeat a gentleman remains one.

He then put all his powers of repartee into a full-dress debate with the other side. Kühlmann, the opposing head, was an able man, though hampered by the distrust of his own Government, which was in fact divided on just how to exploit the new situation in Russia. (Ludendorff was still hoping for a German victory, Kühlmann wanted to try for a negotiated peace.)[11]

In some ways both the Germans and the new Bolshevik leaders were obligated both to submit to each other and to dictate to each other – in the given circumstances they needed each other desperately. If the Germans squeezed the new regime too hard, they might collapse and be replaced by a Russian faction that would resume hostilities. If the Bolsheviks for their part proved intransigent, they might be crushed out of hand by the German Army. The gamble between these two secret allies was still in force – ultimately it hinged on the fortunes of the German Army in the West.

It was, curiously enough, just those circumstances that gave the negotiations the framework of a lofty debate (touching on the self-determination of peoples, the nature of the state, etc.). Such 'principled' discussion was, of course, Trotsky's medium; the German representative also felt at home in it, as did Count Czernin, the urbane Austrian Foreign Minister, acutely conscious of impending disaster for the Central Powers and so all the more sensitive to the urgency of a peace settlement.

Trotsky made a strong impression on both Kühlmann and Czernin. Kühlmann thought him a man of calibre, by no means to be despised: 'His sharp, very characteristically Jewish face was in constant motion through the play of all the muscles.'[12] Years later Kühlmann boasted that it had given him particular pleasure to 'cross swords with Trotsky dialectically, because he wanted to make a point of defeating him at that level'.[13]

Czernin had a similar opinion: Trotsky, he said, 'possesses a quite outstanding oratorical gift, an ... adroitness in repartee such as I have rarely seen, and with it all the impudence corresponding to his race.'[14]

Trotsky stalled for time. A quick settlement might have been natural: both sides had the same interest – the earliest possible peace. Yet Trotsky's determination to inject his own point of view into each clause in fact held up the proceedings for a long time, even though it was manifestly impossible to link his own revolutionary optimism to the 'revolutionary mood' of The Masses in Europe.

Starting out from the impossibility of carrying on the war, but insisting at the same time that the German terms were unacceptable, Trotsky created a formula that was soon to involve the Party in a bitter wrangle.

For the Bolsheviks only The Revolution could bridge the gap between these impossibilities: hence Trotsky devised a formula for the interregnum – 'neither war nor peace!' – and refused to sign anything. He justified the formula by maintaining that the German Army was incapable of launching an offensive.

After the debate at Brest he returned to the Smolny (7 January 1918) to explain himself to the Party. The day before he arrived the Bolsheviks had dispersed the Constituent Assembly – for decades the goal of Russian revolutionaries of all shadings and taken for granted on and off beforehand by the Bolsheviks themselves. The repression of the Assembly was, of course, a logical consequence of the chasm between the composition of any conceivable Assembly and the aims of the Bolshevik putsch. Once the Bolsheviks were committed to a monopoly an Assembly representing the bulk of the population was bound to be hostile.

The elections to the Assembly had produced an absolute majority for the Social-Revolutionaries, and for that matter for the Right wing of this big party, which represented, if anything could, the whole of the Russian peasantry. The support given the Bolsheviks within the Petrograd Soviet had plainly been illusory, even assuming that it could have been interpreted as an identification with the Bolsheviks *as such* and not merely with the peace policy.

The moment the Assembly refused to ratify the Bolshevik transfer of power to the Soviets, as well as Lenin's various decrees (on land, peace, etc.), it was dissolved out of hand.

It was a mere detail – the first confirmation of the Bolshevik monopoly. Trotsky endorsed it without qualification. Under the pressure of the crucial issue of war and peace, in any case, not much time could be spent on it – those who were for the Assembly were now automatically as it were incorporated within the vast number of those whom the new regime was beginning to suppress.

The Party was in any case taken up with the life-and-death question of a possible German advance: Lenin was for peace at any price; a great many others, led by Bukharin and Dzerzhinsky, (a Polish landowner turned Bolshevik who was to be the first head of the Political Police), were for carrying on a 'revolutionary war' against the monarchies of the Central Powers. Trotsky was rather in the middle, since his formula of 'neither war nor peace' – essentially a balance between the 'realistic' assessment of possibilities and a longing for an extension of The Revolution – retained its viability only as long as the Germans did not budge.

Because of this the two factions, in wrangling with each other inside the closed circle of the Central Committee, could, up to a certain point, meet for quite different reasons in support of Trotsky's formula; he was finally authorised (by only a couple of votes) to go back to Brest with his formula worded as a resolution: 'We interrupt the war and do not sign the peace – we demobilise the Army.'

Emotionally, the formula meant nothing. The leading Bolshevik intellectuals were still tremendously eager to carry on the 'upsurge' against the *ancien régime*. This was particularly characteristic of Trotsky, who exploited his aura to fill his speech to the Third Congress with revolutionary pathos:

The great speech of the evening was made by Trotsky . . . all eyes were upon him, for he was at the zenith of his influence . . . the man who incorporated the revolutionary will of Russia, speaking to the outer world. . . . When Trotsky had ended his great

speech, the immense assembly rose and ... solemnly sang the
Internationale. The outburst [was] as spontaneous as it was soul-
stirring.[15]

Behind the backs of the Central Committee, meanwhile, he and
Lenin made a private agreement – there was not the smallest reason
to think the *Germans* were going to be bound by Trotsky's formula:
why, after all? When Lenin asked this sensible question it was
agreed that if the Germans insisted on moving ahead, despite
Trotsky's optimism, then Trotsky was authorised to sign peace
terms. This way out of the ambiguity inherent in Trotsky's formula
was itself somewhat ambiguous: at what *point* could Trotsky sign?

Lenin thought, as it later emerged, that he could sign on the
presentation of the threat, Trotsky only after the fact of an advance;
and indeed, even at that point, too, Trotsky later was to claim he
could not go beyond the terms already offered by the Germans,
though of course common sense would indicate that once an
advance was successfully launched any subsequent terms were
bound to be worse.

In mid-January Trotsky went back to Brest with this conjunction
of ambiguities. The strikes and the movements for peace that had
previously reinforced his optimism had been smothered or had
simply died down: in the face of the increased self-assurance of
Kühlmann and the others Trotsky was reduced to some theatrical
gestures – demanding that the German negotiators at Brest ask
Socialists from their countries to join in the conference, that he be
given time to consult Victor Adler in Vienna and so on. The only
concession he could get on this score was a trip to Warsaw; there he
was welcomed because of his support of Polish independence.

The Ukraine, as well as Poland, had been a natural object of
negotiation: in the debate between Trotsky and Kühlmann much
ado had been made about national self-determination. This was now
turned against Trotsky, since the Ukraine had not yet been subju-
gated by the Bolsheviks in Petrograd and Moscow and there were
not enough local Bolsheviks to take it over. Some Ukrainians who
had been against independence now reversed themselves out of
hostility to the Bolsheviks, whereas the Bolsheviks who had made
'ethnic independence' one of their slogans now found reasons for
ingesting the Ukraine.

The Germans' motives in pretending to support Ukrainian
independence were, of course, primarily practical: the Ukrainian

granary seemed vital. The pretence also made Trotsky's arguments a
little feeble. Thus, at the second round of talks, when he was
informed that the Germans were coming to an agreement with the
quasi-parliamentary Ukrainian Rada that still controlled Kiev,
Trotsky was in an embarrassing position. He was not yet inured to
compromises imposed by contingency.

When the delegates of the Ukrainian Rada flung Trotsky's
principles into his teeth by ferociously denouncing the Bolsheviks'
policy of disregarding Ukrainian Rights and imposing their own
representatives by force, he

> was so distraught it might have made one sorry for him. Com-
> pletely pale, he stared fixedly before him and doodled nervously
> on his blotting-pad. Heavy drops of sweat trickled down his
> forehead. He must have felt deeply the pain of being vilified by his
> own countrymen in the presence of the enemy.[16]

In explaining his disarray on this occasion Trotsky himself, to be
sure, refers to his pain not at seeing his compatriots denouncing him
in the presence of foreigners, but at seeing people who in spite of
everything were true revolutionaries debasing their own ideals in the
presence of 'aristocrats who despised them'.[17]

Between his rhetorical tussles with Kühlmann and the other
negotiators Trotsky relaxed as usual by writing, this time a brief
aperçu of Soviet history – already! – that adumbrated the full-dress
History he was to write in exile not much more than a decade later.

In the very midst of the debate Trotsky learned (21 January 1918)
that the Rada had been wiped out and that the Bolsheviks now
controlled the whole Ukraine: he could return to his principles.

This was to prove a breaking-point. The Germans, who were not,
of course, particularly interested in the actual existence of the Rada,
chose to go ahead with their project for an alliance with an 'independent' Ukraine. Their relations with Trotsky and his aides snapped a
few days later.

In the final rupture Trotsky's grandiloquence came into play:

> We are getting out of the war. We are announcing this to all
> peoples and governments. We are issuing an order for the total
> demobilisation of our armies. . . . At the same time we declare that
> the terms proposed to us by the governments of Germany and
> Austro-Hungary are in fundamental conflict with the interests of
> all peoples. They are repudiated by the toiling masses of all

countries. . . . To the Russian people these terms are a permanent
threat. The masses of the whole world, guided by political consciousness or moral instinct, repudiate them. . . . We refuse to
endorse the terms that German and Austro-Hungarian imperialism is inscribing with the sword in the flesh of living nations. We
cannot put the signature of the Russian revolution under a peace
treaty that brings oppression, woe and misfortune to millions of
human beings.[18]

A British historian records the general stupefaction:

When the echoes of Trotsky's powerful voice died away no one
spoke. The whole conference sat speechless, dumbfounded before
the audacity of this *coup de théâtre*. The amazed silence was
shattered by an ejaculation of Hoffmann 'Unheard-of!' he
exclaimed, scandalised. The spell was broken. Kühlmann said
something about . . . a plenary session. . . ., but this Trotsky refused,
saying that there remained nothing to discuss. With that the
Bolsheviks left the room, and in gloomy silence, still scarcely be-
lieving what they had heard and wholly at a loss as to what to
make of it, the delegates of the Central Powers dispersed.[19]

In this atmosphere, of course, the only thing the Germans could
do, just because their position was desperate, was to start moving
into Russia again, though even now Trotsky dismissed this as
rhetoric: he disdainfully refused to answer Kühlmann's question
about how the Central Powers could maintain contact with the new
Russian Government.

On his way back to Petrograd Trotsky thought his display of
forensic virtuosity had scored a major coup; he was still en route
when the German Army was ordered into the field. By 17 February*
it was pushing forward with no resistance anywhere.

In the Smolny the Party debate became murderously acrimonious;
the Bolsheviks were in mortal danger.

The alternatives, from a practical point of view, were plain – fight
or surrender. But the fighting itself was conceived of in theory as
special – as a 'revolutionary war' against a 'bourgeois' power.

The Central Committee was split between the peace faction led
by Lenin and the war faction led by Bukharin, Radek, Dzerzhinsky,
amongst others.

*Dates henceforth are given according to the calendar now in general use:
it was adopted in the Soviet Union a few days before the event noted.

Trotsky hovered in the middle: his passions led him, like the others, to the idea of a 'revolutionary war'; common sense inclined him, as it did Lenin, to the perception that it was hopeless. A vote had to be taken at once, between 17 and 18 February: Trotsky's was the balancing vote.

Trotsky gave an impression of vacillation: on the first day of the discussion, for instance, he voted both against Lenin's resolution calling for immediate peace and against the partisans of the 'revolutionary war'. He also made a motion of his own calling for a postponement of all negotiations until the scope of the German advance could be clarified. His own vote was enough to carry this; it suited the 'revolutionary warriors'.

The background of this wrangling was the stark fact that the Russian front had practically no defences: the news about the German advance was likely to provide a shock from one hour to the next. In fact in a single day, 18 February, the Russian position on the front deteriorated alarmingly. Hence Trotsky's hesitancy on this prime question was blatantly dangerous. Even after the news of this advance, he still hesitated – he wanted to ask the Germans what they wanted, but *not* to ask them to negotiate.

The next day Trotsky unexpectedly switched round to support Lenin, now even more insistent on immediate peace negotiations; it looked as though Trotsky's formula – which, had The Revolution broken out, might have seemed astute – had been in fact pernicious. In any case his vote made a majority: on 19 February the Bolsheviks formally requested peace negotiations.

Their position was now far worse. The Germans took their time about answering; they gave the Bolsheviks four sleepless days and nights. In addition, the Party wrangle itself was still more envenomed.

During Trotsky's initial attempts to arrange an armistice with the Germans, he had been given a very chilly response by the Allied Governments, when he had asked them whether they would help the Bolsheviks if they were to go to war in effect on their side. Now they had become friendlier; the British and French proposed to co-operate.

Now the Party huffily rejected this Allied proposal, for different reasons.

The peace group thought it might hurt the prospects of a separate peace; the 'revolutionary warriors' were, for reasons of purity, against an alliance with the 'Anglo-French imperialists'. Threatening to resign, and with Lenin's backing, Trotsky talked the Party Committee round.

The German answer made the Bolsheviks desperate; it was much harsher than the proposals in Brest-Litovsk. It called for the total cession of Latvia and Esthonia and the abandonment of the Ukraine and Finland, with only two days for an answer and three for talks. When the Central Committee met on 23 February it did not have even a day to talk it over.

Once again the two camps were so evenly divided that Trotsky's vote swung the decision, again with a maximum of ambiguity because of the gulf between his theoretical principles and his practical recommendations.

His view was that, although he had agreed with Lenin that a peace offer should be made, he had not bound himself to these worse terms which were now so bad that he veered around to the war camp, disagreeing meanwhile with Lenin about the total indefensibility of the Bolshevik positions. Then once again, after doing his best to destroy Lenin's arguments, he supported his proposals nevertheless and swung the vote in favour of the peace group.

The two camps were divided, of course, largely by the angle of approach to their common revolutionary optimism. Lenin's optimism was expressed by the long view that *even* at the cost of territory The Revolution would not be halted; hence the Bolsheviks would be playing space for time. The others, less hopeful about the loss of space, were more hopeful about immediate prospects of resistance, again because of the same revolutionary optimism. Both sides were depending on their example, combined with their struggle, whatever form it took, to move the hearts of The Proletariat outside Russia.

At this crucial session of the Central Committee on 23 February, the peace faction won, this time because of the abstention of Trotsky and the three leaders of the war camp, two of whom had been strongly influenced by Trotsky's warnings against the dangers of schism. The war group, led by Bukharin, resigned.

Consequently, the Central Committee on 23 February 1918, agreed to the Germans' demands, while at the same time voting – unanimously – to begin preparing at once for a war later on.

The opprobrium attached to peace even by its partisans was so great that it was very hard to find anyone to go back to Brest: a personal talking-to by Lenin was needed.

It was Trotsky's over-optimism, his assurance that the Germans would do nothing, that had led to the crisis in the party. He seems to have vanished for a few days after the crucial meeting that accepted the German conditions; when he reappeared, on the evening of 27 February, to address the Central Soviet Executive, he was 'so overcome with mortification that he broke down and wept' after his speech.[20]

The treaty of Brest was signed on 3 March, though not ratified. The Germans, having seized all major points including Kiev and immense stretches of the Ukraine, Bolshevik Russia was substantially truncated and also politically humiliated. By upholding the pretence of Ukrainian independence and forcing the Bolsheviks to accept the pretence at face-value the Germans had put them in the position of overtly abandoning their revolutionary commitments to their Ukrainian partisans.

At a secret Party congress on 6 March Trotsky had to defend his luckless policy of 'neither peace nor war', as well as his shifting away from the moral support of the 'revolutionary war' as a matter at least of principle. He was driven to the point of allowing a possibility of 'Marxist disillusionment' to peep through the perspectives of the new regime. In denouncing the humiliating German demand that the Bolsheviks sign a treaty with the German puppet Ukrainian regime, he brought into question the essence of the Bolshevik putsch. For if the Bolsheviks were forced to sign such a treaty with the German puppet in the Ukraine – forced, that is, to leave the Ukrainian 'workers and peasants' in the lurch – the Bolsheviks might then have to come out and openly confess. 'We have come before our time.'[21]

This phrase is pregnant with what for Marxists replaces fate. The forward thrust of History laid down by Marx is supposed to be articulated through interlocking phases on the basis of large-scale developments; if someone, mistaking his phase, undertakes to do something he is incapable of, he has made an historic blunder.

Trotsky did not, however, generalise this possibility of 'disillusionment' further, nor was he scarcely ever to refer to such a possibility again.

Trotsky expressed an idea at this Congress that in retrospect sounds strange : he seems to have assumed that he might have taken Lenin's place in the Party, since Lenin's position had been undermined by the tensions of the crisis. He explained his backing of Lenin despite his disagreement with him on the 'Holy War' idea as due to his revulsion against the idea of replacing him.[22] He intimated that the consequences of a split in the Party might be so momentous – the guillotine! – that it was worth a 'great act of self-restraint', his own 'sacrifice of the Ego',[23] not to fight Lenin's peace policy tooth and nail.

What is extraordinary about this is, perhaps, first the admission as such, and then the indication that he drew back for the sake of the cause – Bolshevik unity, a concept that was soon to govern his fortunes.

It was in connection with the Brest policy that Trotsky's personality became, as it were, politicalised.

Some sympathisers wanted him to be praised for his Brest policy, though this was put formally as a motion endorsing the Brest policy precisely at a moment when it seemed to many that, whether or not Trotsky alone was responsible for it, it was also just what had got the Bolsheviks into such hot water. Also, the motion was put up by the 'revolutionary warriors', which made it look as though they were seeking compensation for their defeat on the issue itself.

Now identified with the Brest policy, Trotsky had, in any case, a natural tendency to defend all his decisions. When the Congress rejected this motion his feelings were hurt; he resigned from all his posts.

This gave rise to a chaotic set-to on the floor of the Congress; Lenin kept aloof. There was some concern about Trotsky's position, since the question of his becoming War Commissar had now come up; the Congress leaders were eager to soothe him. There was a flurry of vague, ambiguous and contradictory motions; their inconclusiveness so piqued Trotsky that, very characteristically, he proposed a motion – denouncing his own policy!

This sarcastic *démarche* was also shrugged aside by the Congress: Trotsky walked out.

The whole squabble was meaningless: Lenin and Trotsky were elected to the Central Committee again by a demonstratively high number of votes.

The Brest treaty was crushing; it inaugurated a painful era for the Bolsheviks. The parvenu regime was ringed round by assailants of all kinds – the Allies, together with the Japanese and Germans, and for that matter the Czechs occupied enormous stretches of the country, from Vladivostok in the east to Murmansk in the north west and the whole of the Ukraine, including the Crimea and the shores of the Black and Azov Seas.

The foreign interventions, ultimately nullified by dilatoriness, naturally dovetailed with the campaigns of the Russian anti-Bolsheviks: civil war and foreign invasion moved in tandem.

Lenin, while continuing to broadcast his message to The Workers, including the German and Austrian workers, was still more or less upholding the disastrous treaty of Brest: he refused to countenance an out-and-out attack on the German Army.

The Bolsheviks were obliged to move the capital to Moscow, partly to secure the Government against attack, partly to make Petrograd itself a less tempting target. Trotsky, together with the rest of the Council of People's Commissars, moved into the Kremlin. He was now War Commissar; in his own phrase he had begun, as he put it, 'arming the revolution'.

The family's living quarters were rather informal, though not uncomfortable. When Trotsky moved in he could say: 'At last – a nice flat.'[24]

Stalin, withdrawn and remote, occupied another flat opposite Trotsky's. His relations with Trotsky and Natalya were restricted to the minimum necessary for business. He was rather grouchy, often rude. He scarcely greeted Natalya, or not at all, though his young wife, Nadya, was charming to her.

Trotsky was well known for orderliness. Natalya records a wifely view:

Trotsky was always very methodical: his main traits were punctuality, attention, time-tables adhered to and imposed on others. He would not allow lateness for meetings or appointments; he had a horror of *laissez-aller*, chatting, and neglect of work; he always succeeded in surrounding himself by serious collaborators, so that at a time of disorder the officers he was in charge of and his personal secretariat gave an example of efficiency that was commented on, sometimes with praise, sometimes with hostility.

He got up at 7:30 and was at the War Commissariat at 9 precisely; he often returned to the Kremlin for lunch, toward 1:30, and sometimes would snatch a respite to laugh and joke within the family; the afternoon and evening were taken up by sessions and the work of the Commissariat.

The food in the Kremlin was bad, but Trotsky never permitted himself or his family to take advantage of his position. In his own words: 'We must not eat better than we did in the emigration.' Once, noticing some unexpected butter, he flared up: 'Where does *this* come from?'[25]

As Natalya reminds us, this was at a time when bureaucrats were already wangling themselves privileges; many functionaries lived much better than the Bolshevik leaders.

While they were living in the Kremlin Trotsky's father, now over seventy, came to see them. A rich landowner, he had lost everything; he had left Yanovka and crossed the 200 kilometres between Kherson and Odessa on foot, in jeopardy all the way. For the Bolsheviks he was a rich man, for the White Guards he was the father of their principal enemy.

Natalya says that if he was proud of his son he didn't show it: instead he said, with a little spark of malice: 'the fathers work, work to get some ease in their old days, then the sons make a revolution. . . .'[26]

Natalya described him as big-boned, sturdy, with strong features, a white beard and deep blue eyes, full of vitality. He could not, doubtless because of Trotsky's puritanism, take advantage of his son's position: he found work on a nationalised farm and died around 1922, almost seventy-five.

Despite Trotsky's qualms about the purity of a settlement with German militarism, he was now identified with Lenin's policy of peace at any price; the Bolsheviks who still believed in a 'revolutionary war' were more or less disoriented; in public at least they subsided.

To make up for this the junior allies of the Bolsheviks, the handful of ardent Left Social-Revolutionaries, were now denouncing more savagely than ever the duplicity of the Bolsheviks in signing a peace treaty of any kind with the German 'imperialists'.

It was up to Trotsky, accordingly, in the beginning of July (at the Fifth Congress of the Soviets), to defend a policy he himself was in two minds about: seething with indignation, the Left Social-Revolutionaries had plumped for a complete rupture with the Bolsheviks.

Emotional infants – though some of their leaders, like Spiridonova, the famous woman bomb-thrower, were aged – the Left Social-Revolutionaries were the sort of fanatics whose purity of purpose generates glamour and also serves as touchstone for the consciences of others. Trotsky had to defend the practical decisions of Brest against the tug of martyrdom.

One of the S.R.s, for instance (Kamkov), turned on Count Wilhelm Mirbach, the German Ambassador there as a spectator, and flung a torrent of abuse at 'German militarism', using essentially the same

approach Trotsky had paraded at Brest. This was also a reminder
that some months before Trotsky had staked his honour and that of
The Revolution on a sustained fight, and a little later had said he
would be prepared to go 'underground' again because of the Bolsheviks' premature arrival on the stage of history rather than have them
turn their backs on the Ukraine.

Since then he had, for reasons of Party unity, as he said, sided with
Lenin; now, as Commissar of War, he was beginning to play the role
of disciplinarian on behalf of a Party that was now obliged, from a
public relations point of view, to harmonise its principles and its
responsibilities.

Trotsky's 'logical' approach was based on the need to conform
with a policy laid down by the constitutional authority. He summed
up the terrible dangers of private citizens waging war in defiance of
authority; already some Bolshevik commissars had been murdered
by those in favour of a 'revolutionary war'.

Threats of assassination began to heat the atmosphere. Tiny
Spiridonova sneered at Trotsky's 'militarist, Bonapartist style', she
got a very uncharacteristic apology:

> I myself, Comrades, am by no means a lover of the military style
> as such; in life and in literature I am accustomed to the style of the
> publicist. . . . But every activity has its consequences, including
> stylistic ones, and as people's Commissar for War, who forbids
> hooligans to shoot our representatives, I am no longer a publicist;
> I cannot express myself in the same lyrical tone in which Comrade
> Spiridonova spoke here.[27]

Here is an eyewitness description (Sadoul's) of Lenin's and
Trotsky's reactions to the chorus of vilification from the Left Social-
Revolutionaries:

> Lenin gets to his feet. His strange, faun's face remains calm as
> ever, and mocking. He has never stopped and will never stop
> laughing under the insults, attacks and direct threats pouring
> down on him from the platform and from the hall. In these tragic
> circumstances, when he knows what is at stake – his entire work,
> his goal, his life – this vast laughter, full-bodied and sincere,
> which some find out of place, makes on me the impression of
> extraordinary strength. Every now and then a sharper word, a
> more stinging insult, manages for just a second to chill this laugh-

ter, so offensive and exasperating to the adversary, to tighten his lips, narrow his eyes, and harden the pupil, flicking out darting flames from his slitted eyes.

At Lenin's side Trotsky, too, tries to laugh. But anger, emotion, tension change his laughter into a painful grimace. Then his lively expressive face seems extinguished; it blurs and vanishes under a Mephistophelean, terrifying mask. He does not have the master's sovereign will, his cool head, his absolute mastery. Yet he is better, I am sure of it, less implacable.[28]

Mirbach was murdered a couple of days later (6 July).

The background of this episode is unusually murky.

The Bolshevik version (uncontested for decades) put it about that the murder, carried out by two young S.R.s, was the signal for the Left S.R. uprising, intended to provoke a rupture between the Bolsheviks and the German 'imperialists'. The Left S.R.s themselves vigorously denied any intention of an uprising, but accepted, and to some extent boasted of their complicity in the murder.

Yet the discrepancies inherent in this version ultimately destroyed it.

At a moment when the Left S.R.s might have been expected to be staging their coup, the 400 Left S.R. delegates – all 'brawny peasant lads'[29] – were sitting peacefully in the Moscow hall of the Fifth Congress of the Soviets.

Blumkin, the prime murderer, was never really prosecuted: he re-appeared in 1919, giving a manifestly irrelevant and uncheckable story both of the murder and of his escape; for years he worked as a Bolshevik close to Trotsky.

For a short while the Left S.R.s had played a role that for the Bolsheviks was invaluable: they had camouflaged the Bolshevik monopoly from the beginning.

Trotsky's handling of the putsch itself had made use of Vlazimir, the eighteen-year-old Left S.R., as the Chairman of the Military Revolutionary Committee, which was, in theory, a non-party 'Soviet' organisation.

Later on, the dissolution of the Constituent Assembly was facilitated by Lenin's claim that the Assembly majority – Right S.R.s – had been elected before the Left S.R.s had split off. That is, that the majority, presumably representing the bulk of the peasantry, might really have been composed of Left S.R.s altogether.

The Left S.R.s had been rewarded with government jobs.

But their 'revolutionary' ardour soon outweighed their usefulness to the Bolshevik summit, especially since it coincided with the feelings of the more 'Left' Bolsheviks themselves. It was natural, also, for the Left S.R.s, in accordance with their 'revolutionary position', to present themselves as champions of the peasants. Since the Bolsheviks had begun squeezing the peasants for the food needed so desperately by the cities, this intransigence of the S.R.s had become more and more exasperating, especially in that they were numerically strong (a third of the delegates to the Fifth Congress) and very responsive to the hysteria of Spiridonova and her entourage.

The Bolsheviks were still in terrible jeopardy; they might be thrown out of power from one moment to the next. In the course of this tense July Trotsky characterised their situation: 'We're actually dead already, all we need is someone to bury us.'[30]

The relationship of the Bolshevik Party to its German sponsors was naturally aggravated by its weakness: the German Legation in Moscow was pressuring the German Government to shift its support from the Bolsheviks to moderate monarchists and other anti-Bolshevik elements (as indicated in Mirbach's final memorandum). From June 1918 on, indeed, the Germans had been transmitting huge sums – some forty million gold marks – both to the Bolsheviks and to their various rivals, whom the Germans wanted to keep on a string in case the Bolshevik regime, as seemed to be likely, collapsed after all.[31]

Thus the Bolsheviks resorted to a combination of cynicism and brutality in handling the impetuous Left S.R.s. Lenin's attitude was reported 'with profound revulsion' by an intimate, Leonid Krasin, to a Soviet functionary (G. A. Solomon):

'Although I know Lenin well,' Krasin told me, 'I had never been able to suspect him of such profound and cruel cynicism. Talking with me about the projected solution of the situation he would tell me with a crooked smile – note, *with a crooked smile*, "We are going to make an internal loan among the Left S.R. comrades; thus we shall preserve our innocence and get all the benefit." '[32]

It is clear from the context that the 'projected solution of the situation' by means of an 'internal loan' could only mean foisting the responsibility for the Mirbach murder on to the guileless Left S.R.s.

Lenin used the Mirbach murder, in short, as a lever to extinguish the Left S.R.s. The 'uprising' was no more than the resistance of some Left S.R.s to the Bolshevik 'reprisals' that presented them to 'public opinion' and in particular to the German Government as the assassins of Mirbach.

A Russian observer, reacting to the scene described above, in which Lenin and Trotsky were the targets of the Left S.R.s' savage vilification, was much struck not so much by Lenin's 'vast laughter', as by his utter 'indifference' to the proceedings.[33] Perhaps Lenin's indifference, and Trotsky's 'anger, emotion, tension' were produced by their knowledge that the Left S.R.s were about to be dealt with. Trotsky's lesser 'implacability' might have made it painful for him to concur.

In the event it proved quite simple to arrange a bogus version of the episode. As in the case of the German subsidy to the Bolsheviks, neither side had any interest in disclosing the facts. The Germans were still dreaming about victory; the Bolsheviks were gambling, as before, on a German collapse. Hence the awkwardness that might have been expected to arise out of the assassination of a diplomatic envoy had no chance to materialise. The Germans protested, complained; the Bolsheviks shrugged, apologised. Both sides played suitable roles.

The 'mutiny' was remarkably puerile, in any case; the handful of Left S.R.s who evaded the Bolsheviks long enough to withstand the 'reprisals' managed to snatch Dzerzhinsky and others and to occupy the Posts and Telegraphs building.

Their resistance was quickly suppressed: by 9 July Trotsky could make the final 'public relations' presentation. He called the mutineers 'children who had run amok . . . no room for such children' was possible any longer. 'The party demanded enough . . . to rise against the will and the knowledge of the overwhelming majority of workers and peasants . . . committed suicide once and for all on 6–7 July. That party cannot be resuscitated!'[34]

This was the final echo of the imbroglio over the Brest treaty with the Germans; for a time the turbulence in the Bolshevik Party died down.

But the Bolsheviks were still in mortal peril: self-defence was imperative.

It was now that Trotsky performed his paramount service for the Bolshevik Party, aside from the putsch. He created, very nearly from scratch, the structure of an army. Appointed Commissar of War in March 1918, he had almost a free hand for a year.

Immediately after the putsch Kerensky and a few loyal Cossacks at his command were quickly defeated. The apathy shown at this time by the Bolshevik forces had been exceeded by the apathy of the Cossacks. By the end of October the Cossacks had given up, though Kerensky managed to escape. There had been a few skirmishes in Moscow, badly organised: the Bolsheviks won easily. In some other cities partisans of the Soviets also reported victories.

The ferocity of the Civil War that now flared up had been hinted at as soon as the putsch was over: during the fighting with Kerensky's troops, when some military cadets had come out against the Bolsheviks, Trotsky had spoken ominously about hostages and the abolition, in the name of The Revolution, of taboos on the seizure of property.

For a time the Bolsheviks' military position looked well-nigh hopeless. The old armies had simply evaporated; practically nothing was left. The tiny remnants, mainly a few friendly units on the Don and elsewhere, were valueless. They were dismissed; it was better to start with nothing.

In fact no Russians were soon left under arms at all; there was only one division of Latvian sharpshooters; the only Russians more or less organised, though very sketchily, were the Red Guards, which had not been added to since October 1917.

By the summer of 1918 the regime seemed powerless.

From the very beginning Trotsky was obliged to find military talent outside the Bolshevik enclosure. Trotsky himself, of course, had no training at all; he functioned as a top executive.

Moreover, mere exhortation, which had sometimes been effective during the build-up of the atmosphere that enveloped and concealed the putsch, had soon shown diminishing returns.

In the wake of the putsch Trotsky and Lenin had asked some of the regular officers (systematically vilified by the Bolsheviks) to rally round; at that stage they nearly all refused; a few able opportunists accepted.

The Revolution was still in its idealistic, 'principled' phase: the very fact that officers had to be used at all, especially the few careerists Trotsky finally found, deeply disturbed the Soviet, especially the Bolsheviks themselves and the naive Left Social-Revolutionaries. Yet at this point no choice was possible; Trotsky was obliged to use even 'natural' enemies; his only control was strict surveillance.

The use of the Tsarist officers' corps was plainly a ticklish point in 1918: the Tsarist officers could not, after all, be counted on to rush to the defence of the Bolsheviks. Contrariwise, idealistic Bolsheviks were maddened by the idea of using the old officers' corps, for that matter by the very concept of a centralised permanent army. Moreover, many Bolsheviks who did not object to centralisation or discipline felt suspicious, very often for selfish reasons, of the Tsarist officers. These feelings were reinforced by the reluctance of the countless new heroes who objected to any form of subordination altogether.

The original *espirit de corps* of the Bolshevik Party, extravagantly stimulated by the dreamlike ease of the putsch, had swiftly congealed into a sort of caste arrogance, based largely on a plebeian provincialism masked by revolutionary chauvinism.

The question was a broad one: how could the new state hope to survive if it alienated all the qualified people in society – doctors, scientists, technical people, engineers, writers, in fact the intelligentsia in general?

Trotsky's views were the natural consequence of a fact – without the Tsarist officers there would have been *nothing*. Yet Trotsky was distressed by the crass formulation of the Bolshevik view that the Party would harness the Tsarist officers only in order to 'squeeze them like lemons and throw them away'[35] (Lashevich, head of the military section of the Party).

This not only impeded the recruiting of the vitally needed officers, it offended Trotsky's dignity, rooted in the sincerity he always felt through his identification with an idea that in the name of a principle could ennoble a fact. He was sincerely upset over the disdainful treatment of individuals; on principle, also, he was naturally against waste.

It gave his recruiting campaign great elan. Addressing the officers, he would paint the revolutionary transfiguration of the common man in glowing terms:

People who aren't used to The Revolution and to its psychology may view with some horror, if not with revulsion, that licentiousness and anarchic violence that has been seen on the surface of revolutionary events. Yet in that licence, in its most negative manifestations, when a slave of yesterday – a soldier found himself in a first-class carriage, and tore off the velvet upholstery to make puttees for himself – in that display of vandalism there was nevertheless the awakening of a personality. That down-trodden, abused Russian peasant, who used to be slapped in the face and reviled in the foulest language, came into a first-class carriage, perhaps for the first time; he saw the velvet, and in his own boots there was nothing but stinking rags; he tore off the velvet, saying he, too, had the right to a piece of velvet. A day or two, a month, a year later, no, a month, he understood the ugliness of plundering national property. But his awakened personality, his individuality . . . his human personality have been fixed within him forever.[36]

There is no record of the officers' reaction to this lyricism.

Trotsky's personal high spirits, his own morale as it were, and his intellectual self-confidence enabled him to make an impression on many Tsarist officers, whom he would speak to with no trace of pomposity, arrogance, or vindictiveness: but calmly, earnestly and above all intelligently. This general attitude also enabled him, on the other hand, to subject them to penetrating criticism, often with salutary effects. He also set about creating a renovated officers' corps out of the former non-commissioned officers and rankers.

There was also a still more basic question: in calling for volunteers Trotsky had been burdened by the necessity of briskly reversing the traditional Marxist denunciation of militarism. He had to give the establishment of an army a new rationale.

Brute necessity facilitated the discovery of a new 'ideology'. The Bolsheviks were defending their lives while 'representing' a cause: self-defence coincided with idealism.

Trotsky attacked the problem. The month after he became War Commissar he had laid down at least a structure for recruitment by sectioning off his own commissariat. A decree of 15 January 1918 – calling for an army of volunteers – had been, of course, a dead letter, like practically all the legislation of the early Soviet regime; if only because the entire administrative apparatus had simply fallen apart, it had remained a purely ornamental statement.

As part of the volte-face on militarism Trotsky had also to restore the notion of a chain of command, practically meaningless since the Tsarist collapse in February 1917. The Party discarded the idea of electing commanders and running the army by means of soldiers' committees. True democracy, it proclaimed, did not mean that The

Masses actually *ran* the army; they merely 'supervised' the government 'representing' them.

Trotsky instituted a system that had a long life under the Soviet regime: he assigned commissars to parallel the normal army chain of command. The system, modelled after the political commissar system in the French Revolution, had been used by Kerensky; Trotsky's innovation was to make the parallel precise, from company commanders up, with functions defined accordingly.

As it did in the French Revolution, the system ensured both military effectiveness and political reliability. The White Guard general, Denikin, an outstanding victim, indicated as much: 'The Soviet government may be proud of the artfulness with which it has enslaved the will and the brains of the Russian generals and officers and made of them its unwilling but obedient tool.'[37]

Though worded with revolutionary emotionality, Trotsky's appeal for volunteers was not merely visionary. Camouflaged by the screen of the Soviets, the Bolsheviks could claim legitimacy, a legitimacy that, despite the parliamentary squabbling of the past, was not denied them by their former Socialist colleagues. They were thus given an umbrella that encompassed most of the peasantry as well as the working class.

They had not yet elaborated specific solutions of social and economic problems; these were not, indeed, to be applied until much later. Just as a great many ordinary people were 'pro-Bolshevik' before the actual putsch, in the sense merely of adhering to the Bolsheviks' 'democratic' slogans – peace, bread, land – so, too, many people were pro-Bolshevik in the sense of defending 'Soviet democracy' against the *ancien régime* and its partisans.

Thus the Bolsheviks, as the apparently legitimate expression of the Soviets, could make a fairly broad appeal. On the other hand, they had to be sure of people. Those whom they could depend on were, primarily, the working class. It was not until the later summer of 1918 that Trotsky began applying in practice the conscription laid down in principle by the new regime at the very outset.

The recruitment of the first 10,000 industrial workers was regarded as an unusual achievement. The system was gradually extended, very cautiously, until the beginnings of a new army were eventually laid down in the form of a dependable core associated with decreasingly reliable flanking units. Each major army unit was based on a core of proletarian elements that could be more or less depended on and that could serve as a fulcrum for moving the great mass of soldiery of peasant origin. (The latter was often unreliable and, during the Civil War, deserted on occasion in a body.)

Trotsky also centralised the army under a unitary command, suppressing often with great difficulty and against violent opposition, the countless roving guerilla units, anarchists and others. This was to continue to be a source of opposition, sometimes furtive, to Trotsky's policies, especially when it involved Bolshevik submission to former Tsarist generals.

Trotsky also gave full expression to the ferocity inherent in civil war; in the nature of things anything short of the death penalty can be thought rectifiable by the victory of one's own side.

Trotsky's wholehearted identification with an Idea made him implacable – 'merciless' was a favourite word of his own. He had a certain admiral (Shchastny) executed on an indictment of sabotage.

This admiral had been appointed by the Bolsheviks themselves; he had saved the Baltic Sea Fleet from the Germans and with great difficulty brought it from Helsingfors to Kronstadt and the mouth of the Neva. He was very popular amongst the sailors; because of his strong position vis-à-vis the new regime he behaved quite independently. This was what annoyed Trotsky, who was, in fact, the only witness to appear against him, and who denounced him without itemising any charges; he simply said in court that he was a dangerous state criminal who ought to be mercilessly punished. Many Left-wing people, as well as the sailors, were upset by what they took to be a political assassination.[38]

Trotsky also instituted a savage general measure – the keeping of hostages: he had a register made up of the families of officers fighting at the fronts.

The regime was salvaged by the German defeat in the autumn of 1918 and by the rapid subsequent collapse of the monarchies in Germany and Austro-Hungary. The Bolsheviks could devote themselves to the evolving Civil War.

Lenin, absorbed by political and economic affairs, knew little about the army beyond generalities; he sponsored Trotsky's general approach to centralisation, but was unsure of the wisdom of using Tsarist officers; he was flabbergasted when Trotsky told him that as many as 30,000 were serving in the Red Army. On this scale a random case of treason was negligible; Lenin praised Trotsky for 'building communism' with the bricks left over from the old order.[39] He said to Gorky: 'Show me another man able to organise almost a model army within a single year and moreover win the respect of military experts.'[40]

Both sides were remarkably dilatory in organising their respective military forces, but the problem was much simpler for the Bolsheviks, who, though they had to defend a 5,000-mile front held an interior position. There was an alternating series of thrusts and counter-thrusts, in which the White Guards engaged in three major movements – a springtime offensive from Siberia under Kolchak against the Volga area in Moscow itself, a southern movement against Moscow in the summer under Denikin, and an advance against Petrograd under Yudenich in the autumn.

These movements were not co-ordinated. Each was separated from the others by thousands of miles, evolving at its own pace and in pursuit of the often egotistic objectives of each commander.

Though essentially a civilian, Trotsky was bound to get entangled in the front. His first crisis as military commander came about through a contretemps.

The Czech Legion, formed during the war by prisoners of war who wanted to fight Austria-Hungary, was supposed to be disarmed by the Bolsheviks after the treaty of Brest; the Legion had in fact been deprived of most of its arms, and after being moved back and forth beyond the Urals and around Siberia, learned that it was about to be handed over to the Germans. It leaped into action; since there were no armed forces to speak of in Asiatic Russia it was soon in control of a large territory, where it wiped out the Soviets and joined Kolchak's White Guards. It swiftly took Samara on the Volga, and went on to take some other towns, notably Yekaterinburg, where the Imperial family were interned.

The Bolsheviks had originally determined to stage a sensational 'trial' of the Tsar by a 'revolutionary tribunal' (as in the French Revolution). Trotsky, looking forward to putting the trial on the highest possible philosophical level, confronting the luckless Tsar in an open courtroom, had assigned himself to the office of Chief Prosecutor.

But as the Czechs and their White Guard allies were advancing on Yekaterinburg, the Bolsheviks, just before rushing off, killed the Tsar and his whole family, later saying that local Bolsheviks had made a spot decision confirmed after the fact. It seems that despite the obvious risks Trotsky had wanted the family to be evacuated, to permit the trial, and had been overridden by the Politburo.

The killing itself was a matter of course for the Bolsheviks; as a symbol the Tsar was obviously dangerous. Justifying the killing *post facto*, Trotsky remarked years later that 'judicial procedures' were naturally out of the question.[41]

In any case, by 6 August 1918 Kazan, the major outpost on the eastern shore of the Volga, was evacuated by the Bolshevik forces: if the Whites crossed the Volga, they would have a straight run to Moscow.

The very next day Trotsky went to the front in person, in the train that he was not to leave again, except for flash trips to Moscow, for two and a half years. (As Trotsky said, the 'Train of the Chairman of the Revolutionary Military Council' was indissolubly bound up with 'my personal life during the most strenuous years of the Revolution. The train was inseparably linked with the life of the Red Army. It connected the front and the rear, solved urgent problems on the spot, educated, appealed, supplied, rewarded, and punished.'[42])

He learned of the fall of Kazan en route.

When he got to Svyazhsk, on the Volga across from Kazan, he found a state of chaos – desertion en masse, collapse amongst both the officers and the Bolshevik commissars. Within the range of the enemy artillery, his powerful voice flooded them with eloquence. He spoke at first hand to soldiers in the grip of panic, and led them back to the firing lines in person. Accompanied by Kronstadt sailors, he even made a night raid on Kazan on a broken-down torpedo boat; the little collection of ships brought down the Volga by the Kronstadters closed down the enemy artillery on the other shore. Trotsky came back unharmed; his presence had had a decisive effect.

This otherwise negligible but in the circumstances crucial battle was the beginning of Trotsky's military schooling. This first lesson, lasting a month, was spent holding back the surge of retreat, since new detachments, arriving in high spirits, were at once swamped by the slack mood. At Kazan Trotsky saw at first hand the potentialities of effort and determination in the teeth of what he called 'cowardly historical fatalism'. The area held by the Bolsheviks was by now the size of what had once been the Grand Duchy of Moscow: they had almost no army and were beleaguered on all sides by the enemy. 'The highway to Moscow almost without obstacles lay before them. In critical moments everything depended on a battalion, on a company, on the tenacity of a single Commissar, i.e. on a thread. . . . The enemy's strength consisted of military organisation, just what we lacked. And it was this art that The Revolution learned at Kazan.'[43]

The agitation conducted by Trotsky from Kazan, in the form of countless telegrams, churned up the Party leadership. Thousands of men were rushed to Kazan.

Trotsky was both unusually meticulous and unusually harsh – The Cause justified everything. His correspondence with Lenin shows both the details he found time for and the instances of extreme rigorousness in his approach to what he considered matters of principle: he would not, for instance, let the Red Cross through the lines, partly because he wanted no rumours started about any reconciliation with the enemy, and partly because he did not want to see the 'burning and scorching' of Kazan's 'bourgeois quarters'.[44]

An impressive euphemism. . . .

Within a month the Bolsheviks were in a position to retake both Kazan and Simbirsk; the Volga area came under their control once again. This heartening victory coincided with the setting up of an openly acknowledged system of terror in the wake of the assassination of a Bolshevik official (M. Uritsky) and the attempted shooting of Lenin by a woman Social-Revolutionary (F. Kaplan).

In Moscow, at the end of September 1918, Trotsky set about reorganising the Supreme War Council into the Revolutionary War Council; in doing this he was hampered by Voroshilov in the Tenth Army, the most powerful unit in the south of the country, where the White Guards were now concentrated.

This was to be a prime source of friction. The Tenth Army, under the sponsorship of Stalin, was blocking Trotsky's general plan for the streamlining and harmonising of the army as a whole; Stalin had been at Tsaritsyn most of the summer of 1918; in September he had been the principal commissar for the southern front.

By the time Kolchak was defeated – his abortive offensive had taken in a wide front towards the Volga and towards Moscow – Trotsky had more than half a million new men under arms, with some one and a half million men in the army as a whole after a fifty per cent conscription carried out by the trades-unions on their own membership.[45]

After Kolchak fell back the question arose of chasing him into Siberia. Trotsky opposed pursuit: he wanted to secure European Russia rather than run the risk of being trapped by Kolchak in Siberia, where it was thought he might have a reserve force; the establishment in the spring of 1918 of new Soviet regimes in both Hungary and Bavaria – a tremendous stimulus for the Bolsheviks – had made it still more advisable to buttress the European front.

Party commissars on the eastern front appealed directly to Lenin; Trotsky was reversed. He had made a strategic error, as it turned out, that was to play into the hands of the many enemies he had been making as a commander.

After Kolchak's retreat Trotsky went to the Ukraine, where Denikin's thrust had been very successful. The Bolsheviks, thoroughly unpopular there, were harassed, in addition, by the anarchist bands, guerillas, unorganised Red Guards, and other lawless elements that were roving about in conditions of almost complete chaos.

Trotsky had made a mistake about Kolchak's Siberian reserve; there was none. In early July 1919 he went to Moscow to defend himself on this point, and also to explain away the Bolsheviks' reverses in the Ukraine.

Stalin had been in charge of the southern front; he was doing his best to utilise these setbacks and mistakes against Trotsky; he had succeeded in reversing Trotsky on two major matters – the breaking of a commander on the eastern front who had been sponsored by Trotsky (K. S. Kamenev) and the revamping of the Revolutionary War Council.

Trotsky himself was left as chairman, but his associates were ousted and replaced by commissars who had fallen out with Trotsky and been sponsored by Stalin.

Piqued by what was in effect an official rebuke, Trotsky instantly resigned from his major posts. The Party, alarmed by the prospect of a public rift in the midst of a big emergency, had to save his prestige. Upon Lenin's urging the Politburo refused to accept Trotsky's fit of pique; instead it unanimously praised him in a fulsome motion; Lenin, also alarmed by the prospect of losing Trotsky's talents, gave him as army commander *carte blanche*.

Trotsky was humiliated once again on the third major front – Denikin's in the south, where the White Guard front extended from the Volga and Don as far as the Ukrainian steppeland in the west. The forces under Denikin were Don Cossacks and White Guards: Trotsky wanted to attack the White Guards, who were moving along the central and western sections of the front, rather than involve the Don Cossacks. He thought the inherent lack of solidarity between these two segments of Denikin's armies could be exploited, and recommended an attack on Kharkov and the Don Basin to separate the Cossacks and the White Guards, to take advantage of a pro-Soviet and relatively industrial population. He was trying to override his own commander-in-chief, in fact, on the basis of general socio-economic considerations. He was again over-ridden by the Politburo, which decided to push a major campaign in the east instead.

This particular setback was consummated later in 1919, when, undoubtedly at the instigation of Stalin, Vatzetis, the former commander-in-chief, was gaoled on a charge of high treason. Vatzetis had been backed by Trotsky against K. S. Kamenev in the matter of the advance against Kolchak in the east, when Stalin and K. S. Kamenev had been proved right; at that time, in fact, he had been replaced by K. S. Kamenev on Stalin's insistence.

Hence the charge of treason against Vatzetis – otherwise unsub-stantiated, since nothing happened to him and he went on to serve as a highly placed army officer for years – was a direct blow at Trotsky, whose position was complicated further by the terrible state of affairs in the Ukraine, where the fight against Denikin remained bogged down in countless difficulties.

The ramified difficulties were interlocked; they revolved around the complete impoverishment of vast areas against the background of a military situation in which the Red Army, because of K. S. Kamenev's general strategy, had been concentrated on the eastern front.

For all practical purposes, the Ukraine – the central and western sectors of the front – was abandoned.

Trotsky had to nag the Politburo both for simple reinforcements and for supplies to send to the forces in the Ukraine, which were in a state of chaos. It was easy to interpret Trotsky's demands as his way of emphasising that the operational strategy he had been overridden on was the right one – that the White Guards should be fought in the central sector, not in the east.

A couple of weeks later the front collapsed; Denikin held almost all the Ukraine, including Kiev; he was moving on to Moscow by the shortest route.

The new regime was once again on the brink of disaster: Moscow might well be taken. Trotsky renewed his appeal to shift the mass of the army away from the east and back towards the centre, for the defence of Moscow. His view was reluctantly accepted at last: by the beginning of October 1919 Denikin's army had come as far as Tula, the major town before Moscow, while at the same time the White Guards under Yudenich, armed and backed by the British and their navy, were already near the suburbs of Petrograd.

Trotsky's views had been borne out after a dangerous delay. The Politburo swung round: Stalin joined in a blanket condemnation of the previous strategy. Trotsky's spirits soared: he had another accession of the energy he could generate when tension and danger combined to place him in the forefront of controllable events.

Trotsky's operational plan was applied; the front was radically shortened; supplies flowed copiously to the troops. Now the enemy lines were spread too thin. The factor of morale, which was, so to speak, Trotsky's speciality, also came into play. The soldiers were called on to perform heroic feats; Trotsky's powers of oratory were tapped once again.

The Politburo had a gloomy session on 15 October: it seemed that Petrograd had to be abandoned. Lenin wanted to defend Moscow at all costs, but both Trotsky and Stalin energetically presented the defence of *both* cities as imperative, Trotsky partly because the abandonment of Petrograd would have the most depressing effect on the partisans of the Soviets.

Trotsky proposed to handle the defence of Petrograd personally; he laid before the Politburo some urgent measures entailing full mobilisation; he was en route the next day even before the Politburo had approved his plans.

On his arrival in Petrograd he found a situation of chaos, both spiritual and material: Yudenich had already seized Krasnoye Selo, just outside the city. Here is Trotsky's comment:

I found the most frightful confusion. Everything was cracking up. The troops were retreating, disintegrating. The army staff were looking at the Communists, the Communists at Zinoviev. Zinoviev was the hub of the confusion. Sverdlov said to me: 'Zinoviev is panic itself.' In quiet times, when, as Lenin said, 'there was nothing to be afraid of,' Zinoviev very easily climbed into seventh heaven. But when things went badly Zinoviev usually lay down on the sofa – not metaphorically, but literally – and sighed. Since 1917 I've convinced myself that Zinoviev doesn't know any intermediate moods: It's either seventh heaven or the sofa. This time I found him on the sofa.[46]

Trotsky was notified by Lenin that his plan for mobilising all resources in the defence of the city, even from within, street by street, had been approved; he flung himself into the task with abandon.

He had an electrifying effect. Here is an account of it by an eyewitness:

> Like fresh reinforcements arriving . . . Trotsky's presence at once showed itself: discipline was restored. . . . Whoever was inefficient was demoted. . . . Trotsky's orders, clear and precise, sparing nobody and exacting from everybody the utmost exertion and accurate, rapid execution of combat orders, at once showed a firm directing hand. . . . The inward rallying had begun. . . . Liaison, hitherto defective, became satisfactory. The supply departments began to function. . . . Desertion from the front was radically reduced. In all detachments field tribunals were in session. . . . Everybody began to realise that only one road was left – forward. All avenues of retreat had been cut. Trotsky penetrated into every detail, applying to every item of business his seething, restless energy and his amazing perseverance.[47]

Trotsky, on horseback, now personally rounded up frightened men in headlong flight; a panic caused by the surprising sight of British tanks outside the city was overcome when workshops started improvising their own imitations of tanks. The whole Petrograd front, in Yudenich's words, resisted to the point of 'heroic madness', regular soldiers, amateurs, Red Guards, women. . . .

A week after Trotsky came to Petrograd the Bolshevik forces had gained the initiative.

The White Guards, their morale shattered by corruption, apathy, internal disarray, and inflamed by pogroms against the Jews – which, as Denikin said, 'also affected the spirit of the troops, warped their mind and destroyed discipline'[48] – were crumbling everywhere.

From the end of 1919 on Trotsky's involvement with the army contracted radically. Though he had created it, he had, from the very outset, been distracted by the irritations of a divided command, with its inevitable tangles and intrigues.

The Civil War was still going on, but it was plainly won: the regime was anchored. It was possible to relax the constraints that had been due, many Bolsheviks thought, to the implacable exigencies of the Civil War. Tolerance for other parties – at any rate other Socialist parties – seemed possible.

In January 1920 the Bolsheviks did away with a couple of

measures of constraint: the death penalty was abolished; the authority of the Political Police was restricted a little.

Trotsky spent his fortieth birthday in Moscow; it was the second anniversary of the October putsch.

At the zenith of his career and doubtless, too, at the high point of his life, Trotsky, reporting to the Central Executive of the Soviets on the Bolshevik triumph, was hailed as its architect, and vociferously awarded the Order of the Red Banner.

Yet even in the celebration of his unique role there was a curious note – Stalin, who was not at the ceremony itself and had played no role in the last-ditch defence of Petrograd, was given the same honour.

Trotsky was to record the incident with manifest vexation.[49]

Trotsky's Jewish origins played a certain role in the Civil War. All those who opposed the upheavals of February and October reacted, classically, by 'blaming the Jews'.

Curiously enough, with the exception of isolated, more or less 'emancipated' individuals like Trotsky himself, Zinoviev, Sverdlov, and Kamenev (a half-Jew), the Bolsheviks had practically no Jewish followers. Jews as a group were not to accommodate themselves to the new regime for years.[50]

The Bolshevik putsch, in fact, ruined the Jewish community. The loss of tangible wealth has been estimated as between four and five billion roubles.[51] Ultimately, since eighty per cent of the Jews were shopkeepers, small businessmen and the like, 'the nationalisation of private enterprises and particularly the prohibition of free commerce, cut the ground . . . from under the feet of the Jews.'[52] As far as their civil status was concerned, 'thirty-five per cent of Russian Jews were . . . deprived of all rights; the corresponding class among the non-Jewish population did not exceed six per cent.'[53]

As Jacob Mazeh, Chief Rabbi of Moscow, said : 'The Trotskys make the revolutions, the Bronsteins pay the bills.'[54]

The epigram was prompted by Trotsky's telling him, as he turned down some request of Mazeh's on behalf of the Jewish community: 'I am a revolutionist and a Bolshevik, and I am not a Jew.'

It may be curious that Trotsky, after making a point of his Jewish origins in declining Lenin's proposal that he become Commissar for Domestic Affairs, did not, apparently, even mention it again when he was made War Commissar, a position that in the midst of a life-and-death struggle was far more conspicuous.

It is also, no doubt, a crowning irony that the Jews, often held 'responsible' for the Bolshevik putsch by people outside Russia, were destroyed by it, while the German General Staff and Foreign Office, which had played a vital role in supporting the Bolsheviks both before and after the putsch, never admitted this. Ludendorff himself, a prime mover in this partnership, was later to become a follower of Hitler's, whose cardinal obsession revolved, of course, around a archetypal 'Jewish-Bolshevik' plot to run the world.

The key role played by Helphand, a Russian Jewish Marxist, rounds off this historic irony.

CHAPTER VIII

The Apparatus

AFTER THE CIVIL WAR Trotsky settled down in his Kremlin apartment. His drivers, mechanics, machine-gunners and secretaries scattered; his military train was put in a museum.

Already nostalgic for the recent past, he took a short breathing-spell and plunged into work.

He was unquestionably the outstanding figure in the country, second only to Lenin as a state personage. He was publicly, moreover, far more *evident*. Until well into the Twenties, in fact, his celebrity might well have seemed unchallengeable. The most versatile luminary of the Party, he had countless interests aside from politics. Writing voluminously, addressing mass-meetings, he seemed the very emblem of the Bolshevik regime.

Yet it was politics that was soon to undo him.

Reeling out of the Civil War, the Bolsheviks confronted a complex problem.

The putsch itself had been easy: the Civil War, too, despite its appalling losses, had posed no problems of programme – the institutions and ideas being defended by the Bolsheviks were quite general, even national, since the Bolsheviks presented themselves as champions of the great mass of the population and had not yet proposed any unpopular transformations.

But what were they to *do* now?

They had, after all, slipped into power under the cover of a slogan – 'Bread, Peace, Land' – that was independent of their long-range hopes as Socialists: they were still waiting for a successful proletarian uprising in the industrial West. For some time they were to remain in the grip of the illusion that had prompted them to take power – that the putsch was simply the first step in The World Revolution.

This seemed plausible for some years; the First World War brought about so many upsets that their dreams often seemed to be coming true. From November 1918 on large portions of Central Europe were churned up by agitation, especially in Germany, the chief hope of Marxist dreamers.

Until the end of the Civil War Trotsky had been too busy to think very much about general prospects; his energies were exhausted in the putsch itself and its aftermath, then in the Brest negotiations, and then, most strenuously, in the Civil War.

His scattered comments on foreign affairs had been expressed with extravagant optimism: the few barricades in Berlin in January 1919 inflamed his enthusiasm : 'No longer is it the spectre of Communism that is haunting Europe. . . . It is Communism in flesh and blood that is now stalking Europe.'[1]

Lenin was equally euphoric: in January 1918 he had said that 'for the success of Socialism in Russia a certain period of time of *at least a few months* is necessary'.[2] Before the Bolsheviks moved the capital back to Moscow Lenin had said over and over that 'within half a year Socialism would rule'.[3]

In founding the Third International in March 1919 he said the same :

Not only in Russia, but even in the most advanced capitalist countries of Europe as, for instance, in Germany, civil war has become a fact. . . . Revolution has begun and is gaining strength in all countries. . . . The Soviet system has won not merely in backward Russia, but even in Germany, the most developed country of Europe, and also in the oldest capitalist country – England.[4]

Yet after an abortive putsch or two, the 'uprisings' in the West fizzled out. The Bolsheviks, despite their conviction that Russia would soon be buttressed by advances that would place the vast resources of developed capitalism in the service of The Revolution, were ringed round by hostility. The mere founding of Socialist regimes elsewhere did not herald the collapse of capitalism; the Bolsheviks were alone.

They clung to hope for a time : the hopeless Berlin putsch of

January 1919, which had so inflamed Trotsky and which had been put down with such ease – its leaders, Rosa Luxemburg and Karl Liebknecht, were murdered – was misunderstood: in Bolshevik jargon it was only an 'episodic' setback.

But illusions were fading rapidly; the Third International, grotesquely enough, was founded just as they were coming to an end. By the summer of 1919 Bolshevik euphoria was evaporating: in Munich and Budapest miniature uprisings fizzled out as the proletarians of Berlin and Vienna looked on.

At a moment when the prospects were dimmest Trotsky's imagination soared aloft: he abruptly called for an 'Asian re-orientation' – on to India! He suggested to the Central Committee (5 August 1919) that the Politburo – still fighting for their lives in the Civil War – ought to set up:

An industrial base in the Urals (to obviate dependence on the Don Basin); a revolutionary academy beyond the Urals; the creation of military and political staffs in Asia to guide the struggle for The Revolution, with the help of technical personnel, including planners and linguists.

He thought this of particular interest to the Ukrainian Communists: with their country lost, they might move on to Siberia to promote The Revolution there.[5]

These imaginative suggestions of Trotsky's seemed at the time to highlight his powers of extrapolation, so to speak, as well as the breadth of his horizons. The reactions of the Politburo are harder to visualise.

Some experiments had been made in 'carrying abroad The Revolution on the bayonets of the Red Army', but except for Georgia all hopes were dashed.

There was an adventure in Poland, due largely to inadvertence: the breathing-spell granted the Bolsheviks at the end of 1919, with White resistance and foreign intervention ended and southern Russia and the Ukraine in their hands, was cut short by Pilsudski, the Polish dictator, who took advantage of the defeat of the White Guards to move his troops into the Ukraine at the beginning of March 1920.

Though Trotsky had been for flinging the Poles out with a 'resounding blow', he was vehemently opposed to pursuing them into Poland. He wanted to show that the Bolsheviks had no claims outside Russia and were a refulgent example to The Proletariat everywhere: his optimism about The Revolution made him pessimistic about the feasibility of forcing it down people's throats.

Lenin was greatly heartened by the Bolsheviks' success in retaking Kiev from the Poles (12 June 1920), only a few months after losing it. He thought it preposterous not to exploit a bona-fide victory; he was also convinced that the Polish 'workers and peasants' would acclaim the Red Army as liberators.

The idea was, of course, shared by all the Bolsheviks, including Trotsky. Lenin was enthralled by this euphoria not only about Poland, but about Germany too, in his eyes still the great hope of the movement despite all setbacks. He thought a Red Army holding Poland would be 'in contact' with Germany: there, he thought, The Masses were still effervescing: he wanted to 'probe Europe with the bayonet of the Red Army'. That was why he had wanted a 'furious speed-up' of the Polish campaign.

The Bolsheviks were now in the somewhat awkward position of fighting a national war, naturally disguised as a 'struggle against landlords and capitalists' who *happened* to be Polish.

Two army sections headed toward Warsaw in the north and Lvov in the south, in an advance authorised by a majority vote of the Politburo: Trotsky had been against it, but said nothing in public.

This was the limit of the Red Army thrust into Poland. The Second Congress of the Comintern (mid-July to 7 August 1920) was gripped by the tension of large-scale action; Lenin, standing before a big war map, gave impromptu daily comments to the foreign delegates.

With the Red Army standing outside Warsaw, Trotsky delivered to the Congress a Manifesto he had composed: since he said nothing about his opposition on principle to the Polish invasion it was assumed that he deserved most of the credit for an advance the delegates were delirious about. Devoting himself to the usual blistering attack on capitalist putrescence and democratic hypocrisy, Trotsky was acclaimed as conqueror of Poland.

Unfortunately the victory never took place; a few days later the Red Army, treated as an army of alien invaders, was routed at the Vistula. A peace establishing the border was signed that autumn.

In the case of Georgia, at least, the Red Army managed to pull off a victory.

Trotsky first heard in February 1921 that without informing him a section of the Red Army had simply broken the treaty signed during the Polish campaign with the Menshevik Government of Georgia and advanced into Georgia.

Stalin had persuaded the Politburo that the army was going in only to help a 'spontaneous' Bolshevik uprising – it would really have nothing to do. In the event it took the Red Army two weeks of bitter fighting to take the capital; its occupation was accompanied by great ferocity.

After a century of Russian oppression the Bolshevik reannexation of this small neighbour was to arouse a great deal of bitterness amongst Socialists (to say nothing about the Georgians).

Trotsky was already in a position he was to become familiar with. He could not, after all, disavow the Government; he was obliged to defend the regime at all costs, and to express that defence on the highest possible level of principle.

For Trotsky the isolation of Russia was even more painful than for most of the other Bolsheviks: the problem of navigation for a Socialist party running a country unfit for Socialism was utterly intractable.

Why *had* The Revolution broken out in the wrong place?

Rationalisation was, naturally, easy enough: in his *History* Trotsky was to say that 'capitalism had snapped in its weakest link'.

This simple phrase – disregarding as it does the elementary Marxist idea that The Revolution perforce breaks out, for Dialectical reasons, in the most *advanced* industrial country – was plainly contrived to accommodate, in theory, a fact of life : the Bolshevik Party, claiming to represent The Proletariat, had taken power.

With respect to The Revolution that was supposed to be ripening vigorously abroad, Trotsky was obliged to make another accommodation of fact : 'History,' he said, 'is unwinding her skein from the other end.'[6]

This meant merely that a fundamental prognosis of 'classical Marxism' had been destroyed by real events; it did not solve any problems.

The Bolshevik predicament was made acutely painful by the state of the country they were forced to cope with in isolation. Could Socialism be installed at all?

For all the discussion of the advisability of a Socialist party taking power in a backward rural country, the question of realising Socialism had never even been raised : *that* was considered sheer madness by all Marxists.

Here, of course, Marxism converges with horse-sense: if in the nature of things Socialism requires abundance, it is plain, from both a Marxist and a common-sense point of view, that only an advanced industrial economy can guarantee that. And the Bolsheviks, isolated in the wrong country to begin with, were now facing a desperate situation to boot: the disasters of the Civil War had compounded the economic ruin brought about by the First World War.

In short, rationalisation or not, the Bolsheviks had to confront the dilemma of *programme*.

Granted that Socialism could not be realised in Russia before it took over throughout the civilised world, could anything be done to enable the Bolshevik Party to wield power while clinging to its principles?

It was like squaring the circle: put very broadly, the Bolsheviks' alternatives were freedom or constraint: while waiting for Socialism to sweep industrial Europe, should the Bolshevik State manage the economy or install a free market? And if the State were to manage the economy, on behalf of just which elements of the people should it do the managing?

The Bolsheviks had inherited a frightful legacy.

By 1919 the Red Army had run out of most of its supplies; the industries still in the hands of the Bolsheviks could do practically nothing to make good the fuel shortages. Southern Russia, generally the source of fuel, metals and raw materials for the rest of the country, was held by the Bolsheviks rather spasmodically. By the time the Bolsheviks got back there in 1919 the industrial plant was paralysed: the coal mines of the Don Basin were inundated and many other industries simply wiped out. Transport was also crippled: railways everywhere had been exploded; the rolling stock had been neither renewed nor repaired since 1914. The same applied to agriculture: since the beginning of the First World War the peasants had been unable to replace their tools, to say nothing of the grinding up of the fields and the loss of horses to the rag-tag armies surging back and forth across the great plains.

It was just this economic ruin of the country as a whole that obliged the Bolsheviks, almost powerless, to rule with an iron fist. Industry, practically non-existent, was nationalised; private enterprise was banned. Food for the cities and the army was collected by drafted workers. Since there was no administrative machine to collect taxes endless quantities of paper money were ground out; it rapidly lost its value. The black market installed itself as a matter of course; workers would barter what they were producing.

A disaster was plainly looming; the peasants, receiving no pay of any kind for their produce, abandoned the non-existent market economy altogether and went back to subsistence farming, leaving less and less for the requisitioning squads to lay their hands on. Town dwellers streamed back to the land, where at least they could eat.

This dragooning of the population against a background of practically unrelieved misery was known as War Communism; having arisen on the basis of a pulverised national economy it resembled, as it were abstractly, the centralisation that was supposed to be a feature of Socialism *once established*; since the advent of Socialism was supposed to entail the obsolescence of the market economy, an affliction of capitalism, its suppression during the first few years of the Bolshevik regime was considered, by converse reasoning, to be the same somehow as the establishment of Socialism itself.

In theory, of course, the market economy was bound to decline because Socialism, based on a higher productivity, was supposed to elevate the economic level on a titanic scale.

Yet even when the market economy was abolished by force in circumstances that were the direct opposite of Marxist prescience, the Bolsheviks, including Lenin, thought that a beginning had nevertheless been made. They remained obsessed by War Communism.

Constraint had to be endlessly increased: the requisitioning squads had to be made effective by putting teeth into the controls. Peasants had to be forced to grow more; workers had to be forced to produce more.

From the very first moment of power Trotsky felt the bite of the Bolshevik dilemma more acutely, perhaps, than others in the regime, if only because of his addiction to sweeping, 'logical' solutions. In the logical cage constituted by the necessity of doing something that could not be done he flung himself back and forth in administrative systematisations.

He, too, had been wholeheartedly for War Communism, at least as the starting-point of a managed economy. He used all his ingenuity in contriving a whole schedule of controls: while still War Commissar he had, in mid-December 1919, proposed the comprehensive militarisation of labour, which at the time seemed a common-sense extrapolation of the solution of the Government's dilemma and also appropriate to the current mythology of War Communism.

But though Lenin thought the idea first-rate, since the War Commissariat, already handling so much manpower, could just as well apply its procedures to civilian life, the public uproar about it embarrassed the Bolshevik leadership.

At a big conference of trades-unions (12 January 1920) Trotsky made his 'case', based on rigorous 'logic' – *if* War Communism, then *this*. But his logic merely exacerbated the conference. In the event the soldiers were drafted into labour battalions before the civilians were drafted into the army. The armies working in industry and on the land worked under military discipline: reports were regularly sent in on progress along the various 'food fronts', 'mine fronts' and so on (this habit, to flourish luxuriantly in Soviet usage, was invented by Trotsky in this period of War Communism). Trotsky used all his rhetorical powers and his passion to glamorise what were, of course, depressing and generally intolerable makeshifts; he appealed to his audiences as though they were all as devoted as he.

Here is an instance of an Order to the Labour Armies:

> Display untiring energy in your work as if you were on the march or in battle.... Commanders and commissars are responsible for their detachments at work as in battle.... The political departments must cultivate the spirit of the worker in the soldier and preserve the soldier in the worker.... A deserter from labour is as contemptible and despicable as a deserter from the battlefield. Severe punishment to both! ... Begin and complete your work, wherever possible, to the sound of socialist hymns and songs. Your work is not slave labour but high service to the socialist fatherland.[7]

But when he saw that War Communism was merely a phrase, irrelevant to realities, Trotsky switched to the other extreme and rediscovered the market. In February 1920, after returning from a trip to the Urals in which he saw with his own eyes the incompetence of the regime, he proposed that War Communism be replaced by the open market, at least partially: the peasants were to be encouraged to grow surpluses and make a normal profit on their sale.

At this time his proposals were premature. When his proposals for a return to the market were rejected, he went back again to War Communism, in an attempt to make it work *regardless.*

While on his trip to the Urals he had been given another job – as it happened, his last major one. Lenin had asked him to take over the administration of the transport system : as head of this he integrated his ideas about the militarisation of labour into a general plan for laying the foundations of some sort of Socialism. These measures, all draconian, revolved around incentive wages, Socialist 'competition', harsh punishment (including concentration camps) for absenteeism, in fact, an application to Soviet conditions of the American pseudo-science of 'efficiency' expertise.

His view of the trades-unions was a simple, 'logical' extension of his attitude toward The Revolution and the workers' role within it. Since The Revolution had been made by the workers, and since the Soviet state was their handiwork, they were *really* working for themselves, and not for the old capitalist exploiters.

At the Ninth Congress Trotsky's rigorous ideas for speed-up, check-up, etc. were endorsed by a big majority, in the teeth of a vociferous minority that denounced his authoritarianism.

In defending his draconian measures, culminating as they now did in a systematic application of what was plainly forced labour, Trotsky made out a 'case' that led him very far along the path of defending, very nearly, forced labour as a matter of principle. By the use of Marxist historicism – one stage inevitably leading to another, 'higher' stage – he was able to demonstrate that at any given histori-cal stage forced labour had played a 'progressive' role :

> We are moving towards the type of labour that is socially regulated on the basis of an economic plan obligatory for the whole country, i.e., forced on every worker. This is the basis of socialism. . . . The militarisation of labour, in this fundamental sense I have indicated, is the inevitable basic method for the organisation of our labour forces. . . . Is it true that forced labour is always unproductive? . . . That is the most wretched, vulgar liberal prejudice; even chattel slavery was productive, it was higher than slave labour. . . . Forced labour did not grow out of feudal lords' ill-will. It was a progressive phenomenon.[8]

This controversy – fundamental, of course, in the genesis of the Soviet state – was overlaid for a time by the Polish war: it re-emerged in full force later.

Trotsky flung all his energies into the chaos of the railways. Told by the director of the transport system that only a miracle could prevent its extinction, he set to work to perform the miracle.

He demonstrated unusual executive ability. Martial law was declared; he harangued the workers in the repair shops; he got the rolling-stock rehabilitated and replaced. He treated the whole operation in the military manner, replacing trades-union leaders who baulked and forcing harsh remedies down the throats of the membership, disregarding superfluities like the vote. He was so successful that the time-table laid down for the recovery of the transport system was beaten; he was acclaimed for reviving the 'blood circulation of the economic organism'.

When the Polish war was over, however, he overreached himself by precisely the extremism his logic drove him to; he now menaced the workers of the other trades-unions with his treatment of the railways.

This time, however, he was thought to have gone 'too far': he was contradicted in public and forbidden to speak at all on this question of the interaction between the State and the trades-unions.

But though gagged in public, he defended his views with charac-teristic intransigence: as against the idea of allowing elected rep-resentatives a decisive voice, on which he was particularly un-yielding, he emphasised the need for a rational bureaucracy that would get things done. (He had expressed his views at the beginning of December 1920, at a closed meeting of the Central Transport Commission, formed by him in September in order to centralise his control of all transport.)

He thought, of course, that ultimately The Masses, too, would see that his policy was right, but in the present crisis of the regime there was simply no time for The Masses, if only because of their general backwardness, to catch up with this process and judge it democratically.

On this question of bureaucracy Trotsky had, so to speak, also come 'before his time': a large-scale centralisation of state controls was not yet envisaged. By solving a socio-economic problem in its abstract form Trotsky had in effect jumped the gun, just as he had been premature in sketching out the potentialities of the market before the Party executive was resigned to the hopelessness of War Communism. Hence he was disavowed by the Central Committee on this point, too.

He now had a deep, though inexpressible resentment against the

Politburo: he complained in private that though he had been told, when given his assignment, to be governed solely by considerations of efficiency and to disregard all 'democratic' scruples, the Central Committee was now behaving in public in a 'disloyal' way. *He* was bound to silence, but in public the Committee could pretend that they were in favour of democratic methods as against him.[9]

The economic problems of the regime, solved by constraint, were naturally all-pervasive.

By 1921 the Bolsheviks had blanketed the country with propaganda to such an extent that their still-legal rivals – Mensheviks and Social-Revolutionaries – were incapable of contesting the original act of genesis, the October putsch. This was due primarily to the success of Trotsky's original camouflage of the Bolshevik putsch with the mantle of the Soviets, which theoretically represented the bulk of the population. Thus even when the Bolshevik regime was criticised – as was possible for a year or two after the Civil War – the putsch itself had to be paid lip-service. The attitude that had to be displayed was an acceptance – in principle – of the 'conquests of October'.

At first, of course, the only 'conquest of October' was the brute fact of Bolshevik power, however disguised it might have been by the Soviet label.

After the Civil War the desperate plight of the country gave even the Bolsheviks' sympathisers endless material for resentment. Many strata of the population, whether or not they accepted 'October', were enraged about all aspects of life under the new regime.

In particular, the working class, many of whom must have hoped for something from 'October', were by 1921 in a mood, as Trotsky put it, of 'menacing discontent'.[10]

It was the 1920–21 disputes on the 'trades-union question' that highlighted the paramount enigma of Marxism: whom do leaders represent?

For Trotsky, and for Bolshevik theoreticians in general, the very notion that the working class might not sponsor The Revolution was as bizarre as it was indigestible. The theory of The Revolution, after all, implied that the working class was behind The Party that was performing on its behalf the indispensable function of carrying out a mere detail – the putsch. But what if the working class turned aside afterwards?

Trotsky had thought – on the level of theory – that in 1917 the Russian working class, modernised by Socialist thought and by technological advance, had got to the point of being able to overcome the historic lassitude of Russian society: this made it possible for the Bolsheviks no longer merely to 'represent' the working class, but to be an integral part of it.

It was, of course, just this myth – of the Party *being* the working class – that had borne the Bolsheviks aloft, at least as far as the consciences of the many individual idealists among them were concerned. And once the Party could not satisfy the material needs of the working class – to say nothing of the population as a whole! – it was bound to come up against the dilemma of authority, not mythologically, but concretely.

For the Bolsheviks, of course, there could be no question of abandoning their monopoly: that option had been rejected, on the constitutional level, by the very nature of the putsch and by the subsequent dispersal of the Constituent Assembly, and, on the practical level, by the repression of the 'bourgeois' parties and the *de facto* exclusion of the Mensheviks and Social-Revolutionaries, soon to be repressed.

Thus the raising of the trades-union question confronted the Party with what was for the idealists – especially for Trotsky – a crisis of conscience: the trades-union controversy masked the far more fundamental question: whom *did* the Bolsheviks represent?

The Party had never 'represented' the working class in a concrete, numerical sense at all; rather, it represented the Idea of The Proletariat; that is, it made claims *about* the working class. But though this obvious fact could be disguised as long as mere ideas were under discussion, the moment the 'Dictatorship of the Proletariat' became a fact the chasm between the two aspects of 'representation' yawned very wide.

As the flesh-and-blood proletarians increasingly contradicted any identification with the 'Dictatorship of the Proletariat', the Bolsheviks found themselves in the classic dilemma of minorities 'representing' majorities – they had to force the *workers* to accept the Workers' State.

During the trades-union disputes Trotsky, too, took it for granted that the Bolshevik State represented the Idea of The Proletariat: if flesh-and-blood workers demanded something contrary to the Idea, the solution was simple – they had to be reconciled to the Idea. In 1920–21 this boiled down to the claim that the State representing the workers would tell them what to do and how much to produce on behalf of the State. In short, it would discipline the workers, and concomitantly involve the trades-union leadership in the management of the national economy.

The 'Workers' Opposition' within the Party took the opposite view: it was the workers' own unions that should run the national economy.

When Trotsky, at the Tenth Congress in 1921, said it was 'illogical' for the trades-unions to interpose themselves between the workers and the Workers' State, the 'Workers' Opposition' simply accused the State of being no more than a branch of a new exploiting caste.

The Workers' Opposition really believed in the ideal state The Revolution was supposed to be leading to. They insisted that all workers' needs be met *at once*: complete equality of wages, the free provision of countless social services (free food, clothing, housing, medicine, travel and education).[11]

The logic of this claim was grounded in a corollary of the Bolshevik putsch.

The Revolution leading to Socialism was inevitable when economic relations under capitalism were ripe for the transition – when there was an economy of abundance. The Bolsheviks having made a Socialist revolution, the workers were entitled to the fruits of abundance.

This tidy syllogism could be shattered only by saying there was no abundance in sight – but that would imply something quite unthinkable – that The Revolution had come at the wrong time! i.e., the Bolsheviks had miscalculated and Socialism was currently impossible.

The clash of principle, or rather the clash of attitudes towards principle came to a head at the Tenth Party Congress in March 1921. Here is the kernel of Trotsky's views:

The Workers' Opposition has come out with dangerous slogans, fetichising the principles of democracy. They seem to have placed the workers' voting rights above the Party, as though the Party did not have the right to defend its dictatorship even if that dictatorship were to collide for a time with the transitory mood of the workers' democracy. . . . What is indispensable is the consciousness, so to speak, of the revolutionary historical birthright of the Party, which is obliged to maintain its dictatorship in spite of the temporary vacillations in the elemental stirrings of the masses, in spite of the temporary vacillations even in the workers' milieu. That consciousness is for us the indispensable cement. It is not on the formal principle of workers' democracy that the dictatorship is based at any given moment, though the workers' democracy is, of course, the only method by whose help the masses are increasingly drawn into political life.[12]

This style shows that Trotsky had long since abandoned an argument that might have seemed to compete, as it were, with 'bourgeois' democracy, as when he had said, for instance, that Soviet methods were superior because they were able to represent far more quickly and accurately changes in the views of the electorate; his defence of 'proletarian democracy' had now, in fact, tacitly shifted to a defence of the Idea: the Party is 'obliged to maintain its dictatorship . . . regardless of . . . vacillations even in the working class', which, are, of course, 'temporary'.

The little word 'even' sums up his hypostatisation of the Party as the instrument of historic change *regardless of results*.

But by putting the matter so bluntly – despite its fundamentally euphemistic style – Trotsky was as it were congealing the split between the Party and the population: he was giving it a 'principled' basis. He was, in short, being too outspoken.

Between the extremes of Trotsky and the Workers' Opposition there stood the main mass, led by Lenin himself, who were toiling to bridge the yawning chasm between the real situation of authority and its ideal pretensions.

Lenin thought that in view of the essential fluidity of the situation – things were, he hoped, changing – it was foolish to concretise matters so unmistakably. It was perfectly obvious, after all, that the Party had to smash resistance from any quarter whatsoever – why make it an aspect of *theory*?

Lenin thought that constraint, while no doubt inevitable, should come only after trying persuasion. The trades-unions should not be turned into *open* tools of the state, but should retain some autonomy, in order to correct the 'distortions' of bureaucracy, and enable the workers to defend themselves at least a little bit, especially since the Bolshevik State had to deal with the peasants, too. The whole administration, in fact, was bound to be chaotic for the time being.

Trotsky's point of view, with its straightforward espousal of a monolithic and unmasked dictatorship, was defeated at the Tenth Congress in favour of Lenin's somewhat gentler or, perhaps, more hypocritical formulation.

During the Tenth Congress the disciplinarian side of Trotsky's nature came to the fore even more explicitly than it had in his organisation of the railways and his handling of the trades-unions.

There was a sudden, major political explosion at the Kronstadt naval base, during the revolutionary period itself one of Trotsky's own most solid-seeming 'constituents' – an audience that had always been receptive to his eloquence and often taken his orders.

The crews on the warships had been inflamed by political passions, as it seemed, ever since the end of February 1921; the strikes in Petrograd had infected them with enthusiasm, and since they were, moreover, now being led by the anarchists – open enemies of the Bolshevik regime – this political inflammation was transformed into action.

At tempestuous meetings the sailors raised the issue of a new approach to the peasants and also, even more irritatingly for the Bolsheviks, of workers' freedom; moreover, they insisted on free elections to the Soviets. All this was put, in fact, as a call for a Third Revolution, aimed at the ousting of the Bolsheviks and the creation of a new democracy. A group of representatives sent by the sailors to Petrograd was simply arrested.

Kronstadt was gripped with a new slogan: 'Down with Bolshevik tyranny!' Some Bolshevik commissars at the base were gaoled; an anarchist committee took over the command of the fortress. The innocent sailors proclaimed new slogans – 'freedom and the brotherhood of nations'.[13] There was not much more 'formulation' than that!

The Bolsheviks reacted instantly: they put it about that the Kronstadt sailors were counter-revolutionaries who were, moreover, under the orders of a White Guard general. With large areas of the country still in turmoil even after the defeat of the White Guards, the revolt was plainly dangerous. Under the slogan of a 'new revolution' there had been uprisings in the Volga area, where the peasants were starving. Tukhachevsky, with twenty-seven rifle divisions, was sent to crush the revolt. Against a background of grinding poverty, the country was still seething.

Trotsky rushed to Kronstadt; on 5 March he gave the rebels an ultimatum – unconditional surrender: 'Only those who (surrender unconditionally) can count on the mercy of the Soviet Republic. Simultaneously with this warning I am issuing instructions . . . for the suppression of the mutiny by armed force. . . . This is the last warning.'[14]

The sailors, reinforced by some maverick Bolsheviks, disregarded the ultimatum.

The fortress obviously had to be taken while the ice in the bay was still solid. Shock troops were rushed off; they were joined by some delegates from the Tenth Congress, flabbergasted by this explosion amidst debates in which the very principle of Bolshevik sovereignty had already been challenged. The Workers' Opposition, though in theory close to the sailors, were also infuriated by their violent flouting of the Bolshevik Government.

As the picked troops, their uniforms covered by white sheets, moved on the fortress across the ice-covered bay, they were raked by fire; the ice collapsed and the Bolshevik forces perished by the score in the icy water under the fire of the naval guns. More columns were brought up; they were mowed down sliding and creeping over the treacherous ice.

The battle was more gruesome than any of the notoriously ferocious Civil War battles. The Bolsheviks, with heavy losses, reacted with fury: on 17 March, when they finally burst into the fortress, clambering up the walls after an all-night march across the iced-over bay in a tempest, they butchered the sailors.

A couple of weeks later Trotsky reviewed a victory parade: it was now possible for him to call the defeated and massacred sailors 'comrades' and to sympathise with the purity of their motives.

The rebellious sailors had naturally been presented to the Communist press at large as White Guard insurrectionists; a few months later foreign Communists who took it for granted that Kronstadt was just another episode in the blood-stained Civil War were surprised by the tenderness with which the Bolshevik leaders referred to the sailors (this did not, to be sure, help the sailors much!). This was the first time that bona-fide sympathisers, celebrated indeed, for their ardour, had been massacred.

As Victor Serge, a baffled sympathiser, said, it was 'Kronstadt' – a combination of bloodshed and mendacity – that institutionalised totalitarianism even before the word itself came into vogue.[15]

The slaughter of the Kronstadt rebels was an extreme instance of the dilemma Trotsky had been in ever since the October putsch or perhaps, more precisely, since the Civil War, when he could still, as the shield of The Revolution, act without inhibition.

He had been impaled on this dilemma just because he was plainly bound to do *something* despite his conviction that in a country like Russia Socialism was simply unthinkable. Though full of faith in the

imminence of another and more fruitful phase of The Revolution in
some industrial country outside Europe, he had to cope with the
practical problems of the Bolshevik Party.

When War Communism was finally dropped at the Tenth
Congress, at the very moment the Kronstadt sailors were under
attack, Lenin took up the concept outlined by Trotsky the year
before – a retreat to the open market: the New Economic Policy
(N.E.P.).

The year before Trotsky, casting about for a way out of War
Communism had proposed a market economy. When this was
rejected, he explored the possibilities of War Communism *regardless*: intensifying the militarisation of labour, he had come out for a
crushing control of the trades-unions. He had, in fact, formulated
the concept of a monolithic state.

It is true that he had done all this as it were in theory, as part of
his habit of driving propositions to their logical extremes, then
defending the abstract formulation by the full deployment of his
rhetorical abilities. Yet he was, after all, a topmost figure in the
Government; his theoretical excursions might have practical consequences.

Now, in March 1921, it was this disciplinary monolithic approach
of his, the 'logical' over-extension of War Communism, that was
shelved, at least for the time being. The internal economy was
liberalised by restoring the market, largely along the lines suggested
by Trotsky himself, although without giving him credit for it; during
the mixed economy inaugurated by the N.E.P. the militarisation of
labour was obviously out of the question.

The Bolshevik dilemma could not be surmounted so long as ideal
circumstances had not come into being – so long as there was no
economy of abundance. Trotsky adumbrated both the monolithic
state and the mixed economy – both in versions that represented
desperate attempts by ideology to accommodate reality. During the
first years after the Civil War, when Bolshevik hopes, and for that
matter all Russia seemed on the threshold of extinction, he had
boldly tried to think his way out of the impasse.

When it looked as though more force were needed, he had
pounced on the notion of ruthlessly disciplining the working class.
Then he swung to the contrary extreme. At a time when Lenin and
the Bolsheviks were still enthralled by the infantile illusions of War
Communism, Trotsky's common sense, geared to his gift for far-
reaching, clear-cut generalisations, came up with the adumbration

of a proto-N.E.P. Overruled by the Party, he then went back; he made his notion of control still *more so* : straitjacketing was to be total. But once again he could not take the Party with him, perhaps because these flights of logic were too 'abstract'.

His logic was couched in administrative terms – he was after all in the Government – but precisely because of its sweep the logic was irrelevant to any real administrative potentialities. Indeed, that he could not carry the Party at all meant, if nothing else, that his presentation was misdirected.

His abstract logic was really the antithesis of administrative logic, which must take account of possibilities and potentialities. Given a problem to solve in the abstract, Trotsky would create a structure to solve the abstract problem, but immediately collide with the resistance of the mass; then, to defend his abstract position, he would use his talents to create an army of counter-arguments. Officials would simply be infuriated by arguments that might have been 'unanswerable' but were felt to be dead wrong.

The Bolsheviks, still sheltered by the fanciful 'authority' of the Soviets, had not yet suppressed their fellow-Socialists (except in special circumstances). But with the restoration of a normal economy under the N.E.P., their enemies could obviously generalise their opposition. The Kronstadt rebellion had been welcomed, indeed, by all the opposition groups still at large. A revived bourgeoisie, now made likely by the N.E.P., plus an intelligentsia and countless peasants associated with it, would plainly bring about a radical social shift against the Bolsheviks. The revival of some form of anti-Bolshevik force loomed up nightmarishly.

In this way the economic liberalisation of the economy reinforced the political despotism entailed by the very concept of the Bolshevik monopoly.

Trotsky thought the prohibition on opposition parties was going to be ended the moment Soviet life had become more stable. This was obviously another way of saying the millennium; it begged the question by assuming that the Bolshevik dictatorship *could* bring about a stable situation while remaining a dictatorship.

In fact, the suppression overflowed practically immediately into the Bolshevik Party too; this was a consequence of the feeling in the Bolshevik Party that any dissent from the Bolsheviks' political monopoly was a natural prelude to counter-revolution. It was merely another way of saying that the Bolsheviks were opposed by the great bulk of society, and since they claimed to embody The Revolution anyone against them was *ipso facto* against The Revolution too.

This formula inevitably entailed the suppression of *all* opposition. The Bolsheviks' fears, explicitly expressed immediately after the Civil War, were to lead first to the suppression of factions, then to their expulsion, and finally to their physical annihilation.

That the Workers' Opposition could even come into existence was already a danger. If the Party could not tolerate opposition outside, how could it be allowed to break up into factions inside?

At the Tenth Congress of the Party in 1921 the first formal step, sponsored by Lenin himself, was taken to prohibit all forms of 'factionalism'. The motion did not put an interdiction on the expression of opinion, but on activity : discussion was to be open but *unorganised*. Dissidents were asked to express their ideas in the Bolshevik press openly. The main point, however, was unequivocal – *no organisation of opinion,* the indispensable prelude to political organisation in general.

Lenin put this in the form of a motion with a clause – kept secret for some time – giving the Central Committee the power to expel anyone, regardless of his prestige, who broke the ruling.

Trotsky wholeheartedly supported the motion. Though its immediate application was against the leadership of the Workers' Opposition, the motion had, of course, far greater potential scope.

Lenin's prohibition of factionalism might not chafe as long as differences of opinion remained minor : but like all such devices it could not on the one hand eliminate any really serious source of split, and on the other, for that very reason, fail to promote a monolithic tendency with the ruthlessness generated by the seriousness of the issue.

A couple of years later Trotsky's adherence to Lenin's outlawing of factions was to rebound.

War Communism had been such a fiasco that the Bolsheviks, with the N.E.P., leaned over backwards; for a short time they fawned on the middle-class elements now summoned to the rescue. To be sure, the theory behind the N.E.P. was a little vague : it had not yet been worked out and had to contend with the general chaos. The Bolsheviks were hoping that by creating a proper background for a later transition to Socialism that N.E.P. would foster peaceable competition between the state-owned and the private sectors of the economy.

The 'private sector' established its vitality immediately; its success coincided with a first-class crop, almost normal, that is, about seventy-five per cent of what it had been before the war. This ended the horrible famine following the Civil War and also the pestilence. It seemed as though the country, still overwhelmingly agricultural, might breathe again.

Yet the Bolsheviks had not, after all, taken power to demonstrate the virtues of capitalism. The success of the N.E.P., in fact, aroused instant alarm about the dangers of a too-successful capitalism, particularly since private enterprise in such conditions could not be expected to fulfil a major objective of the regime – the establishment of heavy industry, which was still paralysed. There was simply no steel, coal or machinery, a factor that in its turn paralysed any further growth of light industry. This reacted still further on the agricultural economy; there was no reason for the peasants to produce surpluses for towns that had no means of paying.

Against this general background Trotsky's status was swiftly being eroded, at first, imperceptibly, by a cluster of factors revolving around the isolation of the Bolsheviks, the consequent need for terror in self-defence, and the philosophical premises that gave the self-defence a theological form. Lenin's ban on 'factionalism' in 1921, endorsed at the time by Trotsky, was the specific device that was to finish him.

It was during Lenin's lifetime, after all, that the regime was given a monolithic structure, based on a homogeneous single party plus a bureaucracy and a political police.

When the ban on factionalism suppressed any possibility of genuine differences of opinion within the Party the effect on Trotsky was to be fatal, if only because he remained, essentially, a newcomer to the Party. As early as 1922 it was possible for a quite unknown Bolshevik (A. Mikoyan) to call Trotsky a 'man of the State but not of the Party'.

This remark was made in a discussion of Trotsky between Lenin and Zinoviev, in which they indicated some dissatisfaction about the fusion of the State and the Party; they thought it might be a good idea to keep the two bodies distinct.

Mikoyan's point – in this slightly humorous discussion – was that it was no surprise to hear an outsider like Trotsky say such things, but the *real* Bolsheviks?

This was, of course, a piece of sycophancy on Mikoyan's part (he was in his twenties); yet for him to single out Trotsky as an alien, *without any protest*, illustrates its acceptability.

Publicly what undid Trotsky at first was the hagiography instantaneously launched by the victorious Party. The moment the Bolshevik veterans were safely in power they had to start manufacturing their pasts for public consumption.

Quite unknown people were now ruling scores of millions of people. These plainly had to be told who was who; in the course of the lush pseudo-biographical literature that began to pour out it was only natural for these men, fondly re-assembling their pasts, to recall that Trotsky himself had not, after all, been in the Party very long.

Singing their own praises as Party-men, they could not, at this stage of the dictatorship, set themselves apart from their fellows as individual heroes; once the Party past as such was referred to it naturally stopped, with Trotsky, on the very threshold of his glorification in 1917. Most of Trotsky's career had been spent not only outside the Bolshevik Party but as an ally of the Mensheviks, who, having formally been members together with the Bolsheviks of the same party – until 1919 – were now bound to be their most vindictive enemies.

The polemical savagery of Marxist intercourse had been luxuriantly displayed in the remarkably virulent exchanges between Lenin and Trotsky for years before the putsch. Such savagery was so routine that it was, to some extent, a matter of style, but, more important, it also reflected the Marxist tendency, demonstrated par excellence in Marx himself, to *annihilate* opponents. It was quite easy to segregate murderous epithets exchanged by Lenin and Trotsky over many years.

These 'personal differences' had long since been overlaid by the success of the Party, the very success, to be sure, that now inspired the torrent of current hagiography. But since that same success had given rise to the immediate splitting up of the ruling coterie it made it all the easier to delve into the past for the background of the success, in which the apparent enmity, mutual abuse and so on of the two present leaders could be presented in a light that fitted into the movement that was to begin against Trotsky the moment his last major assignment – the Civil War – was over.

Against this background all Trotsky's personal qualities – his actual abilities – played against him. His brilliance as a speaker, his remarkably adroit and fertile pen, his 'logic', his polemical resourcefulness, his unflagging volubility on all subjects, some of them far beyond the orbit of even the top Party intellectuals, naturally set him apart from the grey mass that the Bolshevik leadership turned into within the first few years of power. These abilities, allied to his energy, his administrative zeal, his punctiliousness, his devotion as a taskmaster, which meant demanding from subordinates what he, a man of exceptional vigour, took for granted in himself, meant that his immediate associates and subordinates were a little uncomfortable just being near him.

But this psychological isolation of Trotsky was swiftly given a specific political expression: something took place that was so simple, so matter-of-fact, so altogether obvious that the failure of the Bolshevik leaders, including Trotsky, to foresee it has something almost miraculous about it.

It is a Marxist cliché that the 'economic base determines' the spiritual superstructure. Put so broadly, this is a mere banality – material factors are important, and people with material interests may be expected to defend them.

It was obvious, accordingly, that once the Bolsheviks took power they would cease being a group of intellectuals, agitators, conspirators and bohemians, twirling about in a world of their own outside settled society, and would instead become a corps of administrators – a bureaucracy.

They were wielding power, after all, in a big country; since they had, moreover, a rather broad-gauge approach to its problems they were bound to interfere with society more than other governments. There could be no question, after all, of their relinquishing state power.

All this together meant that they were going to become one more vested interest, indeed the Paramount Interest in the country, and since by taking power while retaining their Socialist doctrines they had made enemies of the bulk of the population, they would, as a Paramount Interest, have to govern by force.

Thus it was plain from the very outset that an administrative edifice based on force had to be erected – in short, an apparatus.

At the beginning of April 1922 Stalin was made General Secretary; the office was thought of as a mere executor of decisions reached on high. It was taken for granted that as General Secretary Stalin would crush any intra-Party opposition (as agreed to at the Tenth Party Congress).

But what it meant was something far more fundamental – the allocation of jobs, in other words the control of personnel, all of which was dependent on the office of the General Secretary.

The dependency of a given appointment on the central Secretariat in and for itself fortified the centralisation already inherent in the

Trotsky's second wife, Natalya

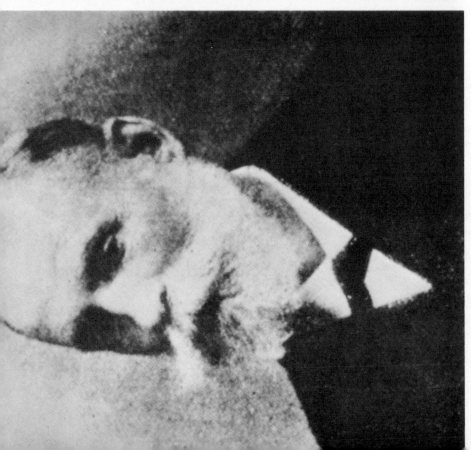

David Bronstein, Trotsky's father

Trotsky in his civil war train

Trotsky addressing Red soldiers in Moscow in 1917

Trotsky aged eighteen

Trotsky in his cell before the trial of the Soviet, 1906

Portrait from life, made at Brest Litovsk, January 1918 (artist Hans Stabcer)

Portrait on French passport in 1917

Trotsky

Trotsky in about 1920

Trotsky, Lenin and L. B. Kamenev during the Second Congress, 1920

Lenin and Trotsky in 1920

Natalya and Trotsky on arrival in Mexico

Trotsky dying

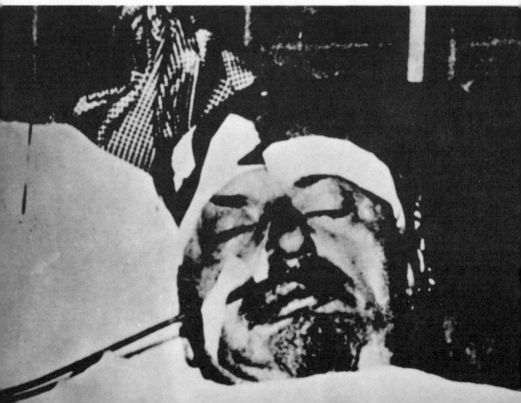

Bolshevik Party; an official in a remote area took it for granted that his appointment had nothing whatever to do with the area, but came directly from the centre – Stalin.

Regional and local Party secretaries thus came to constitute a dense network whose core was in the hands of the General Secretary in Moscow. This in itself was, of course, no more than a logical extension of the process whereby the Moscow apparatus already determined even policy. The network of Party secretaries throughout the country represented in miniature the hegemony of the apparatus over the country as a whole. The Bolshevik theory by which the Politburo was elected by a congress had never been anything more than a fiction to begin with; from now on the Politburo itself was increasingly to function through the Party secretaries. Even formally, for that matter, only they could nominate delegates.

This process, plainly fundamental, was never properly assessed by the top Bolsheviks, perhaps not, for a time, even by Stalin!

In April 1922, when Stalin was appointed General Secretary, Lenin tried to have Trotsky appointed a Vice-Premier, perhaps as a counterweight; Trotsky refused, apparently out of pique at being merely one of a number of Vice-Premiers. He also pointed out that Lenin was making him a mere figurehead, which was, of course, true; only a few months after becoming General Secretary Stalin was already in control of the government apparatus, in fact, substantially in power. This fundamental fact was not itself grasped for some time; in any case Stalin still lacked the crowning attribute of power – acknowledgment.

Trotsky's refusal to become a Vice-Premier meant that in effect he was excluding himself from any practical activity. He made himself a mere complainer: in the summer of 1922, for instance, when Lenin repeated his proposal that Trotsky become a Vice-Premier precisely in order to deal with the bureaucratic misuse of authority, Trotsky contented himself with pointing out what was, to be sure, obvious: that the root of evil lay in the Party structure. By limiting himself to pointing this out, he made it impossible for anything to be done about it. Since Lenin could not act on this complex matter alone he made what was in effect a psychological decision – he went on depending on Stalin's administrative expertise!

Something of the same sort happened on the 'nationalities question', on which Stalin, as a Georgian, was the Party expert.

Trotsky had been against the conquest of Georgia in 1921, though he defended it after the fact. But early in 1922 Stalin, as Commissar of Nationalities, repressed the Mensheviks, long since banned in Russia, in Georgia too. Trotsky now defended the Georgian Mensheviks, because of their greater 'representative' quality, though since repression was the rule in the Soviet Union it was hard to see why Georgia, once it was forcibly incorporated into the Soviet federation, should be an exception.

If one surveys Trotsky's behaviour immediately after the Civil War, it is plain that after beginning as a rigid champion of Bolshevik 'discipline' and authoritarianism, as part of the defence of The Revolution, he had imperceptibly switched over, within a year, to a defence of abstract ideas.

As early as the end of 1922 he had turned into a champion of principles whose sole interest for the apparatus, which was in the process of emerging as an organisation above principle, was as camouflage. In fact, as the Party began diverging from its visions under the pressure of the facts, Trotsky became the defender of the Party's ideals *against the Party.*

It was only in 1922 that Trotsky became aware of the degree to which a cleavage in the Government, obscured to some extent by Lenin's prestige, had taken shape.

It was not a real cleavage, but a progressive isolation of Trotsky. The clash of personalities was bound to become, with the administrative articulation of the regime as a whole, a competition between factions.

And just this was the nub of the matter – Trotsky had no faction! Though prominent, he was no longer powerful.

Some of his opinions, to be sure, attracted others; he had sympathisers. But he was to prove entirely incapable of organising his partisans into an effective force within the government structure.

This was far from evident, at least for a while. Trotsky could still express himself; he was still a member of the Politburo; Lenin was still the paramount authority. True relationships, defined by the evolving Party structure, were still masked. Helpless within that structure, Trotsky depended, in fact, on Lenin's favour; but as Lenin's health began to fail – he had his first stroke in May 1922 – Trotsky began plummeting to disaster.

The Party-State apparatus, rapidly solidifying in Stalin's embrace, was creating its own momentum : this fundamental process no doubt underlay a poignant metaphor coined by Lenin at the Eleventh Party Congress in 1922 – the strange feeling he had at the helm of the Soviet Government like that of a driver who suddenly notices that his 'machine has got out of control'.

Trotsky records a conversation with Lenin in early December 1922. Informally and privately, Lenin proposed to him once again that he become one of his deputies. Trotsky pointed out that in all fields of activity the difficulties stemmed from the apparatus itself, whereupon Lenin said: 'Yes, our bureaucratism is monstrous,' and went on to suggest, using an old remark of Trotsky's, that Trotsky 'shake up' the apparatus. Trotsky said he meant not only the State apparatus, but that of the Party, too, since the whole trouble lay in the interlocking of the two apparatuses and the 'mutual shielding' of the 'influential groups clustering around the hierarchy of Party secretaries'.

Summing this up, Lenin then said that Trotsky meant, accordingly, to wage a 'struggle' against the Organisational Bureau of the Central Committee – that is, against Stalin's office. Trotsky, who 'burst out laughing at the unexpectedness' of this, agreed, whereupon Lenin offered him a 'bloc' against 'bureaucratism in general and against the Organisational Bureau in particular'.

In his own account Trotsky ends this interchange with an urbane acceptance: 'With a good man it is flattering to form a good bloc.'[16]

Lenin was doubtless preoccupied by 'bureaucratism' toward the end of his short life. A few days after this conversation with Trotsky he had another stroke; a little later, on 23 and 25 December 1922, he communicated his preoccupations in a letter to his followers. It was a kind of Testament; though quite meaningless judicially, of course, it was given great weight by his unique authority.

The Testament gave a streamlined sketch of great issues. It singled out the main traits of the six men at the apex of the Party; within the framework of the polarisation that was taking place between Trotsky and Stalin, the cardinal point of the Testament was Lenin's assessment of these two.

He called them 'the two most eminent leaders of the present Central Committee' and intimated that a split between them was a cardinal danger. He regarded Trotsky as the 'ablest' – when the document was eventually published, very much later, the word for 'able' was put into all authorised Soviet translations as 'cleverest'! – and said that the Party was not to hold against him his previous non- or anti-Bolshevism. He criticised Trotsky's attraction to the 'purely administrative aspect of affairs', his 'excessive self-confidence', and his 'individualism' vis-à-vis the Central Committee.

His comments on Stalin were brief; they sounded a little trivial: 'Having become General Secretary, Stalin has concentrated immeasurable power in his hands; I am not sure that he will always know how to use that power with sufficient caution.'

This curiously barren criticism was supplemented a week and a half later – on 4 January 1923 – by a rather strong postscript about Stalin's 'rudeness', which was 'becoming unbearable in the office of the General Secretary'; Lenin advised the Party to 'remove Stalin' and replace him with 'another man ... more patient, more loyal, more polite, more attentive to comrades, less capricious.

He indicated that if this were not done the clash between Stalin and Trotsky would become still more embittered and be very dangerous for the Party.

A cursory glance is enough to indicate the contradictions of the Testament; Lenin's mind seems to have been already clouded. His soul-searchings with respect to the very validity of the Bolshevik enterprise no doubt inhibited him.

On what basis, after all, could he have mentioned Stalin and Trotsky as the 'two most eminent men' of the Central Committee and counterposed them? Clearly – since it could hardly be a question of personal *talents*! – it was because of the 'immeasurable power' in Stalin's hands, i.e., a direct reference to the apparatus Stalin by now had a stranglehold on.

Thus it was not at all a mere clash of personalities, but a fundamental phase in the evolution of the Party.

Lenin's confusion on this point is illuminating. He mentions Trotsky's foible for the 'administrative aspect of affairs'. This must refer to Trotsky's overpunctiliousness, indeed pedantry in superficial things and plainly *is* a personality trait; the status of Stalin, who had transformed his own 'administrative' interest into a vast apparatus capable of circumventing the Politburo in countless matters, is, equally plainly, a different matter entirely.

It seems clear that Lenin himself could not quite digest what was happening – the transformation of people into 'forces'!

This may account for the curiously wishy-washy form of the Testament.

In so far as it was a summation of character it was natural for Lenin to put it forth rather diffidently and inconclusively, hoping that his moral authority would be decisive.

But if Stalin's power really was 'immeasurable' how could Lenin's thumb-nail character sketches have had any effect?

Lenin must have been too ill to envisage playing a role in the clash between the two men if that clash were not temperamental friction but a fundamental conflict; hence, with a quite uncharacteristic weakness due to illness and depression, he put it as though it were a personal clash – it was, of course, that *too*! – and gave gentle advice.

The blurring of Lenin's normally direct mind is indicated – a little ironically – in his summation of Bukharin, 'the favourite of the Party' and its most 'outstanding theoretician', who was at the same time, however, rather 'scholastic' and lacked a real 'grasp of the Dialectic'.

The Dialectic – the crown of Marxism! Its essence!

Years later Stalin, undoing Bukharin, was to cite this remark. It was to flabbergast his innocent audience: how *could* the greatest theoretician of the Party not grasp the Dialectic!

Lenin's 'succession' was, of course, quite unprovided for, just as his authority had no formal warrant.

By December 1922 his death seemed fairly imminent; the following month, in any case, he could not attend the Politburo meetings. As Lenin's presence began to fade, Trotsky found himself confronting an altogether alien constellation: it was not one he could cope with.

Obviously, Stalin now had to get the Politburo to sanction the *de facto* authority he was already wielding as General Secretary; the nominal, 'constitutional' power was naturally held by the Politburo. He allied himself with two of Lenin's oldest henchmen – Zinoviev and Kamenev. It was an alliance of admirable simplicity: it consisted merely of an agreement to vote in unison.

Without Lenin the Politburo consisted of half a dozen people: if only one other person voted with the Trio they would have their way; since the others had no such alliance there was no problem. A further charm of the relationship was that it remained secret for some time, until in fact the Trio itself broke up!

It was aimed, of course, against Trotsky, still considered the most eminent individual in the Party after Lenin, with what seemed to be a formidable following among The Masses, including the rank-and-file of the Party, workmen, soldiers, students.

Zinoviev was essentially an orator and agitator, with a virtuosity considered second only to Trotsky's and the idol of countless mass meetings. But he was not in any sense able or energetic; in addition he was well known to be somewhat vacillating, indeed cowardly in times of crisis.

Kamenev, rather colourless, was married to Trotsky's younger sister Olga: he was considered a conscientious and intelligent worker, very cultivated and far less volatile than Zinoviev. He had a reputation for moderation.

The two men were regarded as political twins, bound together by complementary qualities.

The secret caucus was headed, ostensibly, by Zinoviev, with Kamenev as his ally and Stalin, at first, as a junior. Trotsky was not only outvoted, but if only because of his celebrity, his gifts, and his relentless volubility was now bound to be radically undermined.

From the very beginning Trotsky was checkmated by this caucus. None of the Politburo members was *bound* to him in any way; he could sway them only by argumentation, at which his skill, unfortunately, often cut both ways – skilful arguments that cannot be accepted are bound to be irritating.

With his voting arrangement Stalin could emerge at once as Trotsky's chief opponent, as soon as the imminence of Lenin's death was taken for granted and Lenin himself did not appear at the meetings.

Perhaps the most curious psychological aspect of this is Trotsky's unawareness of the caucus. It marked the beginning of his exclusion from the centres of power. At a time when he thought he was engaged in a bona-fide, though unfortunately unsuccessful attempt to sway the opinion of his colleagues within the Politburo, he was in fact quite helpless. Within the tiny circle of the Politburo and *a fortiori* within the Party apparatus, he had no points of support beyond his personal talents – none of them now functioning relevantly.

In the course of 1923 it became plain that Stalin was master of the overwhelmingly important apparatus, though even then the pre-dilection of the Bolshevik intellectuals, primarily Trotsky, Zinoviev, and Kamenev, for 'ideas' made them systematically underestimate his role.

An ex-secretary of Stalin's (Bajanov) recalls his own amazement that intelligent men like Zinoviev seemed to be totally indifferent to a fact that Bajanov himself thought interesting – that Stalin was appointing all top personnel throughout the country.[17]

In any case, since Trotsky neither suspected the existence of the caucus nor even attempted to create a grouping of his own, in the

Politburo or elsewhere, he was reduced to defending his 'position' merely in debates – in debates, moreover, that took place amidst the handful of men running the country. Since his ideas, moreover, were predicated on a broader, and in the event unrealistic perspective of The Revolution, it was simply impossible for him to persuade them.

Hence, with no faction, Trotsky was obliged to rely on appealing to the Trio, secretly bound to each other, to endorse more generalities – intra-Party democracy, etc. – while remaining incapable of influencing their behaviour.

Thus it was child's play for even Stalin, considered a little inarticulate, to attack Trotsky quite straightforwardly. Trotsky in his more or less sincere articles and speeches, was giving a more or less honest appraisal of the terrible mess the country was in; Stalin could 'charge' him with pessimism, defeatism and so on. He would even point to Trotsky's total inability to manoeuvre as showing a lust for power! When Trotsky refused to become one of Lenin's deputies it was easy to claim that it was his overweening ambition that made the job seem inadequate.

Whenever a proposal made by Lenin – who while incapacitated was still active – diverged from Trotsky's specific views, Stalin and his allies easily spread rumours among the Party strata just below the Politburo to the effect that Trotsky was working *against* Lenin. When Trotsky threatened to expose this at the forthcoming Twelfth Congress, in April 1923, Stalin had plenty of time to prepare himself for a public move that was an idle threat, in any case, since Trotsky was really depending on Lenin's recovery.

Lenin, though very ill, was now determined to crush Stalin on the 'nationalities question', on the basis of Stalin's highhandedness in Georgia.

On 5 March 1923 Lenin got in touch with Trotsky for the first time since offering him the 'bloc' in December 1922. Trotsky realised he was even angrier about Stalin's conduct than he had thought; Lenin actually said he was preparing a 'bombshell' against Stalin at the April Congress; he implored Trotsky to say nothing about the bombshell, and to reject any 'rotten compromise'. Kamenev told Trotsky, in addition, that because of Stalin's coarse behaviour toward Lenin's wife – who had been gathering some data about the Georgian background of the 'nationalities question' – Lenin had written Stalin a letter 'breaking off all personal relations with him'.[18] Lenin's wife told Kamenev, in fact, that Lenin was going to 'crush Stalin politically'.

When Kamenev came to see Trotsky on 6 March with an offer of peace,[19] Trotsky said he would be satisfied with a mere statement from Stalin, inserted into a report to the Congress, to the effect that the Party was against the old-fashioned idea of 'Great Russian chauvinism', plus an apology to Krupskaya, and a promise of good behaviour. All would then be well.

Trotsky's gallantry was instantly accepted by Stalin, now facing a serious public attack from Lenin. But just at this point, a month before the April Congress, Lenin had another stroke: until his death in January 1924 he was to be nearly always mute and generally paralysed.

Trotsky had relied on Lenin completely: he assumed that even if Lenin died he could always disclose Lenin's true views in the form of notes in Lenin's hand. Hence, as Stalin suggested, since Trotsky's 'conditions' for a peace had been accepted, why bother telling the Congress about the differences of opinion at all? Why not have the Politburo decide on how to present it?

In a word, why fight me when you might win!

This hushing-up was so successful that Lenin's views of the treatment of the ethnic minorities in the Soviet Union were not, in fact, to be published until 1956.[20] Thus it was possible for the Politburo to suppress important views of its founder during his lifetime.

At the Twelfth Congress itself it was easy for Stalin to trip Trotsky up still further: he proposed that as the 'most popular member of the Central Committee' Trotsky must as a matter of course make the policy speech hitherto given by Lenin. Trotsky declined, since it might look as though he were taking Lenin's place, and said Stalin could give the speech as General Secretary, that is, not in a personal capacity. In his turn Stalin said that would be misunderstood; playing his own modest role, he put Trotsky in the position of declining something quite appropriate.

The Congress still looked fairly open: delegates were not yet handpicked. Trotsky came into his own again as a public figure. Throughout the country Party cells, trades-unions, workers' and students' groups and so on cabled greetings: almost every message mentioned Lenin and Trotsky, disregarding the others. Zinoviev's reputation in the provinces was fading; Kamenev had never been a glamorous figure: Stalin was still unknown outside Party circles.

Trotsky played a magnanimous role in suppressing any suggestion of friction between the Politburo members: Lenin was not there with his 'bombshell'; Trotsky remained well out of the way.

This did not prevent the Trio from circulating rumours about him, his insatiable ambition, about his desire, secret perhaps but unmistakable, to become a Bonaparte.[21]

It would almost seem as though the Trio themselves, in spite of their more practical attitude, still had a slight hangover of 'ideas'! They thought Trotsky's public prestige might still be turned to his partisan advantage. It was his very prominence, in fact, easily presentable as a danger, that facilitated his undoing.

The cult of Lenin, the cornerstone of Soviet orthodoxy to this day, was established at this Twelfth Congress. It was to have its first tactical application in the elimination of Trotsky.

The Trio's appeal to the Congress was simple: they were the humble disciples of the matchless Lenin; Trotsky, a newcomer, had private ambitions. Thus the homage paid the dying Leader was institutionalised and aimed, so to speak, at Trotsky.

With Trotsky standing diffidently to one side, Stalin, Zinoviev and Kamenev dominated the Congress. The first actually controlled the structure of the Party, the other two served as window-dressing – enunciating what had to be enunciated!

The very fact of Stalin's running the machine gained him some approval. Zinoviev, whose prestige was declining rapidly, had attracted many of the critical shafts loosed at the Congress. Thus, in relationship to Stalin, humble Party servant, Zinoviev was already slipping!

The suppression of the 'Georgian question' played into Stalin's hands in another way.

The Georgians had been hoping for some recognition of their special rights as an ethnic minority; at the Congress Stalin, who had been responsible for the harsh treatment of the non-Russian nationalities, came out in public *against* it; as part of his 'compromise' with Trotsky he had naturally included some formal condemnation of Great Russian high-handedness. The Georgians were baffled by this rhetorical expression of support at a moment when nothing was, in fact, being done for them. Lenin's notes on this matter were known to exist, but the Politburo were all close-mouthed, from the Georgians' point of view quite incomprehensibly.

Bukharin, to be sure, attacked Stalin's 'defence' of the ethnic minorities as mere hypocrisy, but the effect was pathetic. The Congress, which represented, after all, the Party elite, was already committed to Bolshevik centralisation; Stalin's hypocrisy was swallowed as lip-service to an ideal outmoded by events. Bukharin's remarks met with stony indifference.

Thus there was already a dovetailing between the mood of the Party elite and the aims of the apparatus. With Trotsky playing into his hands Stalin found it a simple matter to dismiss the notion of any disagreement with Lenin and to attack all 'deviators'.

This Congress – Trotsky's first open clash with factional intrigue – created a pattern. It illustrated the primary reasons for the decline of his influence, a decline that within the Party was almost instantaneous and was masked only by the persistence of his public celebrity, which meant that the victors in the Party skirmishes, while handling him, in fact, with great ease, merely had to take pains to keep up appearances.

In spite of Lenin's warning Trotsky had struck a 'rotten compromise' with Stalin: Trotsky was allowed to make a major speech as official Politburo spokesman on a focal issue of the regime – centralised economic planning.

His views on this have some historical interest; he projected perspectives for a long time ahead. In the *current* situation, however, it merely emphasised his isolation.

To put economic planning in the right historical perspective, Trotsky had to elaborate the idea of 'primitive Socialist accumulation'; this was so far beyond the grasp of his audience, and moreover so harsh a prospect, that it put him in the most depressing light.

In Soviet circumstances 'primitive Socialist accumulation' simply meant squeezing the workers. With his characteristic straightforwardness, Trotsky put this in such brutally explicit terms that it chilled his audience; at the same time its lofty intellectual framework made it unintelligible. His remark, for instance, that 'there may be moments when the Government pays you no wages, or when it pays you only half, and when you, the worker, have to advance (the other half) to the state',[22] was impossible for a mass audience to swallow.

Just as his central theme was bound to seem alarming to the workers, so it did to the peasants. A moment's thought would indicate that squeezing the workers implied a further squeeze on the peasants, to make them go on producing for the towns.

Most important of all, Trotsky exasperated the elite, the people actually managing the economy. It was so easy to point out shortcomings, blunders, and the general inefficiency of the infant Soviet economy that when this was done within the framework of a broad

general scheme based on a philosophical concept, the effect –
rhetorically – was crushing. It infuriated the administrators by
sounding like a personal attack while reinforcing the view that
Trotsky was, after all, a perfectionist doctrinaire.

In this way Trotsky buttressed his failure as a factional fighter by
a failure as a demagogue; he had managed to frustrate even the
people he supported.

He had failed to defend Lenin's position. He had been silent when
it came to defending in public the Georgians and the Ukrainians; he
had defended them in the privacy of the Politburo, where he was
already outmanoeuvred. He had not supported even the fundamental demand for intra-Party freedom; above all, he had sponsored
– to a public incapable of understanding its 'philosophic' scope – the
idea of planning before winning any support for it from the Party
summits.

Trotsky had, in fact, cleared the way for his own elimination.
When the Central Committee, enlarged by the Twelfth Congress, put
Stalin back as General Secretary – since he controlled it this was no
surprise! – without Trotsky, despite his knowledge of Lenin's mind,
even mentioning Stalin's replacement, it was a simple matter for
Stalin to carry still further the potency of his office. He now started
getting rid of all members of the apparatus both in the centre and in
the hinterland who might be sympathetic to Trotsky. As vacancies
cropped up he filled them with people beholden to him; he did all
this very modestly, justifying each change on its merits. Lenin had
already laid it down that seniority was a criterion; this in itself
benefited the Party veterans for whom Trotsky remained a newcomer.

This was the year that Stalin, hitherto merely very influential
within the Party, now became its boss.

The Party was getting more and more tense because of the
increasingly gloomy international scene: since The Revolution
stubbornly kept hanging fire, Bolshevik foreign policy took on
special importance.

The Comintern was pathetically feeble; the tiny Communist
Parties in Europe had no impact on The Proletariat; they were
plainly incapable of even contemplating an attack on The Bourgeoisie, which seemed to have recovered rather elastically from the
First World War. On the other hand, local leaders kept hoping; the
Comintern had to make them accommodate themselves to the new
situation.

Meanwhile a different set of tactics had to be devised, to enable the Communist Parties to manoeuvre in the 'bourgeois parliamentary' world without losing their revolutionary purposefulness.

It boiled down to the tactic of the 'united front', elaborated by Trotsky and Lenin. This implied the possibility of collaboration between the still feeble Communist Parties with the vastly larger Social-Democratic Parties on the basis of day-to-day workers' demands. The Communists were, of course, to agitate for piecemeal reforms only in the perspective of The Revolution, in contrast with the acceptance of the parliamentary system by the Social-Democrats, but within that narrow framework they could nevertheless work together quite peaceably – in theory. For the time being 'ultra-radicalism' was out of fashion

Helpless within the Party, Trotsky was in a state of exasperation. An outbreak of effervescence in Germany abruptly seemed to offer him a way out of his impasse.

When Zinoviev, for instance, suggested placing Stalin on the Military Revolutionary Council still headed by Trotsky, the latter was so upset he threatened to resign at once from *everything* – the War Commissariat, the Council, the Central Committee, and the Politburo. He wanted to be despatched to Germany as a simple 'soldier of The Revolution'.

This theatrical, or perhaps, romantic proposal – so plainly a desperate escape from Trotsky's *real* problems – was reduced to an absurdity. Zinoviev, President of the Comintern, said it would be still better if *he* went to Germany as a 'soldier of the revolution'. Then Stalin spoke up, in his usual sensible style, saying the loss of either one of these distinguished popular members of the Politburo was out of the question, nor could Trotsky leave the War Commissariat and the Central Committee, which obviously would cause a sensation.

The temperature in the Politburo was feverish; Trotsky lost control of himself:

The scene took place in the Throne room, the door to which is huge and massive. Trotsky pulled it with all his strength, but the heavy panels opened only with killing slowness. Trotsky should have given up immediately. . . . There are some doors that can't be banged. But in his fury he didn't notice this, and he made one more effort, a violent one, to close it. But the door, alas! was as killingly slow to close as it was to open. Thus, instead of a moving gesture pointing up an historic rupture, one saw a puny, helpless figure struggling vainly to close a door.[23]

What was most striking about the crumbling of Trotsky's position was the contrast between his sustained passivity and the abundance of his opportunities.

The Party was simmering; people could still speak up. When some forty-six eminent Party members, many of them Trotsky's sympathisers, called for freedom of speech within the Party, Trotsky was inevitably involved. Yet having bound himself not to attack the Trio, all he could do, while standing off to one side during the mutiny of 'the Forty-Six', was to expostulate.

Though incapacitated by recurrent fevers, he became willy-nilly the natural centre of this ferment, without leading it.

The apparatus was by now so powerful that it was possible for the Trio to absorb, as it were, the protests of the Forty-Six and Trotsky's own critical attitude in a quite simple way – by agreeing with them! In a proclamation (*The New Course*) trumpeting a return to intra-Party democracy, they merely duplicated the protests of the Forty-Six and presented the proclamation to Trotsky to sign. He naturally did so, since in spite of being aware that such verbal assurances were worthless he could not say so in public.

His idea of campaigning against the Trio boiled down to the issuance of a series of rational arguments presented *to an amorphous audience*; hence he had no riposte whenever he was agreed with *in words*. Without organised support he could not accommodate the plain fact that the Trio manipulating the administration might assent to something in words and then simply fail to translate them into deeds.

Thus, in signing the Trio's *New Course*, he once again sacrificed his effectiveness as speaker and writer. Since the proclamation was put forth in the name of the Politburo, which he was still a member of, he could not speak against them. He was deprived of any tactical leverage by accepting the slogan of Party unity at the very moment it was being used to disembowel him politically.

By the beginning of December 1923 it was all over: the Politburo unanimously passed a resolution[24] guaranteeing everything Trotsky wanted: all he had managed to do, as a condition for his signing it, was to insert a few amendments making *clear* what was at issue. At that point, of course, there was no reason for the Trio not to include those too!

By now the clamour against Trotsky had a peculiarly vindictive quality, quite nightmarish and to him utterly incomprehensible. He was still in the position of having to defend his arguments, but there was no way for his articles, for instance in the series collected under the title of *The New Course*, to drown out the din manufactured by the government media.

His recurrent fever obliged the Politburo to meet in his little apartment. Natalya's *Diaries* record the emotional flavour of the set-to – *within* the Politburo!

He was alone, ill, and he had to fight them all. Because of his illness the meetings were held in our apartment; I would sit in the adjoining bedroom and listen to his speeches. He spoke with his whole being; it seemed as though with every such speech he lost some of his strength – he spoke to them with so much 'blood'. And in reply I heard cold, indifferent answers. Everything, after all, had been decided in advance: why should they get excited? Each time, after such a meeting, L.D.'s temperature jumped up, he would come out of his study soaked to the bone, get undressed and go to bed. His linen and clothing had to be dried as though he had been drenched in a rain-storm. At that time the meetings took place often, in L.D.'s room, with the faded old carpet, which appeared in my dreams night after night in the shape of a live panther: the daytime meetings became nightmares.[25]

Trotsky gives his own account:

It was a real conspiracy. A secret political bureau of seven was formed; it comprised all . . . the official Politburo except me . . . All questions were prejudged in this secret centre, where the members were bound by mutual vows. They bound themselves not to attack each other and at the same time to seek opportunities to come out against me. There were similar centres in the local organisations, and they were connected with the Moscow 'seven' by strict discipline. . . . Special codes were used, It was a well-organised illegal group within the Party, directed initially against one man. Responsible functionaries . . . were systematically selected according to a single criterion: Against Trotsky. During the prolonged 'interregnum' created by Lenin's illness this work was carried on tirelessly but still warily in a camouflaged way, so that if Lenin recovered the mined bridges could be preserved intact. The conspirators acted by hints. Candidates for one job or another had to guess what was required of them. Those who 'guessed' went up. In this way a special kind of careerism was developed that later on was openly called 'anti-Trotskyism'.[26]

'A real conspiracy', indeed. . . .

Thus, by 1923, the last year of Lenin's life, the harmony of the Bolshevik nucleus was destroyed.

As Lenin sank into his terminal illness, the Party was not so much sundered as absorbed by Stalin's office. Though Trotsky thought it an adequate description to say that the Trio were 'struggling with the Party', the reality was far simpler – they were shaking Trotsky out.

1923 marked the turning point in Trotsky's career. It was the watershed between Trotsky the eminent Soviet statesman with a great past, who might have had differences with other eminent leaders, and Trotsky the man who was *in essence* an alien. His reputation was pulped. Because of the change in tone this implied, the campaign against Trotsky in 1923 marked the beginning of the extinction of *all* opposition.

During this crucial period Trotsky did not recover from his debilitating illness. At the end of 1923, while the unprecedentedly venomous campaign against him and his sympathisers was at its peak, his health grew still worse. He was in a state of perpetual exhaustion, with a persistent low fever; he could not work anywhere near his usual pace, had no appetite, and was losing weight. He was thus in a state of both high tension and lethargy.

When his doctors advised him to rest in the warmer climate of the Caucasian Riviera, he pounced on the occasion. The decision was momentous, since the Thirteenth Party conference was scheduled for 16 January 1924. Had Trotsky been in better health, he might have remained to appear there, since practically the whole Conference was devoted to smashing him.

Nothing could be done. A few of his sympathisers – Pyatakov, Preobrazhensky, V. Smirnov, Radek – presented their 'case': the vast entourage now managed by the Trio responded with unheard of virulence. Trotsky was roundly condemned, together with the Forty-Six, on charges of 'petty-bourgeois deviation from Leninism'.

Trotsky, apathetic and remote, did not bother waiting for the results; on 18 January 1924 he started off south, moving very slowly;

a few days later, while his train was in Tiflis, he got a wire from Stalin that Lenin was dead.

Though more or less expected, the news stunned him. Aside from personal feeling, his future was at stake: he had been consoling himself with the hope that Lenin's support would enable him to evade the tightening pressure of the Party apparatus. According to Lenin's widow, 'on learning of his death Trotsky fainted and did not recover for two hours'.[27]

The immediate question was, of course, whether he should go back to Moscow for the funeral – plainly a state occasion of the most formidable kind. Adept at ceremonial, the Bolsheviks could not fail to do something stupendous to commemorate the death of the Founding Father: in any case the question of the succession was now vital.

Trotsky sent the Kremlin a coded wire; he was told at once that since the funeral would take place before he could possibly get back he should simply go on to his treatment. In fact, he could easily have got there in time; the funeral was postponed. But what was significant was the source of the information – Stalin!

And what was no doubt still more significant was that in relating the incident years later – in 1929 – Trotsky said: 'Incredible as it may appear, I was even deceived about the date of the funeral. The conspirators surmised correctly that I would never think of verifying it.' This after more than a year of mounting, soul-destroying tension.

Listless, feverish, Trotsky lingered on in the peaceful sunshine of the Caucasus until the springtime.

In the absence of any real data, it would no doubt be presumptuous to psychologise Trotsky's chronic, low-key illness, yet the temptation is irresistible. In *My Life* he refers to it as cropping up repeatedly during emotional crises. Whatever its somatic sources, it manifestly incapacitated him in the conflict he found himself immersed in. It will be worth discussing after that conflict ended.

The question of Lenin's Testament emerged in May, shortly after Trotsky came back to Moscow.

Lenin's Testament was now his only credential. Though evasive, understated, and ambiguous, it proposed something that Lenin's prestige made quite crushing – the ousting of Stalin.

The Testament was read aloud by Kamenev to the Central Committee of the Thirteenth Congress (at the end of May 1924); the effect was shattering. Stalin, sitting on one of the benches on the dais of the Praesidium, looked shrunken and pathetic; he was plainly forcing himself to look composed, but his face clearly showed what was at issue.[28]

Zinoviev and Kamenev fell over themselves in his defence. Using all their prestige and abilities, they presented – of course with ulterior motives – a strong case to show that Stalin had 'reformed' since Lenin's death.

The Testament was nullified.

Trotsky was in an embarrassing position; he was the natural beneficiary of Stalin's discomfiture.

It was not a position he could handle. He remained mute; all he could do was to show, by gesture and grimace, that he was far above the sordid spectacle; at the end he seemed to be congealed with disgust.[29]

Thus, without a word from him, a decision was made – Lenin's Testament was to be ignored! This meant that it could not be published at all; such highhandedness about a clearly expressed opinion of such a deity would be incomprehensible in any other context.

The Thirteenth Party Congress reproduced in a more systematic style the denunciations of Trotsky that had been the main point of the Party Conference in January.

For months, Zinoviev had been demanding Trotsky's expulsion; he now denounced him more extravagantly than anyone else. He insisted that the Party be more 'monolithic' than ever, and that it could not be pacified without Trotsky surrendering by 'recanting' (this was the first time such a demand was made).

Trotsky, outmanoeuvred once again, had to commit *hara-kiri* on the altar of unity.

His speech in 'self-defence' was couched in the same pious style of Party loyalty that had already demolished him vis-à-vis the Trio. It was, moreover, put in the same form of an appeal to a general audience – the same symptom of his inability to manoeuvre in the jungle of the Party apparatus.

Nothing could be ... morally and politically easier than to admit ... one or another mistake. ... Comrades, none of us wishes to be or can be right against his party. In the final analysis the Party is always right, because it is the only historic instrument given to the working class for the solution of its fundamental tasks. ... One can be right only with the Party and through the Party, because history has not created any other way for rightness to be realised. The English have an historic saying, 'My country, right or wrong.' With much greater historic justification we can say: 'My Party, right or wrong' – wrong on certain partial, specific issues or at certain moments. ... It would be absurd, perhaps almost indecent, to make any personal declarations here, but I hope that, if it comes to it, then I too will not be the last soldier on the last Bolshevik barricade![30]

The key sentence is doubtless: 'The Party is always right.' It sums up Trotsky's central attitude – in lieu of personal authority, an identification with an idea to the point of desperation. It made it impossible for him, *regardless of what the Party had become*, to move against anyone claiming its support.

The final phrase – 'not the last soldier' – with its mixture of pathos and self-abnegation, discloses the very nub of his helplessness.

CHAPTER IX

The Muezzin

By THE END OF 1923 Trotsky's eclipse was well-nigh complete; Lenin's death in January 1924 confirmed it; a year later he was ousted as War Commissar.

In May 1925 he was given a few jobs – on the Electro-Technical Board, the Scientific-Technical Board of Industry, the Concessions Committee.

As he said later on, these jobs had nothing to do with each other; they had been contrived to 'isolate me from the Party, to submerge me in routine, to put me under special control. . . . Nevertheless, I made a conscientious effort to work in with the new arrangements. When I began my work in three institutions quite unfamiliar to me, I plunged in it up to my ears. . . .'¹

Priceless words: 'nevertheless', 'conscientious' . . . Stalin must have snickered – Trotsky, once again a prize pupil.

Trotsky's docility was to prove futile: only a few years after he had 'plunged up to his ears' in unfamiliar work he was thrown out of the Party altogether; in January 1928 he and Natalya were exiled to Siberia; a year later they were deported from the Soviet Union.

That was five years after Lenin's death.

If one looks back over Trotsky's career as leader, one is bound to be struck by its brevity.

Beginning with the midsummer of 1917, when he joined the Bolshevik Party and together with Lenin led it through the putsch in October–November, it ended with the Civil War. It lasted about three years.

Throughout this period he was used, as it were, for assignments:
the putsch itself, the negotiations in Brest-Litovsk, the Civil War,
the reorganisation of rail transport. When these assignments were
over it became plain that he had no roots in the Party.

Consequently, when Trotsky, after brilliantly performing his
assignments, found them terminated by the tidal wave of Soviet
evolution, a tidal wave he could not be shielded against since his
hopes for The Revolution never materialised, he was dismissed. In
Schiller's phrase: 'The Moor has done his duty, the Moor can go.'

Trotsky's explanation of his defeat was to be that Stalin, himself a
mere mediocrity, 'represented' the reaction away from The Revolution, a reaction due to Russian backwardness, the failure of The
Revolution elsewhere and so on: hence, since these stultifying
forces were on the upgrade the forces 'represented' by Trotsky were
bound to go under for a time.

This explanation, plausible only within its restrictions, makes it
simply vulgar to ask why Trotsky couldn't have done something to
stop it, say, arrested the Stalin coterie, organised his sympathisers –
acted.

Yet this vulgar question must be asked if only because Trotsky
had acted in the past; it was, after all, his leadership as well as
Lenin's that had changed History.

Why, in the Twenties, could he not have changed History
again? If Stalin and his entourage were backsliders why could not
Trotsky, the true representative of The Revolution, amputate the
excrescence?

For in spite of his insistence on the omnipotence of 'social forces'
Trotsky was preoccupied with the role of personality. This is most
obvious in his discussion of Lenin's role after his return to Russia in
April and in the Bolshevik seizure of power in October 1917.

In 'classical Marxism', of course, individuals don't amount to much
as compared with the play of 'forces'. At best they 'sharpen' or
'deepen' some historical tendency; they cannot do more than modify
a general movement.

The point was put with classical pithiness by Plekhanov in his essay
on *The Role of the Individual in History*: the example Plekhanov
gives is Robespierre, who, no matter how 'absolutely indispensable' a
force, was not the 'only one': if he had been killed by, say, the
'accidental fall of a brick' his place would 'of course' – Plekhanov says
sublimely – 'have been taken by someone else'.

This view – a banality for deterministic schools of thought – was shared by Trotsky.

Yet in the Russian upheaval he faced a problem that from precisely this point of view was altogether baffling: suppose *Lenin* had been hit by a brick – what then?

Here the evidence is unambiguous: all accounts testify to the plain fact that when Lenin turned up in April 1917 he found his own Party totally unreceptive to the idea of taking power: in spite of his immense authority it took him weeks of agitation to persuade them.

Even after swinging them over, he had to make the *decision* to go ahead, which he did in October: moreover, there can be no doubt that no one else could have managed it; no one else had the combination of will and authority.

The *actual* putsch was child's play, but a decision to make it was indispensable; hence it was Lenin's personal initiative that made him a world-shaker.

But what does that do to the Marxist claim of the paramount, indeed unique importance of historical 'laws'? What about the brick?

Trotsky had to admit all this; outside his *History* he gives answers that are quite unequivocal: in his *Diary*, for instance, he says:

Had I not been present in 1917 in Petrograd the October Revolution would still have taken place – on the condition that Lenin was present and in command. If neither Lenin nor I had been present in Petrograd, there would have been no October Revolution: the leadership of the Bolshevik Party would have prevented it from occurring – of this I have not the slightest doubt![2]

The same view is expressed in the *History*, too, though with a wariness better called evasiveness:
He asks the question:

Is it possible . . . to say confidently that without him the Party would have found its road? We would by no means make bold to say that. . . . A disoriented and split party might have let slip the revolutionary opportunity for many years.[3]

Here Trotsky uses the slipperiness of the Dialectic to establish two quite different things at the same time.

On the one hand 'Lenin did not trust the Central Committee' and was, indeed, 'not so wrong in his mistrust'; on the other, 'Lenin did not oppose the Party from outside, but was himself its most complete expression'.[4]

This was in spite of the well-known fact of the Party's being at odds with Lenin on even the *general* question of taking power, and the even better-known fact that on the very eve of the insurrection his two acolytes, Zinoviev and Kamenev, were absolutely against the whole thing, while the rest of the Politburo were swept along only by Lenin's self-assurance.

The Marxist point of view is, in fact, contradicted by Trotsky's explicit admission in his *History*: without Lenin a 'disoriented and split party might have let slip the revolutionary opportunity for many years'. But, since conjunctions of events are constantly shifting, 'many years' might mean forever. Even if a pious Marxist were to retain his faith in the outbreak of The Revolution, why in Russia?

Trotsky has thus effaced a plain contradiction by a rhetorical patchwork: on the one hand Lenin was not 'a demi-urge of the revolutionary process' – where would Marxism be? – he is nothing but a link – of course a 'great' link! – in a chain of 'objective historic causes'.

On the other hand, without him things would have been very different!

This is of a piece, to be sure, with the contrast Trotsky habitually establishes between the marvels of Marxism as a philosophy of reality and the deplorable performance of countless Marxists. Just as he had been struck, before 1917, by the German Social-Democrats' 'non-revolutionary' incomprehension of true Marxism, so he is mesmerised by the contrast between ideal Bolshevism and wretched ordinary Bolsheviks.

Lenin surpassed his closest disciples so immeasurably that in his presence they felt themselves freed once and for all from the need to solve theoretical and tactical problems independently. Separated from him at a critical moment they were bewilderingly helpless. So it was in the autumn of 1905. So it was in the spring of 1917.[5]

In a word, individual Bolshevik leaders – except Lenin! – are wayward and fallible. Zinoviev is shifty and feeble, Kamenev no better: Stalin is primitive, coarse, limited, indeed obtuse, in any case 'mediocre'.

Yet these nonentities could actually have 'prevented' the whole October Revolution! And at the same time, in another context, they were the leaders of the splendid Bolshevik Party!

Trotsky bridges this gap by leaping over the heads of the 'disciples' to 'The Masses', to the 'rank-and-file of the Party' that 'sensed the correct line of action much better than did their semi-leaders when the latter were thrown on their own resources',[6]

Similarly, in discussing the evolution of the apparatus, he is obliged to highlight the supremacy of personality, at least potentially, at the very moment he skips over the potentiality of his own role.

In reporting his conversation with Lenin, for instance, about the dismaying growth of 'bureaucratism', Trotsky, while perceiving it to be a massive social phenomenon, thought that 'at that moment Lenin would undoubtedly have been able to carry out the regrouping in the . . . direction he had planned'.

This really implies that if only Lenin had lived – with his broad horizon, vision, and moral refinement – he could have forestalled the entire creation of the Soviet apparatus.

[His and Lenin's] joint action against the Central Committee would without the shadow of a doubt have brought us victory. And what is more, I had no doubt that had I come forward . . . in the spirit of a 'bloc of Lenin and Trotsky' against the Stalin bureaucracy, I should have been victorious even if Lenin had taken no direct part in the struggle.

After saying this, he bows to Marxism, to be sure, when he discusses the 'solidity' of such a victory, mentioning, namely, the necessity of taking 'into account a number of objective processes in the country. The thing that matters is not Stalin, but the forces he expresses without even realising it.'

But *then* he says: 'In 1922–3, however, it was still possible to capture the commanding position by an open attack on the faction then rapidly being formed of national . . . usurpers of the apparatus, of the unlawful heirs of October, of the epigones of Bolshevism'.

In the context of ruthless Marxist analysis these words – 'unlawful', 'usurpers', 'epigones' – have a strange ring, since *in any case*, as he says, 'the chief obstacle was Lenin's condition'.

No matter how it is put, the ascription to Lenin of a unique role is unmistakable : just as Lenin was indispensable for the seizure of power so he was also, in that stage of bureaucratic formation, indispensable for checkmating Stalin's influence. The 'objective processes' were to come only later.

If Trotsky's admission that Lenin had been indispensable twice – in taking power and in being able to forestall Stalinism – was sound, it meant that Trotsky, too, might have brought about a different historical outcome by *personal action*.

Hence the question must suggest itself: What if, after all, Trotsky, too, had. . . ?

It is, in fact, in examining his answer to the question he was asked so frequently – 'how did you lose power?' – that his character comes into focus.

For what must be explained, in solving this problem of Trotsky's 'loss of power', is his radical inability to form a faction.

An assessment by a friend, Lunacharsky, sheds some light on this :

Trotsky was very bad at organising not only a party but even a small group. He had practically no partisans of his own at all: he was hampered by the extreme definiteness of his personality . . . if he was impressive within the Party it was exclusively because of his personality. . . . An enormous authoritativeness, and a sort of inability or unwillingness to be in the least caressing and attentive to people, an absence of that charm that always enveloped Lenin, condemned Trotsky to a certain solitude.[7]

This 'solitude' was due to traits of character that Trotsky was no doubt reluctant to acknowledge : perhaps they were too intimate.

Here is an instance of Trotsky's 'aloofness' : an old friend found him sitting alone in a cafeteria (after his release, in the aftermath of the 'July Days') :

I felt compassion for him. We had been so attached to each other in the past. . . . I approached him, but immediately felt that a wall of estrangement divided us. . . . In the corridor . . . I came over as an old friend; in a tone half-facetious, half serious I scolded him . . . instead of answering in the same tone he drew himself up (like) a speaker at a mass-meeting and began orating loudly . . . I resented this . . . and never met him again.[8]

Max Eastman describes Trotsky's appearance at a merry, lusty, drinking, talking, singing party in the Kremlin in the early Twenties:

Trotsky wandered among all those old revolutionists, of whom he was then still the chief, like a lost angel, faultlessly clad as always, with a brand-new shiny manuscript case under his arm, a benign sort of Y.M.C.A. secretary's smile put on for the festivities, but not an offhand word to say to anybody. . . . He reminded me of Little Lord Fauntleroy.[9]

An unmistakable impression!

Here is Trotsky's own account of such parties:

If I took no part in the pleasures that were becoming more and more customary in the new ruling stratum, it was not because of ethical principles, but because I disliked subjecting myself to the torment of the worst kinds of boredom. Making the social rounds, assiduously attending the ballet, the collective drink-fests with the tittle-tattle about those absent, could by no means attract me. The new summit felt that I did not fit this way of life. Nor was any attempt even made to draw me in. It was just because of this that group conversations would stop whenever I appeared and the people taking part in them would separate, with a little embarrass-ment toward each other and some hostility toward me. This meant, if you like, that I was beginning to lose power.[10]

Trotsky hastens to follow this up by generalising it, so to speak, out of existence – more 'social forces'!

Apart from such observations Trotsky's specific answer to the elusive question of his defeat is illuminating. It displays with a technical precision the two conditions that made it inevitable: on the one hand, the objective circumstance that Trotsky had no faction; on the other hand, his subjective qualities – diffidence plus a theatrical hyper-sensitivity to appearances.

Any action of mine might have been understood, or rather represented as my personal struggle for Lenin's place in the Party and the State. I could not think of that without shuddering inside. . . . Would the Party understand that it was a question of Lenin's and Trotsky's struggle for the future of The Revolution, and not of Trotsky's struggle for the place of the ailing Lenin? Thanks to the special position occupied by Lenin in the Party the indefiniteness of his personal condition was transformed into the indefiniteness of the condition of the entire Party. The provisional situation went on being prolonged. And the prolonging played completely into the hand of the epigones, since Stalin as General Secretary was naturally transformed into the majordomo of the apparatus throughout the 'interregnum'.[11]

This boils down to saying it was impossible to fight because people would think you were fighting. Linked to Trotsky's short-comings as an intriguer, it really implied that no fight could even be started, that *only* 'objective forces' could come to the rescue.

Trotsky's very wording is revealing: his 'independent action . . . would have been interpreted, or, to be more exact, represented. . . .'

This takes us into the very heart of his own attitude; his wording shows that he thought of himself as a *public* performer instead of a combatant within the Party. It implies his taking it for granted that he *could* not have a faction.

For if he had been capable of putting one together, it would not have seemed to him that the initiative for 'representing' his attitude was bound to be in the hands of his enemies alone: his whole passivity in this matter arises out of the knowledge that he had no way of doing anything *but* proving, claiming, demanding etc., his right to be Lenin's successor.

Yet with a faction, and with all the moves possible in the chess-game of factionalism, he would simply have been manoeuvring against the other factions – the epigones! – and done as best he could. For that matter Stalin contrived to *look* unusually diffident in the very process of becoming an unprecedentedly powerful boss.

Thus Trotsky's phraseology, with its passivity, its obsession with abstractions and generalities, compounded by his 'self-love', which doubtless made him peculiarly susceptible to a *charge* of vanity, entails precisely what we know in retrospect about his performance – this remarkably active man was, in such relations, remarkably passive.

All his writings about this tragic period of his life speak only of what *others* did; he was so totally outdistanced, so completely out of his element, that his entire description of Stalin's victory is in the passive mood – this is what *they* did to *me*, the scoundrels!

This passivity comes out most strikingly, perhaps, when he is

recommending action: after pointing out that Zinoviev and
Kamenev, with whom he was later to form a somewhat flabby
alliance, lacked 'that little thing called character', he says he
'repeated to them dozens of times: "We must aim far ahead, we
must prepare for a long serious struggle." '[12]

It is plain from the very formulation of these words, from their
seeming far-sightedness, as well as from the personalities they were
addressed to, that Trotsky's idea of a 'long and serious struggle' was
to – wait!

To wait for a change in the times. . . .

The very thought of exercising power seems to have been intrinsi-
cally distateful to him: his comment on this, recalled from the
moment after the putsch, is revealing:

> The conquest of power brought up the question of my govern-
> ment work. It's a strange thing – I had never even thought about
> that. Never once had it happened to me, in spite of the 1905
> experience, to link the question of my own future with the ques-
> tion of power. From my earliest years, or more precisely from my
> boyhood on I had dreamed of becoming a writer. Later on I
> subordinated my writing, as I did everything else, to revolutionary
> goals. The question of a conquest of power by the Party was
> always before me. Scores and hundreds of times I wrote and spoke
> about the programme of a revolutionary government. But the
> question of my own personal work after the conquest of power
> never crossed my mind. Because of this it caught me unawares.
> After the insurrection I tried to stay out of the government, and
> offered to assume the direction of the Party press. It is possible
> that a nervous reaction after the victory played a part in this. The
> preceding months had been bound up for me too directly with the
> preparation of the insurrection. Every fibre in me was taut. . . .
> the 25th of October brought a let-down. I had the feeling a
> surgeon has after a difficult and dangerous operation – I had to
> wash my hands, take off my apron, and rest.[13]

It seems to point up a theme of his autobiography: 'The longing
for study never left me, and many times in my life I had the feeling
that The Revolution was preventing me from working in a systematic
way.'[14]

As a vehicle for abstractions, Trotsky's talents were powered by
immense energy. Enamoured of Marxism as an adolescent, borne

aloft on an impulse that channelled his energies in a direction that was, so to speak, impersonal, he had shown unusual initiative. His goal was the promotion of an Idea, in which, to be sure, his gifts could naturally come to the fore.

Then, having become a public figure in 1905 through his virtuosity as a performer in a democratic arena, he lapsed back into a spectatorial role. During the decade preceding 1917 – from the age of twenty-seven to thirty-seven – he remained essentially a hanger-on of a movement, a journalist with a political speciality.

In 1917 circumstances once again enabled him to perform in a public arena, this time, however, with the added dimension of action made possible by the attrition of Tsarist society, which created potentialities for all performers. Trotsky's virtuosity was now conjoined with action aimed at specific goals. He was able to perform this action through his identification with a vehicle – Lenin's Party.

In Bolshevik harness, Trotsky distinguished himself. His energy, his commitment, his intelligence enabled him to carry out unusual feats of organisation, both in the putsch and in the Civil War, as well as in his administration of transport. Trotsky was at his best, in fact, as an *adjutant*.

Squeezed out of the Party, he was in the wide world once again, this time in a position that precluded spectatorship. There was no longer a democratic arena: events, and responses to events were shaped by a team. Trotsky, called upon to act in defence of his person as well as of his ideas, could no longer promote mere abstractions. To attain a goal he had to promote himself.

Yet just as his rationalism, while buttressing his organisational gifts, prevented him from descending, as he called it, into the mire of vulgar, day-to-day politics in an intra-Party struggle for power, so his personal temperament – haughty, aloof, reserved, *noble* – debarred him from the rough-and-tumble of intrigues, in which accords are reached, after all, against a background of material and psychic exchanges.

It is plain that, despite Trotsky's *theory* of voluntarism, his own personal voluntarism did not at all consist of the ambition – like Lenin's – of imposing his will, but of displaying his gifts.

When Lenin referred to Trotsky's 'ambition' as keeping them apart in 1915 he himself had mistaken Trotsky's style for his character: the test of power clarified the two kinds of ambition.

Before 1917 Trotsky's eminence had come to him with effortless ease. A gifted younger son, the only child of distinction, the apple of his father's eye, he could meet all the expectations of his milieu without strain. He became a prize pupil merely through acumen. Later on his singular virtuosity as a speaker, reinforced by his literary fluency, poured rewards into his lap. A display of talent might have seemed to make superfluous a thrust of will.

It was, perhaps, just this essential passivity of will that led to his over-estimation of the power of ideas. Trotsky's 'loftiness' was really a way of soaring above practical reality and the decisions it demands. An over-concentration on ideas obviates action by transferring the fulcrum of change to an abstract sphere. Ideas, after all, can work themselves out automatically!

Trotsky's inability to make primary, as distinct from subordinate decisions enabled him to function with energy only when the framework of his activity was *right* – when the stage was set for him. He could not, by putting forth his will, create his own stage.

Before 1917 he had found stages ready-made: the democratic arena of 1905, then the pleasant life of the emigration, where he devoted himself essentially to writing essays, chatting with like-minded friends, and speaking to casual audiences. In 1917 the democratic arena was supplemented by a functioning team in which he could subordinate himself to a leader. His artistic gifts, plus his energy and brains, functioned on two levels – public performance and supervised administration within a tightly-knit organisation.

This concept of a situation being 'right' before he could act may be the broad psychological category that clarifies another quality he was celebrated for – a certain finickiness about detail, an obsessive pedantry and orderliness that Lenin apparently had in mind when he referred, in his Testament, to Trotsky's preoccupation with the 'administrative side' of things.

What Trotsky's aloofness surely meant was that despite his apparent peremptoriness he was really *shy*. Coming out in public under his own aegis, *alone*, he felt ill-at-ease.

He was incapable of developing a party of his own, indeed of leading a party, and incapable of putting himself forward under his own authority.

In a curious way his behaviour after Lenin's death recalls the frantic paralysis of the Mensheviks during the turbulent period prior to the Bolshevik putsch – when they held the *de facto* power in their hands yet could not make up their minds to wield it. Trotsky's sneer at them in his *History of the Russian Revolution* as lacking, quite simply, the character to exercise authority is even more striking if it is turned against Trotsky himself – they were *all* shy!

This is particularly paradoxical, of course, in the case of Trotsky, notorious for self-assurance or for that matter arrogance. Energetic and intelligent, he might have used his gifts of oratory and physical magnetism to become a leader had he had, in fact, the inner composure to put himself forward as one.

A friend, Angelica Balabanoff, puts it with feminine perceptiveness: after pointing out that if Trotsky 'had from the beginning fought the repression of honest dissent, the calumny of opponents . . . how much more sympathy he would have found!' she sums him up: 'He was simply too weak and too self-conscious.'[15]

A woman's eye has pierced the camouflage of ideas! It has cloven beyond Trotsky's presentation of 'social forces' to the core of his character.

Could Trotsky's shyness have been linked to his Jewish origins?

This notion would, no doubt have been repugnant to him. He claimed to have transcended tribalism – an attitude that was, indeed, a banality amongst all those Jews who had discarded their background in the pursuit of cosmic aims.

In common with so many Jewish Marxists he leaned over backwards disclaiming his roots. He summed up his identity as a very young man: at the age of twenty-three, when asked to classify himself, he heatedly denied that he was *either* a Russian *or* a Jew – he was 'a Social-Democrat, that's all!'[16] Years later, at the summit of the new regime, he made essentially the same remark to some Jewish petitioners: 'I am a Bolshevik, and I am not a Jew!'[17]

The very fact that he had, in spite of everything, a strong sense of Jewish identification can only mean that his Jewish feelings had to be suppressed all the more dynamically. For cerebrally speaking, his view of this whole question was infinitely lofty:

> Even in my early youth . . . national prejudices had aroused in me only a rational perplexity that in certain cases . . . even turned into a moral nausea. My Marxist education deepened these feelings and transformed them into an active internationalism. My life in so many countries, my acquaintance with their languages . . . and cultures only helped me to absorb that internationalism into my very marrow.[18]

This is, no doubt, a very 'Jewish' attitude: no other people, after all, is indifferent to its own 'national prejudices'. Only Jews, indeed, are 'absolute' internationalists, in contrast with French, German, English etc. internationalists!

To drive the point home Trotsky tells a curious anecdote about a Cossack during the Civil War who, irritated at taunts about taking a Jew's orders – Trotsky's – retorted hotly: 'Nothing of the sort – Trotsky is not a Jew! Trotsky is a fighter, it's Lenin who's a Communist, a Jew, but Trotsky is one of us – a fighter – Russian – our own!'[19]

Against a Russian background, in short, in which the Bolshevik Party, overwhelmingly non-Jewish despite its few Jewish luminaries – themselves detached from their background – and the Soviet intelligentsia as a whole were sensitive on the 'Jewish question' – as they have remained – Trotsky's aura was unmistakably Jewish, pace the confused Cossack.

Trotsky's memoir of his childhood has already shown us a global rejection of everything his parents stood for. He also, plainly, rejected his parents themselves.

For Trotsky there was 'no creature more disgusting than a petty-bourgeois engaged in primary accumulation'.[20] And in Trotsky's ostentatious disdain for money, in his contempt for 'bourgeois' values, in his disavowal of his earliest language and his religious training, in his bookishness, in his desire for the disappearance of his people, we see an image of his father in reverse.

Fashionably called 'alienation', this thoroughgoing rejection of origin was summed up in Trotsky by the sweeping contrast between his father's intense parochialism and his own cosmopolitanism.

If we accept a factor of shyness as a source of the adult Trotsky's inadequacy in personal relations, we are bound to acknowledge the shyness itself as arising out of the process of his self-identification.

At bottom Trotsky was incapable of forming the basic act of maturity – taking responsibility. He could not accept himself as a leader because his own ego was not a sufficient source of authority.

Genuine authority arises, after all, only on the groundwork of a personal integration in which the whole man, having overcome his adolescent rebellion against his parents, is capable of achieving, through the absorption and sublimation of hostility toward his father, an identity of his own anchored in the fusion of unconscious strivings, the ambitions of the ego and the ideals of the super-ego.

It was, perhaps, the unconscious disdain he felt for his father –

petty-bourgeois, illiterate, provincial, Jewish – that prevented
Trotsky from realising the confluence between ambitions and
personal history that should, ideally, take shape when the adolescent
rebellion has yielded to the maturing of an adult who can perceive,
accept, and love his father as another adult and can thus assimilate
a balanced, purified, and harmonious version of him as a model.

Trotsky's rejection of his father made it impossible for him to
become a father in his turn: he remained a son – a lost boy.

Harmonious integration is radiated in personal relations; the
superiority of a gifted person makes itself felt without arousing
resistance. It is not imposed, it is accepted. It requires no external
props; it is not bureaucratic. The self-assurance felt by the integrated individual is not registered by others as haughtiness, but as
wholeness. It becomes an object, in fact, of deferential love.

This is, plainly, just the opposite of Trotsky's aura. During his
brief term as a member of the governing coterie his authority
depended on impersonal relationships – namely, his being an agent
of the Bolshevik Party vis-á-vis members and outsiders. Within the
Bolshevik enclosure itself he was obliged to establish a network of personal relations based on his authority, which failed him precisely
because it was dependent on external attributes – 'office' and 'status'.
Because of his lack of inner composure his power did not embed
itself within the hearts of his peers, it merely put their backs up.

Their submission, accordingly, was hypocritical – it lay in wait for
an opportunity to reverse itself. The 'authoritativeness' attributed to
Trotsky was, in short, the antithesis of true authority.

Any psychoanalysis of Trotsky would be presumptuous: it is
impossible. No unconscious material is available, no dreams, no
intimate information.

Yet it would seem likely that what amounts to Trotsky's disavowal
of his origins – of his family background as well as of his family –
stitched a kink into the very fabric of his being – an inability to
radiate a personal charm gladly internalised by his peers. His fundamental self-rejection forestalled his exercise of an authority based
not on his position but on himself. And it was during the grotesquely
misnamed 'struggle for power' in the Twenties that his recessiveness
reached a peak.

Historically, it is of some interest that in the Jewish community of
Eastern Europe the erosion of traditional Judaism by the secular
ideas stemming from the French Revolution had the effect of
channelling a pervasive religiosity into projects of world-reform.

Trotsky's passionate rejection of his parochial background, which served as springboard for a leap into the stratosphere of sweeping abstractions, was characteristic of many contemporaries and compatriots. The impulse to treat Marx's writing as Holy Writ, typical of Russian Marxism and especially common among Russian Jewish Marxists, was plainly a translation of old traditions into a new idiom that despite apparent secularisation retained the aroma of a millennial piety.

Trotsky's cluster of shortcomings, all rooted in the unconscious sources of his character, obliged him to concur in the ikonisation of Lenin.

Lenin whilst alive had became his only bulwark, as it seemed, against his obliteration by the evolving apparatus: after Lenin's death Trotsky hoped that Lenin, incarnate in the 'legacy of Lenin', would go on playing the same role.

Having for most of his youth shielded his ego against Lenin's pre-eminence, Trotsky had to accommodate the fact of the putsch and *submit.* He then seemed to internalise his submission – he made it sincere. He developed an adulation of Lenin that paralleled, though with a different flavour, the burgeoning state cult.

It would no doubt be easy to establish an unconscious pattern in this process: Lenin, though only nine years older, had been the head of the Party that now claimed Trotsky's allegiance, and also the head of the State, thus a father on at least two counts. His death made it all the easier for Trotsky to find him in the paternal prop that in the abstract had been given him by Marx, but that in the organisational jungle he was floundering it had to be reinforced by a more palpable anchor.

Hence the crux of the matter is this: *Did* he adulate Lenin? Was his adulation genuinely integrated with his essential uprightness in order to safeguard, unconsciously, his sincerity? Or was it merely expedient?

After all, Trotsky desperately needed some psychological support within the Party, since his own personality could not create it. During the turmoil that followed the October putsch Lenin could serve as the archetypal symbol for Trotsky's psychological and strategic requirements equally.

This made it natural for him to ikonise the Idea of the Party as well as his relationship with the dead Lenin. He could quote, with pride, Lenin's commendation of him as one of the finest Bolsheviks, as indeed absolutely *all right.*

The essay he wrote on Lenin after his death in 1924 was restricted to a sketchy review of his political relationship to him. It omitted all frictions: in view of his ultimate union with Lenin these had, of course, been no more than 'episodic'.

In *My Life* Trotsky takes pains to show that he and Lenin were *always* close. He gives a sketch of their views during the First World War in order to demonstrate the gravitational tug that brought their ideas together in spite of their absence of contact. The contrast is highlighted between the convergence of his ideas and Lenin's and the line of the local Party leaders in Petrograd at the time – Stalin – that was to be reversed by Lenin the moment he arrived in April.

This is incontestable; yet at the very moment of using this convergence in the realm of ideas to 'defend' himself against the charge of a non-existent 'Trotskyism', Trotsky failed to claim his due – namely, that Lenin too had once been against Permanent Revolution, and had adopted it only in April, in the heat of the tussle.

Trotsky could defend himself only by showing that he had always been a good boy, unlike what was being said in the slanders circulated about him – a good boy who had independently come to the same views as The Teacher, Lenin.

He transmits a sort of good-conduct report by Lenin himself, who said that at the crucial moment 'Bolshevism drew to itself all the best elements in the currents of Socialist thought nearest to it.'

Trotsky asks: 'Can there be even a shadow of a doubt that . . . Lenin had foremost in mind what is now called "historical Trotskyism?". . . . To Lenin . . . Trotskyism was no hostile and alien current of Socialist thought, but, on the contrary, the one closest to Bolshevism.'

The weakness of this is plain.

First of all it acknowledges, in a way, that there is such a thing as Trotskyism – thus conceding the major, utterly bogus point made by Stalin. Secondly, Trotsky throws himself on Lenin's authority, and since Stalin was running the government and owned, as it were, Lenin's corpse, Trotsky was already in the position of appealing to *someone else's* ikon.

And this was after the insurrection that had made the Bolsheviks a world force, an insurrection stage-managed by Trotsky himself in accordance with his own theories!

It would no doubt have been futile to attempt to disavow these theories and his own role in implementing them, yet he had to tone down their importance in one way while at the same time recalling them to his audience. His writings in exile were to sustain a note of pathos: it was painful for him to remind the Movement what he had done for it.

Trotsky tended to admire in others only those qualities he took seriously in himself – his cluster of gifts. Thus he had originally under-estimated Lenin because of the latter's colourlessness; he under-estimated Stalin because of Stalin's coarseness and inarticulateness.

In over-estimating Ideas, in rationalising his refusal to 'stoop', 'deign' and 'demean himself', he was evading the unmistakable fact that he was simply incapable of navigating in the protean relationships of a large organisation. While capable of expressing with mystical conviction the generalisations of Marxism, he was blind to the real-life interests of his opponents, who exploited such generalisations in order to make them dovetail with their private ambitions.

A realistic view of this fundamental process would have obliged him to assess his own chances not as reflecting a clash of 'ideas' but as a contest between individuals. This was just what he would not 'deign' to do.

He remained capable, politically speaking, of only one thing – soliciting the attention of multitudes unstructured by administration.

It was no doubt his lofty – indeed, in the philosophic sense 'idealist' view of politics that made Trotsky misunderstand what was actually happening. It astigmatised him, as it were, with respect to the power of the actual apparatus, and made him regard himself as a Bolshevik paragon merely because of his identification with the Idea of the Party: he disregarded his failure to be identified with its *personnel*. It was as though a tightly knit band of men inspired by an Idea and linked by common experiences over a period of time were to be approached by a convert to the Idea, and expected to accept him on the basis of the Idea alone. It was this blind spot vis-à-vis people – as individuals, not as exemplifications of Ideas – that made him misconceive the fragility of his position.

Tied hand and foot by the dogma of 'unity', Trotsky could not contest Bolshevik mythology without coming out against the leadership. Once the apparatus had emerged, in fact, it could be influenced only from within, which was just where Trotsky, incapable of forming alliances, was helpless. As the apparatus expanded it became a world unto itself, consequently less and less a medium for Trotsky.

Trotsky's account of his conversation with Lenin, (see page 275), after it had become clear that the 'machine was getting out of control', illustrates his under-estimation of the apparatus at the very moment he was grappling, as he thought with the problem.

Lenin's offer of a 'bloc', at that time, just before Lenin's stroke of December 1922, had seemed to be based on the notion that Trotsky himself could, in fact, 'shake up the apparatus' – already the most concentrated government in history. If the conversation had been really serious it could have meant only that in the very midst of discussing the perniciousness of the apparatus, both Lenin and Trotsky were disconcertingly unaware of the magnitude of the forces that had engendered it.

This contrast is heightened by the irony that Lenin had originally offered Trotsky no more than the Education portfolio – a long jump away from any power centre!

This blind spot on the part of Lenin helps explain the curious turgidity of his Testament, with its recommendation that Stalin, 'rude and disloyal', be 'removed' to avoid a 'split'. Aside from the fact that Stalin did not 'split' with his colleagues but wiped them out, it is bewildering to see Trotsky's inadequate assessment of the titanic 'social force' that was, after all, embodied in the apparatus.

Trotsky despised intrigue to the point of incomprehension. If he could have allowed his intellect to grasp what was, after all, obvious, he would have felt obliged to take action in a field he could not handle. His seeming obtuseness was no doubt another rationalisation of his ineptitude in personal relationships.

He records a trivial episode from the Civil War.

One Menzhinsky was, Trotsky says, a complete nonentity: 'He seemed more like the shadow of some other unrealised man, or rather like a poor sketch for an unfinished portrait. . . . Only now and then would an ingratiating smile. . . . betray his eagerness to emerge from his insignificance.'

Stalin was a sponsor of his. 'Stalin generally gave his support to people who existed politically only through the grace of the apparatus.' Ultimately, Menzhinsky became not merely the head of the Political Police but a member of the Central Committee.

Trotsky tells how, long before rising in the hierarchy, Menzhinsky was looking for another job – under Trotsky, then War Commissar.

Menzhinsky came to me in the train with a report.... After finishing . . . he began to stammer and shuffle about, with that ingratiating smile of his that makes one feel alarmed and puzzled at the same time. He ended by asking me: 'Was I aware that Stalin was conducting a very complicated intrigue against me?'

'What?' I asked in sheer bewilderment – I was far from . . . such thoughts.

'Yes, he is insinuating to Lenin and others that you are grouping men about you who are especially hostile to Lenin.'

'You must be out of your mind, Menzhinsky, please wake up. I don't want to talk about it.' Menzhinsky left, coughing, his shoulders hunched up. I think it was from that day on that he began looking for other fish to fry.

But after an hour or two of work I began feeling uncomfortable inside. This man, with his quiet, blurred speech, had planted a malaise within me just as though I had swallowed a piece of glass while eating. I began recalling things, putting them together. Stalin came out in a different light.... On a short visit later on to Moscow I went to see Lenin first, as usual. We talked about the front.... We laughed. Lenin was usually merry. Nor would I call myself gloomy. Towards the end I told him about Menzhinsky's visit on the southern front: 'Could there really be any truth at all in it?'

I noticed at once that Lenin had got excited. The blood even surged into his face. 'Just trivialities,' he kept repeating, though without assurance. 'I'm interested in one thing only,' I said, 'could you possibly allow yourself, even for a minute, to have such a horrible idea as that I could be picking up people to oppose you?'

'Trivialities,' retorted Lenin, but this time with a firmness that instantly reassured me. The little cloud hanging over our heads seemed to be dissipated, and we said our good-byes with special warmth. But I realised that Menzhinsky had not been talking at random. If Lenin had denied it while leaving something unsaid, it was only because he was afraid of . . . a personal fight. Here I was in complete sympathy with him. But Stalin was obviously sowing trouble.[21]

This simple phrase about Stalin 'obviously sowing trouble', written years afterwards, seems illuminating. Trotsky ascribed to personal vileness alone an incident that bears the unmistakable outlines of a classical intrigue.

There was certainly an element of personal antipathy in Trotsky's attitude toward Stalin from the very beginning of their association. It comes out vividly in an anecdote told by Trotsky:

> On overhearing a lovers' conversation immediately after the putsch between Alexandra Kollontai (a Menshevik recruit to Bolshevism), an aristocrat over forty-five, and a twenty-nine-year-old jolly, self-confident giant sailor . . . Stalin, with whom until then I had not carried on a personal conversation, came up to me with a kind of unexpected jauntiness and, pointing with his shoulder toward the partition (behind which the sailor was speaking by phone with Kollontai), said, smirking: 'That's he with Kollontai, with Kollontai!' His gestures and his laughter seemed to me out of place and unendurably vulgar . . . I don't remember whether I simply said nothing, turning my eyes away, or answered drily, 'That's their affair'. But Stalin sensed that he had made a mistake. His face changed, and in his yellow eyes appeared the same glint of animosity I had noticed in Vienna. From that time on he never again attempted to engage me in conversation on personal themes.[22]

Across the decades the reader can sense Trotsky's flesh crawling . . . *Stalin* had made a mistake!

Stalin, evidently, had much to overcome later on in his efforts to woo Trotsky, whom at one time he needed: Stalin himself, after all, was not always sure of himself either!

Trotsky, repelled by Stalin's 'interior servility',[23] found himself obsessed by his 'mediocrity' to the point of discounting the very 'forces' he embodied.

If Trotsky's analysis was accurate, and 'Stalin rose to his position as the supreme expression of the mediocrity of the apparatus',[24] he might have been expected to see that anyone who could master an apparatus with the capacity to manhandle millions of people with such ferocity had to have qualities that dovetailed with the 'historical process'.

'Mediocrity' is a great 'social force'!

It was all these qualities of Trotsky's, both public and private, that might have given him a distinguished career in a democratic society, the antithesis of the streamlining that reshaped the Bolshevik Party after the putsch.

A fish out of water, Trotsky nevertheless, in the middle of the Twenties, still had a public aureole.

Here is a glimpse of him at the age of forty-seven:

A simple brotherly handshake; his gaze clear and direct, a smile unexpected and celebrated: a voice of bronze, modulated between sweetness and a rap.

His hair already going grey, brushed back high, continuing the line of a forehead steep as a cliff. Jutting jaws, their angle softened by the goatee. . . . The lips, flat and broad, turn the mouth into a moving millstone that breathes, tramples or shatters his words. The moustache is thrown back on both sides with vivacity. In this sculptured face the simple and sky-blue eyes, glinting behind the spectacles, cast a gaiety, even a joyousness that give his whole head an indefinable touch of some intelligent and faithful pride, the very hallmark of courage and self-possession.[25]

In public nothing was known of his vanished power. For that matter it was never really disclosed: the initial propaganda of the regime merely yielded to the shifts of later propaganda as the regime itself evolved. Before Lenin's death in 1924 all was veiled: Trotsky was still the most versatile luminary of the Party, outside the apparatus Stalin's name was scarcely known.

Trotsky kept working like a beaver; Natalya records his manifold concentration and, above all, the nervous strain he was labouring under:

Trotsky's capacity for work was always exceptional. He was living literally under constant pressure, following up twenty subjects at the same time, studying, documenting himself, dealing with literature, economics, domestic and international politics. Nevertheless, his health began flagging; he suffered from malignant debilitating fevers that quite often made him take to his bed or take refuge in Caucasian rest-houses. Physicians diagnosed a form of malaria. . . . It seems indeed that the nervous temperament, the very lively sensitivity of L.D. showed itself – against his powerful will – in these discomforts during periods of intellectual hypertension. He had suffered from gastric troubles, often on the eve of speaking in public. He was never cured of the fevers that

laid him low at moments in the course of the struggle with the
Politburo, the Party, and later in exile. In bed, he went on
working, reading, taking notes and dictating.[26]

Trotsky's liking for the Caucasus 'rest-houses' has a certain
interest, especially since it is glided over rather rapidly by Trotsky
and Natalya as well as by others.

He spent a quite unusual amount of time – months and months –
in the Caucasus during the crucial phases of his political eclipse.

There life was very different! In 1923 and 1924 no one realised the
troubles Trotsky was having in Moscow: in the provinces his
portraits were still hanging next to Lenin's in the clubs and government offices. Most of the Communists on vacation in the Caucasus
were delighted to meet him and ask him to lecture.

In rocky, green Sukhum, on the Abkhasian coast, studded with
palm-trees and cedars, Trotsky and Natalya could relax; the intrigues
and machinations in Moscow, above all the crippling passivity his
temperament and position condemned him to, could be forgotten.

Trotsky's energies had always been poured into a variety of
outlets; he always found it congenial to deal with the 'problems' of
culture. During the long periods when, in his own eyes, the political
'struggle' was quiescent – that is, while the Party summit was jelling
without him – his unflagging concentration took on an extraordinarily
wide range.

During the summer of 1922, he had taken a vacation, after fitting
himself into the routine of government as distinct from the army.
He spent most of his time criticising literature. A decision already
taken by the State Publishing House to publish his collected Works,
a series that was to comprise some thirteen volumes, led to an idea
for a current project: an obviously much-needed preface for his
numerous pre-revolutionary articles on literature, constituting a general survey of the literary results of the Soviet upheaval.

What began as a preface rapidly swelled to the dimensions of a
book, which he spent all his vacation time on but could not finish. He
took it up again the following summer – when the question of The
Revolution in Germany seemed to be a burning issue, and while he
himself was spun into a cocoon of futility by Stalin, Zinoviev and
Kamenev – and now managed to turn it into a major work, *Literature and Revolution.*

In the summer and autumn of 1923 he devoted his energies to the
analysis of trade cycles in the nineteenth and twentieth centuries; he

also wrote on the conflict between the Freudian and the Pavlovian schools of psychology. He believed in 'tolerating' research in general, and more especially in freedom for Freudians to speak up.

He also found time to express that side of his nature that can only be called priggish: in the late summer of 1923, in which no doubt his political fate, and eventually, indeed, his very life, were at stake, he devoted a series of essays to the normal behaviour of ordinary people. In addition to such subjects as family life he wrote articles on such things as 'Civility and Politeness', 'Vodka, the Church and the Movies', 'Russian Swearing' etc.[27]

To educationalists, librarians, journalists and so on, he gave countless speeches on the terrible standards of the press, the crying need of the Russian language whose beauties were now being polluted by the flood of Party bilge.

His puritanism was outraged:

Foul language is a legacy of slavery, degradation, and disrespect for human diginity . . . our Russian foul language is especially so. One would have to question philologists, linguists and folk-lore specialists as to whether other people have such unbridled . . . coarse swearing as we do. . . .

In our lower classes swearing came from despair, embitterment and above all slavery, without hope or escape. But the swearing of the upper classes, through the throats of the gentry. . . . was the expression of class-rule, slave-owners' arrogance, and the unshakability of the base. It is said that proverbs are the expression of folk-wisdom – not only wisdom, however, but also darkness, prejudice and slavery. . . . Two streams of foul language in Russian – of rulers, officials, and police, full-throated and fat, and the other, of the hungry, the desperate, and the tormented – have coloured the whole of Russian life with loathsome patterns. And it was this legacy, among much else, that The Revolution inherited.

But primarily, after all, The Revolution is the awakening of a human personality in The Masses that beforehand were thought to have none. The Revolution, despite all its occasional cruelty and the bloodstained mercilessness of its methods, is primarily and above all the awakening of humanity, its movement forward, the growth of respect for one's own dignity and for the dignity of others, the growth of sympathy for the weak. The Revolution would be no Revolution if, with all its power and all its resources, it did not help woman, doubly and triply enslaved, on to the path of personal and social development. The Revolution would be no Revolution if it did not show the greatest sympathy to children – it is they who are the future in whose name the Revolution is to be made. But can a new life . . . be created . . . in the atmosphere filled with the roaring and bellowing of Russian swearing? The struggle against 'language' is just as much a prerequisite of spiritual culture as the struggle against dirt and vermin is a prerequisite of material culture.[28]

Not only did Trotsky fail as governess, but the very phenomenon, later to be called Stalinism – though not by the Stalinists – that defeated him, came to concentrate within itself just those qualities of coarseness, violence and obtuseness he considered it his duty to combat tooth and nail.

The cultivated classes had faded away after the putsch, at least during the ensuing violence. The intelligentsia, in particular, almost uniformly hostile to the Bolsheviks, evaporated after the Civil War, in which many were wiped out. Of the new rulers practically none but a handful of the topmost stratum had any education to speak of at all. Outside the narrow circle of the relatively cosmopolitan Bolshevik leaders, Marxism was regarded as a sufficient catch-all.

If Marxism, after all, could serve even a cosmopolitan like Trotsky as the Great Key, how rapidly was it bound to degenerate, in the minds of the Party orang-outangs, into a mere talisman!

Consequently those intellectuals who did stay on to serve the new regime, some of them even with genuine zeal, found themselves being lectured by the topmost orang-outangs; the orang-outangs, on the other hand, sometimes unsure of themselves in the presence of these outsiders with cultural pretensions, vented their uncertainty in callous bullying.

Trotsky's haranguing of the local commissars, Party secretaries, and so on, to be more lenient with the old fashioned Russian intellectuals, a harangue in which he was joined by the other Bolshevik luminaries – Lunacharsky, Bukharin, Leonid Krasin and Lenin himself – was possible only at the very outset.

As the Bolshevik apparatus ramified and solidified, as the new structure was established as a genuine social stratum, the chasm between the old intelligentsia and the parvenu intelligentsia now sprouting under the Bolshevik dictatorship, which a few Bolshevik intellectuals like Trotsky had been doing their best to reconcile, began to yawn still further. As the dictatorship jelled, in short, it was only natural for its functionaries to lay down the law in culture as well as in administration. This was just as natural as the process that was simultaneously converting the Bolsheviks from a party of quasi-intellectuals into a corps of bureaucrats. There was nothing surprising in the bureaucracy's imposition of its own primitive ideas on everyone else: the former intelligentsia, helpless and outcast, were bound to submit.

Trotsky's energies were directed far more against philistinism, conformism, slavishness, and authoritarianism in cultural matters than they were against his political adversaries. As targets, indeed, they suited his general gifts far more – in particular his addiction to abstract moralising. Far from spending his time intriguing within the Party, it would seem, on the contrary, that he was almost wholly preoccupied by culture and by his desperate longing to bring about The Revolution, as it were, in the hearts of men.

From the very beginning of the Bolshevik dictatorship it was no doubt inevitable for the more simple-minded Bolsheviks, 'dizzy with success', and even more for the flocks of hangers-on that began pouring into the Party, to hand down authoritative opinions on all subjects including 'culture'.

The Proletariat, which had little to do with the Bolshevik putsch to begin with, soon had its name pinned, equally fictitiously, to a wide variety of ideas – 'proletarian' culture, art, literature, as well as military strategy, much spoken of during the Civil War. This concept was summed up in the cant coinage – 'Proletkult', which by the end of the Twenties, and especially during the Thirties, was to blossom forth in the grotesque extravagances of the Stalin era, most of which have survived to this day.

As a 'subtle' Marxist, Trotsky saw that all this was eye-wash, and did his best to counteract it. This attitude of his probably made him more unpopular with the Party orang-outangs than his purely political postures. Just as peasants thought nothing of destroying the libraries and paintings that represented the 'values' of the upper classes, so the plebeians who accepted the Bolshevik Party saw no reason they should not kick aside the heritage of 'the past', which still meant for them the way of life of the upper classes. As this attitude solidified into the cocksureness of the parvenu bureaucracy the old cultural values were replaced by a new, half-baked, streamlined, stripped-down and sloganised form of Marxism that was enforced, moreover, by the club.

Both Lenin and Trotsky opposed the whole theory underlying Proletkult, Trotsky, as it were professionally – Lenin was busy with other matters. But the Proletkult itself represented so pre-eminent a socio-cultural *fact* – its appeal to the parvenu ruling stratum – that fighting it was a strenuous and ultimately hopeless enterprise. When Trotsky was reduced, in the general field of 'culture', to exhorting vast numbers of people to behave differently from the way in which they were well-nigh bound to behave, he acquired even more of a governessy look.

With respect to the old-fashioned 'liberal' intelligentsia itself, on the other hand, it was natural for him to make out the contrary 'case'. With his messianic goals anchored in 'classical Marxism', he could, nevertheless, as one who was at the same time a cosmopolitan intellectual, implore them not to be *too* scornful of the Bolshevik dictatorship.

He was in an ideal position : he could explain his own views, now officialised by power, to the world at large, especially to the old-line intellectuals it might have given him some pleasure to impress.

Since Marxism has always claimed to be a science, it was neces-sarily thought compatible with other sciences, and indeed, because of its broad-gauge claims, a guide to *all* sciences. Trotsky was bound to be preoccupied, accordingly, by the philosophical background of the new technicians and scientists in the Soviet Union : he kept addressing meetings on the relationship between the Master Science of Marxism and the ordinary sciences.

It is ironic, perhaps, that his own preoccupation with this, natural to him in the past as a Marxist, was renewed and given a topical twist after his expulsion from the Government into inconsequential jobs.

These jobs were a political disaster for Trotsky, indeed the prelude to his destruction, but they could also, of course, be looked upon as technically very interesting. They enabled him to make the limited efforts of the experts dove-tail with the more comprehensive views of scientific Marxism.

Throughout 1925–6, accordingly, Trotsky, whose welfare might seem to have been already compromised beyond redemption, com-posed a great many essays in this field. Though science itself requires some virtuosity or at least some expenditure of time, the philosophy of science is far more accessible. It was here that Trotsky could make his mark.

Trotsky was not at all pompous about his Marxist training: he was not exactly a *scholar*, after all, but a gifted exponent of the general ideas of others, especially those of his twin mentors, Marx and Engels.

On the other hand it was natural for him to maintain that scientists, however talented, must not remain bogged down in their narrow disciplines; it was plain that they must have a general philosophical framework out of which new advances could be made; he naturally thought Marxism just such a framework. In September 1925, for instance, he made a speech to the All-Russian Congress of Scientists on Mendeleyev, the celebrated pioneer in chemistry. Trotsky thought Mendeleyev exemplified the dilemma of modern science: the very necessity of acquiring information through fragmented procedures entailed the necessity of having a broad philosophical framework to organise disjointed data – thus the greater the fragmentation the more urgent is the need for an organising view of the whole, without which the Scientist was bound to become closeted within his own corner, and even there be hampered.

An outsider might, to be sure, have considered it a little peculiar for Trotsky, sitting in an exalted office, to use his journalistic versatility to tell a group of topmost scientists that one of their luminaries would have been still *more* distinguished if he had been a Marxist!

He even mentioned the fission of the atom, which in this March 1926 comprehensive speech he predicted as flowing inevitably from the evolution of physics. He associated this prediction with a parallel and indeed contingent prediction, that of a 'social revolution' that would 'coincide' with it.[29]

As for defending, not Freudianism, but tolerance with respect to it – he thought Freudianism itself 'capricious' – Trotsky found himself involved in the same sort of tangle he was in with respect to politics in general.

Freud was blocked both by the puritanism of the Bolsheviks, who as primitive Marxists thought Freud carried on too much about sex in a way that made it somehow incompatible with Marxism, and by the native Russian school of Pavlovians, conservative in politics but naturally monopolistic with respect to their own field. Thus, even though the Pavlovians were not Marxists, their theories seemed to the Bolsheviks much more 'materialistic', and thus acceptable as against what seemed to them Freud's mystical or at any rate non-materialistic, personal, and 'unconscious' explanations. The combination of the two reactions – both, moreover, true-Russian! – was enough to bury Freud's work. It was violently attacked from the early 1920s on and finally suppressed.

Trotsky had been upset by this early on: in 1922 he wrote to Pavlov[30] asking him in a nice way to sponsor a little broadmindedness and come out for general freedom of enquiry. If Pavlov got the letter he paid no attention; for the next few years Trotsky let the whole subject lie. When he returned to it in 1926, on the eve of his exclusion from the Party, it was to become just one more of the countless phenomena of Soviet life he was protesting against – in this case the obsequiousness surrounding the school of Pavlov as it did all Soviet institutions.

In his letter to Pavlov he had defended Freud's theory as such, claiming it was all right because it was at bottom materialistic too: his defence of Freud seems to have been based on the claim that philosophically it was just as legitimate as Pavlov's theory – both being materialistic.

Here is his comparison of the two approaches:

The idealists hold that the 'soul' is a bottomless well. Both Pavlov and Freud think its bottom is constituted by physiology. Pavlov, like a diver, plunges down to the lowest depth and diligently investigates the well from the bottom to the top. Pavlov's approach is by experiment: Freud's is by guesswork, sometimes fantastic.... An attempt to declare psycho-analysis 'incompatible' with Marxism and merely turn one's back on Freudianism is too simple, or rather, simple-minded. But in any case we are not obliged to adopt Freudianism either. It is a working hypothesis that can and indubitably does give rise to conclusions and surmises pointing toward a materialist psychology. In due time experimentation will put it to the test. Meanwhile we have no right or justification to ban another approach that, even though it is less reliable, tries to anticipate results towards which the experimental approach leads only very slowly.[31]

Presumably, if Freud's theories *had* gone beyond materialism, or been 'incompatible' with Marxism, Trotsky – and a government, say, led by him – might have 'turned their back on it', perhaps proscribed it. When Trotsky says that 'meanwhile' they did not have the right to 'ban' it the implication must have been that at some other time a ban might well be in order!

The situation, to be sure, never arose. The suppression of Freudianism was shortly followed by that of Einstein's theories, which Trotsky also championed (the ban on Einstein was not lifted until after Stalin's death in 1953; Freud is still proscribed).

Trotsky's real *métier* was literary criticism, where amateurism can scarcely be said to exist. Here too he expressed a tolerant humanism. He could not bear the philistinian, arrogant contempt for the past and the even more arrogant self-complacency of the new Bolshevik orthodoxy, which rapidly dominated and eventually monopolised all artistic expression in the Soviet Union. The 'orthodox' stance in life embraced, naturally, all coteries in both art and literature : in a more normal society they would have gone in for the usual tug-of-war between would-be innovators struggling to impress the more or less inert mass of outsiders, but in the Soviet Union, with power swiftly coagulating about the Party summits and en route taking on the attributes of moral righteousness and total *exclusiveness*, the coteries themselves soon began flinging their weight about as 'truly revolutionary', etc.

All this was taking place against a background of almost complete emptiness; there was no large educated public at all; the heritage of the past was still being denied, very nearly totally; what the great revolutionary upsurge stimulated in the arts was very nearly nil.

It was in this wilderness that the Proletkult was propagandising vigorously for a monopoly. Bukharin, as editor of Pravda, and Lunacharsky, the urbane Commissar of Education, were its champions; Lenin had sneered at it, thus very nearly crushing it. The Proletkult thought Trotsky might back them, but he agreed with Lenin that art must not be forced within official slogans.

After the putsch had been ramified into a state mythology as well as a state apparatus, there was no end to the effervescence of the tiny elite; it gave rise to strange literary formations.

Trotsky's attitude toward literature was, of course, positive. He was essentially, after all, a writer – a writer with a commitment that coloured his views, but wholly receptive to the literary medium as such. Though this sometimes exasperated him about specific writers his temperament was generous enough to sustain a certain urbanity that precluded spitefulness.

Morally, or perhaps aesthetically, Trotsky was in a strong position. Though always 'orthodox', he was in practice not at all fanatical: he was quite sympathetic to the 'fellow-travellers' – a word he invented to refer to those writers who were able to 'travel a stretch of the road with The Revolution' without being converted to Communism.

By a sufficient contortion of the mind these fellow-travellers could even 'reject' Communism while 'accepting' Bolshevism: Bolshevism being the characteristically Russian i.e., savage, primitive even Asiatic aspect of The Revolution, Communism being the contemporary, working-class, 'European' factor.

Trotsky's attack on Proletkult (the core of *Literature and Revolution*) singled out just that element in it that was to become the cultural axis of Stalinism.

His acumen and humaneness enabled him to see what was, to be sure, obvious: though influenced by social factors, art essentially transcends them. As he put it:

> It is fundamentally wrong to oppose proletarian culture and proletarian art to bourgeois culture and bourgeois art. The former will never exist at all, since the proletarian regime is temporary and transitory. The historical meaning and the moral grandeur of the proletarian revolution lies in this, that it is laying the foundations of a classless culture, the first that will be truly universal.[52]

Using the Marxist time-table, Trotsky was bound to visualise the 'proletarian' period in this perspective; it fitted in with his general view that the Dictatorship of the Proletariat, especially in a primitive country like Russia, was justified only because it ensured the swift transition to the economy of abundance that with Socialism would then make a classless society not only possible, but inevitable. Thus it *had* to be 'temporary and transitory'. With technology being developed by the Dictatorship as fast as it could within the straitjacket of Bolshevik controls, even the ancient legacy of barbarism would soon yield to the tug of history; hence the talk about 'proletarian' art was stupid as well as reactionary.

Trotsky could give free rein to his imagination:

> Having rationalised. . . . his economic order, man will totally demolish his present-day warped, debased domestic life. The cares of feeding and rearing children, a gravestone weighing on today's family, will be swept away together with it, and become an object of social initiative and inexhaustible collective creati-

vity. Woman will emerge, finally, from her semi-barbarous status. Alongside technique, pedagogy, in the sense of the psychological formation of new generations, will become the queen of social thought. Pedagogical systems will rally round themselves mighty 'parties'. Socio-educational experiments, the competition between different methods, will achieve dimensions that today are not even conceivable. Communist life will not be shaped blindly like coral reefs, but will be consciously constructed, tested by thought, directed and corrected.

Not only that: man will finally harmonise himself in earnest. He will set himself the task of implanting within the movements of his own organs – in working, in walking, in playing – the greatest precision, purposefulness, economy, and hence beauty. He will want to master the semi-conscious and then, also, the unconscious processes of his own organism – breathing, blood circulation, reproduction – and . . . subject them to the control of reason and will. Life, even in its purely physiological aspects, will be experimented on collectively.

This lies wholly in the line of evolution. Man first drove out the dark elements from production and ideology: he overcame barbaric routine by scientific technique and religion by science. Then he drove out the unconscious from politics, overthrowing the monarchy and class-society by democracy and rationalistic parliamentarism, then by a transparent, Soviet, out-and-out dictatorship. The worst of the blind elements was in economic relations – he eliminated even those through the socialist organisation of the economy. . . .

Finally, in the deepest and darkest corner of the unconscious . . . there lurks the nature of man himself. Isn't it obvious that the greatest efforts of the inquiring mind and of creative initiative will be directed at that? The human race will not have ceased creeping about on all fours before God, Tsars and capital in order to bow down docilely to the dark laws of heredity and blind sexual relations! Liberated man will want to attain . . . a more balanced evolution in the breakdown of his tissues . . . there can be no doubt that it is just this extreme anatomical and physiological disharmony in man . . . that gives to the life-instincts the . . . hysterical . . . fear of death that darkens reason and nourishes stupid and humiliating fantasies about an existence beyond the grave.

Man will set himself the goal of mastering his own feelings, of raising his instincts to the summit of consciousness, of making them transparent, of extending his will-power to the subterranean . . . and thus lifting himself to a new stage, making himself a higher socio-biological type – Superman, if you like.

The average human type will rise to the level of Aristotle, Goethe, Marx. And above these heights still loftier pinnacles will rise.[33]

These long-range analyses, based on ideal conditions, wildly irrelevant to what was actually going on, were just what made Trotsky a misfit. His vision collided with the crystallisation of the upper strata of the parvenu society – the Party orang-outangs and the titanic bureaucracy. By elevating art beyond their comprehension as well as their controls he was breaking a primal law of organisational behaviour.

For there were no ideal artists at all in Trotsky's sense; by definition, in fact, they could not yet have come into existence. In cultural life, too, Trotsky was without a faction! He was simply the spokesman, once again, for abstract ideas, in a situation where such ideas had found no embodiments.

During the Twenties politics – in the sense of a rapidly evolving straitjacket – was bound to engulf all aspects of life. The Party General Line laid down for economics and politics could not ignore the humanities.

Trotsky's vision outstripped both the prejudices of his colleagues and the 'public opinion' of the elite. Since his views on culture had a general unity – cosmopolitanism, humanism, tolerance – it was natural for them to be lumped together with his opinions on politics and economics. Just as the 'official' attitude began to be institutionalised and to encompass very nearly everything, so it also became natural to stigmatise whatever Trotsky said about almost anything as part of something that toward the mid-Twenties rapidly became a 'heresy'.

As the working-class ingredient of the Bolshevik Party vanished, as it did very nearly altogether by the early Twenties, it was natural, in fact, for the attack on Trotsky's views on culture to single out his rejection of Proletkult as the primordial element of that heresy.

Just as Trotsky had failed to grasp the transformation of the Bolshevik Party into a vested interest, so in attacking Proletkult and its adherents among the upstart elite he was again attacking one more vested interest, with no vested interest of his own to shield him.

It was a reflection of his 'alienation' from the new society.

CHAPTER X

The Toboggan

AGAINST THE BUSTLING background of his own versatility, Trotsky, after his diminishment in 1923, was politically quiescent. In public he said nothing about the issues churning up the Politburo and the Central Committee.

Yet under a regime that was rapidly being consolidated along monolithic lines he could scarcely insulate himself.

The first Congress after Lenin's death (the Thirteenth) had gagged him on two fundamental topics – economics and the intra-Party regime. But though debarred from discussing policy, he could not keep quiet. To express himself he resorted to – a discussion of history.

Before his downgrading the Party had authorised the publication of his *Works*. In 1924 he took advantage of this to write a new preface to a volume of speeches and writings in 1917 : it was called *Lessons of October.*

This volume, whose publication coincided with the anchoring of the Lenin cult as the foundation of Soviet orthodoxy, was to prove fatal for Trotsky. By bringing about a broad philosophical confrontation it obliged his enemies to systematise their enmity. They had to accommodate Trotsky's powers of generalisation : the need for systematisation entailed the creation of canons of orthodoxy, already inherent no doubt, in Marxism, and ineluctable against the Soviet background.

The Party hagiography had established Trotsky, for the Party rank-and-file, as more or less a Menshevik, because of his semi-Menshevik past before 1917. In the framework of the rapidly evolving Bolshevik orthodoxy this charge was lethal.

Bolshevik mythology had long since obliterated the actual events of 1917. By 1924, moreover, less than one per cent of the Party had been in it since 1917. Thus the putsch itself was quite unknown to most of the younger generation. In particular, it was known only via the Party, since whatever might have been the real memories of its participants, these were a handful compared with the scores of millions of people now the targets of Party propaganda.

Hence the publication of Trotsky's actual speeches and articles from 1917 was a first-rate opportunity to correct the impressions being formed of Trotsky as an inherent opponent of the Bolshevik Party: young people, distressed to learn that the Commissar of War had once sympathised with the Mensheviks or indeed been one, could then be given Trotsky's own account. This would naturally expose the mendacity of the campaign now being waged against him. Since the putsch was Trotsky's chief revolutionary credential, it was natural for him to make use of it.

On the other hand, it was – equally naturally – bound to enrage his opponents.

Once again he was using the method of appealing to a mass audience in his public capacity. He wrote a lengthy preface that also came out as a brochure. This was not merely a reminder of his heroic role in 1917, but a sustained attack on his current opponents – the whole leadership!

By highlighting his own role in the putsch, by downgrading the whole of the Party leadership in April 1917 – when the Party had had to be won over to the putsch by Lenin – and by then going on to the present, to discuss principles of revolutionary leadership with special reference to the German crisis of 1923, *Lessons of October* constituted a violent attack on the Politburo. Trotsky established an organic contrast between the revolutionary leadership offered by Lenin and himself and the passivity of the other leaders; he attributed the defeat of The Revolution in Germany to that same passivity.

Trotsky's raising of this fundamental question – historical only superficially – was the trigger for a campaign of self-defence on the part of the leadership that created a paradigm at first for the slanting, then for the distortion and finally for the outright fabrication of history. In order to smother this version of Trotsky's, Stalin,

Zinoviev, and Kamenev organised a vast movement involving even foreign Communists.

At first Trotsky's version of his own pre-eminent role was not denied but merely put 'into proper perspective': then, as whole throngs of writers were involved, it became possible to invent things outright.

The key fabrication was doubtless Stalin's. He came out with an account of the central event flatly stating that the putsch had not been made by the Military Revolutionary Committee, presided over by Trotsky, but by a quite different 'centre' that Stalin was in but not Trotsky.

Up to this intervention of Stalin's in the fight – in Bolshevik jargon the 'literary debate' – no one had ever said this, not in a single one of the countless historical accounts composed by the Party. Insiders apparently greeted it with some levity at first, but it swiftly made its way into all histories and textbooks; in fact it remained the only official account of the putsch throughout Stalin's lifetime.

Thus the attempt to outmanoeuvre Trotsky in the bizarre conditions of the Bolshevik jungle took this roundabout form: history had to be rewritten to defend those Trotsky had been attacking. This was so easy it has served as the model for Soviet historiography to this day.

There is some slight irony to be enjoyed, perhaps, by recalling that when this started in 1924, the people, aside from Stalin, who were most assiduous in obliterating Trotsky were themselves to be wiped out in a little more than a decade, as victims of the Moscow 'Show Trials', produced by Stalin via the same fabrication-mill, vastly expanded and streamlined.

Yet at that time re-writing history was not quite adequate: it was difficult to single out the putsch as the sole touchstone for running down Trotsky; there his role could not be *entirely* obliterated. Trotsky's current depravity had to be integrated into a long history of depravity in the past. The no-good Trotsky of 1924 had to be equated with a Trotsky who had always been no-good.

Trotsky's non-, or even anti-Bolshevik past was interwoven with the concept of the General Line of the Party – Stalin's handiwork. It was the General Line, established during the Twenties, that laid the foundations of Soviet orthodoxy.

It was, essentially, a device enabling the dominant faction of the Party to impose interpretations of theory. As a 'science' Marxism has so many elusive elements that without some sort of ritual any decision might generate endless debate. The evolving 'official' attitude laid it down that only one mode of behaviour in any given situation was correct: ergo, all others were wrong. Hence a 'deviation' from the General Line was pernicious.

The notion of the Line was given a theological definition much like original sin: people who were anti-Bolsheviks by nature could not be anything else : they might *seem* to be struggling to be Right, but their Wrong nature was bound to assert itself.

Thus Trotsky's old disagreements with Lenin could be made much of as displaying an inherent irreconcilability. In the aftermath of the putsch, also, their fallings-out – of which only two, the dispute about Brest-Litovsk and the trades-union question, had been of any consequence – could be blown up as showing that even after Trotsky seemed to have become a Bolshevik he was still *really* an enemy alien. This was done, of course, in order to show that he was attacking Lenin's legitimate heirs today just as yesterday he had attacked Lenin himself.

The great 'literary debate' ranged far and wide, all the way back to 1905–6. It finally brought forth one central idea that from then on was to brand Trotsky himself and anything labelled 'Trotskyite'.

This was his theory of Permanent Revolution, which until 1924 had been just as much of a Party dogma as the Party's other dogmas; it had, in fact, been the theory used, within sophisticated Party circles, to justify the putsch itself.

By now, however, the German collapse of 1923 was very much to the fore in discussions; as it became plain that the prospects of World Revolution were for the time being, at least, utterly nil, and as the Bolshevik Party was definitely thrust back on its own resources, the problem of current programme, more acute than ever, was still further away from any hope to be found in The Revolution.

In this situation, Trotsky's theory was seized on as the hallmark of his depravity.

Since Lenin, though he had accepted this theory in 1917, had also attacked it before, it was easy to dredge up a few such attacks – from 1906! – to show that Trotsky's theory had been pernicious from the outset.

In 1906 Lenin had said that Trotsky had been too optimistic about the Socialist consummation of The Revolution – Trotsky had 'jumped over' the Bourgeois phase and had in addition 'underestimated the peasantry'. These two charges were now, in this initial phase of Trotsky's annihilation, to become clichés. They then had to

be reconciled, to be sure, with other clichés about his being a
Menshevik (the Mensheviks had not wanted to go *beyond* the
Bourgeois phase), but in order to do this it was necessary to generate
and systematise a simply stupendous amount of verbiage that was
altogether beyond even the most sophisticated Bolsheviks, to say
nothing of the rank-and-file.

In addition, of course, the denunciation of Permanent Revolution
was a natural form of demagogy, in view of what Russians had been
through for the previous decade. By talking of the Permanent
Revolution as a piece of incendiarism they could easily discredit it
among all those now hoping to settle down at last.

Permanent Revolution was anathematised: it was made the
counterpart of the True Doctrine, Socialism in One Country, which
was launched by Stalin during this singular 'literary debate' in the
autumn of 1924, scarcely six months after he had said, with the rest
of the Party, the precise opposite – i.e., that the attempt to construct
Socialism in Russia could be successful only as a prelude to world
revolution.

Willy-nilly, accordingly, by indulging himself in the only form of
political response he was capable of, Trotsky gave rise to a campaign
that precisely because of his literary gifts found in him a target of
sufficient substance to transform into a heresy.

There was something blood-curdling about the mobilisation of the
State's resources against one of its founders. Here is Trotsky's
description of what happened shortly after Lenin's death:

When the secret preparatory work was finished, a campaign
against Trotskyism burst forth, at a signal from *Pravda*, simultaneously from all sides, on all platforms, in all newspapers and
columns, in every single nook and cranny. Of its kind it was a
grandiose spectacle. The slander took on the appearance of a
volcanic eruption. The broad mass of the Party was shaken up. I
lay in bed with a temperature and kept my mouth shut. Journalists
and speakers were taken up with nothing but the exposure of
'Trotskyism'. No one knew just what that meant. Day after day
episodes from the past were served up, polemical quotations from
Lenin's articles of twenty years back: they were jumbled up,
falsified and twisted, but the main thing was as though it had all
happened the day before. No one could understand anything. If it
had all really happened, then Lenin, after all, was bound to have
known about it. The October Revolution, after all, had happened

subsequently. The insurrection, after all, had been followed by
Civil War. Together with Lenin, after all, Trotsky had created the
Komintern. Everywhere pictures of Trotsky were hanging, after
all, alongside pictures of Lenin. After all . . . after all . . . but
slander poured forth like a cold stream of lava.

Natalya's *Diary* around this time is poignant; not only does it show
Trotsky ill, it casts into high relief his spiritual inadequacy:

The second attack of L.D.'s illness coincided with a monstrous
campaign of harassment against him that we endured as though it
were a most virulent disease. The pages of *Pravda* seemed enormous, endless; every line of the paper, every single letter in it was
a lie. L.D. kept silent. But what that silence cost him! Friends
dropped in on him throughout the day, and sometimes even at
night. I recall someone asking him whether he had not read the
day's paper. He replied that in general he was not reading newspapers. He really did just take them in his hands, scarcely glanc-
ing through them and throwing them aside. . . . He knew only too
well the cooks who were preparing this dish, and the same dish
every single day to boot. Reading the newspapers of that time, he
would say, was just like sticking a funnel brush into your throat.
. . . But he remained silent. His cold dragged on, because of his
grave nervous condition. He grew terribly pale and thin. In the
family we avoided talking about the harassment, yet there was
nothing else we could talk about either. I remember how I felt
every day on my way to work at the Commissariat of Education:
it was like running a gauntlet.[1]

It is disconcertingly obvious that Trotsky simply did not know
what to do. Later on he was to say, falling back on his characteristic
loftiness, that the campaign of 'unflagging slander, bellowing furi-
ously . . . howling rabidly, drowned out its own contradictions, its
own emptiness. It won by mere volume.'[2]

By the mid-Twenties Trotsky had been established as a dangerous
alien – a 'passive' anti-Bolshevik and at the same time an incorrigible
mischief-maker masquerading under mock-radical phrases.

The scope of this campaign – its general tendency no less than its
content – was in its nature altogether different from the mere
polemics that had once given the Marxist milieu its impenetrability.
As soon as it was observed that outright falsification was successful,

that no account whatever need be taken of what Trotsky had actually said, in what context, and so on, it was possible to paint an arbitrary portrait to fit the tactical requirements of the dominant faction at first, and later on to establish it more broadly, as the linchpin of an entire view of the cosmos in which Trotsky was, quite simply, equated with the Devil.

The long-range consequences of his *Lessons of October* were thus fatal for Trotsky; the more immediate ones were also disastrous.

By showing that Lenin's disciples had disagreed with him Trotsky really shocked the pious who thought the leaders all acted in unison. In addition, this kind of attack was very good for Stalin, who as a practically inarticulate Bolshevik was spared most of Trotsky's ferocious analysis, while Zinoviev and Kamenev, voluble intellectuals, were torn to shreds. Thus Stalin, relative to the others, looked more and more like the Arch-Bolshevik – very pure!

By breaking ranks, moreover, with the mass of senior Bolsheviks, whose Bolshevik pasts could not, after all, be taken from them, Trotsky tended to shelter all sorts of non-Bolshevik dissidents now being repressed. This made it all the easier for Trotsky's opponents to point to him as being, in fact, a rallying-point for enemies of the Party just when the Party tops insisted on 'unity' above all, a unity that Trotsky himself had leaned over backwards stressing.

His status was still imposing: he was still Commissar of War, with a close control, one might have thought, over the army. A year before, when he had offered his resignation from this office as well as from all others, Stalin, Zinoviev and Kamenev had not yet been sure enough of themselves to accept it. Now they were more than prepared to oust him altogether.

The theory of Trotsky as a Bonaparte is grimly amusing if one recalls what a stickler he was for correctness: he forbade any attempts to involve in the bitter polemics of 1923 and 1924 the military cells, which had a special voice.

Hence, when some of the most important posts within his own Commissariat were given to other nominees, and Trotsky's own sympathisers were simply dismissed, he did nothing to defend them and nothing to stop the Politburo from trampling all over his Commissariat. There too the Party was right.

In 1924 he lost all control of his own Commissariat, his last line of defence. By the time the Trio had thrown their net over all the political commissars assigned to the army, it was easy for *them* to involve the army cells in their undermining of Trotsky, who was duly condemned by the army cells for the *Lessons of October* and whose ouster as War Commissar was duly voted: the same thing happened in the Military Revolutionary Council, which he had been chairman of since its inception.

Trotsky did nothing; he was suffering from malarial fever again. On 15 January 1925 he wrote the Central Committee, whose plenum was to meet two days later, that he was off to the Caucasus for his health. He also gave a terse summary of his answer to the chief charges aimed at him in connection with *The Lessons of October* – his only reply in this whole 'literary debate' – and resigned as president of the Military Revolutionary Council.

He was now out of all strategic positions, retaining only his position on the Politburo itself and on the Central Committee; in both he was utterly outmatched.

The Central Committee plenum that came together on 17 January 1925 reserved its chief discussion for the 'Trotsky case'. Zinoviev and Kamenev tried to have him expelled from both the Politburo and the Committee; once more Stalin, moderate and wise, blocked them. Trotsky was to remain a member of both bodies, but was put under a threat of formal expulsion if he carried on any more public argumentation. The Committee formally cut short the 'literary debate', at the same time sending out directives to all its ideological sections to carry on with the 'enlightenment of the whole party . . . about the anti-Bolshevik character of Trotskyism, beginning from the year 1903' – when Trotsky was twenty-four! – 'and ending with the *Lessons of October*'. The Committee also initiated a parallel propaganda movement to make it clear to the whole population, as well as the Party, how vile 'Trotskyism' was.

The Central Committee session was tranquil: it ended with his removal from the Military Revolutionary Council. His connection with the institution in which, aside from the putsch, he had played the most effective role was terminated by a summary dismissal couched as a blanket denunciation.

He might now have seemed retired: he was leading the life of a government functionary with what amounted to a literary hobby.

He had plainly given up whatever ambitions within the Party he might have had. If his desire, immediately after the putsch, to leave the Government is recalled, it might even be taken for granted that he was now willing to slide into retirement and resume his more natural pursuit of literature.

He seemed, in any case, to be indifferent to Party conflicts: he signalised his contemptuous detachment by reading a book – a French novel, to boot![3] – in the Central Committee. His aphorism about Stalin as the most 'eminent mediocrity' in the Party summed up his attitude toward the Government as a whole. He was subtracting himself, so to speak, from the historic process.

His passivity was all the more striking because of the ferment of the Party elite during just this period of the mid-Twenties.

They were being harrowed by the tension inherent in the contrast between Bolshevik goals and the successful N.E.P., with its restoration of more or less normal farming, industry, and social stability.

Industry was too primitive to make it worth the peasants' while to supply the towns; about a third of the population, accordingly, (including the towns and cities) were eating only about two-thirds of what they had eaten under the Tsars, and only half as much meat.

The Bolsheviks had not yet co-ordinated the peasants, who had recovered from the famine in the early Twenties and were eating again, though they had to pay twice as much for inferior industrial goods as before 1914 without getting much more for their own produce. The peasants constituted a cardinal problem for the Bolsheviks, who had nationalised the land after expropriating the landowners. The peasants living on the nationalised land did not own it. They were still stratified in the traditional categories of well-to-do peasants who occupied a good deal of land and could employ labour – perhaps ten to twenty per cent of the total – the small holders who did their own work – another thirty to forty per cent – and the remainder, peasants with perhaps a small plot of their own but with no horses or equipment, which they had to hire from the richer peasants and pay for by their own work. A decade after the Bolshevik putsch the wages of landless farm labourers were forty per cent lower than they had been under the big landowners; they worked much harder. They were, in effect, serfs. The 'poor' farmers were still worse off.

The Bolshevik apparatus was in chronic crisis. The collision between the private sector of the economy and the large-scale expansion of industry via 'primitive Socialist accumulation' was about to split the Party ideologues.

It was this collision that drew Trotsky out of his retirement and sealed his fate.

In the intensely political milieu of the Party elite it was, of course, difficult to be inert. Trotsky's name was still associated with strong views on all the questions churning up the ideologues. By the beginning of 1926, to be sure, those sympathetic to his views amounted to no more than a handful of people: in Moscow he had a few energetic, intelligent sympathisers, including his friend Christo Rakovsky and men like Pyatakov, Preobrazhensky, Radek and Krestinsky. In Leningrad a small group of friends met at the flat of his first wife, Alexandra. In the provinces there was practically no one.

Trotsky preserved his silence even as the conflict between the two schools of thought about the country's economy turned into a head-on collision. His views on industrialisation were expressed by others, notably Preobrazhensky, with the difference that whereas Trotsky still thought full industrialisation possible only against a background of international revolution, Preobrazhensky thought it could be done with Russian resources alone (this ultimately reconciled him to 'Socialism In One Country').

These views were counterposed to those of men like Bukharin, who believed in backing the peasants, especially the rich peasants, since they were the only ones who could grow a marketable surplus. Bukharin and his sympathisers held that private enterprise had to be rewarded within the framework of a Socialism that at this point depended on a growth of prosperity for the nation as a whole; hence it was natural to reinforce agriculture as the biggest portion of the private sector.

Stalin himself always behaved in sharp contrast with the Party ideologues: he made a point of blunting the 'logic' behind ideological clashes, of skirting jagged edges and indeed ideology in general. His practical attitude enabled him to pick any argument that suited his immediate purpose. Thus he could ally himself with Bukharin's arguments without going to extremes: the main point of agreement – Socialism in One Country – was fundamental; on that basis they were allies for a time.

This radical disagreement on basic policy now split the Trio.

The Leningrad Party was most sensitive to the terrible state of industry; the city's industrial plant was idle. Moreover, the relatively sophisticated Leningrad workers were alive to the need for industrialisation as a general thing; they disliked the notion that Soviet economic recovery had to depend on the pace of agricultural convalescence.

Zinoviev, still at the head of the Leningrad Party, was a natural leader of this 'anti-peasant' tendency; the whole of the Party, as well as the Young Communist League, aired their views freely in the Leningrad press.

There had been no spiritual unity between Stalin and his fellow-triumvirs; they had been forced together, in fact, by their over-estimation of Trotsky as an adversary. With Trotsky dislodged from the War Commissariat and gagged, there was no rationale for their coalition.

Stalin and his entourage began referring to themselves as the 'Centre'.

The conflict between what now appeared to be two wings of the Party jutting out, as it were, from Stalin's 'centre', was hotting up to such a degree that an open clash could not be avoided. Led by Zinoviev and Kamenev, the new opposition to Stalin at first involved Trotsky as a merely passive object.

A statement signed by Zinoviev, Kamenev, Krupskaya, and Sokol-nikov calling for an open discussion on fundamental controversies was submitted to the Central Committee: the discussion was to precede the Fourteenth Party Congress scheduled for the end of 1925. It was an open attack on the Party machine in an effort to by-pass Stalin, allied at the moment with Bukharin, via the Party membership (something like Trotsky's own futile attempts before his previous defeat).

The simple mechanism that had gagged Trotsky now worked again: the Central Committee forbade the discussion that traditionally preceded any Congress: they thus gagged Zinoviev and Kamenev as they had Trotsky.

A violent fight now broke out between the former partners in the Trio: passions ran high. When the Fourteenth Congress opened (18 December 1925), Zinoviev attacked the Bukharinites openly, and by implication, Stalin.

Zinoviev's position might have seemed strong: he was not only President of the Comintern – which meant little – but he had his own base, the powerful Leningrad Party.

The Congress was tempestuous: Trotsky was mute. Zinoviev and Kamenev violently attacked Stalin and his entourage; Krupskaya attacked the Lenin cult.

The concept of Socialism in One Country was given a systematic exposition: Trotsky sat on in silence. The wrangling was so intense that the former Trio washed all their dirty linen in public, giving a detailed account of all their squabbles, including those involving

Trotsky. Zinoviev mentioned disbanding the Young Communist Central Committee after a big majority vote in it for Trotsky; Stalin reported his rescue of Trotsky's person from the lethal intentions of Zinoviev and Kamenev.

The Fourteenth Congress witnessed, in short, a genuine clash of opinion: the general issues of The Revolution and the very shape of the regime were wrestled over in public. The quarrelling was carried on, to be sure, in a theological idiom far beyond the rank-and-file of the Party, to say nothing of The Masses!

Trotsky was actually praised by both sides, and lavishly at that. It was plain, because of the Politburo split, with a chasm yawning between Stalin and his former allies, that Trotsky might make some practical use of his previously ineffective public stance.

As usual Stalin presented himself as a conciliator, chiding Zinoviev and Kamenev with wishing to start a process of 'amputations' and 'bloodletting' in the Party by proposing Trotsky's exclusion. Mentioning some incidents in which Bukharin had come under fire, he suddenly cried out: 'And now they want Bukharin's blood!'

It has been suggested that this abrupt, unexpected mention of bloodshed – still remote – was meant to emphasise the innocuousness of the merely political sanctions now inflicted on the losers.[4]

The violent Congress ended with a bitter defeat for Zinoviev: he was expelled from the Leningrad Party and replaced by a protégé of Stalin's (Sergei Kirov). The Opposition were severely disciplined, and lost control of the Party newspaper in Leningrad. The news of all this gave rise to stormy manifestations in Leningrad; they came to nothing.

Kamenev was expelled as leader of the Moscow Party; his successor saw to it that Trotsky was denied access to the Party cells on a variety of pretexts: the prohibition was accompanied by the usual propaganda to the effect that this was his own choice: just then Trotsky was making cultural speeches to various groups of intellectuals, including scientists; the workers were informed that Trotsky preferred 'bourgeois' audiences.

Characteristically, the moment the Congress was *over*, Trotsky came out in defence of the Leningrad Opposition, on the basis of *general principles*. He considered the repression bad *as such*, but did nothing to help the Opposition practically.

Stalin now began to lump together the sympathisers of both Trotsky and Zinoviev. Their Jewish origin served a useful purpose: it enabled the official propagandists to say, sinisterly, that 'it was no accident' that Stalin was opposed by Jews. I.e., Stalin's entourage, leaping lightly over Stalin's own Georgian origins, claimed to be native, authentic, true-blue Russian; others were enemy aliens.

Throughout this entire upheaval Trotsky had said nothing whatever. Much later he was to say that he had been caught completely unawares: the 'situation (had) . . . appeared absolutely unclear' to him.[5] This was partly, as he said, because he had no idea of what the Trio had been talking about privately. But it must also have been, surely, because of his state of mind.

The basic question of Socialism in One Country, outlined by Stalin and Bukharin a year and a half before, was not commented on at all by Trotsky for still another year and a half. Yet it was a key principle that he regarded as the quintessence of the 'vulgar Marxism' he detested and that he was to devote the rest of his life to fighting.

Trotsky had been so embittered by his previous relations with Zinoviev and Kamenev that he could not envisage joining forces with them. He thought of them as 'right wingers', because of their opposition to the October putsch itself and because of their identification with those old Bolsheviks he thought guilty of 'bureaucratic degeneration'. Also, very naturally, he was suspicious of their opportunism – something he himself was so inept at. For years – ever since 1923 – he had been cutting both Zinoviev and Kamenev and vice versa; it was a difficult habit to overcome, especially in the case of Kamenev, his brother-in-law.

Months were to go by, in fact, before there were any signs of a *rapprochement*, which came about only when it was forced on all three men by the evolution of Stalin's career.

In the Spring of 1926 they began supporting each other at a Central Committee session as it were spontaneously; then they met, reluctantly, for a practical chat.

They had a secret, rather emotional meeting. Now forty-three, Zinoviev and Kamenev were in their prime. Zinoviev was running a bit to fat: he had a rather pale, round face, a massive and somewhat dishevelled mane, with grey-blue eyes. Kamenev, with his 'middle-class', look, had a thick beard, already turning grey.

They did their best to charm Trotsky, and to banish the horrors of the recent past, with its nightmarish invention of 'Trotskyism'. They told him, cosily, how they had invented the whole idea: 'If you hadn't written your *Lessons of October* we should easily have found some other pretext. We had to attach the old disagreements to the current ones.'

Afterwards there were constant meetings in the Kremlin, sometimes in Trotsky's flat, sometimes in Kamenev's, Zinoviev's, or Radek's. Zinoviev and Kamenev complained of the circumstances of their collaboration with Stalin, how mistrustful of him they had to be, how his primitive culture, his poor grasp of ideas, his different intellectual background had weighed on them so heavily.

They gave Trotsky a novel re-assessment of Stalin's character seen close-up, and demonstrated the difference between his marvellously effective modest, sober, unassuming demeanour and his real nature – wily, perverse and sadistic.

Kamenev even revenged himself by imitating Stalin personally – his awkwardness, his accent, his elementary language. Trotsky found this distasteful, Natalya recalled; he would make an effort to change the subject. He disliked lowering the debate to quirks of behaviour.

As Trotsky said: 'The man is disagreeable enough as it is to meet . . . if it's necessary to go on and imitate him when he's not there, that's too much!'[6]

In fact, they gave Trotsky a lurid account of all Stalin's sinister qualities – he was not *merely* absurd! Both Zinoviev and Kamenev had written, and safely deposited somewhere, letters accusing Stalin personally, in case they were to die abruptly without a good explanation; they counselled Trotsky to do the same.[7]

Curiously enough, it took Trotsky years before he could believe the direct, immediate, human, convincing testimonies of the two former members of the Trio, one of them his brother-in-law. Their story showed the Kremlin to be a Borgia's lair: Trotsky's high-mindedness had made him disregard it.

Zinoviev and Kamenev were curiously optimistic; they, like Trotsky, had been quite baffled by the growth of the vast government apparatus; they thought their loss of 'popularity' was a sort of grotesque accident, an historical 'misunderstanding' easily rectified.

All three intellectuals looked upon Stalin in a purely personal way, assessing his qualities from their own rather parochial point of view. Despite the plain fact that he had been the prime ruler of the country for some years, since even before Lenin's death, they persisted in regarding him as a sort of lout, well below the level of them all and especially, of course, of Trotsky – as the former Triumvirs said to him winningly.

Trotsky was more pessimistic: he was by now inured to futility. Yet he, too, thought that if they all put out some joint 'statements' sponsored by some talented sympathisers they could somehow galvanise the Party against the background of a renewed 'upsurge' in the working class.

This was, of course, precisely the reasoning that lay behind Trotsky's previous defeats, in so far as those had been rooted in or at least defended by mere reasoning; a belief in the charismatic effectiveness of personality, plus a faith in development deduced from analysis and both together bypassing the real determinant of the whole situation – the looming apparatus!

Throughout this time Trotsky's strange illness plagued him. His persistent and unaccountable fever, his lassitude and sleeplessness, all no doubt due to 'hypertension', which had cropped up for years in critical moments were worse than ever. He would often say, 'My head is empty.' The whole family, indeed, had insomnia.

During the winters of 1924 and 1925, until well into the spring, Trotsky stayed in the Caucasus. The Soviet physicians, baffled, recommended their German colleagues; in the middle of April 1926 Trotsky went to Berlin with Natalya and a small escort.

Most of the time he was in a private clinic, without his beard and under a false name; in between examinations and a minor operation he roamed about the city incognito.

It did not last long; rumours of an attempt made on his life by White Russians were passed on to the clinic by the German police; he moved to the Soviet Embassy under heavy guard and then went back to Russia, with no improvement in his fever. His trip had lasted six weeks.

He now tried to make a deal with Zinoviev and Kamenev; one of his difficulties was that he had very few sympathisers. Since 1923 his following, however it might have been defined, had dwindled away. Moreover, their animosity with respect to Zinoviev was often insurmountable. Zinoviev's supporters, for their part, who had taken all the blather about 'Trotskyism' seriously, were bewildered by the switch: when Zinoviev and others explained that the whole campaign against 'Trotskyism' had been a mere ruse, innocents were shocked.

Thus the two coteries, of varying degrees of strength, cohesiveness and enthusiasm, were uneasy at the idea of a *rapprochement*. In addition, the leaders themselves were still at odds on many theoretical topics : this hampered their practical collaboration.

Immediately after Trotsky's return at the beginning of June 1926, Stalin attacked him in the Politburo on some minor points. Trotsky responded, following up his self-defence at the meeting with a provocative Open Letter[8] to the Politburo – threatening it with the likelihood of being taken over by a dictator unless it was completely overhauled.

An all-out attack on the closed circle he was attacking – conducted by a letter!

This time the conflict between Stalin and the 'Joint Opposition' led by Trotsky and Zinoviev was to be conclusive. It lasted about a year and a half; for Trotsky it came to an end with his banishment to Siberia.

Outside the tiny group of men at the Party summit no one heard about it; not a whisper ever made its way to The Masses whose destinies were the objects of the 'debate' within the Party. Thus the numbers involved were negligible; Stalin, with the government apparatus in his hands, was simply sparring with his utterly out-matched opponents in such a way as to keep up appearances in public.

Hence the Oppositionists – especially Trotsky, the most outstanding as a theoretician and orator – were obliged to carry on a debate in its nature hopeless without outside action. Their rhetoric, restricted to a tiny audience they could not possibly convince, was once again, like all Trotsky's *démarches*, dependent on the intervention of History.

And while Trotsky and his allies were totally insulated within the Party – the dogma of unity kept them locked up – Stalin completely controlled the Party structure and its elections, as well as all appointments and promotions. Because of this focal control of his, his own 'position' was indistinguishable from the Government's – it *was* the Government's!

A curious debate!

After Trotsky's declaration of war in his Open Letter the Oppositionists made some attempt to organise their disparate entourages. Stalin's office reacted at once by instructing the regular Party Committees to break up any Oppositionist meetings as illegal; if they persisted thugs were to break them up.

Hence all meetings had to be held secretly – fatal, in case of failure!

Nevertheless they managed to get together a few thousand followers: numbers have been assessed at some figure in between 4,000 to 8,000,[9] considered to be roughly divided between 'Trotsky-ites' and 'Zinovievites'.

The Joint Opposition was eager to bring together all dissidents *within* the Party regardless of any divergence of view in the past. Thus the assembly of a few thousand dissidents, not even sharing the same views, looks trivial against the background of the Party as a whole, which numbered about three-quarters of a million members.

The Joint Opposition was proclaimed within the Central Committee and the Central Control Commission. A policy statement ranged over all the questions vexing the regime: wage-policy, proposals for taxation reform with respect to the peasantry, for the acceleration of industrialisation, for the moderate, balanced collectivisation of farming, and in general for the strengthening of the Socialist sector of the Soviet economy. At the same time it explicitly condemned Socialism in One Country, optimistically assessing the chances of The Revolution abroad.

These ideas – all well-exposed views of Trotsky and the others – were expressed for the first time here in the form of a rounded policy statement presented to the dominant faction.

There was an outburst of violent polemics, highlighted by a two-hour hysterical denunciation of Kamenev by the Politburo Police Chief Dzerzhinsky, who on leaving the rostrum collapsed and died of a heart attack.

The Party framework was impenetrable: the Central Committee merely turned down Trotsky's 'policy statements', not on the basis of theory, but on the basis of Party discipline – Stalin simply accused the Joint Opposition of factionalism, i.e., of breaking the interdiction on the formation of factions laid down by Lenin and accepted by everyone in 1921.

He attacked Zinoviev for misusing his authority as President of the Comintern and, among other blows directed at less prominent Oppositionists, proposed that he be expelled from the Politburo at once.

Kamenev had already been demoted to alternate membership of the Politburo at the disastrous Fourteenth Congress; now Zinoviev was off it altogether and hence bound to leave the Comintern.

Stalin, in short, while taking pains to keep to all the rules, had instantaneously got rid of the President of the Comintern.

He had doubtless moved against Zinoviev out of prudence, since he was weaker as a figure, in some ways, than Trotsky, at least now that he had lost his stronghold in Leningrad. It sounded and in a way was 'moderate' on Stalin's part to do nothing for the moment against Trotsky.

The Politburo was obviously a cul-de-sac: argument there could accomplish nothing. Hence Trotsky and Zinoviev willy-nilly had to appeal to the rank-and-file against the Party leadership; during the summer of 1926 they told their sympathisers to start talking up the Party cells, telling the Party members of their arguments, 'theses' and so on.

This was catastrophic; even if the involved, tortuous, high technical, quasi-theological debate could have been carried from the Politburo to the Party cells to be defended there by workers, it would have been merely quixotic.

In any case the apparatus nipped the idea in the bud: they simply broke up all such meetings, and for the first time organised street disturbances on such a massive scale that even an accomplished, forceful, experienced orator like Trotsky, with a powerful voice and great wit, found it impossible to address meetings in factories and in railway workshops. The most famous orator in the country, he was checkmated by catcalls, hissings and booings. Other oppositionist speakers were handled still more savagely.

Throughout this suppression the crowds themselves, whatever their feelings might have been, were quite lethargic: in fact the apathy of The Workers confronted the Oppositionists with a stone wall.

This lethargy was endlessly reinforced by a rather obvious aspect of the dominant faction's behaviour, which had always been evident in Stalin's own manoeuvring. It consisted of blunting all 'principles' by applying them in a modulated form.

Thus, for instance, when the Joint Opposition called for a rise in workers' wages, they found themselves forestalled, when about to make an appeal to the Party membership, by Stalin's and Bukharin's promises along exactly the same lines. Similarly, with respect to industrialisation, Stalin, without giving Trotsky 'credit' for the idea, simply talked in the same vein; he also completely blurred the highly technical discussion of the peasantry by seeming to borrow some phraseology directed against the well-to-do peasant – the 'kulak'.

The Opposition in short, having been reduced to using nothing but arguments, could not, in the first place, get those arguments heard in the right context, and secondly, could not get their point across in such a way as to inconvenience the dominant faction.

Even if, ideally, an argument appealed to some segment of the population, the Opposition could not benefit when it was led by Stalin – it could only have the moral satisfaction of having been 'right'!

But what was still more fatal to the Oppositionists, and what was to prove infinitely beneficial to the faction in power, was the actual style of the argumentation.

It was incontestable that as late as 1924 the idea that Socialism was impossible in one country had been a Party axiom; there could be no doubt that Lenin himself had thought it an elementary implication of 'classical Marxism'.

Things had simply turned out wrong!

But that could not be admitted: the Party was in its nature *right*.

Hence, to refute the Opposition's references to 'classical Marxism' Stalin's entourage – equally devout, of course – was obliged to cover up its own inevitable and, as it were, materially determined lapses from classical Marxism by spinning a remarkable web of hairsplitting definitions, deductions, qualifications and so on, that in being refuted by the Oppositionists naturally collided with their own fine-spun web.

Neither side, of course, questioned the Party dictatorship as such: the Bolshevik monopoly remained a tacit axiom. And perhaps the main, though unconscious function of the flood of Marxist 'dialectics' was to camouflage that simple fact. The upshot was an impenetrable tangle of casuistry that was, above all, unbearably boring.

How, for instance, could an ordinary worker, peasant or for that matter Party member be expected to follow an intricate argument propping up a difference between Trotsky's idea, on the one hand, that Socialism could be fortified in Russia only through the world-wide spread of The Revolution, and the official claim that The Revolution was best served by the fortification of Socialism in Russia?

It was plainly out of the question. Yet since the Oppositionists – out of power – had to *persuade* the Party membership, they were bound to stupefy them.

Marxist polemics have always borne a heavy mortgage of in-accessibility: in the tussle between the dominant faction and

Trotsky in this era of the Twenties they achieved a gargantuan indigestibility that guaranteed the extinction of the Opposition.

On 4 October 1926 they proposed an armistice; Stalin accepted it at once, but made a point of wording the terms himself. The 'armistice' amounted to a total surrender: the Opposition were forced once again to accept the fundamental source of their tactical impotence – the binding quality of the Central Committee's directives.

They were barricaded within the same logical box; having tried to appeal to the Party cells after their failure within the Central Committee, they were now obliged to retreat to the confines of the Central Committee, which they were incapable of influencing by mere arguments, and thus to accept its straitjacket.

Spiritually, too, this retreat weakened them substantially: one of the surrender terms was the disavowal of their allies and sympathisers abroad as well as in Russia.

A week after their surrender had been broadcast,[10] Stalin nullified the truce: he added a report on the Opposition to what had been otherwise innocuous agenda for a Party conference. This was obviously a way of raising the issue all over again.

Trotsky naturally demanded that Stalin live up to the terms agreed on. No attention was paid to this. Stalin played a simple trick on the Opposition: he took advantage of another indiscretion of Trotsky's.

About a year before, Max Eastman (in his book *Since Lenin Died*) had printed some extracts from Lenin's Testament, at the time formally denied by Trotsky; this year Eastman had the entire document reprinted in the *New York Times*[11] giving an explanation of the characteristic light-mindedness of the whole operation. He later explained[12] the full publication as having been authorised, more or less, by a sympathiser of Trotsky's in France, and by the 'Opposition as a whole . . . a good many consciences in Moscow were troubled by Trotsky's disavowal of my book'.

What had happened is plain: when Trotsky found himself trapped into public opposition to Stalin, the publication of Lenin's Testament naturally suited him; it was merely a misfortune that his opposition did not last even long enough to benefit by the later publication, which coincided with his second, more massive defeat. Zinoviev and Kamenev had also been for the publication of Lenin's Testament at the Fourteenth Congress, independently of Trotsky;

when they all joined forces it was obviously high time for them to arrange for the document to be published.

Of course, had things gone better for them it would have appeared in *Pravda*; that was naturally out of the question now. When it appeared in a highly 'bourgeois' publication it made another *de facto* breach of discipline that Stalin, as a consummation of his blanket victory, could make them pay for all over again.

Thus, by the time the Central Committee met, on 23 October, the world press was full of the exposé: it aroused extravagant interest. Stalin came down on the Opposition in a full-dress onslaught on them as a 'Social-Democratic deviation', and this time, furthermore, called on them all to 'recant'.[13]

Maddened by helplessness at the Politburo meeting, Trotsky lost his temper: he made a violent speech culminating, as he turned to Stalin, in an outcry:

'The First Secretary is putting himself up for the post of the gravedigger of The Revolution!'

Stalin turned white, held on to himself for a moment, then rushed out of the room, banging the door shut.

This was the first time, with all the ferocity of Bolshevik polemics, that this particular kind of moral epithet had been used; it marked the overt transition between discord, however savage, and moral obloquy.

Here is Natalya's account of the reaction to Trotsky's outburst, while some friends were waiting in his flat for him to return from the meeting:

Pyatakov was the first to return. He was very pale and shaken. He poured out a glass of water, gulped it down, and said: 'I've been under fire, you know, but that, *that*! That was worse than anything! And why, why did Trotsky say that? Stalin will never forgive him, down to his great-great-grandchildren!' Shattered, he could not even explain clearly just what had happened. When Trotsky finally came into the dining-room Pyatakov lunged at him: But why, *why* did you say that?' Trotsky waved aside the questions. He was drained and calm. (He had yelled at Stalin 'Gravedigger of The Revolution!') We all understood that the rupture was irreparable.[14]

Next day, at a session of the Central Committee – many of whose members had witnessed the scene in the Politburo – Trotsky was thrown out of the Politburo altogether, and Zinoviev's elimination as President of the Comintern was formalised by his removal from the representation of the Soviet Communist Party on the Comintern executive.

The denouement was at the Fifteenth Party Conference at the end of October. The Oppositionists did not defend themselves *at all*; they were simply taunted, baited, and mocked. On the seventh day Stalin gave a remarkably zestful, occasionally comical and bitingly sarcastic account of the curious alliance between his current opponents. Zinoviev had once called Trotsky, in a rather routine way, the 'arch-eneny of Leninism', while Trotsky had sneered at him and Kamenev as the 'strike-breakers of October'. Stalin very effectively – to a hand-picked audience, to be sure! – poured scorn on the 'amnesty' they had given each other.

Trotsky himself made one of his strongest speeches, even to this hostile, but nevertheless, for a moment, respectful audience. It was so comprehensive, sober and at the same time penetrating, that he was allowed to speak much longer than his allotted time : he went over the whole ground once again, putting all disagreements and clashes and agitational action in his own characteristic perspective – that of The Revolution as a whole.

The calm surrounding Trotsky's speech did not last long; the assembly resumed the ferocious tone characteristic of Party 'debate'. Stalin himself was quite restrained; there was no need for him to be anything but heavily sarcastic. But his followers displayed the extraordinary thuggishness typical of the Central Committee, the topmost mass institution of the Party. Bukharin, in particular, the best 'theoretician of the Party', as Lenin said, now spoke in a style that was as brutal as it was extravagant: with Stalin's support he indulged himself in all sorts of malicious sallies – the Control Committee was convulsed with merriment.

Trotsky had been drawn out of his retirement by external circumstances. Practically passive when drawn into the Joint Opposition, he plainly lacked either the will or the ability to carry on a real 'fight' against the apparatus.

Now out of politics completely, he was back again in his natural medium – writing, editing, studying.

Yet with the Party now becoming more and more the sole mouthpiece of opinion, his tendency to comment on policy in the most comprehensive style possible kept leading him into one collision with the Party rulers after another.

It is difficult for the outsider, with no knowledge of Trotsky's inmost thoughts, to know whether he was consciously carrying on a 'struggle'. It would seem, rather, that he was reluctant to play a positive role, but on the other hand could not merely remain mute. The result was a characteristic falling between two stools – with no faction to influence the Party from within, all his diffuse, unfocused, roundabout 'appeals' to the Party rank-and-file and indeed to The Masses, served only to inflame his opponents.

Trotsky remained, in short, riveted to the dilemma that had already dislodged him from the Party summits and established him as a literary amateur.

He was now to be eliminated altogether, through two unrelated crises – in China and in Great Britain, respectively.

Immediately after the 1917 putsch some Bolshevik leaders had been fascinated by the potentialities of the colonial and semi-colonial areas; after the 'liberation' movements began in eastern Asia in 1920 the Bolsheviks instructed the small Chinese Communist Party, formed in 1921, to support the Kuomintang, founded by Sun Yat-Sen. Even after the Communists were doing quite well on their own the Bolsheviks retained great confidence in the Kuomintang; when the latter was alarmed by the growth of Communist influence the Soviet authorities – by now Stalin – still instructed the Communists to support the 'patriotic, nationally-minded bourgeoisie', and Sun Yat-Sen's philosophy for good measure.

Stalin and Bukharin soothed the Party by pointing out – on the basis of 1905 in Russia – that The Revolution in China still had to be 'bourgeois', that the Kuomintang was leading a Bourgeoisie hostile to the Western imperialists and hence should be supported. Meanwhile they admitted the Kuomintang to the Comintern in 1926 and put its leader, Chiang Kai-Shek, on the executive.

Chiang's own aims were thoroughly anti-Communist; he exploited the Comintern's endorsement to move against the Communists, who in spite of their renewed fears of a civil war were again bullied by Stalin into yielding to the Kuomintang regardless.

These complex events in a remote country – handled by agents of Stalin without even a pretence of expertise – took place outside the Party squabbles.

Trotsky had never paid much attention to China: he had been, of course, against any alliance with the Kuomintang, but had mentioned China only once or twice; during the crucial years

1924–6, when he was still unmuzzled, he had never brought it up at all in the Comintern.

In 1926 he had been the chairman of a commission dealing with diplomacy in China; in April he had attacked the official conduct of affairs. Nothing had come of it; for a year he said nothing.

But in March 1927 Chiang turned on his former allies; then, on 12 April 1927, he massacred tens of thousands of Communist and non-Communist workers in Shanghai.

This was the background of bloodshed and fumbling when Trotsky, bound and gagged within the Party, aired the scandal.

The day of the first Shanghai uprising (22 March 1927), when Kuomintang troops entered the city, he noted 'the danger that in the Central Committee they would turn the matter into a factional squabble instead of discussing it seriously'. And yet, he asked, 'how can one keep silent when nothing less than the head of the Chinese proletariat is at stake?'[15]

This surely highlights his essential guilelessness, or at least a strange confusion between ideal and practical situations.

If Stalin and Bukharin, now facing a strong attack because of their blunders, had confessed to these blunders, their opponents would have gained a tremendous 'factional' advantage : how could it have been otherwise?

Trotsky's *démarche* was of a piece with his behaviour throughout the fateful period he was plummeting away from power; it illustrated once again his inability to make a bridge between his 'classical Marxist' ideas and any procedure for implementing them. Once again, he could not go *over the heads* of his opponents to some force outside, and swing that force against them as he had tried to do, so ineffectually, in his previous 'appeal' to the Party cells. He could only argue with his opponents behind closed doors, and in a situation, moreover, in which they simply could not acknowledge their mistakes.

The fiasco was in any case the result of three years of inept floundering about with incalculable forces in a strange country : Trotsky could scarcely have expected to rectify it in a few weeks, especially since there had already been a denouement that from the Kremlin's point of view was catastrophic.

The atmosphere was further envenomed by another fiasco, much smaller, in Great Britain.

In 1925 the Soviet chiefs had been hopeful about the prospects of

co-operation with the British trades-union movement, which early in
the year had sent a delegation to Moscow and in May had joined the
Soviet Government in establishing the Anglo-Soviet Trade Union
Council. The previous 'ultra-Left' stance of the Comintern was for
the time being obsolete.

Trotsky had just finished one of his shorter books: *Where is
Britain Going?* The book, written in his liveliest style, was based on
the perspective of an imminent 'revolutionary situation' in Great
Britain, a view that even at the time seemed extravagant and a few
years later looked merely silly. In the framework of this perspective
he had naturally condemned as pernicious any Soviet policy based
on án agreement with the trades-unions: from his point of view they
were hopeless anachronisms.

By the time of the denouement of the Chinese crisis, the arrangement with the British had evaporated: the Anglo-Soviet Trade
Union Council collapsed, on British initiative. There was, moreover,
a huge amount of diplomatic agitation based on resentment of the
Soviet Government in Great Britain.

Using one fiasco to obliterate the other, Stalin's entourage
exploited Trotsky's criticism to terminate his career.

The whole discussion of China was simply cut short: war was
jeopardising the regime!

This made it easy to start brandishing the threat of Party expulsions. Krupskaya implored Zinoviev and Kamenev to keep quiet
about 'China'. Trotsky and Zinoviev asked for a secret session of the
Central Committee: the Politburo refused.

Trotsky again tried to break out of the magic circle of the Party
summits to a relatively wider audience – of all things to the Comintern Executive. Formally, the Comintern Executive was a higher
instance: any member of any Communist Party could appeal to it
against his Party. That had never been the *de facto* situation, of
course; even the formality had never been bothered with.

A minor success won by Trotsky now became a weapon against
him: some eighty-four people signed a document backing his stand
on 'China'; it was soon concurred in by some 300 other well-known
members.

This gave Stalin a useful lever – once more the Opposition had
formed a faction!

Then, while Trotsky at the Comintern Executive was denouncing
the Chinese fiasco (on 24 May), the British broke off relations with
the Soviet Government.

Stalin could now make a point of Trotsky's 'untimely' onslaught, using an odd but deadly phrase: a 'united front from Chamberlain to Trotsky'.[16]

The Kuomintang itself finally kicked the Communists out. Stalin, linking this painful fact to an 'ultra-Left' switch in strategy, now began to break up the Opposition, adroitly using the classic device of distributing honorary positions abroad – ambassadorships, diplomatic missions and so on – in order to remove outstanding Oppositionists from the centre. The so-called 'Eighty-four' who had come out with Trotsky on the 'Chinese Question' were obliterated as a political force. In addition to the resounding titles handed out to the leading Oppositionists – Kamenev, for instance, was sent off to Mussolini as ambassador! – lesser ones were moved around the apparatus or punished in various administrative ways. This, too, followed a sort of protocol: only notables got embassies; small fry were often just kicked out. When the Opposition complained – all they could do – the Party tops were annoyed even more: they could now regard the most trivial complaint as a pretext for venting their spleen.

Then another piece of gaucherie exacerbated the Party tops. In mid-June an outstanding sympathiser of Zinoviev (I. Smilga, head of the Baltic Fleet during the October putsch and an eminent political commissar during the Civil War) was being deported to some job on the far-off Manchurian frontier. He was seen off at the Yaroslavl Station in Moscow by thousands of friends.

The assembly was very nearly a manifestation if only because of its location; it was politicised still further by the presence of Trotsky and Zinoviev, who made speeches – naturally – and turned the assembly into a demonstration against the Stalin entourage, even though Trotsky, out of tact, made a point as it seems of not raising any 'issues' at all; indeed he referred to the taut international situation and to the duty of all good Bolsheviks and Soviet citizens to rally behind the Party.

Intended or not, this 'Yaroslavl Station meeting' was the first public manifestation the Opposition had as yet made against Stalin. From his point of view it was a move to bring what had been an intra-Party clash into the open. It was enough for a rank-and-file Oppositionist to have been present for him to be summarily kicked out of the Party. The uproar about this meeting continued for the whole of the summer, aggravating the pervasive war panic.

Trotsky appealed by letter to the Central Committee on 27 June

1927[17] asking them once again to review the entire situation, to restore, as he put it, the 'Leninist regime' within the Party, for which an occasion lay near at hand – the preparations for the Fifteenth Party Congress. Trotsky thought this would be a good opportunity to stage, at last, an open *debate* that would include all the Oppositionists.

While this letter was still en route, the official Soviet press repeated the charges that the Opposition was collaborating with 'foreign imperalists'; Trotsky wrote the Central Committee *another* letter, telling them about this, too, and charging Stalin with the intention of destroying the Opposition physically. Some of Zinoviev's sympathisers were so startled at the language of this letter, and also so unbelieving, that they asked Trotsky to tone it down, but he remained adamant – he wanted the truth to be formulated with precision.[18]

Stalin by now controlled the Central Committee well-nigh completely: vehemently rejecting Trotsky's charges, he had both Trotsky and Zinoviev formally indicted by the end of the month (June) for bypassing the Party leadership via the Comintern Executive and for the 'Yaroslavl Station meeting'. He wanted to have the Party's highest court expel them at first from the Central Committee, a necessary preliminary to barring them from the Fifteenth Congress, where they might expose the Chinese fiasco. Since the Congress had been announced for November 1927 Stalin had to lean on the Party tribunal, constituted by the Presidium of the Control Commission.

Trotsky appeared before it on 24 July 1927: he defended himself by a sort of legalism, pointing out that the Control Commission itself was subject to the Comintern Executive, and so could not judge him for what he had said there.

He also said there was nothing to be blamed for at all about the 'Yaroslavl Station meeting'.

Had his judges not claimed that Smilga's transfer to Siberia was mere routine, and no punishment? Why then should a farewell to him be interpreted as a 'demonstration' against the Committee? If, on the other hand, Smilga was being punished, then the Control Commission itself was guilty of – 'duplicity'!

Then he denounced the 'Stalinist regime' root and branch, gave a survey of the great issues at stake – emphasising as he was to do for the rest of his life, the metaphor of 'Thermidor', i.e., the unconscious shift of the Jacobins to the 'Right' in the French Revolution – and at the same held out a hope that the mortal split could be forestalled if, somehow, the 'Party were allowed to . . . form its opinion freely'.[19]

His performance seems curiously unrealistic: if such splits were really due, as Trotsky thought, to titanic social conflicts, why should his adversaries, who in the popular press had already accused him of actual collusion with 'foreign imperialists' allow the Party to 'form its opinion freely'?

Trotsky now gave Stalin still another pretext to move against him: it was in the form of an historical analogy drawn from Clemenceau's famous action at the beginning of the First World War. In a tense situation, with the Germans only eighty kilometres from Paris, Clemenceau had savagely attacked his Government for its 'flabbiness': in doing this, Trotsky said, he 'did not betray his class, the Bourgeoisie'; on the contrary, he served it more faithfully.

Trotsky seemed to be announcing that he intended to take Clemenceau as a model (an article was submitted to *Pravda* in late July 1927). He was immediately denounced for having practically admitted he was ready to start a putsch even if the enemy were to be only eighty kilometres from Moscow.

Trotsky's 'Clemenceau statement' was to be turned against him for years; it was brought up, in fact, whenever the Party rank-and-file had to be impressed with his depravity, which was done all the more easily since they could hardly have had the faintest idea of who Clemenceau was.

The Party court met again (1 August 1927) to review Trotsky's expulsion. He was vilified again in a practically all-inclusive way from the very beginning of his career as a youth of twenty-three. The charges now culminated in the 'Clemenceau statement', to show that whenever the Soviet Union was in danger he was inherently treacherous.

Their reasoning reflected his own dilemma.

If he could not defeat the dominant faction within the Party, was the danger not inevitable that he would attack it from outside, i.e., by means of the Party's enemies? Was he not then *potentially* an enemy of the Party?

His defence sounded like sophistry: in pointing out that Clemenceau had not staged a putsch but had simply been elected, he had to go on to say that the parallel to this in Soviet life was the intra-Party regime: *theoretically* the Party could vote him in and Stalin out, hence appealing to the Party was *not* disloyal.

But since his standard criticism of the intra-Party regime was its complete phoniness, it was mere logic for the Stalin faction first to deny his charges as a matter of form and then to emphasise the obvious conclusion that since ousting Stalin constitutionally was out of the question, Trotsky would in the nature of things be forced to make a putsch.

Thus the basic situation extracted a sort of inner logic from the mere metaphor of the 'Clemenceau statement': the polemic behind closed doors – Trotsky's whole problem – obliged him to admit he would be implicitly for force in overthrowing Stalin's forcible control of the apparatus.

The court was still reluctant to oust Trotsky. The theory of Bolshevik solidarity, though long since eroded, retained some sentimental force; it called for keeping up appearances at least. Trotsky and Zinoviev submitted to a mere vote of censure, after solemnly proclaiming their unqualified loyalty to the regime and to the 'unconditional defence of the Soviet Union' (indeed, this remained Trotsky's basic stance to his dying day).

Trustingly, Trotsky and Zinoviev produced for the first time an actual platform to present to the forthcoming Fifteenth Congress.

Stalin's real power emerged at once: though he had not been able to move the high court to pass an open vote of expulsion, he used his unchallenged administrative power to harass the Oppositionists on the pretext that the Platform was itself an act of renewed aggression. He also postponed the Congress for a month, to gain time for backstage arrangements.

When Trotsky complained, repeating his request that the Central Committee authorise an open discussion and distribute, moreover, the Opposition Platform throughout the Party, the demand was not only rejected, but the Opposition were forbidden to do it themselves.

This was their last chance: if they did not want to risk another charge of breach of discipline they simply had to knuckle under as they had done before.

In a corner, Trotsky and Zinoviev made up their minds to defy the ban. They summoned their sympathisers to sign the Platform individually: it was a crucial decision: they had never before risked such a test of strength.

Stalin responded in his own fashion.

The small print-shop run by the Opposition was broken into; those printing the Platform were picked up and some of them declared by the Police to have been plotting with a former White Guard officer.

The same day Trotsky left for the Caucasus again: a number of sympathisers[20] accepted responsibility; they were instantly expelled from the Party.

Zinoviev, Kamenev and Trotsky, who had rushed back to Moscow, explained to the head of the Political Police (Menzhinsky) what it had all been about. Harmless! A few young volunteers, some of them, admittedly, not in the Party, had been duplicating mere typescripts of the Platform. A former White Guard had said he would help distribute it.

Later on it turned out – the Political Police head made no bones about this to Trotsky and Kamenev, and then to the Central Committee – that the White Guard was simply a cat's-paw of the Political Police.

The Opposition were baffled: when this point came out Stalin, with a poker-face, merely argued the right of the Government to make use of ex-White Guards in general, with the aim of unmasking counter-revolutionaries in particular. Stalin could argue in two directions at once – defending the right of the Government to use White Guards and denying that right to 'counter-revolutionaries'.

The mere rationalism of the Oppositionists was no use. By the time these details were 'cleared up' – as though the Political Police had not known what they were doing! – the impression desired by Stalin had been made: the Opposition had been blackened ideologically; ordinary Party members had been warned.

In retrospect, the most suggestive element in this curious affair of the print-shop was its deliberate use of a White Guard to *create* a charge of conspiracy. It was in effect a concretisation of the otherwise merely polemical accusation already launched at the Opposition, of establishing a 'united front from Chamberlain to Trotsky'. The White Guard was a living bond between the real people in the Opposition and – in the imagination of the Party stalwarts – the 'foreign imperialists'. It was a warning that the Opposition was no longer a tolerable variety of Bolshevism, but an *evil* tendency – to be stamped out. It advertised that all 'varieties' of Bolshevism were intolerable but *the* variety – the orthodox Bolshevism incarnate in the summit.

This tiny detail in the 'conspiracy' of 1927 was to be amplified titanically in the Great Charades of 1936–8, the Moscow 'Show Trials'.

Stalin now made an announcement that the Government was

going to commemorate the tenth anniversary of the putsch by
launching a seven-hour day and a five-day week.

This was out of the question not only at the time but for decades;
yet as a 'public relations' manoeuvre it had the effect of soothing
Party members who might have felt that this part of the Opposition's
criticisms had some sense.

When Trotsky – again at a meeting of the Central Executive
Committee held in mid-October to confirm Stalin's announcement
(he had made it on his own initiative) – pointed out how unrealistic
the whole idea was, he was hamstrung once again by the character
of his audience – adamant adversaries.

This was all the more striking since this economic issue was the
only one for years that had any connection with the real problems of
Soviet workers: the other issues – 'China', 'Permanent Revolution',
'Socialism in One Country', the 'Clemenceau statement', 'Thermidor'
– were Greek to one and all. And this, a bona-fide bread-and-butter
issue, was also effortlessly turned against him.

Trotsky describes a big parade that month in Leningrad, to
celebrate this meeting of the Central Executive Committee. During
a contretemps the car with Trotsky, Zinoviev and some other
Oppositionists in it was held up; the crowd, seeing who was in it,
thronged around, leaving the first platform, reserved for the official
leaders, a 'vast gulf of emptiness': even when the official leaders
climbed on to the Oppositionists' platform the people kept shouting
names, and those 'names were not those of the official masters'.

Zinoviev was flooded with enthusiasm; he expected the most
spectacular results from the demonstration. I did not share his
impulsive assessment. The working masses of Leningrad were
manifesting their dissatisfaction in the form of platonic sympathy
for the leaders of the opposition, but they were still incapable of
preventing the apparatus from settling accounts with us. On this
score I had no illusions whatever. On the other hand, the
demonstration was bound to suggest to the ruling faction the
necessity of accelerating the suppression of the opposition in order
to confront the masses with an accomplished fact.[21]

Despite Trotsky's common-sense scepticism about the significance
of this mass support, and his realistic appraisal of Stalin's immediate
reaction, both he and Zinoviev were inflamed: that evening they
said to each other: 'The Masses are with us!'[22] Filled with euphoria,

or, in Trotsky's case, perhaps, a resigned desperation, they took a chance on summoning these 'Masses' to a show-down during the celebration of the October putsch a few weeks later.

Stalin, 'speeding up the destruction of the Opposition', as Trotsky, with his passive insight, had predicted, once again proposed that Trotsky and Zinoviev be expelled from the Central Committee.

The scene this time was nightmarish: there were constant outbursts of the foulest language, vulgar abuse reinforced by the actual throwing of things at Trotsky as he spoke – heavy books, inkpots, a glass.

Stalin himself was wholly calm: cold-bloodedly, he repeated all the now classical accusations. Trotsky, too, in spite of the flood of abuse he was subjected to, and in spite of the objects being thrown at his head, seemed self-assured: he placed himself again on the side of History, claiming that the Bolsheviks had brought about 'gigantic' results' by violence against the old ruling classes and the representatives of lost movements like the Mensheviks and Social-Revolutionaries, but that it would do them no good against an Opposition that stood for 'progress'.

His peroration – 'expel us – you will not prevent our victory' – was the last thing he ever said to any Party institution, and they alone were to hear these words of what was, in fact, his curtain-speech.

The Opposition now suffered the consequences of their defiance. Zinoviev counted on 20,000 or 30,000 signatures for their Platform; he thought that would intimidate Stalin. On top of such evidence of 'mass support' the Opposition could then launch their appeal to The Masses.

Yet their dilemma was the same.

If they came out unequivocally with slogans, statements, demands, etc., that would succeed in inciting The Masses' against the dominant faction – there they would be again, guilty of a breach of discipline. If, on the other hand, they spoke too softly or ambiguously, the whole point would be lost.

The same circle: it could not be squared.

Here is a typical gathering of sympathisers, of the kind Trotsky and Zinoviev spent most of their time in: it is described by a friend, Victor Serge:

Some fifty people filled a wretched dining-room around Zinoviev, thickened now, pale, curly-haired, his voice low. There was something soft yet very appealing, too, in his whole bearing.

At the other end of the table was Trotsky, visibly aging, grey, massive, stooping, his features sharply chiselled, kindly, always ready with an intelligent response. A woman worker, cross-legged on the floor, asks them abruptly: 'And if we are expelled from the Party?' 'Nothing can prevent Communist proletarians from being Communists,' Trotsky replies, 'Nothing can really cut us off from our Party.' Zinoviev, with a half-smile, explains that we are entering an era of struggle when around the Party there will be many expelled and semi-expelled people worthier of the name of Bolshevik than the organisation secretaries. It was simple and moving to see the men of the Dictatorship of the Proletariat, the most powerful of yesterday, coming back in this way to the quarters of the poor, looking for support and for comrades. Volunteers stood guard on the outside staircase, watching the passages and approaches; the intervention of the Political Police was possible at any moment.

Once I was accompanying Trotsky when he left such a meeting. . . . In the street he put up the collar of his coat and pulled the peak of his cap over his eyes so as not to be recognised. He looked an old intellectual still erect after twenty years of wear and tear. We went over to a cabman. 'Bargain over the fare,' Trotsky said to me, 'I have hardly any money on me.' The cabman, a bearded peasant of Old Russia, leaned toward him and said: 'For you there is no fare, get in, Comrade. You're Trotsky, aren't you?' The cap had not been enough to mask the man of the battles of Svyazhsk, Kazan, Pulkovo, Tsaritsyn. A faint, reassured smile lit up Trotsky's face: 'Don't tell anyone about this, everyone knows cabmen belong to the petty bourgeoisie whose favour can only discredit us.'[23]

Both Trotsky and Zinoviev thought the elimination of the Oppositionists en masse would not be a relief to the Party but a stunning blow; that a 'great debate' could at last be begun throughout the cadres of the Party and hence that Stalin and the dominant faction would be obliged to take this into account, if only because the expulsion of a great many Oppositionists as counter-revolutionaries meant gaol, which would endanger the 'proletarian dictatorship'.

This was plainly a misunderstanding: the Party did not show the smallest inclination to do anything against its own apparatus. It had already shown countless times that it could swallow with ease the official vilification of Trotsky.

Trotsky, Zinoviev and their sympathisers were being cut out of the Party in accordance with a procedure in which Stalin's preoccupation with appearances was possible just because his tactics, combining sledgehammer and poison-dart, were, in fact, accepted by the Party without protest of any kind.

The Platform Trotsky and Zinoviev were busily collecting signatures for was now under blanket condemnation as actual subversion: not more than 5,000 to 6,000 people at the outside signed it.[24] Moreover, because of the terror that was beginning to make itself felt, most of the names were kept secret.

Thus, despite their caution, Trotsky and Zinoviev found themselves in the worst position possible: obliged to come out *openly* against the leadership, they had shown up the weakness of their own following. They had provoked a reaction and simultaneously shown their inability to withstand it.

Trotsky was suffering from his characteristic cluster of afflictions: depression, headaches, sleeplessness. The nervous tension he was under throughout this period was kept at a height by the torrent of incredibly venomous abuse he was now being subjected to by the whole Soviet press, which also reproduced cables alleged to come from the whole world. Natalya, relatively apolitical by nature, naturally underwent the same ordeal.

Of their two sons only one, Sedov, shared Trotsky's political life. For him his father was the incarnation of greatness: twenty-one at this time, it was a matter of course for Sedov to take more or less automatically to the same path, as it seemed to him, that his father had taken at his age – the course of revolutionary self-sacrifice. He had wholeheartedly identified himself with the ideals represented by his father: he had added to his age to get into the Young Communist League, and had tried to join the army as well; he had left his parents' flat in the Kremlin to live in a sort of commune with young down-at-heel student workers. As the Opposition took shape he was in it automatically. Sedov had personally experienced the transformation of the Young Communist League, which before being worked over by the Party machine had more or less idolised Trotsky, into a hotbed of anti-'Trotskyism'. He had even become an agitator while that was still possible, canvassing Party cells and haranguing meetings in the provinces.

Now, as the crisis kept hotting up in the autumn of 1927, with the atmosphere surrounding his father growing more and more poisonous by the day, he clung more closely than ever to his father's person, both as aide-de-camp and as guard.

The other son, Sergei, only nineteen, avoided politics altogether. Thus a burden that was to afflict his older brother – the too-great awareness of Trotsky's personal gifts – was spared him. Sergei preferred the 'lighter' aspects of life – sports and amusements, including the arts: he even ran away for a year or two with a circus troupe. As the crisis began gathering in 1927 he was back at home, still ignoring politics and applying himself to his father's youthful studies, science and mathematics. But as the crisis came to a head Sergei, too, found himself entangled by loyalty.

Trotsky's two daughters by Alexandra, Nina and Zinaida, were also enmeshed in the net that was strangling him: they were passionate partisans. Now well over fifty, Alexandra was the focal point for the handful of Trotsky's sympathisers in Leningrad; the two girls, in their middle twenties, were active in Moscow. Both young women had tuberculosis: their husbands had already been barred from all jobs, and very nearly ousted from the Party altogether, or about to be: both families had two children each. The two branches of Trotsky's small family were being put through the same wringer.

The denouement was swift.

The Opposition kept flinging itself at the same brick wall: Trotsky and Zinoviev instructed their sympathisers to participate wholeheartedly in the November 1927 celebration of the putsch, but in such a way as to suggest to the onlookers what they *really* thought: their slogans had to be clearly distinguishable as *their* slogans, but at the same time innocuous enough not to inflame Stalin.

The slogans they carried into the 7 November parade accordingly were worded in such a way that only a rather astute political scientist could have grasped their inwardness.

They had selected unexceptional mottoes such as 'Preserve Bolshevik unity!' and 'Beware of a split in the Party!' side by side with platitudes like 'Down with opportunism!' and also the slightly more revealing slogan 'Carry out Lenin's Testament' which, while much more dangerous, was, of course, still more unintelligible, since outside a small circle no one even knew what Lenin's Testament was.

The slogans were, in fact, aimed only at the most knowledgeable Party veterans, though at the same time they were witnessed, of course, by multitudes.

It all turned out rather unfortunately: Stalin had instructed the police and Party apparatuses to smash the slightest attempt at any independent demonstration. He was one of the few people who could understand the slogans.

Accordingly, the slightest initiative on the part of any of the marchers in the huge parades collided with instant action on the part of the Political Police as well as of the large stratum of the Party orang-outangs, now called 'activists': anyone with a flag or a picture of Trotsky or Zinoviev, or heard voicing some unconventional motto was simply ordered to leave or pounced on and beaten up. In Moscow the collisions were even more violent than in Leningrad. In neither city was there any real contest.

All special banners were simply torn to ribbons whenever seen; in the parade itself any Oppositionists were forced to march along with the procession as a whole, deprived of their banners, keeping step with the others in total silence; whenever a window started display-ing a portrait of Zinoviev or Trotsky it was torn down with great efficiency and the people in the flats ruthlessly manhandled. Natalya herself was beaten up.

Trotsky and Kamenev drove around Moscow: in Revolutionary Square Trotsky tried to address a column of workers parading toward Lenin's tomb: he was pounced on by policemen and orang-outangs: there were some shots; shouts could be heard: 'Down with Trotsky, the Jew, the traitor!'

The Oppositionists' effect on the crowds was, in short, nil. It was in fact quite impossible to determine what the effect might have been; there was no way it could be expressed, and no way of knowing what individual workers were thinking about. There was no reaction whatever from those participants in the parade who were not already committed to the Opposition. The countless small tussles between the police, the activists, and the sympathisers of the Opposition did not, as far as could be seen, move the others at all.

A week later both Trotsky and Zinoviev were expelled from the Party on a charge of counter-revolution. Some of the other Opposi-tionists (Kamenev, Rakovsky, and others) were thrown out of the Central Committee. Countless rank-and-file members – at least many hundreds – were summarily expelled.

Now a private citizen, Trotsky prudently left his Kremlin flat the evening of 7 November: he was spared the humiliation of eviction, unlike the other Opposition leaders.

Though determined to exile them all, Stalin did so as unobtru-sively as possible: appointments to 'important work' in the hinter-land were haggled over. Trotsky and his friends finally agreed, for instance, to accept such jobs only if they were genuine, due consideration being given to climate, family welfare, etc.

In January the whole pretence suddenly stopped: the Political Police abruptly told Trotsky (12 January 1928) that he was being deported in four days to some place near China.

The last few days were spent in a feverish rush: last-minute conferences, meetings, instructions, farewells – the day itself.

Here is Serge's description of the atmosphere:

> I went up a service staircase.... He whom we referred to among ourselves as the Old Man, like Lenin before him, was living in a small room facing the courtyard and furnished only with a field-bed and a table covered with maps from the entire world. Wearing a threadbare waistcoat, brisk, massive, his high shock of hair almost white, his colour sickly, he was displaying, caged, a ferocious energy. Messages he had dictated were being copied out in the next room. Comrades arriving from every corner of the country were received in the dining-room – between 'phone calls he was chatting with them hurriedly. All of them might be arrested at any moment – and after the arrest what? No one knew ... but all were rushing to take advantage of these last hours, for they were surely the last.[25]

The final day the tension was extreme. The little family was supposed to start off on its long journey at ten in the evening – they sat around waiting till well past the hour: finally the Political Police phoned to say the departure was delayed two days.

The story given out was that the whole arrangement was voluntary on Trotsky's part. The original day of departure Rakovsky and some friends, tremendously excited, had come back from the station, where thousands of people had gathered to say goodbye. A huge portrait of Trotsky had been set up and cheered. The demonstrators had run out in the front of the locomotives, climbed on to the cars and called out for Trotsky. A rumour was circulating that he had been smuggled into the train by the Police, who were preventing his admirers from seeing him. Some demonstrators had prostrated themselves on the line to hold up the train with their bodies.

Hence the Police changed their plans once again; they unexpectedly arrived on the seventeenth, a day ahead of time. Since Trotsky's flat was not being watched by his sympathisers, the Police found only Trotsky and Natalya, the two youths, Sedov and Sergei, Yoffe's widow, and another woman.

Trotsky resorted to the device he had often used before – nonviolent resistance. There was some bargaining through the door, which he had locked; impatient, the officer gave orders to burst in. It was the same officer who had been a bodyguard of Trotsky's during the Civil War on the famous army train; he was beside himself, crying out: 'Shoot me, Comrade Trotsky, shoot me!' Trotsky found himself soothing him, even exhorting him to obey his instructions.

But Trotsky would not get dressed; the soldiers were obliged to take off his slippers and dress him, then, since he refused to walk, to lift him up bodily and take him downstairs – as the family and Yoffe's widow shrieked and booed.

The two boys, as well as Yoffe's widow and the other woman, had been held for a moment in the flat, but had slipped out: Sergei, very athletic, had used his muscles. Sedov, running downstairs, had rung at each door, yelling: 'Comrade Trotsky is being carried off!'

The house was reserved for high functionaries: frightened faces appeared and vanished in the doors and on the steps.

In the full light of day Trotsky, Natalya and the two boys were squashed into a police-car; it started off towards the Kazan Station, but in the wrong direction – a different station altogether: Yaroslavl Station again! This time quite deserted.

Once again Trotsky would not walk: the Political Police agents simply yanked him out of the car and carried him as they had before. Sedov called out to a handful of railway workers, famous at one time, of course, for their revolutionary ardour: 'Comrades, look! They're carrying off Comrade Trotsky!' Not a peep from a single one.

Finally they were in the train. Fifty kilometres from Moscow their car was coupled to a train headed for Central Asia. Sergei left to go back to Moscow.

Trotsky was on his way to banishment with only Natalya and Sedov, together with a small police guard.

After all their precautions they had been arrested so precipitately that for the first time in his life Trotsky had brought along nothing to write with. They did not even have any change of underclothing or the most primitive necessities, not even medicine for Natalya, who had a fever. They had to sit or lie on wooden benches, in a sombre, candlelit little compartment.

Yet, as Natalya said, Trotsky was 'in a good mood, almost merry. The situation had cleared up.'[26]

Trotsky was still on Soviet soil, still a public figure: he had to be handled diplomatically. He was deposited in Alma-Ata, a tiny Mongol town in Eastern Siberia, where he was to live a year.

It was as far away as it could be. The climate was severe – hot and cold, with blizzards in winter and heat waves in summer. That summer it teemed with rabid dogs.

For a while Trotsky was not disturbed much. He was finally sent a whole truckload of his books and papers. After being put in an ancient, broken-down little tavern, the family was given a four-room flat, allowed to go hunting, even sent a pet dog. Externally, in fact, his circumstances were once again idyllic.

He describes a hunting-trip:

We brought back more than forty ducks and a brace of geese. . . . The trip gave me enormous satisfaction, whose essence lay in a temporary return to barbarism: sleeping in the open air, eating under the open sky some mutton cooked in a pail, not washing, not undressing and so not dressing, falling off a horse into a river (the only time I had to undress, under a hot noonday sun), spending almost entire days on end on a small log in the midst of the water and reeds – it all made a rare experience.

Natalya gives some details:

In June and July, in the little thatched cottage in the apple-orchard, work was in full swing; the typewriter clattered without let-up, something unheard of in those parts. L.D. was dictating a critique of the Comintern programme; he would make corrections and give it back for retyping. The mail was heavy – 10 to 15 letters a day, all sorts of theses, critiques, internal polemics, news from Moscow, and a great many telegrams about political questions and about our health. Great world problems were mixed up with local and trivial matters that also, however seemed to us important . . . Rakovsky's remarkable letters were copied and sent on to others. The little low-ceilinged room was crammed with tables, covered with piles of manuscripts, files, newspapers, books, copied-out excerpts, clippings. For days at a time little Lyova would not leave his little room alongside the stables, typing, correcting the typists' copy, making packages, sending out the mail, receiving it, and looking up the necessary quotations. . . . Toward evening L.D. would often go up to the mountains with a gun and dog, sometimes accompanied by me, sometimes by Lyova. We would come back with quails, pigeons, mountain-fowl or pheasants.

So we spent a year in Alma-Ata, a town of earthquakes and floods . . . on the borders of China, 250 kilometres from a railway and 4,000 from Moscow, in the company of letters, books and nature.[27]

Trotsky studied hard: just as in Moscow, after being shunted into a cul-de-sac, he had set to work diligently learning about electrotechnique, so in Alma-Ata he applied himself to books:

I'm spending a lot of time on the study of Asia – geography, economics, history and so on. . . . There's a simply frightful shortage of foreign newspapers. I've already written away asking for newspapers to be sent me even if they're not so fresh. Mail gets here after a long delay, and gets lost, apparently, very often.

The role of the Indian Communist Party is very unclear. There have been despatches in the newspapers about the activities of 'workers' and peasants' parties' in various provinces. The name alone gives rise to the most legitimate alarm. In its time the Kuomintang, too, after all, was called a workers'-peasants' party. It might prove to be a repetition of the past.

Anglo-American antagonism has finally come out into the open. Now even Stalin and Bukharin seem to be catching on to what it's all about. Yet our newspapers simplify the question very much when they describe it as though the antagonism between Great Britain and the United States, by increasing steadily in intensity, will lead to war directly. There can be no doubt that there will be a number of turning-points in this process. For both sides war would be too great a danger. They will still make more than one effort for agreements and peace. But in general the development is heading toward a bloody denouement with gigantic strides.[28]

Between April and October 1928 Trotsky sent out about 800 political letters from Alma-Ata and 550 telegrams; he received 1,000 letters and 700 telegrams.

His ordinary writing consumed a great deal of time. He was, in fact, a professional writer again, back at his desk. His government pittance, inadequate at best, fell laughably short of his demands.

The publication of his Works by the State Publishing House had naturally been halted after some thirteen had appeared: these were already proscribed. His mind teemed with ideas: his memoirs, suggested to him by many people, were soon to appear as *My Life*; he started work on this only a few months after arriving in Alma-Ata. But these writing ideas could not yet bring in money; he resorted to translating – Marx and Engels!

His fees as translator, editor and proof-reader supported his family, and even covered the vast correspondence he was still allowed to maintain. During the first phase of his exile in Alma-Ata, it was easy to think that anything might happen. He was still receiving letters from friends and acquaintances, still hearing the gossip of the Kremlin. For the time being at least, things were tolerable.

His personal life was filled with more and more pain. When Nina's husband was gaoled and exiled she collapsed; Trotsky heard about it in the spring of 1928. She was twenty-six. Some time later he learned that she had died on 9 June, while he was still asking Rakovsky by mail about her health. The censors had held on to one of her last letters to him for more than ten weeks: he dedicated to her – a little oddly, perhaps – the attack on the Comintern programme he had been writing while she lay dying.

The older daughter, Zinaida, had meant to join him in Alma-Ata; her husband, too, had been exiled, and her already shaky health had been consumed tending Nina. Zinaida had to keep putting off the long trip until it was too late: at last Trotsky and Natalya learned that she was too ill to travel, and in addition had a serious illness of the kind called 'nervous'. Sergei nevertheless did come for a holiday, bringing Sedov's wife and small child: they stayed a few weeks.

Trotsky's illness descended on him again in the summer of 1928: the fevers, headaches and stomach 'catarrh' that had plagued him all his life.

The state of his health had some political significance; he could still be thought of as representing some potential in Soviet life. But his status was worsening rapidly. By the autumn of 1928 the censorship, which had been relatively lenient, now began waging a sort of psychological warfare – only discouraging letters, say, from Oppositionists preparing to reconcile themselves to the Party, were given to him: his own mail was never delivered. Even wires about Zinaida's illness went unanswered. The eleventh anniversary of the October putsch went by with none of the customary greetings being delivered.

An Oppositionist or two, hitherto unmolested, vanished. Rumours drifted in – Stalin had special plans. For a time Trotsky belittled the idea of another deportation – where to? Something was brewing in the Kremlin.

After Trotsky's exile the 'Zinovievites' had capitulated at once, on the understanding that they would keep quiet. But the moment their surrender was accepted they were told they had to announce a real change of mind – recant, and support Stalin publicly.

The argument for this was simple : it would look odd if eminent members said nothing about their aberrations of the day before – what would the rank-and-file make of it all?

Thus, in the Bolshevik milieu the first surrender led to a second, the prelude to physical extinction.

Stalin, having eliminated the various exponents of high-speed industrialisation, could now implement the idea himself. Discarding his association with the 'Bukharinite' support of the market economy during the year Trotsky was in Alma-Ata, he took over Trotsky's original proposals for speeding up industrialisation.

This switch-over to a crash programme was heralded by the slogans for the eleventh anniversary of the putsch : 'The danger is on the Right!' 'Speed Up Industrialisation!' 'Strike out against the Kulak!'

These proposals, originally made by Trotsky in an administrative vacuum, were now to be implemented by the massed weight of a consolidated apparatus and its chief arm – the Political Police.

For the first period of this massive drive (until about mid-1929) Stalin's new programme was practically a copy of Trotsky's proposals : there was simply nothing for Trotsky's sympathisers to get their teeth into.

Why, in fact, should Trotskyites – however the term was understood – exist at all? In the Soviet Union, at least, where life was now an ordeal for all dissidents, there was, in fact, not much reason for remaining politically distinguishable as long as the central faction, on top of being successful organisationally, had gone over to the basic position of the Left opposition. Great numbers of Oppositionists were seduced by the plausibility of a reconciliation with Stalin.

Why fight? they said. He is doing what you want! To be sure, the existence of the terror made it quite clear that another cardinal demand of the Opposition – intra-Party democracy – was not about to be restored so very quickly; still, they actually said that since

Stalin had applied the Left programme in agriculture and industry why shouldn't he do so in the Party, too?

As long as intellectuals straitjacketed by abstractions could be bamboozled by their inability to distinguish between a programme Stalin was promoting and Stalin as the agent of *any* programme, it was perfectly natural for them to accept as a formula of reconciliation the claim that they should support Stalin because he was putting forth the *right* programme – theirs!

Such a formula, within the context of real politics, was plainly either naive, even stupid, or hypocritical. Yet it was a formula that persuaded thousands of Oppositionists to return from the penal colonies to the centre.

They were in a box. They could either have gone on languishing, quite helpless politically, or else return to real life under any conditions whatever. For the losers *there was no choice*.

Moreover, it was still possible to nourish illusions: though harassed and terrorised, Party members were not yet being killed. As yet Stalin would not, it was felt, go that far. The idea of a reconciliation to be worked out by negotiation could still be defended sincerely.

It was to be a few years before this whole idea of negotiation sounded like adolescent sentimentality!

There were also Oppositionists – including Trotsky's friend Rakovsky – who thought Stalin's 'Left' switch 'insincere' – a mere 'temporary manoeuvre' that was bound to be followed by a further jump to capitalism in the form of another N.E.P. Such people did not have to change their 'programme' at all: they thought that if Stalin continued 'Leftward' he would be forced – by logic – to stop persecuting the Left Oppositionists! If on the other hand he turned 'Right' again and backed 'capitalist elements', he would get into such trouble he would need Trotsky's help.

This was the 'orthodox Trotskyite' approach. In naiveté it is hard to distinguish it from the other attitude, based on Stalin's 'sincerity', that made it so tempting for some of Trotsky's former sympathisers to rally behind Stalin.

Those who felt like going back to active politics found themselves whittling away their minimum demands in the 'negotiations' with Stalin they were looking forward to; finally what they were doing was, in fact, capitulating totally, though they would doubtless have done so in any case through *force majeure*. Those whose Bolshevik fanaticism proved unyielding on the ideological plane, developed such manic intransigence toward Stalin that they drifted away from politics altogether.

As was natural in a Marxist milieu, the divergence of intellectual views became a moral question: Bolsheviks split by differences of interpretation treated former comrades as moral degenerates, turning on each other the vocabulary of Marxist anathema – flunkeys, traitors, petty bourgeois counter-revolutionaries. . . .

The pros and cons of all this were wrangled about unflaggingly in all the penal colonies. Trotsky was naturally the final arbiter. He kept maintaining that Stalinism, though unprincipled, hated the Opposition for *theoretical* reasons. He could not believe in the quest for *power*: he thought the conflict reflected authentic intellectual differences.

An outsider, to be sure, might ask: why is the elimination of rivals not a natural consequence of any struggle for power? And might not one attack opponents *with the same ideas* more ferociously than others?

By the end of 1930, hardly any Oppositionists were still outside the Party. About a thousand individual sympathisers were still in evidence in gaol and exile, before the massive surrenders led, in stages, by Radek, Preobrazhensky, Smirnov and others, and by Rakovsky and others, mopped up the whole Opposition.

Trotsky was now in his classic posture: 'Let there remain in exile not three hundred and fifty people faithful to their banner, but only thirty-five. Let there remain even three – the banner will remain, the strategic line will remain, the future will remain.'[30]

There were at this time thousands of individual Oppositionists for whom Trotsky retained some authority. With Stalin embarked on an immense enterprise derived in part from Trotsky's well-known writings, Trotsky's presence might, conceivably, prove embarrasing. With the Party situation bound to become still more tense, Trotsky's presence was obviously an irritant.

Yet it was still out of the question to kill him: this would have been an abrupt departure from Stalin's posture of sobriety and moderation, also a little embarrassing vis-à-vis the topmost strata of the Party and any idealists still around. Gaoling was not much better: the same embarrassment would not even have had the *fait accompli* of a corpse.

With his habitual misdirection Stalin spread rumours that Trotsky was about to be banished from the Soviet Union; then he had the rumours contradicted; then he started them all over again.

By the time this had happened once or twice it was clear, first of all, that the 'public' was paying no attention whatever; also, that it was easy to accustom 'public opinion', already apathetic, to the idea that the co-founder of the regime and the organiser of the Red Army was about to be deported.

The denouement was far more rapid than in 1927. In mid-December 1928 a high official of the Political Police handed Trotsky an ultimatum – he was to stop his 'counter-revolutionary activity' forthwith on pain of 'complete isolation from political life' and an 'enforced change of residence'.

Trotsky responded in a lengthy letter – five printed pages – couched in his characteristic style:

> The demand that I refrain from any political activity means demanding that I give up the struggle for the interests of the international proletariat that I have been carrying on for thirty-two years without a stop, that is, throughout the whole of my conscious life. . . . Only a bureaucracy rotten through and through could demand from revolutionaries such a renunciation. . . . Only contemptible renegades could make such a promise. . . . We know our duty. We shall do it to the end.[31]

He addressed the letter to both the Party heads and the Comintern: for a month nothing happened; the Political Police official hung about Alma-Ata waiting for instructions. The Politburo had not made a decision. There were violent objections to extreme measures, made by three of the Politburo members, especially Bukharin, who had a hysterical fit when the final vote was taken.

By 20 January 1929 Stalin could force a majority: Trotsky's little four-room apartment in Alma-Ata was encircled and occupied. The Political Police functionary handed Trotsky an order for deportation 'from the entire territory of the USSR'. Trotsky's receipt read:

'The Political Police decision, criminal in substance and illegal in form, was communicated to me on 20 January 1929.'[32]

The gaolers had been ordered to disarm Trotsky and remove him within twenty-four hours. He was not to be told where he was being banished until he was travelling. Two days later, at dawn, a large escort conducted the little family through a wilderness in the midst of the worst winter in generations.

En route the family was placed on a train for Russia: they were told the place of banishment was to be Istanbul. Trotsky protested:

he asked at least to see Sergei and Sedov's wife in Moscow. This request was complied with: they came to join the exiles on the train: Trotsky dug his heels in again and declined to go to Istanbul at all: his Political Police escort asked for further instructions.

For twelve days the train went back and forth; after being taken off the main line it was finally halted near a 'dead little station', in Trotsky's description:

> There it expires between two strips of thin woodland. Day after day goes by. The number of empty tins surrounding the train keeps growing. Crows and magpies gather for the feast in larger and larger flocks. Wasteland, solitude.... A fox had laid his stealthy track up to the very train. The engine and one carriage make a trip once a day to a big station for our lunch and for newspapers. There's an outbreak of grippe in our carriage. We reread Anatole France and Klyuchesky's *Russian History*.... The cold hits 53 degrees below zero; our engine keeps rolling back and forth to avoid freezing.... We have no idea where we are.[33]

Finally, the train went ahead at a normal speed to Turkey. Sergei and Sedov's wife left once again for Moscow: it was the last time Trotsky, Natalya and Sedov ever saw them.

His last look at Russia came to Trotsky through the windows from the pitch-black night outside; the train made its way through the city of Odessa and its port; the pier had a large tight cordon of troops; the ship waiting to transport him was named after Lenin: *Ilyich*.

There was no longer any reason for finickiness. Stalin still kept up appearances, but the actual expulsion was executed with a curious combination of flat-footedness and bizarrerie.

By moving administratively Stalin put a stop to the manoeuvrings Trotsky's celebrity still made necessary within the Politburo; Stalin had learned to avoid even the appearance of discussion; this time the whole banishment was clandestine; the troops quietly stationed in the Odessa port could forestall any public outbursts, if such were still conceivable.

Trotsky did not have the slightest idea what was happening to him. He had no inkling of Stalin's plans, nor any way of guessing. The Political Police had constantly been breaking promises to him; he had no way of checking. Since the word of any officer, even if sincerely given, could always be overridden by Stalin, Trotsky was unable to maintain even ordinary human relations.

Publicly, Stalin had not yet committed himself even now. If any outcry about Trotsky's expulsion had been made Stalin, because of its secrecy, could always have invented some other explanation.

This final banishment was, in fact, the beginning of a protracted process of depersonalising Trotsky; this time there were to be no witnesses to impede the fabrication of an official version. There was no question of fellow-passengers to be impressed by anything Trotsky's ingenuity might devise – he was kept insulated even from the ship's crew. The circumstances of the expulsion were, in fact, arranged precisely to put an end to Trotsky's public career; he was simply an individual boarding an empty ship.

The *Ilyich* left Odessa in a powerful windstorm, in the blackness of the night; the winter was so cold that year that the Black Sea, very unusually, was partly frozen over; an ice-breaker hacked out a passage.

CHAPTER XI

The Hero

ON THE VOYAGE Trotsky wrote a protest to the Politburo against the 'conspiracy' between Stalin, the Political Police, and the 'national fascist' police of the Turkish head of state, Kemal; he also warned them they would sooner or later be called to account for this 'treacherous and shameful deed'.

Stalin had carefully sustained the initial ambiguity of the banishment by sending the consular officials ambiguous instructions; since no announcement had been made they had no idea of what was happening. Trotsky was taken at once to the Soviet Consulate and given full honours; a whole wing was set aside for the small family. Some officials who had served under him during the Civil War and the Political Police officers themselves treated him with great deference, complying with all requests and trotting about the city on errands. His voluminous archives were delivered intact.

He could not, of course, be left to stay long: during the second half of February a series of articles treating the Soviet authorities very aggressively and giving his own account of the factional 'struggle' that had culminated in his exile appeared in the *New York Times*, the *Daily Express* of London and some other newspapers. The Soviet press could now write about him openly.

He was ordered out of the Consulate – the Political Police could no longer vouch for his safety! Still escorted by Political Police Officers, Natalya and Sedov started house-hunting. In a few days they found something on the Prinkipo Islands in the Marmara Sea, an hour and a half from Istanbul.

A few weeks after his expulsion from the Soviet Union, Trotsky had become a householder in a remote Turkish suburb, deserted except for a few islanders tending their flocks and fishing.

A private citizen now for more than a year, Trotsky had recovered his freedom of action. All he had to do was make a living.

The situation he had been ejected from had been acutely painful: its torment, beginning with at least Lenin's death had been growing for some six years. He was, in a way, free: healthy, vigorous, a little over forty-nine, a new life was easily imaginable.

Might it have been possible for him to resume a way of life that was characteristic of him for far longer than his relatively brief spells of organised activity – the putsch, the Civil War, the first period of intense activity in the new regime?

He had spent, after all, a decade before 1917 as a free-lance writer with a certain viewpoint: his 'revolutionary' journalism had co-incided and merged with that; his actual political activities were really no more than a hobby. While the professionals, his sometime colleagues, had been putting together organisations as well as carrying on agitation, he had been writing, speaking . . .

And even more recently, after he had been shunted away from authority, had he not, once again, resumed his congenital pursuits? Had he not remained passive within the apparatus until others had burst in on his detachment, a detachment that in different circumstances might have continued indefinitely? In fact, now that he was his own man once again, might it not have been *natural* for him to retire?

It was out of the question. Now he *stood* for something: moreover, his commitment to his ideals had been reinforced by the experience of state power. Despite his inhibitions about being a leader in his own name, despite his demonstrated inability to create an organisation, Trotsky remained nailed to his myth.

At the age of fifty, on the eve of his final exile, he expressed his defiance.

He quotes Proudhon:

'The movement is, no doubt, neither regular nor straight-forward, but the tendency is constant.

'What every government in turn does in favour of revolution becomes irreversible; what is attempted against it passes by like a cloud.

'I enjoy this spectacle, in which I understand every scene; I witness these changes in the life of the world as though I were receiving an explanation from on high; what oppresses others exalts me more and more, inspires and strengthens me: how then can you want me to blame Fate, to bemoan people and to curse them?

'Destiny – I laugh at it; and as for people, they are too ignorant, too shackled for me to be offended by them.'

Despite the slight flavour of ecclesiastical rhetoric, these are very good words. I subscribe to them.[1]

Forced into this heroic posture, forced to remain a professional, Trotsky was able to view the future with professional hopefulness.

It was possible for him to believe that though The Revolution had suffered a setback in Russia its prospects were still bright: the imminence of a major upset in industrial Europe might be regarded as a counterweight to the victory of repression under Stalin.

He could have hoped for recruits for his own views among the ranks of the foreign Communist Parties, not yet frozen in the conformism that toward the end of the Twenties was only just setting in.

What had been happening in Russia, after all, was still obscure: the dense web of lies now dominating the expanding Soviet apparatus, plus its rapidly growing army of careerists, had not as yet had its full impact on the international movement.

For the mature generation of the end of the Twenties Trotsky was still famous in the Left-wing and 'progressive' part of the political spectrum. His abilities, reinforced by his role as military leader, had moved many individuals of the younger generation in Europe: doubtless he had helped make them Communists.

In the 'bourgeois' world, too, his name had a special cachet among small circles of the intelligentsia, both of the diffuse Left wing and at large. The streak of boyish romanticism in Bernard Shaw, for instance, combined with his connoisseur's appreciation of Trotsky's literary talents – plus Shaw's desire to startle the squares! – echoed the enthusiasm of a wide variety of intellectuals throughout Europe and America. It was natural for young men like, say, André Malraux, the French adventurer and writer, and Edmund Wilson, the American literary critic, to be magnetised by Trotsky's emblematic uniqueness, by his intellectual powers, by his cosmopolitanism. Since they were generally artists or writers Trotsky's name became highly publicised, though the notoriety surrounding him was not to have any effect on his organisational prospects.

On his arrival in Prinkipo Trotsky thus felt himself engaged in three different tasks.

He had already begun explaining his differences with the Stalin Government; this had to be linked to his articles and correspondence as the organiser of a movement; he also had to attend to his literary work – the articles he was to write for the 'bourgeois' press, his autobiography, begun in Siberia, and his *History*.

News of his political elimination had leaked abroad in a somewhat lopsided way. He now produced four books: *The Real Situation in Russia, The Stalinist School of Falsification, The Third International After Lenin,* and *Permanent Revolution.* Anyone paying sympathetic attention to these books might be considered a partisan. By the early autumn of 1929 the whole of *My Life* had been sent to his various translators (German, French, English) and was appearing serially in newspapers. By November 1929 he was well launched on his *History*. In addition he was immersed in what rapidly became a torrent of correspondence with various sympathisers.

Prinkipo was a small island set off by red cliffs against the deep-blue sea: there were no cars. In summer middle-class families would come out from Istanbul for a few weeks to lounge about the beaches. When they left the desolation was well-nigh total.

Trotsky's house, his home and his headquarters, was a large villa on the outskirts of Büyük Ada, the centre of Prinkipo. It was completely broken-down and filthy. The whole family, organised by Natalya's aesthetic passion for cleanliness, pitched in and began sweeping, scouring and painting the whole place. They had no intention of making it really comfortable; it was thought of only as a way-station to civilisation. The paint they used on the floors was so cheap that for months shoes would cling to it.

There was a somewhat grotesque contrast, never overcome, between what had been the original pretensions of the villa – owned by a bankrupt Turkish notable – and the barren functionalism of Trotsky's headquarters. There was a sad clash between the 'dingy marbles, sad bronze peacock, and humiliated gilt'² of the owner, and the 'bare barrack' created by Trotsky and Natalya.

The centre of both floors of the house is a vast hall – not a hall exactly, but a room twenty feet long and fifteen feet wide with great double doors opening on a balcony which looks outward to the richly deep blue sea and downward to his bright red-cliffed island that crouches in the sea like a prehistoric animal drinking.

In these vast rooms and on these balconies there is not an article of furniture – not even a chair! They are mere gangways, and the doors to the rooms on each side are closed. In each of these rooms someone has an office table or a bed, or both, and a chair to go with it. One of them, downstairs, very small and square and white-walled, with barely space for table and chairs in the dining-room. The garden surrounding the villa is abandoned to weeds and these are running to seed. 'To save money,' Natalya explains. Through sheer indifference to beauty, I should say. Trotsky talks a good deal about art in his books and lays claim to a cultivated taste, but he shows no more interest in art than in that garden.[3]

This account by Max Eastman, the American writer who for some time was a sympathiser of Trotsky as well as his chief translator, emphasises Trotsky's aesthetic 'deadness'. Even the garden surrounding the villa was left abandoned: depite Natalya's remark about 'saving money', from a purely financial point of view Trotsky's writing quickly began bringing in money so quickly that for house-holding purposes he was far from penury.

It was to be Trotsky's home for four and a half years. His nostalgia for Europe was quite frustrated: he was boxed in.

For the world at large Trotsky's conflicts with Stalin, for years shrouded in mystery anyhow, could not outweigh his own symbolic potency. The Soviet regime seemed quiescent within Stalin's formula of 'Socialism in One Country'; it was regarded by many observers as normal, even respectable. Trotsky remained the in-carnation of blood-thirsty extremism.

At this time, to be sure, the Bolshevik undertaking was unique, and above all, recent. The biggest empire in the world had been toppled in a few days in 1917; the Provisional Government that followed it had been undone in a few hours: all had been brought about, as it seemed, by a handful of people against a background of mysterious social forces.

The Bolsheviks had attributed their triumph to the potency of their ideas – they had created a myth that could be propagated by the resources of a big government. It was a myth that found a counterpart, curiously enough, in the minds of those who thought the Bolsheviks demons. A panicky fear of ideologically inspired conspiracies was only natural; it was also natural for the chief architect of the Bolshevik victory, as well as its most articulate exponent, to be identified with the forces of disruption.

Hatred of the Soviet Government abroad was compounded by the systematic distortions inherent in the monopoly of the dictatorship. The simplest aspects of Soviet life were, in fact, hidden by a practically impenetrable jungle of ignorance and confusion persisting, indeed, to this day.

At first there was no way of knowing whether Trotsky had been *really* banished or whether the whole thing was not a mere ruse on the part of the wily Bolsheviks to stir up mischief. Trotsky was refused asylum everywhere: though willing to give all conceivable assurances that he would not 'interfere' in the domestic politics of any country he could not, after all, stop writing. Despite his helplessness he remained in the public mind a potentially explosive factor.

His first application for a visa had been made from the Soviet Union to the German Social-Democratic Government in power in Germany. It was refused once, but after Trotsky's exile the question was re-opened by Loebe, the speaker of the Reichstag, who actually offered him asylum in a public speech. When Trotsky instantly re-applied for a visa, he was then asked to accept three successive restrictions on his activity: first on his freedom of movement, to which he said he would be willing to live in 'complete seclusion', doing nothing but write; he was then asked whether he might not, after all, come just long enough for some medical treatment; when he said he would if he had to he was told he really wasn't ill enough.

I asked whether Loebe was offering the right of asylum or the right of burial. . . . In the course of a few weeks the democratic principle was truncated three times. First the right of asylum was turned into the right of sojourn on an exceptional basis; then into the right of medical treatment, finally – into the right of burial. But that meant that I could appreciate the advantages of democracy to their full extent only as a corpse.

The reaction in Great Britain was the same, though there Trotsky had some powerful support: Bernard Shaw, the Webbs, Lloyd George, Sir Herbert Samuel, H. G. Wells, J. M. Keynes and many others. Curiously enough, in this case it was the Labour Party, all Socialists, that refused him; his supporters were all outside the Labour Party.

It stood to reason, to be sure, that while ordinary people might be impressed by Trotsky's personality, actual Left wingers were bound to be hostile. The combination of hostility with the cant of democracy enabled the Labour Party in power to perform miracles of hypocrisy, and to give Trotsky an occasion for another shaft that even took in one of his backers:

It sometimes seemed as though a one-act comedy on the theme of democracy were being given an 'all-European' production. Its text could have been written by Bernard Shaw, if the Fabian liquid flowing in his veins had been added to by even five per cent of Jonathan Swift's blood.[4]

This comment on Shaw, while in harmony with Trotsky's attitude towards him, was a little unkind, since Shaw actually went to considerable pains to help him, intervening, to be sure vainly, with important officials, writing letters and statements on behalf of a man whom he could, after all, only consider to be an enemy.

Shaw had the highest opinion of Trotsky's abilities: in his letter to the Home Secretary he referred to the

ironic situation . . . of a . . . Socialist government refusing the right of asylum to a very distinguished Socialist while granting it . . . to the most reactionary opponents. Now, if the government by excluding Mr. Trotsky could have also silenced him . . . but Mr. Trotsky cannot be silenced. His trenchant literary power and the hold which his extraordinary career has given him on the public imagination . . . enable him to use every attempt to persecute him . . . He becomes . . . the hero of all the militants of the extreme Left of every country. He should be allowed into England by anyone with an unreasoned dread of him as a caged lion . . . if only to hold the key of his cage.[5]

Throughout these frustrations he was extremely active. His productivity began to pay off very quickly. As his household came to include a team of permanent secretaries and more or less long-term guests, his correspondence attained staggering dimensions, while in spite of everything his expenses amounted to only one thousand to one thousand five hundred dollars a month.[6]

As a journalist Trotsky was very popular. His very first articles, for instance, before he had even settled down in Prinkipo produced ten thousand dollars; a little later that year he got seven thousand dollars as an advance against the American rights for his autobiography. His *History of the Russian Revolution* was published in serial form by the *Saturday Evening Post* – of all magazines! – for the sum of forty-five thousand dollars,[7] which in 1932 represented what is generally referred to as a tidy sum.

This does not, of course, give a clear view of Trotsky's personal finances: substantial chunks of his income were poured into his political activities in so far as they were reflected in periodicals: the Russian-language *Bulletin of the Opposition* for instance, as well as some others, consumed six thousand of the ten thousand dollars he got for his first articles from Istanbul.

Indeed, it may be a commentary on Trotsky's movement that it was financed to such an extent by his earnings as a popular writer: after all, if the *Saturday Evening Post*, long regarded as a bulwark of the squarest segment of the suburban middle class, could advance a huge sum for a work like the *History*, whose style may safely be said to be one not often encountered by its readers, it is plain that Trotsky's talents, combined with his celebrity, gave him a fairly lucrative vantage-point in bourgeois society, though his income was to remain rather spotty and eventually to dwindle away.

With his exile his personal tragedy began sharpening its point.

Zinaida, it was now plain, was mentally unstable: her sufferings, aggravated by the painful death of Nina, the banishment to Siberia of her husband, and the difficulties of making ends meet, was heightened by her tuberculosis and by Trotsky's persecution.

Nina's children, whose father was in gaol, were being taken care of by Alexandra; Sedov's wife and family – a wife and child – had been abandoned in Russia. All four families in Trotsky's immediate circle had been broken up, to say nothing of the fate of dozens of individuals associated with his political fortunes, some of whom were friends.

Oppressive as his personal situation was, it was to go on steadily deteriorating.

He was never molested in Turkey: his suspicion of Kemal Atatürk as an accomplice of Stalin's was baseless. More important, the Soviet Political Police seemed quite inactive, though it was to come out that an agent sometimes penetrated Trotsky's intimate circle with notable ease. It was quite simple, of course, for anyone to get close to him by a pretence of sympathy. Nothing could be done about it: in fact it could never be known who had or had not been a secret agent. Only a few were to be exposed.

This was plainly a condition inherent in the life of a political exile;

at one time Lenin had a lecture circle of some five people, of whom three later turned out to be Tsarist secret agents. He had used this incident to claim that the tug of history shows which side was bound to win – what good did it do the Tsarist regime to monitor his lectures?

In the stance of professional revolutionary now imposed on him it was natural for Trotsky to model himself on Lenin-in-exile. One man against the world, he seemed to radiate the conviction that the world, properly understood, was with him as it turned out to have been with Lenin : that he was aligning himself with the forces of *at least* tomorrow. His professional optimism, at any rate, obliged him to cling to this posture.

During the Twenties occasional attempts had been made by Soviet leaders to consolidate followers in foreign Communist Parties, though with hindsight it is plain that only the desperation of their position in the Soviet regime had driven them to this expedient, which in any case proved futile.

In exile, Trotsky had no alternative. In France, Italy, Germany and Spain, Holland and Belgium, indeed even in China, the United States and Mexico, individuals and tiny coteries, clinging to Trotsky's name as a symbol of tenacious activism and alienated, perhaps, from the primitive orthodoxy of Moscow, aligned themselves, somewhat fitfully, with the new current of opinion.

He was in a dilemma about a name for this new 'tendency' : what, indeed, could he baptise it?

Trotsky never claimed a special role for himself : all he was doing throughout his life, was 'applying' Marxism to different situations. He had even been obliged to soft-pedal the originality of his Permanent Revolution, a genuine though doubtless peripheral contribution to Marxism.

During the process of his elimination from the Party he had been flung back on a frantic insistence on his 'Bolshevik' orthodoxy and on his identificaton with Lenin. This diffident posture with respect to the Party was maintained nearly all his life : it was this connection, to be sure, that had made him a world figure ! It was only natural for him to cling to it in exile – he called his movement 'Bolshevik-Leninist'.

In spite of that, however, his partisans were more generally called 'Trotskyites' plain and simple. Within his small following his own personality was so outstanding that he instantly became its oracle. His authority was to constitute a kind of orthodoxy.

The notion of setting up an actual movement, that is, an independent organisation of his 'tendency', was obvious enough.

He had been ejected from the Soviet Government, from the Party, and from the International – what should he do about it?

His reply was plain – his followers were to regard themselves as loyal members of the institutions that had flung them out : they had not, that is, been expelled by the institutions themselves, but merely by *usurpers within*. Forced into the status of a faction, they would not regard themselves as founders of a new party – that would have been an acknowledgment that the usurpers had been successful.

Consequently, just as Trotsky insisted to his dying day on 'defining' the Soviet Union as a 'workers' state' despite its 'bureaucratic deformations', so he remained loyal to the Third International for years. Expelled or not, he refused to abandon it.

Alas! It was the same dilemma as before : just as Trotsky had been trapped into proclaiming his loyalty to 'Party unity' at a time when the Party had been engulfed by the apparatus, just as he had succumbed to the ikonisation of Lenin, so in exile he went on regarding the Communist Parties of Europe as the 'vanguard of The Proletariat'.

This made his position, of course, all the more hopeless. For this massive 'vanguard' remained within the Soviet Union. It was that bureaucracy, arising on the groundwork of the titanic overhaul of Soviet society and shaped by Stalin as his own personal Government, that with mounting brutality was now forbidding the slightest flicker of 'Oppositionist' sentiment within the International as well as in the Soviet Union.

Thus the dilemma Trotsky was impaled on would seem to have had all the rigour of an ineluctable condition of History – a fact of life.

Both within the Soviet Union and abroad, in fact, Trotsky's hopes were to prove singularly unrealistic.

By the end of his first year of exile the factional victory so easily won by Stalin in the early Twenties was to blossom into an unprecedented magnification of Stalin's person.

In April 1929 a torrent of adulation began that by Stalin's fiftieth birthday in December launched a movement that with extraordinary rapidity expanded into the most extravagant personal cult in history. Stalin's glorification went far beyond that of Marx and Engels, far beyond Lenin. For a quarter of a century he was the paramount and indeed unique authority in the Soviet Union on almost literally all areas of knowledge.

'Genius' was the minimal epithet linked to his name; from 1930 on it was so routine that its omission was automatically ascribed to concealed hostility.

Though Stalin fell short of deification – in this respect he was outstripped by Jesus – Mohammed and Buddha were a short distance behind him.

As his cult was consolidated during the onset of the Thirties it consummated the repression of heterodoxy and became the spiritual framework of Soviet society as a whole. Dissidents were treated in ways unheard of in Tsarist goals, which had been, indeed, rest-homes compared with the punitive regime established so swiftly by the Bolsheviks.

Though for a short while the Political Police passed over the outstanding moderates, they sent the intransigent Oppositionists to the cruellest treatment, short of torture and death, in the gaols – freezing, crowded cells, terrible food, with no light, nothing to read, and no way of writing to friends or families. They were treated far more harshly than out-and-out anti-Bolshevik prisoners after the Civil War; by March 1929 Trotsky's *Bulletin of the Opposition* was comparing the treatment of obstinate 'Trotskyites' with Dostoyevsky's *House of the Dead*.

The experience of the next few years was going to make *that* look like a picnic!

Nor did martyrs spring up, as they had under the incomparably milder regime of Tsarism. Even granted the more efficient use of force during the Thirties, an overriding reason for this is to be found, not in the intimidation of the population, but in the propaganda of the regime, echoed by the demoralisation of its opponents.

In contending with the Soviet regime during the Thirties, Trotsky was hampered by an inability to keep up with the gargantuan efflorescence of the Stalin cult and in particular by his having been the chief and indeed the earliest champion of its own paramount achievement – centralised planning. Though Stalin's implementation of this concept was to arouse his furious criticism, Trotsky could never dissociate himself from its principle.

At first Stalin had been a little tentative in copying Trotsky's proposals. Even in April 1929, at the Sixteenth Party Conference that initiated Stalin's quasi-deification, though a speed-up was called for it was announced that small private farms would remain the chief agricultural factor for a long time to come. Only twenty per cent of the small farms were to be collectivised by 1933, in the first Five-Year-Plan; the richer peasants – the 'kulaks' – were not yet scheduled for 'liquidation'.

By the end of 1929 all this was forgotten: a frenzy of zeal obliterated all moderation. The target figures of the Five-Year-Plan were revised upwards over and over again; by November 1929 private farming was condemned altogether. The current slogan was 'immediate and wholesale collectivisation'. Some months later Stalin announced that half – about thirteen million – of the small farms had already been collectivised: the 'kulaks' had been exiled and butchered, and millions of others had been clubbed into the new economic framework.[8]

In human terms what this meant was unbelievable. The peasants, with no weapons to use against the small mobile units of heavily armed Political Police detachments except, quite literally, clubs, scythes and pitchforks, were herded into enclosures and often massacred wholesale. What had begun as an administrative decree had instantly, because of peasant resistance, become a well-nigh military campaign against millions of peasants that in the space of a couple of years, produced at least some ten million dead, including women and children.

Stalin gave this figure to Churchill after the Second World War:[9] though a heavy silence enveloped the operation while it was in train the rough reliability of the figure is confirmed by all other accounts.

Simultaneously Stalin rammed the urban sector of the country into breakneck industrialisation at a pace and on a scale Trotsky had never dreamt of. Trotsky's own sombre predictions of the cost of 'primitive Socialist accumulation', though timed by Trotsky himself so clumsily as to alienate the Party, were now to be beggared by the horrors of the drive started by Stalin with a matchless fanfare.

This vast and violent transformation, so extravagant in tempo and methods, took everyone by surprise, including the Bolshevik leaders.

The frenzied campaign was, of course an attempt to ensure the Bolshevik leadership against two consequences of its natural isolation – to provide a high wall behind which 'Socialism in One Country' could maintain itself against the encirclement of capitalism, and more immediately, to create a socio-economic structure that could obviate the capitalist restoration inherent in the success of the

N.E.P. The Bolshevik regime, 'representing' the people of the Soviet Union, was defending itself.

Once Stalin moved against the peasants so murderously he could not turn back. Terror became commonplace; the Political Police became the basic fact of Soviet life.

In fact the violence unleashed by the social upheaval at the end of the Twenties and beginning of the Thirties far surpassed the rough-and-ready brutality of the Civil War, which was a straight contest between two sides.

The well-organised army put together by Trotsky had the support of large segments of the working class that had been influenced by Socialist ideas and that accepted the destruction of Tsarism as such, while the rather badly organised forces of the White reaction, which could not, after all, offer much to the peasants, were debarred in advance from competing with the promises scattered about by the Bolsheviks.

Now the terror was directed at the whole population by a Party that had meanwhile produced its own veteran elite and had embarked on a large-scale programme of overhaul and construction directed at the bulk of the working class and especially the peasantry. Its principal levers were, of course, the police power ruthlessly applied, and, on the positive side, the messianic elan of a minority of youth and of idealists gripped by the thrill of construct-ing utopia in their own lifetime.

This utopian elan was, in fact, the hallmark of the very first phase of the Five-Year-Plan: the Young Communists and the 'Shock workers' were *enthusiastic*: they really thought, in the beginning, that fervour alone could – in the celebrated slogan – 'overtake and outstrip' Western capitalism in a few years, make a heavily pro-tected enclosure of Socialism in One Country, and thus justify, as it were, Stalin's decision.

But the elan did not last long; it was simply not possible to 'overtake' let alone outstrip any industrial country in a few years. And since that too could not be admitted the elan had to be replaced by the terror that, with only a few pauses, was to last for decades.

Yet it was not the terror based merely on inequality, but the specific problem of carrying out the collectivisation programme that gave the terror of the Thirties its singular murderousness.

The Big Jump of the Stalin regime was aimed at the creation of a stable base in the countryside, that is, on herding the peasants into a controllable economic situation by means of the collective farms. Since the collective farms were initially incoherent from an economic point of view – they had not, in Marxist terms, replaced the preceding system because of their superior productivity! – they had to be maintained in existence by fiat plus guns, demonstrating in an extreme form, indeed, the pattern laid down by the Bolsheviks in their fundamental act of statehood – the seizure of power itself. The only thing that could stop the peasants from resuming their millennial tilling of the soil were the execution brigades led by the Political Police.

Stalin's decision to collectivise the peasantry at the pace he had fixed on – 'immediate and wholesale' – meant that throughout the year – ploughing, sowing, harvesting, reaping and delivering the harvest to the state – the peasants had to be confronted at every single stage by machine-guns. The massacre of ten million peasants – including women and children – was thus accomplished by a more or less constant application of brute force: since the peasants were still well over sixty per cent of the population it meant that a tiny minority – the Political Police – backed by a slightly larger minority – the Party – bore the whole burden of applying that brute force.

The hatred of the regime generated by this mass brutality infected not only the towns, where countless workers were still only one jump from the farm, but the regime itself, by now fighting for its life amidst the pretence that all was well – countering the crude, unsophisticated violence of the countryside with a technically expert, sophisticated violence of its own.

For his part Trotsky, in order to avoid being outflanked by 'bourgeois' critics, was obliged to laud to the skies the vast potential of Soviet planning even while attacking the details of the actual plans. He had to fend off 'Left' criticism of himself for being too harsh on the Soviet regime, and hence to play up the gigantic revolutionary dynamism that made it possible for Stalin to accomplish anything at all. In the contemporary condition of the European working-class movement, that was to prove a mortgage Trotsky was incapable of paying off.

Trotsky's polemical isolation was highlighted by the rise of Hitlerism, which destroyed the Central European working-class movement and precipitated the Second World War.

Trotsky's reaction to Hitlerism no doubt constituted his major achievement in exile. He was practically the only observer who perceived the drive of the Nazi movement and its threat to the

Soviet regime. Throughout the Thirties this was his predominant theme; it produced some of his best writing.

The doom of capitalism is of course a Marxist article of faith. But the 'collapse' of such a complex edifice cannot be instantaneous: the succession and interaction of its stages create an immense area for analysis and prediction.

In the early Twenties – roughly 1923–8, between the N.E.P. and the breakneck drive for industrialisation and collectivisation – the Comintern had taken a 'soft' line on capitalist 'collapse': it decided capitalism would for the time being 'stabilise itself'.

At that time Trotsky had been criticising the Stalin 'line' from what was called the 'Left': he recommended various forms of activism, thus becoming identified with a 'Left' line in general and turning into a symbol of intransigence within the Communist sphere.

By the summer of 1929 the notion of the 'stabilisation' of capitalism was replaced by the 'Third Period' theory.

According to this theory the 'First Period' was one of revolutionary turbulence: it lasted, after the First World War, until the 'Second Period' in 1923, when capitalism began stablising itself. This lasted until 1928, the beginning of the 'Third Period', which was guaranteed to see the extinction of capitalism and its offspring, imperialism.

This had a corollary: if capitalism was now definitely on its last legs, if all its 'contradictions' were about to 'explode' and finally bring to fruition the apocalyptic vision of the youthful Marx, the task of the Soviet Party was clear : any seemingly casual friction, the most trifling conflict between 'classes', had a vast explosive potential that made it possible to discard 'reformist illusions', take advantage of the tremendous thrust of the revolutionary movement possible in such an epoch of decay, collapse, and explosion, and embark on a decisive contest for power.

Since this climactic contest for power was now inevitable, according to the Kremlin seers, there was no point fooling around any longer with the Social Democratic Parties. According to Bolshevik cliché such Parties were inherently counter-revolutionary: in any genuine crisis there was only one side for them to be on – the side of reactionary capitalism, where they were all the more dangerous because of their *pretence* of Socialism, which could only deceive innocent workers.

In this 'Third Period' jargon, in short, Social-Democratic Parties were 'social-Fascist' – *really* Fascist behind their Socialist rhetoric. Hence Communists spent most of their time denouncing Social-Democrats.

This view of the great Social-Democratic parties of the Continent was to dominate Soviet policy throughout the rise of Nazism, the Great Depression, and the collapse of the Spanish monarchy.

The 'Third Period' theory constituted, of course, a complete right-about-face vis-à-vis the previous theory of capitalist stabilisation; it was carried out with the usual Soviet fanfare and cocksureness.

It had a disastrous effect on Trotsky. Beforehand, he had been regarded as a 'Left' critic of official policy; now, since he was made to sound as though he were criticising official policy from the *Right*, could he be presented as a flibbertigibbet. Just as before, when it was not rhetorical persuasiveness that decided issues, but the clout of the apparatus, so it was easy for the apparatus, with its myriad outlets, to present the exiled Trotsky, battling with his pen alone, as being inconstant: look, first he was so-called 'Left', now he is Right!

As a Marxist Trotsky, naturally, also thought capitalism on its way out. But his acumen prevented him from regarding complex, long-term developments as immediate tactical perspectives. It was both senseless and dangerous to base directives for immediate action on journalistic effusions.

Trotsky showed that the notion of stabilisation had *always* been wrong (for instance, the Chinese revolution took place in that era as well as the British General Strike of 1926: Marxists took that very seriously). Contrariwise, even though capitalism was doubtless going through crises, it was plainly quite capable of going from slumps to booms as well as from booms to slumps. He made the perhaps obvious point that descriptions of epochs were meaningless as guide-lines; seeing a 'civil war' in any clash made genuine guidance impossible. Trotsky described all this as mechanical, doctrinaire, lifeless Marxism – opposed, of course, to his own!

Trotsky was no doubt pointing out an ambiguity inherent in Marx's and more flagrantly in Engel's original formulations. Though concerned, in fact, with immediate outcomes they had had a habit of making timeless predictions. Consequently when some particular prediction failed to come off – which happened consistently – it was always possible for themselves and their sympathisers to revert to the timelessness of their style, and to maintain that even though a particular event had misfired the validity of the scheme as a whole remained unimpaired.

Similarly, at a later date, the Kremlin simply took its own rhetoric about the inevitable, guaranteed decline of capitalism at face-value, and rather obtusely linked general predictions to specific events.

It had been possible for Marx to be euphoric because as a young man he had really believed that capitalism was going to 'explode' from one month to the next. Thus the stylistic timelessness of his prophecies did not necessarily conflict with what he could conceive of as concrete likelihoods or indeed certainties.

But a century later a new social regime had come into existence, a regime wedded both to his ideas and to his jargon: for the Bolshevik Party to blur the distinction between overarching generalities and tactical manoeuvres merely because of a misapprehension as to the immediate validity of Marxism was positively confusing.

Part of the reason for this confusion, of course, was also what checkmated Trotsky. The Revolution was not, in fact, advancing. The 'objective' development of capitalism as a whole was not accompanied by any rise in 'self-consciousness' as the industrial working class matured in tandem with it. There was no spontaneous evolution in the European working class that could provide a matrix for the genesis of a revolutionary spearhead that might have rallied to Trotsky. This same failure of The Revolution to move forward had to be coped with by the regime in power – by now, after all, a vested interest – in the only way it could – by fiat. The initial blunder of analysis – i.e., the stupidity of the Kremlin analysts – was compounded, in fact, by their 'inorganic' relationship to events.

Unable to base themselves on real politics, in the sense of spontaneous shifts in society, they were bound to hand down, within the framework of their 'theoretical' analysis, tactical decisions that were naturally put as dogmatically as ever but being in the event quite wrong had the effect of paralysing followers and discouraging potential recruits.

Yet none of this was to do Trotsky any good. The tide itself, after all, was against him: he could not counter it merely by being correct. It could not even be claimed that the seeming 'radicalism' of the 'Third Period' theory corresponded with an upsurge of revolutionary sentiment in Moscow. The Stalin faction was not lashing out at the world in a recrudescence of messianic fervour.

Trotsky was unable to work up enough of a following to take

advantage of what he called, characteristically, the 'Third Period of the Comintern's blunders'.

Trotsky was hamstrung. The ability of the official spokesmen to do this was in its own way a reflection of the weightiness the regime had acquired merely by virtue of being a regime. It carried so much weight, in fact, as to constitute an entire universe: those living within that universe could not see so clearly that there had been a shift of position – their own position was shifting too! They were being carried along with the whole of their horizon. To all those within the orbit of Soviet-style Communism – the same ones who constituted Trotsky's only possible audience – it could be made to seem that it was not they who had made the right-about-face, as Trotsky said, but Trotsky himself.

In the election of 14 September 1930 Hitler, who since his abortive putsch in 1923 had generally been written off as a crank, was voted for by six and a half million Germans: since the last election, in 1928, in which his party had won 800,000 votes and been the smallest in the Reichstag, it had become the second biggest.

The Soviet leadership, committed to the 'Third Period' theory, swallowed the Hitler victory with a degree of complacency that remains unbelievable.

Since the Communist Party had also increased its vote from about three million to better than four and a half, it was possible, by disregarding the proportions of things, for the Communists to preen themselves on their own victory, and to continue the 'Third Period' line that precluded any co-operation with the Social-Democrats, who for their part also refused, with equally incredible obstinacy, to take Hitler seriously. While frightened by his rhetoric into supporting a conservative regime, they did nothing to rally their own followers against Nazism.

Trotsky's reaction to Nazi agitation, while at first contemptuous, as he was of all irrationality, matured into an unusual appreciation of Hitler as strategist, agitator and organiser.

In Germany he was dealing with a dynamic flux quite different from the rigidity of the Stalin dictatorship; he could watch Hitler manoeuvring in the open against many contenders for the allegiance of a vast public. Trotsky's intelligence and passion came into play; long before it became even remotely fashionable anywhere else, and especially not in the Soviet Union, he produced penetrating analyses of German politics.

He underestimated, no doubt, Hitler's positive appeal – the

apocalyptic vision of a new world that inflamed countless young people, as well as their elders, disgusted by the depressing spectacle of parliamentary corruption and 'babbling'.

For Trotsky the cardinal factor was the attitude of the Communist Party. He took it for granted, of course, that the Social-Democrats or at least their leaders would do nothing to stop Hitler.

It was just this that made the responsibility of the Communists all the more fateful; he hammered away at the smugness of their pseudo-radical theory of the 'Third Period', a theory that by lumping all non-Communist Left wingers together as tools of the bourgeoisie and hence, as at the very least crypto-Fascists, made it impossible to make a useful distinction between potential allies and outright enemies.

In 1931 and well into 1932 the Communist press was full of savage descriptions of the Social-Democrats as Fascists – the 'Left wing of Fascism'. A *fortiori*, the Centre parties were Fascists too, indeed absolutely everyone in the country was Fascist, except, of course, the Communist Party.

Trotsky pointed out what madness it was for working-class leaders to fail to recognise the differences between 'bourgeois' democracy and Fascism: as a 'consistent Marxist' he too had to admit that both were 'forms of capitalist rule', but it could not be denied that differences of procedure were vital. In a parliamentary democracy the 'bourgeoisie' kept itself propped up on concessions to the proletariat, i.e., it allowed the existence of independent working-class organisations, including, of course, parties and trades-unions, the 'islands of proletarian democracy within bourgeois democracy'.

Trotsky gave a graphic picture of how Hitler would do away with all forms of workers' autonomy – trades-unions, parties, press, everything. Solely because of this, in fact, the workers should defend themselves by safeguarding their 'islands of proletarian democracy' against the onslaught of the Hitlerites.

Trotsky's warnings were timely and persuasive; they were filled with all the dramatic urgency his talent could infuse them with.

They persuaded no one.

Trotsky was vilified right and left as a sort of malevolent nut: – the Communist press, both in the Soviet Union and in Germany, called him a 'panic-monger', an 'adventurer', 'an ally of the counter-revolutionaries' and so on. His predictions, which in this case all came true, earned him nothing but abuse. His powerful appeal fell on deaf ears.

His own following, tiny to begin with, remained a helpless sect. The vast organisations of the working-class movement, the Social Democratic and the Communist Parties that could chalk up thirteen million votes, with countless newspapers and trades-unions, indeed a whole social complex that paralleled society as a whole, simply did not react.

Trotsky took it for granted that without a civil war the prospect of power was altogether beyond Hitler, whose intentions had been unequivocally expressed for years and who was the leader of a movement combining both ideological fanatics and romantic idealists, with a huge contingent of out-and-out thugs. For Trotsky the vital question was the organisation of the working class for that civil war.

Nothing happened. On 30 January 1933 Hitler, quite legally, became chancellor, long before the Socialists and Communists together, after years of confronting the obvious, had even begun to prepare their limitless resources for a contest.

Even then Trotsky thought it was not too late: Hitler was still only chancellor, head of a mere coalition. Only a little more than a month later, on 5 March 1933 – after the Reichstag fire – in elections that were held with the Nazi tidal wave spreading a general terror throughout the countryside, the Nazis were still unable to organise themselves sufficiently to prevent twelve million votes going to the Social-Democrats and the Communists, and another nearly six million to the other (Catholic) opposition to Hitler.

This was to say nothing of the frictions within the German ruling coalition, not only between Hitler and his ephemeral partners but even within the Nazi Party, frictions that Trotsky successfully deduced in his Prinkipo burrow.

To no avail: his last summons, written a week after Hitler's accession to power, was not even printed before the countless institutions of the working-class movement in Germany were pulverised.

Trotsky thought the German fiasco would surely lead to a re-orientation in the Soviet leadership and in the Comintern – they would *have* to admit their errors, just as he thought they *had* to about China.

The defeat of the biggest working-class movement in the world – including the Soviet Union – was plainly a catastrophe. To Trotsky's mind the failure of the Comintern paralleled the Second International's failure to stop the First World War – the failure that had led to the establishment of the Comintern itself.

Yet there was a difference between the two defections – a difference that made the Comintern look even worse than the Second International.

Unlike the surrender of the Second International to chauvinism – which to Trotsky, impervious to the tug of nationalism, seemed almost like a moral betrayal – the collapse of the Comintern and of the German Communist Party in the face of Hitlerism was plainly due to the ossification of the Communist cadres in both the Soviet Union and in Germany.

This ossification transcended mere treachery – it cast doubt on the validity of Marxist training

Hitler was, after all, confronting generations of Marxist-trained workers, a gigantic organisational network at the disposition of both the Social-Democratic and the Communist Parties, to say nothing about the resources of the Soviet state, with its batteries of propagandists and theoreticians. His onslaught, moreover, had been unmistakable from the outset.

Yet the great heritage of the German working class was extinguished overnight, and its extinction was acquiesced in by numerous, well-equipped, well-trained leaders of the German Communist Party and the Comintern.

Not merely had there been no struggle against Hitlerism, but – what from Trotsky's point of view was even worse – there was not a ripple of complaint!

One might have thought that the whole working-class movement, which Trotsky had congratulated for having created the Russian Revolution and the Workers' State, to say nothing of the institutional efflorescence that made the German working class such a formidable factor, would have displayed its rage – would have mutinied, at least, against a leadership that had shown itself to be so innocent, cowardly and stupid.

Nothing!

No doubt Trotsky had a right to expect that now he would be listened to. His pamphleteering, the best of his career, would be able to play a role at last among at least the more intelligent and independent working-class elite.

Yet it was doubtless naive to expect the rigidity of the Third International to accommodate the admission of a blunder any more than it had been able to in the 'China question'. The structure that

Stalin had been building for several years now rested, indeed, precisely on his infallibility: the quasi-deification of Stalin the Genius was the fundamental element in Soviet orthodoxy.

At the first meeting the Comintern Executive held after Hitler's triumph it not only failed to question its past policy, instead it proclaimed that the German Communists had behaved splendidly – Hitler's triumph was meaningless!

The Executive reinforced this decision, characteristically, by prohibiting its discussion.[10] Nor was the interdiction challenged by a single member of the Comintern.

Trotsky was staggered by this most of all: despite his belief that the Comintern itself was moribund, he retained his faith in the vitality of the individual Communist Parties.

He was forced to say: 'An organisation that has not been awoken by the thunderbolt of Fascism . . . is dead and cannot be resurrected.'[11]

He felt helpless: he might just as well abandon his futile efforts to reform the Communist movement from within. He now had to make up his mind about a break with the Third International.

Trotsky's inhibitions about leadership under his own name were now put to the test with particular urgency. He had both to cut himself adrift from his spiritual anchor, the Soviet regime that had made him an actor on the world stage, and to set up an organisation of his own.

For years he had stubbornly maintained that since the Comintern was a mere outgrowth of the Soviet 'Workers' State', the 'proletarian' leadership throughout the world was bound to support it on behalf of The Revolution. The rupture with the Second International during the First World War had at least produced that 'Workers' State': but where could Trotsky go?

In the blind alley of the Thirties he had to summon up more faith than ever, or greater semblance of faith, to sustain his public stance.

For months after the Nazi triumph he grappled with the problem of institutionalising his authority in a new International. His secretaries saw him pacing his room for hours at a time: 'His face streamed with sweat; one sensed the physical exertion of his thought and of his hesitancy.'[12]

He stalled as long as he could: in the spring of 1933 he called for no more than a new German Communist Party free of Stalin's paralysing hand. Still hoping for atonement by analysis, he waited for the German defeat to shake up other Communist Parties in

Europe, notably in the countries bordering Germany – initially Austria, Czechoslovakia, Poland, the Netherlands and above all France – and to force them, through scrutinising the past, to abandon the Soviet network.

This was just as visionary as his hopes for the German Party; by July 1933 he was cornered: he set about creating a New (Fourth) International.¹ᵃ

Even now he baulked at the ultimate step – telling his adherents that the New International would function within the Soviet Union.

This was a thorny problem: could he attack the Stalin regime openly? Abandon, at last, Party unity?

He hesitated: for a time he said that since the Soviet Union was no longer the 'key to the situation' in the international working-class movement, it was legitimate to agitate only outside it.

It was certainly impossible to agitate against Stalin inside the Soviet Union! For that matter any hope of agitating within the Soviet Party – 'factionalism' – had been altogether utopian since 1927 at least and really long before.

Yet it was plainly silly to launch a New International and bar it from the Soviet Union; in October 1933 he finally yielded to 'logic' and proclaimed his International on Soviet soil.¹⁴

He could still hope that with the advance of The Revolution in the West the Stalin coterie might be eliminated by a mere 'police operation'. As he put it, there were 'no normal constitutional ways . . . left for the removal of the ruling clique' – i.e., a vote would not do it! On the other hand, if the working-class forces were regrouped on a world scale, they would leave 'the Stalinite apparatus suspended in a vacuum'.

Despite his ferocious attacks on the Stalin bureaucracy he thought it was merely a 'malignant growth on the body of the working-class, not a new possessing class'. Its 'deformations' were due, accordingly, not to a new social situation but to the primitiveness of the old society that it had not yet pulled out of the mire. In short, Trotsky's view of the Soviet Union as the repository of the 'conquests of October' was still summed up in his slogan of 'unconditional defence'.

What frustrated him fundamentally was the manifest fact that faith in the Stalin cult was *reinforced* by setbacks.

In 1932, for instance, after the slaughters of the collectivisation drive, murmurings against Stalin had become more and more savage; it looked as though opposition might be organised. Nothing materialised: partly by a slowdown in the breakneck pace, partly because of a good harvest, Stalin not merely restored his position, he had more prestige than ever, if only because his apparatus of terror managed to bull its way through his monumental blunders.

The defeat in Germany, the very fact that such a powerful state had been taken over by a fanatical enemy of the Soviet Union consolidated Stalin's position still further: he seemed needed more desperately than ever.

Indeed, the number of Soviet sympathisers in general, outside the Stalin cult, had been increased by Hitler's victory. Liberals had always been susceptible to Soviet propaganda; since Hitler's victory the Soviet Union became the darling of multitudes of well-wishers, soon to be endlessly amplified by Stalin's launching of the People's Fronts – the discarding of the 'Third Period' – as a belated riposte to Hitler.

Trotsky was reaping the harvest he had been obliged to sow, and indeed, had sown with enthusiasm ever since his identification with the Bolshevik Party in the crucible of 1917. By accepting Lenin, by accepting the Party as the 'only instrument of history', by accepting the Soviet Party as the trustee of The Revolution, he had put himself in a position he could not extricate himself from.

The calcification of the Soviet apparatus, the creation and consolidation of the cult of Stalin the Genius against a background of more and more rigid Marxist dogmatic orthodoxy had had their effect. The ikonisation of the Party, State and Leader represented, for pious Communists everywhere, a new Trinity. Its enemies were only too easily anathematised.

Stalin, as architect of the apparatus and inspirer of the new orthodoxy, had managed to establish a functional identification between the Soviet bureaucracy and the heritage of 'Leninism'.

If Trotsky's only conceivable audience had disregarded his exhortations on behalf of reform *within* the movement, why, after all, should they listen to his call for a systematic rupture with the big parties?

That might have been possible if a powerful current had animated the working-class movement, as at the founding of both the Second and the Third International, but this was just what was lacking. The reason Trotsky was calling for a new International – the degrading defeat of the old Internationals – was the same reason it was so difficult: the whole movement was at its lowest point in generations – just what had ensured Hitler's victory!

Trotsky was now in the situation he was to remain in for the rest of his life: he was swept to one side by currents that neither his personal influence nor his powers of analysis could contend with.

The Soviet regime was evolving differently from the way he had predicted; the organised working-class movement remained indifferent to his ideas. More particularly, the cult of Stalin the Genius now flourished as never before.

In 1932, for instance, some Oppositionists (Zinoviev, Kamenev, Preobrzhensky among others) had been deported (as in 1927); they had been asked to extol Stalin's genius, his incredible infallibility and so on, and had refused. But by May 1933 they were ready to accept this formalised obsequiousness as a condition of capitulation : recantations, systematised according to formulae of ecclesiastical penitence, now had to include the dithyrambs made commonplace by the cult of Stalin the Genius.

It was doubtless such recantations, in addition to Stalin's remarkable recovery from the frightful crisis of 1929–32, that enabled Trotsky to amputate himself from what had been his anchorage. In his despair he decided to sponsor a new International.

Yet even now Trotsky never thought that the scattered groups of his sympathisers could themselves be that International. He still could not quite launch a new organisation on an independent basis : his followers were far too few and uninfluential.

He was obliged to stall on the actual organisation of an International, as distinct from proclaiming it in principle. He thought it would have to wait, once again, until it made its own way as an idea among the many former Communists and Socialists whose disillusion with their leaders might finally persuade them to turn toward Trotsky.

This was, of course, just another way of rephrasing the same dilemma. Just as Trotsky's ideas had misfired, so now the idea of a new International 'in principle' made no headway to speak of. Even though he found some sympathisers in many places – from China and India to America – they were to acquire only 'episodic' influence, and then only much later as elements in the politics of small countries against a background of more or less democratic agitation (Ceylon, Greece).

Within the old movement, in short, Trotsky remained paralysed, and he could not get a foothold outside it.

He did no better in broadcasting his analysis of German affairs to 'bourgeois' opinion.

Hitler's primary task was to put himself over as a misunderstood moderate – all he wanted was peace, his real enemy was the Soviet Union alone.

It was easy for Trotsky to point out that Hitler required Western indulgence in order to rearm Germany. But it was far easier for Hitler to bamboozle Western leaders. Trotsky summed it up neatly:

> Anyone who expects to meet a lunatic brandishing a hatchet and instead finds a man hiding a revolver in his trouser-pocket is bound to feel relieved. But that doesn't prevent a revolver from being more dangerous than a hatchet.[15]

Yet his wit could not nullify Hitler's diplomacy – that worked. Whether Hitler's objective was the destruction of the Soviet Union or a German reorganisation of Europe, as long as the Western Governments were afraid of war and in half a dozen minds about the pace, scope or even advisability of large-scale rearming, Hitler's holding out a flag of peace while intimating an attack on the Soviet Union later on was bound to be seductive.

Spain, too, was a major preoccupation of Trotsky's in exile.

The Spanish monarchy had been extinguished in April 1931: a republic had ripened, to be succeeded by a social upheaval Trotsky thought similar to the Russian breakdown in 1917, and toward the end of Trotsky's life by the Franco dictatorship.

From the Communists' point of view the course of events in Spain might have been thought the opposite of what was happening in Germany – there was a substantial development on the 'Left' side. Yet the Comintern, enthralled by its 'Third Period' obsession, handled both arenas the same way.

Just as the German Communist Party shrugged aside the conflict between the Nazis and the Weimar Republic, so the Spanish Communist Party dismissed the clash between the ancient monarchy and the republic as a triviality. In Spain, for that matter, the question of the Party's *benefiting* by the clash was not even raised: it had no ambitions at all.

The Comintern thinkers considered Spain too backward for any question of the 'proletarian dictatorship' to be raised. For that matter the notion of a 'proletarian dictatorship' in a rural country like Spain sounded rather like Trotsky's 'Permanent Revolution', and since that was now being presented to the Comintern's clients as his paramount heresy, the Soviet leadership had to avoid anything similar.

Thus a quite irrelevant piece of outmoded 'factionalism' produced an artificial barometer for Spain. The contradiction of Trotsky's theory, required in order to stigmatise him as an outcast, was applied mechanically even where it was superfluous.

In any case Trotsky's views had little influence : the Spanish Party, puny and confused to begin with, had succumbed to Soviet-style orthodoxy, with its concomitant of 'heresy' and the merciless harassment of all aspects of non-conformism on its own side.

Trotsky predicted that the corrosive divisions among the managers of the working-class movement would lead to a Fascist victory; in Spain, as in Germany, he exhausted himself calling for unity. In both countries he was to have the bitter satisfaction of Cassandra's role.

Eventually, with the victory of Hitler, the 'Third Period' of the Comintern's philosophy was finally eclipsed by the new constellation in Central Europe : the Soviet Union plainly needed allies. The rest of the Thirties was to be dominated by the People's Fronts.

By the autumn of 1932 Trotsky had been working at his back-breaking pace for more than three and a half years : he had been remarkably productive despite a finickiness that made him not only re-draft but re-write practically every sentence of each book.

He had not only not been able to leave Turkey, but had visited Istanbul only a couple of times, to see the Santa Sophia Cathedral and – a dentist.

Now he slipped his leash : on the anniversary of 'October' he went to Copenhagen to give a lecture to some Social-Democratic students. Though he had received such invitations before, he had never got a visa. This time the Social-Democratic Government in Denmark gave him one : he hoped he could use it to slip out of coming back.

In vain : it was to be no more than a brief respite.

In mid-November 1932 he left for Europe under an incognito – 'Mr. Sedov, a stateless passenger'. His identity was broadcast immediately; the European press was filled with rumours about the intentions of the 'caged lion', *Pravda* sneered at the 'escaped lion'.

He was not allowed into Athens; he saw Pompei under police escort; he was not allowed off the ship at Marseilles; he had to take a motor-boat, land outside the port and be hustled through France at top-speed, with only an hour allowed him in Paris.

Press people struggling to catch up with him managed to do so only at Dunkirk, where he got on a ship for Denmark : the Right-

wing French press kept up a steady barrage of denunciation throughout his lightning trip through the French countryside.

In Denmark he was a nuisance to everyone, especially, of course,
to his Social-Democratic hosts. He had been told to disembark
outside Copenhagen, to be brought into the city as furtively as
possible – 'by the backstairs entrance', as a leading newspaper
(*Politiken*) described it. He was jeered at by organised Communists.

The Danish Royalists castigated him as the 'murderer of the Tsar's
family' (the Tsarina had been a Danish princess); on the other side
the Soviet ambassador voiced Stalin's displeasure.

Yet 'the moment Trotsky showed himself there was a deep
silence – the sense of an historic personality and perhaps of an
historic occasion.' His 'perfect calm' was commented on.[16]

In a rather donnish style – to avoid 'disturbances' – Trotsky gave a
two-hour lecture summing up to an audience of two thousand the
thesis of his three-volume *History*. It was the last public speech he
was to make.

Nothing happened during the week's stay in Copenhagen. He
gave some interviews and made a broadcast in English to the United
States. There was an immense amount of talk in his entourage,
which had immediately been swollen by the arrival of twenty-five of
his German, French and Italian followers. In fact, an impromptu
'international conference' was held, at which 'everyone talked endlessly except Trotsky, who worked hard nearly all the time in his
room, either writing or dictating'.[17]

At this time Zinaida's health had been worsening visibly; Sedov,
who could not get a visa out of Berlin, was on the phone every day
about the frustrating situation – he could not rejoin his parents even
for a moment, help Zina get her child and so on.

Trotsky spent a week like Laocoon, entangled in red tape, its
maddeningness compounded by malevolence. When the eight days
of his visa were up he tried to manoeuvre : hoping in desperation
that something would somehow happen to enable him to stay – to
see Sedov, to get Zina's child to her, *anything* – he insisted that he
was simply not ready to leave.

By now the Danes were determined; he was hustled out by motor-
car, to make sure he did not overstay his visa. When Trotsky, Natalya
and his secretaries left this time there was no one in the port either
to wave goodbye or for that matter even to jeer.

The ship, which left Denmark on 2 December 1932, sailed via
Antwerp; the port was teeming with police; Trotsky was questioned

aboard ship by border police, a little strangely, since he was in transit only; there was a quarrel, 'threats of arrest'. No one was permitted ashore.

Trotsky used the stopover to write a defence of Bolshevism and to taunt Vandervelde, the well-known Socialist who had been Belgium's Prime Minister, with the inadequacies of democracy. He reminded Vandervelde that he had once let him into the Soviet Union to defend the Social-Revolutionary who had tried to kill Lenin in 1922, and that Vandervelde had been allowed to attack the Soviet system to his heart's delight in open court. Trotsky's satisfaction in his 'polemic' was rhetorical only; there was no way for Vandervelde to respond, still less to get him a Belgian visa.

They came to Paris on 6 December 1932; here they had a tiny breathing-spell. Sedov had been given a visa to meet them; he was waiting for them in the Gare du Nord, together with a police cordon.

When Trotsky heard at the frontier that he would have to hang about Marseilles for nine days until there was a boat to Istanbul he was delighted – nine days in France! His delight was cut short immediately; the moment he arrived in Marseilles he was forced aboard a cargo steamer sailing the same night.

Once aboard he learned that there were, in fact, no provisions for passengers; the trip was going to take a fortnight. Though it was now midnight, he and Natalya left the ship at once. Actual force, though apparently no violence, was tried, but to no avail – the Trotskys were so frightened of being trapped on such a long trip they actually fought the police. The odd little group spent the night in the port area; even the weather was disagreeable.

Trotsky wired everyone he could – Herriot, Blum, even the Communist leader Thorez. Then he asked Rome for a transit visa; the Fascist Foreign Ministry gave him one at once.

He had to wait for hours for Paris to show some signs of life. He and Natalya were tucked away in a hotel before dawn; once they got the Italian visa they were hastily forced on to the first train going to Italy. Sedov was still there – they had seen him for one day only, in atrocious circumstances; they embraced across the police line.

Inside Italy, Natalya and Trotsky 'sat long, long ... in the dark compartment and wept. . . .'[18]

A few days later they were back in their Prinkipo cage.

He felt more helpless than ever. His European 'organisations' were plainly futile: in Germany especially, with the Nazi movement expanding mightily, his cluster of devotees was standing still. There his chief outlet was a tiny new monthly (*Permanente Revolution*): it was ineffectual.

Though his longer articles, his brochures and so on, were read in many languages by many people outside any movements and his reputation as a journalist kept growing, it had no political significance for him.

His little *Bulletin* had been moved from Paris some time before: he proposed to set up an International Secretariat in Berlin. It was natural for Sedov to go there.

Sedov was no doubt the most poignant element in Trotsky's ordeal. Able, intelligent, and unservile, he was wholly identified with his father – his lieutenant in all respects. Yet the pressure of his father's personality was overwhelming; it was exacerbated by an unmistakable though inexpressible emotional ambivalence.

Though a man of immense control with strangers – famously courteous, indeed, and restrained – Trotsky's nervous tension was in the very nature of things extreme. The rarity of his physical outlets – sailboating, walking, etc. – made it natural for him to lose his temper. He would express himself sharply to Sedov, painfully criticising the devoted young man for 'disorder', 'sloth and sloppiness', and even of 'letting down' his father.[19]

There was also an emotional element in the decision to send Sedov to Berlin. Jeanne Molinier, the wife of Molinier, one of Trotsky's chief French sympathisers, and the one, moreover, whom Trotsky had apparently some special warmth for, had left her husband and moved in with Sedov. This added a personal quirk to the tangle of insoluble political problems; Sedov's departure together with Jeanne Molinier quieted the atmosphere.

After some seven or eight months, Sedov succeeded in getting a German visa, in February 1931, for the purpose – only partially exaggerated – of studying at a technical institute. Before he left in mid-January his half-sister Zinaida arrived in Prinkipo, having been delayed for months by the Soviet Government. She came together with her five-year-old son Seva; her other child, a girl six to seven years old, had been left behind as a hostage, being cared for together with the two children of her deceased sister Nina by Alexandra.

Zinaida, sharp-featured, with blazing eyes, looked most like Trotsky. She resembled him temperamentally, too: she had his gift for abstract identification; politics was as natural for her as for him.

In her mother's words, 'she was more public-spirited than family-minded'.[20]

Trotsky had never had any time for his children; as he had said about Alexandra, whom 'life had separated' him from, life had also separated him from their two daughters. It was by now, in fact, almost three decades since, only a little over twenty, he had left Alexandra and their two small children in his first exile at the eastern tip of Siberia.

Until 1917, in fact, he had seen these daughters of his very briefly and only a couple of times; in the turmoil of the years that followed, there could be no question of a 'normal' family life, to say nothing of time to spare for two girls he was not even living with. During the turbulence of 1917 they had yearned at him adoringly from among the throngs he had fascinated. After Nina's death, during Trotsky's exile in Alma-Ata, Zinaida was prevented by illness from coming to see him when he was expelled from the Soviet Union.

Now, in Prinkipo, her psychic imbalance soon emerged. Full of exaltation at the reunion, she flung herself into Trotsky's politics. She involved herself completely in the life of the tiny, slightly obsessed household: her pet name for her father was Churchill's phrase – the 'Ogre of Europe'.

Temperamental and high-strung, she at first seemed no more than that. Natalya was exceptionally kind: she soon saw that Zinaida was ill, and made a point of taking her to physicians. She went out of her way to leave her alone with Trotsky.

Within the first few months after Zinaida's arrival fire swept the household twice: the first time a little while after she got there, the second a few months later. On both occasions a suspicion of arson was routine – what else? Everyone was upset, as a secretary was to write later, 'except Trotsky himself'. Trotsky's sang-froid in fact was already a fixed element in his manner; when the whole household made its way to a local hotel Trotsky started dictating the very next day as 'though nothing had happened during the night'.[21]

Zinaida's nervous disorder, exacerbated by consumption, re-asserted itself; she was in a state of great turmoil – worried about the little girl she had left in Moscow, by her husband in Siberia, by the heat; she also needed some operations.

She began succumbing to what in today's cliché would be a nervous breakdown – fits of hysteria that enabled her to express the cluster of resentments that had doubtless been accumulating since her early childhood, when she had been *de facto* abandoned by Trotsky. As a child she seems to have suffered a tremendous shock on finding a dummy in Trotsky's bed after his escape from exile in eastern Siberia. She wrote that she had clung to the idea of him all her life, while suffering immeasurably not merely from the enforced gulf between them, but even more from his inability to express his own emotions.

Trotsky naturally evaded scenes by becoming still more retiring. This equally inflamed Zinaida's feelings of unwantedness, especially since her desire to show her devotion by helping with Trotsky's political drudgery was also frustrated.

A vicious circle, in short, swiftly arose – her emotional instability, rooted in feeling unloved, made it impossible to 'trust' her in technical matters; the failure to trust her was taken to be another sign of being unwanted, and so on. In the summer of 1931, she left for a lung operation, which though successful did nothing to help her spiritually.

Enclosed in his own emotional carapace, while aware of Zinaida's suffering, Trotsky also suffered: there was a great gulf between the magisterial passion he poured into his endless writing on abstract questions and the bafflement he felt at her anguish.

Trotsky had to do something positive. Though sceptical of psychoanalysis, he felt it might help his sick daughter; he had written about it to friends in Berlin. In fact the last thing Zinaida wanted to do was to plunge into 'the filth' of her unconscious; nor could she bear the idea of being taken from her father once again, and this time from her small son, as well, whom she could no longer care for. Nevertheless, in the autumn of 1931 she left for Berlin, leaving her small son Seva with his grandfather.

A few months later Trotsky's Soviet citizenship was cancelled. The decree, which appeared in *Pravda* on 20 February 1932, also took away the citizenship of all those relatives who were in exile together with him; this included Zinaida, who was thus deprived of any chance of seeing her exiled husband and small daughter.

On top of that the doctors she had come to see found themselves helpless. She simply would not allow herself to be psychoanalysed; but since the first few months in the turbulent capital had exhilarated her a little they had been deceived by her seeming high spirits.

Zina's relations with Sedov, her only real connection in Berlin, were also exacerbated both by his natural preoccupations – with politics and with his technical institute – and by the fact that his political preoccupation was itself, after all, due to his intimacy with their father. His natural reserve, moreover, appeared to her unfeeling; 'Every time I see him I suffer a nervous breakdown', she wrote Trotsky.[22]

With the loss of her citizenship, hence the loss of her daughter and her husband, she was worse off than ever. Her doctors thought she should go back to Russia and lead a normal life! It didn't help much.

Nor was it possible to carry out another recommendation of her doctor, that her child be brought to her from Prinkipo. The same decree that had taken away Trotsky's and Zinaida's citizenship had taken away the child's: all applications were rejected on the claim that the child had to travel with a parent or grandparent. The child's health was also affected by the separation from his mother, especially when she sent him effusive messages that she would soon be back and begged him to remember her.

Sedov's life too, was wretched. He was completely overtaxed with his vast private and organisational burdens. The wife and child he had left behind in the Soviet Union constituted a tragedy in and for themselves; his wife kept writing him painful letters about the grimness of her life and the child's; she had been very upset, of course, when he left them, but at that time his excuse had been that he had to help his father; now here he was in Berlin, away from his father and mother, as well as away from her and their child; she threatened suicide.[23]

He was always unhappy with Jeanne. In fact his personal life was terrible; it was exacerbated by the gruelling work he was doing for his father. At least so Trotsky, himself in a frenzy of nerves and irritability, altogether dependent on his son for both human and political contact, would think in periodic bouts of bitterness. Sedov was his father's principal, indeed almost sole political agent: in this curiously lopsided movement he had countless chores, all indispensable.

First of all, he had to maintain liaison with the numerous splinter groups of sympathisers, get the *Bulletin* printed properly, supervise the German publication of everything his father wrote – vital in Trotsky's eyes because of the critical situation in Germany, the centre of the European working-class movement – and also act as his father's literary agent.

He also spent hours moving around Berlin, hoping to run across someone from the Soviet Union on a trip, to get information from or give a message to. Meanwhile he kept attending the technical institute, studying, somewhat pathetically, the mathematics and physics he had some gift for. All this was in addition to his extensive correspondence with his parents.

Trotsky's irascibility, generally under control, was for that reason all the more upsetting to Sedov when it exploded: in his correspondence with his mother, which was far more open and emotional than with his father, he would learn that his father, despite his actual behaviour, was merely reacting to solitude when he lost his temper. It was Natalya, indeed, herself in bad health, who acted as natural buffer and lubricant between them: she helped each in turn, explaining each to the other and struggling to help them all endure their ordeal.

The denouement of Zinaida's distractions was as tragic as might, perhaps, have been foreseen.

Her small son had finally been brought to her; his arrival apparently intensified her psychic strain. She gassed herself, barricading her room with remarkable energy so that a rescue was out of the question; she left a terse note mentioning 'the approach of her terrible disease'.

Sedov cabled his parents on 5 January 1933; the cable was terse but, according to Trotsky, 'with unbearable moral tension in every line': he was 'alone with the corpse of his elder sister'.[24]

Trotsky sent an *Open Letter* to Soviet Leaders: he interpreted Zinaida's suicide as an act of despair she had been hounded into by Stalin; he vowed vengeance in the future from a 'revived party'.[25]

Alexandra had now lost both her children; she was undone. In one of her last letters to her, Zinaida had blamed her illness on the 'discord' between herself and Trotsky. Now Alexandra, perhaps with a tinge of embittered wifeliness, reminded Trotsky of what she had written Zina: 'all this comes from your character, from your finding it so difficult to show your feelings even when you would like to.'[26]

Trotsky was shattered. He and Natalya withdrew to their room. He did not emerge for several days; his hair had turned much greyer.[27]

CHAPTER XII

The Agony

IN THE SPRING FOLLOWING the Nazi victory things started loosening up after all. Trotsky's cage was about to be opened.

His French sympathisers had been trying to get an annulment of the 1916 order expelling him from France in perpetuity. Trotsky was sceptical; he assumed the Radical Socialist French Government would not want to irritate the Soviet Government. Nevertheless he aggravated his financial plight by deferring some big publishing projects just when his German income dried up completely. He had also had to spend money for the Copenhagen trip; in addition, the moment the Nazis came in Sedov had gone into hiding and slipped into France; the *Bulletin* had been shut down at once. Trotsky had to pay for moving both Sedov and the *Bulletin* to Paris.

By mid-July 1933 Trotsky was finally let out of his cage, though the visa he got from the French was qualified by restrictions: he was allowed into the south of France on condition that he remain incognito under police observation and never come to Paris.

On 17 July 1933 he left Prinkipo for good. He boarded a steamship for Marseilles, with Natalya, Jean van Heijenoort and two other secretaries, and Max Shachtman, an American follower. It took a week to get there; the world press devoted its usual speculation to the *real* reasons for his trip. Reporters were told only that the Trotskys needed medical attention.

They scarcely budged from their cabin; Trotsky wrote and read as usual. (He wrote a review of *Fontamara*, by Ignazio Silone, an Italian sympathiser; it was to enjoy a certain vogue and in fact launch Silone, who had abandoned the official Communist movement.)

Near Marseilles he was smitten by lumbago. Loaded with difficulty into a tug outside the port, he could scarcely move without groaning. Sedov and Molinier had been waiting for them; the sight of them soothed Trotsky's and Natalya's apprehensions. Bypassing the throngs of journalists, they landed in Cassis, a short distance from Marseilles: a French security officer officially put into his hands an annulment of the police order of 1916. Trotsky's humour peeped out: 'It is a long time since I acknowledged the receipt of any official document with so much pleasure.'[1]

Moving very circumspectly, the little group left for the Atlantic coast. All Trotsky's impedimenta – archives and luggage – were sent on to Paris, to throw the Soviet Political Police agents off the track. Almost immediately a fire broke out in their villa: it was accidental, but Trotsky was so sensitive about his incognito that to avoid the big crowd that had sprung up to watch the fire he dashed out of bed and into Molinier's car on the other side of the road. When spoken to he passed himself off – oddly, in view of his terrible accent! – as an American tourist. Next morning he and Natalya were described in a local paper as an 'elderly American couple' (Trotsky was fifty-three).

Racked with lumbago, he had to keep to his bed for more than two months. He could hardly get up for a walk on the beach or a look in the garden; even when he was a little better he could not carry on a conversation for more than fifteen or twenty minutes; he sweated and seemed on the verge of fainting.[2]

But he could not evade the pressure created by his accessibility: in the space of two months and a bit he received some fifty visitors at the villa: prominent Left-wing Europeans, in addition to sympathisers. Some, like Paul-Henri Spaak and André Malraux, were to become famous.

A good part of Trotsky's time was now to be taken up with a conference, scheduled in Paris towards the end of August, meant to found a new International. Though he could not attend it, he was more active than ever preparing for it, writing resolutions and 'Theses'.

Yet the various little groups interested in the idea of the new International did not do much to realise it. Trotsky could not persuade any of those attending the Paris conference in August that they must launch a Fourth International. Even those who agreed with him would not go beyond setting up a mere preliminary organisation, not the thing itself. Trotsky kept up appearances by saying that the conference, however puny as a beginning, might be just as important as the celebrated Zimmerwald conference at which the Bolsheviks had broken with the Second International.

Privately he was more dejected than ever. Natalya went to Paris to see some doctors after they had been in the villa for more than a month; his letters to her, very personal, are all the more depressing because of the general condition he was now to be more and more reminded of – his failing powers. In one letter he wrote that Sedov, after seeing off some visitors, had come back to see him, kissed him and said: 'I love you, father'. Then he wrote to tell her that he had woken up from sleep and called for her 'like an abandoned child ... didn't Goethe say old age catches us by surprise and finds us children?'

Natalya tried to cheer him up: 'How sad you are ... You have never been like that ... I see you pale, weary, doleful – it's terribly depressing.'[3]

Yet he soon recovered; by the end of October 1933 he was back in harness again, more or less: he wrote to his British publisher, Gollancz, that he would now embark on the life of Lenin that Gollancz had been eager for; the advance was put at one thousand five hundred pounds.[4]

Life was more pleasant; he had kept his incognito so carefully that no one had the least idea where he was except for visitors, who were never quite clear about his exact address anyhow: Sedov was very painstaking.

The little household was permitted to establish itself near Barbizon, a town near a forest about an hour out of Paris, famous for the school of painting.

Trotsky had a house in a corner of the forest, in a secluded little park watched over by guards and dogs. Messengers kept shuttling back and forth to Paris to his followers; during the winter he slipped into the capital a number of times with an escort.

This interlude, which was not to last long, was idyllic: his energies back to normal, Trotsky re-established his usual schedule. He would work from six in the morning till noon, interrupted only by breakfast; after resting for an hour after lunch, he would start in again: everyone stood up over tea, which was at four, then went back to work again until dinner, or rather supper. After the meal there would be discussion, characteristic of such a milieu: it was in effect a general debate with Trotsky as natural chairman.

He was now concentrating on his *Life of Lenin*; he had to go back into Lenin's family background and early life, and study the Russia of the period just preceding his own birth, of the 1870s and '80s. This was to be the only part of the book he ever rounded out.

In spite of his lengthy stays in prison and in exile, Trotsky's education had been a trifle spotty; he had to go over a great deal of philosophical terrain, since Lenin had based himself squarely on Marx who had primarily, after all, been a philosopher.

Organisationally the outlook remained obdurately sombre. The number of sympathisers – to say nothing of followers! – remained pathetic : in France – the only possible centre – the grand total of all sympathisers, in various tiny groupings, came to no more than a hundred. The circulation of the official organ, *Vérité*, numbered fewer than 3,000.

As for their revolutionary elan, that was still more depressing : he wrote a sympathiser two years later (1936) that he considered the bulk of his French following 'Philistines' plain and simple : 'I have been in their homes and have smelt their petty-bourgeois life – my nose has not deceived me.'[5]

He was soon on shaky terms with his outstanding followers : Alfred Rosmer, a man he was devoted to and vice versa, did not see him for the two years Trotsky was to remain in France. Trotsky found Molinier 'politically irresponsible', another follower, Pierre Navile, 'arrogant' and 'lacking revolutionary spirit'.[6]

On the other hand he chatted for hours with Simone Weil, who for her own, doubtless morbid reasons regarded herself as a 'Trotskyite' : Trotsky found her, not surprisingly, with 'no understanding for working-class politics and Marxism'.

Later on she was to become a convert to a form of mystical Christianity; during the German occupation she starved herself to death as part of her obligation to share the suffering of others.

This situation was to remain chronic with Trotsky : precisely because his organisation could never find its way 'To the People' he had to cultivate all sorts of middle-class dilettantes who for personal reasons found his presence, enhanced by his historical aureole, exciting.

Trotsky's hopes of organising his followers in a new International were fading : in the turbulence of French politics his own coterie required now more than ever roots in *some* mass movement : Fascist and semi-Fascist violence was growing against the Radical

Socialist Government; there was even an abortive Fascist putsch (6 February 1934).

With the Communist Party insulated against his ideas, only the French Socialists seemed accessible. He advised his little coteries to join the Socialists, not because of any conversion to 'reformist' ideas, but to 'carry the revolutionary programme to The Masses'.

This was feasible because the French Socialist Party was a loosely organised confederation; since its lively intellectual atmosphere was quite free of the conformism of the Comintern Parties, it was not unreasonable to imagine that Trotsky's sympathisers might win some support for the Fourth International.

In the conventicles of his would-be movement this was known as the 'French turn'. Down to the Sixties, indeed, this recommendation of Trotsky's in the mid-Thirties was discussed among the small groups professing allegiance to the Fourth International (it has been calcified in the jargon as 'entrism').[7]

It was, of course, a lapse, though unavowed, to the older tactic of conversion 'from within' that Trotsky had been so loath to give up. The original scheme of creating a new International that would of itself attract the vanguard of The Proletariat was tacitly dropped: splinter coteries grouped, really, around no more than Trotsky's name and his writings were thus advised to go back to the organisations with mass memberships and use *them* as a point of departure.

It was to work no better than the attempt to set up a new International independently; how could it, indeed, especially in France?

The necessity of resorting to a big party implied that there were not enough potential targets of propaganda outside; in its turn this implied submission to a central organisation, however loosely organised, that felt strong enough to let them in to begin with, with a programme, moreover, that was bound to collide with the very tradition that held the whole organisation together – in the case of the French Socialist Party and of Social-Democratic Parties generally an atittude of more or less placid 'reformism'. The French Turn compounded the previous mistrust of Trotsky's position and the rooted Communist antipathy to Social-Democrats into an alloy characterised by an intense animosity to himself.

Before the People's Fronts were launched Trotskyites could denounce the Stalinists from French Socialist platforms, but afterwards the Trotskyites went on attacking 'reformism' in general and

in addition the 'illusions' of the People's Front itself. Since the
Socialist Party was part of the People's Front these attacks led to the
expulsion of the Trotskyites from the Socialist Party, and once the
Stalinists joined the People's Front they had a splendid opportunity
to promote these expulsions.

Less than six months after Trotsky had set up his study in the
forest of Fontainebleau his incognito was cracked. By sheer accident
a messenger – a German refugee – was picked up by the local police
for a traffic offence; the police soon learned about Trotsky.

The news broke: Fascists and conservatives at one end and
Communists at the other set up a hullabaloo about Trotsky, for them
both, of course, an arch-criminal from diametrically opposed points
of view. To add to the clamour the Nazi regime put out a rumour
that Trotsky had come to France to launch an insurrection.

The uproar was so general that the Government was harassed into
expelling Trotsky out of hand, though for a short while his expulsion
was to remain a dead letter – there was a little problem: what country would have him?

He was forced to take to his heels in a highly humiliating way. In
mid-April, a few days after his incognito was exposed, he was
ordered out of his Barbizon house; prudently frightened of an
onslaught from either Fascists or Communists, he shaved off his
celebrated goatee, disguised himself as best as he could and stole
into Paris, where his son had him put up in some student's attic. This
was plainly a makeshift; a few days later he took off with Molinier's
brother and with his chief secretary, van Heijenoort. They drifted
south.

For the next fourteen months he was to gypsy about; occasionally
he would stay in an out-of-the-way Alpine village. He could not stop
in any one place for more than a few days. It was practically
impossible to conceal himself; his arrival would be regarded by the
local press as a scoop.

Since he could not stay near the border, he had to look for some
place at least 300 kilometres from Paris. After Natalya joined him at
Chamonix, near the Swiss frontier, they had to start back. They
finally put up at a boarding-house; this was a little awkward since he
was not allowed to use a false name and could not, of course use his
own. They were reduced to a charade: pretending to be a Frenchman of foreign antecedents, he went with Natalya into a boarding-
house under the pretence of deep mourning, to ensure privacy; van
Heijenoort, standing guard, passed himself off as a nephew.

This particular boarding-house happened to be the centre for the monarchists and Fascists of the area; the police agent who was following the Trotskys around and who was, characteristically, an ardent republican, would get into violent arguments with the locals, duly reported by van Heijenoort to the amusement of the Trotskys. They reinforced their 'image' by pretending to go to mass; this gave them an airing.

They finally settled down, more or less, a few months later: a school-teacher put them up outside Grenoble. They stayed here for almost eleven months in a state of almost perfect seclusion, with no secretaries or guards. Once a month they received mail; a secretary would come from Paris once in weeks; their social life was made up of visits paid to their host by fellow-teachers for chats on school matters. It was a kind of imprisonment: to avoid being seen they went out during the day for a short walk. They were more restricted than on Prinkipo or for that matter in Siberia.

Trotsky's work naturally fell off. There could be no question of finishing his *Life of Lenin*: instead he wrote a short pamphlet on French politics, which like generations of Russian intellectuals Trotsky always had a weakness for.

The pamphlet (*Whither France?*) was closely modelled, unfortunately, on his view of Germany; since things turned out quite differently in France this pamphlet must be thought of as a failure even of analysis, despite its characteristic sparkle. His blackness of mood extended to the People's Front, which from 1935 until the Hitler-Stalin Pact in 1939 was to dominate Left-wing politics. His cardinal point – that the 'reformist illusions' of the People's Front would pave the way to Fascism by disarming the vanguard of the Socialist and Communist workers – misfired; France did not turn Fascist either then or later.

Until the end of 1932 Trotsky had been able to keep up a few scattered contacts with sympathisers in the Soviet Union. He had actually been receiving communications from gaols, camps and so on, smuggled out by all sorts of clever devices on the strangest kinds of paper, dealing both with 'issues' and with personal relations; the correspondence (conserved in the Trotsky Archives) is full of torment, at the same time of optimism. Yet even before he had moved back to the West these communications had dwindled to a full stop.

Thus by 1933, when he came to France, he was out of touch with anyone in the Soviet Union; in February 1934, while he was still living outside the forest of Fontainbleau, this state of solitude was personalised by the final capitulation of one of his most stalwart sympathisers – Christo Rakovsky, who had been more intimate with him than any other associate.

Rakovsky had withstood the growing pressure of Stalin's machine; practically every issue of Trotsky's *Bulletin* had given him some space.

Trotsky notes the surrender in his *Diary*:

Rakovsky was virtually my last contact with the old revolutionary generation. . . . Now nobody remains. For a long time now I have not been able to satisfy my need to exchange ideas and discuss problems with someone else. I am reduced to carrying on a dialogue with the newspapers, or rather through the newspapers with facts and opinions.

And I still think that the work in which I am engaged now, despite its extremely insufficient and fragmentary nature, is the most important work of my life – more important than 1917, more important than the period of the Civil War or any other.

One is obliged to assume that Trotsky's heroic bearing was a form of whistling in the dark: in connection with Rakovsky's defection the above passage (after calling himself and Lenin indispensable in the October putsch, noted on page 293) goes on to say:

I cannot speak about the indispensability of my work even about the period from 1917 to 1921. By now my work is 'indispensable' in the full sense of the word. There is no arrogance in this claim at all. The collapse of the two Internationals has posed a problem which none of the leaders of these Internationals is at all equipped to solve. The vicissitudes of my personal fate have confronted me with this problem and armed me with important experience in dealing with it. There is now no one except me to carry out the mission of arming a new generation with the revolutionary method over the heads of the leaders of the Second and Third International. And I am in a complete agreement with Lenin (or rather Turgenev) that the worst vice is to be more than fifty-five years old! I need at least about five more years of uninterrupted work to ensure the succession.[8]

He stoutly disregarded what to an outsider might well seem an element of futility in his preoccupations. A passage in his *Diary* for early 1935 allows something to slip out:

> For the very reason that it fell to my lot to take part in great events, my past now cuts me off from chances for action. I am reduced to interpreting events and trying to foresee their future course. At least this occupation is more satisfying than mere passive reading.[9]

This admission is, perhaps, unique in his writings.

Though Trotsky lived beyond the five years he needed to 'ensure the succession', his work was interrupted: his career was about to be radically transformed.

In the Kremlin there had been, it seems, a mood of reconciliation in 1933-4 with respect to the Oppositionists: the Party had managed to weather the slaughter of the peasantry during the crisis of collectivisation.

It was illusory: Stalin had different plans. The atmosphere of reconciliation, authentic or not, was abruptly dispelled.

On 1 December 1934 it was announced that Sergei Kirov, head of the Leningrad Party and a member of the Politburo, had been assassinated. This inaugurated a new phase in Soviet history; it also opened the final phase of Trotsky's life.

This was not, however, to become clear until a year or two later.

During the first few weeks after the assassination the Soviet press published a number of contradictory accounts.

The first one said the assassin – a former Communist, one Nikolayev – had been the hatchetman for some White Guard terrorists, with a foreign consul who had received money from Trotsky acting as go-between. Then it was announced that 104 White Guards had been executed. Then it was said that Nikolayev was a partisan of Zinoviev and Kamenev, no mention being made of the executed White Guards. Then it was announced that Nikolayev and fourteen others, all Young Communists, had also been executed: Zinoviev and Kamenev were expelled from the Party again – the third time – and gaoled to await trial.

Then Trotsky was placed squarely in the centre of what was announced to be a full-dress conspiracy: linked to Zinoviev and Kamenev, he was named the chief plotter.

Meanwhile a campaign of terror was launched against the whole bloc of 'Kirov's assassins' – thousands of Party men, evidently listed as former Oppositionists, were deported to concentration-camps.

The last stage in the public presentation of the Kirov killing was the announcement that some high officials of the Leningrad Political Police had been accused of 'neglect of duty' and given gaol sentences of two to three years apiece.

In his Alpine cul-de-sac Trotsky was transfixed: all he knew was what he heard from the Moscow radio. He realised at once that the hullabaloo about Kirov portended something far bigger than the killing itself. He assumed it was a pretext for some large-scale scheme of Stalin's. It never occurred to him that Stalin had staged the killing; that was not to come out for many years, long after Trotsky's own murder.

He thought the Political Police had been using Nikolayev as a cat's-paw and that the young man had used his gun prematurely: this explained the contradictoriness of the official accounts, the secrecy surrounding Nikolayev's trial (if there had been one), and the strangely mild punishment of the Political Police.

Since Zinoviev and Kamenev had been given mild sentences, too – ten years in gaol for Zinoviev, five for Kamenev – Trotsky thought the Political Police would now try to get bogus evidence against him from them, since they had been obliged to accept a 'spiritual' responsibility for the assassination, based on the idea that their long-past criticisms of Stalin might have maddened Nikolayev!

Trotsky thought a deal had been made: Stalin would rehabilitate his two former allies if they denounced Trotsky. Accordingly, Trotsky now predicted that the Kirov killing had put Stalin in a dilemma: the 'amalgam' – from now on a favourite word of his – linking Trotsky to Nikolayev was so defective that it would have to be covered by new 'amalgams' on a 'world-scale'.[10]

The Kirov killing affected his family immediately. His two sons-in-law, banished since 1928, were re-arrested and given still longer sentences. Alexandra, his first wife, by now well over sixty, was deported from Leningrad, ultimately to a remote province. She had been taking care of three grand-children, who had been handed over to an aunt; it was hard to learn what was happening to them.

Trotsky's younger son was also finally affected: Sergei had ceased all communication with Trotsky, ever since 1929 writing to his mother alone about everything but politics: the week following the Kirov killing he wrote referring to his 'grave' general situation; this was followed by silence. An old friend's widow, now living abroad, made inquiries; she was ordered out of the country immediately.

Nothing further was known. Sergei's fate remained a source of torment, and also, no doubt, a source of guilt on Trotsky's part: it was Trotsky's political destiny, after all, that had brought so much misery on innocent relatives.

> Every time I recall Seryozha, it is with a sharp pain. But Natalya does not 'recall' him, she always carries a deep sorrow inside her. 'He put his trust in us . . .' she said to me the other day (her voice still echoes in my heart). . . . 'He thought that since we left him there, it was the way things had to be.' And it has turned out that we have sacrificed him. That is just what it is . . .[11]

At this time his *Diary* in general records a depressing picture of melancholia, partly due to the advance of age. It has lengthy entries about his ailments – blood-pressure, sclerosis, etc. – mixed in with politics.

Trotsky was at the lowest point of his life. Though he was still to have bursts of elan the Kirov affair and its aftermath flung him on to an inclined plane he was never to get off.

During the eleven months Trotsky and Natalya spent outside Grenoble, in the tiny village of Domesne, they were more isolated than they had ever been. Trotsky's *Diary* reveals an unusual depth of feeling for Natalya. Perhaps it also marks a certain turning aside to the more personal side of life.

> Today on our walk we went up a hill. Natalya got tired and unexpectedly sat down, quite pale, on the dry leaves. . . . Even now she still walks beautifully, without fatigue. . . . Her gait is quite youthful, like her whole figure. But . . . her heart has been playing up now and then. She . . . sat down all of a sudden – she obviously just *could not* go any further – and smiled apologetically. What a pang of pity I felt for her youth.[12]

Natalya, though utterly identified with Trotsky's fortunes, was not herself a political figure. Yet to save her younger son she became a sort of agitator. She wrote an *Open Letter* on Sergei's behalf; a purely human document, it pointed out that not only the Political Police, but Stalin, 'whose son was a frequent guest in our boy's room', must have known perfectly well how remote Sergei was from politics.

She solicited the intervention of public personages like Romain
Rolland, André Gide and Shaw; she asked for an international
commission to examine the consequences of the Kirov killing. . . .

In the midst of her appeal to compassion she had to turn back to
politics. It was to be the fate of the Trotskys that their most intimate
suffering was inextricably intertwined with their politics – abstract,
inaccessible and fruitless.

> Concerning the blows that have fallen to our lot, I reminded
> Natasha the other day of the life of the archpriest Avvakum. They
> were stumbling on together in Siberia, the rebellious priest and his
> faithful spouse. Their feet sank into the snow; the poor exhausted
> woman kept falling into the snowdrifts. Avvakum relates: 'And I
> came up, and she, poor soul, began to reproach me, saying: "How
> long, archpriest, is this suffering to be?" And I said, "unto our very
> death." And she, with a sigh, answered: "So be it, let us be getting
> on our way." '[18]

The Kirov murder signalised the onset for Trotsky – and for
others – of a long-drawn-out era of anguish. He now became far
more systematically than before the synonym for all that was pernicious – the very incarnation of 'counter-revolution', with a ghoulish
twist of murder and depravity thrown in.

In the turbulence of French politics at this time anything that
strengthened the Communist Party – i.e., anything countering a
Right-wing move – necessarily heightened Trotsky's jeopardy. As
early as the month of the murder itself the party organ, L'Humanité,
carried an article by Jacques Duclos about 'Trotsky's hands covered
with Kirov's blood'. It was the keynote of a frenetic Communist
campaign.

The People's Front was germinating: in the spring of 1935 Stalin
agreed to support the defence policy of the Radical Socialist French
Government; the French Communists naturally rallied at once to the
suddenly-fashionable patriotism. It was plain that there was no
longer anything to stop the French Government's placating their
new-found allies by putting into effect the deportation order they
had already handed Trotsky a year before. Since he was still unacceptable anywhere else he faced the prospect of deportation to
some outpost further away from Europe than Prinkipo. His remoteness in an Alpine village was no longer worth anything.

For a moment luck favoured him. The Norwegian Labour Party, a member of the Comintern until 1923 and not in the Second International, was in a neutral position; the esteem felt for Trotsky by some of its members could be expressed. He applied for a visa.

In June he learned that a sympathiser in Norway had the ear of a Left-wing Norwegian leader: Trotsky could find refuge there. But he collided with the obduracy of Norwegian officialdom in Paris: after he left his Alpine village (10 June 1935) they simply refused to produce a visa.

The French police instantly assumed the whole thing had been a ruse to get to Paris; Trotsky was given forty-eight hours to leave the country.

He was also refused permission to go to a clinic while waiting for Oslo to respond to further pressure: both he and Natalya were ill. For a couple of days they were put up by a Paris physician; Trotsky sent the Norwegian Prime Minister a desperate wire.

On top of everything else he was completely impoverished; he could not even pay their fare. To make matters completely hopeless the Norwegian officials, in a masterpiece of redtape, had insisted that he get hold of a French re-entry permit before he could enter Norway at all! A grim joke.

Finally the Norwegian Government was cajoled into giving him a six-month visa: he could leave.

The excitement of departure, reinforced, perhaps, by Trotsky's heroic stance, enabled him to describe his humiliating departure as a momentous occasion – in much the same style, in fact, as he had described his deportation to Siberia in 1928.

At that time, of course, with the future still unknown, with many thousands of sympathisers still in existence, and when he was merely facing exile on Soviet soil, hasty farewells to partisans could be dramatised.

In Paris, with the kind-hearted physician's rooms turned into an impromptu political conference room by the dropping in of all sorts of friends, the occasion, seen in retrospect, was no more than a playback of that fateful scene in Moscow. In Paris it must have been plain that his hasty departure for Norway – *Norway* – was merely a steeper drop into a general decline.

It was his last stay in France.

The meanness with which the Norwegian Government had accepted Trotsky was now complemented by its keeping him under wraps. He was under the same sort of restrictions as in France; he was nailed down some distance away from Oslo.

He was turned into a constant source of embarrassment for the Labour Party Government. From the day of his arrival (18 June 1935) his presence in the country was hotly debated; conservatives, naturally, opposed it; even ordinary people would not put him up. He was requested, as a matter of course, to stay out of politics; he assented, thinking the request conventional.

The Norwegian Labour Party considered itself hostile to Soviet Communism: what was involved was no doubt a simple, rational fear of Soviet power.

Individually, Labour Party people went out of their way to show friendliness to a man whom as Socialists and former Comintern members they respected. The announcements in the Party press were full of generous sentiments; the drawbacks of Trotsky's stay in Norway were estimated to be mere details.

A Socialist editor, Konrad Knudsen, was delegated to help Trotsky find lodgings; when this proved impossible he put him and Natalya up in his own house.[14]

Three Party leaders, including Trygve Lie (later Secretary-General of the United Nations), came to see Trotsky. In a friendly atmosphere Lie emphasised Trotsky's obligation to avoid politics.

The conversation grew animated: Trotsky was asked to explain the Kirov terror campaign, his views of Stalinism and so on. An idyll began between Trotsky and the Norwegian Left wing.

Knudsen's house was in a little village thirty miles outside Oslo. Politics was never even touched on: Knudsen was simply a kind-hearted moderate Socialist.

Trotsky's working routine was as usual remarkably concentrated: when not actually ill, Knudsen reports, he

used to get up at 5.20 or 5.30 in the morning, go down to the pantry, take a little food, and set to work. He did it all very quietly, on tiptoe, so as not to disturb anyone. I have no words to describe his tact and consideration for all who lived in our house. Natalya's behaviour was the same; we nicknamed her affectionately 'the little lady of the big house'. Their needs were quite incredibly modest.[15]

Trotsky's life was relatively normal: it was really the first time he had been free of an escort, friendly or not, since the Bolshevik putsch. The gate to the house was always open; people could drop in. All sorts of friends from different parts of the world came to see him, including a number of Americans. One of those, Harold Isaacs, had made himself something of a specialist on China and was to be helpful to Trotsky, for whom China had become a favourite subject. French sympathisers and followers, especially, made several trips to Norway, bringing him their more or less chronic feuds to umpire.

Trotsky kept up his already vast and rapidly growing correspondence with his far-flung little groups of followers; in the midst of the staggering amount of work this involved he started putting together his last, complete major work, *The Revolution Betrayed*.

His health was upsetting him. In September, despite the comfort of the Knudsens' big family house, he had to go to hospital : his fevers were now complicated by an unusual attack of overall enfeeblement. Check-ups gave no information; he left with no cure in sight, indeed no diagnosis, and spent most of December 1935 on his back.

His health was no doubt affected by his complex relations with his followers, of whom the French, with their greater numbers, were the principal source of annoyance. He was torn between the literary work he was still capable of and the exhaustion of personal relationships.

In addition he was still constantly hard up : he was obliged, for instance, to ask Isaacs for money to avert a 'financial catastrophe' in the hospital in September.[16] Yet he bounced back in his characteristic way, baffling his physicians, and finished *The Revolution Betrayed* in another half-year.

In spite of his vexations his circumstances were almost ideal; he could work very steadily, relaxing once a week with the Knudsens at the village cinema.

In this lull storm-clouds began gathering. With elections scheduled for the autumn, some pro-Nazis, headed by Quisling, had been organising; they attacked the Government for sheltering Trotsky. Far more sinisterly, the Norwegian Communist Party, evidently on Soviet instructions, accused him for the first time, of making Norway a terrorist base.

Around this time, too, Trotsky's connection with the Fourth International – hitherto a secret – came to light. Though the Fourth International was not formally articulated his secretaries could easily be designated by the Norwegian police as 'agents'.

Meanwhile Trotsky was leaning over backwards to avoid embarrassing the Norwegian Socialists, especially his host : he started using a pseudonym for his articles in the *Bulletin* ('Crux'), refused to

be interviewed by foreign papers, and would not even attend his
host's election meetings. His behaviour was impeccable; the Government extended his residence permit twice as a matter of course.

Some information had leaked out of the Soviet Union, from some
followers and sympathisers who had just got out of Soviet
detention.[17] One of them[18] reported that would-be capitulationists
had been offered a surrender formula: 'Do you agree that Trotsky is
the chief of the vanguard of bourgeois counter-revolution?'

There was another ominous piece of news that summer of 1936:
the Norwegian Foreign Minister (Koht) had been invited to Moscow
and given a tremendous reception. Against the background of the
new surrender formula in the Soviet Union Trotsky found the
fanfare suspicious: he told Knudsen that at the Kremlin they were
'bargaining' over his head.

His jitters were more than justified; they fell, in fact, far short of
the mark.

The surrender formula was a detail: the mass terror unleashed by
the Kirov murder was attaining unprecedented ferocity and volume.
It far transcended the ranks of former Oppositionists.

Huge concentration-camps had become commonplace; the prisoners were treated with systematic brutality. What was still more
important, a conventional technique had been amplified: bogus
confessions were extracted from prisoners by various kinds of psychological manipulation. The formula establishing Trotsky's crimi-
nality was the standard.

He was beginning to get a new picture of Soviet conditions;
despite his pessimism he had been unable, since the beginning of the
Thirties, to keep up with the scope of Stalin's terror: the terror he
had personally been aware of had been relatively modest. Now he
was confronted with something whose outlines, gradually becoming
clearer during his exile, constituted a phenomenon of a plainly
different order.

The reports of the escaped Oppositionists had been utterly
sombre: harassed, tormented, and humiliated, individual Oppositionists in the Soviet Union could not even agree on an understanding of what was happening. They were completely disoriented.[19]
In the gaols and concentration camps the 'defence' of Trotsky
revolved around a moral question – his honour: 'programme' had
gone by the board.

Before the end of 1935 tens of thousands of ordinary Party
members, generally stigmatised as 'Trotskyites' and 'Zinovievites',

had been expelled from the Soviet Party and Young Communist League. For a moment Trotsky regarded this with an optimism that in retrospect seems poignant: if all these people – apparently some 40,000[20] and more throughout the country, in addition to those expelled from the Young Communist League – had been thrown out as 'Trotskyites', why, that meant there were lots of Trotskyites! In 1927, on the eve of Trotsky's final rout within the Party, only some few thousands – four to six – had signed the Platform of the Joint Opposition, hence the figures for 1934–5 were terrifically encouraging – ten times more!

Trotsky could still manage to sound optimistic. In France, for instance, he was convinced that a titanic revolutionary movement was swiftly ripening. Everything looked good: the economy was collapsing, the 'possessing classes and their parties' were panicking: 'the whole working class' had 'begun moving'. In fact, as he said in the title of an article he wrote for *The Nation* (New York), 'The French Revolution has begun.' Thus even with Nazi Germany busily rearming and deafening the world, and despite the news from the Soviet Union about the fate of his partisans, real or alleged, he could make a bold show.

But a new factor now made its appearance: the consequences of the Kirov murder were about to come to a head.

On 4 August 1936 Trotsky and Knudsen drove off for a fishing holiday to an uninhabited islet in a southern fjörd. Knudsen noticed some men following them; he recognised some Norwegian Nazis. They were shaken off at a ferry, which he and Trotsky took to the islet. They went to bed.

In the morning they were woken up by some one from Knudsen's house – some of Quisling's men had smashed their way into the house, passing themselves off as policemen: when Knudsen's daughter and son aroused some neighbours and resisted, the raiders had fled, taking only a few typewritten sheets of paper. Later they admitted they had intended to force their way into the house when Trotsky was away. They had known the right time by tapping the phone; they wanted indications of illegal activity on Trotsky's part to help Quisling in the autumn election; they claimed to have been successful.

This little expedition seemed odd; from Trotsky's point of view it was almost a joke. What evidence could they have obtained? Even his archives, which might have given them something to get their teeth into, had been safeguarded. It seemed, in fact, so trivial, though grotesque, that Trotsky, after years of this sort of contre-temps, merely shrugged his shoulders; he and Knudsen stayed on to fish, rock-climb and rest. The next week they had a visit by plane: the Norwegian police chief had come to question Trotsky as part of the trial of Quisling's people; he left the same day, to tell the press there was nothing against Trotsky.

The morning after the police chief had left, Knudsen was the first to listen to the little radio, run by batteries; he could not hear very distinctly. But he heard enough; he rushed to wake Trotsky up.

Moscow was announcing that Zinoviev, Kamenev and fourteen others were about to be tried on charges of high treason, conspiracy, and attempts on Stalin's life. The lengthy indictment culminated in the charge that Trotsky was the architect of the whole terrorist plot. Knudsen thought the Gestapo had been brought into it as well.

This flabbergasted Trotsky: 'Terrorism? *Terrorism?*' he kept repeating: 'Well, I can still understand that. But Gestapo? Did you say *Gestapo?*'[21]

This was the first Moscow 'Show Trial'; it was to be supplemented by two more within the space of the next year and a half; they were all part of a general plan.

There is no need now to 'refute' them: Khruschev's 'Secret Speech' to the Twentieth Party Congress in 1956, and the official rehabilitation, generally implicit, of all the prisoners, confirm the conclusion that arises in any case from a scrutiny of the transcripts – the 'Show Trials' were, quite simply, fabricated.[22]

They ushered in a tidal wave of repression – the Deep Comb-Out of the Soviet population, a 'Great Purge' that destroyed between eight and nine million people as 'Trotskyite agents'.

Though the 'Show Trials' were frenetically publicised, the Deep Comb-Out was relatively clandestine; disclosed only much later through memoirs of defectors and survivors, it has never, indeed, been officially acknowledged.

The 'Show Trials' were not trials in any sense of the word. They are most properly called Charades – theatrical productions designed to convey a certain kind of propaganda in a certain way: the *form* of a trial was intended to conceal just that – it was an essential ingredient of the propagandistic design. The very words 'defendant', 'prosecutor', 'confession', 'judge', 'courtroom' and so on were elements of the fabrication.

The Great Charades were a masterpiece not merely of political creativity but of myth-making: they constituted an effective instru-

ment for the smothering of all dissidence within a theological structure that camouflaged the vast blood-bath systematically taking
place throughout the Soviet Union.

None of this was to be known for years: in 1936 it was beyond
anyone's powers of divination – except, perhaps, Stalin's.

What Trotsky had to listen to during the week beginning 19
August was a wholly unprecedented phantasmagoria.

The sixteen prisoners, headed by Zinoviev and Kamenev, as well
as Trotsky himself and Sedov, were charged with fantastic crimes
designed to restore capitalism.

No material evidence to speak of was presented: the first Great
Charade was based only on the prisoners' statements. All of them not
only pleaded guilty, but went far beyond even the vehemence of
Vyshinsky, the 'Prosecutor' and heaped abuse on their own heads to
the point of dementia. The five days of the performance were given
over to scenes of incredible self-vilification.

It was this element of 'confession' and extravagant self-denunciation, in fact, that evoked the most comment in the world press
during the next few months. Granted that these old-time Bolsheviks
had done all they were charged with, why had they suddenly
confessed, and why so spinelessly?

It was to remain an enigma for a long time.

The prisoners were all sentenced to death and immediately
executed. Trotsky and Sedov were to be arrested and tried at once if
captured in the Soviet Union.

Trotsky's situation had changed overnight. By the second day of
the Moscow performance he had started making statements to
journalists and news agencies; he insisted on being extradited to the
Soviet Union; he wired the League of Nations his readiness to
submit to a Commission on Political Terrorism proposed by the
Soviet Government itself; he sent messages to a mass-meeting in
New York. ...

He desperately needed a breathing-space to get his self-defence to
the public before it was flooded by the torrent of propaganda from
Moscow.

That breathing-space was just what he was now to be denied; he
was, in fact, shut up immediately. The 'Show Trial' was scarcely over
when two senior policemen came to tell him he had violated his
residence permit; they insisted on his signing an agreement not to
meddle in 'political questions current in other countries'.[23]

Trotsky refused; he was immediately put under house arrest and forbidden to make a public statement. Guards were stationed outside his doors.

A sharp right-about turn had plainly taken place in the official attitude toward Trotsky. The Soviet Government was demanding his expulsion. The Norwegian cabinet, appalled at the prospect of difficulties with the Soviet Union, and even more afraid, perhaps, of losing an election, gave in.

The Soviet Government never requested Trotsky's extradition; it merely wanted him deported from Norway.

Extradition was a first-class legal point. Asking for Trotsky to be handed over at once to the Soviet Union would have been the 'natural' thing to do, but it meant that the courts of the extradition country had to be satisfied of the case, i.e., Trotsky could have defended himself in an open court beyond Stalin's control. The risk was far too great for Stalin's purpose.

But no country would accept Trotsky; hence, since the Norwegians couldn't deport him they at least had to stop him from defending himself in public. As an alternative to deportation they decided on internment.

Yet how could they lock up a man whom they had welcomed, whom many of them admired and whose innocence they had confirmed in public? And in their own country! It would have looked like cowardice; the government chiefs were bound to find some other pretext.

They came up with the accusation that Trotsky had gulled them by attacking friendly governments and by working for the Fourth International; though none of that was illegal it gave them a public case against Trotsky for abuse of confidence.

The technique for this somewhat flimsy legal shift proved difficult, since they had no 'evidence' even of that. In an Oslo court some of Quisling's Nazis were on trial for breaking into Trotsky's house; they had actually filched some papers attacking the People's Government in France.

But while this was, to be sure, an attack on a friendly foreign government, it was all quite public: the attack was, in fact, the article that had appeared in *The Nation* as well as in two Trotsky publications. Besides, how could Norwegian Socialists ally themselves with Nazis to attack someone who was, after all, a fellow-Socialist?

As for Trotsky's Fourth International activities, the well-informed authorities had already extended his residence permit only the preceding June.

Yet though as men they were ill-at-ease, as officials they had no choice.

Trotsky was obliged to testify a second time (28 August) at the trial of the Norwegian Nazis. He was questioned more severely than they; after Trotsky said 'yes' to various questions put to him about corresponding with his followers abroad – questions irrelevant to the trial itself, which had to do only with the charge of breaking and entering laid against the Nazis – the judge said Trotsky had admitted to violating the terms of the agreement underlying his entry into Norway. When Trotsky started to say he had never agreed not to express his opinions to the public and to his followers and that he had never done any plotting, the judge made him step down from the stand.

A melodramatic scene ensued.

Trotsky was escorted by policemen to the building of the Ministry of Justice. In the presence of high officials the Minister of Justice handed him a statement, ordering him to sign it then and there. It was the corollary of the government claim that he had been conspiring with followers and attacking foreign governments; he had to bind himself to do nothing whatever of any kind to 'involve' himself, Natalya and his secretaries 'in political questions current either in Norway or abroad'; none of his 'writings of a theoretical nature' was to be 'directed against any government of any foreign state'. He was, moreover, to agree to live wherever the Government directed him and to allow all the mail and his phone calls to be censored.

Signing such a shameful document, amounting to an outright repudiation of a political role of any kind, was out of the question.

Trotsky's theatrical gifts came to the fore. He drew himself up; his eyes 'flashing with scorn'.

He forced Trygve Lie to admit that he, Trotsky, had never meddled in local affairs, had never conducted any terrorist activities from Norway, had never, in fact, done anything whatever against Norway. The government case against him for having broken a 'pledge' to refrain from *any* political activity was ridiculous; he had never given such a 'pledge', nor indeed could any Socialist or Communist of any kind have done so. For that matter how was his article on France in *The Nation* any worse than the interview he had

given Lie himself for the official government organ? And how could
they take their line from what had been done by a gang of burglars,
Nazis to boot, in smashing into his house?

He raised his powerful voice; it rang through the building:

This is your first act of surrender to Nazism in your own country.
You will pay for it. You think yourselves secure, and free to deal
with a political exile as you please. But the day is near – remember
this! – the day is near when the Nazis will drive you from your
country, all of you together with your old fogey of a Prime
Minister.

This warning – surely in harmony with the most ancient traditions
– was to be remembered: when the same Government was driven
into exile by the Nazis four years later King Haakon reminded Lie,
as they stood about waiting for a ship to England, of 'Trotsky's
curse'.[24]

Trotsky and Natalya were now put under strict house arrest. Lie
had to be given special powers for it: a few days later (2 September),
after Trotsky's secretaries were expelled from the country, Trotsky
and Natalya were escorted out of Knudsen's house to a little place
in Hurum, on a fjörd twenty miles outside Oslo. They were under a
twenty-four hour guard; the house was filled with twenty policemen
in jack-boots, smoking pipes and playing cards.

No visitors whatever were allowed except for a Norwegian
lawyer; Trotsky was not even permitted to exercise or take walks, a
routine privilege of ordinary convicts. He needed special authorisation to get a newspaper; all letters were censored, moreover by a
Nazi! Two officers guarding him were also Nazis.

This harsh treatment was meant to gag Trotsky; he kept writing
article after aricle, tearing the first Great Charade to pieces: he kept
sending his son and his followers instructions on how to go about
responding to Vyshinsky's lengthy courtroom tirades.

Nothing ever appeared; nothing was sent. The censor simply kept
it all without telling Trotsky.

All Trotsky and Natalya could do was listen to a radio that with
much difficulty Knudsen had managed to get to them. The Moscow
radio was making a big thing out of the first Charade: the accusations published in the courtroom were repeated and commented on
in all the media available to a big government.

Trotsky's internment was, in fact, the first step in the tidal wave of propaganda that now rose to obliterate him. With no response from Trotsky for weeks on end, it was natural for many people to wonder: might there be something in it? The mere fact of his internment had an effect on many: after all, would a neutral government, a Socialist one, too, have done that, unless ... ?

He thrashed about like a mink in a snare. He was powerless, at least in the international arena; he tried to do something locally. He sued a couple of Norwegian newspaper editors who had repeated Vyshinsky's 'charges'- the Government simply stopped the whole thing.

This was plainly illegal: Lie had to contrive another special decree to stop Trotsky, as 'an alien interned under the terms of the decree of 31 August 1936,' from appearing 'as plaintiff before a Norwegian court without the concurrence of the Ministry of Justice'. Trotsky was the sole 'alien' to whom both decrees applied.

He then made an attempt to get his case before some foreign courts, by suing various Communist editors in a number of countries for defamation. The Norwegian Government, this time without even a shadow of justification, stopped this on the basis of an impromptu statement by Lie.

Trotsky was now tied hand and foot and gagged. He could communicate, in letters with scarcely any content, only with his son Sedov, now his father's sole champion against the venom billowing out of Moscow.

Sedov was, of course, equally involved: his name was invariably coupled with his father's as 'co-defendant'. He was the mainstay of the 'terrorist plot'; his implication gave the Soviet 'Prosecutor' far more freedom to claim contact between the various elements of a fabrication that was to become increasingly ramified.

For Sedov the situation was peculiarly trying, more distressing even than for Trotsky. As a young man, after all, he had venerated some of the men who had appeared in the Moscow courtroom. Kamenev was his uncle (a relationship scarcely mentioned by Trotsky). The children of the Bolshevik leaders had grown up together; Sedov knew them perfectly well, Stalin's children, too, Now the leaders of Sedov's ardent youth were being defamed and destroyed.

The work he produced – Le Livre Rouge sur le Procès de Moscou – came out a few weeks after the first Charade. It was the first time the charges made in Moscow were refuted on a factual basis. Sedov destroyed, very effectively within the 'legal' context, the sole two pieces of material evidence that had been presented: the claim that the Hotel Bristol in Copenhagen had been the place where Sedov had met his father to further their conspiracy, and that he had ever been with his father in Copenhagen at all. This was one of the few *overt* mistakes made by the stage-managers of the first Charade; it showed the danger of factual detail, at least in places beyond the reach of the Soviet Political Police.

Trotsky and Natalya received their son's defence with joy; in what had become practically solitary confinement it was the first sign of help. As Trotsky put it: 'Our brave dear Lyova (Sedov), my wife and I said to each other, "We have a defender".'[25]

Under a great strain now, Sedov was physically far more vulnerable than his father who was at least more or less secure in his solitude. As the most accessible target of the Soviet Political Police he was in constant apprehension: he had the feeling, eventually to be confirmed, that someone unknown was watching his every move.

Among Sedov's friends in the French Trotskyite coterie, he was comforted most of all by Mark Zborowski, a young man known as 'Etienne'.

Zborowski was very helpful: a student of medicine and philosophy, he helped to edit the *Bulletin*; he was also a member of a small Russian Committee that kept in touch with the Opppositon in the Soviet Union. Sedov and Trotsky trusted Zborowski completely; he was even detailed to pick up Sedov's mail; he kept Trotsky's most secret papers in his own house.

Long afterwards it was to turn out that Zborowski was an agent of Stalin's; he had been assigned to the job of keeping the French Trotskyites under surveillance.[26]

It was Zborowski's presence, in fact, that explained why the Soviet Political Police had never raided Trotsky's archives, which Trotsky regarded as constituting his political identity.

There was one tiny attempt, to be sure: at one time, in early November 1936, under financial pressure, Trotsky sold some part of his archives to the Netherlands Institute for Social History. Some files were duly delivered to its Paris branch, then in the charge of Boris Nicolaevsky, the eminent Menshevik archivist, though the bulk of the archives were kept by Zborowski in his flat. The files had scarcely been deposited when the premises of the building were burgled and some of them taken. The burglary was executed with a competence pointing far beyond the abilities of a petty thief; on the other hand nothing of any value was removed – merely trivia like newspaper clippings.

It was plainly the Soviet Political Police: but on enquiry Sedov completely exonerated the only three people who could have known about the operation, Nicolaevsky, a Mrs. Lola Estrine (a Menshevik refugee), and Zborowski – especially the last!

This little mystery was cleared up years later when Zborowski's true role was revealed: he had been so intimately involved with Trotsky and Sedov for so long that the Soviet Political Police had never had to worry about what was in Trotsky's archives: photostats were enough. The tiny burglary was, no doubt, designed to make him look even better in Trotsky's eyes – the attempts by the Political Police misfired, while Zborowski stood there, a faithful watch-dog!

Trotsky was to linger in Norway for a few more months, in painful solitude. Friends in the United States were doing their best to get him into Mexico, a perilous prospect, though he had no choice. He still had no access to the world press, where he was constantly being denounced by all Stalin's media.

He was given only one opportunity to defend himself, when he had to testify once again in the case of the Norwegian Nazis.

Escorted by a big police detail, he appeared (11 December 1936) and took the witness stand. The Minister of Justice had ordered the courtroom to be kept clear of the public and press; Trotsky could speak to a mere handful of people. It was the only audience he had had for a long time: in German, he made a lengthy, signified statement[27] as though he were on a genuine rostrum, with his usual lucidity and controlled passion.

He bore his life in Hurum stoically, he was courteous to the guards, to whom he would make a point of protesting – in correct Norwegian![28] – about the various restrictions inflicted on him.

He was visited only two or three times by Lie. Once, on 11 or 13 December, Lie noticed a book of Ibsen's plays on the table (Trotsky was a great admirer of Ibsen); he mentioned it: Trotsky made a corrosive parallel between the position he and Lie were in and some characters in Ibsen's *Enemy of the People*.

Trotsky, perhaps unkindly, identified Lie with the Burgomaster Stockman, who sacrifices even his brother on the altar of the *status quo*: 'Your Government has all the vices of a bourgeois government with none of its virtues.'

Lie was a little upset; he said it was a 'silly mistake' to have let Trotsky come to Norway; Trotsky said, 'and this silly mistake you now wish to make good by a crime?' and went on to declaim a speech from the *Enemy of the People*: 'We shall yet see whether meanness and cowardice are strong enough to close the mouth of a free and honest man.'

This obviated any further chitchat: Lie got up; he turned back to shake hands; Trotsky declined.[29] It didn't matter – Trotsky was about to leave Norway.

A week later Lie came back to tell him he could go to Mexico; he and Natalya were to sail the next day on an oil tanker Lie had engaged. They were to be escorted by the Nazi chief guard from Hurum.

Trotsky was alarmed by the hastiness of the operation: he did not even have enough time to put his affairs in order, communicate with friends, or inform the Mexican Government. For that matter he was not even being allowed to go by his own route and to ensure his own security. He was being chivvied from one bolthole to another – what might not happen to him and Natalya in an unknown ship on the high seas!

Lie refused to help him, but gave him some reassurances about the safety of the voyage itself: he told him none of Stalin's people could know about the plan, which was known only to himself and the owner of the tanker.

Trotsky asked to go by way of France; this was also refused: Lie said he had to get Trotsky out of Norway before the whole imbroglio came up once again in the parliament. This time too, Trotsky prophesied doom to Lie's Government: 'In three to five years . . . you will all be émigrés!' Again he declined to shake Lie's hand.[30]

Trotsky was sure he would never survive the sea-voyage: dated 18 December 1936, his last letter to Sedov 'from Europe' had, as he said 'testamentary value'.[31]

One of his final acts was to write still another article in self-defence (*Shame!*); he lacked the smallest assurance that it would be seen. It dealt with one of the more repulsive by-products of this whole extraordinary epoch – the great variety of middle-class liberals assiduously defending the Great Charades.

He was leaving his article for publication 'as the shipwrecked sailor leaves a bottle in the sea'. He had written it in invisible ink.[32]

He had a final visit: bills were handed him by his doctor, his lawyer, and the tax collector; his bank account had to be attached.[33]

The oil tanker left Norway on 19 December 1936. Its only passengers were the Trotskys and their police guard. They sailed in total secrecy; their tiny quarters in Hurum were to remain under sentry patrol for several days afterwards, to put people off.

For a while the weather was bad, they lolled about their cabin, reading about Mexico. As the weather improved Trotsky resumed his writing: the first Great Charade, together with its sequel, was to preoccupy him for years.

The ship had been told to avoid all normal routes; it dodged about for three weeks. By now the secret was long since out; the world press kept trying to interview Trotsky by wireless; he was not allowed to say anything.

On New Year's Eve he wrote in his *Diary*: 'This was Cain's year.' But even that was being optimistic.

The Trotskys were still prisoners; at meals their police guard stood over them. There was a curious nervousness aboard ship: despite the general calm and the absence of any other ships, the captain and crew kept dropping hints about the Soviet Political Police.

Trotsky had last left Europe two decades before, in the midst of the First World War.

At that time the great danger had come from submarines.

CHAPTER XIII

The Release

THE SHIP DOCKED IN Tampico on 9 January 1937.

Trotsky and Natalya would not budge until they saw some friends; they were about to be forced ashore by their guard when a boat came alongside and disgorged a group of Mexican officials headed by President Cardenas.

What a relief!

Natalya describes their feelings:

> New faces . . . smiled at us. Diego Rivera couldn't come, but his wife . . . was there, also journalists, some Mexican officials, comrades, friendly and affectionate and happy to welcome us. . . . We were breathing purified air. . . . A motor-car took us to the train, offered by the Mexican government; it carried us across the fields of palms and cacti to the suburbs of Mexico City; a blue house, a patio filled with plants, airy rooms, collections of pre-Columbian art, paintings all over: we were on a new planet, in Rivera's house.[1]

For the first time in his exile Trotsky found something pleasurable; his first letters to Sedov were full of satisfaction with the country, its climate, its plants.

The political atmosphere, too, was agreeable. With the Mexican revolution in full swing Cardenas could afford a gesture of solidarity: Trotsky, he said, was a guest, not a refugee.

Trotsky and Natalya were in a real home; the only source of friction at first was Rivera; he fancied himself a political leader. But in the beginning, at least, both he and Trotsky avoided abstract issues.

Rivera had been a founding member of the Mexican Communist Party; he left it in 1927 (after the elimination of the Zinoviev-Trotsky sympathisers), at the same time falling out with another Mexican painter, David Siqueiros, who had sided with the winners.

On the personal plane Rivera was at first impressed by his proximity to a man he had juxtaposed to Lenin in his Rockefeller Center mural. Trotsky's relations with Rivera's wife, Frida Kahlo, a mysterious-looking former model, were later to be gossiped about.

The clamour broadcast by the first Great Charade was only now building up real momentum. Trotsky was being threatened daily by the Soviet Government, faithfully echoed by the local Communists.

Only a few days after his arrival the second 'Show Trial' was staged. Some more Old Bolsheviks (notably Pyatakov and Radek) appeared in a 'courtroom', charged with fantastic plots.

Trotsky and Natalya were again riveted to the radio, listening to a torrent of outrage and falsehood on a scale that dwarfed even the first Charade.

Again the prisoners were accused, this time in conjunction with Hitler and the Mikado of Japan, of scheming to destroy the Soviet Union, while Trotsky, again the Arch-Plotter, was busily arranging titanic calamities in all branches of the Soviet economy, poisoning workers en masse and making one attempt after another to assassinate Stalin and the Politburo. As before the prisoners 'confessed' with incredible vehemence.

This time both Trotsky's sons were implicated: Sergei was mentioned in the indictment as following Trotsky's instructions to kill off masses of workers by poison; Sedov was noted again as his father's chief agent.

This Charade lasted a little longer than the first; Radek and one other prisoner were not executed, but given ten-year gaol sentences.

As with the first Great Charade, both Trotsky and Sedov were preoccupied by the task of refuting the torrent of slanders broadcast by the Soviet media and reprinted by the world press. Having set himself the goal of disproving statements made in the form of allegations in a court, Trotsky had been driven into an attempt to set up a full-dress 'counter-trial'; he had projected this for the spring of 1937; he naturally required his own 'legal' material.

Rivera's Blue House was buzzing: the whole little group – Trotsky, Natalya and his secretaries – were busily shuffling countless papers. There had to be a vast labour of translating and copying in preparation for Trotsky's counter-case. All this was on top of Trotsky's normal work – the endless explanations and analyses of events in general and of his own 'position' that he had to keep the world press supplied with. He was also struggling to establish his own 'Commissions of Enquiry' in a number of countries.

Trotsky exhausted himself demonstrating what was, in fact, no more than a complex alibi, agonisingly encumbered by the difficulty inherent in the very attempt to gather an immense quantity of data covering all his movements for years and drawing on the testimony of countless eyewitnesses – acquaintances, friends-turned-enemies, policemen, landlords, etc.

Trotsky exhausted his small circle, too, demanding of them the same superhuman energy he was pouring out himself. He became a demon: he even turned on Sedov, bearing the bulk of the burden in Paris. Despite gruelling effort Sedov was unable to keep up with his father's demands.

Trotsky's reproaches became extravagant: he referred to Sedov's 'excuses', to his 'sloppiness bordering on treachery':

It is difficult to say which are the worst blows, those coming from Moscow or those from Paris; I have not yet had a day as black as this one, when I opened your envelope confident I would find the affidavits ... and instead found only apologies and assurances.[2]

Sedov had naturally expected the burden he had been carrying during his father's Norwegian internment to be lightened somewhat after Trotsky recovered his freedom. Instead he found himself the agent of a task that from the point of view of mere labour was still more onerous, aside from his doubts as to its point: he thought Trotsky's lively book, *Stalin's Crimes*, a much more effective rebuttal.

Not merely was the friction between rival groups of partisans a constant source of delay, but Sedov had to secure testimony from people Trotsky had formally broken off friendly relations with. A delicate business! There was also the factor of mere distance: because of faulty communications, for instance, Sedov went on trying to put together a counter-trial in Switzerland, on the basis of Trotsky's instructions from Norway, when Trotsky had meanwhile decided to arrange it in America.

Sedov, now thirty, wore himself to the bone: he kept writing on his own, handled Trotsky's relations with publishers and agents, acted as his financial agent, published the *Bulletin*. He was living under a fearful strain; his sleeplessness became chronic.

Natalya describes the strain Trotsky himself was under: 'With pencil in hand, over-tense and overworked, often in fever, yet tireless, [Trotsky] lists the forgeries that have grown so numerous it becomes impossible to refute them.'[3]

Trotsky was reduced to going back – a millennium! – to the idea of working-class solidarity. He tried to get the Second International, full of enemies he had been denouncing for years, also the Trades-Union Internationals, to attack the 'Show Trials'. Some were willing – Friedrich Adler, Secretary of the Second International, had needed no prompting to denounce the 'Show Trials' as 'medieval witch hunts' – but it was a simple fact of politics that during the era of the People's Front many politicians needed Stalinist support.

Leon Blum, *de facto* head of both the Second and the Trades-Union Internationals, also needed it. When the Second International, at Adler's initiative, finally passed a luke-warm condemnation of the Charades – declining to do anything more – Blum, politically ill at ease, prevented any further action of even this innocuous kind.

Thus the People's Front made the European Social-Democrats condone the Great Charades by silence; some Social-Democrats even whitewashed Stalin explicitly.

Trotsky was reduced to the support of a handful of intellectuals; this was a little embarrassing, since he had spent a good deal of time sneering at the efforts of the various 'peace' and 'anti-Fascist' operations that the Stalinists, once again, had been so successful in rallying platoons of right-thinking liberals behind. For that matter, though Trotsky had little choice and would have been grateful for sympathy from any quarter, the response even from intellectuals and liberals was for all practical purposes non-existent.

By this time, with Hitler at his zenith, the vanguard of liberal as well as Left-wing sentiment everywhere rallied to the defence of the Great Charades with stupefying verve. The list of cultural luminaries – writers, artists, professors – was endless.

It was perhaps inevitable for Soviet intellectuals to say what they had to – the terror was *there* – but in the West, where the constraint was largely spiritual, the enthusiastic adherence to those fabrications was breath-taking.

Trotsky never succeeded in rallying to his 'counter-trial' even people like Gide and H. G. Wells, who had initially been sympathetic. The Webbs were, of course, hopeless; they had long since become the most obtuse of Stalin's devotees.

Nevertheless by the spring of 1937 the foundations were laid for a counter-trial. The individual Committees of Inquiry set up by American, British, French and Czech sympathisers created a Joint Commission. The best-known member of it was its head, John Dewey, who had a world reputation as a philosopher and was unblemished, politically speaking, by any anti-Soviet record.

Dewey was well-known as an old-fashioned liberal; he believed in democracy and truth. At the same time he was completely honest. In the feverish atmosphere of the era, among at least the liberal and intellectual milieux, his willingness to head the commission instantly brought him a torrent of vilification from Stalinites and their fellow-travellers. He resigned from *The New Republic,* which he had helped found and whose editorial board he had been a member of for almost twenty-five years. He was the centre of a variety of intrigues, all of which strengthened his resolve to take up the defence, not of Trotsky as a theoretician, but of the rights of such a man to a fair trial.

Shelving a major work on logic, Dewey steeped himself for months in the official accounts of the Great Charades, Trotsky's voluminous production, and vast quantities of documentation: he became an expert on the whole case.

He did all this in the face of an unflagging campaign to scare him off. He was told that going to Mexico – necessary since Trotsky would plainly never be let into the United States – involved him in the likelihood of actual violence from the Mexican workers' union, heavily infiltrated by Stalinists.

None of this had any effect; he was quite impartial and determined to prove it. He remained impartial in the sense that though sure the Great Charades in Moscow had not shown Trotsky to be guilty, he was not as yet sure he was innocent.

When the 'counter-trial' – a mere hearing before an unauthorised investigating body – opened on 10 April, Dewey presided. The hearing was held – to save money and public upsets – in Trotsky's study in Rivera's Blue House; it lasted a whole week, broken up into thirteen extended sittings. (It is embodied in *The Case of Leon Trotsky.*)

At the end of the inquiry, Trotsky, worn by the ordeal, summed up the essence of the Great Charades – the first two – that had already been put on. He demonstrated their incoherence through the articulation of his opening point – either he himself and practically the whole of the Politburo group around Lenin were renegades, or else Stalin and the present Politburo of the Soviet Union were counterfeiters.

He ended his statement with a profession of faith:

> The experience of my life, in which there has been no lack either of success or of failure, has not only not destroyed my faith in the clear bright future of mankind, but, on the contrary, has given it an indestructible temper. This faith in reason, in truth, in human solidarity, which at the age of eighteen I took with me into the workers' quarters of the provincial Russian town of Nikolayev – this faith I have preserved fully and completely. It has become more mature, but not less ardent.[4]

Despite his fatigue his performance made a strong impression on those present: after a simple treatment from Dewey – '. . . anything I can say will be an anti-climax' – and a few technical remarks, the inquiry was over.

Trotsky had subjected himself to many disadvantages in order to forestall criticism. Not merely did he often express himself in an uncharacteristically moderate manner, to avoid irritating the Mexican authorities, but he also forced himself to transcribe Marxist jargon – gibberish for outsiders – into something intelligible. He did this, moreover, in a very rough and ready English, i.e. without the aid of his principal gift – verbal power. Nevertheless his passion and his logical powers made a persuasive impression of intellectual and spiritual solidity: years later Dewey was to speak of 'the intellectual power with which Trotsky had assembled and organised the mass of his evidence and argumentation'.[5]

It is curious to observe that in spite of the tremendous amount of trouble Trotsky and his entourage had gone to in arranging this inquiry, the final result was simply based on common-sense criteria that could have been applied without it. Its effect was achieved not by the parade of technical alibis, but by the purely political-cum psychological analysis of the issues raised in the Great Charades, and their resolution through the demonstration of their essential, not technical incoherence.

Contrariwise, from Stalin's point of view, the purpose of launching the Great Charades was achieved, very nearly, by the mere fact of the launching. Those who 'sided with' the Soviet regime, by and large, swallowed the Charades. The regime's enemies rejected them out of hand, while at the same time often using them as proof that *everything* to do with the Soviet regime was pernicious – a plague on both your houses!

After the Dewey Commission had finished its inquiry it had to digest the evidence to produce a 'verdict'; while this was going on – it took months – Trotsky did not relax the pressure on his little band in Mexico and abroad. He still felt he had to round out the evidence he had submitted to the Commission, and kept everyone plugging away at it. He himself succumbed to the strain; for months afterwards he had chronic headaches and other symptoms of high blood pressure.

The 'counter-trial' made practically no impression. In Great Britain and France it was scarcely mentioned, nor did it ever excite a ripple of interest outside the Left wing and to some extent the liberal milieu in the United States, the only groups interested in such matters to begin with.

The pressure that had culminated in the Dewey Commission was only just beginning. As usual Sedov complained in full only to his mother; to his father he merely expressed wounded dignity. His life was even more frustrating, if possible, than Trotsky's: his countless functions drained him. In addition, his personal inadequacies were brought home to him.

A letter to his mother discloses this aspect of his depression:

> Writing . . . comes with difficulty to me – I have to read, study, reflect, which requires time. . . . Yet since I have been in emigration I have been burdened almost continually with technical and other chores.
>
> I am a beast of burden, nothing else. I do not learn, I do not read. I cannot aspire to do any literary work: I do not have the light touch and the talent that can partly replace knowledge.[6]

On top of all this large-scale frustration Sedov mentioned to his mother the likelihood that he would soon need a 'small operation'.

In some ways, of course, the life Trotsky was leading with his small household and entourage in the Mexican suburb might have been thought quite pleasant. The house was comfortable; there was a garden; his routine, heavy though it was, was running along on the rails that he was by now quite accustomed to and that was, perhaps, his favourite style of life.

Yet something came up to disturb marital harmony – Natalya became jealous. The woman was, at it seems, Rivera's wife Frida.

This episode is a little difficult to fill in; in the ambiance of the Russian intelligentsia such things are scarcely even mentioned, let alone discussed. Trotsky had always been attractive to women; through his looks, his physique, his brilliance, and a masculinity that while often expressed in a high, impersonal and theatrical style was nevertheless permeated with vigour.

In any case, Natalya's letters refer to someone with the initial F; some friction was noticed between the two women that seemed to parallel some drawing apart between Trotsky and Rivera. Natalya was now fifty-five, only a couple of years younger than Trotsky; Frida much younger. Natalya and Trotsky had been married thirty-five years.

This curiously poignant contretemps made Natalya suffer intensely.

While this passing coolness was at its height Trotsky went on a trip to the mountains, to do some riding and hunting. He wrote to Natalya every day: in a reference to Tolstoy – an established sexual athlete – he mentions Tolstoy's account of his simmering with lust for his wife at the age of seventy after coming back from a long ride. Comparing himself with Tolstoy in this department, Trotsky writes Natalya how he too found himself in the same state of mind, so to speak, at the age of fifty-eight when returning from *his* rides. He even – incredibly – uses some sexy language, apologising of course immediately. He brings up an incident of twenty years before – a love-affair of Natalya's! – and asks her not to reproach him, since he had done nothing to warrant her jealousy, just as he had never reproached her.

If one is to take the letter at its face-value, and assume that as long as Trotsky sounds frank about it he is also telling the truth, it can only mean that he did not, in fact, have what would today be called an 'affair' with Rivera's wife – it was just flirtatiousness.

In any case Natalya clarified this antiquated non-affair, and resumed her role as prop: 'You will still carry me on your shoulders, Nata, as you have carried me throughout our life.'[7]

The 'Jewish question' had not cropped up explicitly in the Great Charades. Long after Trotsky's murder – for the purposes of the 'Show Trials' staged in some Soviet satellites after the Second World War – the formula underlying the Charades was extended to encompass Jews as such: 'Zionism' was added to 'Trotskyism' as an element of complex and increasingly satanic conspiracies.[8]

Trotsky had pointed out, to be sure, strands of anti-Semitism in the Great Charades, too, both in some trivial details as well as in their background and psychological build-up. In the first Charade, for instance, he was supposed to have sent four obviously Jewish agents to the Soviet Union as terrorists; typically, they were said to be working for the Gestapo at the same time.

Now, in connection with the second Great Charade in January, 1937, Trotsky expressed his mature view of the 'Jewish question'.

In an interview with the American-Jewish daily *Forwards* he said he no longer believed that his former hopes for the disappearance of the Jews ('assimilation') would be realised; they would need, after all, a territory of their own. He did not, of course, believe that a Jewish state in Palestine could accommodate the problem, or for that matter that it could be solved under capitalism at all.[9]

The first two Great Charades were still being bickered about in Left wing and liberal milieux when, in May 1937, observers of the Soviet regime were given another jolt.

A bald statement was published that the outstanding Soviet military figure, Marshal Tukhachevsky, together with a handful of other eminent generals, had been guilty of high treason and, except for one suicide, had been executed. They were all accused of plotting with Trotsky and Hitler to sabotage the Soviet Union. Their execution triggered, as was later to come out, the killing of tens of thousands of Red Army officers (25–30,000) that came to an end only just before the war with the Nazis. There was no claim that they had been tried at all; they seem to have been shot shortly before the announcement.

Some attempts have been made to ascribe the killing of Tukhachevsky to a successful operation of the Gestapo, which is thought to have prepared the documents, arranged for their transmission to Stalin via their own Soviet Political Police contacts, and thus to have lured Stalin into killing off his own high command and a substantial segment of the upper officers' corps.

There seems to be no evidence of this; in any case it would not explain the killing of so many officers.

The wiping out of the bulk of the officers' corps was, in fact, part of the broader process already mentioned, in which all the 'apparatuses' of the Soviet Union – the Party, the Political Police, the government administration and the army, together with large strata of the population as a whole, went through the Deep Comb-Out, which destroyed five to ten per cent of the total population between the summer of 1936 – the summer of the first 'Show Trial' – and the summer of 1938, when the 'Yeshov era' (after the then chief of the Political Police) came to an abrupt end.

Trotsky had no idea of the scope of this movement. For him a 'purge' still meant mere exclusion from the Party: what was most to be feared was harsh treatment in remote gaols and in concentration – or hard-labour camps.

The news of the raking out of the major Soviet 'apparatuses' did not emerge till much later, when it was learned that countless veteran Stalinists were, just like the Oppositionists, thrown out of the Party, secretly killed off and later denounced as spies. Of the Stalin faction itself, numerous members of the Politburo were simply killed out of hand. What was soon to be a campaign of terror reached out not only to the countless foreign Communists seeking refuge in the Soviet Union; it extended far beyond the borders of the Soviet Union: the foreign sections of the Soviet Political Police were also combed out.

In Spain the Soviet Political Police had created a specially strong base; using the dissensions on the Republican side of the Spanish Civil War to advance its own policies, it embarked on a campaign of heresy-hunting, assassinations, defamations of character, and kidnappings.

Because of the secrecy surrounding this whole Comb-Out, it came as a sensation when Ignaz Reiss, a senior Soviet agent in Europe, resigned from the Political Police before being called back to Moscow. He told a Dutch sympathiser of Trotsky's (Sneevliet, in the Netherlands parliaments), that Stalin was in the process of 'liquidating Trotskyism' abroad as he had already done inside the Soviet Union. He described to Sneevliet (who passed all this on to Sedov) the tortures, physical and mental, the horrible debasement, the blackmail, the general aim of literally wiping out the entire generation of Old Bolsheviks; he also gave a note of hope: he said there were countless young Communists who went to their deaths crying 'Long Live Trotsky!'[10]

One of the last of the 'ideological' policemen, Reiss himself was, apparently, sufficiently naive to retain some faith in gestures – a hangover from another life. He wrote to the Party headquarters on 18 July 1937, saying he was through with Stalinism and was joining the Fourth International. Almost seven weeks later his corpse was found on a road near Lausanne. He had been trapped by an agent of the Soviet Political Police, which had, apparently, known all about his defection long before receiving his dignified letter.

The police on both sides of the border quickly learned that the murderers had belonged to an association under the aegis of the Soviet Embassy in Paris. The trackers had been keeping Sedov, too, under surveillance: for a few months before this he had noticed that his shadows were slacking off; they had evidently been concentrating on Reiss, and would soon come back to Sedov.

Sedov was perturbed: who, indeed, had been keeping tabs on Reiss?

It was plain that there was a finger-man in Sedov's immediate milieu, plain, also, that he could be, in fact, only Zborowski – no one else could have known such details. He too had been on the payroll of the same Soviet agency as the assassins.

The Reiss murder was effective in 'encouraging the others' to go back to Moscow. They were all wiped out.

Only two foreign officers seem to have defected around now: Walter Krivitsky and Alexander Barmine, who both fled the service (Krivitsky was a veteran Political Police officer, Barmine a chargé d'affaires.) Though without an Oppositionist past they made some attempt to join Trotsky, who, as Krivitsky explained, was 'surrounded by an aureole' even for the agents assigned to fight his ideas.

Zborowski himself sailed through the growing pall of generalised suspicion with great aplomb; though many members of the Trotsky coterie in Paris were now quite suspicious, Trotsky himself and Sedov trusted him to the end of their lives. For all Krivitsky's knowledgeability he never mentioned him either, though he agreed with Reiss that there was an agent in the Paris centre.

Zborowski calmly went on collecting all Trotsky's correspondence and systematically generating misgivings about everyone in the organisation. At one time Sedov himself came under suspicion![11]

The police gave Sedov special protection; Sedov's life in Paris was becoming exceptionally risky – it seemed natural for him to think of going to Mexico. Trotsky was against this, as indeed Sedov was too. Despite Sedov's actual physical and moral exhaustion they both agreed he must stay on 'at his post'. Trotsky thought the Soviet Political Police just as dangerous in Mexico as in Paris or more so.

The whole question of whether Sedov should go to Coyoacan was particularly depressing because of the hopelessness of the position in both Paris and Coyoacan. But the latter was the 'outpost' – whether the immediate target was Trotsky or Sedov.

In September the general depression was lightened a little by the report of the Dewey Commission – *Not Guilty!*

In accordance with the title itself the report came out quite unequivocally, even forcefully, with a 'verdict' absolving Trotsky and Sedov completely and referring to the first two 'Show Trials' – of August 1936 and January 1937 – as 'frame-ups'.

The Dewey Commission Report made no more impression than the hearing itself. While Dewey's authority had some validity in the United States, though not on this subject, political opinion, both in the United States and far more so in Europe, showed no reaction whatever. Those who might have been interested in Trotsky and the Charades were far more interested in Nazi politics, in French politics, the People's Front, the Spanish Civil War.

Trotsky's disappointment – he set great store by the public effect of the Commission's report – was again reflected in his irritation with Sedov, this time because the *Bulletin* came out a little late with the Commission's report. 'I am utterly dissatisfied with the way the *Bulletin* is conducted and I must pose anew the question of its transfer to New York.'[12]

Sedov was in a terrible state. Aside from his grinding life as chief of his 'outpost', he was increasingly dismayed by the Great Charades. So far from looking for an explanation of what they *meant*, he seems to have become morally entangled in the substance of the scenarios – how *could* these men confess!

He was desperate. His fever and sleeplessness were now aggravated by an attack of appendicitis. A letter written to Coyoacan in early February reported a momentary uplift: the *Bulletin* had finally brought out the Dewey Commission's Report; he enclosed the proofs.

It was his last word to his parents: on 8 February he had another onset of appendicitis. This time it seemed dangerous; an operation had to be arranged, very cautiously: the Political Police had to be deceived. The person to discuss details with was, of course, his 'best and most reliable comrade' – Zborowski.

They discussed it weightily. It was too risky for Sedov to go to a French hospital under his own name: it would be much better to go to an obscure clinic, managed by Russian refugees, as a Monsieur Martin, a French engineer. This was not to leak out to anyone; he was to speak nothing but French.

This whole arrangement looks preposterous, not merely in retrospect. Sedov could not possibly pretend to be French, least of all
among Russians. Indeed, it was obvious that Russian refugee circles
were the worst possible milieu for him. Elementary common sense,
and for that matter Trotsky's insistent advice, warned him against
homesick Russian exiles 'on whom the Soviet Political Police might
have a hold'. Sedov himself had treated such people as lepers,
especially since the Reiss killing.

Zborowski helped make all these arrangements and got hold of an
ambulance; Sedov, not even feverish, docilely got in with his wife
and Zborowski; the operation was performed at once.

For a while he seemed to be recovering: he was visited by his
wife and by Zborowski. They had a lively discussion about – politics.
Zborowski was pressed to visit him again as soon as possible: he told
some French sympathisers he had to keep them in the dark about
Sedov's whereabouts because of the Soviet Political Police.

Four days later Sedov fainted after suffering acute pain; he was
found roaming about at night through the empty hallways, half-
undressed and raving in Russian.

The next day his wife was asked whether he might have attempted
suicide: in sobs she said no, and mentioned only the possibility of
poisoning at the hands of the Soviet Secret Police.

A couple of days later, after a protracted bout of agonising pain,
Sedov died. His death was officially attributed to 'complications'
and, of course, heart failure: poor resistance was also mentioned. He
was thirty-two.

There is, naturally, a good deal of obscurity about all this. The
Soviet Political Police had some interest in removing Sedov, and also
any number of opportunities in this little clinic managed by refugees, some of whom were working for the same Soviet agency that
had killed Reiss.

The circumstances that came out in the police inquiry could
scarcely be more suspicious: the staff pretended they had thought
Sedov French, though eyewitnesses said they had heard him
maundering and for that matter arguing in Russian. Though the
doctors denied poisoning, the first question they asked the morning
after his delirium had been about suicide; his widow said the same
surgeon had later been terrified during the inquest and used 'medical
ethics' to excuse his reticence.[13]

Trotsky was staying at a house belonging to one of Rivera's friends
(he had moved from the Blue House after some suspicious men were

seen around it) when the report of Sedov's death arrived. He heard it from Rivera: he lost his temper at first and ordered him out of the house; when he recovered they both went to Coyoacan to tell Natalya:

I [Natalya] was just sorting out old pictures, photographs of our children. . . . The bell rang; I was surprised to see Leon coming in: I went out to meet him. He entered, his head bowed as I had never seen it, his face ash-grey and his whole look suddenly ageworn. 'What has happened?' I asked in alarm. 'Are you ill?' He answered in a low voice: 'Lyova is ill. Our little Lyova. . . .'[14]

For days they were shut up in his room: they saw no one. A week later Trotsky came out: he had not recovered his voice; his eyes were puffed. Some weeks later he wrote to Jeanne: 'Natalya . . . is not yet capable of answering you. She is reading and re-reading your letters and weeping, weeping. When I manage to free myself from work . . . I weep with her.'[15]

His third child, the only human being aside from Natalya he could think of as a friend, was now gone. Moreover, he felt responsible: Sedov had stayed in Paris largely on his insistence; there had been friction between them.

Trotsky's obituary for his son must be the most personal of his writings. At the same time its introduction highlights his own view of himself:

. . . The older generation in whose ranks . . . we once took to the road of revolution . . . has been swept off the stage. . . . What could not be done by the hard-labour gaols of the Tsar, by the deportations, by the poverty of the years of emigration, by the Civil War and by illness, has been accomplished during the past few years by Stalin, the worst of the scourges of The Revolution. . . . The best part of the middle generation, those aroused by 1917 . . . has also been wiped out. The best part of the younger generation, Lyova's contemporaries, has also been trampled down. . . . During the years of our last emigration we made many new friends, some of whom became intimately involved in the life of our family. . . . But we met all these only during the last few years, as we were nearing old age. Only Lyova knew us in our youth. . . .[16]

There was no news of Sergei; Trotsky and Natalya took it for granted he was dead. It was to come out that he had been badgered for months by the Political Police in 1936 to abjure his father, and on refusing had been given a concentration-camp sentence; he was reported killed, though in 1939 Trotsky heard he had been alive in 1937.[17]

The only one of Trotsky's progeny surviving was Zinaida's son, Seva, now twelve. Seva had been brought up by Sedov and Jeanne; he played a special role in her childless life. After Sedov's death Trotsky invited Jeanne to come to Mexico with Seva; if she could not bring him at least to come for a visit.

This rather natural suggestion instantly bogged down in the bickerings of the French sympathisers. The inquiry into Sedov's death had been so unsatisfactory that an inquest had been requested: Jeanne – who belonged, curiously enough, to a different political alignment from Sedov's – had given the representation of the next-of-kin's interest to a lawyer who belonged to her own shading: the other followers of Trotsky – the Trotskyites proper, so to speak, who included Trotsky's own lawyer – claimed that the whole procedure was illegal. The dispute made it easy to disregard the petition for the inquest itself; nothing happened.

This curious byplay was duplicated, in a somewhat more 'political' context, by Jeanne's refusal to release Trotsky's archives; which, having been in Sedov's care to begin with, were now naturally passed on to Jeanne and through her – also naturally, against this background! – to her coterie, the 'Molinier group'.

Trotsky's attitude toward Jeanne underwent a sudden chill: his most precious possession was being withheld by a *follower!* He did not get hold of his archives for some time; a special American emissary had to be sent.

Now Jeanne would not join the Trotskys or send them their grandson either. Her relations with Trotsky and Natalya also got entwined in the squabbles of the Trotsky coteries in Paris; there was well-founded feeling that Jeanne was a little disoriented – in the jargon of our own day, disturbed.

Trotsky was actually reduced to suing for his grandchild, the lawsuit went on for a year; it was also part of the squabbling.

Jeanne's attachment to Seva gave her mental imbalance a sharp point. She claimed Trotsky had no standing in the matter – both his marriages were illegal!

Trotsky was obliged to disprove this strange claim formally, though he indicated his indulgence for Jeanne's suffering. He repeated his offer to have her accompany Seva; he even offered to consider sending the child back after he had seen him. The courts found in his favour twice; Jeanne simply kidnapped the child. It was not, in fact, until the autumn of 1939 that Seva was finally brought to Trotsky by his friends the Rosmers, who in spite of political differences had remained faithful to him personally.

At the beginning of March 1938, scarcely a fortnight after Sedov's death, the third Great Charade was staged. This time Bukharin and Rykov appeared, also Rakovsky (this shattered Trotsky). Henry Yagoda, the police chief who had staged the first Charade, also turned up as a prisoner.

The third Charade extended the first two to such a degree of fantasticality as to sound deranged, especially since the technique of hysterical self-denunciation remained the mainspring of the performances.

Once again Trotsky had organised a vast conspiracy; this time it included Bukharin, who had never been associated with him and had been, in fact, an outstanding ideological adversary. Sedov was given still more prominence as a plotter, now not merely with the Mikado and Hitler, but with British Military Intelligence and for good measure the Polish Secret Service. Trotsky was charged not merely with trying to kill Kirov, Stalin and others, and with the usual catalogue of disasters – train-wrecks, mining accidents, mass poisonings – but also with the death of Gorky and for that matter of a well-known Bolshevik (Sverdlov) in 1919.

This time the 'plot' was pushed much further back into the past; Trotsky was accused of plotting with the German Army in the early Twenties. He was also accused of having directed the activities of Yagoda, who for a whole decade had been organising the harassment of Trotsky's sympathisers.

Trotsky's imagination was overwhelmed by the scope and virulence of Stalin's latest project. In its breadth of conception, in its disregard for material evidence, the last Great Charade soared far beyond its predecessors.

At first Trotsky likened it to the murder of an individual, Rasputin, an illiterate Siberian, with physical and mesmeric powers, who had become the confidant of the Tsar and Tsarina and had finally been killed by some aristocrats. The scandals preceding his assassination had concentrated on his sexual exploits with noblewomen and on his business deals.

The third Great Charade involved scores, indeed, by implication thousands of people, associated within a general conception that was a pure fabrication, a genuine scenario composed by Stalin that created a new universe.

Trotsky had been sufficiently stunned by his afflictions to compare this monstrosity of political creativity with the murder of Rasputin – an escapade!

It is also irony of a kind, no doubt, for Trotsky to have reacted to the Charades by comparing their 'indictments' with the Dreyfus Case, with the Beilis blood-libel case of 1913, and with the accusations made by the Kerensky regime against Lenin as a German hireling.

The Dreyfus Case was a mere miscarriage of justice, after all; the accusations were not in their nature impossible. The Beilis case was a reflection of pathological anti-Semitism exploited for superficial, obvious political purposes. The claim that the Bolsheviks had received a subsidy from the German Government was true, and even if not was not implausible.

The Great Charades constituted a form of theological victimisation in the service of a cult – the cult of Soviet orthodoxy anchored, at the time, in the personality of Stalin the Genius.

Thus Trotsky's lumping them all together is, to use a favourite epithet of his, an 'amalgam' of his own.

By the time of the third Charade Trotsky was caught up in his technique of rational response: he proceeded with the demonstration of his alibi, proving, quite satisfactorily, the impossibility of his or Sedov's having been able to do what they had been accused of.

He ended his first major article on the third Charade with another apocalyptic prediction, that 'Cain-Djugashvili' – Stalin – would himself one day be judged in a trial, a 'genuine one' in which 'no words will . . . be found in human language to defend the most malignant of all the Cains to be found in history'.[18]

Stalin and his cult flourished for another decade and a half; they survived the Second World War and its aftermath. The personality of Stalin himself was to be denigrated later on, but the cult of Soviet orthodoxy has remained powerful to this day, to say nothing of the more eccentric orthodoxies derived from Marxism in Asia, Africa and the New World.

The last phase of 'Trotskyism' as a world movement, at least during Trotsky's lifetime, was played out in the United States.

In January 1938 various splinterlets formed the Socialist Workers'

Party; this had two regular publications (the *New International* and the *Militant*) and was soon to be the 'strongest section' of the Fourth International. It was even, most unusually, prominent in some trades-unions.

In addition, the movement converted some writers and critics on a scale similar to the development in France some years before but with more articulate and better-known individuals.

The American intelligentsia had been 'radicalised'; the Great Depression and the rise of Hitlerism, coupled in the later Thirties with the Spanish Civil War, had heightened an interest in politics, especially in New York. A small group had gone into Communism, but as the Soviet regime itself seemed to be settling down on the one hand into the respectability of an established state and toward the end of the Thirties, on the other hand, into the unintelligible grotesqueries of the Great Charades, some Left-wing types found themselves repelled, finally, by the rigidities of Stalinism. A small Trotsky cult sprang up.

Trotsky was confronted again with his classic situation in exile – the admiration of people without the smallest working-class connection. He was to find himself more and more often engaged in discussion of tactics, and finally of principles, with well-meaning intellectuals who though attracted both to his aureole and to the conversational mileage to be gained from his eccentric point of view could not do much for The Revolution.

His relationship with the literary Trotskyites did not sit well with the leaders of the Socialist Workers' Party, who were irritated by the glamour Trotsky made available to rootless intellectuals, who had, moreover, come to their own version of 'Trotskyism' from a lengthy immersion – equally literary! – in Stalinism.

The honeymoon between Trotsky and the American intellectuals did not last long. Frozen in opposition to all existing institutions, Trotsky was incarcerated in an isolated fortress; as the fortress showed no signs of being relieved most of those originally fascinated by him found themselves disconcerted on the one hand by his single-mindedness, and on the other by his failure, as it seemed, to harmonise his conception of The Revolution with the development of the Soviet regime.

Trotsky was assaulted from the rear – Marxism itself came up for a broad-gauge discussion. It was to consummate the crumbling away of his American following.

In the winter of 1937–8 some critics (former sympathisers like Max

Eastman, Boris Souvarine and Victor Serge) singled out the Kronstadt massacre as the turning-point in the 'degeneration' of Bolshevism. The 1917 putsch itself was not challenged: they baulked only at the repression of the sailors' mutiny four years later.

The discussion of 'Kronstadt' naturally turned into an attack on Trotsky: he had, after all, been on the Politburo and had sponsored the slaughter. Now, of course, he was the only one around to discuss it.

The discussion took place in the midst of the furore about the Great Charades; it was all the more irritating to Trotsky since on the broad canvas of the Civil War in Russia and the massacres of the crash programme of 1929–32 Kronstadt was no more than a fleabite.

Trotsky felt he was being stabbed in the back: while he was straining every nerve to counteract the Great Charades his seemingly sympathetic critics had revived an extinct question: his conduct in power.

What was the relevance, in the Thirties, of an act of violence in the Twenties? Why, when Trotsky was attacking the Stalin regime for killing the wives and children of Oppositionists in the Soviet Union, should these critics pounce on him for executing hostages during the Civil War?

The discussion of 'Kronstadt' inevitably took in other acts of violence. It was plain, in fact, that in its very nature such a discussion had to fan out into a general debate on principle – abstract morality, or ends and means, and more specifically, the divergence between the original aims of the Bolsheviks and their handling of power. His critics were really saying that certain things were simply *not done*.

Trotsky was forced back into his stance of 1924: 'My Party – right or wrong'. He had to prove that the Bolshevik dictatorship, which he was convinced had a right to exist, had a concomitant right to defend itself.

He summed up the issue in a lengthy essay, *Their Morals and Ours*, widely reprinted in many languages. He accepted, partially, the charge of 'Jesuiticism' so often flung at the Bolsheviks – desirable ends *did* justify means that genuinely led to them.

But this raised a more specific question: did the Bolshevik dictatorship have a *right* to exist in the first place? Was Marxism correct in claiming that the means of change deduced from its study of History – the class struggle – did in fact bring about the desired results?

In Marxism the 'revolutionary class struggle' is 'justified' because it leads to Socialism; on the other hand, it leads to Socialism because that is simply the way History works.

It is, accordingly, an axiom: this enabled John Dewey, also involved in this high-level debate, to point out the fundamentally religious core shared by 'orthodox Marxism' with 'traditional idealism'.[19]

But aside from questions of abstract morality, Trotsky's treatment of the Bolshevik enterprise as a whole, especially as it embarked on the great transformations of the Thirties, failed to satisfy many critics.

If The Proletariat had really conducted The Revolution through its first phase, 'October', if the 'class struggle' had really brought about the Dictatorship of The Proletariat, if Russia really were still in the grip of a 'revolutionary' upheaval, the Twenties and Thirties in the Soviet Union were impossible to explain.

It was difficult, in fact, to see how, with Trotsky's explanations, Stalinism could have emerged at all. The Masses, passively victimised by the Party fiat via the Political Police, had remained torpid.

Where was The Revolution? More particularly, what was the use of Marxism?

For Trotsky, an unbending Marxist, this was to be an indigestible and for the matter unacknowledged conundrum. 'Classical Marxism' did not help him explain Stalinism.

He could explain neither the titanic growth of the bureaucracy, nor the ferocity of the crash programmes of the Thirties.

By pulverising peasant resistance Stalin had consolidated the parvenu dictatorship: he smashed small-farming, forestalling the democratic erosion of the dictatorship through the revival of capitalism and simultaneously promoting the industrialisation required to strengthen the regime.

Since Trotsky also thought it 'progressive' to destroy small-farming and to industrialise the economy, he regarded the ferocity of the crash programme as a mere 'deformation', and the Soviet bureaucracy as representing the 'degeneration' of the Workers' State.

The problem remained: on behalf of which 'class' was the Stalin dictatorship lashing out?

The dictatorship was, after all, confronting not a question of Marxist analysis, but a brute fact – the explosive flux of a parvenu regime. As head of a conspiratorial elite whose elan was buttressed

by the police power, Stalin could not dawdle: he had to counter-
feit a Revolution by a crash programme.

If there was a 'Revolution' at all, it was not the October putsch,
but the shake-up in the Thirties.

The putsch itself had merely put into power a few men with
certain views, perhaps intentions, at the time not well defined in
practical terms. Had the Bolsheviks chosen, for instance, to apply a
different programme they might have been spared a great deal of
trouble. Had they chosen, say, to take in their Socialist colleagues,
had they chosen to promote the Constituent Assembly, nothing
would have been changed in Russia that had not come about
through the dissolution of the Monarchy and the events of
February–March 1917.

The crash programme produced a new industrial structure, much
bigger than that of Tsarist Russia, on top of a smaller agricultural
base. The urban population – doubled in the first decade of the
breakneck drive – had to make do with less food; a fundamental
lopsidedness was unavoidable.

Trotsky's Permanent Revolution had been caricatured.

The lunging forward of an elite, grounded, according to his
theory, in the tug of elemental forces, in the bubbling over of
impersonally accumulated techniques, in the gradually swelling
cosmic forces within the peasantry, had been replaced by the fiat of
a clique.

By refusing to acknowledge the putsch and the crash programme
of the Thirties decisons of small groups, not an upsurge of The
Masses, Trotsky had to snipe at the titanic crash programme
peripherally – pointing out mere errors of scale and momentum.

Trotsky misunderstood the scope of the terror and the cult of
Stalin the Genius. His 'position' was too subtle to retain the recruits
attracted by his otherwise mordant criticism.

The true rationale of the crash programme could not, after all, be
admitted by the regime, which naturally maintained that everything
it did flowed ineluctably from the finest, indeed the only type of
Marxism conceivable. Since the 'classless society', the professed goal
of the regime, required an economy of abundance that was out of
the question the chasm had to be plastered over. Mere mendacity,
mere propaganda was not enough – terror was needed.

This was essential in establishing just that cult of orthodoxy that
beginning with the Twenties expanded in the Thirties together with
Bolshevik programmes of social transformation.

Trotsky's bewilderment was consummated by the Great Charades.

The Great Charades – Stalin's macabre Masterpiece – congealed 'Trotskyism' as the perfection of that heresy on the basis of which Trotsky himself had already been extruded from the Party. 'Trotskyism', a catch-all for every variety of 'heresy', became the polar opposite of Soviet orthodoxy.

The parabola of intensity in the vilification of Trotsky makes this clear.

From the middle of the Twenties on it was normal to denounce Trotsky as a 'deviator', normal for Stalin to be praised as the only authentic interpreter of 'Leninism', already a bogus though indispensable supplement to Marxism.

The lightning-like ikonisation of Stalin at the end of the Twenties developed a reverse process – the satanisation of his opponents. By 1931 it was necessary to show that Trotsky had *always* been a counter-revolutionary, practically demented into the bargain.

The systematic falsification of documents and incontestable facts was at first useful for the Stalin faction; then it became the counterweight to the apotheosis of Stalin's person. By the mid-Thirties it had become an integral part of the new theological institution: as Stalin became God Trotsky became the Devil.

This had nothing to do with the wiping out of Trotsky's *real* sympathisers, whom Stalin had obliterated by the end of the Twenties, simultaneously insulating the Communist movement as a whole against 'Trotskyite' ideas.

The defamation of Trotsky as a Gestapo agent was a mere detail in the general anathematisation of 'Trotskyism' as the essence of Evil.

Trotsky's rationalistic, logical, common-sense efforts to withstand the effect of the Great Charades were doomed: 'Trotskyism', once a routine epithet in Marxist mud-slinging, had been integrated into the cult of Soviet orthodoxy.

Trotsky had been perplexed by the emergence of this cult at its very inception, with the adumbration of the General Line in the early Twenties. While still at the summit of the Party, he found the mummification of Lenin's corpse repugnant:

The attitude toward Lenin as a revolutionary leader was replaced by the attitude toward him as the head of an ecclesiastical hierarchy. Over my protests a mausoleum, unworthy and offensive to any revolutionary consciousness, was erected on Red Square. The official books about Lenin were also turned into mausoleums. His thought was cut up into quotations for lying sermons. His embalmed corpse was used as a weapon against the living Lenin and – against Trotsky. . . . Thanks to their quantity, ignorant fabrications took on political quality. They were deafening, oppressive, demoralising. The Party was condemned to silence. A regime consisting of an outright dictatorship of the apparatus over the Party was enthroned. In other words, the Party was ceasing to be a party.[20]

The phrase 'ignorant fabrications' is surely an outcry of juvenile rationalism: it was, after all, the systematic, though of course unconscious foundation of just this cult that was to achieve gargantuan proportions by the end of the Twenties, recast all Soviet society by the end of the Thirties, and in our own day shape the Soviet universe.

Caged within an ideal theory, Trotsky failed to assess first the true weight of the apparatus as it emerged, then its consequences, at home and abroad, then the elan of the cult that imposed an iron constraint on all its members and created a matrix for the slaughter of millions of people within the framework of a heresy formalised by police procedures.

Thus, by failing to explain first the establishment of the bureaucacy and then the cult of Stalin the Genius, Trotsky was unequipped to explain the Great Charades and the Deep Comb-Out.

It is true that the news of the Deep Comb-Out emerged only after Trotsky's murder. Yet in a way that heightens the triviality of his fundamental analysis.

If his explanation of the ferocity of the crash programme was inadequate, how much the more would he have been nonplussed by the decapitation of all the apparatuses of the Soviet regime, as well as by the wiping out of millions of ordinary people, during the Deep Comb-Out?

His assessment of Stalin, flimsy even during the Twenties, in the Thirties was irrelevant altogether.

Trotsky has a graphic phrase for Stalin's ascension: 'At a certain moment his figure, in the full panoply of power, suddenly stepped away from the Kremlin wall, and for the first time the world became aware of Stalin as a ready-made dictator.'[21]

This surely seems to imply a neglect of the real power 'panoplying' Stalin in favour of the theatrical effect of its publicisation.

Stalin had not, after all, created the Soviet state; in his position first of Party administrator, then Party boss, then Dictator, then Sub-God, he was merely solving, as it were, the problems presented to him, as Trotsky might have said, by History. These problems were the fruits of the interaction between collective interests against a given historical background.

Thus, even though Stalin's character was an element, perhaps essential to the construction of his eerie solutions, still it was bound to be subordinated to external events.

In his biography of Stalin, which Trotsky was in the midst of writing when assassinated, Trotsky's bafflement by the moral problem of Stalin's existence makes him slip into a psychological contradiction.

On the one hand it was his favourite observation that Stalin was nothing much. His remark that Stalin was the 'most eminent mediocrity of the Party' became a classic; it remained the expression of Trotsky's ripest consideration. Perhaps this was true; at least Trotsky was bound to look down on a talentless thinker, a cowardly man of action, and an arch-intriguer.

On the other hand, Trotsky was trying to explain how such a mediocrity managed to control a vast apparatus, to create indeed a whole private government, to carry out the slaughter of millions via an agency also perfected by him, to reorder the institutions of a big country, to create a religious cult around himself – to establish, in short, a new society.

It is plainly essential either to show his qualities or else to analyse the edifice in which such a mediocrity had ensconced himself in a crucial position.

It is just here that Trotsky's general inability to accommodate intellectually the role of personality deflects his assessment of the interaction between the individual and the social process.

His assessment of Stalin's ability in terms of intellectual dexterity alone was strangely provincial, especially from someone whose chief distinction was just such dexterity.

Administration doubtless calls for qualities, whatever they are, that are different from abstract thinking. Yet could Trotsky have thought Stalin found himself at the summit of the apparatus 'by accident'? That he did nothing to shape that apparatus? That he had been, in fact, as passive as Trotsky?

Perhaps under the influence of the nightmarish Charades and the bloodbath that was beginning to be rumoured about, Trotsky, outraged to the depths of his rationalistic being by the matchless surge

of hypocrisy and ferocity in Russia, was blinded to the figure of
Stalin himself. In the blaze of Trotsky's indignation Marxist 'forces'
went up in smoke.

Trotsky refused to blame the putsch itself, still less the 'conquests
of October' for the 'deformations' and 'degenerations' that followed.

Nor could he bear giving Stalin any personal credit for them, so to
speak, at the very moment of emphasising their scale.

Yet in spite of himself he allows an unusually high estimate of
Stalin's importance to slip in.

He makes much in his *Stalin* of a suggestion, for instance, that
Stalin poisoned Lenin: Trotsky makes a strong case – means,
opportunity, and motive. All that is lacking, in fact, is evidence.

It is part of a general design in which Stalin is made to seem a
grotesque figure of evil from his earliest days on – vindictive,
devious, small-minded, treacherous and cruel.

Yet before the Great Charades Trotsky had not always had such a
sombre view: he had once called Stalin a 'brave and sincere
revolutionary'.[22] That might have been diplomacy, of course; still,
Trotsky had never remotely suspected the iniquities Stalin was capable of.

Hence, in discussing the possibility of Stalin's murdering Lenin,
he is so distracted by the problem of historic responsibility that he is
again obliged to abandon a 'materialistic' explanation of history in
order to ascribe unique importance to Stalin:

Trotsky writes:

Whether Stalin sent Lenin the poison he asked for with the
hint that the physicians had left no hope for his recovery, or
whether he resorted to more direct means, I do not know. But I
am firmly convinced that Stalin could not have waited passively
when his fate hung by a thread, and the decision depended on a
small, very small, motion of his hand.[23]

This is a curious repetition in miniature of his evasive admission, in
his *History*, that without Lenin the putsch would have been out of
the question. He now appears to be saying that without that 'very
small motion' of Stalin's hand the entire subsequent history of the
Soviet Union would have been different – no ten million peasants
slaughtered in the breakneck collectivisation, no murderous 'Purges'
or 'Show Trials', no cult of orthodoxy.

At the same time the impression is unavoidable that, by summing up both Lenin's and Stalin's fate as dependent on a 'small motion', Trotsky was also overwhelmed by a sort of narcissistic self-pity: it was that 'small motion', practically an accident, that brought about his own destruction!

Since Stalin went on to far more grandiose killings Trotsky's interest in this obscure incident seems excessive. It parallels, oddly, the theme of 'Bolshevik Judases' displayed in the Great Charades and some of the 'Show Trials' in Soviet satellites after the Second World War – the satanising motif of people seeming to be Bolsheviks but *really* traitors since birth.

Plainly, Trotsky's intellect baulked at the problem: how, indeed, could a monster like Stalin have been produced by the Workers' State?

It warped Trotsky's summing-up to the point of worthlessness.

His characterisation of the relationship between Stalin and the Bolshevik Party is illuminating if only through his simile: 'Of Christ's twelve Apostles Judas alone proved to be a traitor. But if he had acquired power he would have represented the other eleven Apostles as traitors.'[24]

Trotsky was far from the perception of Stalinism as a secular cult.

Nor did his last complete book, *The Revolution Betrayed*, help him retain his temporary recruits at the end of the Thirties.

Essentially an argument – though its analysis of Soviet society is still lively – the book was a desperate attempt to salvage *something* from Stalin's Russia to sustain 'classical Marxism'.

It rotated around a confrontation that was at bottom quite unreal – the contrast between the ideals of 'classical Marxism' and the sinister fact of Stalinism. Its point of departure was the Soviet proclamation – in the late Thirties – that Socialism had already been *achieved* by the Stalin regime.

But neither Marx nor Engels, nor any one else, had ever said exactly what Socialism was to be like; it was to be brought into being by the play of cosmic forces. It was so vague, indeed, that Lenin himself had been able to say, in the immediate aftermath of the putsch, that Socialism had been achieved *even then,* and Trotsky had endorsed it.[25] Now, more than a decade later, Trotsky was putting himself essentially in the position of a scholastic proving that a definition did not fit – Stalinism was not Socialism!

By now, of course, Soviet society was a far cry not only from Socialism, however that was interpreted, but in some respects from

any form of civilisation ever known. Stalin was not 'defining' Socialism – he was clinging to power. His cult was all-inclusive for good
reasons – historical, theological, *practical*.

Thus Trotsky's exposure of the contrast between ideal Marxism
and the facts of Soviet life was merely abstract: it did not explain
how the whole mess had come about.

To be sure, Trotsky's analysis succeeded in encouraging some non-
Communist Left-wing intellectuals as well as, of course, the somewhat diffuse milieu of Trotsky's scattered conventicles.

George Orwell, for instance, caricatured him as a Jew, and in 1984
counterposed him, somewhat mysteriously, to Big Brother. Some ex-
Marxists picked out what they could from its ambiguously presented
material.

But none of this helped him retain the allegiance of his American
sympathisers. He lost most of the 'parlour pinks' whose revulsion
against Stalinism had made them dally a moment with Trotsky
before resuming their headlong flight from Marxism.

More generally, Trotsky's mind, despite the breadth of his
interests in later life, never broke out of the parochial framework of
his early absorption of Marx. He never freed himself, indeed, from
the structure of Marxism as worked out by Marx and Engels in their
own early youth.

He reveals this unmistakably in an essay he wrote in 1939, where
he emphasised the most primitive strand of Marxism – the notion
that the process of revolutionary 'ripening' was inexorable. Even if
the sophisticated capitalist clique running society *studied* Marx they
simply could not get round the 'iron laws' working themselves out
with 'astronomical certainty'. Any attempt *at all* to reform capitalism
was no more than 'reactionary, hopeless quackery'.[26]

Moreover, just as American technique dominated production relations, so it also guaranteed, sooner or later, a spectacular advance of
the American working class toward – Marxism.

Trotsky's conviction that the agrarian Far East would never
become revolutionary was also linked to this same faith in The
Proletariat as the vanguard of The Revolution.

Instead, of course, the American working class was to become the
outstanding obstacle to all Marxism, while new regimes professing
their own brands of 'Marxist Socialism' were to proliferate in overwhelmingly peasant countries – like Russia itself.

Trotsky's discouragement led him, after the outbreak of the

Second World War, to envisage, for a moment, the possibility that his entire career had been rooted in an illusion.

In one of his last articles, after making a conventional bow to his ideals by predicting a 'proletarian revolution' as a result of the war, he went on to strike a more realistic note:

> If . . . it is conceded that the present war will provoke not revolution but a decline of the proletariat, then there remains another alternative; the further decay of monopoly capitalism. . . . The inability of the proletariat to take into its hands the leadership of society could . . . lead to the growth of a new exploiting class. . . . This would be . . . a regime of decline, signalising the eclipse of civilisation. . . .
>
> However onerous the second perspective may be, if the world proletariat should actually prove incapable of fulfilling the mission placed upon it by the course of development, nothing else would remain except openly to recognise that the socialist programme based on the internal contradictions of capitalist society *ended as a Utopia.**[27]

Yet this conclusion was so painful he did not refer to it again. Instead, whistling in the dark more desperately than ever, he was obliged to fall back on a Marxist mannerism traditionally resorted to whenever long-range predictions fail to accommodate short-term facts.

It would be difficult to ascertain, from Trotsky's writings at the end of the Thirties, whether his eye was fixed on the horizons of eternity or on next year's likelihoods. Sometimes he seemed to be speaking for the aeons, in writing that 'all great movements have begun as "splinter groups" of old movements' – Protestantism a splinter of Catholicism, Marxism a splinter of the Hegelian Left, the Third International a splinter of the Second.

Success sounds a long way off!

Yet the programme he composed in the summer of 1938 for the Founding Congress of the Fourth International sounds just the opposite, like a tactical guide for a functioning movement.

On a gramophone record he made – in English – for a New York mass-meeting in connection with the Founding Congress he said: 'Our Party is now the greatest lever of history'; he ended his

*My italics. J.C.

recorded speech with a prediction – 'in the course of the next ten years the programme of the Fourth International will become the programme of millions, and those revolutionary millions will be able to storm heaven and earth.'[28]

In the spring of 1937 he had even said that in only a few years – 'three to five', in fact – the Fourth International would be a 'great force in the world'.[29]

Trotsky's real tragedy, perhaps, lay not in his personal ordeal but in the collapse of his intellectual framework: even more – in the inhibitions that prevented him from perceiving this.

Just as 'classical Marxism' was embodied, practically, in the macabre handiwork of the Bolshevik Party, so in its 'pure' form it failed to help Trotsky either to influence events or ultimately to understand them.

Impoverished by Marxism, Trotsky's thinking was unhinged by the 'conquests of October'.

The Founding Congress of the Fourth International was held on 3 September 1938; Trotsky had spent the summer after the third Great Charade preparing for it. He wrote its Draft Programme and many resolutions.

The Congress was no more than a get-together of twenty-eight of Trotsky's sympathisers, who spoke for organisations in eleven countries. They met in Alfred Rosmer's house outside Paris, in the shadow of the recent martyrs, Sedov and two of Trotsky's secretaries (Rudolf Klement and Erwin Wolf), killed in 1936 in Spain by the Soviet Political Police.

In this atmosphere of killing and spying it was thought prudent to have only one full session; hence the conference went on all day with no interruptions; no one was allowed in. The 'Russian Section' of the Fourth International was ably represented by – Zborowski.

A couple of outsiders were also present, one of them Sylvia Agelof, a young woman from New York who acted as interpreter. She had turned up in Paris a little while before and had become involved with a man called Jacques Mornard, who hovered outside the meeting room waiting for her.

The conference was chaired by Max Shactman; the reports and resolutions Trotsky had spent the summer drawing up were passed.

A 'progress report' presented by Pierre Navile indicated – inadvertently – the hollowness of the enterprise. Behind the panoply of titles – Executive, International Bureau, Secretariat – there was, plainly, very nearly nothing. The harassment of the Political Police had converged with the failure of the movement to expand.

The membership of the whole ensemble of the little 'national' groups was somewhat pathetic: the biggest section, the American, did not even pretend to more than a formal membership of 2,500. The Internal Bulletins of the Party gave it as 1,000; other sources indicate still fewer.[30]

There was near-unanimity on most major points; the conference voted nineteen to three for a proclamation to the effect that the Fourth International had launched itself. When an Executive Committee was elected Zborowski complained that no place had been authorised for the 'Russian Section': Trotsky was at once put on the newly elected Executive of the Fourth International as a member both 'secret' and 'honorary', but since he could not, of course, appear, the 'Russian Section' was to go on being represented by – Zborowski.

It may be premature to assess the prospects of the Fourth International. Trotsky naturally identified his enterprise with the history of Bolshevism – a tiny group, of no obvious consequence, changes History.

This is the hope of all small movements. Yet of itself unimportance is not, of course, a *guarantee* of importance. And in the case of Trotsky the impression is hard to avoid that History is not likely to grant his brain-child the opportunity of duplicating Lenin's victory. If the regime that destroyed the democratic successor to Tsarism is to be replaced it is hard to envisage the role of Trotsky's Marxism.

He never, after all, claimed more than fidelity to Marx and Engels; hence any activity linked to his name could only be a form of 'pure' Marxism – distinct from that claimed by any actual regime. And since his personal contributions were restricted to the horizons of the Twenties and Thirties they would seem to be inherently irrelevant to any subsequent development.

It is only Trotsky's person, in short, that can be taken as an inspiration. It was essentially, in fact, as a symbol that his name was to survive his death.

Aside from scattered groups who consider at least some of his writings authoritative, who may even call themselves 'Trotskyites' – that would surely have embarrassed him! – there are many today for whom Trotsky's name has acquired the glamour of an off-beat mentor.

Dissociated from the monuments of 'classical Marxism', from his learning – indeed, fom his brainpower! – Trotsky was to become one of a small pantheon of folk-heroes who stand for the purity of revolutionary intentions. His very failure to cling to power – the proof of his own purity – was to make his name a slogan.

Thus the destiny of the Fourth International is bound up with the future of Marxism. Encompassing as it does the political activities of well-nigh half the human race, that is sure to withstand prediction and, perhaps, analysis.

The dispersion of Trotsky's following of American intellectuals was reflected in a worsening of his finances.

Among those he was now 'breaking with' right and left was Rivera, who toward the end of the 1938 Mexican elections attacked Cardenas, who was in effect Trotsky's host, in favour of a Right-wing general. Rivera also became a Stalinite, the only one close to Trotsky who ever did *that*.[31]

Trotsky had to disown Rivera publicly; he had been living in his Blue House, after all, for two years. Now he left it, and had to pay rent again.

He was bogging down, moreover, in his writing. He had never finished more than the first part of his *Life of Lenin*; his *Stalin* was coming along very slowly. His American publishers had been rather generous: in 1936, for instance, Doubleday had given him five thousand dollars for his *Lenin*, as well as two thousand dollars for his *Revolution Betrayed*, which had not earned its advance. They began to drag their heels: by the second half of 1938 Harper was declining any further advance for the *Stalin*.[32]

Trotsky had been very reluctant to write this book in the first place: he would have preferred almost any other subject, especially his long-dreamed-of joint biography of Marx and Engels, never even begun, or for that matter friendship, love, etc. Stalin's life was, in addition, peculiarly obscure, especially its beginnings, and even his role in 1917.[33]

Nor was he selling his articles normally, even though the era was full of hotly debated crises – the rise of Japan, Munich, Soviet armaments.

He had to start borrowing again. He began negotiations with various universities for the sale of his archives, but even though his asking price was very low nothing was to happen for more than a year.

He sold a few articles to *Life* magazine – a sketch of Stalin the man and something on Lenin's death. It produced a curious tangle:

the first article (October 1938) annoyed some fellow-travelling liberals, who wrote to the magazine saying some rude things about him. He regarded these as slanderous and also as having been composed by a Soviet Political Police 'factory' in New York. The second article was turned down: the editors wanted 'more unquestionable facts' about Stalin's sinister role in Lenin's death. Trotsky thought of suing *Life*; finally it gave him the money anyhow. The article itself came out in *Liberty*.

In the winter of 1939 Trotsky rented a large, ruined house far outside the little suburb of Coyoacan; it was surrounded by a spacious garden dominated by tall leafy plants, and filled with great cacti and agaves; it was alive with birds twittering in the mornings on the old trees. A large stream ran down one side when it was not dried up; on the other there was a dusty highroad with a few adobe shacks.

Trotsky and Natalya reconstructed it very simply. A wall encircled the whole property; visitors would enter by a solid iron door that a guard would open after inspecting them through a peephole.

The police built a small brick hut some thirty paces from the entrance. Strong bars were placed in front of the doors, the walls were protected by sandbags, alarms were put in. There was an around-the-clock detail of policemen – five – patrolling the street outside the walls. Inside Trotsky had his secretarial staff – eight to ten, nearly all Americans, as protection. As at the Blue House the youthful Trotskyites were given duties at first at the entrance gate, which was later on to have a watch-tower installed; then inside the house where they worked as secretaries, helped out with the household chores, and also, of course, took part in the regular evening discussions.

A huge room off the entrance was arranged as a library and secretariat: it was full of filing cabinets, books, newspapers, and typing tables. A door opened into the dining-room: there was a big table made of white wood, chairs painted in the hispano-Indian style, and cupboards. Trotsky's work-room, at the left, was a square room with a high ceiling; it was well lighted, airy, and furnished only with the basic necessities – a table also in wood and the works of Lenin bound in red and blue cloth. The light came from a balcony window that Trotsky would keep his back to while working. His work-room communicated directly with the dining-room, furnished just as simply.[35]

Trotsky's routine remained the same: he would get up early, while the light was fresh and before the sun began to blaze. He had retained his proud, majestic bearing, his forthright gait, his vivacity. Though his mane, with its rebellious locks, was white, he did not seem to be aging.[36]

Trotsky had always been physically powerful, in contrast with a common stereotype that made him out to be a puny bookworm. Since he liked activities with a purpose, he had organised country excursions for the gathering of enormous rare cacti in the mountains. He was quite capable of exhausting his far younger bodyguards as he ascended a sharp decline carrying a heavy collection of these 'bayonet-bladed' cacti. He used to rush about in the scorching sun among the great boulders, dressed in a blue French peasant tunic, his mane of white hair tossed by the wind.

These hiking expeditions now declined: it was becoming too dangerous for him to expose himself so ostentatiously amidst the gathering ferocity of the Stalinite press. He was reduced to exercise in his garden, where he began raising out-of-the-way cacti and taking care of chickens and rabbits. His sole relaxation, very nearly, was to come from feeding his rabbits, in a strictly scientific, painstaking and organised way: 'when his health was poor the feeding of the rabbits was a strain; but he could not give it up; he pitied the little animals.'[37]

Natalya describes his manner during his final incarceration:

He would generally receive visitors at his work table, leaning forward slightly to hear them better, his blue-eyed gaze very intent; he spoke in a voice that was always clear, carefully spacing out his sentences and doing his best, even in English, German or French, to construct them lucidly. He was courteous, and took pains to avoid creating, even voluntarily, trivial misunderstandings that can . . . mar personal relations. . . . In spite of his habit of judging people with an objectivity that might seem rigorous, his starting-point was fundamentally benevolent. He avoided telling me anything unfavourable or displeasing, and he himself preferred not to hear it. He easily grew enthusiastic about a person, about a piece of writing, about an ideal. But since he himself subordinated himself so completely to the rigour of ideas, and did not admit that they might be . . . separated from action, he never hesitated with the friends, comrades and individuals he liked most, to carry on discussions with intransigence and, when the argument led to it, to note an ideological rupture. For him ideas did not constitute parts of some lofty intellectual game; they were alive, they absorbed one's whole person, they demanded an appropriate response.[37]

Trotsky used his voice expressively: his chief secretary van Heijenoort describes it:

> With the people fairly close to him, (secretaries, well-known persons), Trotsky's voice was ordinary; when he spoke French he rolled his 'r's a little. As soon as the occasion was a bit out of the daily routine (a group of visitors, people coming for a few days from abroad), his tone became more didactic; there were gestures with the hands and fingers. The delivery was slower and more articulated. Finally, in public speaking, the delivery became metallic, with extreme force. When speaking with Natalya in Russian his voice became almost a whisper; it was hard for a non-Russian to understand it. When dictating in Russian his voice was extremely clear, but without great effects. There were many voices. . . .[39]

In Coyoacan, except for Natalya, there was no one close to him. When not in the presence of visitors for whom they had to keep up appearances he and Natalya had the atmosphere of a lonely old couple. There was scarcely ever even anyone to speak Russian with. Natalya describes Trotsky's manner in private:

> I would sometimes hear [him], alone in his study; heave a deep sigh, and speak to himself – 'What weariness, what weariness!' he would murmur. 'I can't bear it any longer.' That he would have said to no one. The demented humiliation, the moral undoing of the old revolutionaries he loved, who had died heaping infamy on him and on themselves, ravaged him with an inextinguishable pain. . . . All died an atrocious death, all had betrayed themselves, all had betrayed the conscience of The Revolution! Alone, Leon Davidovich would sometimes pronounce their names. . . . The endless spaces of Mexico scarcely lightened his burden.[40]

There was, to be sure, a trickle of visitors, generally Americans now. Aside from a more or less steady flow of partisans from the American organisation there was a motley throng of academicians and journalists, even Congressmen.

Hospitality was by now Trotsky's chief entertainment; he was remarkably accessible to new people. The discussions in the fortress covered the endless range to be expected from his broad horizons.

In October 1939 the Rosmers, the only survivors of the springtime of his life, came to visit the strange fortress in Coyoacan. They left the following May. The Trotskys and the Rosmers had a relaxing time chatting about the past and arranging its documents – Trotsky's extensive archives.

Another refugee came for a visit – Otto Rühle, a well-known Marxologist and a founder of the German Communist Party he was also one of the first to abandon. It was Rühle who made a small anthology – *The Living Thoughts of Karl Marx* – for which Trotsky wrote his Introduction about the marxification of the American workers.

A suggestion was made by Trotsky that all three revive the now classic document, the Zimmerwald Manifesto – composed by Trotsky – proclaiming revolutionary resistance to war. Characteristically, they could not come to an agreement: Rühle was not, after all, a partisan of Trotsky's, still less of Rosmer's: the idea of reviving that classic Manifesto remained one more conversation.

Trotsky's grandson, Seva, after all the grotesque, painful, wrangling with Jeanne, had finally been brought by the Rosmers to Coyoacan.

Since being sent away from Prinkipo some seven years before, Seva had had a peculiarly tempestuous personal life: different countries, different schools, different languages, different caretakers. He could scarcely speak Russian. As an infant he had lost his father; as a child his sick mother by suicide; Sedov, his uncle and foster-father, had also vanished mysteriously; and suddenly he had become the pawn of a baffling family fight. Kidnapped and hidden, he had now been snatched away to live with a man who was a sort of legend, in a peculiar fortress thronged by strangers.

In February 1940 Trotsky, who had on odd occasions written a number of short, essentially technical drafts of wills wrote a genuine Testament, to ensure the transmission of his copyrights.

It was only a page and a half: it started off by saying his life had been wholly that of a dedicated revolutionary and Marxist, and could not be sullied by the 'vile and stupid slander of Stalin and his agents'.

Then Natalya is mentioned:

Fate, in addition to the happiness of being a fighter for the cause of Socialism, gave me the happiness of being her husband. During the almost forty years of our life together she has remained an inexhaustible source of love, magnanimity and tenderness.

The Testament ends on an emotional note:

Natasha has just come up to the window from the courtyard and opened it wider so that the air may enter more freely into my room. I can see the bright green strip of grass beneath the wall, and the clear blue sky above the wall, and sunlight everywhere. Life is beautiful. Let the future generations cleanse it of all evil, oppression, and violence, and enjoy it to the full.[41]

A few days later – 3 March 1940 – Trotsky seemed to be preparing for the end:

The nature of my illness (high and rising blood pressure) is such – as I understand it – that the end must come suddenly, most likely – again, this is my personal hypothesis – through a brain hemorrhage. This is the best possible end I can wish for. It is possible, however, that I am mistaken (I have no desire to read special books on this subject and the physicians naturally will not tell the truth). If the sclerosis should assume a protracted character and I should be threatened with a long-drawn-out invalidism (at present I feel, on the contrary, rather a surge of spiritual energy because of the high blood pressure, but this will not last long), then I reserve the right to determine for myself the time of my death. The 'suicide' (if such a term is appropriate in this connection) will not in any respect be an expression of an outburst of despair or hopelessness. Natasha and I said more than once that one may arrive at such a physical condition that it would be better to cut short one's own life or, more correctly, the too slow process of dying. . . . But whatever may be the circumstances of my death I shall die with unshaken faith in the Communist future. This faith in man and in his future gives me even now such power of resistance as cannot be given by any religion.[42]

This seems strange: after all, Trotsky was being very productive. Though his health was somewhat uncertain it had been so for some time; there was no reason, one might have thought, to be so sombre, or at any rate to record the mood.

Perhaps the conjunction of the implacably gloomy political outlook and the depression of his vital forces had given rise to forebodings. Something ominous was, in fact, being prepared, though Trotsky could not have known of it. His chronic suspicion of the Soviet Political Police had become calloused; he could not pinpoint any particular machination.

Yet one was now to encompass him.

After Franco's victory in Spain some of the Soviet Political Police sections specialising in extirpating the Opposition moved to Mexico; they were sheltered there by the massive Stalinite influence.

At the beginning of 1940 the stridency of the campaign against Trotsky was heightened. On May Day some 20,000 Communists in uniform paraded through Mexico City calling for his expulsion.

Against this background of systematic agitation against Trotsky's person a man called 'Jacson' began frequenting Trotsky's house. He was the man one of Trotsky's secretaries had become involved with in Paris just before the Fourth International Founding Congress at the Rosmers'.

'Jacson' was thought to be a well-to-do 'bourgeois', a playboy with a penchant for sports: ostensibly working for an oil company, he had come to Mexico around the same time as Rosmer, in the autumn of 1939; for some time he had had no particular contact with the fortified villa in the outskirts of Coyoacan.

His acquaintance with Sylvia Agelof, the secretary, as it came out much later, had been far from fortuitous; some planner in the Soviet Political Police had conceived it.

Both Sylvia and her sister were 'Trotskyites'; the sister had sometimes acted as secretary and messenger for Trotsky.

Sylvia was of a type made familiar by countless crime-thrillers, both fictional and real-life. A lonely, plain bluestocking, she had a linguistic gift that included Russian.

'Jacson' (known in Paris as 'Mornard') was to be identified much later as Ramon Mercader, a Catalan Spaniard whose mother, Cuban by birth, was a Stalinist 'militant' living in France; she was a familiar of the Soviet Political Police.[43]

Handsome, well-dressed, urbane, Mercader smothered Sylvia with attention. Flinging money around, he whirled her through France: she explained it all by his 'bourgeois' background.

In retrospect his 'cover-story' does not seem to have been worked out very well by the script-writers in the Political Police; even at the time Sylvia was occasionally puzzled by hitches in his exposition. Also, his indifference to politics seemed extravagant even for a businessman being condescended to by a 'Trotskyite'. It was no doubt this condescension, to be sure, that made her swallow his cover-story so easily.

Bemused, Sylvia went home in February 1939; the following September Mercader rejoined her in New York. Here again his cover-story slipped a little; perhaps because of technical difficulties in the supply department of the Political Police, he had a rather strange passport – a bogus Canadian one with the improbable spelling of 'Jacson'; he explained it as a ruse to evade the Belgian Army. Mercader was slipshod again in New York, too; he said he had never visited New York, yet he seemed very knowledgeable and, rather strangely, let Sylvia see this.

She sometimes asked him for explanations; though very careless in his actual behaviour he found it quite simple to satisfy her more or less. At no point did she ever conceive any suspicion of him on political grounds; she thought him at worst a frivolous *bon vivant* and show-off. She even tried to reform him : her efforts met with apathy.

Since he pretended to be in the import-export business, there was nothing odd about his going to Mexico. It was natural for him to ask her to join him.

In fact he left for Mexico early in October; a couple of months later she was there too. Very naturally she went to Trotsky's fortress; equally naturally she was put to work as a secretary. Mercader would drive her to the villa in a plush motor-car and pick her up after work.

This aroused no suspicion. Mercader became quite friendly with the guards, without making any effort to enter the enclosure. It was natural for him to collide with the Rosmers as they went in and out of the gate; as 'Sylvia's husband' he became friendly enough with them to ask them out to dinner and drive them around the countryside.

He had begun, as it seemed to Sylvia, to work up a little interest in her revolutionary activities; this was, of course, gratifying to her.

He still kept up appearances as a businessman by spending time, as he said, working as a sales-agent; later it was to emerge that he was keeping in contact with Political Police agents and, apparently, with his mother, who seems to have been in Mexico around then. Sylvia was never, of course, taken to meet her.

Mercader kept making slips: even the happily unaware Sylvia thought them strange. He once, rather needlessly, told her where his 'business-office' was; when she caught him out he rectified the blunder with another address. Sylvia's memory finally began working; she recalled the same thing in Paris.

At her wit's end she turned to Marguerite Rosmer, who was apparently lulled into confidence when she found out that the address was genuine – in the sense that it existed. The Rosmers thought the only thing strange about Mercader was his political uninvolvement.

Not the smallest investigation of Mercader's 'office' was ever made. Later on it emerged that it was a rendezvous of some prominent Mexican Communists; one might have thought an investigation easy.

Sylvia was in her own way rather circumspect. Since Mercader had said his passport was bogus she felt embarrassed at having him taken into the Trotsky villa; she may also have thought it hard for the Trotskys to swallow an effete member of the bourgeoisie!

She went back to New York in March; Mercader promised her explicitly never to go into Trotsky's fortress while she was away.

All this was long before he met Trotsky. Mercader was sufficiently sure of the household for an occasion to crop up when he had a plausible pretext for going into the villa: when Rosmer was ill it was Mercader, with his plush car, who naturally took him back and forth to a hospital in Mexico City and to do various errands. It aroused no suspicion that an energetic businessman was able to spare the time for this sort of thing.

Mercader was now on quite friendly terms with many of the people in the household, three months before he met Trotsky. His assignment at this time does not seem to have been the killing; he was a scout.

Meanwhile a totally different operation was also being planned by the Soviet Political Police – an armed assault on the villa.

This assault was to be conducted by David Siqueiros, a mining chief as well as a prominent Communist. He had come back from the Spanish Civil War the year before; he had commanded several units. He thought killing Trotsky a laudable assignment.

Siqueiros designed the assault on the Trotsky villa; he got hold of some survivors from his Spanish units, as well as some local miners, to carry it out.

The heightened campaign in the Stalinite press had had the effect of a covering barrage; by now the little household in Coyoacan was more or less waiting for some such move. The wires encircling the house had been electrified, machine-guns installed; there were in addition the heavy bars across the doors and the alarms; the villa, an armed fortress, was guarded by some ten local policemen inside and out. There was a twenty-four-hour sentry-patrol at the gate inside; four or five young men, sometimes American college graduates, were on the alert in their section of the house. Of course, the guards could not be expected to stay on indefinitely, and there could scarcely be any question of getting any experienced workers from the handful attached to the Trotsky organisation.

The night the armed raid on the villa took place a college-boy was on sentry duty at the entrance door. His name was Sheldon Harte; he had been at Coyoacan for some six weeks; handsome, good-natured and popular, he was rather simple-minded. Shortly after coming to Coyoacan Trotsky himself saw him hand over the key to the front gate to one of the construction men; he rebuked him for his carelessness in giving a key to some unknown person. Later on Harte was recalled as having got rather quickly on good terms with Mercader; they were frequently seen leaving the villa together.

Neither Trotsky nor Natalya, who might have been thought to be more inquisitive about human relations, was in the least bit perplexed by a relationship that was on the face of it quite odd – the attraction a plain spinster like Sylvia might have exerted on a personable playboy like Mercader, and equally, why Mercader could have found a sentimental dullard like Harte worth spending time with. Trotsky and Natalya were plainly a little reckless; one is bound to consider the possibility of their disheartenment, indeed, of downright defeatism.

At about four in the morning of 23 May 1940 Trotsky, after a hard day's work, nevertheless needed a sleeping pill, which he took after going to bed late. He was woken up by the sound of machine-gunfire, which to his dulled senses sounded for a moment like the fireworks common on Mexican holidays. The next second it was plain what it was: 'the explosions were too close, right here within the room, next to me and overhead. The odour of gunpowder became more acrid . . . we were under attack.'[44]

By the time Trotsky woke up, Natalya was already out of bed – protecting him with her body. There was a hail of bullets a second later, she forced him down on the floor, where they wedged themselves between the bed and the wall. In the dark they lay there still as mice; a sustained enfilade poured through the windows and the doors. Later an estimate of 100 shots was made, close to and on the beds. Seventy were noted in the walls and doors. They kept quite still; Natalya stirring a little, to be yanked down by him again.

All of a sudden the child, Seva, screamed out 'Grandpa!' from his room; the assailants had burst into it. Natalya wrote: 'This cry chilled us to the marrow.' There was a moment's deep silence. 'They have kidnapped him,' Trotsky murmured to her.

The explosion of an incendiary bomb in Seva's room suddenly lit up the outline of a man: 'the curve of a helmet, shining buttons, an elongated face'. This man paused for a moment between Trotsky's room and Seva's, let loose another volley at the beds, and disappeared.

Seva's room was now blazing; there was a din of gunfire in the courtyard; Natalya saw drops of blood going into the patio; Seva had vanished.

Natalya thought to herself:

Where can I hide him safely? ... I was losing my strength from the tension and the hopelessness. Any moment now they will return to finish him. ... We felt the stillness of the night, like the stillness of the grave, of death itself. ... And suddenly there came again the same voice, the voice of our grandson; but this time it came from the courtyard; it sounded quite different – it rang out like a staccato passage of music, bravely, joyously: 'Al – fred! Mar-gue-rite!' It returned us to the living!

It turned out that Seva too had concealed himself under the bed; he had thought Trotsky and Natalya had been killed and had gone out with a wounded toe to look for the Rosmers.[45]

The raid, in spite of the care that had gone into it and the many people involved, had been a fiasco.

A few minutes after the gunfire had stopped, everyone in the villa rushed out into the courtyard. Nothing had happened; no one was hurt; the guards themselves were befuddled. No one had even looked to see what had been going on with the police in the street outside. Trotsky hurried out; the sentries were trussed up, disarmed.

The story was simple: some twenty men, dressed as policemen and army soldiers, had taken the sentries completely unawares; they were overcome without a sound. The attackers, under the command

of someone dressed as an army major, went up to the gate; Harte
opened the gate immediately; the attackers swooped through the
courtyard, took the other guards unawares and forced them to
submit by threats; they installed machine-guns so as to cover
Trotsky's bedroom, and simply started shooting at Trotsky, Natalya
and Seva.

The whole thing had lasted only twenty minutes; it seemed
inconceivable that any of the Trotskys could have survived the
shooting; the attackers rushed out, having tossed some incendiary
bombs into the house itself and another bomb – a dud, as it turned
out – into the courtyard. Some of them took off in a couple of
Trotsky's cars, which had their keys in place, as they generally did,
ready for instant take-off. Harte, his arms gripped and offering no
resistance, left with them.

For a moment Trotsky's acute sensitivity to irony was inflamed –
how ridiculous! The Soviet Political Police, accustomed to manhandling millions, baffled by his climbing under a bed! Still, a
moment later misgivings justifiably manifested themselves.

For one thing the attackers seemed to know the house intimately.
Also, the role of Sheldon Harte was disturbing: could even a fool
have let in such strangers? He must have known one of them. But
why was he taken away?

The whole thing looked mysterious. In an account of the episode
given by Colonel Salazar, the head of the Mexican Secret Police, he
reports being dumbfounded by the 'surprising calm' of both Trotsky
and Natalya.

Trotsky smiled, with his eyes bright and clear behind his
tortoiseshell glasses – eyes always keen and piercing – his glance
sharp and penetrating, with a jesting, sarcastic, slightly Mephisto-
philian air. He was of medium height, strong, and carried himself
well. His mouth was large, his lips thin, the lower one slightly
prominent. His hair, his moustache and his small pointed beard
were grey, almost white. His hair seemed a little untidy, thrown
back from his forehead, with stray locks falling at the sides. . . .
His features, still young, firm, energetic, without a single crease in
the strong brow, compelled attention. . . . Natalya's face, with
delicate features, expressed great sweetness. Sadness rather than
the years had prematurely aged her. What a contrast. . . ! He,
energetic and authoritative; she, sweet, calm and almost
resigned.[46]

What Salazar was struck by, of course, was just the futility of the whole enterprise – it was so *very much* a fiasco! The suspicion was unavoidable that it was a frame-up, stage-managed by Trotsky for his own purposes.

He asked Trotsky a routine question: Did he suspect anyone?

'I most certainly do!' he replied in a very decided tone of voice. 'Come . . .'

He put his right arm on my shoulder and slowly led me towards the rabbit hutches . . . He stopped, glanced all round him to make sure that we were alone, and, placing his right hand near his mouth, as though wishing to make the confidence more secret, he said in a low voice with deep conviction:

'The author of the attack is Joseph Stalin.'[47]

Salazar, without rancour, thought he was being bamboozled: Trotsky's and Natalya's calm seemed to him ridiculously unnatural. After he counted seventy-three bullet holes over Trotsky's bed the idea of such a 'miraculous escape' looked quite fishy; Trotsky's sardonic remarks also struck him as suspicious. Moreover, the extravagance of the raid itself, if one were to take Trotsky's explanation seriously, seemed to go beyond even the effrontery of the Stalinites, who were, moreover, backers of President Cardenas.

There could, in fact, be no question about its being an inside job, in the jargon of the crime-thriller; but Salazar could not be expected to know this. Neither could Trotsky – the 'insider', Mercader, was not even suspected.

Harte had certainly been up to something, despite Trotsky's vigorous, though apparently groundless assurances of his innocence. Trotsky was to remain convinced, a little strangely, perhaps, of Harte's innocence to the end. On 25 June, a little more than a month after the raid, Harte's corpse was discovered in the soil of a farm just outside the capital: the house on the farm had been rented by two Stalinite painters. To Salazar's astonishment Trotsky wept at the sight of Harte's corpse.

From then on the atmosphere in the armed villa was somewhat oppressive. Trotsky had a little joke: every morning he would say to Natalya: 'You see, they did not kill us last night, after all; and you're *still* dissatisfied!'[48]

His activities remained the same: he still showed the same energy, writing, discussing the same range of social and political questions; he played the same energetic role in helping out the police inquiry.

It was suggested to him that he go underground altogether: hide, change his name and appearance and vanish somewhere in the United States. He turned a deaf ear to such suggestions; the only concession he made was to strengthen the Coyoacan fortifications. These were now, in fact, substantially improved: higher walls, some other watchtowers, armouring on the doors and steel shutters on the windows.

He found these improvements repugnant. He seems to have assented to them only under pressure, to do his aides and friends a favour.

He was given a bullet-proof vest; he found it annoying, and recommended it to a sentry, Nor would he have his guests searched for arms when they came to see him in his study; he was manifestly irritated when his bodyguards hovered about while he was talking to people.

The strengthening of the fortifications and the merely statistical, so to speak, improvements in Trotsky's protection after the abortive raid in May are, of course, a classic instance of locking the stable after the horse has gone. Why, after such precautions were taken, should the Political Police use the same cumbersome methods all over again?

Nor did they. They resorted to the opposite technique, that of the Trojan Horse. They might have been keeping it in reserve.

The Trojan Horse was 'Jacson', the import-export man.

A few days after the abortive raid Mercader saw Trotsky for the first time. Very generous with his services as usual, he had proposed driving the Rosmers to Vera Cruz, from where they were finally, after an almost eight-month visit, going back to France.

Mercader turned up early to pick the Rosmers up; he was told to wait for them in the courtyard.

Trotsky was feeding the rabbits as usual; as Mercader came into the courtyard he shook hands with him while carrying on with the rabbits. Urbanely, Mercader did not linger; he went into the house directly to give Seva a toy glider; Natalya then invited him to sit down with them all, the Rosmers, Trotsky and herself at the table.

That was the first time. Mercader took the Rosmers to their ship; he did not go back to the fortress for another fortnight. This time he stopped just long enough to say goodbye on his way to New York; he lent his car to Trotsky's guards.

Mercader came back to Mexico in July, but did not show himself at the villa for a few weeks. Trotsky invited him and Sylvia to tea on 29 July. They stayed chatting for more than an hour.

This was the only real contact, such as it was, between Mercader and Trotsky. In fact, during the three months following the May fiasco, according to the guards' carefully kept records, he went through the gate of the fortress ten times. He actually saw Trotsky only a few times.

His impersonation, remarkably defective, aroused no suspicion. With Sylvia he had passed himself off as redoubtably apathetic on political questions, yet when chattering with the guards he would drop names, referring to eminent sympathisers from various countries in such a way as to imply intimacy with the movement. He would also speak freely about giving the Party money. He had already given money to some French 'Bolshevik-Leninist' periodicals.[49]

It has, in fact, been plausibly suggested that Trotsky's poverty – both personal and organisation – was taken advantage of by Mercader. The trap Trotsky fell into, in short, had been baited with money.

The sums mentioned by Mercader were carefully calculated: his casual gift of three thousand dollars to Sylvia was attuned to the psychology of the household – not too much, not too little. The information that Mercader's 'boss' had sixty million dollars was also well contrived: Mercader was not *too* rich himself – else he might have been expected to contribute more – but could hold out the promise of cash.[50]

In speaking with Natalya and with Trotsky the few times he saw him, Mercader, shuffling shyly from one foot to the other, successfully impersonated an outsider on the verge of being taken inside. His reasons for entering the fortress were always genteel – he would be bringing gifts to Natalya on behalf of his 'wife', Sylvia.

What was, perhaps, most curious of all, granted the Trotskys' strange imperviousness to Mercader's aura, was that he also took part in what one might have thought the somewhat rarefied discussion at the table. At this time, during the summer of 1940, the burning issue within the coterie was the great 'split' – the defection of James Burnham and Max Shachtman. Sylvia herself was, of course, up to her ears in coterie politics.

It was possible for Mercader, despite his role of businessman, to take part in the hot debating around the table and come out for – Trotsky! He took pains not to overplay this, to be sure; he was performing a highly sophisticated function – showing his 'wife' the light.

No one noticed anything out of the way. During the two decades he was to spend in gaol he was to maintain his anonymity quite successfully; until the moment of action, however, his play-acting was strikingly mediocre.

His composure began to be eroded as the crucial moment drew near.

On his return from New York his whole manner was different; this was recalled, of course, only later. Beforehand he had seemed to be rather merry; now he was jumpy, with a curiously unwholesome complexion. He was in bed most of the time, quite withdrawn, not speaking to anyone, including Sylvia. His moodiness would alternate with bursts of febrile gaiety: he bragged about his mountaineering and his muscular prowess; he would make a point of showing off his dexterity in dismembering a chicken; he would boast of his business connections, his employer's acumen, talk about making money on the Stock Exchange for the Fourth International.

Once, while looking at the fortifications being added to the villa, together with Trotsky and the chief body-guard, Joseph Hansen, Mercader made a sensible remark: he said there was no reason to think the Soviet Political Police would try the same operation again. Trotsky and Hansen asked for no details.

At the time no one noticed these points; they were put down to Mercader's cranky nature.

In short, perfect insensitivity reigned. It was remarked to Trotsky with some annoyance, for instance, that Mercader had failed to visit the little Party's headquarters in New York, though he was not supposed to be, really, a 'Trotskyite' at all. Trotsky defended him as a potential recruit, anyhow, yet was irritated by Mercader's boastful chatter about the Stock Exchange and his 'boss's' flair for finance.

Trotsky's annoyance took a curiously ethical turn: 'Who is this very rich "boss"?' he said to Natalya: 'One should find out. It may, after all, be some profiteer of the Fascist type – it might be better for us not to receive Sylvia's husband any more.'[51]

Since to a Marxist all capitalists were profiteers the remark sounds odd: why should Mercader's boss have to be a 'Fascist' to make money on the Stock Exchange? And if there was something eerie about Mercader, why did it have to have something to do with business?

Since Mercader was by now on a friendly footing in the trustful household he could not, of course, be insulted by questioning.

By now Mercader had worked out a plan for being closeted with Trotsky. It was a simple one – he would show him an article! On 17 August he came to the villa saying he had written something about the 'split' in the American party: would Trotsky help him? Look at it, make some changes. . . .

Though the weather was warm, Mercader had a hat on, and was clutching an overcoat in his arms. He and Trotsky walked into the study; as Trotsky looked over the draft of his 'article' Mercader sat down on the table, well above Trotsky's head, without budging and without taking his hat off.

Ten minutes later Trotsky came out of the study; he was very upset. He told Natalya he was through with Mercader: something had finally aroused his suspicions, apparently both Mercader's curious manner – Trotsky interpreted it as discourtesy – and, rather suddenly, the realisation that he did not behave at all like a Frenchman, or even a Belgian raised in France.

Natalya was startled: this was a novelty to her. Since she knew Mercader much better, indeed, had had tea with him often enough, she was disconcerted. Mercader's nationality had also passed muster!

Even now no one paid much attention: a couple of days later Trotsky told Hansen the same thing. Trotsky's intuition had finally stirred; it was too late.

At the 'literary consultation' on 17 August Mercader had been armed to the teeth, with an ice-axe, a dagger and a pistol. That accounted for his heavy clothing in such hot weather.

Mercader had set the stage for a dry-run: by establishing the positions of the two principals he had arranged the basic elements of the simple act he was now to perform.

The day came.

Three days after that strange interview in Trotsky's study, and a day after Trotsky had conveyed his misgivings about Mercader to Hansen, Mercader had another closed session with Trotsky.

On 20 August Trotsky got up feeling splendid. The weather was fine; after taking his usual pill he had slept very well. He couldn't wait to get down to a good day's work. He made his ritual joke with Natalya: 'You see, they didn't kill us again last night,' and said the sleeping-pill had done him a world of good. Like other wives,

Natalya pointed out the true state of affairs: 'It isn't the drug that does you good, but sound sleep and complete rest.'

Trotsky quickly put on his clothes and 'vigorously walked out into the patio to feed his rabbits': he spent two hours with them.

At breakfast he was still optimistic and energetic; he was looking forward to resuming work on his 'poor book, *Stalin*'; he had shelved it a few months before, after the near-fatal assault on the fortress in May; his time had been taken up with the police investigation. This was all over now: his real work had to be returned to – his main book and a big article.

In his study he learned to his satisfaction that the archives whose disposition had been troubling him were now to be accepted by Harvard University; he answered a few letters, and settled down to dictate his final article on a recorder.

The article was never finished. It remains a shapeless mass of notes about a problem – the contemporary significance of the classical slogan: 'revolutionary defeatism'. During the First World War that had been good for the Bolsheviks, but now? With the Nazis overrunning Europe? Trotsky was modifying the Bolshevik 'position' of more than twenty-five years: he and his little party were supporting the seventy per cent of the American workers who in a public-opinion poll had come out for a draft.

Throughout the day Trotsky's routine was normal; he had a siesta and was soon at work again. He stood in the patio for a moment; Natalya brought him his white cap, against the sun. A moment later he was back in his study. Natalya looked in on him as usual, 'so as not to disturb him': he was 'in his usual position, bent over his desk, pen in hand.'

In the late afternoon, he fed the rabbits again; looking down at him from the balcony, Natalya saw 'an unfamiliar figure' close to him; a moment later, as the figure drew nearer, she suddenly recognised Mercader, looking very peculiar. She went down; Mercader asked her for a glass of water; she suggested tea, but he declined in an oddly tense manner: 'No, no, I dined too late and still feel the meal there' – pointing to his throat – 'it's choking me.'

He kept hugging his overcoat to his body. He had a 'grey-green', nervous look; Natalya recalled that it had been one of his boasts never to wear a coat or hat even in bad weather.

'Why are you wearing a hat and carrying a raincoat in the sun?' she asked. 'It might rain,' he said.

'Put out', Natalya didn't express her own thought – it was surely *not* going to rain.

'How is Sylvia?' Natalya asked. The question seemed to confuse Mercader: he looked distrait. Natalya then asked about his article: hanging on to his coat, he indicated some typewritten pages he was carrying in one hand.

Natalya walked over to the rabbit-hutches together with him. Polite as always, Trotsky suggested to her in Russian that it might be suitable to invite Mercader and Sylvia to a meal: they were going back to New York the following day. Natalya said Mercader was feeling ill; he had just turned down tea. Trotsky turned to him: 'Your health is poor again, you look ill. That's no good.' They stood for a moment.

'Trotsky was reluctant to leave his rabbits and had no interest at all in the "article". Controlling himself, he said: "Well, what d'you say, shall we go over your article?" Unhurriedly, he fastened the hutches and took off his work-gloves. . . . He brushed his blue jacket and slowly, silently, walked with me and "Jacson" toward the house. I accompanied them to the door of the study; the door closed.'

A few moments later Natalya heard a 'terrible, heart-breaking cry': for a second she didn't realise whom it came from. She rushed out to find Trotsky 'standing in the doorway, between the dining-room and the balcony, leaning against the door-frame. His face was covered with blood, through which his blue eyes, without his glasses, were shining clearly; his arms were hanging limply at his side.'

Alone with Trotsky, Mercader had taken his ice-axe out from under his overcoat. As he said later: 'Closing my eyes, I brought it down on his head with all my strength.' It smashed through Trotsky's brain.

Mercader had expected to kill Trotsky on the spot; he could have made his escape unmolested, but Trotsky had leaped to his feet, flinging everything he could lay his hands on at Mercader, including the recording-machine, then had hurled himself at him bodily.

Before Natalya and the guards, stunned by his 'terrible, heart-breaking cry', could recover and rush to the study, Trotsky had struggled like a madman. Grappling with his assassin at close quarters, he bit his hand and yanked the ice-axe out of his grip. Mercader had been stunned; he had used neither his pistol nor his dagger.

'What's happened,' I [Natalya] asked, 'what's happened?' I put my arms around him. . . he did not answer at once. For a second I wondered whether something had not fallen on him from the ceiling – repairs were being made in the study – *and why was he standing here?* Calmly, without anger, bitterness, or sorrow, he said: 'Jacson.' It was as though he had wished to say: 'Now it has happened.' We took a few steps, and slowly, aided by me, he slumped down on to the floor.

'Natasha, I love you.'

He pronounced these words in such an unexpected manner, so grave, almost severe, that I found myself suddenly bereft of all force. I leaned over him. . . .

'You know, in there' – he turned his eyes toward the door of the study – 'I felt I understood what he wanted to do . . . he wanted to . . . again . . . but I did not let him.'

In that 'I did not let him' I sensed a kind of satisfaction.

'He . . . must not . . . be killed . . . he must . . . talk,' he said slowly, spacing the words.

When [the guards] were manhandling him, the assassin had cried out: 'They made me do it . . . they're holding my mother . . . they've put my mother in gaol.'[52]

In English, Trotsky said to Hansen: ' "This is the end: take care of Natalya, she has been with me many years." The Old Man pressed our hands convulsively, tears suddenly in his eyes. Natalya cried brokenly, bending over him, kissing his wound.'

While he was being put on a stretcher later, he whispered to Hansen again: 'I want everything I own to go to Natalya . . . you will take care of her.' In the hospital he asked Hansen in a mutter whether he had his notebook: Hansen took down some broken phrases:

I am close to death from the blow of a political assassin . . . struck me down in my room. I struggled with him . . . we . . . entered . . . talk about French statistics . . . he struck me . . . please say to your friends . . . I am sure . . . of victory . . . of Fourth International . . . go forward.[53]

Trotsky's last words to Natalya, as the nurses began undressing him, were: 'I do not want them to undress me . . . I want you to undress me.'

After Natalya finished undressing him she leaned over to kiss him:

'He returned the kiss. Again. And again he responded. And once again. That was our final farewell.'[54]

Trotsky lost consciousness that evening; twenty-four hours later, after an operation carried out by five surgeons, he died. He was sixty years old.

His brain had been massively damaged: the autopsy showed it weighed two pounds thirteen ounces.

'His heart, too, was very large.'[55]

BIBLIOGRAPHY

Mark Aldanov, *Novy Zhurnal* (New York, 1942), (Ubiistvo Trotskogo, pp. 338–66).

B. Bajanov, *Avec Staline dans le Kremlin* (Paris, 1930).

Angelica Balabanoff, *My Life as a Rebel* (London, 1938).

Winifred Baumgart, *Deutsche Ostpolitik 1918* (Vienna and Munich, 1966).

Alexander Berkman, *Der Aufstand von Kronstadt*, reprint *Der Monat* (n.d.).

Theobald von Bethmann-Hollweg, *Betrachtungen zum Weltkrieg*, 2 vols. (Berlin, 1919–20).

Karl Bernhard, Freiherr von Bothmer, *Mit Graf Mirbach in Moskau* (Tübingen, 1922).

R. P. Browder and A. F. Kerensky, (Eds.) *The Provisional Government 1917*, 3 vols. (Stanford, 1962).

Louise Byrant, *Six Red Months in Russia* (London, 1919).

Sir George Buchanan, *My Mission to Russia* (London, 1923).

J. Bunyan, and H. H. Fisher, *The Bolshevik Revolution 1917–1918* (Stanford, 1934).

Joel Carmichael, *Stalin's Masterpiece* (London and New York, 1974).

W. H. Chamberlin, *The Russian Revolution*, 2 vols. (New York, 1960).

Victor Chernov, *The Great Russian Revolution* (New Haven, 1936).

Winston Churchill, *Great Contemporaries* (London, 1939).

The Second World War, Vol. IV (London, 1951).

A. Ciliga, *Au Pays du Grand Mensonge* (Paris, 1937).

Robert Conquest, *The Great Terror* (New York and London, 1968).

Count Ottokar Czernin, *Im Weltkriege* (Berlin, 1918);

In the World War (London and New York, 1919).

Theodor Dan, *Proiskhozhdeniye Bol'shevizma* (New York, 1946); translated as *The Origins of Bolshevism* by J. Carmichael (New York and London, 1965).

General A. I. Denikin, *Ucherki Russkoy Smuty,* Vols. I–IV (Paris and Berlin, 1921–6).

Isaac Deutscher, *The Prophet Armed,* Vol. I (London and New York, 1954).

The Prophet Unarmed, Vol. II (London and New York, 1959).

The Prophet Outcast, Vol. III (London and New York, 1963).

John Dewey, 'Means and Ends', *New International* (New York, 1938).

Max Eastman, *Since Lenin Died* (London, 1925).

Leon Trotsky : Portrait of a Youth (New York, 1925).

The End of Socialism in Russia (London, 1937).

Great Companions (London, 1959).

Heroes I have Known (New York, 1942).

Michael T. Florinsky, *Russia: A History and an Interpretation,* 2 vols. (New York, 1947, or 1953).

O. H. Gankin and H. H. Fisher, *The Bolsheviks and the World War* (London, 1940).

Julian Gorkin, *Como Asesinó Stalin a Trotsky* (Barcelona, 1961).

Maxim Gorky, *Lénine et le Paysan russe* (Paris, 1924).

H. Grebing. *Politische Studien* (Munich, 1957), pp. 221–34 ('So macht man Revolution').

Leonhard Haas, *Carl Vital Moor* (Zurich, 1970).

W. Hahlweg, (Ed.), *Lenins Rückkehr nach Russland 1917* (Leyden, 1957).

Karl Helfferich, *Der Weltkrieg* (Berlin, 1919).

Gustav Hilger, *The Incompatible Allies* (New York, 1953).

General Max Hoffmann, *Aufzeichnungen,* 2 vols. (Berlin, 1929).

Michael Karolyi, *Memoirs* (London, 1956).

George Katkov, *Russia 1917: the February Revolution* (New York, 1967).

International Affairs, Vol. XXXII (April, 1956), pp. 181–9 ('German Foreign Office Documents on Financial Support to the Bolsheviks in 1917').

St. Antony's Papers, No. XII (Soviet Affairs No. 3) (London, 1962).

Karl Kautsky, *Sozialisten und Krieg* (Prague, 1937).

A. F. Kerensky, *Izdaleka (Sbornik Statei)* (Paris, 1922).

The Catastrophe (New York, 1928).

Count Harry Kessler, *Diaries of a Cosmopolitan* (London and New York, 1971).

N. Krushchev, 'Secret Speech' to the Twentieth Congress of the Soviet Communist Party (in the *Manchester Guardian* Edition 1956: 'The Dethronement of Stalin').

Major General Sir Alfred Knox, *With the Russian Army 1914–1917* (London, 1921).

N. K. Krupskaya, *Memories of Lenin* (London, 1942).

Richard von Kühlmann, *Erinnerungen* (Heidelberg, 1948).

V. I. Lenin, *Sochineniya*, Vols. I–XXXV, 4th ed. (Moscow, 1941–50). *Leninskii Sbornik*, Vols. IV–XX (Moscow 1925–32).

Isaac Don Levine, *The Mind of an Assassin* (New York, 1959). *Eye-Witness to History* (New York, 1973).

Bruce Lockhart, *Memoirs of a British Agent* (New York and London, 1933).

Erich Ludendorff, *Meine Kriegserinnerungen, 1914–1918* (Berlin, 1919).

Anatoli Lunacharsky, *Revolyutsionnye Siluety* (Moscow, 1923).

Eugene Lyons, *The Red Decade* (New York, 1941, 1970).

Dwight Macdonald, *Memoirs of a Revolutionist* (New York, 1958).

Vladimir Medem, *Fun mein Leben*, 2 vols. (Yiddish) (New York, 1923). *Zum Zwanzigsten Johrzeit* (New York, 1943).

S. P. Mel'gunov, *Zolotoy Nemetskii Klyuch' Bol'shevikov* (Paris, 1940).

P. N. Miliukov, *Istoriya Vtoroy Russkoy Revolyutsii* (Sofia, 1921).

A. Morizet, *Chez Lénine et Trotsky* (Paris, 1922).

Rudolf Nadolny, *Mein Beitrag* (Wiesbaden, 1955).

Pierre Navile, *Trotsky Vivant* (Paris, 1962).

Joseph Nedava, *Trotsky and the Jews* (New York, 1972).

B. I. Nicolaevsky, *Power and the Soviet Elite* (New York, 1965).

Alexander Orlov, *The Secret History of Stalin's Crimes* (London, 1953).

George Orwell, *1984* (New York, 1963).

Perepiska Sekretariata, Central Committee, Moscow.

M. Price Philips, *My Reminiscences of the Russian Revolution* (London, 1921).

Parvus (A. I. Helphand), *Rossiya i Revolutsiya* (St. Petersburg, 1906).

Robert Payne, *The Life and Death of Lenin* (New York, 1964).

Stephen T. Possony, *Lenin: The Compulsive Revolutionary* (New York, 1964).

Pyat' Let Vlasti Sovietov, Central Executive Committee (Moscow, 1922).

John Reed, *Ten Days That Shook the World* (London, 1934).

Kurt Riezler, *Tagebücher, Aufsätze, Dokumente* (Göttingen, 1972).

A. Rosmer, *Moscou sous Lénine* (Paris, 1953).

Russian Jewry 1917–1960 (G. Aronson and J. Frumkin, Eds.), (New York, 1967).

Jacques Sadoul, *Notes sur le Révolution bolchévik* (Paris, 1919).

L. A. S. Salazar, *Murder in Mexico* (London, 1950).

Leonard Schapiro, *The History of the Communist Party of the Soviet Union,* 2nd ed. (New York and London, 1970).

Paul Scheffer, *Sieben Jahre Soviet-Union* (Leipzig, 1930).

Philip Scheideman, *Memoiren eines Sozial-Demokraten,* 2 vols. (Dresden, 1928).

David Shub, *Lenin* (Pelican edition) (London, 1966).

Politicheskiye Deyateli Rossii (New York, 1969).

Novy Zhurnal (June, 1959) ('Lenin i Vil'gelm II: Novoye o germano-bol'shevistskom zagovore 1917').

Victor Serge, *Vie et Mort de Trotsky* (Paris, 1951) (Natalya Sedova part author).

Mémoires d'un Révolutionnaire (Paris, 1951).

Le Tournant obscur (Paris, 1951).

G. A. Solomon, *Sredi krasnykh vozhdei* (Paris, 1930).

Alexander Solzhenitsyn, *The GULAG Archipelago* (New York, 1974).

J. Stalin, *Sochineniya,* Vols. I–XIII, (Moscow, 1946–51).

I. N. Steinberg, *Als ich Volkskommissar war* (Munich, 1929).

Gewalt und Terror in der Revolution (Berlin, 1931).

In the Workshop of the Revolution (New York, 1953).

N. N. Sukhanov, *Zapiski o Revolyutsii,* 7 vols. (Berlin, 1922–3); translated, abridged and edited as *The Russian Revolution 1917* by J. Carmichael (London and New York, 1955).

L. D. Trotsky, *Nashi Politicheskiye Zadachi* (Geneva, 1904).

Istoriya Revolyutsii 1905–6 (St. Petersburg, 1917).

Our Revolution (New York, 1918).

Itogi i Perspektivy (Moscow, 1919).

Terrorizm i Kommunizm (Leningrad, 1920).

Between Red and White (London, 1922).

Die Russische Revolution 1905 (Berlin, 1923).

Kak Vooruzhalas' Revolyutsiya, Vols. I–III (Moscow, 1923–5).

Sochineniya (several volumes published in Moscow, 1923–7).

Literatura i Revolyutsiya (Moscow, 1923).

Voprosy Byta (Moscow, 1923).

Problems of Life (London, 1924).

Pyat' Let Kominterna (Moscow, 1924).

Lenin (Paris, 1924).

Pokoleniye Oktyabrya (Moscow, 1924).

Where is Britain Going? (London, 1926).

Moya Zhizn, Vols. I–II (Berlin, 1930).

Permanentnaya Revolyutsiya (Berlin, 1930).

History of the Russian Revolution, Vols I–III (London, 1932–3).

Vie de Lénine, jeunesse (Paris, 1936).

The Third International After Lenin (New York, 1936), the American edition of the Critique of the programme of the Third International, written in 1928.

The Stalin School of Falsification (New York, 1937).

Stalins Verbrechen (Zurich, 1937).

The Case of Leon Trotsky (London, 1937).

The Revolution Betrayed (London, 1937).

Not Guilty! Report of the Dewey Commission (London, 1938).

Their Morals and Ours (New York, 1939).

Stalin (New York, 1946).

Literature and Revolution (New York, 1957).

Diary in Exile (London, 1958).

The Real Situation in Russia (the English version of the Platform of the 'Joint Opposition', co-authored by Trotsky and Zinoviev).

The Case of Leon Trotsky (The Dewey Commission) (New York, 1938).

I. G. Tsereteli, *Vospominaniya o Fevral'skoy Revolyutsii*, 2 vols., (Paris and The Hague, 1963).

G. Urutadze, *Vospominaniya Gruzinskogo Sotsial-Demokrata* (Stanford, California, 1968).

Vera Vladimirova, *Revolyutsiya 1917 Goda (Khronika Sobytii)* (Moscow and Leningrad, 1923–4).

N. V. (Valentinov) Volsky, *Vstrechi s Leninym* (New York, 1953).

John W. Wheeler-Bennett, *Brest–Litovsk, The Forgotten Peace* (London, 1938).

Bertram Wolfe, *Three Who Made a Revolution* (New York, 1948).

Khrushchev and Stalin's Ghost (New York, 1957).

A. Yarmolinsky, *The Jews and Other Minor Nationalities in the Soviet Union* (New York, 1928).

Z. A. B. Zeman, (Ed.) *Germany and the Revolution in Russia 1915–1918* (London, 1958).

Z. A. B. Zeman and W. B. Scharlau, *The Merchant of Revolution: The Life of Alexander Israel Helphand (Parvus)* (London and New York, 1965).

G. A. Ziv, *Trotskii, Kharakteristika po lichnym Vospominaniyam* (New York, 1921).

Periodicals:

Bolshevik, Bulletin Oppozitsii, Izvestiya, Pravda, Sotsialisticheskii Vestnik, Kommunisticheskii Internatsional.

Internationale Presse-Korrespondez, Unser Wort, Permanente Revolution.

Militant, New International, Fourth International, Partisan Review, The Reflex (New York).

The Moscow 'Show Trials' :

Stenographic Report of the Trotskyite-Zinovievite Terrorist Centre (Moscow, 1936).

Stenographic Report of the Anti-Soviet Trotskyite Centre (Moscow, 1937).

Stenographic Report of the Anti-Soviet Bloc of Trotskyites and Rights (Moscow, 1938).

KPSS v Rezolyutsiyakh, Vols. I–II, (Moscow, 1953).

CONGRESSES :

2 Syezd RSDRP, Moscow 1932
5 Syezd RSDRP, Moscow 1933
6 Syezd RSDRP, Moscow 1934
7 Syezd RKP (b) Moscow 1923
8 Syezd RKP (b) Moscow 1933
9 Syezd RKP (b) Moscow 1934
10 Syezd RKP (b) Moscow 1921
13 Syezd RKP (b) Moscow 1924

NOTES

Books referred to are listed in the Bibliography. Translations are the author's unless otherwise noted.

Chapter I: The Nursery

1 Trotsksy, *Moya Zhizin'* (My Life), Vol. 1, pp. 106-7. Henceforth *Life,* referring to the Russian edition (Berlin 1930) unless otherwise noted.
2 Ziv, p. 41
3 *Life,* Vol. I, p. 36.
4 Ibid., pp. 59-60.
5 Ibid.
6 Ziv.
7 *Life,* Vol. I, ch. 4, p. 86.
8 Ibid., Preface, pp. 14-15.
9 Ibid., Vol. 1, p. 60.
10 Ibid., Vol. I, pp. 100-1.
11 Ibid., Vol. I, pp. 104-5
12 Ibid., Vol. I, pp. 105-6.
13 Ibid., Vol. I, p. 108.
14 Ibid., Vol. I, p. 80.
15 Ibid., Vol. I, p. 83.
16 Ibid.
17 Ibid., Vol. I, p. 79.
18 Ibid., Vol. I, p. 67.
19 Ibid., Vol. I, p. 94.
20 Ibid., Vol. I, pp. 94-5.
21 Ibid., p. 109.
22 Ibid., p. 110.
23 Ibid.
24 Ibid., pp. 110-11.
25 Ibid., pp. 111-12.
26 Ibid.
27 Ibid., p. 99.
28 Ziv, p. 10.

Chapter II: The World

1 *Life,* Vol. I, p. 117.
2 Ibid., p. 120.
3 Ibid., p. 126

4 Ibid., p. 120.
5 Ibid., p. 121.
6 Ziv, p. 7.
7 *Life,* Vol. I, pp. 118-19.
8 Ibid., p. 121.
9 Ibid., p. 122.
10 Ibid.
11 Ibid., p. 123.
12 Ziv, p. 16.
13 *Life,* Vol. I, p. 124.
14 Ibid., p. 125.
15 Ziv, p. 8.
16 Ibid., pp. 9-10.
17 Eastman, *Trotsky, Portrait* . . . p. 68.
18 Ziv, p. 35.
19 *Life,* Vol. I, pp. 121-2.
20 Ziv, p. 15.
21 Ibid.
22 Ibid., p. 10.
23 *Life,* Vol. I, p. 128.
24 Ibid., pp. 128-9.
25 Ziv, p. 19.
26 Ibid., pp. 18-20.
27 Ibid.
28 *Life,* Vol. I, p. 130.
29 Ziv, p. 21.
30 Eastman, op cit., p. 70.
31 *Life,* Vol. I, pp. 130-1.
32 Ziv, p. 21.
33 *Life,* Vol. 1, p. 127.
34 Ibid, pp. 141-2.
35 Ibid.
36 Ibid.
37 Quoted in Wolfe, p. 208.
38 Ziv, p. 54.
39 Serge, *Vie* . . . , p. 43.
40 Ziv, p. 33.
41 *Life,* Vol. II, p. 146.
42 Ziv, p. 35.
43 Ibid., p. 38.
44 Ibid., p. 39.
45 Ibid., pp. 36-7.
46 *Life,* Vol. I, p. 148.
47 Ziv, p. 40.
48 *Life,* Vol. I, pp. 148-9.
49 Ziv, p. 41.
50 *Life,* Vol. I, p. 151.
51 Ibid.
52 Ibid., p. 154.
53 Ibid., p. 156.
54 Ibid, pp. 157-8.
55 Ziv, pp. 25-6, 46.
56 *Life,* Vol. I, p. 160.

Chapter III: The Stage.

1 Serge, *Vie* . . . , p. 40.
2 Medem, *Fun mein Leben,*Vol. II, pp. 7-8.
3 *Life,* Vol. I, ch. 11, p. 166.
4 Serge, *Vie* . . . , p. 40.
5 Ibid.
6 *Life,* Vol. I, p. 172.
7 Ibid., p. 176.
8 Nedava, pp. 50-1.
9 Lenin, Sochineniya 4th ed., Vol. 34, p. 114.
10 Wolfe, *Three* . . . , p. 239.
11 Ibid., p. 235.
12 Ibid., p. 240.
13 Ibid.
14 Ibid., pp. 235-6, from the summary of minutes, generally approved by speakers.
15 Krupskaya, *Memories of Lenin,* p. 99 (Verney's translation from second Russian edition).
16 Quoted in Deutscher, Vol. I, p. 45.
17 Nedava, pp. 54-7.
18 Trotsky, *Sochineniya,* Vol. II, Book I, pp. 42-8; Nedava, pp. 54-7.
19 Nedava, pp. 195-6.
20 *The Spark,* No. 56, January 1st, 1904.
21 Trotsky, *Nashi Politicheskiye Zadachi, p.* 54; Deutscher, Vol I, p. 90.
22 Ibid., p. 75; Deutscher, ibid.
23 Ibid., p. 95; Deutscher, ibid., p. 92.
24 *Life,* Vol. I, p. 194.
25 Ibid.
26 Beginning in No. 59, February 10th, 1904.
27 *The Spark,* No. 80, January 1st, 1905.
28 Quoted in Wolfe, p. 293.
29 Serge, *Vie* . . . , p. 43.
30 Trotsky, *Sochineniya,* Vol. II, Book I, p. 51.
31 *Life,* Vol. I, ch. 13, p. 192.
32 Deutscher, Vol. I pp. 112-13.
33 Lenin, *Sochineniya,* Vol. 8, pp. 262-3.
34 Nedava, pp. 60-1.
35 *Life,* Vol. I, p. 200.
36 Ziv, p. 50.
37 Lunacharsky, p. 20.
38 Serge, *Vie* . . . , p. 50.
39 *Life,* Vol. I, p. 206
40 *Izvestiya,* No. 7, November 7th, 1905: Trotsky, *Sochineniya, Vol II,* Book 1, pp. 290-3.
41 Deutscher, Vol. I, p. 142.
42 Ibid.

Chapter IV: The Free-Lance.

1 Lunacharsky, pp. 20-1.
2 Leading St. Petersburg daily newspapers: *Novoye Vremya, Rech', Strana, Oko, Birzhevye Vedomosti.*
3 Ziv, p. 53.

4 Volsky, p. 92.
5 *Life*, Vol. I, pp. 216-17.
6 Ibid., p. 227.
7 Ziv, p. 56.
8 Morizet, p. 101.
9 *Life*, Vol. I, pp. 233-4.
10 Ibid., p. 263.
11 Ibid., pp. 264-5.
12 Ibid., pp. 252.
13 Ibid., pp. 278-9.
14 Nedava, pp. 73ff.: *Die Neue Zeit*, November, 1913.
15 *Life*, Vol. I, pp. 243-4.
16 Ibid, pp. 236-9.
17 Ibid.
18 Ibid.
19 Ibid.
20 In a letter, curiously enough, to the publishers, Simon and Schuster: Deustcher, Vol. III, p. 269.
21 *Life*, Vol. I, pp. 239-40.
22 Deutscher, Vol. 1, p. 192, quoting *Bol'sheviki, Dokumenty Okhrannogo Otdeleniya*, Vol. 1, p. 42.
23 *Pravda*, No. 21, 1910, in Deutscher, ibid., p. 197.
24 Lunacharsky, p. 23.
25 *Life*, Vol. 1, p. 251.
26 A memoir in *The Archives*, September 22nd, 1939: quoted in Deutscher, Vol. I, p. 209.
27 Stalin, Sochineniya, Vol., VII, pp. 271-84: quoted in Deutscher, Vol, p. 210. p. 210.
28 Serge, *Vie . . .*, p. 57.
29 *Life*, Vol. I, p. 276.
30 Zeman and Scharlau, p. 128.
31 Zeman, Document #1 et seq.
32 Ibid., Appendix I.
33 Zeman and Scharlau, pp. 125-224.
34 "An Obituary on a Living Friend", *Our Word*, #15, February 14th 1915 (quoted in Deutscher, Vol. I, p. 220).
35 Ziv, pp. 62-3, 76-7.
36 Zeman and Scharlau, p. 155; Shub, *Novy Zhurnal* June, 1959, pp. 226-7.
37 Zeman, p. 86; also, Transcript of the 'Case against the Anti-Soviet Bloc of Rights and Trotskyites, Moscow 1938, pp. 300-1.
38 E.g., Lunacharsky, Pokrovsky, Ryazanov, Lozovsky, Manuilsky, Pavlovich, Antonov-Ovseyenko, and Rakovsky himself.
39 Kautsky, also, Shub, *Politicheskiye . . .*, ch. V.
40 Balabanoff, pp. 175-6.
41 *Life, Vol.* I, p. 298.
42 Serge, *Vie . . .*, pp. 60-1.
43 *Life*, Vol. I, p. 309.
44 Ibid.
45 Ziv, pp. 72-6.
46 Ibid, pp. 80-1.
47 Ibid.
48 *Life*, Vol. I, p. 313.
49 Balabanoff, pp. 176-7.

Chapter V: The Star.

1 Sukhanov, p. 340.
2 Ibid., pp. 272-4.
3 Ibid., pp. 277-89.
4 Ibid.
5 Ibid.
6 Ibid.
7 Ibid., pp. 290-1.
8 Lunacharsky, pp. 24-5.
9 *Life,* Vol. II, p. 56.
10 Serge, *Vie . . .* , p. 92.
11 Lunacharsky, p. 24.
12 Sukhanov, pp. 430-1.
13 Ibid., pp. 446-7.
14 *Rech'* and others, July 19-20th, 1917.
15 Tsereteli, Vol. II, pp. 332-41.
16 Ibid.
17 Zeman and Scharlau, p. 231; Zeman, Document #94.
18 N.K. Krupskaya, *Vospominaniya o Lenine* (Moscow, 1957), pp. 273-6.
19 Kühlman, Ludendorff, Bethmann-Hollweg.
20 Sukhanov, p. 472.
21 Trotsky, *History . . .* , (Russ.) Vol. II, p. 116, (Eng.) p. 95.
22 Sukhanov, pp. 471-2.
23 Trotsky, *History . . .* , Vol. II, ch. IV; *Life,* ch. 26.
24 Zeman and Scharlau, p. 231; *Vorwärts,* Zentralorgan der Sozial-Demokratischen Partei Deutschlands: 'Ein dunkles Kapitel' January 14th 1921), 'Meisterstück und Meisterschuld' (January 20th, 1921).

Helphand's business activities cannot be described in detail. Before his death in 1924 he destroyed practically all his papers (Zeman and Scharlau, p. 4).

Yet there can be no doubt of the magnitude of his enterprises or of his having been granted large sums of money for the support of all anti-war elements in Russia and more especially, after March 1917, of the Bolsheviks (Schapiro, pp. 177-9).

Helphand had become a Prussian citizen in 1916; he was an open 'agent' or 'ally' of the German Government.

In the spring of 1915 he had set up an institute in Copenhagen for the ostensible purpose of making scientific and statistical studies; the institute employed various Russian exiles. He had also set up a strictly business organisation there: at the height of the war a lively trade between Germany and Russia passed through Scandinavia (between August 1915 and July 1916 it came to more than eleven million roubles). Helphand's German connections enabled him to get special import and export licences.

In the spring of 1916 Helphand organised a coal combine to undercut the export of British coal to Denmark by replacing it with German coal; in the autumn of that same year he organised his own freight company. Both enterprises entailed close collaboration with the Danish Socialists and the Danish trades-unions. He made a substantial fortune out of the coal business alone.

As part of his legitimate business activities Helphand was able to create a business network in Russia that could encompass subversive activities. His chief assistant in this repect was Jacob Fürstenberg, better known as Haniecki, son of a rich family from Poland. Fürstenberg was a confidential assistant of Lenin's; he had lived with him for two years before the war. In the summer of 1915 he moved to Scandinavia, about the same time as Helphand. Ostensibly working for Helphand's 'Institute', Fürstenberg was managing director of Helphand's Copenhagen export company and his main link with Lenin. Fürstenberg was to remain a high functionary of the Soviet Government until at least 1932; he was head of the Soviet National Bank.

Lenin also used Kozlovsky, an otherwise undistinguished Petrograd lawyer and former member of the Polish Social-Democratic Party.

Helphand and Fürstenberg conducted an extensive exchange of goods between Germany and Russia. Helphand would get from the Germans, for instance, commodities like surgical instruments, medicines (especially 'salvorsan', a contemporary panacea for syphilis), and chemicals, for which there was a Russian demand; Fürstenberg exported them to Russia in a variety of ways. The money to pay for these goods did not go back to Germany, but from the early spring of 1917 on was used to pay for Lenin's propaganda requirements (Zeman and Scharlau, p. 165, quoting H. Grebing in Politische Studien (Munich, 1957), p. 234).

In the spring of 1917 Fürstenberg was joined by Karl Radek, another confidant of Lenin's. Together with V. V. Vorovski (Orlovski), an engineer by training, all three made up the Bolshevik Foreign Mission, which published, on the side, the Bote der russischen Revolution and Korrespondenz Prawda.

Vorovsky had started to work with Fürstenberg after the collapse of Tsarism in February. At the turn of the century he had studied in Munich at the Polytechnic, where he might have met Helphand.

Radek (who was to survive in the summit of the Soviet Government until eliminated, though not executed, in the Moscow 'Show Trials' of 1936-8) was the most active member of the Bolshevik Foreign Mission in Stockholm.

Lenin, on his return to Russia in April 1917, had refused to meet Helphand personally during a stop-over in Stockholm on 13th April. Radek arrived that same day to act, apparently, as go-between; Helphand spent most of 13th April with him.

Helphand was authorised by the Germans to promise substantive support to Lenin's party; Radek was authorised by Lenin to accept. Radek stayed on in Stockholm, to direct the Bolshevik Foreign Mission; Helphand went to Copenhagen to confer with his chief German contact, Count Brockdorff-Rantzau, Minister to Copenhagen (Zeman, Document No. 50). Helphand then went to Berlin to meet with German Social Democrats and also with State Secretary Zimmermann. Then he returned to Scandinavia, shuttling back and forth for some weeks between Copenhagen and Stockholm, where he spent most of his time with the Bolshevik Foreign Mission.

The chief activities of the Foreign Mission revolved around transmitting money to the Bolsheviks in Russia. Helphand was the main, though perhaps not the sole immediate paymaster. The Germans put their diplomatic communications system at the disposal of the Bolshevik Foreign Mission, which could also make occasional use of the Russian diplomatic bag for communications with Petrograd. Helphand's business net-work was a fundamental element.

Eduard Bernstein's report that the German subsidy amounted to more than fifty million gold marks would give a figure, in today's currency, of two thousand million Deutschmarks (reckoning an average of forty Deutschmarks per gold mark of 1917) in purchasing power. This would come to roughly six hundred and sixty-six million dollars, or two hundred and thirty-five million pounds.

The subsidy was largely consumed, no doubt, by the Bolshevik press. By August 1917 the Bolsheviks were publishing forty-one newspapers and journals (twenty-one in Russian, the rest in various minority languages). Newspapers were coming out at a rate of one and half million a week, or 320,000 a day. The production costs were substantial, especially since the newspapers were very often distributed for nothing. A daily newspaper that printed 4,500 to 4,800 copies might lose as much as two hundred to two hundred and fifty roubles *daily*. Nor could the Party income, theoretically based on the ten per cent allocation of the Party dues, revenue from local organisations, etc., conceivably have covered the costs. Bolshevik income from avowable sources was negligible (Schapiro, pp. 176-7; *Perepiska Sekretariata*, Vol. I, pp. 50-1, p. 339).

It is quite inconceivable that a Bolshevik propaganda network could have been established without Lenin's sponsorship. Hence, despite the absence of hand-written receipts, his primary role would seem incontestable.

Trotsky, too, must have been familiar with the source of the vast Bolshevik funds, at least after he joined the Party in the summer of 1917. He must have known of the close links between Helphand and Radek, Fürstenberg, and Vorovski. As Commissar for Foreign Affairs Trotsky must have known that Vorovski was also connected with Riezler, Counsellor of the German Embassy in Stockholm (Riezler, also Scheidemenn, Vol. II, p. 127). As War Commissar he must have known that the Bolsheviks were receiving substantial sums from the Germans down to the eve of their defeat on the Western Front.

As indicated, the Bolsheviks, including Trotsky, always denied with great vigour all charges of complicity with the Germans. Yet there were some illuminating slip-ups.

Eduard Bernstein, at the time an Under-State-Secretary in the German Finance Ministry, was called a liar by the *Rote Fahne*, the official organ of the German Communist Party, after his first article in *Vorwärts* on January, 14th, 1921; in his second article he offered to defend himself before any court chosen by the Party. They never responded. (Bernstein himself abandoned his exposé, no doubt at the urging of the German Social-Democratic Government, to avoid damaging relations between Germany and the Soviet Union).

Amidst blanket denials of complicity with the Germans Lenin also specifically denied any monetary dealings with Fürstenberg and Kozlovsky. He signed and published two letters to this effect in *New Life* July 11th (24th), 1917 and July 26th (August 8th), 1917; the letters were reprinted in Vladimirova, Vol. III, pp. 329 and 360 respectively.

Nevertheless two letters he wrote Fürstenberg in April 1917 survive. In the first Lenin, said, notably: 'We still haven't received any money from you . . .' and, in the second: 'We have received the money (2,000) from Kozlovsky.' Both letters were reproduced in *Proletarskaya Revolyutsiya* (No. 9/21, pp. 227-32, Moscow, 1923) with an anodyne explanation.

Further, the 'controversial affairs' of Fürstenberg and Kozlovsky were discussed eight times, in the course of August and September 1917, in the Central Committee of the Party, but all accounts were omitted from the verbatim reports of the Central Committee for the period. (There is a note by the Institute of Marxism-Leninism (in *Protokoly Tsentral'nogo Komiteta*, p. 250) to the effect that the material was insufficient to 'ascertain the subject matter of the questions discussed'. (Schapiro, pp. 177-9.)

Radek himself, at the time the scandal broke in July 1917, was obliged to account for Fürstenberg's well-known connection with Helphand by saying (in *Korrespondenz Prawda*, 31 July) that Fürstenberg had worked for Helphand not only in order to 'support his family, but also because he could give powerful financial help to the Polish Party organisation in Russian Poland'. This 'explanation', in conjunction with the well-known fact that the 'Polish Party organisation' was a mere puppet of Lenin's, disclosed the essence of the relationship between the Germans and the Bolsheviks, namely, that the Helphand organisation, ostensibly a business enterprise, was really used to transmit funds to Lenin's purely political organisation (Zeman and Scharlau, pp. 227-8).

25 *The Catastrophe*, New York, 1928.
26 *Life*, Vol. II, p. 30.
27 Shub, *Lenin*, p. 248.
28 Sukhanov, pp. 528-9.
29 Serge, *Vie* . . . , pp. 91-2.
30 *Life*, Vol. II, ch. 29, p. 62 (quoting Lunacharsky).

Chapter VI: The Gamble.

1   *Protokoly Tsentral'nogo Komiteta*, p. 5; Deutscher, Vol. I, p. 288.
2   Lenin, *Sochineniya*, (4th ed.), Vol. xxvi, p. 162.
3   Ibid., p. 21.
4   Ibid., p. 55.
5   Ibid., pp. 154-5.
6   Ibid., p. 164.
7   Trotsky, *Sochineniya*, Vol. III, Book I, pp. 321-3.
8   Sukhanov, p. 541.
9   Ibid., p. 556.
10 Ibid., p. 578.
11 *Protokoly Ts. Kom.*, pp. 110-25; Lenin, *Sochineniya*, Vol. xxvi, p. 165.
12 Trotsky, *Sochineniya*, Vol. III, Book 2, pp. 31-2; *Rabochii Put'*, #41, October 20th, 1917.
13 Ibid., p. 37.
14 Sukhanov, pp. 587-8.
15 Ibid., pp. 584-5.
16 Ibid., p. 595.
17 Trotsky, *History* (Russian), Vol. III, p. 227, (English) p. 205.
18 Sukhanov, p. 614.
19 Deutscher, Vol. I, p. 310.
20 Knox, Vol. II, p. 711 (Note).
21 Sukhanov, pp. 639-40.
22 Ibid., pp. 642-3.
23 *Life*, Vol. II, p. 46.
24 Ibid., pp. 48-9.
25 Serge, *Vie* . . . , p. 106.

Chapter VII: The Pinnacle.

1   Sadoul, p. 76.
2   *Life,* Vol. II, pp. 59-60.
3   Ibid.
4   Sukhanov, Vol. VII (Russian), p. 266.
5   *Life,* Vol. II, pp. 62-3.
6   Trotsky, *Stalin,* pp. 242-3.
7   Sadoul, p. 91.
8   *Life,* Vol. II, ch. 29, pp. 65-6.
9   Zeman, Documents Nos. 72, 75, 92 *et al.*; Zeman and Scharlau, pp. 235-59.
10 Trotsky, *Sochineniya,* Vol. III, Book 2, p. 138.
11 Katkov, in *St. Antony's Papers* #XII.
12 Kühlmann, p. 530.
13 Kessler, p. 361.
14 Czernin, pp. 234-5 (German, p. 319).
15 Price, pp. 224-5.
16 Czernin, p. 246.
17 *Life,* Vol. II, p. 104.
18 *Mirnye Peregovory v Brest-Litovske* (Records of the Peace Conference in Brest-Litovsk) Moscow, 1920, pp. 207-8.
19 Wheeler-Bennett pp. 227-8.
20 Price, p. 251.
21 *Sedmoy Syezd RKP,* p. 71.
22 Ibid., p. 69.
23 Ibid., p. 72.
24 Serge, pp. 127-8.
25 Ibid.
26 Ibid., p. 129.
27 Trotsky, *Kak . . . ,* Vol. I, p. 269.
28 Sadoul, p. 396.
29 Lockhart, p. 292; Katkov, *St. Antony's Papers,* #XII.
     Blumkin, one of the two murderers – not the actual one, he lost his head and fired wildly – seems to have been controlled by the Bolsheviks.
     He had been in touch with them before the murder; Trotsky indicated as much years later (Case of Leon Trotsky), when he said that Blumkin 'appeared before us *again*' (my emphasis, J. C.). Trotsky also indicated that the Bolsheviks had to seem to prosecute Blumkin in order to placate the Germans *pro forma.* This need naturally became obsolete after the German collapse.
     Blumkin was in Trotsky's confidence for years, until, in the Thirties, he brought a message from Trotsky's son to Radek at a time when Radek was co-operating with Stalin in the theatrical fabrications known as the Moscow 'Show Trials' aimed at destroying all opposition as 'Trotskyite'. (Carmichael, Conquest.) (See Chapters XII and XIII.) He was shot out of hand.
     The timing of the Mirbach murder arose out of the confrontation between the Bolsheviks and a political opposition organised by the Left SRs at the Fifth Congress of the Soviets that opened July 4th, 1918. The Left SRs attacked the Germans with extravagant fanaticism, thus putting themselves in a position of responsibility for the murder.
     On the eve of the Fifth Congress Blumkin approached Spiridonova with an offer to kill Mirbach. It is not clear whether Blumkin thought of

himself as really acting to promote Left SR policy, but, at a time when heads were beginning to roll freely, the Bolsheviks helped him escape and never punished him. Neither Radek, an intimate of Blumkin's, nor Trotsky could have undertaken such a responsibility without Lenin's approval.

Spiridonova accepted full responsibility for the murder; she did so as a matter of principle and, no doubt, of comradely solidarity. Other Left SRs co-operated with the Bolsheviks by accepting the Bolshevik 'reprisals' as justified. Others boasted of it as a laudable act of terrorism.

The fogginess of so many details in successive official versions indicates a defectively contrived cover-up.

30 Bothmer, quoted in Baumgart, p. 216; paraphrased in Riezler, p. 719, in a top-secret letter to Reichskanzler Count Hertling. The remark was recorded by Bothmer on July 13th, 1918.
31 Zeman, Documents Nos. 133 and 136; Katkov, St. Antony's Papers No. XII, Riezler, p. 101.
32 Solomon.
33 Katkov, St. Antony's Papers, #XII, quoting Yefim Zozulya, in the VIII Syezd Sovietov, the daily bulletin of the Congress published by the VTsIK, #13, January 1st, 1921, p. 4.
34 Trotsky, Kak . . . , Vol. I, p. 284.
35 Quoted in Deutscher, Vol. I, p. 412.
36 Trotsky, Kak . . . , p. 165.
37 Denikin, Vol. III, p. 146.
38 Ziv, pp. 90-1.
39 Lenin, Sochineniya (1st ed., 1920-6), Vol. XVI, p. 73.
40 Gorky, pp. 95-6.
41 Trotsky, Diary, p. 82.
42 Life, Vol. II, pp. 140-1.
43 Ibid., p. 126.
44 Leninskii Sbornik, Vol. XVIII, p. 186; Trotsky, Kak . . . , Vol. I, p. 244; Trotsky (Archives), quoted in Deutscher, Vol. I, p. 421.
45 Pyat' Let Vlasti Sovietov, pp. 156-7.
46 Life, Vol. II, ch. 35, p. 158.
47 Lashevich, Borba za Petrograd, pp. 52-3, quoted in Deutscher, Vol. I, p. 445.
48 Denikin, Vol. V, p. 146.
49 Life, Vol. II, p. 165.
50 Russian Jewry, 1917-1960.
51 The Reflex, Vol. I, No. 5, November 1927.
52 Yarmolinsky, pp. 50-1.
53 Nedava, p. 105.
54 The Reflex, Vol. I, No. 5, November 1927: S. Melamed, St. Paul and Leon Trotsky, pp. 7-8.

Chapter VIII: The Apparatus.

1 Trotsky, Sochineniya, Vol. XIII, p. 14.
2 Trotsky, Lenin, p. 148 (English): Trotsky's emphasis.
3 Ibid.
4 Lenin, Sochineniya, Vol. XXVIII, pp. 433-4.
5 Deutscher, Vol. I, p. 457.
6 Pyat' Let Kominterna, p. 430.
7 Pravda, January 16th, 1920; Deutscher, Vol., p. 495.

8 *Tretii Syezd Profsoyuzov,* April 6-13th, 1920 (Moscow, 1921), pp. 88-9.
9 *Desyaty Syezd RKP,* p. 215; Deutscher, Vol. I, p. 503.
10 Trotsky in a letter of April 14th, 1926: The Archives, quoted in Deutscher, Vol. I, p. 504.
11 *Desyaty Syezd RKP,* pp. 690-1.
12 Ibid., pp. 350-1.
13 Berkman, pp. 10-11.
14 Trotsky, *Sochineniya,* Vol. XVII, Book 2, p. 518; *Pravda,* No. 51, March 8th, 1921.
15 Serge, *Mémoires . . . ,* p. 146.
16 *Life,* Vol. II, pp. 215-17.
17 Bajanov.
18 Khrushchev's 'Secret Speech' in 1956, cited from Wolf, *Khrushchev . . . ,* pp. 98, 100.
19 *Life,* Vol. II, pp. 223-4.
20 In *Kommunist,* June 1956.
21 Rosmer, p. 283.
22 12 *Syezd RKP,* p. 315.
23 Bajanov, pp. 76-7.
24 *Pravda,* December 7th, 1923.
25 *Life,* Vol. II, pp. 240-1.
26 Ibid.
27 Karolyi, p. 265.
28 Bajanov, p. 44; Trotsky, *Stalin,* p. 376.
29 Bajanov, p. 46.
30 *13 Syezd RKP,* pp. 156-9.

Chapter IX: The Muezzin.

1 *Life,* Vol. II, pp. 261-2.
2 *Diary* pp. 45-6.
3 Trotsky, *History,* Vol. I, pp. 341-2.
4 Ibid.
5 *Life,* Vol. I, p. 202-3.
6 Ibid.
7 Lunacharsky, pp. 21-5.
8 Nedava, p. 251, quoting Dr. Mandelberg, a fellow-delegate with Trotsky to the Second Social-Democratic Congress, from *Me-Hayyai (Out of My Life),* (Tel-Aviv, 1942), p. 103.
9 Eastman, *Heroes . . . ,* p. 247.
10 *Life,* Vol. II, pp. 244-5.
11 Ibid., pp. 219-20.
12 Ibid., p. 266.
13 Ibid., p. 62.
14 Ibid., Preface, Vol. I, p. 15.
15 Balabanoff, p. 276.
16 Medem, *Zum Zwanzigsten . . . ,* pp. 10-11.
17 Cf. Note No. 54 to Chapter VII.
18 *Life,* Vol. II, p. 63.
19 Ibid., p. 86.
20 Trotsky, *Diary,* p. 10.
21 *Life,* Vol. II, pp. 182-3.
22 Trotsky, *Stalin,* p. 244.
23 Serge, *Vie . . . ,* p. 181.

24 *Life*, Vol. II, p. 241.
25 Navile, pp. 15-16.
26 Serge, *Vie* ..., pp. 182-7.
27 Published in one volume as *Problems of Everyday Life*.
28 *Pravda*, May 16th 1923; Trotsky *Sochineniya*, Vol. XXI, pp. 26-31.
29 Ibid., p. 413.
30 Ibid., p. 260.
31 Ibid., pp. 430-1.
32 Trotsky, *Literatura i Revolyutsiya*, 2nd ed., Moscow 1924, p. 11.
33 Ibid., pp. 192-4.

Chapter X: The Toboggan.

1 *Life*, Vol. II, p. 256-8.
2 Ibid.
3 Deutscher, Vol. II, p. 249.
4 Serge, *Vie* ..., p. 197.
5 In 1938: *The Case of Leon Trotsky*, pp. 322-3.
6 Serge, *Vie* ..., pp. 200-1.
7 Trotsky, *Stalin*, p. 417.
8 June 6th, 1926; Deutscher, Vol. II, p. 269.
9 Deutscher, Vol. II, p. 274, giving the lower figure as 'Stalinist' and the upper as 'Trotskyite'.
10 *Pravda*, October 16th, 1926.
11 *New York Times*, October 18th, 1926; Levine, pp. 195-7.
12 In a letter to Deutscher, Vol. II, p. 295.
13 *Pravda*, October 22nd, 1926.
14 Serge, *Vie* ..., p. 213.
15 Deutscher, Vol. II, p. 329.
16 Stalin, *Sochineniya*, Vol. IX, pp. 311-12.
17 In the Archives, quoted in Deutscher, Vol. II, p. 339-40.
18 Ibid.
19 Trotsky, *The Stalin School of Falsification*, pp. 126-48; Deutscher Vol. II, p. 345.
20 Preobrazhensky, Mrachkovsky, Serebryakov.
21 *Life*, Vol. II, p. 279.
22 Serge, *Mémoires*, p. 239; *Life*, Vol II. p. 278.
23 Serge, *Tournant* ..., pp. 113-14.
24 Serge, *Mémoires* ..., p. 243: the figure comes from the Opposition.
25 Serge, *Tournant* ..., p. 155.
26 *Life*, Vol. II, p. 289.
27 Ibid., pp. 296-9.
28 Ibid.
29 Ibid., p. 469.
30 Deutscher, Vol. III, pp. 81-2.
31 *Life*, Vol. II, pp. 309-13.
32 Ibid.
33 Ibid., p. 315.

Chapter XI: The Hero.

1 *Life*, Vol. II, pp. 337-8.
2 *Manchester Guardian*, March 17th, 1931.
3 Eastman, *Great Companions*, p. 117.
4 *Life*, Vol. II, pp. 318-33.

5   In the Archives, quoted in Deutscher, Vol. II, pp. 17-18.
6   Eastman, *Great Companions,* p. 116.
7   Deutscher, Vol. III, p. 27.
8   KPSS v Rezolyutsiakh, Vol. II, pp. 450-69, 593 ff.
9   Churchill, *The Second . . . ,* Vol. IV, p. 498.
10 *Kommunisticheskii Internatsional,* 1933: No. 36, p. 17.
11 *Bulletin of the Opposition.*
12 Pierre Frank, a French sympathiser; quoted in Deutscher, Vol. III, p. 198, Note 2.
13 *Bulletin of the Opposition,* #33, 1933.
14 Ibid.
15 Ibid, #35, 1933.
16 Deutscher, Vol. III, p. 184.
17 Ibid., p. 187.
18 Natalya to Sedov, December 16th, 1932, quoted in Deutscher ibid., p. 193.
19 Ibid. p. 145.
20 Ibid., in a letter from Alexandra to Trotsky, January 31st, 1933.
21 Jan Fraenkel, in *The Militant,* January 2nd, 1932.
22 Deutscher, Vol. III p. 177.
23 Ibid., p. 180.
24 *Bulletin of the Opposition,* #64, March 1938.
25 Ibid., #33, March 1933.
26 Letter dated January 31st, 1933: Deutscher, Vol. III, pp. 198-9.
27 Deutscher, ibid., quoting Pierre Frank.

Chapter XII: The Agony.

1   Deutscher, Vol. III, p. 262, from The Archives.
2   Ibid., p. 263, quoting depositions in The Archives by Natalya, by Klement and by 'Erde'.
3   Ibid., p. 265.
4   Ibid., p. 266, a letter to Gollancz of October 23rd, 1933.
5   Ibid., p. 270: a letter to Serge of July 30th, 1936.
6   Ibid., Trotsky to Sedov of December 27th, 1935, quoted in Deutscher, Vol. III, p. 270.
7   Ibid., p. 272.
8   *Diary,* pp. 45-6.
9   Ibid., p. 3.
10 *Bulletin of the Opposition,* #m 42, February, 1935.
11 *Diary,* p.134.
12 Ibid., pp. 51, 56.
13 Ibid., p. 135.
14 Deutscher, Vol. III, p. 293-7.
15 Ibid.
16 Ibid.
17 *Bulletin of the Opposition,* Nos. 45, 47-9 and 51 (1935/6), citing A. Tarov, A. Ciliga, and V. Serge.
18 E.g., Tarov.
19 Ciliga.
20 Deutscher, Vol. III, p. 328.
21 Ibid., p. 331.
22 See notably Carmichael, Conquest, Solzhenitsyn, and other entries in the Bibliography.

23 Trotsky, *Stalins Verbrechen;* Deutscher Vol. III, p. 336.
24 Deutscher, Ibid., pp. 431-2.
25 *Bulletin of the Opposition,* No. 64, March 1938.
26 The story of Zborowski, now living in the United States – as an academic anthropologist! – has been told in the *New Leader* (H. Kasson, November 21st, 1955; David Dallin, March 19th and 26th, 1956); also Hearing before U.S. Senate Sub-Committee on Internal Security, Part 51, February 14-15th, 1957, pp. 3423-9.
27 Trotsky, *Stalins Verbrechen,* pp. 37 ff.
28 Deutscher, Vol. III, p. 351.
29 Trotsky, *Stalins Verbrechen,* pp. 77-8.
30 Ibid.
31 Deutscher, Vol. III, p. 353.
32 Ibid.
33 Ibid.

Chapter XIII: The Release.

1 Quoted in Rosmer's appendix to the French translation of Trotsky's autobiography (p. 618).
2 Letters of February 1st and 15th, 1937: Deutscher, Vol. III, p. 364.
3 Serge, *Vie . . . ,* p. 258.
4 Dewey Commission, quoted in Deutscher, Vol. III, p. 380.
5 Ibid, p. 382.
6 June 29-30th, 1937: Deutscher, op. cit., p. 383.
7 July 18th, 1937: ibid. p. 386.
8 Carmichael, *Epilogue.*
9 *Forwards,* New York, January 26-28th, 1937.
10 *Bulletin of the Opposition,* Nos. 60-1, December 1937.
11 Deutscher, ibid, p. 392.
12 January 21st, 1938: The Archives, Deutscher, ibid., p. 394.
13 Ibid., pp. 397-8.
14 Ibid.
15 March 10th, 1938: Deutscher, ibid.
16 *Bulletin of the Opposition,* #64, March, 1938 (In English, as a pamphlet: Leon Sedoff, Son, Friend, Fighter).
17 Sergei was seen in February 1937 in a Moscow prison by Joseph Berger, a founder of the Palestinian Communist Party who had spent twenty-three years in Soviet prisons and concentration camps. Nedava, p. 256 (on the basis of a conversation with Berger in December 1961); cf. Deutscher, Vol. III, pp. 401-2.
18 *Bulletin of the Opposition,* #65, 1938.
19 Dewey, 'Means and Ends', *New International,* August 1938.
20 *Life,* Vol. II, p. 257.
21 Trotsky, *Stalin,* p. 336.
22 To Max Eastman, *Since Lenin Died,* p. 55.
23 Trotsky, *Stalin,* p. 381.
24 Ibid., p. 416.
25 In his *Lenin,* 1924.
26 Introduction to *The Living Thoughts of Karl Marx.*
27 *New International,* 'The U.S.S.R. at War', November 1939.
28 *Bulletin of the Opposition,* #71, November 1938, pp. 15-16.
29 *New Stateman,* November 10th, 1937, p. 582 (to Kingsley Martin).
30 Macdonald, p. 17; Deutscher Vol. III, p. 420.

31 Serge, *Vie* . . . , ibid., p. 250.
32 Deutscher, p. 445.
33 Serge ibid., pp. 247-8.
34 Deutscher, ibid., p. 446.
35 Serge, ibid., pp. 247-9.
36 Ibid.
37 Ibid., also Natalya Sedova, *Fourth International,* August 1941.
38 Serge, ibid., pp. 249-53.
39 Private communication to author, May 2nd, 1969.
40 Serge, ibid.
41 *Diary,* pp. 165-6.
42 Ibid.
43 Gorkin.
44 Trotsky's own account (June 8th, 1950), published posthumously in the *New International,* August 1941.
45 Serge, *Vie* . . . , pp. 309-10.
46 Salazar, pp. 6-7.
47 Ibid., pp. 9-10.
48 *Bulletin of the Opposition,* #85, March 1941.
49 Salazar, p. 89: Trotsky's statement.
50 Aldanov.
51 Serge, ibid., p. 264.
52 Ibid., pp. 266-7.
53 Joseph Hansen, 'With Trotsky to the End', *Fourth International,* October 1940.
54 Serge, ibid., p. 268.
55 Salazar, ibid., p. 110.

INDEX